Liberation in Southern Africa– Regional and Swedish Voices

Interviews from Angola, Mozambique, Namibia, South Africa, Zimbabwe, the Frontline and Sweden

Edited by
Tor Sellström

Nordiska Afrikainstitutet, Uppsala

Indexing terms
Sweden
Angola
Mozambique
Namibia
South Africa
Zimbabwe
National liberation movements
Interviews

Cover: Adriaan Honcoop
Language checking: Elaine Almén

Second edition 2002
ISBN 91-7106-500-8
First published 1999 (hard cover) (ISBN 91-7106-438-9)

Printed in Sweden by
Elanders Gotab, Stockholm 2002

Contents

Maps.. 5
Preface and Acknowledgements 7
An Introductory Note 9
    The Context of the Interviews................................ 9
    Interviews in the Context of Oral History 11

Angola

Paulo Jorge	15	Alberto Ribeiro-Kabulu	27
Lúcio Lara	18	Holden Roberto	30
Ruth Neto	21	Jorge Valentim	34
Miguel N'Zau Puna	23		

Mozambique

Joaquim Chissano	38	Marcelino dos Santos	47
Janet Mondlane	41	Jacinto Veloso	52
Jorge Rebelo	45	Sérgio Vieira	54

Namibia

Ottilie Abrahams	59	Mishake Muyongo	86
Ben Amathila	62	Festus Naholo	89
Hadino Hishongwa	67	Zedekia Ngavirue	92
Peter Katjavivi	71	Hifikepunye Pohamba	94
Charles Kauraisa	75	Andreas Shipanga	97
Dirk Mudge	80	Andimba Toivo ya Toivo	99
Aaron Mushimba	84	Ben Ulenga	100

South Africa

Jaya Appalraju	103	Billy Modise	156
Alex Boraine	107	Kay Moonsamy	161
Roelof 'Pik' Botha	111	James Motlatsi	165
Gora Ebrahim	118	Sankie Mthembi-Mahanyele	168
Gerald Giose	122	Indres Naidoo	173
John Gomomo	127	Beyers Naudé	181
Rica Hodgson	131	Barney Pityana	186
Lindiwe Mabuza	134	Walter Sisulu	190
Reddy Mampane	142	Garth Strachan	192
Trevor Manuel	149	Craig Williamson	197
Thabo Mbeki	153		

Zimbabwe

Canaan Banana 206	John Nkomo 223
Dumiso Dabengwa 209	Sydney Tigere Sekeramayi 226
Kumbirai Kangai 213	Ndabaningi Sithole 231
Didymus Mutasa 216	Josiah Tungamirai 233
Abel Muzorewa 221	

Zambia, OAU and the Soviet Union

Kenneth Kaunda 238	Vladimir Shubin 248
Salim Ahmed Salim 243	

Sweden

Roland Axelsson 252	Tomas Ledin 300
Birgitta Berggren 256	Sören Lindh 303
Tore Bergman 262	Stig Lövgren 309
Stig Blomquist 266	Åke Magnusson 315
Pär Granstedt 269	Ernst Michanek 320
Birger Hagård 272	Hillevi Nilsson 326
Sven Hamrell 277	Pierre Schori 330
Gunnar Helander 281	Bengt Säve-Söderbergh 336
Carl-Henrik ('C.H.') Hermansson 289	Carl Tham 340
Lena Hjelm-Wallén 292	David Wirmark 345
Anders Johansson 295	Per Wästberg 352

List of Acronyms 358
Name Index 361

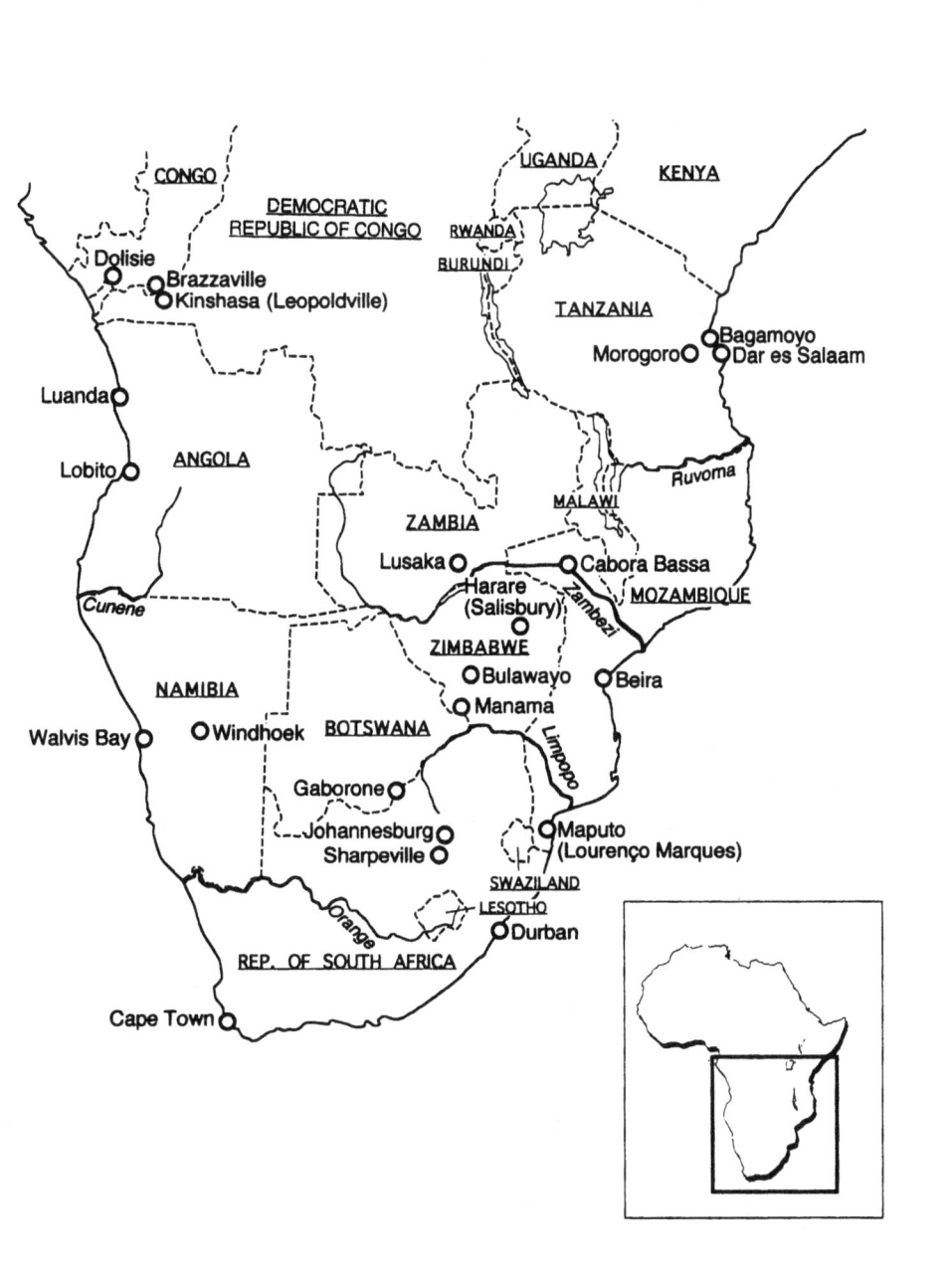

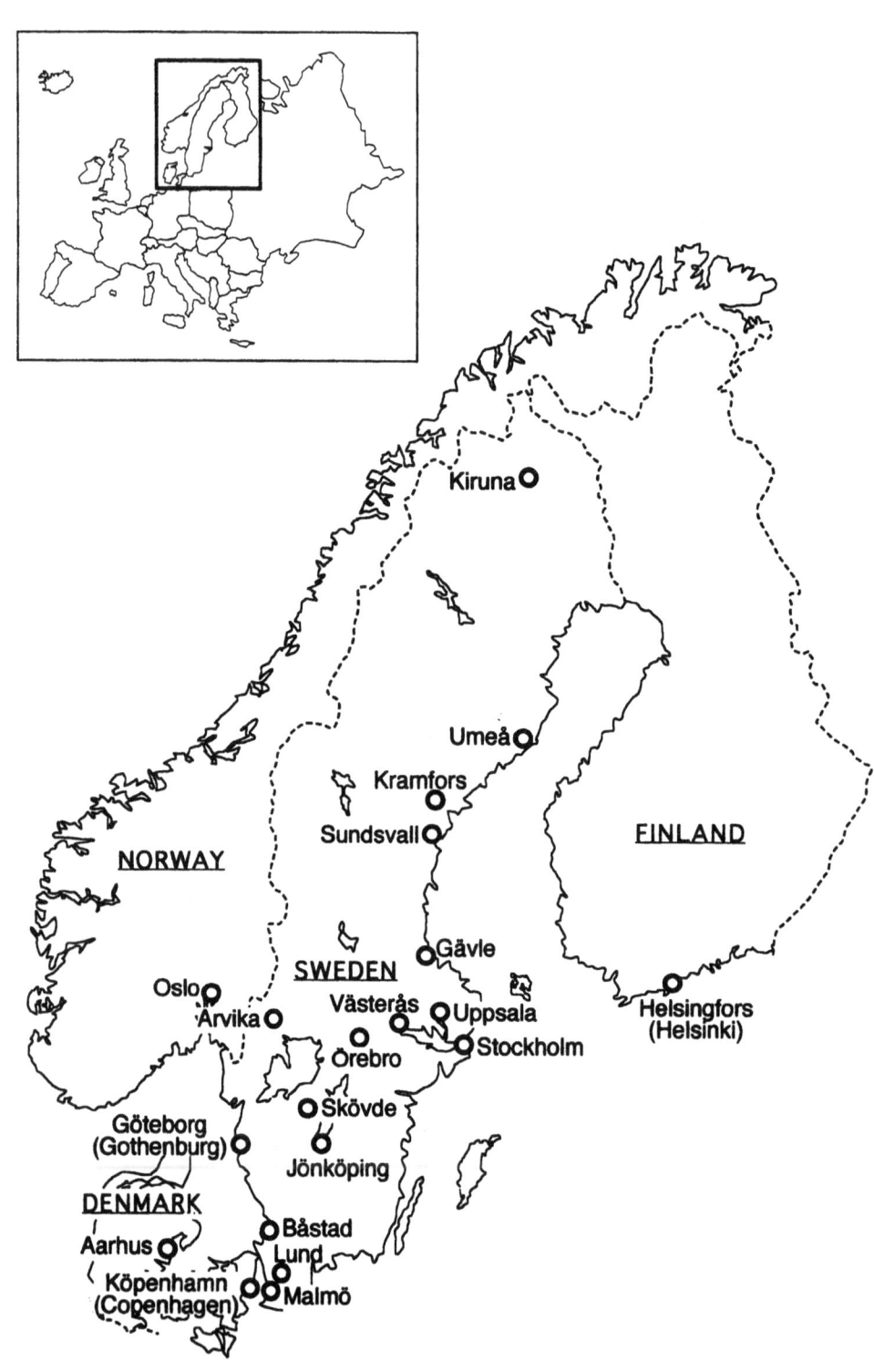

Preface and Acknowledgements

The interviews contained in this book were conducted for a project on *National Liberation in Southern Africa: The Role of the Nordic Countries*, which had as its main objective to document and analyse the involvement of the Nordic countries in the struggles for majority rule and independence in Angola, Mozambique, Zimbabwe, Namibia and South Africa. Focusing on the relations between the Nordic countries and the Southern African liberation movements, the project findings are published by the Nordic Africa Institute in the form of separate studies on Denmark, Finland, Norway and Sweden.[1]

This book is both a companion to the Nordic studies and a reference source. When designed, it was found that the project would benefit from personal inputs by people with a direct experience from—or knowledge about—the relations between the Nordic countries and the Southern African liberation movements. Oral testimonies could inform the studies and add texture to the presentation of a relationship that for reasons of security had largely developed outside the public arena and of which there was little evidence in open sources.[2] There was, in particular, a lack of 'voices from the South' in the form of statements and comments by representatives of the liberation movements and their allies.

During the course of the project, it became increasingly apparent that the testimonies should be made available to a wider public. Generally found to contain relevant information and express important opinions on the relations between the Nordic countries and the Southern African nationalist movements, they, for example, ought to be useful for further studies on a number of related questions.

The title—*Liberation in Southern Africa: Regional and Swedish Voices*—indicates that the book primarily covers Sweden's involvement in the liberation process.[3] Formal interviews were used differently and to varying degrees in the Nordic studies. In addition to the testimonies collected in Southern Africa, more than twenty tape-recorded and transcribed interviews were carried out in Sweden. A smaller number of similarly documented interviews were done in Denmark and Finland, while informal exchanges were conducted in Norway. The interviews done in Sweden are here published with those from Southern Africa.

It has been a time-consuming and arduous task to prepare, transcribe, edit and clear the more than eighty interviews contained in this volume. To state that it has only been possible with the assistance of many and that the book is the result of a collective effort is far from a cliché. My thanks go to all those involved.

---

[1] Iceland forms part of the Nordic group of countries. Due to its marginal involvement in the liberation process in Southern Africa, no particular Icelandic study has, however, been undertaken. The Danish study is authored by Christopher Morgenstierne; the Finnish by Pekka Peltola and Iina Soiri and the Norwegian one is edited by Tore Linné Eriksen.

[2] See the introductory chapter to Volume I of the Swedish study: Tor Sellström: *Sweden and National Liberation in Southern Africa: Formation of a Popular Opinion (1950-1970)*, Nordiska Afrikainstitutet, Uppsala, 1999.

[3] On the 'Swedish bias' of the interviews conducted in Southern Africa, see the Introductory Note.

To begin with, it would not have been possible to arrange the interviews in Southern Africa without the assistance and good offices of Sten Rylander and Anna Wahlström at the Swedish embassy and Carolin Guriras at NEPRU[1] in Windhoek; Elisabeth Dahlin at the Swedish embassy in Lusaka; Ibbo Mandaza and the staff at SARIPS[2] in Harare; Garth Strachan and his colleagues at FCR[3] in Cape Town; Gunilla von Bahr at the Swedish embassy in Pretoria; Jaya Appalraju at Matla Trust and Pumla Mtyeku at ANC in Johannesburg; Lena Sundh and Marie Andersson at the Swedish embassy and Ilda Carreira in Luanda; and Ann Stödberg and Pamela Rebelo at the Swedish embassy in Maputo. Jan Cedergren at the Ministry for Foreign Affairs in Stockholm and Lennart Wohlgemuth at the Nordic Africa Institute in Uppsala similarly facilitated a number of interviews in Sweden.

I am in this regard deeply indebted to professor Carl Fredrik Hallencreutz, who kindly accepted my questionnaires and on my behalf conducted the interviews with Canaan Banana, Abel Muzorewa and Josiah Tungamirai in Zimbabwe.

Above all, I am deeply grateful to the persons whose voices appear in the book. In spite of important responsibilities and busy working schedules, they not only found the time to sit down and freely give of their personal experiences and opinions, but also to proof-read the transcripts. I am particularly impressed by the support granted me in Southern Africa, both by representatives at the highest levels of government and by members of the political opposition. Without exception, they all showed a keen interest in shedding light on the relations between Southern Africa and the Nordic countries. Their generous contributions are invaluable.

A number of students in Uppsala performed the onerous task of transforming several of the tape-recorded interviews into draft transcripts. My thanks go to Ulrika Eckstrand, Anna Hamrell, Fia Nilsson, Jenny Rosendahl, Erik Sellström, Jeanette Sävström and Johanna Vintersved. In the case of the interviews carried out in Portuguese[4], the same task was performed by Ana Cristina Pires-Hagman and by my colleague António Lourenço at the Nordic Africa Institute.

Special thanks go to Annelie Borg-Bishop and Charlotta Dohlvik at the Nordic Africa Institute. More than any others, they made this book possible. Struggling outside working hours with transcriptions, corrections and correspondence with the interviewees, their enthusiasm and support will always be remembered.

The financial support granted by the governments of Denmark, Finland, Norway and Sweden to the Nordic project, as well as the general assistance extended by Lennart Wohlgemuth and his staff at the Nordic Africa Institute, are, finally, recorded with gratitude.

Uppsala, August 1998
Tor Sellström

---

[1] The Namibia Economic Policy Research Unit.

[2] The Southern Africa Regional Institute for Policy Studies.

[3] The Foundation for Contemporary Research.

[4] The interviews with Paulo Jorge, Lúcio Lara, Ruth Neto, Miguel N'Zau Puna, Holden Roberto (Angola), Marcelino dos Santos and Jacinto Veloso (Mozambique) were carried out in Portuguese.

An Introductory Note

The Context of the Interviews

In May 1969, the Swedish parliament endorsed a policy of direct official humanitarian assistance to the national liberation movements in Southern Africa and Guinea-Bissau. Followed by the other Nordic countries,[1] Sweden thereby became the first industrialized Western country to enter into a direct relationship with movements that in the Cold War period elsewhere in the West were shunned as 'Communist' or 'terrorist'.

Although geographically and culturally far apart, during the protracted struggles for majority rule and national independence in Angola, Mozambique, Zimbabwe, Namibia and South Africa a close relationship would evolve between the Nordic countries and the Southern African liberation movements, both at the official and at the non-governmental levels. Over the years, an increasing proportion of the liberation movements' civilian needs was covered by the Nordic countries, involving a wide range of organizations, from the official aid agencies to churches, trade unions, solidarity groups etc. To this should be added assistance extended to organizations aligned with the liberation movements, such as the South African United Democratic Front. In the case of Sweden—which extended official support to MPLA of Angola, FRELIMO of Mozambique, SWAPO of Namibia, ZANU and ZAPU of Zimbabwe and ANC of South Africa—a total of 4 billion Swedish Kronor in current figures was disbursed as official humanitarian assistance to Southern Africa until the democratic elections in South Africa in 1994. Of this amount, not less than 1.7 billion—over 40 per cent—was channelled directly to the six liberation movements under bilateral agreements.[2] As stated by the American scholar William Minter,

> in the 1980s, the international right wing was fond of labeling SWAPO and ANC as 'Soviet-backed'. In empirical terms, the alternate, but less dramatic, labels 'Swedish-backed' or 'Nordic-backed' would have been equally or even more accurate, especially in the non-military aspects of international support.[3]

Talking about Sweden, the ANC leader Oliver Tambo—who from 1960 regularly visited the Nordic countries and perhaps more than any other Southern African politician contributed himself to the close relationship[4]—characterized the

---

[1] Denmark did not extend direct official support to the Southern African liberation movements, but channelled considerable resources to them via Danish and international non-governmental organizations.

[2] Based on disbursement figures according to the annual accounts of the Swedish International Development Authority (SIDA), established by Ulla Beckman for the Swedish study.

[3] William M. Minter: Review of *The Impossible Neutrality* by Pierre Schori in *Africa Today*, No. 43, 1996, p. 95.

[4] Denmark was the first European country to receive the ANC leader. Barely one month after going into exile, Tambo was invited by the Danish trade union confederation to address the Labour Day celebrations in Copenhagen and Aarhus on 1 May 1960.

unusual North-South dimension as follows in a tribute to the late Prime Minister Olof Palme in 1988,

> There has [...] emerged a natural system of relations between Southern Africa and Sweden, from people to people. It is a system of international relations which is not based on the policies of any party that might be in power in Sweden at any particular time, but on the fundamental reality that the peoples of our region and those of Palme's land of birth share a common outlook and impulse, which dictates that they should all strive for the same objectives.[1]

To document and analyse the involvement of the Nordic countries in the Southern African struggles for national independence and majority rule, a project on *National Liberation in Southern Africa: The Role of the Nordic Countries* was launched at the Nordic Africa Institute in August 1994. Focusing on the direct relations with the liberation movements, the four studies on Denmark, Finland, Norway and Sweden have to a great extent made use of hitherto restricted primary material at both Nordic government and NGO archives. The Swedish study, in particular, has in addition drawn largely upon oral testimonies by people in Southern Africa and Sweden. The formal interviews carried out for the Swedish study are published in the present volume.[2]

The interviews were conducted to give guidance to the Nordic studies and add texture to the presentation of a relationship that during the liberation struggles for reasons of security developed largely outside the public arena and of which there is little evidence in open sources. When and why did, for example, leading representatives of the Southern African liberation movements enter into contact with the Nordic countries? How was the Nordic support perceived in the prevailing international context? Was it extended with conditions attached? What significance did it have? And in the case of Sweden and the other Nordic countries: How did the involvement with Southern Africa begin? What were the motives behind the support? Why were certain liberation movements assisted and others not? How did different domestic political actors view the support in the Cold War context?

Reactions to these and other questions could, naturally, only be sought from a limited number of people. The ambition was to interview people who had direct experience from—or knowledge about—the relations between Sweden/the Nordic countries and the Southern African liberation movements; who could speak with authority on behalf of their respective movements, parties, organizations or social sectors; and that the interviews in each country would cover a politically relevant spectrum.

A number of requested interviews could for different reasons not take place. Nevertheless, the voices that appear below conform to a great extent to the set criteria. The testimonies from Angola are, for example, given by leading repre-

---

[1] Oliver Tambo: 'Olof Palme and the Liberation of Southern Africa' in Kofi Buenor Hadjor (ed.): *New Perspectives in North-South Dialogue: Essays in Honour of Olof Palme*, I.B. Tauris Publishers, London, 1988, p. 258.

[2] Only the tape-recorded and approved testimonies published below appear as 'interviews' in the Swedish study. Non-formal consultations are referred to as 'conversations'.

sentatives of MPLA, FNLA and UNITA, while the South African voices *inter alia* represent ANC, PAC, BCM, SACP, UDF, the churches and the trade unions. Prominent white opponents to the nationalist movements are also included, such as the former South African Foreign Minister Roelof 'Pik' Botha—who served at the South African embassy in Stockholm between 1956 and 1960—and the security officer Craig Williamson—who infiltrated the International University Exchange Fund and became close to a group of Scandinavian Social Democrats in the late 1970s. In the case of Sweden, there are interviews with leading representatives of the five traditional parliamentary parties,[1] the Ministry for Foreign Affairs and SIDA, solidarity pioneers and veteran members of the Africa Groups in Sweden, the Church of Sweden, the trade union movement, the world of popular music and Swedish export interests.

Around 80 interviews conducted between March 1995 and March 1997 are included in this volume. Out of these, 13 are from Angola and Mozambique, 9 from Zimbabwe, 14 from Namibia, 21 from South Africa and 22 from Sweden. In addition, testimonies by the former President of Zambia, Kenneth Kaunda; the Secretary General of the Organization of African Unity, Salim Ahmed Salim of Tanzania; and the former head of the Africa Section of the International Department of the Communist Party of the Soviet Union, Vladimir Shubin,[2] appear outside the direct relationship between Sweden/the Nordic countries and the Southern African nationalist movements.

The interviews are primarily reproduced as texts accompanying the Swedish and the other Nordic studies. They are, however, in their own right a reference source to quite a unique contemporary North-South relationship, often extending beyond the direct support to the liberation movements. Students of the Southern African labour movement, for example, will find in the testimonies authoritative evidence of a little known involvement by the Swedish Mineworkers Union/LO-TCO Council of International Trade Union Cooperation in the initial build-up of both the South African National Union of Mineworkers and the Mineworkers Union of Namibia.[3]

Interviews in the Context of Oral History

The role of interviews in social science research is not unproblematic. Before turning to the testimonies from Southern Africa and Sweden, brief comments are thus warranted regarding the methodology used and the general issue of context in oral history.

---

[1] Although a member of the Swedish parliament, Birger Hagård could not be considered a leading representative of the Moderate Party. Mobilizing support for UNITA in the 1980s, his views do, however, represent a real dissentient Swedish opinion.

[2] Approved by Shubin, the tape-recorded transcript has been arranged according to specific themes and is, exceptionally, referred to as a 'conversation'.

[3] See interview with Stig Blomqvist, Bro, 29 January 1997; interview with James Motlatsi, Johannesburg, 25 April 1996; and interview with Ben Ulenga, Windhoek, 16 March 1995.

The interviews followed written questionnaires, which—whenever possible[1]—were submitted in advance. All the interviews were tape-recorded, transcribed as verbatim accounts, roughly edited and submitted to the interviewees with a copy of the original tape-recording for proof-reading, possible corrections and approval.[2] It may thus be argued that the spontaneity of the original exchange has been lost. On the other hand, the information and opinions given have been reconfirmed and validated by the interviewees. Before inclusion in the present volume, the interviews conducted in Portuguese were, finally, translated into English, all texts were submitted to a language check and—when required for reasons of clarity—additional editing was carried out. In some cases the draft transcripts were shortened and in others restructured. Facts and opinions expressed were, naturally, never altered. Nevertheless, it should be borne in mind that the texts below—as is almost invariably the case with published interviews—are the end result of a process in which amendments to the original verbatim accounts have been introduced.

Interviews are, in addition, generally subject to a number of non-verbal influences. Both the social and the physical setting have, for example, a bearing upon the exchange between the interviewer and the interviewee. The most important consideration in this regard is that the author in many cases—particularly in Namibia, South Africa and Sweden—personally knew several of the interviewees beforehand and that the documentation submitted when requesting the appointments made his Swedish background known to all of them. During the actual interviews, this often translated as an unintended 'Swedish bias', where the answer to a question on the Nordic countries mainly or exclusively was given in relation to Sweden.[3]

This example is indicative of a deeper issue concerning oral history testimonies. The goal of oral history is, obviously, to elicit information about past events. However, in addition to the fact that memories become blurred and even distorted with the passing of time, oral history interviews necessarily produce a dialogue between the past and the present. "Interviewees interpret the meaning of both the past and the present, including the interview itself. Each query presents them with the task of searching through their memories to see which recollections bear on the question and then fitting this information into a form that will be seen as answering the question."[4] That oral interviews about the

---

[1] This was not always the case in Southern Africa, where interviews were sometimes arranged at very short notice.

[2] Surprisingly few interviewees did not comment on the draft transcripts and in only one case was the author asked to delete a statement made. The tape-recordings and verbatim transcripts are available to interested scholars at the Nordic Africa Institute.

[3] In some cases, the focus on Sweden was, however, explicit. When asked to discuss the involvement of all the Nordic countries in the liberation struggle in Southern Africa, Kenneth Kaunda, the former President of Zambia, thus replied that "it was Olof Palme who led the Nordic countries in this process. It was his contribution which aroused the interest and the feelings of the other Nordic countries. They also made very wonderful contributions, there is no doubt about that. But I am merely being factual when I say that it all started with Sweden" (interview with Kenneth Kaunda, Lusaka, 15 July 1995).

[4] Charles L. Briggs: *Learning How to Ask: A Sociolinguistic Appraisal of the Role of the Interview in Social Science Research*, Cambridge University Press, Cambridge, 1986, p. 14.

past are directly related to the present should be particularly relevant in the case of the testimonies which follow. A majority of the people interviewed are still politically active, often holding leading positions in their respective countries, political parties or organizations. Asked to comment upon past international Cold War relations and ideological positions, there is, for example, reason to believe that their answers—albeit unconsciously—are adjusted to the circumstances created after the demise of the Soviet Union and the achievement of majority rule and national independence in Southern Africa.

While post-rationalization of the past due to present considerations should thus not be discounted, a necessary awareness of the limitations inherent in *all* oral history interviews should, however, not cast particular doubts over the testimonies contained in this volume. On the contrary, the people interviewed were generally keen to openly, sincerely and constructively shed light on the relations between Sweden, the Nordic countries and the Southern African liberation movements. In several cases—particularly in Southern Africa—the interviews were approached and acknowledged as significant opportunities to reflect upon a little known, but close historical relationship, not least for the benefit of the people in the region.[1] On a number of important issues, the views expressed by the various actors in the different countries are also strikingly similar.

Published as a companion to the Swedish and Nordic studies, the present volume is, as stated, a reference source in its own right. As such, it is simply arranged according to the countries covered. Within each country section, the people interviewed appear in alphabetical order. As they are either well known to students of Southern African affairs or—mainly in the case of Sweden—their relations to the liberation process will be evident from the texts, they are only introduced through brief presentations, indicating the liberation movement, political party or organization that they represent—or have represented in the past—as well as the principal positions that are relevant to the main subject. In addition to date and place, the position of the politically active people at the time of the interview is also given. More detailed information on the interviewees appears in Volume I and Volume II of the Swedish study.

---

[1] See, for example, interview with Peter Katjavivi, Windhoek, 20 March 1995 and interview with Marcelino dos Santos, Maputo, 3 May 1996.

Angola

Paulo Jorge
MPLA—Director of Information
Former Minister of Foreign Affairs
(Luanda, 15 April 1996)

Tor Sellström: When did you come into contact with the Nordic countries?

Paulo Jorge: After fleeing from Portugal, I started to work for MPLA in Paris in 1962. I then became aware of the contacts that our organization had with solidarity groups in Sweden. From 1968-69, I was sent to Sweden to meet them. One was the Africa Groups. I formed part of a delegation that also established contact with people from the Swedish Social Democratic Party. But it was not until 1971 that I got a deeper knowledge of the relations between MPLA and the Swedish solidarity groups and the Social Democratic Party. At that time, I had been transferred to our eastern front, which covered the province of Moxico (the so-called third political-military region), the Lundas (the fourth region) and Bié (the fifth region). I had left the second political-military region in the Cabinda province. Between 1971 and 1973, I learned about the aid from Sweden and other Nordic countries, such as Finland and Norway.

TS: Was the support from Norway for the Ngangula school?

PJ: Precisely. It started to arrive at the same time as the support from Denmark. It was humanitarian assistance, such as clothes and school equipment. Of course, as a matter of principle, there were no military items. Only humanitarian.

TS: Including means of transport, vehicles?

PJ: Yes. The humanitarian assistance and the vehicles were very important and added to other support that we were receiving. Whenever deliveries arrived from a country—such as Sweden and the other Nordic countries—MPLA would inform its soldiers and members about the assistance so that they would understand the meaning of solidarity and know which countries were our friends. We always gave this information through our radio broadcasts. We had two programmes, one from Brazzaville and the other from Lusaka, called 'Angola in Combat' ('*Angola Combatente*').

TS: How did you explain then that two of the Nordic countries were members of NATO?

PJ: It was very simple. To avoid problems, we always said that the assistance came from solidarity organizations, support committees and so on. We never spoke of parties or governments. When we received assistance, we said: 'We received this from solidarity organizations in friendly countries'. Up to a certain time, we never mentioned the name of the parties.

TS: But how could MPLA's leadership explain that the movement received humanitarian support from the Nordic countries, which were part of the Western bloc?

PJ: Our understanding was the following: These governments had their relations, accords and agreements. It was not for us to tell them that they could not be part of this or that European organization. Our interest was that they found a way of helping us and that they did not interfere in the war. We knew that the Nordic countries never interfered directly in the military process on Portugal's side. That was the most important aspect. There was a kind of neutrality from the Nordic countries, as well as others, towards the war and Portugal's military actions against us.

TS: Did you experience any political conditions related to the Nordic support?

PJ: No.

TS: Was it strictly humanitarian?

PJ: Absolutely. There was never any condition imposed on us. We received the assistance and we stayed in contact. I went to Sweden a couple of times, once to Norway and once to Finland before independence. Of course, the assistance opened a channel for discussions. We held meetings without major publicity, because we did not want to cause any trouble for those who supported us. We also received some support from other European countries. I should underline that as far as I know the assistance from Sweden was always larger than that from Norway, Denmark or Finland. We received the goods and distributed them. There were never any conditions attached. In our contacts with the political parties, it sometimes also happened that there was some monetary support involved. For example, when we visited Sweden there were certain groups that paid for our stay.

TS: The Swedish Social Democratic Party gave MPLA financial contributions from its solidarity fund.

PJ: Exactly. I remember very well that our President Agostinho Neto informed us about the financial support from the Nordic countries and that he mentioned precisely that fund.

In the period between the end of 1971 and 1974, we received a lot of humanitarian assistance from the Nordic countries, in particular from Sweden. The largest amount was from Sweden and a considerable part from Denmark. The Africa Groups played an important role for the mobilization of these funds and also with regard to the financial help that the Social Democratic Party gave us.

TS: Do you think that the fact that Sweden assisted Cuba and Vietnam facilitated your relations with the Nordic countries?

PJ: Yes, but it was not only that. Sweden also attracted our attention because it already had close relations with the liberation movements in Mozambique, Guinea-Bissau and Cape Verde, namely FRELIMO and PAIGC. We were aware of these relations. It is also true that a certain independence and neutrality concerning, for example the Cuban question, helped. It made it easier for us to receive the support. In the case of Angola, the information we had, moreover, was that the support from the Nordic countries was basically for MPLA and not for the other movements.

TS: As regards Sweden, Holden Roberto visited a couple of times, but FNLA never received official assistance from the government.

PJ: Exactly. That clear position of independence—I call it an independent position—by Sweden and the other Nordic countries helped the liberation movements that were really fighting. Sweden was very wise in this regard because it supported those that they knew were fighting, that is PAIGC, FRELIMO and MPLA. That was important. We could see that Sweden's position was in favour of the authentic movements, those which really were involved in the struggle for independence and the creation of a new independent state. Sweden took a very clear and wise stand. We saw that.

TS: Do you believe that Olof Palme played an important part in this context?

PJ: I had the privilege of meeting Olof Palme a couple of times. It was obvious that he took a very special position towards the liberation movements on the African continent. There was a very interesting episode. I do not recall the year, but at that time I was Foreign Minister of Angola and there was a meeting in Maputo. Prime Minister Olof Palme attended that meeting.

At a dinner given by President Samora Machel, I was seated at a table with Machel, Palme, Joaquim Chissano, the Foreign Minister of Mozambique, and other leaders. On that occasion, something happened that underlined Palme's involvement for the liberation of the African continent. And because of his involvement and commitment towards the liberation movements, he was given an honorary title. We began to address Prime Minister Olof Palme as an 'honorary freedom fighter'.

TS: Despite the fact that Sweden never supported the armed struggle?

PJ: Of course. The aim of the assistance was to help the people. There was never any military support. When that dinner took place in Maputo, Angola and Mozambique were already independent countries. In this context, I also remember something which it is important to point out. In 1978, I made an official visit to Sweden as Foreign Minister. At the end of the visit, the first cooperation agreement was signed between Angola and Sweden. At that time, Ola Ullsten from the Liberal Party led the Ministry of International Cooperation. We signed the first agreement, through which SIDA pledged to give Angola a non-reimbursable grant of 50 million Swedish Kronor. I was Minister of Foreign Affairs from 1976 until 1984. When my mandate ended in 1984, the assistance from SIDA was close to 200 million. It was increased a little every year. It was almost automatic. SIDA's assistance constituted an extraordinary economic and social support. I was pleased because the first agreement between independent Angola and Sweden was signed by me and the minister from the Liberal Party.

TS: Do you believe that Amílcar Cabral played a part in the establishing of relations between MPLA and Sweden?

PJ: I do not know if there was a personal intervention by him. What happened was that MPLA, PAIGC and FRELIMO—later also CLSTP of São Tomé and Principe—had very close relations within CONCP. Amílcar Cabral, Eduardo Mondlane and Marcelino dos Santos used to go to Sweden and, of course, they also discussed the struggle in Angola. If it was a leader from MPLA—Mário de Andrade, Agostinho Neto or Lúcio Lara—who went, they would, naturally, similarly discuss the progress of the struggle in Guinea-Bissau or Mozambique. There was a very close relationship. We met annually and we discussed strategies together. It was quite natural that when Amílcar Cabral went to Sweden he would talk about MPLA and support for MPLA. He would certainly make the same contribution as Marcelino dos Santos when he went to Sweden and talked about PAIGC and MPLA.

TS: In a letter from Agostinho Neto to Olof Palme, written after the Inter-Regional Conference in 1974, Neto mentioned a certain 'misunderstanding' that had occurred at the level of the Swedish embassy in Lusaka. Do you know what that was about?

PJ: There was the so-called Eastern Revolt led by Daniel Chipenda. At that time, he belonged to the Steering Committee of MPLA on the eastern front, where he was one of the main leaders. He was the person who on MPLA's behalf was in contact with various organizations, including international support organizations and the embassies. When the problem of the Eastern Revolt occurred—initially created by the dissatisfaction of a small ethnic group in the area of Moxico—Chipenda wanted to take advantage of the rebellion to challenge the leadership of Agostinho Neto. But the Eastern Revolt did not have any great chances of succeeding. It did not have sufficient support. However, when this took place there was a kind of paralysis. The diplomatic missions and the solidarity organizations in Zambia suspended their assistance for a while in order to understand what had happened.

TS: Did the Soviet Union also suspend its assistance?

PJ: Yes, they did. As far as I know, one of the countries that did not suspend assistance and maintained its position was Yugoslavia.

TS: And Cuba?

PJ: Naturally. Cuba was always completely behind us. But even the Soviet Union suspended its assistance. We had to explain the situation to them. Meanwhile, after the Eastern Revolt the Active Revolt broke out in the area of Cabinda and Congo-Brazzaville. The underlying cause of both the Eastern Revolt and the Active Revolt was an offensive by the Portuguese army on the eastern front. Using chemicals and defoliants, the Portuguese army forced the MPLA soldiers and the people living in the liberated areas to withdraw to Zambian territory. It involved a large number of people and during the first days it was very difficult for us to organize food supplies. We had to make a great effort to arrange the financial means and the food to be able to receive these people.

This situation led us to organize a congress between MPLA and those two factions, the Eastern Revolt and the Active Revolt in Zambia at the end of July 1974. As we did not reach an agreement, MPLA decided to leave the congress and move inside Angola and hold a new conference there. It was exactly 1 August 1974. It was also the day that the constitution of FAPLA, the Popular Armed Forces for the Liberation of Angola was declared. We all went inside Angola and in the middle of September the Inter-Regional Conference of Militants was organized. It elected a new Central Committee and established a course of action for an independent Angola, because the coup of 25 April 1974 had already taken place in Portugal.

Lúcio Lara
MPLA—Secretary for Organization and Cadres
Former President of the National Assembly
(Luanda, 16 April 1996)

Tor Sellström: Representing MPLA, when did you come into contact with the Nordic countries?

Lúcio Lara: The first contact was with Denmark. We built a kind of educational institute at Dolisie in Congo-Brazzaville, close to the border with Cabinda. We received support from SIDA and the Danish organization WUS. The students from World University Service helped us to build that educational centre. They sent us construction materials and an administrator, Peder Sidelmann, who still works with us in Cabinda.

TS: At that time, you served as MPLA's Secretary of Organization and Training?

LL: Yes. I still have the whole educational collection that we managed to produce. The mathematics book was one of the books printed in Sweden. That was the first contact we had. In 1971, Peder Sidelmann and the General Secretary of WUS invited me to Denmark for discussions. While I was in Denmark, I took the opportunity to establish the first contact with SIDA in Sweden.

In 1972, I went to the Swedish Social Democratic Party congress as a delegate of my party. We were in Stockholm during the congress and we established very good relations. It was very interesting. The main personality was Mme Binh from FNL of Vietnam. Amílcar Cabral from PAIGC was also there. I do not recall who was there from Mozambique. We had a march in Stockholm in favour of the liberation movements. The only photograph I have is with Prime Minister Olof Palme.

TS: Mário de Andrade had by then published some articles in the Swedish newspapers and President Neto had already visited Sweden. There was some knowledge about MPLA. But the first concrete support was to the Dolisie school?

LL: Yes. With a lot of help from Sweden and Denmark and with the government of Congo as an intermediary.

TS: Norway also supported schools for Angolans in Zambia. Were they run by MPLA?

LL: Yes.

TS: Were they of the same kind as the Mozambique Institute in Dar es Salaam?

LL: No. Our curriculum was both for children and freedom fighters.

TS: Was this part of MPLA's Centre of Revolutionary Training (CIR)?

LL: Yes. The Dolisie school was at the same place, but separate, because there we had programmes connected with classical training. We had two types of training, revolutionary and classical.

This year I am going to have an exhibition of the books that we edited at that time. I have them all. I lost one set. When I came to Luanda, I loaned it to the Ministry of Education, but they lost it. However, I kept one at home. They want me to have an exhibition on education because of the 40th anniversary of MPLA. An exhibition of the books we used. Among the books is the mathematics book edited in Sweden. I was there to correct the drafts. Alberto Neto was our representative in Sweden.

TS: You are a mathematics teacher by training?

LL: Yes, of physics and mathematics. I even worked as a physics and mathematics teacher when I was in exile in Conakry.

TS: Coming from a very different world, how did you view the Nordic countries then?

LL: In the Nordic countries, we were pleased and encouraged to find complete understanding. At the time, we were very anti-American. It is only now that we have good relations with the United States. The Americans were our main enemy, but Germany and France also supported Portugal a lot. Germany had aeroplanes at the Beja airbase and gave weapons to Portugal. France created political difficulties for the liberation movements. We had to pass through France clandestinely. We had passports from Guinea-Conakry and Congo.

Neto once came to Paris, but they did not let him enter the country. They saw his name on the screen and refused him entrance. France made it difficult for us. The Nordics were very co-operative, understanding and dynamic. There was an active solidarity, not only speeches or words. They showed a kind of equality and comprehension that we were also to find with the Dutch in the Angola-Committee. They were also very dynamic, although not as generous because they did not have the same means as the Nordics. Above all, the Nordics gave us concrete support and materials. For the Dolisie school they assisted us with machetes, hoes and seeds, because that was also a part of education. It was very useful.

TS: Later Sweden donated trucks and other means of transport for MPLA's eastern front activities. Was that not strange to you? After all, Sweden and the other Nordic countries were part of the Western world?

LL: Their attitude showed total understanding. Actually, they had the same attitude towards Guinea-Bissau. It even made us a little jealous. They assisted PAIGC much more. We compared the figures in terms of the size of the countries and saw the difference. The reason was the presence of Amílcar Cabral. He was very dynamic and always on top of events. That was very important.

TS: There were strong links between Sweden and PAIGC.

LL: Yes, and also with Vietnam.

TS: Did that help you to understand why Sweden assisted MPLA?

LL: Yes. It was a natural solidarity, without conditions and demands. It was much appreciated. We were regarded as Marxists, Communists etc., but Sweden never gave us any problems.

TS: Olof Palme wanted practical results. Is it also your opinion that Palme was a man of achievements?

LL: Yes. First of all, he was in favour of active support to the liberation struggles and he had the ability to understand the root of the problems. He did not fall into the traps others did. He did not hesitate. At the same time, he was very humanistic and that helped him in the choices he made.

TS: But many criticized Palme. They said that he was more interested in the Third World than in Sweden?

LL: That characterized his active solidarity. He sometimes sacrificed domestic issues, just as we did in the struggle against apartheid. Angola sacrificed a lot to defend a cause that concerned the whole of Southern Africa and the entire world. The Angolan people sacrificed the most.

TS: Sweden and the other Nordic countries channelled a lot of support to ANC and SWAPO in Angola. Did you never see this as interference in your internal affairs?

LL: No, not at all. Solidarity has a broader dimension. Precisely because Angola had earlier benefited from this kind of solidarity on the part of Sweden and the Nordic countries, we understood perfectly well that Sweden wanted to assist those that Angola was also supporting in our country. We did not see that as interference at all.

TS: However, Sweden and the Nordic countries did not support the armed struggle. At the United Nations, for example, they could not vote in favour of resolutions that made reference to violence. Did you see this as a problem or did you understand the position of the Nordic countries?

LL: From the beginning of the armed struggle, we were used to being very careful with that aspect. For example, we gave a signal for the insurrection of 4 February 1961 at a press conference in the House of Commons in London attended by Mário de Andrade, Viriato da Cruz, Américo Boavida, Aristides Pereira and two persons from Goa—which was also part of our Anti-Colonial Movement (MAC). We worked together. We had not yet separated into national movements. We just called ourselves MAC. Although PAIGC of Guinea-Bissau and MPLA already existed, we did not present them to the public because many people had been imprisoned in Angola.

When we had that press conference, Fenner Brockway and Basil Davidson—who supported us in London—asked us not to talk about armed struggle. We therefore talked about 'direct action'. We learned very soon to deal with the sensibility of assemblies, members of parliament and national oppositions in countries that wanted to help us. We always understood that.

TS: At the time of Angola's independence, MPLA had problems with the Socialist Party of Portugal (PSP) while the Nordic Social Democratic Parties supported PSP. How did you look upon that?

LL: Well, in Angola we call it *'makas'* (problems). But the problem was not with the Socialist Party, which was almost non-existent at that time. It was Mário Soares' preconceptions, which lasted until the end, well, until today. Wrongly, he always believed that we were agents of the Portuguese Communist Party (PCP), which is untrue.

When we were preparing for MAC, the Communist Party invited us—not as MAC, because we never said anything to the Portuguese, but as a group of revolutionaries from the colonies—to send an observer to the fifth congress of PCP in 1957. We chose the poet Noémia de Sousa. But at the last moment she was unable to go and I was appointed to attend. It was in Lisbon, somewhere near Cascais. We went in a special kind of taxi that was very big and normally used for weddings, lying on the floor. The car drove into a garage. We went through a tunnel which they had dug from the garage to the house. We only saw the roof of the tunnel and then we were in the house where the congress took place. I stayed there for about five days. At that fifth congress, the Portuguese Communist Party for the first time took a clear position in favour of freedom and independence for the Portuguese colonies. Before that they wanted to help us to organize, but we never let them.

I knew Joe Slovo of the South African Communist Party very well. We were very good friends. His party's philosophy was South African. It was not paternalistic. It was nationalist. The Portuguese Communists did not understand that. They more or less tried to recruit us to work in the colonies as members of the Portuguese Communist Party. But I was contacted by the *Angolan* Communist Party, through Viriato da Cruz. Yesterday I found the credentials, with the photograph he gave me of the person I should contact here. It was the *Angolan* Communist Party. We never even considered working in Angola as Portuguese.

I fled from Portugal because I had been to that PCP congress. After almost two years, the police found out who had been there. There was a man from the Central Committee who betrayed us and someone from the party warned me. He was also fleeing and came to my house for shelter. He told me that 'so-and-so betrayed us. He gave the police a list of everyone present at the congress, so we have to leave'. Our guiding principle was not to let ourselves be taken by the Portuguese secret police, PIDE. It was better to flee to a foreign country than to be sent to a Portuguese jail. I therefore went to tell Agostinho Neto. I had a Communist colleague and I also told him: 'Look, I am going to leave, because I know that someone betrayed the Portuguese Communist Party and gave away the names of those who were at the congress. My street is already being watched and in a day or two they will take me'. That guy then went to tell the leaders of the Portuguese Communist Party. He returned and said: 'You cannot do this. It is a mistake. We will protect you. We will be responsible for your security. Go underground and we will take care of you'. But I said to him: 'We do not want to be dependent on you and be your responsibility. We have to take care of our own lives'. They never understood that. And they became very upset.

TS: Maybe the difference between Olof Palme, Mário Soares or Álvaro Cunhal was colonialism? Sweden did not have a colonial heritage.

LL: Of course. But Álvaro Cunhal was a very wise man and in touch with the people. He easily learned what was wrong in his ideas. You discussed with him and he saw what was wrong and then he corrected it. That is very important. Mário Soares always saw us as connected to the Portuguese Communist Party, but there was never any connection. There was not, because we were the colonized people and we accepted neither the Communist Party nor the Portuguese government.

Having colonies immediately conditions the outlook—even the revolutionary thinking—within the colonizing countries. Of political parties as well as of countries. Talking in Marxist terms great perception is necessary in order to overcome the myths and the determinants that the colonial system imposes on the working classes. In our struggle, we said that the whites in Angola generally had an attitude against the indigenous people. It was necessary to overcome that and some did.

Not having colonies represents an advantage over the colonizing countries when we talk about revolutionary parties, which have to struggle against and overcome many constraints.

TS: Do you think that there were conditions attached to the support given by the Nordic countries to MPLA?
LL: No. Absolutely not. The natural respect and sympathy that we always enjoyed from our friends in the Nordic countries in general is explained by the fact that they in their expressions of material support and solidarity never imposed any conditions, demanding that we did this or that. We ourselves were informed by that. We were affected by the idea of non-conditional support. SWAPO and ANC were here and we never imposed any conditions upon them.
TS: Did Angola co-ordinate policy at the United Nations and within the Non-Aligned Movement with the Nordic countries?
LL: Yes, especially in the Non-Aligned Movement. The Nordics always gave us very important support. Policies were co-ordinated. There were meetings where we discussed strategies for every document and each position.

TS: Do you believe then that in relation to Zimbabwe, Namibia and South Africa, the Nordic countries enlarged the political space for the liberation movements?
LL: Yes, of course. It was an opening and more or less an alliance of beliefs. The Western countries were generally colonialist and reactionary, but the Nordic countries offered us support in the midst of the Western world. That was necessary to break through some barriers and carry some resolutions and votes.
TS: In the case of Sweden, the first official support to MPLA was given in 1971. In that way, Sweden *de facto* recognized MPLA as a government-in-waiting?
LL: Yes. I myself was received at the Ministry for Foreign Affairs for a meeting with SIDA to present our projects.
TS: Did you feel that Sweden recognized MPLA as the representative of the Angolan people?
LL: Yes, and that was very early.

Ruth Neto
MPLA
President of the Organization of Angolan Women (OMA)
(Luanda, 16 April 1996)

Tor Sellström: When did you come into contact with the Nordic countries?
Ruth Neto: I started to participate directly in the struggle in 1968, and I think that in 1968-69 there were people from the Nordic countries—particularly from Sweden—who came to Dar es Salaam to make contact with the liberation movements, and in our case with MPLA. At that time, I got to know some people from Sweden who not only visited Dar es Salaam, but also our eastern front in Angola.
TS: When did you go into exile?
RN: I left Luanda in 1956. I only returned in 1975. I spent the first years studying in Portugal. I also attended a religious course. I lived at an evangelical home where Graça Machel later lived. In 1960, I left for Germany, because I could not return to Angola due to the persecution from PIDE. They had already imprisoned my brother and my family advised me not to return.

I went to Germany—to Lüdenscheid—a town close to Cologne, where we knew a family who received my fiancé and me. At first, I worked in a factory. Thereafter, I moved to Frankfurt, where I took a training post as a nurse. I wanted to become a clinical analyst. Later, I went to Freiburg to enrol in a clinical analyst course. At the beginning of 1968, my brother—who was already the President of MPLA—passed through Vienna, Austria, and I went to meet him there. In April of the same year—when our new front had opened in the east—I went with his family to Dar es Salaam. I stayed in Dar es Salaam for some time, working in the MPLA office. Later I was transferred to our third political-military region at the border between Angola and Zambia.
TS: At that time you had not yet visited Sweden?
RN: No, not yet. My first visit to Sweden took place in 1976, after independence. We

were invited by the Left Association of Swedish Women (SKV). The contacts with the women were mainly in the form of seminars, meetings and exchange of experiences between not only Swedish women, but also women from other African and European countries. These contacts were always very good, because there were new experiences for us to acquire. They also served to inform about the situation of the women within the liberation movement.

TS: What were your impressions from the culturally so different Nordic countries?

RN: Well, they were not only culturally different, but in every way. For example, the climate. During the first couple of meetings, we suffered tremendously because we went there during winter. The difference between Dar es Salaam or Luanda and Stockholm is huge. We also noticed that there was little knowledge about Africa and our work, our struggle. Especially from those who had never had any contact with women from other countries. Anyhow, these meetings had a positive effect. That was proven by the interest in helping us that was shown later. At each meeting we explained who we were and what the reasons behind our struggle were. That contributed to a better understanding of our cause and helped us to gain some solidarity, good collaboration and, above all, comprehension of our problems.

TS: Would you say that the relationship between your brother and Olof Palme was close?

RN: You could say so. They met a couple of times to discuss common interests. The relations were good.

TS: Do you believe that those common interests were related to the nationalist process?

RN: Yes. I believe that Sweden was concerned about our countries. Colonialism was coming to an end and there was a need for great support from honest and known people that could help the pursuit of the struggle for self-determination. On this point Sweden played a very important role. They received nationalists who they helped diplomatically and morally. Later they even helped us materially. I think this was the issue. The other parties and Swedish groups—mainly on the left—also condemned colonialism and imperialism. Those positions helped us.

TS: Did you get to know Lisbet Palme?

RN: I met her two or three years ago. Annie Marie Sundbom had invited us to visit Stockholm. We visited several places, and at the end we were invited to a conference about children where Lisbet Palme was the main speaker.

TS: What kind of projects did the Left Association of Swedish Women support in Angola? Were they also educational?

RN: Yes, some were educational. But the organization that distinguished itself the most was the Africa Groups, which supported various projects and used to visit us many times to see how we used the materials that they sent us. From SKV we got material support for the women, especially things that had to do with household tasks, for example needle-work, linen and machines. There were a number of projects developed by us with the objective to raise funds for our organization, the Organization of Angolan Women (OMA). The Africa Groups gave us tremendous support by sending us used clothes. We gave some to the most needy people and sold others to raise funds.

Unfortunately, after the multiparty elections the cooperation has not been very efficient. SKV argues that OMA continues as MPLA's women's organization, and that it is now important to help all women. Maybe they were hoping that OMA would be established as a non-governmental organization. It is not as yet. At this moment we are trying to establish a women's movement from several parties and various associations. It is a lot of hard work, but OMA manages. We especially manage well in the provinces, but it is very difficult. The situation is very tough. The problems have increased and the women are poorer. They are displaced, widowed, have no homes and their children are missing. There are a series of problems. This is all the result of the war.

TS: A question many ask is how Sweden came into contact with MPLA. Do you think that Amílcar Cabral played a part there?

RN: I do not really know, but it is possible that he could have influenced that.

TS: In a letter from Agostinho Neto to Olof Palme, he wrote after the Inter-Regional Conference in 1974: 'We have reflected on the need to render the relations between our two organizations closer, since our countries in a near future, definitely, are destined to establish important links of cooperation in areas of common interest'. As women from OMA, did you have any contacts with the Social Democratic women in Sweden at that time?

RN: I believe so. For example, Annie Marie Sundbom is a Social Democrat. She was one of the first Swedish women that I knew. There was also a group of Social Democratic women from SKV who kept in touch with us. SIDA too. There are Social Democratic women in SIDA. Those were the contacts we had. What I did not understand was that SKV was a broader organization. I thought that it was a branch of the Swedish Social Democratic women.

I would like to add that I knew the late Bernt Carlsson from the Socialist International. On one of our visits to Sweden, he came to us to know more about MPLA's struggle. I got a very good impression of him. He came looking for us to exchange points of view and that really impressed me.

TS: He died in the Lockerbie air disaster. He was the United Nations Commissioner for Namibia at the time.

RN: Yes, it was very sad.

Miguel N'Zau Puna
UNITA—Secretary General and Political Commissar of the Armed Forces for the Liberation of Angola (FALA)
Leader of the Movement for Democratic Reflection (TRD)
(Luanda, 17 April 1996)

Tor Sellström: Do you remember when UNITA had its first contacts with the Nordic countries?

Miguel N'Zau Puna: I think that it was right after the foundation of UNITA in 1966. In 1965, UNITA started to recruit men and send them for training in China. At the same time, in the beginning UNITA also had some Swedish friends who helped us, such as Lars-Gunnar Eriksson, responsible for student co-ordination at COSEC, and Pierre Schori, who had direct contacts with President Savimbi and other people in UNITA.

Through Eriksson, we used to travel. He helped us with tickets for the journeys from Cairo to Switzerland and back and for the trips to Tunisia, where I was a student. He even arranged the trip from Cairo to Dar es Salaam, Lusaka and our entry into Angola in 1968. Our contacts with Sweden were through Lars-Gunnar Eriksson and Pierre Schori. Eriksson was a great friend of ours. When we were in Cairo, he came to visit us at home in Zamalek. We talked and analyzed the liberation movements. In 1967, Savimbi visited Sweden and the other Nordic countries thanks to the support of Schori and Eriksson and openings by them. They worked a lot. The Swedish funds were arranged through Eriksson and it was he who organized the trip which gave Savimbi the opportunity to visit Sweden, Norway and Denmark. We then started to have more co-operation through Schori, who was closer to the Swedish Socialist Party. Our relations with Sweden from 1966 until 1968 were good.

When UNITA decided to send the leadership into Angola, Savimbi and I had to leave Cairo. Savimbi pretended to be heading for Switzerland and I pretended that I was on my way to an OAU conference. I came to Dar es Salaam first. Through our SWAPO friends—with whom we had good relations—we started to understand that there was a Swedish initiative to support MPLA. MPLA was already based there and recognized by OAU and the United Nations. UNITA was not. With our entry into the interior of Angola, our contacts with Schori and Eriksson were then in practice cut off. After UNITA's second congress in 1968, the leadership wrote a letter to Olof Palme, trying to re-establish the relations with our Swedish friends.

TS: Was it at that congress that you were elected Secretary General?

MNP: Well, it was at the second congress that I was elected Secretary General, a position that I already had, but only in an acting capacity. At the second congress, I was elected General Secretary of the party and

Political Commissar of FALA, UNITA's military forces. From then on, we started to develop the activity of our organization. But the Cold War had started. It began to divide the liberation movements into two camps. There were movements that were supported by the Soviet Union and others by the West. At that time, we were neither supported by the Soviet Union or the West, but by the Chinese. As all the UNITA cadres had been trained in China, we started to receive more Chinese help. It was difficult, because there was polarization. An African group—'the progressives'—supported MPLA because they regarded it as the only movement, while the 'moderates' supported FNLA. This created great difficulties for UNITA's development.

TS: It was at the Khartoum conference in 1969 that the so-called 'authentic' movements were recognized by the Soviet Union?

MNP: Yes. The so-called 'authentics'—or 'the progressives'—were in the Soviet sphere and stated that they were the only ones. The others were CIA agents.

UNITA was prejudiced by the fact that OAU did not adhere to the stipulations in its foundation charter. In the charter, it was written that whenever a liberation movement was created, an OAU commission should go to the country to verify if the movement really existed. Unfortunately, in our case this never happened, despite the letters we sent to OAU, asking them to visit the areas controlled by UNITA. One thing should be underlined: there were several liberation movements—FNLA, MPLA and others—but the only movement with a permanent leadership inside the country was UNITA.

We had to survive and in order to survive we had to find a way to attract the people to our side. Our best defence was the people, because we were not recognized, we did not have any weapons or any external support. We had to buy weapons illegally in Katanga, Zaire, and move them through Zambia into Angola. This is how we fought. From time to time, our friends in SWAPO—which was recognized by OAU and received weapons, but did not have the men in Namibia to fight with those weapons—helped us. That is how UNITA was growing stronger.

We never forgot our first friends. When there was reconciliation between UNITA and FNLA in 1975, Savimbi also went to Kinshasa to seek reconciliation with Mobutu himself. He then went to Dar es Salaam, where he met Agostinho Neto. There was reconciliation, and in 1975 we went to Mombasa to participate in the Mombasa agreement. UNITA was thus reconciled with FNLA and MPLA. There only remained the need for bilateral reconciliation between MPLA and FNLA.

OAU only recognized UNITA after the meeting in Mombasa and when we went to Alvor we had the status of a liberation movement. OAU and the United Nations accepted that there were three liberation movements in Angola, UNITA, MPLA and FNLA, although in the beginning the others claimed that they were the only ones. MPLA said that they were the only one and FNLA said the same. We said: 'We also exist!' Eventually, the international community could verify our existence. Kurt Waldheim, the Secretary General of the United Nations, went to Portugal to discuss with the Portuguese authorities. They confirmed that UNITA was a true liberation movement, because it had areas where it was fighting. After that, there was no other alternative but to accept UNITA as a liberation movement.

However, then the situation became unstable. Instead of finding a common understanding each movement started to build up forces to be ahead of the others. MPLA was looking for weapons, FNLA was looking for weapons and also UNITA was looking for weapons. This cannot be explained by patriotic duty, but simply by hegemony. Each movement wanted to be ahead of the others. That is why in 1975 instead of a united proclamation of independence there were two proclamations. There was the independence proclamation by MPLA in Luanda and the one from the UNITA/FNLA coalition in Huambo. But it was the one in Luanda that was recognized, because it was made in the capital. Internationally, whoever holds the capital represents the strongest force. The issue was not whether MPLA was better or UNITA worse, but that MPLA went to Luanda and therefore was in a better position to get support from everybody.

But what revitalized MPLA was the presence of the Cuban army. It changed the scenario completely, because MPLA, UNITA and FNLA did not have regular armies. When the Cuban army arrived, the whole situation changed automatically. That is why I believe that to achieve peace today, all Angolans have to sit down, turn the page and forget the past. When we speak about our heroes, we have to speak about the heroes of MPLA, the heroes of UNITA and the heroes of FNLA. That is how we can say that we are all represented. But if we only speak about one movement, the frustration will continue and there will never be any understanding.

TS: Considering that the Nordic countries are Western countries, how would you explain that they supported the same movements that were assisted by the Soviet bloc?

MNP: Sweden believed that the African countries had a right to liberate themselves. In spite of threats from NATO and others, they considered it just that the African countries obtained their freedom. The right to self-determination and independence is a right of all peoples. With the contacts that they started to have with the African peoples they noticed that support was needed to achieve what 'we have already achieved'. Therefore, many Africans went to Sweden. I did not go myself. I was supposed to, but I had to go inside Angola. Savimbi went. Other members of UNITA went to Sweden several times and they also visited the other Nordic countries. Sweden influenced all the Nordic countries to support the liberation movements. They even started to give political asylum to many Africans. This allowed them to get established, not only by sending messages to other Africans living in those countries, but also by explaining to the Swedish and Nordic peoples what the objective of our struggle was. The objective of our struggle was not against the Europeans or the Americans, but a just cause.

From Sweden there was much understanding, but from the Soviet Union the support was only ideological. Sweden did not impose an ideology. They said: 'Yes, we can see that you are suffering'. There is also the fact that as Sweden had little knowledge about Africa, it supported certain movements that did not represent anything in their respective countries. But that was due to lack of experience. Sweden's intentions were good. I think that the intention was to support all the movements to see if they could reach their objectives.

I had contacts with China and other countries. From Cairo—and later through African countries—we always had contacts, but our first contacts were really with Sweden.

However, with Savimbi and me inside Angola and not being recognized by OAU, we could not come out. We had to fight from inside. That resistance—and I can say this without being contradicted by anyone—must have been one of the best guerrilla campaigns Africa has ever experienced. Being inside the country and fighting with the people was not easy. The other leaders were abroad and sent others to fight. They sent troops to fight while they were accommodated in neighbouring countries. But we were right in there. When the other movements saw our methods, the courage and the internal organization, they started to say that we were a Portuguese creation. That UNITA had been created by PIDE and other such accusations. President Savimbi may have committed certain mistakes, but in the most essential matter—to mobilize the people, to lead the people and to live with the people—he was outstanding.

Even today, MPLA keeps claiming that 'we are the only ones'. But one can go to Cazombo and ask: 'Who was the first commander who came here?' and the people will answer: 'He was from UNITA'.

UNITA was penalized because the Western countries supported the 'moderates', that is FNLA, while the 'progressives' supported MPLA. We were considered pro-Chinese. But at that time the Chinese had little influence in Africa. There were some movements with pro-Chinese tendencies, such as ZANU of Zimbabwe—the major part of its cadres were trained in China—PAC of South Africa, which was allied with UNITA, and SWANU of Namibia, which was not very efficient at that time.

Now, in spite of having pro-Soviet tendencies, SWAPO had fraternal bonds with us. A common culture and a common past. In those days, we did not go in for ideology. We looked at ethnic affinity and, above all, regional affinity.

TS: Did SWAPO go through areas under UNITA control to enter Namibia?

MNP: Yes. That was the only way that they could get into Namibia.

TS: Was there a tactical alliance between UNITA and SWAPO?

MNP: There was a strategic and tactical alliance. Many soldiers from UNITA fought with SWAPO. We also made some incursions into Namibian territory under UNITA's General Commander Samuel Chiwale, who is now a general. There was Francisco Kulunga, who fought a lot on the other side to help our friends in SWAPO. We also had Commander Lucas Canjimi. He is from Kavango, on the border with Namibia. His nephews are here and his uncles on the other side. It is the same family.

TS: Sweden had good relations with SWANU, SWAPO and the Socialist Party in Portugal (PSP). You also had good relations with SWANU, SWAPO and PSP. Why did you never establish direct contacts with the Social Democratic Party in Sweden?

MNP: We did, with Olof Palme's party. But when we went inside Angola, the contact was in practice broken. But the feelings remained, because they were the first to open the door to us. At the same time, we benefited from the good relations between SWAPO and Sweden, because we had friends like Andreas Shipanga, who used to visit Sweden frequently, or Emil Appolus, who also went there. We also had Peter Katjavivi in Norway. We had a close affinity with everyone in SWAPO and SWANU. After moving to the interior, we got better contacts with SWAPO because they had fighting forces. We also had good relations with Mugabe's ZANU. Mugabe's journey to China was at Savimbi's request as he already had good relations with China. Savimbi had visited and also trained in China. This is how Mugabe managed to go to there.

TS: Later, when the relations with Sweden no longer existed, a Swedish conservative MP, Birger Hagård, visited Jamba. From the mid-1980s, he was very active and co-founded a support committee for UNITA in Sweden. Did you know about that?

MNP: Yes, we did. The person who co-ordinated that was Jorge Sangumba, our representative in London. He was the one who sent Luís Antunes to Sweden and it was through Antunes that the MP visited Jamba.

TS: In September 1987, UNITA kidnapped three Swedes in Quibaxe. It was very difficult for the Swedish opinion to understand why this happened, since Sweden gave humanitarian and development assistance to Angola. Two men were taken to Jamba and the third was killed.

MNP: I remember it very well. At that time we thought that if we kidnapped some foreigners, the international community would perhaps become more aware of our struggle. The UNITA area commander decided to kidnap them without knowing the relationship between the leadership of UNITA and Sweden. They went on foot to the Lunda provinces. One of them died. I think that he died during the ambush in Quibaxe. After that, they went down to Jamba. They were then released through the Red Cross. The buried body was later found and returned to Sweden.

This happened because our soldiers did not know the relationship we had with the Swedes. They thought: 'Well, they are like the others' and kidnapped them. But we told them 'You did wrong, because we have a past relationship with the Swedes'. It was more or less like that. It was not something intentional. It was rather 'if we kidnap these persons, people will talk about us'. No one spoke about the struggle we were fighting. After some time, we stopped the kidnappings. We kidnapped Swedes, Englishmen and many others. But we reached a point where it was not worth it.

TS: Do you think that the Nordic countries contributed anything constructive to the process of national liberation and self-determination in Southern Africa?

MNP: I think so, because the Swedish presence in several African countries supported the liberation movements. It was most notable in Tanzania, where the OAU Liberation Committee was and where all the movements were represented. Sweden did not only support the liberation movements, but also the reconstruction of the countries which had recently obtained independence. That was the case in Tanzania, Kenya and Zambia. We could therefore see that the Swedish presence was important, not only in support of those that were fighting for their freedom, but also for the countries that were developing. I believe that it is a support that should be taken into consideration. In comparison with many other European countries, Sweden played a fundamental part. The African countries which benefited from this assistance must not forget that. They should not only maintain the relations, but improve them even more. That is my opinion.

Alberto Ribeiro-Kabulu
MPLA—Director of the Service for Radio and Telecommunications
Minister of Industry and Energy
Ambassador of Angola to Zimbabwe
(Harare, 5 May 1996)

Tor Sellström: Did you as a young MPLA student in Portugal have any contacts with the Nordic countries?

Alberto Ribeiro-Kabulu: In Portugal, we had a front organization called *Casa dos Estudantes do Império*, which had students from all the former Portuguese colonies, but the biggest group was from Angola. We organized ourselves underground and managed to leave Portugal in 1961, after the outbreak of the armed struggle in Angola. We were together with our comrades from Mozambique, Guinea-Bissau, Cape Verde and Goa. After passing through Paris, we went to Ghana, where we set up a new organization called the General Union of Students from Black Africa under Portuguese Colonial Domination (UGEAN). The first congress of UGEAN took place in Rabat, Morocco, in August-September 1961.

The first contacts that we had with student groups in the Nordic countries, Germany, France and so on was at that congress. From then on, support was extended to us as a student organization via the World Assembly of Youth (WAY) and the World University Service (WUS).

There was very strong solidarity at the level of the students. I got a scholarship from the West German Students' Union to pursue university studies in Germany. I studied to become a telecommunications engineer. After I had finished my studies in Aachen, I worked in West Germany for three years with computers and in telecommunications before going to MPLA's Eastern Front in Angola in 1968.

President Agostinho Neto twice came to see the Angolan students in Germany and when MPLA organized the Eastern Front many cadres joined from different parts of the world. Neto asked me to set up the telecommunications services for the liberation struggle. Of course, the first condition was to find suitable people. I asked Neto to give me all the MPLA students who had been under technical training all over the world. That is how people who had studied in the former Soviet Union and elsewhere came to my squadron. It was a military squadron, called the SRT—Service for Radio and Telecommunications.

TS: I think that you had a petroleum engineer from the Soviet Union in your squadron, José Eduardo dos Santos, now President of Angola?

AR: Exactly. He and all the others who had been studying in the Communist countries. What was interesting was that my case was quite unusual, because I had graduated from a university in West Germany. It was Neto who insisted that I should have this responsibility, but in the days of the Cold War it had its limitations. I had no access to the Communist countries. I was not chosen for further training in the Soviet Union and I was only able to visit the socialist countries after our independence.

TS: It illustrates Neto's position in the bipolar world at the time?

AR: Yes. He was very independent, both in relation to thinking and in the way he was leading the struggle. He wanted to be at a comfortable distance to the countries that could help us militarily, that is the former socialist countries. Telecommunications was a very sensitive area, because it dealt with the codes and the secrets of the movement. We had fronts in Cabinda, in the Dembos region, in central and eastern Angola and offices on the other side of the continent, in Dar es Salaam. My first task was to organize a network of telecommunications so that we could talk from Dar es Salaam to Brazzaville, for instance, and from Brazzaville to the Eastern Front. Neto was always travelling, so this was crucial.

To know what was going on in the military structures of the enemy we also needed intelligence, and intelligence obviously comes from listening to the enemy. My first real cooperation with Sweden came through that. In around 1969, we had captured some radios from the Portuguese units in eastern Angola. They were very useful. I remember when they were brought to me. I immediately informed the MPLA leadership that we for the first time would be able to listen to the Portuguese and so we did. Later, we needed some supplies to change the frequencies. We then put the question to our friends from the Africa Groups in Sweden. That is how we came to know Hillevi and Lars Nilsson and the Swedish engineer who is still working with the Ministry of Defence in Luanda. We got very useful supplies from them.

TS: So, you had early contacts with the Swedish solidarity movement even inside Angola?

AR: Yes. We asked them to provide a good telecommunications engineer who could work with us. To my surprise I met a very quiet person, but a brilliant engineer. He came to see us in Lusaka and immediately started to work with us. We assembled the radios which we captured from the enemy. The main reason for using technology from the Western countries was that it was used by the Portuguese. To understand what was going on and to get intelligence from listening to their radio emissions, we had to have access to that. The second reason was, obviously, that the Western technology was by far superior.

One of the first tools that we used from 1968 was audio-tapes. We went into combat with audio-tapes. For instance, when ya Henda died in action at Karipande everything was recorded on a Philips audio-tape. One of the solidarity groups which supplied us with the necessary equipment was the Swedish Africa Groups. Our reports were mostly made on small tapes. That was completely new in the 1960s. It was something that only came onto the market at that time.

We also had another early form of cooperation which was very sensitive. I was asked by President Neto to protect our communications network as much as I could, because we were talking all across Africa, from Dar es Salaam to Brazzaville. Neto was very clear on one aspect. He asked me to invent something new and not follow the roads given to our trainees in the socialist countries. Our people who went for training in the Soviet Union, Cuba and so on brought us some knowledge of codes and cryptography. But Neto told me: 'Look, I don't want to use this. Try to invent something new'. When I finished my masters degree in Germany I had been working with computers and I had gained some knowledge related to that. However, I needed books on cryptography and mathematics, which I got through the solidarity groups. It was a very useful and little known support, including from Lars and Hillevi. With books for this specific area, we created our own code.

Some of our friends were not at all happy with that. In particular, of course, the liaison officials from the socialist countries. They also wanted to know what was going on. But it was Neto's clear position that 'we have to keep our own secrets and we will use this system'. Until the end of the war we used our own codes. We also used the equipment we had captured in action against the Portuguese to control things. In this connection, one very interesting event comes to my mind. After the April 1974 revolution in Portugal, I talked to our leaders and said: 'We are able to follow what is going on.' Neto was keen to sign a cease-fire inside Angola, not outside the country. So we initiated contacts with the Portuguese through the very same radios that they had used against us. It was really amazing. The Portuguese were very surprised when we met for the cease-fire in Moxico, seeing that we had such a well organized service, not only with regard to communications, but also to intelligence. Again, it was not only through our own achievement, but very much that of the solidarity committees, in this case specifically in Sweden.

Finally, after signing the cease-fire with the Portuguese we came to Luanda. At that time, we had the transitional government. One day President Neto asked me to go with the head of security of the MPLA to meet a Portuguese officer in charge of military intelligence. He was very surprised to learn that we were not using the methods of codification used, for instance, by FRELIMO and the other liberation movements. He wanted to know the reason why...

This is a clear illustration of the fact that MPLA never was completely under the control of foreign military advisers, which was the policy of Neto. He was very independent-minded in relation to that. Even stubborn. Of course, during all these years from 1968 to 1974, he sometimes put me in a very uncomfortable situation. But it is gratifying to know that we really had our own resources and that we used them for the liberation struggle.

TS: In 1969, the Swedish parliament paved the way for official support to the liberation movements. How did you view this development?

AR: Well, the Nordic countries knew that the sources of our struggle were genuine. They knew that from the early 1960s a group of real nationalists were fighting under the banner of MPLA and that it was a broad-based grouping, a front representing different tribes from different regions of the country and different classes, from students to sailors. From the lumpen proletariat to traditional chiefs.

In countries like Sweden, Denmark and Norway we had direct contacts with the civil society at the level of students and support committees. When I recall my personal ties with the Nordic countries—first of all with Sweden, Denmark and Norway—the support always began through the people, students, workers and trade-unionists. It was the civil society in those countries that channelled the message to their governments. In other cases, for instance in the socialist countries, the support came straight from the governments and from parties in one-party states. In the case of the Nordic countries, it first came through contacts from people to people. It was the civil society that was in touch with us. It made a big difference in relation to the support.

In addition, Neto was somehow seduced by Olof Palme, Sweden and the Nordic countries regarding the way that they understood the nationalist interest of their own countries, based on moral principles and independence in the divided bipolar world of the socialist and the capitalist blocs. He was seduced by that and also by the principles of social solidarity which were one of the bases of the Social Democratic Party in Sweden.

I recall a discussion between Neto and Olof Palme when Palme visited Angola with the Socialist International in 1977. At the time, the world was very polarized. It was during the worst days of the Cold War. Olof Palme told Agostinho Neto: 'With your background, your attitudes and the way in which you have led the liberation struggle, I cannot believe that you are a Marxist.' I think that it had some influence on Neto's immediate actions. We had been confronted by the terrible force of apartheid South Africa. To survive as a nation we had had no choice but to look for help where it was available. However, after the meeting with Palme, Neto immediately started to work on an independent settlement, which would include the withdrawal of the Cuban forces and the independence of Namibia. The real beginning of UN Resolution 435—which was negotiated in 1978—was a drive from Neto to have a settlement without the participation of outside forces. An independent settlement of the conflicts in South Western Africa—including Angola and Namibia—without the constraints of the Cold War polarization. I believe that Palme's advice was decisive in relation to this.

The death of Neto was very untimely. It was a sad event. He could have changed the course of history, because he had the blueprint for a solution. When I look back at some of the missions he gave me before his death in relation to the settlement of the conflict in Angola, to our problems with UNITA and to the contacts with the apartheid regime, the Cubans and the United States, I think that if he had had six months more of his life he could have implemented Resolution 435. Ten years thereafter we finally came to a settlement. In December 1988, we signed the agreement in New York. In the meantime we had lost ten years.

TS: There was thus a close relationship between Olof Palme and Agostinho Neto?

AR: Yes. The neutrality of Sweden was very important for this relationship. We were looking for support outside the Cold War polarization and it could only come from the Nordic countries, as indeed it did.

TS: Do you think that there were political or ideological conditions attached to the Swedish, or the Nordic, humanitarian support to MPLA?

AR: No, not at all. I also got the impression that the solidarity groups and the civil society in the Nordic countries—particularly in Sweden, but also in Denmark—were watchful in that context. They knew us very well. They had been with us in the liberated areas and they had played an important role for the official aid from the governments. Even if we sometimes faced constraints and limitations—for instance regarding four-wheel drive vehicles, which could be used for military purposes—the insistence of the solidarity movement always helped us to get things right.

TS: After independence, the Nordic countries continued to support the liberation movements in Angola, particularly SWAPO and ANC. Was this discussed with the Nordic governments? How did you look upon this support?

AR: The Nordic support to ANC and SWAPO in Angola was very welcome and part of our contacts. In the case of SWAPO, the entire leadership was in Angola since our independence.

We were very generous to ANC and, particularly, to SWAPO. SWAPO had almost complete autonomy, for instance, in Kwanza Sul. We had a lot in common with our Namibian comrades-in-arms in SWAPO, including culture, language and ethnicity.

SWAPO really enjoyed a high level of autonomy. I recall when ya Toivo was released from prison. The South Africans tried to bribe him to remain in Windhoek, but he refused and came to Luanda. I got to know him in those days. I was impressed by his courage and determination. At that time, we discussed with SWAPO the possible security arrangements that we could provide for an independent Namibia. That is when SWAPO for the first time started to discuss membership of the Commonwealth. We gave them complete freedom to make contacts at the highest diplomatic level in Luanda to discuss the issue. In my personal view, the only possible umbrella against apartheid South Africa was the Commonwealth, because we could not provide the necessary protection and the guarantees for the survival of Namibia. Anyway, this is an indication of the high degree of independence that SWAPO had. They could work in Luanda as a government. They had access to our government, but they also had access to the diplomatic corps.

TS: Did you coordinate policy at the United Nations with the Nordic countries?

AR: Oh, yes very much so. Martti Ahtisaari, for example, came to Angola many, many times to find out how to implement UN Resolution 435.

Holden Roberto
President of FNLA
(Luanda, 17 April 1996)

Tor Sellström: When did you enter into contact with the Nordic countries?

Holden Roberto: It was in the 1960s through David Wirmark, who is very well-known in African circles. He was General Secretary of the World Assembly of Youth and, later, Swedish ambassador to Tanzania. He knows Africa very well. He had contacts with several political parties and with the liberation movements in all of Southern Africa. Wirmark is well known and also my personal friend.

TS: He represented the Swedish Liberal Party and later defended official support to both MPLA and FNLA.

HR: Absolutely. At that time we looked for democracy. All the democrats in the world wanted to see the Portuguese colonies liberated.

TS: Considering that you are from a country which from cultural, historical and political points of view is very different from the Nordic countries, how did you interpret the Nordic stand on Southern Africa?

HR: I have the impression that the Nordic countries really practise true democracy. In our contacts with Denmark, Norway and Sweden, we noted during our liberation struggle that they also strongly supported our struggle for democracy. The Nordic countries helped a lot through international organizations and NGOs. We in FNLA had friends in Sweden. In 1972—at the head of a large delegation—I participated in the Liberal Party congress in Gothenburg. It was an important occasion for us and we increased our contacts. The Nordic countries know Africa very well, especially the liberation struggle by the African liberation groups.

TS: They are, however, Western countries. How would you explain their involvement in the struggle in Southern Africa?

HR: At the time of our struggle, the Western countries did not assist us. The Nordic countries are based on democracy and that is why they helped us. It may be part of their culture. They also fought to liberate themselves. They took a very positive and important position towards our liberation struggle. They had, in addition, no involvement in commercial or economic interests.

TS: No colonial heritage?

HR: No, there was no colonial heritage. Their major concern was to help the countries to liberate themselves from colonialism.

TS: Did FNLA also have contacts in Denmark, Finland and Norway?

HR: Yes, we did. But not as deep as in Sweden. Because in Sweden we had a friend, a woman journalist by the name of Brundin, who was very active. Unfortunately, she died in 1979 or 1980.

TS: Did she visit your bases?

HR: Many times. She was well informed about our activities and tried to get the Swedish government of the time to support us. But the politics of Prime Minister Olof Palme was more to the left. He had many links to MPLA. I remember when we came to Sweden with a big delegation in 1971. We had great difficulties in contacting the government. At the same time, there was a delegation from MPLA, led by Lúcio Lara. Whenever we tried to contact the authorities, the MPLA delegation was already there. The Secretary of State at the Ministry for Foreign Affairs was very pro-MPLA. All our explanations were in vain. The Swedish government was at that time very committed to MPLA.

TS: How would you explain that the Swedish Social Democratic Party supported movements which were aligned with Moscow?

HR: It is very strange. There was also the case of the World Council of Churches (WCC) in Geneva. It was more inclined to MPLA than to the parties that did not follow a Marxist line. We once received support from WCC and were told that MPLA had received more money than we had. At that time, MPLA was not at war. It was not fighting and had no front. We had 300,000 to 400,000 refugees and MPLA had no activity at all. But they received more money than we did!

I went personally to Geneva to talk with the World Council of Churches. Being a Protestant, I expected a warm welcome. The General Secretary was the Reverend Black, an American. I asked why MPLA had received more money than us. I wanted to know the criteria upon which they based their decision to give more money to MPLA. They said that it was WCC's policy. They received the money from Sweden and the Communist countries and could not do anything else. Later, Reverend Black called me and said that he wanted to have a word with me alone. I went to his house and he said: 'Look, we have a problem at the World Council of Churches. It is that the biggest part of the money that we receive comes from the Communist countries through the Orthodox churches. But that money comes with pre-established conditions. For instance, it must be given to FRELIMO, SWAPO, ANC, MPLA, ZAPU, PAIGC or MLSTP from São Tomé.'

TS: The so-called 'authentics'?

HR: Exactly. He also said 'we do not have much money for the other parties. NGOs from the Nordic countries give us some, but we receive specific orders not to give any money to FNLA. Only to the parties that are revolutionary'.

I then told Dr. Black: 'Under those circumstances, I am not prepared to accept your cheque. I do not believe that the church should be used as a vehicle for Communism in Africa. If the Communist countries give money with conditions attached, it is because they want to impose a certain ideology. We are struggling to liberate our country and, above all, to give our people the possibility to choose the future democratically. I do not agree to our having to commit ourselves ideologically when we are still colonized. I am going to return your cheque and I really regret that the World Council of Churches is a vehicle for Communism in Africa'. He said: 'I understand, but we cannot act in any other way. Otherwise, we will not be able to maintain unity in the World Council of Churches, because the Orthodox churches belong to the Communist countries'. This was a case that I experienced personally and, furthermore a case which had serious consequences. The infiltration of the Communists, of the Soviets, within the World Council of Churches. I returned the cheque and left Switzerland.

TS: In the case of Sweden, did you get an explanation from the Social Democratic Party?

HR: No, we did not get any explanation. They did not want to listen to us.

TS: The Social Democratic Party was a member of the Socialist International, which as a principle defended multi-party systems. In the case of Angola, the support from the Swedish government was, however, to one movement only. How did you look upon that?

HR: In democratic terms, we considered that a big mistake. At that time, we did not struggle for an ideology, but to liberate the Angolan people. To let the Angolan people freely choose their own way and not impose a direction at once. We did not understand the stand taken by the late Prime Minister Olof Palme's government. It was very strange.

TS: Did you have a representative in Sweden?

HR: Yes, we had Mateus Neto. But he did not get any support whatsoever. He had many problems. The support he had was from friends. He worked in order to be able to maintain our representation. We did not receive any government support.

TS: Did FNLA receive any support from the Liberal Party?

HR: Yes, but the Liberal Party was not in power. We had support, especially through Olle Wästberg. He had been to Angola and seen our activities. He wrote in the Swedish newspapers. But it had no effect.

TS: Did Wästberg and Brundin visit the FNLA base at Kinkuzu in Zaire?

HR: Yes, they were at the base. They saw the humanitarian activities, the hospitals and the aid to the refugees. It was very interesting. They took photographs. But there was no response from the Swedish government.

TS: When you visited Sweden in 1971, you spoke to the students at Stockholm University. How were you received by them?

HR: I was met very hospitably. I was very well received. Mrs. Brundin, who was a great friend and supported us a lot by making Angola's problems known in Sweden, was there. Unfortunately, the government had a very different attitude.

TS: In 1976, the Liberal Party formed part of a non-socialist coalition government in Sweden. At that point, was there no support for FNLA?

HR: Unfortunately, this was during the Cold War. The Soviet Union had already intervened in Angola, imposing a government. The Communist regime ruled with Cuban troops and with the presence of all the Warsaw Pact countries.

TS: Were there any Nordic organizations that sent material assistance to FNLA?

HR: We received some assistance—but it was not very important—from Norway. A small gift of medicines. We did not receive anything from Denmark. But I remember very well that we received assistance from Norway.

TS: At the diplomatic level, I understand that you frequently visited the Swedish ambassador in Kinshasa?

HR: Yes, we had contacts with the ambassador in Kinshasa, above all with the help of Mateus Neto, who came to Kinshasa. He talked to the ambassador, who was very impressed as Mateus Neto spoke in Swedish. He was very interested, but maybe the government did not follow up on his work.

TS: How would you describe your relations with the Swedish embassy in Kinshasa?

HR: Very good!

TS: And at the United Nations?

HR: Sweden supported us. In that case, the liberation struggle was well supported. The Nordic delegations were always in favour of self-determination for the African countries, especially in Southern Africa.

TS: But they could never vote in favour of resolutions with a reference to the armed struggle?

HR: Well, that was difficult. I understood that it was very difficult.

TS: Could you co-ordinate your positions then regarding Portugal?

HR: Yes. For the condemnation of Portuguese colonialism in general we always had the support of the Nordic countries. That was clear.

TS: Do you think that there were any conditions attached to the Swedish support to MPLA?

HR: Frankly, I cannot tell. Seeing the commitment by the Swedish government and Olof Palme, I get the impression that there was a 'particular' involvement. We tried to explain that the Swedish government should not ally itself with MPLA only, because we were fighting to liberate Angola. The struggle was to democratize the country, and Sweden—by tradition a democratic country—should support the struggle for liberation and not adopt any special orientation. This was not implemented. It was not understood. There was in fact a very strong involvement for MPLA. Even a certain aggressiveness towards FNLA when we came to Sweden. I personally saw this at the Ministry for Foreign Affairs. There was aggressiveness by the Secretary of State at the time. He was deeply committed to MPLA. Really committed! Mrs. Brundin made all possible efforts, but she said: 'The man has a very open leftist tendency. Therefore, we cannot do anything'.

TS: Do you think that Olof Palme's position influenced the other Nordic countries?

HR: Absolutely. He influenced a lot.

TS: Was the entire Nordic area then closed to you?

HR: Absolutely.

TS: Did the same happen to UNITA?

HR: I do not know. At that time UNITA did not play any role. There were only two parties, FNLA and MPLA. UNITA's connection with South Africa made the Nordic countries avoid close contacts with the movement.

TS: Did FNLA maintain good relations with other liberation movements from Southern Africa?

HR: Yes. For example, the first fighters from SWAPO and the first from Mozambique trained at our base. Nujoma brought the soldiers there. We had good relations with all the parties, but later they sided with MPLA and moved away from us.

TS: In the early 1960s, I think that you shared offices in Algeria with Robert Resha from ANC?

HR: That is true. We had good relations, but only as long as the Soviet Union's influence was not felt through OAU.

TS: Do you think that the 1969 Khartoum conference was a turning point, after which the movements called 'authentic' began to receive support from the Soviet Union as well as from the Nordic countries?

HR: Yes. That was a big mistake. We were not invited, because, obviously, there was an agenda. I do not know what they meant by 'authentic' and 'not authentic' movements. We were conducting an armed struggle. We were against colonialism and we were fighting. But, we were not ideologically part of the group of the so-called 'authentics'. We were not invited. MPLA was present. At that time, MPLA did not have any strength. It did not fight. It did not have a base and no front in Angola. The only movement that was fighting was FNLA. But ideologically, MPLA had more external support. In that way, we did not receive any help from several countries.

TS: For some time from late 1972 FNLA had an alliance with MPLA. Did you not receive any support from the Nordic countries at that point?

HR: No. As I said, MPLA had no front. Then they decided that they should join the movements to accelerate the struggle. But the obstacle was always the ideology. We wanted to be free from all ideologies, but MPLA came with preconditions. They wanted to influence us and talk about imperialism. We understood, but believed that there should be no ideological aspects involved, nor aspects in favour of the Soviet Union. They used a concept—'positive neutrality'—in favour of Communism. We did not accept that. That was always the cause of the failures. We wanted to be completely independent. We were fighting for freedom and democracy. We knew that it formed part of the Cold War—the conflict between the East and the West

blocs—but we did not want to be a part of that. It created many problems for us. We could not receive assistance from the Western countries, because of NATO and the relations with Portugal. We had no support. The little support that we could count upon was from African and Arab countries, such as Tunisia. And Israel, which was very important for us. The Israeli government helped us at that time.
TS: With weapons?
HR: With weapons. It was with the help by Golda Meir. I understood why she did that. The Arab countries already had a strong influence over us and she wanted to counteract that. It helped our struggle. It was very interesting.

TS: Do you believe that the Swedish assistance to MPLA was similarly intended to counteract the support by the Soviet Union?
HR: I do not know. I think that the social democratic policy perhaps diminished the influence of the Soviets within MPLA. But that should not have prevented support to us too. They could help MPLA, but as a non-aligned country Sweden should have also helped us. But they did not. They only assisted MPLA. They gave a lot of assistance to MPLA. A lot of money. Financial and humanitarian support. Really a lot. We tried to explain, but there was no opening at all. Total rejection, especially at the Ministry for Foreign Affairs, where we met real opposition.

Jorge Valentim
UNITA—Secretary for Information
(Luanda, 18 April 1996)

Tor Sellström: When did you first enter into contact with the Nordic countries?
Jorge Valentim: I was the President of the National Union of Angolan Students (UNEA), which was supporting UNITA. There was another organization, called the General Union of Students from Black Africa under Portuguese Colonial Domination (UGEAN), which was connected to MPLA. Their international base was with the International Union of Students (IUS) in Prague, while the National Union of Angolan Students was connected to the Western International Student Conference (ISC) in Leiden, Holland. ISC had a special programme for Africa, preparing cadres to lead the different national student unions. Another section worked with scholarships. It was mainly—maybe to 85 or 90 per cent—financed by the Scandinavian countries. Many students were from the Portuguese colonies. Students from Southern Africa were the main target group. In the 1960s, most of the African students that got scholarships were supported by ISC with funds from Scandinavia.

In around 1964 or 1965, I met the key leaders of the ISC scholarship section. One was from Norway. That man—Øystein Opdahl—is the one who opened the road and created an impact on the Scandinavian countries, arguing that it was wise to be involved with the liberation movements on a humanitarian basis. After him there came another gentleman, Lars-Gunnar Eriksson from Sweden. He continued the project. One source of the money was SIDA. They worked very hard and Eriksson would travel all over Africa. I think that he was the last man that I worked with.

In 1964, we organized a seminar about Southern Africa at the University of Uppsala. I went there and I still have very good memories from that visit. The contact with the Scandinavian countries is also sentimental, because their economic structure and political stability were examples for us. Ever since I worked at the International Student Conference—which was at the time of the Cold War—our reference and model was the Scandinavian countries. You could not point to the United States since it was fighting against Russia. To show the Africans that a democratic society is a good thing we used the slogan: 'Free men in a free society'. In this context, it was essential to give examples and that is where the Scandinavian countries were mentioned.

I would, however, like to raise the contradiction that while SIDA was giving us scholarships irrespective of the political parties that we represented, officially, the

Swedish government had another policy. It was more connected with the older, accepted liberation movements.

TS: Eventually, the Swedish government only gave direct support to MPLA, not to UNITA or FNLA. How did you look upon that?

JV: This dichotomy of behaviour, or approach, would be very interesting for a political analysis. Among the liberation movements there were two groups. Those that were supported by Russia formed a kind of trade union in Rabat, Morocco. Their strategy was that if you wanted to support the struggle in Mozambique, you had to choose a movement that had connections with a movement in Angola or in Guinea-Bissau. They acted as a group. They represented each other and that had some influence. I think that Sweden was getting the impression that it was better to work with those movements rather than to connect ideologically. There was some kind of attitude that 'let us gamble on these movements and forget the rest'. In addition, knowing Prime Minister Olof Palme, I think that he influenced the Swedish position.

TS: You knew him?

JV: Yes, I knew him. He was one of the founders of the International Student Conference. He was not so well disposed towards the United States. Therefore, he gave priority to the movements that were not connected to the USA. I think that he was aware that they had a certain ideology, but not the money. He would gamble with the Swedish support. That is why UNITA as a party never got any support from Sweden, only UNEA for scholarships and so forth.

TS: The Swedish Social Democratic Party was very much involved in the reconstruction of the Socialist Party of Portugal, which had its problems with MPLA but quite good relations with UNITA. How do you explain that?

JV: Well, it is both true and not true. It is true with regard to Mário Soares, but the Socialist Party as such was not favourable to UNITA. As a simple member of the cabinet of the Movement of the Armed Forces (MFA), Mário Soares was in the beginning surrounded by Communists. The MFA was really controlled by Communists and Soares could not express himself freely and strongly at the time of the Alvor agreement. The Socialist Party, on the other hand, belonged to the Socialist International, which was led by Sweden and France. It was therefore very difficult for the Socialist Party of Portugal to have an open policy towards UNITA.

TS: The Socialist International advocated multi-partyism. Against this background, is it not strange that the Swedish Social Democratic Party supported only one liberation movement in Angola?

JV: Well, I think that the Social Democratic Party stayed in power for more than thirty years and that Palme was the boss. He did not listen to all the voices. I think that there were big sections of the population in Sweden that did not agree, but, unfortunately, they also supported the official policy of Sweden. They did not want to show their disagreement outside the borders. The democratic line inside Sweden was biased outside, encouraging one-party systems.

TS: It may also have to do with the close relations between Palme and African socialist leaders such as Nyerere of Tanzania and Kaunda of Zambia?

JV: Yes, it is true, but that brand of African socialism was emotional. It did not mean anything. I praise President Nyerere, who afterwards made self-criticism, and President Kaunda, who ended with the mentality of the one-party system, accepting multi-party elections that the world had imposed on him as a condition for economic support.

TS: Did Savimbi ever visit the Nordic countries?

JV: Yes, he visited Denmark before the military coup in Portugal. He was very well received. Denmark never completely followed the position of Sweden. It had a different policy. We had more support and understanding in Denmark than in Sweden.

TS: In the 1980s, there was a UNITA support group in Sweden which included a member of parliament from the Moderate Party, Birger Hagård. He visited UNITA's headquarters in Jamba and campaigned for support to UNITA in Sweden. Did you notice that support inside Angola?

JV: Yes, there was a tendency in Sweden towards a different approach. I think that there was some weakness of the Social Democratic Party in power, which made it possible for the other side to come out strongly. The members of the Swedish parliament who visited Angola helped us a lot. They helped to change the perception in the world at large, because people were getting the impression that every single Swedish person was against UNITA. Later, they realized that this was due to party politics and that you also would find a different opinion, depending on the leadership. Others have said that the support given to our first representative in Sweden was very useful. We should now try to send a stronger delegation there, because even for the reconstruction of Angola Sweden should help and play a great role. I am pleased that the contacts now are very good.

TS: Did you get any financial assistance from UNITA support groups in Sweden?

JV: I was working in the information department and that kind of foreign policy activities was directly connected to the President, so I cannot answer the question. However, some support was necessary for our representative. First of all, political support, giving him the opportunity to speak for our cause. The strongest embassy of the MPLA government was in Sweden, so if they allowed a different opinion that in itself was important. The financial questions were, however, not part of my responsibility.

TS: Would you like to comment on the incident in 1987 when three Swedish aid workers were kidnapped by UNITA at Quibaxe? One of them died and the other two were taken to Jamba.

JV: Well, I can say that it was not the outcome of any anti-Swedish policy. Before that happened, UNITA had announced that all foreigners should leave the areas of military activity. The MPLA government used them and exposed them to danger. It so happened that some Swedes were found, not captured. An enemy is captured, but they were not the enemy. In addition, kidnapping is when you ask for ransom, but we were not asking for money. We did not get any benefit out of it, apart from some publicity. I am really sorry for what happened to the Swede who died, but the instruction from the President was that they should be treated well. As I said, it was not part of any anti-Swedish policy, but due to the war situation.

TS: Perhaps you were present in Jamba when the Swedes were handed over to the representatives from the Swedish Ministry for Foreign Affairs?

JV: Yes, I was. The message from our President was clearly that we had nothing against the Swedes and that the incident was due to the state of war. I think it is a thing of the past.

TS: In retrospect, do you think that the role of the Nordic countries was constructive for the liberation of Southern Africa?

JV: Well, having worked with international organizations and also according to my education, I want to see things globally. Sweden helped only one side, MPLA, but MPLA represented part of the opinion of Angola. If the support was beneficial to that part, fine. Other countries assisted the other side. This was due to the Cold War configuration of blocs. I would now prefer to learn from the lessons of the past and have a positive perspective. We finally have the Lusaka protocol—I am one of the negotiators—and we should now build confidence between ourselves. In this situation, we ask the Nordic countries to be dynamic, to open the doors to both sides and see UNITA and MPLA as twin brothers. I think that the Nordic countries have great possibilities to assist. They have the know-how and a lot to say.

Mozambique

Joaquim Chissano
FRELIMO—Chief Representative to Tanzania—Secretary of Security—
Prime Minister in the Transitional Government of Mozambique—Minister of Foreign Affairs
President of Mozambique
(Maputo, 2 May 1996)

Tor Sellström: Swedish support to FRELIMO started in 1965 via the Mozambique Institute in Dar es Salaam. As FRELIMO's representative in Tanzania, was this your first contact with the Nordic countries?

Joaquim Chissano: No, not at all. I left Portugal for France in 1961. As students, we tried to have as many contacts as possible to denounce Portuguese colonialism and spread information to the youth and students in all the countries about what was going on in Mozambique. At the time, we had formed an organization called UGEAN, the General Union of Students from Black Africa under Portuguese Colonial Domination. In the process, it happened that I represented Mozambique at the Afro-Scandinavian Youth Congress in Oslo in 1962. That is when I came to know the former Swedish Prime Minister, Ingvar Carlsson. When we later met, I reminded him of that. The late Oliver Tambo of ANC also participated in that congress.

TS: How did you then see the Nordic engagement for Southern Africa?

JC: Well, I could only see it from the point of view of the youth, which, however, was very strong. Actually, they were very alert and knew what was going on. Not so much in the Portuguese colonies, because they were mainly discussing matters related to apartheid and racialism in South Africa. There was a big discussion about whether to support an armed struggle, a violent revolution, or not. It was very interesting, because in Mozambique we were still trying to see if we could fight peacefully for independence, although we could already see that the armed struggle was an alternative. There was also the question whether a struggle for liberation in South Africa was viable without the independence of Mozambique. Some tended to say that Mozambique should be free first so that South Africa could carry out its own fight, while others tended to say the reverse.

We had very interesting discussions. Youth representatives from all the Nordic countries were present. It appeared to me that the Swedes already had a full vision about the whole issue, because Sweden did not belong to NATO. For Norway things were a bit different.

After that congress, I went all the way to Dar es Salaam for good. That was my last job to promote the liberation struggle in Europe.

TS: From 1965, the Swedish government extended support to the Mozambique Institute. It later led to direct support to FRELIMO. How did you in the bipolar East-West situation look upon this support?

JC: We very much welcomed the help of Sweden to proceed with the work of the Mozambique Institute. It came at a time when the Ford Foundation had desisted from supporting it. The whole plan was collapsing. Apparently, the point made by the Ford Foundation was that we were embarking on armed struggle for liberation, which they could not understand. Although Sweden was not in favour of support to the armed struggle, they did understand that the people of Mozambique were free to make their own choice regarding how to liberate themselves. However, Sweden chose to support what they called the humanitarian, or the non-military, side. So, the Mozambique Institute was built regardless of the bipolar divisions of the two camps. The fact that Sweden was in EFTA was irrelevant. The approach was humanitarian.

We did not have much to discuss with Sweden, but we had to try to dissuade Norway from giving help to Portugal through NATO for the wars. There was much discussion among the youth—even from the Scandinavian countries—about how to differentiate a gun used against the Mozambican people and the other colonies and a gun which was not. But, again, we thought that Norway could play an important role within NATO, trying to distance the NATO members from the posture of Portugal regarding the colonies. We tried to use the fact that Norway was a member to make our case from within NATO.

TS: Was it not strange that the Nordic countries—who were not favourable to the Communist ideology—supported the very same movements that were assisted by the socialist bloc?

JC: Well, I think that from China, the Soviet Union and the others there was not a single question about Sweden. The participation of Sweden was welcomed by them. They viewed it positively. For us, it was very much in our interest to have Swedish support. It proved our policy in terms of relationships. It was also our intention to get support from the United States of America through various organizations or the government directly, but we wanted to be as independent as possible. Sweden and the other Scandinavian countries helped us to achieve that goal, which later developed with the participation of Finland and Holland and—when it comes to the general public—of other countries in the West, such as Italy, Britain and even the United States.

TS: At the diplomatic level—in international fora like the United Nations—do you think that the Nordic countries opened up space for you?

JC: Yes. Our struggle was an armed struggle. What used to be the first emphasis from 1962 to 1964, that is, the use of international institutions and of the public opinion in Europe, became in 1964 a second emphasis. We had, however, to have friends to push resolutions in the United Nations General Assembly and Security Council and we were sure that the Scandinavian countries were on our side together with most of the African countries. We used to consult with them and they took positions on our behalf. It was a big support.

TS: Although the Nordic countries could not vote for resolutions that contained references to the armed struggle?

JC: Yes, but we understood that, although we tried to use the influence of the public opinion to change the position. In our view, the humanitarian position of Sweden should be expanded to include an understanding of the nature of our struggle, which was in defence against aggression and violations of human rights by Portuguese colonialism. We tried to influence this, but we also understood that Sweden and the other Scandinavian countries could not just change the opinion without going through a democratic process. They faced a public opinion which should be convinced. They had parliaments and many political parties. They were not obliged to have the same understanding of the situation in Mozambique as we had.

Even among the African countries there were many who did not understand our situation. If you told them about the situation in Mozambique, they would immediately say: 'It is the same as with us. In our country this also happened', but as you talked with them, they became astonished. They started to see the difference. They could not understand, for instance, that we were speaking about a country which was under colonialism and fascism at the same time. They could not understand that we were talking about a country where the indigenous population was almost 100 per cent illiterate. They were speaking about a different situation. The Swedes often had a better understanding of our situation.

TS: When it comes to the question of the armed struggle, the stand of the Nordic countries did not really change until you had built a strong solidarity movement?

JC: Yes.

TS: The new generation of leaders—such as Olof Palme—would also understand this much better?

JC: Yes. Olof Palme was one of our staunch supporters. Also my friend Pierre Schori. He was very close to us and visited Dar es Salaam several times. Later, different Swedish delegations and representatives of the press started to visit the interior of Mozambique. All this contributed to the understanding. Anders Johansson, for example, visited the liberated areas with President Mondlane in 1968. I remember many of these visitors. For example, Lennart Malmer from the Swedish television who visited in 1971.

TS: You also visited Sweden and the other Nordic countries in November 1970. Was it to explain the context of the Portuguese op-

eration 'Gordian Knot' and the military situation?
JC: There were two issues. One was that of the 'Gordian Knot'. The other was to explain the aftermath of the death of President Mondlane. He died in 1969 and the world wanted to know what the situation was regarding the FRELIMO leadership.
TS: You also visited the Swedish solidarity movement?
JC: Yes, we had a big meeting. I worked particularly with Emmaus Björkå, I remember, and with *Afrikagrupperna*. Besides that big meeting, we also had separate meetings.
TS: These groups were very critical towards the Swedish government, wanting it to give unconditional support to FRELIMO. Was that difficult for you?
JC: Well, we knew how to position ourselves. Imagine that we—throughout the struggle until independence—were able to work with the two arch-enemies of China and the Soviet Union! In addition, on the one side we had China and the Soviet Union and on the other the Soviet Union and the United States of America. Although we did not get any formal recognition from the United States, we kept on pushing for support. We also received support from different groups, going from the African-American Institute to the black communities, which were rather extremist in their posture against the government. We knew how to work with them without creating big problems, taking their points of view but making our own approach.

We were in favour of the approach by the Swedish solidarity groups that the help should be unconditional. The only condition was to assist the struggle against Portuguese colonialism. This was particularly problematic when it came to a definition applied by the Scandinavian governments regarding the use of medicines. They gave us medicines to treat civilians, but we said that humanitarianism means that a man with a gun also has a right to life and to be treated when he is wounded. A wounded civilian could come to the hospital for treatment, but a soldier could not be treated with the same medicine. This was shocking to us and on that point we had to be sharp.

TS: Was it not difficult to control if you supplied medicines to the soldiers in the liberated areas?
JC: Well, we used to receive the medicines and we tried to do our best until we could convince the Swedes that this was impossible, particularly in the clinics in Dar es Salaam and at our hospital in Mtwara. The Swedes would visit and say that 'these are medicines from Sweden. They cannot go to that patient, because he is a military'. That was very powerful! It was impossible! We have a soldier, a military, who is fighting. His child is in the Tunduru camp, receiving medicines and clothing from Sweden. When his father comes, he cannot be clothed or fed with assistance from Sweden. It was so strange! The mother and the child could, but not the father!

We tried to say to Sweden that they were supporting a struggle for liberation, but they chose to support just one aspect of it. We could not separate the diplomatic, social or military areas. It was impossible.
TS: Do you then feel that there were ideological conditions attached to the support from the Nordic countries?
JC: No, I do not think that there was any ideological pressure on us. Actually, even ideologically we were close to Sweden. The support constituted a balance to the tendencies of copying what one could see in countries where there had been revolutions, like in the Soviet Union or China. We found a middle point in Sweden which we could refer to.
TS: One contentious issue between Sweden and FRELIMO in the late 1960s was, of course, the involvement of ASEA in the Cabora Bassa project. FRELIMO was very outspoken against the project and ASEA finally withdrew. Do you think that the Cabora Bassa debate influenced your relations with the Nordic countries?
JC: That discussion was very good and interesting. It brought the attention of the world to the immoral side of the Cabora Bassa project. Per se it seemed a very peaceful and progressive project, but there were many bad sides to it which could not have been understood if we had not discussed them with companies like ASEA and the Swedish government, stressing the sacrifices

that countries should make for the liberation of the peoples of the world.

If you give support when things are easy, it does not show real commitment. Support when things are easy has no meaning. But the fact that Sweden took the decision to withdraw, losing some income for its economy, was a big contribution to the liberation struggle in Mozambique. We think that some of these issues have to be made public so our people will know that we should value the support we got from different countries.

TS: After the independence of Mozambique, there was a lot of Nordic humanitarian support to ZANU of Zimbabwe in your country. Did the Swedish and the Nordic governments consult with you in this regard?

JC: Oh, yes!

TS: You did not see the support as interference in your own process?

JC: No, we helped ZANU and ZAPU—all the movements which were here—in their bid to get support. We had refugees, as was our case in Tanzania. We had to take care of both refugees and freedom fighters for a long period until the UN High Commission for Refugees assisted. So, we participated in seeking support for the liberation movements hosted here.

In our case, it was a continuation of a common struggle. From 1972 to 1974, we were fighting together with ZANU, utilizing the same training camps and the same transit points from Tanzania to Zambia and from there to the interior of Mozambique. We helped the Zimbabweans to their border. After independence, it was just a continuation, especially when we had to take the decision to close the border in compliance with the UN mandatory sanctions against Rhodesia. It was a contribution to the struggle for the liberation of Zimbabwe.

TS: There were close relations between Sweden and ZANU. Herbert Chitepo came to Sweden in October 1972, explaining to SIDA that 'we are going to launch the armed struggle from the north-eastern parts of the country, the result of which will be refugees into Zambia, so, can you buy us a farm?' He actually came to a Western country, giving away the military plans and asking for support.

JC: Yes, ZANU started in 1972. They were then utilizing our farm in Zambia, but they were looking for another farm as a transit camp. We knew about that. I was then in charge of the military contacts between ZANU and FRELIMO together with Samora Machel.

We tried to do exactly the same with ANC, but in their case it was more complicated. Their borders were far away. As a matter of fact, it started with ZAPU, but they did not like to go through this side of the border. They wanted to go from the Wankie side, which we had nothing to do with.

Janet Mondlane
FRELIMO—Director of the Mozambique Institute
Former National Director of International Cooperation
(Maputo, 30 April 1996)

Tor Sellström: You and Eduardo Mondlane visited Sweden as early as 1964. Was that on your initiative or were you invited by a Swedish organization?

Janet Mondlane: When FRELIMO was founded in 1962, my husband and I decided that something should be done for the Mozambican refugees in Dar es Salaam and southern Tanzania. We decided to set up a school. As we had lived in the United States we approached the Ford Foundation for assistance. The foundation said that it would support the school and we were funded by them for about a year. Then Portugal made a complaint to the American ambassador, who in turn spoke to the US government. The US government was very concerned about what was going on and that the Ford Foundation was giving money to the Mozambican liberation movement. The result was that the support was cut off very suddenly.

By that time, we were already functioning so it was very difficult. I then turned to Z. K. Matthews at the World Council of Churches and got funding for one year. However, as I knew that it could not go on I searched in my mind, thinking how the world was at the time. I thought about Sweden, in great part because my grandparents were Swedish and I always felt a kind of alliance with the Swedish people. Thinking about that, I decided that I must go to Sweden. I invited myself. I went there looking for funds. My husband joined me later. I cannot remember who I saw first, but it must have been the Social Democratic Party.

TS: Did you also visit the other Nordic countries?

JM: No, it was only Sweden that time around. The relations with the other countries developed later. The Nordic countries worked very much together, telling each other what they were doing. I think that it is more or less how the involvement with the other Nordic countries started.

TS: At the beginning of the 1960s, the Swedish solidarity movement was almost uniquely concentrated on South Africa. Was there any awareness in Sweden regarding the Portuguese territories in Africa?

JM: What happened was that I got very good advice. The actual penetration was done through the Social Democratic Party to the union of secondary school students, SECO. It was an extraordinarily powerful youth organization. I went around, speaking in different schools. The end result was that SECO decided to take Mozambique—in particular, the Mozambique Institute—as a fund-raising campaign. Through their annual Operation Day's Work there was an extraordinary publicity. It was not just the money that was important, but the sensitization of the whole population. These young people went home and talked about what they were doing. It was a big event. Not just in Sweden, but in the other Nordic countries as well, particularly in Finland. That is how a kind of a mass consciousness about what was happening in Mozambique really began. After that, things began to snow-ball as far as Sweden and the Nordic countries were concerned. The awareness about Mozambique's war was really brought to the fore.

TS: In the case of Finland, the students donated a printing press to FRELIMO?

JM: Yes. It is still functioning here in Maputo. It was a fantastic donation.

TS: FRELIMO also distributed good and reliable information about the struggle?

JM: Yes, we did. We managed to make a distinction between the social services and the war effort. It was on that basis that the World Council of Churches were able to help and it was on that basis that the Nordic countries also worked with us. We separated the social services—which were humanitarian, educational and to some degree cultural—from the military struggle. It was accepted, except by the Ford Foundation.

TS: Was the fact that FRELIMO had embarked upon armed struggle a problem in the Nordic countries?

JM: No, it was not. I spoke to the labour unions and to other groups. The support was part of a conscious and really determined effort by the Swedes to make the population aware of what was happening in the Portuguese colonies. I spoke to these groups on their initiative. They were really debating the issue of the Portuguese colonies, looking at it from a moral point of view. The Swedes were very concerned about how they were behaving in the world at that time. For example, we talked about the target of one per cent of GDP for international aid. That debate was going on. In FRELIMO, we really admired this. Sweden was one of the very few countries—later there was Denmark, Finland, Norway and Holland, as well as the World Council of Churches—that really did take a moral decision, defending the right to self-determination. They not only thought about it, but also acted, which was rare. That is where the great admiration for the Nordic countries started.

TS: At the same time, two of the Nordic countries—Denmark and Norway—were members of NATO and, together with Sweden and Finland, also members of EFTA?

JM: Yes, it was an issue, but there was something extraordinarily different about what was going on in the Nordic countries. I certainly did try to get assistance from other countries, but it did not work. It just did not work. But it worked in the Nordic countries. Until this day I am sure that it was due to some moral education.

TS: There must have been a close relationship between some of the Swedish Social Democratic leaders and Eduardo Mondlane. One example is that Pierre Schori wrote to

Mondlane, asking for his points of view on different opposition groups in Portugal.

JM: Yes, there was, but to understand that you have to understand Eduardo Mondlane. He was the key to the relationship. As far as I am concerned, there were two factors behind the relations with the Nordic countries, in particular with Sweden. One was the separation of the humanitarian and the armed activities within the liberation movement. The second was the personality and the leadership of Eduardo Mondlane. He was able to cultivate good friendships and respect on the part of peoples who were not from his culture or milieu.

TS: Would it be fair to say that the close relationship with leaders such as Mondlane made it possible for the Nordic leaders to see beyond the ideological Cold War divisions and more easily understand the nationalist cause of the liberation struggle?

JM: I would say that it probably may have been so. As far as FRELIMO was concerned, Eduardo Mondlane was an extraordinary person. For example, in the Cold War context he was able to manage the Soviet government and the Chinese government, speaking with both of them without causing problems. It was difficult then, because if you were a friend of the Soviet Union, China was not going to have anything to do with you and vice versa. I remember passing his office one day. He was with the Soviet ambassador and the Chinese ambassador was waiting outside. I laughed about it and wondered how many could do that balancing act. I have many letters of his, written from the Soviet Union, in which he—tongue in cheek—talked about the Cold War situation. It is very possible that he mentioned these things in his conversations with the Nordic leaders. Of course, they were much more involved in the Cold War situation than we were, especially in Finland.

TS: Could you say that the Nordic countries recognized the liberation movements as governments-in-waiting? Were they seen as legitimate governments-to-be?

JM: This was one of the things that we talked about, but from my point of view there was another element which was very important. One can reflect on these things politically and at a theoretical level. With the Nordics, I felt a respect towards the peoples trying to become independent. It was not just a theoretical political concept, which is admirable in itself. It went beyond that. I can hear the young Swedish and Finnish people saying: 'If we really knew the Mozambicans, we would probably like them'. That is different from a theoretical position.

TS: Do you think that the question of non-racism was important?

JM: Yes, I think that it was very important. I have often wondered about that. The Nordic countries had not been exposed to a lot of foreign people. Like myself. I grew up in an absolutely white village, so I was positively curious about blacks. Until I was a teenager, I had had no contacts with blacks at all. Fortunately, my family did not colour my attitude, so I grew up in ignorance and innocence. I was a kind of a microcosm of the Nordic society. They were very positive when it comes to race. I always felt that it was on the basis of an equal relationship.

TS: Did you or your husband during the early visits in the 1960s meet Olof Palme?

JM: Oh, yes! My husband much more than I. I went to see Olof after Eduardo was killed. He then told me how they had worked together in a meeting of the Socialist International. It was very much in his mind. They made strategies together. They knew each other very well and respected each other a lot.

TS: Olof Palme said that his first political act was in 1949, giving blood to raise funds for non-white students that were expelled from the white universities in South Africa. Eduardo Mondlane was one of them.

JM: Yes, he was the first student expelled from South Africa, for being 'a foreign native'.

TS: In the beginning, you had quite difficult discussions with the Swedish government regarding whether the support should be given to the Mozambique Institute in the form of goods or as cash. How did you look upon this?

JM: Well, at first I thought: 'They should give us the funds so that we can buy what we want'. But you cannot hit people over the head in the beginning. You have to ease them into the situation. You have to give them confidence. When donations were made in cash or kind to the Mozambique Institute, it was terribly important to have a good reporting system. You had to ask people to come down and visit and you had to make a great effort to inspire confidence. Contributions in kind were very good, because we needed the goods, but they were much more difficult to administer. They had to be packed and shipped. It is much easier to report on money spent than on things received. We were supposed to show how every little thing was distributed. That is hard when you are running a big operation. The Mozambique Institute included the Tunduru refugee centre, Dr. Américo Boavida Hospital and activities in the liberated areas inside Mozambique. How can you put your word on the line and say: 'Yes, I know that those books went off to such and such a place?' But it worked out. We had to go slowly. In the end, a lot of confidence inspired our working relationship and reached such an extent that we received cash funds. But it had to go slowly, because there was no previous Swedish experience in working with the liberation movements.

TS: As the American-born wife of the FRELIMO President, was it difficult for you to negotiate on behalf of the liberation movement?

JM: My position in FRELIMO was not that of a black Mozambican. My position was that of the wife of the President and of a person who could raise material support and a certain amount of respect. I had a lot of really good friends, but I was not generally integrated. There was an argument between some members of the Tanzanian government and FRELIMO after my husband was killed. It concerned my working in the southern part of Tanzania—not to speak of crossing the border into Mozambique—because I was white. This was a problem. A lot of strange things were said about me by some FRELIMO members who we can call the opposition at that time and who were allied with some members of the Tanzanian government. That made my life very difficult. However, I ignored it.

My view of the Swedes, the Danes and the Norwegians was obviously a bit different from that of many people in FRELIMO. I felt more integrated with the Nordic countries than they did. I had another point of view. But I was in a sense able to interpret both sides, if we look at it positively. Of course, my real devotion to FRELIMO existed, but I had also a sincere respect for the Nordic countries. I saw them through very special glasses and I still do.

TS: Do you feel that there were strings attached to the Nordic support?

JM: No, not that I was aware of, but I think that one has to take each Nordic country by itself. Sweden was absolutely the most open, with no strings attached. I was always very impressed by the fact that they talked about it. The Swedish leaders and the people with whom I dealt were talking about how the assistance to the resistance struggle should have no strings attached. Denmark was much more cautious about this. I would not say that there were strings attached, but they did not channel the money in the same way as the Swedes did. There was always a feeling that 'the Danes do not really trust us'. They used different Danish groups to cover their tracks. That was the difference. The Finnish government also found it hard to work directly with us. The biggest relationship was with the secondary school students' movement, which paid for the printing press and sent out a technician. I do not remember how the Norwegians gave us funds.

TS: At the same time, FRELIMO received assistance from the Nordic governments and a lot of support from the various solidarity organizations. The latter were often very critical of the governments, criticizing them from the left. Was that a problem when you visited different milieus in the Nordic countries?

JM: No, that was not a problem. If they had problems, they were kept among themselves, but they never translated into my problems. Maybe I was hard-shelled, but I never really felt a problem. I moved very easily between the two milieus. When you represent a liberation movement, you are different. You do not have to meddle in the internal problems of others. Let them help as they can. But they really fought among themselves. I remember going to European solidarity conferences where you had the far left and the middle-of-the-road, edging over to the right. The liberation movements would just sit back and watch the things that were going on between the various solidarity groups. It really was not our problem. It was theirs.

TS: Do you remember if FRELIMO would liaise with the Nordic countries on the issue

of decolonization in international fora such as the United Nations?
JM: I was not involved in that and I do not know if FRELIMO did. Certainly, Mondlane did. Olof Palme also said so. It was a very interesting time. I somehow feel that it was the last decade of the age of innocence of the Nordic countries.

Jorge Rebelo
FRELIMO—Secretary of Information
Former Minister of Information
(Maputo, 1 May 1996)

Tor Sellström: When the Nordic countries started to support FRELIMO, how did you look upon this?
Jorge Rebelo: It is a question which we at that time—and even now—put to ourselves: Why did the Nordic countries, which were so far away and had a culture completely different from ours, become interested in Africa? What was the reason? I must confess that I do not have an answer. Some people said that it was because they did not have colonies, therefore being more sensitive. It is not an explanation which is satisfactory to me, because there are many countries in the world which did not have colonies. Others said that it was because the Nordic countries appreciated freedom and justice. That is why they were against oppression and exploitation. Still others said that they were white and cold and therefore liked countries which are hot and people who are black.
TS: Was it not strange that the Nordic countries supported the same movements that were supported by the Eastern bloc countries?
JR: Well, we did not mind so much what the motivation was. We wanted as much support as possible, wherever it came from. The reason why we were closely linked to the Eastern bloc was that they agreed to support us. We asked everybody—even the United States and Britain—to support the liberation struggle, but we did not get any support from them.
TS: In the very beginning, FRELIMO received support from the Ford Foundation for the Mozambique Institute. But the US withdrew that support?
JR: Yes. It was due to pressure from the US administration.

In my capacity as Secretary for Information, my main task was to inform the people inside Mozambique and the outside world about our struggle. At the time, there was the polarity between the West and the East. Then there were the African countries, which supported us through the Organization of African Unity, and the Asian and Latin American countries, which were in the non-aligned movement, but not really relevant in terms of influencing world affairs. In fact, there were two blocs. The Eastern bloc—Soviet Union, China, Bulgaria, all these countries—supported us, while the Western bloc was against us. This was seen in absolute terms by our people. The West was the enemy. The East was a worthy friend. But in FRELIMO we knew that it was not because the Soviet Union liked Mondlane or the Mozambicans that they were giving us support. Nor China. They had their geo-strategic interests. There were certain moments—in fact many moments—when their support was given under very strict conditions. The basic condition was to support their policies and condemn—now that expression no longer exists—imperialism.

Mobilizing our people, we wanted them to be aware of the situation. We received support from the socialist countries, but they had their reasons for that. They wanted something in return, either at that moment or later. On the other hand they were our friends and we could not say as much as I am telling now. We depended absolutely on their support for the war effort. If we had questioned the reasons why they were giving the support, it could have been a disaster. But we knew. We also knew that the West was not a monolithic entity and in our mobilization work we told the people that not all the capitalist countries were enemies. There were countries belonging to the Western bloc that supported the liberation struggle. That is why it was important that the Scandinavian countries supported us. Instead of talking in abstract terms, we could show that not all the Western countries were bad. But we had to prove it. When the people through the Mozambique Institute saw the medicines and books, we could say that they came from Sweden or Norway. It then became concrete. It helped us in our effort to break the dichotomy bad-good, West-East.

The support we were getting from the Nordic countries took two forms. One was diplomatic and the other material. The material support was important, although it was not for the armed struggle. In fact, all the support was non-lethal—as it was called at the time—or humanitarian, in the fields of education, health and to a certain extent information. But the vital support to FRELIMO was arms, because we were engaged in a war. That is also why we depended so much on the socialist countries.

The Nordic support—in addition to educating our people that the West was not so bad—helped us to advance and implement our programme of national reconstruction. In education, for example, we needed teachers and we can say that in an indirect way the support also assisted the liberation struggle, because it extended education to people who were able to fight better. It, thus, had implications for the war itself. In the diplomatic area, we were, however, very often confronted with contradictions. Sweden, Denmark and Norway were saying that they were for the liberation of Mozambique, Angola and so on, but in international fora they would say something different. They would take different positions—especially at the United Nations—and that often made it difficult for us. It was incoherent. For example, an article on EFTA in our *Mozambique Revolution* in 1967 reproduced a debate in the Swedish parliament where Mr. Ahlmark said that 'it is quite clear that the increasing trade and foreign investment in Portugal stimulated by EFTA has contributed to the economic development in Portugal and thus to an ever increasing amount of money for the wars in Africa'. In the case of Sweden, there was an important increase in trade after EFTA was formed. The exports from Portugal to Sweden doubled in two years. This was the point: 'The contradiction between the Scandinavian image and the actual government policy is steadily becoming more blatant'.

TS: FRELIMO was more critical than the other Southern African liberation movements, perhaps because of its strong non-alignment. Is that a fair assessment?

JR: It is a completely fair assessment. It came with the first leaders, specifically Eduardo Mondlane. At that time, the basic policy of FRELIMO was to be independent of any bloc and any outside influence. It was perhaps even clearer under Samora Machel, because he was a very strong nationalist, proud of his country and his people. He would not accept being pressurized to do this or that, but, of course, there were moments when we had to. For example, during the conflict between China and the Soviet Union, the Soviet Union would say that 'you have to make a statement condemning China, otherwise we will not give you any more weapons'. There was no alternative. But the basic principle was to be independent and non-aligned.

We used to think about this problem, although the war was going on. We were aware that we could not be successful in the war effort if we did not analyse the country and the world, aiming to be as independent as possible. Otherwise, national independence would not be the kind of independence that we wanted. It would not be real independence.

A very important contribution from the Nordic countries was the printing press that the Finnish students gave to FRELIMO in 1970. It was installed in Dar es Salaam by Kid Ahlfors, who even went to the liberated areas inside Mozambique to see how the support was being used. This donation was really important. It brought about a big change in our information work, particularly concerning *Mozambique Revolution*. It was really fantastic. We could put much more material in each bulletin and the quality improved dramatically.

The printing press still works. We brought it from Dar es Salaam. It is in a printing unit now. It belonged to FRELIMO, but we decided to make it a private company with links to the party.

TS: Did you also publish in Portuguese?
JR: Of course. In *A Voz da Revolução*. The nature of the articles was not exactly the same. For example, in English we would publish a long essay on the cotton regime. For the outside world that was important. But in Mozambique it was not so necessary, because the people knew about it.

In *Mozambique Revolution* we informed the world about the material support to our education programmes in Mozambique and Tanzania. We expressed a great deal of gratitude to some of the Scandinavian governments. At that time, Sweden was more supportive and we had to differentiate between them. Another important area was, of course, the support given by Sweden to the Portuguese soldiers who deserted, as well as to the Mozambicans who ran away and could stay in Sweden.

TS: In retrospect, do you think that the Nordic support left a positive legacy for the relations with independent Mozambique?
JR: Obviously. It is well documented, for example in President Machel's speech at independence, when he mentioned the support and what we owed the Scandinavian countries. He also said that we considered it important to develop our relations with the Scandinavian countries, Finland and Holland.

The Nordic support enabled us to carry out programmes in education, health and information. Through cash contributions—which often were given—we could develop economic activities in the liberated zones. It was important, because it is a fact that you cannot win a war by just firing against the enemy. We wanted to create a new life. For this we needed support. We could mobilize the people to cultivate, to produce maize and products which they could eat, but it was difficult for us to supply soap, medicines and other basics. The support from the Nordic countries filled this gap.

Secondly, it helped us to educate our people and change their image that the West was bad and that all the Eastern countries were our friends. We knew that it was not so, but we needed something to substantiate that with. I think that it was at that moment that the seeds of the future relations were sown. After independence, the Nordic support was thus seen as a continuity, while, for example, if the United States had said 'we want to give you support', the first thing that the people would have asked is 'why, since you were against us during the liberation war?'. People would start thinking that they had other motives.

Marcelino dos Santos
FRELIMO—Secretary General of CONCP—FRELIMO Secretary of External Affairs and Vice-President
Former Minister of Development and Economic Planning, and President of the National Assembly (Maputo, 3 May 1996)

Tor Sellström: When did the contacts between FRELIMO and the Nordic countries begin?
Marcelino dos Santos: First of all, I would like to welcome the initiative by the Nordic Africa Institute, because we believe that it will be a good contribution for us too. We have taken a firm decision to write the history of FRELIMO, which is also the history of Mozambique and partly the history of Southern Africa. We all need to know our history and the history of the relations between FRELIMO, Sweden and the other Nordic countries. It is quite a positive history, which should certainly be recorded. We are proud of having been able to build the cooperation with Sweden and the other Nordic countries, because—especially now—we can see the great political and moral dimension that these relations had.

My memory is too poor to recall when we made the first contacts. I know that we were always interested in Sweden and that it was in Sweden that the Socialist International held a meeting in 1966, in which Eduardo Mondlane participated. At that time, some of us did not have a clear idea about the Socialist International. If I remember correctly, it was at that meeting that the relations with Sweden were initiated.

For me—and maybe for many others among us—there was one aspect that impressed us strongly. It was that the Minister of Education, Olof Palme, participated in a street rally for the people of Vietnam against the war of the Americans. We said: 'That is a person who we have to respect. A minister of a government which maintains diplomatic relations with the United States of America, but shows that it is also his right as a citizen to be present at such a demonstration. That impressed us profoundly and made us feel deep respect for Olof Palme. Later, I had many meetings with him. We often discussed and I could see with my own eyes what he stood for, both during the liberation struggle and after independence. These were crucial times in the relationship between FRELIMO and the Swedish government.

TS: Sweden and Finland were members of EFTA and Denmark and Norway were also members of NATO. How could the Nordic countries have relations with FRELIMO and at the same time be members of those Western organizations to which Portugal belonged?

MS: That question was very important to us. We tried to find its deeper meaning. The way we interpreted it was that each country had its own reasons to establish agreements, links and political relations, but that these political relations could never be allowed to condone a crime. Denmark said: 'We are members of NATO, but because of that we cannot stop condemning a member state that is colonialist'. This moral value was very important. That was our conclusion about the stand of the Nordic countries.

This understanding of the Nordic countries made us speak to the world on many occasions, especially to West Germany, telling them that we were in opposition: 'We believe that it is a country's sovereign right to establish relations with whoever they want. But we also believe that you can never accept that someone embellishes or tries to embellish a crime'. We denounced the attitude of the countries that, because they were members of NATO, never condemned Portugal. During a visit to West Germany, the Social Democratic Party offered us a million German Marks for medicines, but we said that we thought that it was immoral. We would rather see them give the medicines to the Portuguese and instead give us the weapons that they gave to Portugal. They never did. They never accepted our proposal, but the media made a big deal out of it.

The moral value dignified the Nordic countries and that is something we greatly appreciate. Because of that, we never questioned if they were or were not members of EFTA or NATO. We questioned NATO's role in supporting Portuguese colonialism. We did not think that it was necessary.

TS: The conservatives in Sweden saw the official assistance to the national liberation movements in Southern Africa as support for Communism while the left said that it was to guarantee capitalism. How did you see the interests behind the support?

MS: We believed, and we still believe, that the stand by different states could never call into question the fundamental principle of freedom. If I want to fight for a socialist state, should I not have that right? I have the right to do what I want, and not what foreign countries want. This right to freedom is inherent. What is essential is that it is us who want it. That there is consensus among the Mozambican people. We therefore always believed that support extended on condition that the recipients took a certain course was unacceptable. If you have feelings of solidarity for someone, you want him to be free to have the right to become whatever he wants to become, not what you think that he should become.

TS: Did you in FRELIMO notice any ideological or political conditions attached to the Nordic assistance?

MS: No. We never thought that about the Nordic countries. However, we always said that we did not agree with the Swedish position of being in support of peace, and therefore not being able to help us to wage war. We said: 'The war which we are waging, is it not for peace? 'But we also said: 'Sweden is a great country. It has the right to do whatever it wants. If it feels that it should not give us weapons, then it should give us other items instead'.

We never questioned Sweden's right to state that 'since we are in favour of peace, we cannot give you arms'. We never said to Sweden: 'Change your beliefs'. We used to say: 'Look, we have an idea about what a freedom struggle is. It is obviously and necessarily also a struggle for peace'. We had a clear conscience about this, which was different from the Swedish way of thinking.

Fortunately, during the liberation struggle, we never had to buy weapons, and with the support given by Sweden, the other Nordic countries and also by Holland we were able to develop education, health services and production. It was necessary to have machetes, axes, hoes, all that we needed. We received these items from many countries and we always tried to balance support from one side with assistance from another in order to be able to solve all our problems.

I would like to underline that we always said that the principal form of struggle that history imposed on Mozambique was the armed struggle. If we had not waged an armed struggle we would never have come to power. Humanitarian assistance alone was not sufficient to assume real power. We wanted to explain this to various governments, including Sweden. If the principal form of struggle imposed by history on a people is determined and you refuse to recognize that, you will not succeed. Now, if our friends had understood this question, then Sweden—in our point of view—would also have given us arms. They should have understood that humanitarian aid alone would never bring us to real power. This was our basic position. A policy which was the outcome of a sound and clear scientific analysis.

TS: Something that seems contradictory in this context is that Sweden and the other Nordic countries supported the so-called 'authentic' liberation movements, which also were assisted by the Soviet Union. How would you explain that?

MS: I think that we in FRELIMO were able to understand the motives of each country. We always made an effort to organize the cooperation with different states based on a clear understanding of the internal reality of each country. In the case of Mozambique, this meant that we had to demonstrate that FRELIMO was, in fact, the only force that existed.

It is not because a group exists in exile that it is worth something. In the case of Angola, it was obvious that an organization like FNLA through the way it appeared, its methodology and its political ideas was very much turned towards the outside world. That was the main reason why it was never possible to make an alliance with FNLA. If you are a tool of foreign countries you will never succeed, because they have their own politics. Today, I could say the same thing about RENAMO in Mozambique.

TS: Would that also be the case of UNITA in Angola?

MS: We all know very well that UNITA disappeared from the map after 1966-67. When OAU met in Rabat in 1972—where the reconciliation between MPLA and FNLA took place—no one worried about UNITA's absence. UNITA only reappeared after the coup d'état in Portugal. It then became known that UNITA had all along been doing the Portuguese army's work against the people, the liberation struggle and MPLA.

In the case of Zimbabwe, we were, however, wrong. Reality and history showed that ZANU, in fact, was an authentic movement. In 1967-68, ZANU asked us several times if they could move into the interior of Mozambique. We hesitated. When we eventually agreed, we told ZANU: 'Alright, you can go. You want to learn about our struggle, but remember that we have diplomatic relations with ZAPU and not with you. But go anyway'. They went there. For example, Tongogara trained in Mozambique. When in 1970 we opened a trail to the south of the Zambezi river—via the province of Tete—we went straight to the border with Zimbabwe. We also moved into Zimbabwe and the comrades who went there informed us that the entire area was controlled by ZANU. We then spoke to the comrades from ZAPU and ZANU, asking for a meeting, but the comrades from ZAPU refused to come. They said: 'We have been allies for so long. You always talked to us. Why do you now also want to talk to ZANU?' We answered: 'Because now we know your reality better'. As they refused to come to our meeting, we then officially declared that from that time on we supported both ZANU and ZAPU. We saw with our own eyes that ZANU really had bases inside Zimbabwe and from that moment we made all our possibilities available to them.

TS: FRELIMO had strong support from the solidarity groups in the Nordic countries, such as the Africa Groups in Sweden and the Norwegian Council for Southern Africa. They often took critical positions vis-à-vis their governments. You visited the Nordic countries many times. Did the governments ever try to limit your contacts with the solidarity groups?

MS: I think that they never did. For example, I do not remember them telling me: 'You should not see the solidarity groups'. No one has ever said anything like that to me in any Nordic country. I do not think that it was difficult for us to meet the conservatives either. We never felt any obstacles. I am saying that because I compare with Germany, where we had to meet the Catholic church or political forces closely connected with the Catholic church. That was really difficult. But we never had a similar situation in the Nordic countries. We always found good will and a capacity to understand our concerns there. But I have to add that we had facts and examples from our struggle to demonstrate our political quality and fighting morale. The opposition we encountered was from the press in countries like England, Germany, France, Italy etc.

TS: Perhaps more than any other liberation movement, FRELIMO had the independent capacity to receive aid and be critical at the same time. One example is the campaign in Sweden against the Cabora Bassa project. You said that if the Swedes went there you would shoot them.

MS: That was one case, but we also had the Sino-Soviet conflict. It was always a problem for the liberation movements, but not for us. We welcomed our relations with the People's Republic of China and with the Soviet Union. They had their problems and we had our points of view. There were intense discussions between us and the People's Republic of China and between us and the Soviet Union, but they were discussions between comrades that never affected the validity of the common struggle.

TS: Did you consult the Nordic countries about representing your positions at the United Nations and in other international fora?

MS: We cannot say that we had reached that level of agreement, but we always appealed to the Nordic states to present the validity of our positions to the international community. We also asked the Nordic states to do us the favour of telling the world what they were doing. In addition, we requested all countries to take strong action against the whites in Mozambique, Angola and South Africa in order to explain that the blacks were not evil, that they were not beasts and that they did not eat people. We used to say: 'Tell them that you have relations with us and show them these relations! Make propaganda over the radio! Make programmes for South Africa, Mozambique and Angola to show exactly that!' However, Radio Sweden continued as they always had done and I do not think that there were great efforts to do that work. We explained: 'It is important to create the right conditions, so that when the time arrives the transition will go well. It is necessary that the white population knows that we do not have anything against them'. It would have been good if the white population had been prepared, so that they did not have to live under great anxiety and repeat what had happened in other countries, namely, a general exodus. But the radio stations in the Nordic countries never did that work. It was a pity. We never fought against the whites. It was necessary that voices that the whites would listen to had spoken out.

TS: In 1974, you negotiated the last assistance programme from Sweden to FRELIMO. As Minister for Development and Economic Planning, you then continued to have close relations with Sweden and the other Nordic countries. Was the transition a natural process in the relations?

MS: Yes, our relations were completely natural. In both the political and in the material field we tried to receive support from and promote cooperation and solidarity with the Nordic countries. In Europe there were countries that did not want to have anything to do with FRELIMO and there were countries that had relations with us. They were the Nordic countries—Sweden, Norway, Finland, Denmark and Iceland—and also the Netherlands. Not the other countries. That is why they were not present at our independence celebrations. Except England, but that was due to trickery. At that time, England had a woman as Minister of Co-operation and she came to talk to us. Despite the fact that the British government had never had anything to do with us, she managed to infiltrate the independence celebration and get a seat. We said: 'FRELIMO is giving this independence party. We do not have any relations with you. That is why you have not been invited to attend the celebration. When the Mozambican government has been formed—and if you decide to establish relations with us—then we will receive you'. That is what happened.

We naturally felt great respect towards the states that had supported us. For example, between February and April 1975 a delegation from FRELIMO went to all the Nordic countries to thank them. I myself was the head of the delegation and I remember that Júlio Zambete Carrilho, Fernanda Machungo and Joaquim Ribeiro de Carvalho were part of it. We went to thank everybody for the support they had given us during the struggle for national liberation.

I recall that we were a little surprised in Denmark. In our meetings with the support groups, they asked us: 'Now that you are independent, you are going to create new political parties, aren't you?' That was something that really went beyond our understanding. During the liberation struggle we had continuously worked to achieve unity. Why should we create divisions when we were independent? We had to explain the reasons why we would not do this. If Denmark had a history of various parties, that was Denmark's problem. But one should not think that it is the same everywhere. We managed to end tribalism, regionalism, ethnicism, racism and the divisive problem of religion. We were able to build unity. Why should different groups in a country not be able to build deeper unity? This was even necessary.

TS: Via the Socialist International, the Swedish Social Democratic Party was very active in the reconstruction and promotion of the Socialist Party of Portugal (PSP). FRELIMO had on various occasions strained relations with PSP. How did you look upon the relations between the Swedish and Nordic Social Democrats and PSP?

MS: Well, it was first *Acção Socialista* and then the Socialist Party. In 1970, the International Conference of Solidarity with the Peoples of the Portuguese Colonies took place in Rome. For that meeting we decided to do everything we could to stop the Portuguese Socialist Party from attending. Why? Because at the end of 1969, there had been elections in Portugal and we had put pressure on the Socialist Party to use the ending of the colonial wars as a slogan, but they refused. When the conference was being prepared, we therefore said no to the Socialist Party. But our Italian friends had a different opinion. The Italian Socialist Party came to us and said: 'Listen, we are from the Socialist International and so is the Portuguese Socialist Party, or *Acção Socialista*. If you don't want them to be present it will create a big problem for us. We will have to withdraw from participating, even though the conference is taking place in Italy. That would be unpleasant for everybody'. We had to rethink. We met the Portuguese Communist Party and we spoke to the African countries. We finally agreed that *Acção Socialista* would participate. Luckily, they had the good sense to send Tito de Morais as head of delegation. He was very much respected by all of us for his stand.

We did not have much affinity with the Socialist Party. That was not the force that declared its solidarity with us in Portugal. The political force that represented total solidarity in Portugal was the Portuguese Communist Party. After 1957, when at their congress they declared that they recognized the right of all peoples to be independent and that they were ready to establish relations of friendship and solidarity with all the nationalist forces in Angola and Mozambique, they always supported us.

The support given by the Swedish Social Democratic Party to the Portuguese Socialist Party did not worry us. It was never a problem. It was quite normal and natural, in the same way as other Communist parties gave important support to the Portuguese Communist Party. I even know that there were Communist parties from the socialist countries that wanted us to advance in certain directions defined by the Portuguese Communist Party. For example, to give priority to the struggle for democracy and economic development and only in the third place stress the struggle against colonialism. We had many friends who told us to support the positions of the Portuguese Communist Party.

Our answer was: 'We are very close friends with the Portuguese Communist Party, but in this concrete case, we have our own ideas. We believe that they should have their own slogans and carry out their own struggle. We will do ours with our slogans'. Many of our friends were not pleased with us.

TS: Did you never use your good relations with the Swedish Social Democratic Party to discuss your problems with the Portuguese Socialist Party?

MS: No, we never considered asking them to intervene. But the problems were always explained to our friends.

Jacinto Veloso
FRELIMO
Former Minister of Security, Economic Affairs and of Cooperation
(Maputo, 29 April 1996)

Tor Sellström: How did FRELIMO look upon the Nordic countries when you were in exile in Tanzania?

Jacinto Veloso: From our point of view, support from the Nordic countries was very much appreciated. The Nordic countries, as a whole, appeared as countries that were developed, in an advanced stage of internal democracy and with a foreign policy of understanding and support for self-determination. They were clearly anti-colonialist and, therefore disposed to solidarity with the cause of national liberation. For example, for Eduardo Mondlane—with whom I had the opportunity to work many times in Tanzania from 1964 to 1965—they were real allies and maybe even ideal partners for liberation. They did not have any particular interests or were, at least, equidistant from the East – West conflict.

TS: Generally anti-Communist, why do you think that the Nordic countries supported liberation movements which were close to Moscow?

JV: Examining the question today—not only having in mind what was happening at that time—I believe that the analysts designing the politics of the Nordic countries always interpreted a certain inclination by FRELIMO, MPLA or PAIGC in favour of the East, of Moscow, as an apparent—conscious or unconscious—relationship to reach independence, and not as an internal construction by the nationalists. Today, 20 to 30 years later, it is clear that Marxism-Leninism was not rooted in these countries. However, until this day some Western radical anti-Communists do not believe that that was the situation.

TS: Do you believe that personal contacts between leaders like Eduardo Mondlane and Olof Palme facilitated an understanding of the nationalist factor and the question of self-determination in Mozambique and Southern Africa?

JV: I believe that personal contacts facilitated a lot. There were many contacts. There were contacts between the main leaders. There were contacts or visits to our region by individuals, journalists, politicians and officials from the governments of the Nordic countries. I believe that they must have understood and written reports—some of a public character and others more restricted —with analysis where they saw that the East influenced the politics of FRELIMO, MPLA etc. through pressure, aid and even through persons directly involved in those organizations. The Nordic countries had a very special way of drawing attention to the fact that a good solution would not be found in the East—and maybe not in the West—but in something genuine to each country.

TS: Do you think that the support was extended with conditions attached?

JV: I believe that the support was limited and today we can say that it was very limited. But it was non-conditional. The Nordic countries could have done much more. But I think that they did not for internal political reasons. Also because there were some risks involved in the solidarity. At the same time, through their contacts they tried to make us understand that for different reasons complete dependency on the East was not the best policy for Mozambique and its future development.

I heard Swedish leaders—persons involved—saying that it was necessary for us to reflect and debate more internally to find our own course of action, not one imposed from abroad. Therefore, I believe that the support opened a dialogue and that the dialogue made us understand the problems.

TS: In the case of Mozambique, there were frictions between the Portuguese Socialist Party (PSP) and FRELIMO. The Swedish Social Democratic Party supported both FRELIMO and PSP. Did you see this as a problem?

JV: I do not think so, because the Socialist Party of Portugal only appeared later. Those who became leaders of the Socialist Party— the fellow party of the Swedish Social Democratic Party—were in the Portuguese Patriotic Front of National Liberation and had various leanings. There are today distinguished leaders of the Socialist Party who were members of the Communist Party and others who were less to the left, being democrats, republicans, independents etc. In my opinion, that was not an impediment, because the relations with the Patriotic Front were good. I myself was in Algeria and worked with them.

TS: As early as in 1966, Pierre Schori from the Swedish Social Democratic Party wrote to President Mondlane, asking him about his opinion of the Patriotic Front. This would mean that the most important relationship was with FRELIMO?

JV: Yes, because the Patriotic Front was very complex. It was a big mixture, with strong internal frictions. I met Pierre Schori in Algeria. Aquino de Bragança introduced me. De Bragança unfortunately died in the disaster with President Samora Machel. I believe that if he was alive he could tell a lot, because he had very good relations with the Nordic countries and with Pierre Schori. They used to write to each other and discuss questions about future democracy.

TS: Swedish journalists played an active part in bringing Sweden and FRELIMO closer together. Anders Johansson is one example. He formed part of the solidarity movement in Sweden.

JV: Exactly. He used to write for the newspaper *Dagens Nyheter*.

TS: He was also the first Swedish journalist to visit the liberated areas.

JV: Precisely. He was in Cabo Delgado.

TS: Did you go to Algeria after your stay in Tanzania?

JV: Yes, I worked at the Algerian airline company, but after work I was with the FRELIMO office.

TS: What was your view of the Nordic countries from Algeria?

JV: There were very close connections, but the Nordic countries had less impact there. Algeria aspired to be the leader of the Third World. They had close contacts with countries like Cuba. However, even in Algeria the Nordic countries were well placed. I remember that there were very good relations.

TS: FRELIMO was not yet in government but it was part of the non-aligned movement (NAM), so to speak. Did you consult with Sweden and Finland concerning declarations at the different NAM meetings?

JV: Not that I recall, no.

TS: When did you leave Algeria?

JV: I left for good after 25 April 1974. I went straight to the peace negotiations with Portugal. It so happened that many of those behind the revolution in Portugal were old colleagues of mine from the military course.

TS: So you were negotiating with your ex-colleagues?

JV: Exactly. And actually very well. There could have been a reaction against that, but their attitude was, on the contrary, excellent. They said: 'You were right'. It was interesting.

TS: After Mozambique's independence, Sweden and the other Nordic countries continued to support the process of independence in Southern Africa. In your country, they supported ZANU and ANC. What was your view on that?

JV: I do not think that there was any limitation. On the contrary, the open relationship continued after independence.

TS: In 1976, with the change from a Social Democratic to a non-socialist government in Sweden, many believed that the support for Mozambique and the national liberation process in Southern Africa would be affected negatively. But this did not happen. Instead, it increased. Did you have the same contacts with the non-socialist government as with its Social Democratic predecessor?

JV: Well, our contacts were always very good because the cooperation policy remained the same. I believe that a clear notion of international solidarity with peoples that want to liberate themselves is characteristic of the Swedish electorate and that this is independent of the political colour of the parties. Actually, we had times of crisis at the government level when the Social Democratic Party was in power. It was very critical and publicly presented very harsh criticism of the FRELIMO government. In my opinion, this happened for internal Swedish electoral reasons. But the fact is that the moments of major crisis with Sweden occurred when the Social Democratic Party was in power. Nevertheless, the relations were without a doubt always good. Severe criticism such as that often happens when the party in power is politically closer to you and is more to the left. It is a defence mechanism against criticism from the conservative parties. It usually occurs during the months preceding general elections. The rest of the time there is a truce.

TS: You were responsible for national security in Mozambique at the time of the Nkomati Accord with South Africa. Were there any supportive, or critical, reactions from the Nordic countries to the accord?

JV: I think that they were more of the critical kind, if I am not wrong. But, the criticism was not very strong. That came from the East. Until this day, such reactions continue to come from Cuba.

I think that our explanations were accepted. We explained that the accord had advantages for us, but primarily—although it could not be seen at once—that it would have advantages for the liberation of South Africa itself. We set a precedent by concluding an accord on good neighbourliness and non-aggression between South Africa and Mozambique, an independent African country seriously suspected of being an 'agent' of the Soviet Union. At the time, it appeared to us that the accord also would set a precedent for an internal agreement between the black population and the established white power in South Africa. Although this might have seemed utopic, I believe that this was actually what happened. The final downfall of apartheid started with the Nkomati Accord. This kind of action accelerated the process, even though ANC at that point also opposed the accord. I believe that the immediate advantage for Mozambique was that South Africa at least stopped attacking us directly with their military forces and war planes. Had it only been for that, it would have made sense to sign the accord. But the repercussions were much greater. They culminated in the election of ANC to political power in South Africa. The Nkomati Accord lit the light at the end of the tunnel for democracy in South Africa.

TS: Soon after the Nkomati Accord, the Socialist International had a meeting in Arusha where Olof Palme, Samora Machel and Oliver Tambo spoke about its consequences. Palme and Tambo criticized the accord, did they not?

JV: I was there. Yes, they spoke. Tanzania was also against the accord. President Nyerere in particular. They did not think that it was a good step to take, but later they admitted that maybe it was right. I myself heard from high-ranking ANC leaders—at the time detained on Robben Island—that the Nkomati Accord, after all, was entered into for the good of democracy in South Africa and to facilitate the legalization of ANC.

Sérgio Vieira
FRELIMO
Former Minister of Security and of Agriculture
(Maputo, 29 April 1996)

Tor Sellström: As a participant in the liberation struggle—but also a person who has reflected on the struggle and written about its international context—how did you look upon the Nordic countries when they started to give humanitarian support to FRELIMO?

Sérgio Vieira: I saw it as a really serious and fundamental action. I think that the persons who started the relationship with the Nordic countries were Eduardo and Janet Mondlane in the early 1960s. I was a young man when the Swedish Minister of Education, Olof Palme, walked the streets against the war in Vietnam. It was very important for my generation. Here we saw a minister of a European country saying that 'you are right in wanting freedom with independence, freedom with liberty'. From an ethical standpoint, the Nordic countries said that 'we are from Europe and we may be members of NATO, but we disagree with colonialism'. In FRELIMO, we made a tremendous effort to depolarize the issue of the liberation struggle. In the very beginning—under the Kennedy administration—the United States also said so, of course, taking into consideration all the international problems at the time. But after the Kennedy assassination, there was a shift under Johnson. Franklin Thomas of the Ford Foundation told me two years ago that he was very shocked by the pressures from the US State Department to make them withdraw their support from the Mozambique Institute. The involvement by the Nordic countries was, however, a first clear sign that liberation was not an issue of the Cold War. Decolonization was not Cold War.

Secondly—and I do say that it was very important—the Nordic humanitarian support was medicine, clothes and food. There was a tremendous need of all this. I would say as much as weapons. Weapons alone do not change life, but the clothes supplied, for example, helped us to present something to the peasant in the liberated areas. He could get something in return for his production. It was fundamental to create a base of economic development and self-reliance, whatever you want to call it. It was essential. Thus, when we in 1970 managed to call the solidarity conference in Rome—where a broad spectrum of political forces, from Christian Democrats to Communists from all over Europe attended—they went there also thanks to the example set by the Nordic countries.

TS: Would you say that they broadened your diplomatic field of action?

SV: Yes. They were a sort of locomotive in that respect. After independence and during the confrontation with Rhodesia and apartheid, the ethical stand of the Nordic countries was essential. Today, a lot of people discuss how efficient the Nordic support really was. I think that it is a false discussion. Things were done. Trucks were there to carry the products. Agriculture was developing and forests were planted. Of course, we faced problems of management, but fundamentally problems of war. You cannot have good management when things are physically destroyed. However, the economic growth in Mozambique from 1977 until 1981 was also a result of the support given by the Nordic countries, without conditions attached.

TS: You did not feel that there were political conditions attached?

SV: No. We agreed and disagreed in open discussions.

TS: Also during the liberation struggle?

SV: Absolutely. The Nordic governments never told us: 'Do not attack the Portuguese or do not do that.' Never. They said: 'Your struggle is just. Of course, we are in principle in disagreement with the armed struggle, but we do understand that it is the only way, since there is no possibility of dialogue with Salazar'.

TS: I get the impression that FRELIMO—perhaps more than any other liberation movement—was very principled, for example, criticizing Sweden regarding its involvement in the proposed Cabora Bassa scheme?

SV: Yes, but Sweden took a good stand on that issue. It was not our purpose as such to oppose Cabora Bassa. After all, we were one hundred per cent sure that we would be independent and after independence we would need that source of energy. Also, Cabora Bassa made the war much more expensive for Portugal. It weakened the economic base of the colonial war. There is not one particular reason for the collapse of the Portuguese regime. The main reason was, however, the colonial wars. People were killed in the wars, the military expenditure rose, desertions were taking place and the army became exhausted. All of this was involved in the Cabora Bassa issue.

I would like to point out another interesting dimension in our relationship with the Nordic countries, namely the respect that they had for us and the respect that we had for them. For example, in 1977 there was a conservative government in Sweden. The Prime Minister was Mr. Fälldin. I was charged by our government to prepare an official visit and I went to Sweden before Samora Machel arrived. I discussed with our Swedish friends and was received by the Prime Minister. At a certain point I said: 'Mr. Prime Minister, there is something very sensitive that I really would like to ask you. During a long time, Olof Palme was a very close friend of ours and today he is the leader of the opposition. Would it be improper for President Machel to meet Olof Palme?' I received an answer that symbolized what Sweden was for us. He said: 'We would be surprised otherwise. Olof Palme is the one who contributed to the consensus in Sweden around our relationship with FRELIMO. Please, do see him'.

Another important dimension in our relationship with the Nordic countries was that solidarity became a popular movement. For example, I was very touched—many of us were very touched—when we received a printing machine for the Mozambique Institute in Dar es Salaam from Finland. It was through an effort by school children. They collected money for that. It was a clear expression of how they felt about solidarity. The support was not just at the level of states, coming from SIDA, DANIDA, NORAD or FINNIDA, but from the base. From children, churches, trade unions, from all strata of society. I think that this was precious.

TS: FRELIMO probably enjoyed stronger support from the Nordic solidarity organizations than other liberation movements?

SV: Yes. A number of reasons contributed to that. In the first place, nobody doubted who was leading the liberation struggle. It was very clear that there was only FRELIMO and the colonial power. Full stop. Secondly, what very much assisted our dialogue and acceptance by the people in the Nordic countries was FRELIMO's ethical principles regarding treatment of prisoners of war, the total refusal to attack the civilian population and resort to terrorist actions like putting a bomb in a super-market, a cinema or a school. Some of our friends wanted us to engage in that kind of action, but all the time we said no. We refused. Respect for human dignity and human life was an ethical principle of FRELIMO. A distinction between the colonial power and the settlers was always upheld.

TS: You also had a very good information apparatus keeping the international opinion informed about the struggle?

SV: Well, a very small apparatus, but I think that it was efficient. Some of my colleagues who worked in the Nordic countries—for instance, Lourenço Mutaca, who was later killed in Ethiopia—contributed to the growth of the relationship.

TS: After Mozambique's independence, Sweden and the other Nordic countries supported ZANU in your country. How did you look upon this? Did you see it as interference or as continued internationalist involvement in Southern Africa?

SV: I think that the Nordic support to the liberation movements in Southern Africa was coherent. There was no interference at all. They did not come to us saying: 'We want to do that'. They said to us as host country: 'Can we do that?', and we responded: 'Yes, they need the support. We are asking you to support them. Their cause is just. We think that you should support ANC, SWAPO and ZANU'. When it comes to Zimbabwe, a shift occurred, because during a certain period we in FRELIMO thought that ZAPU was the main movement until we started to study the situation in 1970-71. At that time, the Smith forces were already operating inside Mozambique and we wanted to force them out to be kept busy in their own country. We then started to look for ZAPU, but could not find them. I participated in the discussions. We tried with J. Z. Moyo and others but no one was forthcoming. Until Chitepo and Tongogara from ZANU came to us and said: 'Please, can you help us?' We had already studied the situation and knew that they were on the ground, so we said yes.

TS: In the case of Sweden, equal support was given to ZANU and ZAPU. Is it your impression that the Swedish support was more pragmatic than ideological?

SV: I do not know if pragmatic is the proper term. I would say that Sweden tried not to interfere or prejudge. They were not present in the terrain, but they knew about ZANU and ZAPU, saying 'let us have a more balanced approach, because it seems that both of them represent important segments of the population'. I do not think that it was on the basis of cold calculation, which the word 'pragmatic' may suggest, but on the basis of respect.

TS: During the liberation struggle, did you find that the Nordic countries acted on your behalf in different international fora, as at the United Nations? Did you consult with the Nordic countries?

SV: There were consultations and clear signs that they were positive. In NATO, Denmark, Norway and Iceland, for instance, raised the question of NATO weapons going to the Portuguese colonial wars. To a large extent I would say that the solidarity was extended into the global action of bringing an end to the colonial and the apartheid systems.

TS: Similarly, did you, for example, inform the Nordic countries about the Nkomati Accord between Mozambique and South Africa?

SV: Yes, we informed them. During a certain period, a sort of misunderstanding occurred. I remember that we had very long discussions and that eventually Olof Palme and others from the Nordic countries at the Socialist International meeting in Arusha, Tanzania, in 1984 understood our position and decision. They had not understood us properly. Actually, they had not read the documents. They thought that we wanted to stop ANC's armed struggle, but ANC was actually not waging any armed struggle from Mozambique and we were not stopping anything. Samora Machel summarized the situation and said that 'either we march towards a war between South Africa and Mozambique or we try peaceful coexistence. What is your advice? Should we declare war or should we fight for peace? Should we, the Mozambicans, appear to the international community as war-mongers or should we let the South Africans show that they do not respect peace?' Olof Palme replied that 'no country can oppose an effort for peace'.

There was a slight misunderstanding, because people did not know the documents, even thinking that there was a sort of hidden agenda. But there was no hidden agenda, only the text in the documents. Nothing else. We discussed with South Africa. I was in charge of that. On a number of occasions we discussed with P.W. Botha about ANC, the need to release Mandela and the end to apartheid. He was all the time saying that they were going to do something. I remember when Foreign Minister 'Pik' Botha phoned me from Geneva to say that P.W. Botha was going to make an important statement. He was going to 'cross the Rubicon'. I sat down to watch 'the crossing of the Rubicon' on television, but it was not exactly the Rubicon, rather a glass of water.

Anyway, it was an expression of the contradictions existing within the apartheid system. I do not think that the Nkomati Accord was a fundamental element, but it was important for the isolation of the apartheid regime. Reagan had to react to that. It was an element to further depolarize the issues. South Africa was all the time arguing that they were going to be invaded by the Russians, the Chinese and the Communist hordes through Mozambique. After Nkomati, they could not come with that kind of mythology. It helped to further erode the apartheid system and strengthen the internal struggle.

TS: In this respect, was the Nordic support important?

SV: Yes, very important. In conclusion, I would say that the support of the Nordic countries for the liberation of Southern Africa was fundamental.

Namibia

Ottilie Abrahams
SWAPO—Student and SWAPO-Democrats in Sweden—Namibia National Front
Director of the Jakob Morenga Tutorial College
(Windhoek, 16 March 1995)

Tor Sellström: How do you see the development of the liberation movement in Namibia and the relations with the Nordic countries?

Ottilie Abrahams: Namibia has a history of groups like SWAPO and SWANU working together. For example, already at the time when my husband was arrested by the South African police in Rehoboth, SWAPO and SWANU stood ready to go as one body to defend him. Even in exile, SWAPO and SWANU always worked together. If SWANU people arrived in a place where they did not have a representative, they were taken in by the SWAPO people. In the late 1960s, we held talks with SWANU. That was when Moses Katjiuongua and Fanuel Kozonguizi were in Dar es Salaam. We held talks on forming one body. We felt that we were getting very far.

Then we met OAU, because we knew what their concept of 'sole authenticity' would do. We asked OAU specifically not to give money either to SWAPO or to SWANU, but to give it to an organization. The name was SWANLIF, South West African National Liberation Front. We already knew in 1963 that donors were going to use the question of funding to alienate the two groups. There were certain political groups in certain countries which were supposed to be the sole liberators of those countries, and we opposed that view from the start.

TS: Was that view the policy of the OAU Liberation Committee?

OA: Yes. We said that it was a violation of the democratic rights of the people. We foresaw that they would create demagogue people who wanted to colonize the struggle so that any input which was not in line with the 'sole authentic party' immediately would be stifled.

In spite of the oppression, those of us who had stayed in South Africa were brought up in a very democratic tradition in the Non-European Unity Movement (NEUM). You could get up when a leader spoke, ask about anything and tell him that you did not agree with him. In the Cape Peninsula Students' Union we were taught to fight ideas with ideas. We always thought critically. If we agree with you, we do not care whether you are the President or not. If we disagreed, we would say so. We always felt that if people basically were loyal to the party, but had different ideas on how to get to the goal, it was an enrichment.

When we went to Dar es Salaam in 1963—that is, when we went into exile—we came to a place where people were beginning to talk about the 'sole and authentic' leaders of the revolution. The concept was imposed by people from outside. First by OAU. The donors—for their own reasons—then decided that they were going to reinforce the idea. But we felt that it was suppressing any opposition. We felt that if you belong to a party and you see that something is wrong, you have to have the right to criticize and to propose an alternative. But whenever you did that you were put in a prison camp because you were opposing the leaders. I am myself suspended from SWAPO until this day. The reason was 'disrespecting the leadership' when I was Secretary for Education and part of the Executive Committee. My upbringing was politically different. If there was something that I wanted to say, I said it, because you wanted to go with your party. But this business of 'sole and authentic' began to mean that the only opinion that was relevant was the opinion that agreed with what the leaders said.

TS: But you were in favour of one strong Namibian liberation movement?

OA: When one speaks about *a movement* one does not speak about *one party*. A liberation movement includes all groups, whether they are church groups, women groups or political parties. They are moving towards a common goal. That is what I understand by a liberation movement, and that is why we got on so well when we formed SWANLIF. That did not mean that SWAPO or SWANU should dismantle, but that we should meet on issues of common concern and speak with one voice.

We said so in the meeting with OAU: 'We have formed this organization and this is what we stand for.' We gave them copies of documents where we said: 'Please, do not give money to one or the other. Give the money to the movement. Then we can decide how much we are going to use for what item. Each party will have its own share to do with it as it pleases.' After I spoke they got up and said: 'How do we know that you are not forming SWANLIF to get our money?' As naive as I was, I got up and said: 'Look, we were sent out of the country to get this organization going. We are South West Africans and we will do it with or without your help.' And when we left the meeting, the money was immediately given to SWAPO. End of story.

This is what the donors subsequently have also done. We regarded this as interference in the affairs of another country, whether we were free or not. One day when I am old I want to write a book on the birth of the concept of sole authenticity. This is where it started. It is important, because it boosted certain organizations to such an extent that they became little Hitlers. Already in those years we fought SIDA and all those people, saying: 'You are creating a problem for us which will cause the death of many, many people.'

TS: In Sweden, the decision to support SWAPO was taken a couple of years later. At the beginning of the 1960s, there was a close relationship with SWANU.

OA: But after the invention of sole authenticity the others were dropped. Because the elite in Africa said so. All of us had to fall into place with that! The reason why I am delivering this point is that I feel that there is a direct link between that problem and the position of the opposition today. It is like a snowball. You, the authentic party, get the money. Because of that you can get more organizers and because you have more organizers you can get more people. The thing snow-balls! Where we are now, the snowball is so big that everybody else is insignificant. The problems are going to be felt in Namibia, as they have been felt in other countries. This is where it comes from. Right from the start. If you were a person who disagreed, you went to the camps. Later on you went to the holes of ANC, SWAPO and other groups. There is a direct line here. Because of that, these parties became more bigotted than they would have been if they had been left on their own.

The tradition of democracy—which is a prerequisite for health in any country—has slowly been watered down. If you look at the opposition in Namibia, it consists mostly of people who were not there in the beginning. Apart from people like Moses Katjiuongua and so on, they were not there when we started. They do not have this history of the struggle. They do not have that sense of decorum. As a result, even though people do not want to vote for the party in power, there is no alternative. Because with their support OAU and the donors made sure that there should not be any opposition.

TS: In the case of the ruling Nordic Social Democratic Parties, multi-party democracy was, of course, a principle within the Socialist International. It was also a principle supported by the non-socialist, bourgeois parties. When you lived in Sweden, how did they react to your points of view in this context?

OA: Precisely, and that is why we kept asking them: 'If democracy is good for you, why is it not good for us?' We asked them! But they said: 'Africa is different.' They just told us that we are different! The other thing they said was that 'we have to mobilize the Swedish society. The things that you are telling us are not important and if we must put the whole complexity of the argument in front of the Swedish people, they will not understand it.' I said that I did not know that the Swedes were such idiots. This was the country from which Ingmar Bergman comes. If the Swedes could understand the plays of Ingmar Bergman, surely they could understand the complexities of the African political situation. But they said 'No, you are going to confuse the people.' That was the argument. My opinion, frankly, was that the Swedes knew exactly what we were talking about.

If you want democracy you can even go to the pre-schools in Sweden. That democracy reinforced the democracy which we learnt in South Africa. It was that reinforcement of democracy that made us create schools like the one where we are sitting now and where the students are running the affairs. All this started in South Africa. It was reinforced in Sweden and is now even found in rural pre-schools. Not that the Swedes have given one cent to support it. The Norwegians have, but the Swedes have scrupulously avoided giving the Jakob Morenga Tutorial College one cent for the past ten years. These schools come out of their ideas. But in that country—where democracy was even part of the pre-schools—they could not understand that we were asking for democracy. Because we were not first class citizens. We were third class. And the bourgeois government in Sweden at that time, for their own reasons—maybe because they wanted to sell Volvos here after independence or whatever they wanted to sell—agreed to accept it.

But when we were in Sweden we did not experience any discrimination as human beings. Up to this day I have always said that if I could not live in my own country, I would live in Sweden. I do not think that refugees were treated better in any part of the world. My children still think of themselves as Swedish citizens. As human beings we were treated very well, but not at the political level. My little children came back from school telling me that they had learnt that SWAPO was the only political party in Namibia. I said: 'Let the Swedes teach their nonsense to people who do not know, but we know.' Then you had SIDA coming with things like 'liberated territories in Namibia'. We were sitting in the audience, asking them: 'Tell us, where are those places?'

TS: Did not Per Sandén shoot a film there in the 1970s?

OA: Per Sandén. We went to Per and said: 'Just tell us where that place is?' He disappeared! Anything that is based on a lie has to explode some time or other.

TS: When Andreas Shipanga was jailed, he had some support from prominent church people, for example in England. There must, surely, have been voices also raised in the Nordic countries?

OA: We started a hell of a campaign in Sweden and because of that we have been ostracized for years by all the African governments. Even though my husband was the doctor for MPLA—and although we provided money with which they attacked the enemy—those people cannot even invite us for a ceremony. We still have to be ostracized.

TS: When did you launch that campaign?

OA: It was just before SWAPO-Democrats was formed. And just before Shipanga and the others came out of prison. We campaigned for two years, with church people like this man in Germany, Groth, and others. He was also ostracized and is still being ostracized for telling the truth. We pursued the campaign through the *Namibian Review*, which we had established in Sweden with Swedish money. People smuggled out letters from the prison holes in Angola that we published in the *Namibian Review*. They realized that some opposition started to build up about what was happening.

TS: You founded SWAPO-Democrats in Sweden in June 1978. Did the new party have any support there?

OA: There were lots of Swedes who understood our position, but they were not in charge. When Shipanga and these people were freed, they came to Stockholm. SWAPO-D was formed in Spånga, where we lived. But the problem was that by that time we had been in exile for thirteen years and we were totally out of touch with the sentiments of the people in Namibia. The formation of SWAPO-D was a mistake. But the feeling behind it was not a mistake.

We did not want to leave SWAPO, but we wanted the accent to be on democracy. That is the problem we had with SWAPO. Historically, the establishment of that party was an expression of the wishes of some of us who came from South West Africa. We voted for SWAPO, we thought that it was a good party, but we wanted infusion of democracy.

TS: So SWAPO-Democrats did not have any support from a political organization, church or youth movement in Sweden or the other Nordic countries?

OA: No. The mistake we made was that we thought that the people who formed SWAPO-D with us were the same people whom we knew in 1963. We did not know that they were exposed to the same influences as the rest of SWAPO. The people we had in SWAPO in South Africa were real resistance people. The police used to invade their houses at three or four o'clock in the morning. They never revealed names of SWAPO people. They could be locked up, beaten or whatever, but they stuck to their comrades. Now, when we formed SWAPO-D we had not seen each other for thirteen years. But what we obviously forgot was that these people—who had also been in the leadership of SWAPO—were exposed to the same influences and were affected by this. They were thinking very similarly to SWAPO.

TS: Why did you then form SWAPO-D in Sweden?

OA: Because that is where we and other SWAPO people, like the Moongos, were living. We had numerous discussions on this before it was done. We thought that if we returned to Namibia as a group, we would know where we were going. But when we arrived in Namibia, we discovered that people were totally opposed to the formation of anything new. They were also exposed to 'the sole and authentic' concept and people regarded SWAPO, for very good reasons, as the liberating organization. There was no fertile ground for anything else.

TS: Did you notice any difference between the Nordic countries in this respect? What were the reactions in the different Nordic countries to the detention of Shipanga and the formation of SWAPO-Democrats?

OA: I would say that the opinion was predominantly pro-SWAPO, but you had people—even in Finland—who disagreed with the official position. Of course, people around the Beukes in Norway were in opposition to this concept. But some had more sense than we. As my husband said one day: 'We should actually have shut up and got onto the band-wagon.' But there are certain things you just cannot do.

TS: How about Denmark? The Danish government never officially recognized SWAPO as the sole and authentic movement and DANIDA channelled their funds through WUS, IUEF, Africa Education Trust etc.?

OA: In Denmark you also had individuals who were totally opposed to us. In WUS, definitely. I was not really involved there, but I got the impression that they were just as full of 'sole authenticity'. WUS Denmark was terrible. My problem is that there were good projects coming up, real nation-building projects. But because the projects were not launched by SWAPO, they were ditched. This school is a triumph of the spirit of the people in the NGOs. In spite of all the oppression and suppression, it is now ten years old. That is why it is so important to me.

TS: Why did you join SWAPO in the first place?

OA: One can understand why people in Namibia went to SWAPO. We were ourselves very strong SWAPO executive members. SWANU also had a good position as the oldest political party. It is probably an accident that my husband and I were both studying in Cape Town at the time. We decided that it did not matter whether we worked in SWAPO or in SWANU as long as the movement was good. There were, for example, people who did not know how to vote. We took them into the NEUM to open their minds and actually taught them how to vote. By bringing them into the NEUM we thought that influence and tradition of democracy would be brought into Namibia. That is why we joined SWAPO. But if SWANU had been in Cape Town we could probably have joined SWANU. It was a question of throwing the dice as to which organization you would support. To us it was not important who was in SWAPO. We had numerous discussions on this issue. It was a common decision that SWAPO is where we will go, but at the same time we had good relations with SWANU and helped them wherever we were.

Ben Amathila
SWAPO—Chief Representative to Scandinavia, West Germany and Austria—Secretary of Economic Affairs
Minister of Information and Broadcasting
(Stockholm, 19 May 1995)

Tor Sellström: You were the first official SWAPO representative to the Nordic countries, based in Sweden? What was the background to the decision to open a SWAPO office there?

Ben Amathila: When I got my instructions to go to Sweden, they were not very clear. I had to set up a SWAPO office in Sweden shortly after the Tanga consultative congress at the beginning of 1970. The congress was very important and crucial to the effectuation of the liberation struggle. Some of our people had been arrested and their appearance in court raised a number of questions. Our constitution did not make reference to armed struggle. Those who were arrested in Pretoria could not benefit from the Geneva convention on prisoners of war. And whilst the struggle was going on, one of the most important things that we had to tackle was, obviously, to answer the question: 'After liberation: What?'

There was nothing before Tanga that indicated that we were preparing ourselves to take the reins of power after liberation. These were the things which were addressed at Tanga. An administration was set up which made people believe that SWAPO was preparing to declare itself unilaterally as a government in exile.

My coming to Sweden was partly to highlight those issues and the direction in which we wanted to go. Certainly, one has to take note of the fact that Namibia was isolated, cut off from the rest of the world. The only place that Namibians used to know was South Africa, and through South Africa some other countries. To me it was a new experience to come to Sweden. My personal contacts only started through correspondence from Dar es Salaam and with the Swedes that I met there, like Anne-Marie Sundbom in 1969.

My instruction was very vague. It was left to me to devise means of creating the Stockholm office and to make it work. To open the office, I was only given 15 US Dollars as pocket money. The ticket was provided by the Afro-Asian Solidarity Organization in Moscow, which gave it to me to attend a student conference in Helsinki in 1971. It was believed that it would be easier to get a visa to Sweden through Helsinki. But it did not work. After two weeks I had to return to Moscow to await the visa there, which again did not work. I was then obliged to join my wife, who was studying in London, because I simply could not make ends meet any more. I stayed with her for two or three months, living on her stipend until I finally got a visa. I then took the ferry to Gothenburg and the train to Stockholm. While in Helsinki, I had met somebody called Mattias Berg, who was a student leader. He put me up in a hotel for two nights. Thereafter they could not manage, so I had to establish contact with some individuals.

There was a small flat which was used as an office for SWAPO by a Namibian called Paul Helmuth. He had left SWAPO some months before I arrived. However, I got this place. It was just one room. I spent my nights there, cooked my food there and also did my political work in that room at Regeringsgatan No. 5 in Stockholm. The building does not exist any more.

One has to appreciate that SWAPO had to formalize the liberation struggle. One should also take note of the contrast and the sharpness of the conflict between the super powers and the Cold War. The Soviet Union on the one hand and the West on the other. Also China, which was not necessarily in line with the Soviet Union. In its quest for identity, SWAPO was treated with suspicion by the West because of the contacts we had with the Soviet Union. As Namibia did not offer a viable political alternative to SWAPO, both the Chinese and the Soviets agreed that SWAPO was a force to be supported. SWAPO was possibly one of the few movements that had access to both Beijing and Moscow, without offending either one.

TS: This was after the demise of SWANU?

BA: Well, on my arrival, SWANU was still very active in Sweden. Sometimes I found that at the meetings that I organized there were more SWANU people than Swedes.

The conflict between the East and the West was so intense that whoever you chose it cost you a label. The problem was more with the West. I think that my coming to the Nordic countries, especially to Sweden, provided a cushion to absorb the suspicion and hard criticism of where we belonged. I came to realize that the Swedish government already at this time did not really need the public to push it into a certain direction. Most of the people I dealt with were internationalists who understood what was taking place and they formulated a policy in line with SWAPO's expectations. They accepted the Liberation Committee of the OAU. The Swedish government used it as a guide to inform themselves of what was happening in Africa and what position to take.

Within OAU were obviously the countries that hosted the liberation movements in the early 1960s. Tanzania and Zambia were the ones who mainly shared the burden. They were under much pressure from the Portuguese, because of their presence in Mozambique and Angola, as well as from Ian Smith in Southern Rhodesia and from South Africa. The threat of attack, the intimidation and sabotage of the infrastructure in those countries was so severe that it almost made their nationals turn against the liberation movements. It is amazing how these countries stood by their decision to support the liberation movements against the great powers and how they guided their nationals to accept the price of facilitating the liberation struggle.

There was another element of pressure and that was the work of the enemy intelligence. The enemy started to train their agents to get information from the liberation movements and the host governments, which increased tension and suspicion. The most dramatic event was the death of Eduardo Mondlane in February 1969 and the rifts that ensued in FRELIMO, which actually changed the whole political atmosphere and also the political attitude of the governments of Zambia and Tanzania. They did not abandon the liberation movement, but became more cautious.

In 1973, OAU and the Norwegian government held a conference in Oslo on liberation movements, which came up with a resolution that movements with liberated territories should get priority assistance from the Nordic governments. The trust the Nordic governments had in OAU was strong.

TS: All the Nordic countries had close relations with Tanzania and Zambia. It probably explains that trust?

BA: Yes, that is very true. I think that Tanzania was particularly accepted as the soul of the progressive African countries at the time. They were authoritative. Whatever position they took was respected. Nyerere, in particular, became a spokesperson for the liberation movements and for Africa in general. The same goes for Kaunda. These were the few countries who actually stuck their necks out for the liberation movements, also because of their early contacts with Nkrumah in Ghana. That put them in a special light and made them respected by the Nordic countries.

On my arrival in Sweden I had to start from scratch to define what the SWAPO office was supposed to be. I really did not have any briefing on what I was meant to be doing. I had to seek the necessary tools to do my work, because I did not have a budget. It was a very difficult situation.

I was told that Olof Palme had attended a conference on South West Africa in Oxford in 1966 and that it possibly might have brought him to terms with the political situation in Southern Africa, Namibia in particular. You had internationalists like Olof Palme and his colleagues, who stood up against the Americans in areas like Vietnam and by so doing carved out a special place for Sweden in the hearts of the oppressed the world over. By the time I arrived in Sweden, the Vietnamese issue was well embraced by the Swedish public and government, which led to political tensions between the United States and Sweden. It culminated in the threat by the Americans to boycott Swedish products, including Volvo.

By 1973 all political parties in Sweden embraced the question of Vietnam to the extent that while we all supported it, it posed a problem to a newcomer like Namibia. It became a problem of penetration, a problem of getting the necessary contacts to mobilize a group to support Namibia. The issues of Angola, Mozambique and Guinea-Bissau were well embraced as well. And South Africa. People had read about apartheid, but Namibia was unknown. Whilst in the late 1960s, apartheid was definitely a political issue in Sweden, it was overtaken by the events in Vietnam and the OAU criteria of supporting movements with liberated territories. It was generally felt that Sweden was too small to effectively embrace all the issues in Africa and Asia. This was not the attitude of the government, but definitely that of some of the support groups that I came across.

My first experience with something which came close to an official Swedish government policy towards the liberation movements—

verging on recognition—was the policy by Krister Wickman, who succeeded Torsten Nilsson as Foreign Minister. After the conference which was held in Oslo, Krister Wickman held a reception for all the liberation movements' representatives at the Foreign Ministry in Stockholm. After that, Sweden almost recognized the liberation movements as official representatives of their peoples. That was a very significant development towards recognition and support for the liberation movements. By 1969, the only financial contribution that I know existed between SWAPO and Sweden, for instance, was a donation of 30,000 Swedish Kronor, which was given to SWAPO in Dar es Salaam and in Lusaka to buy office equipment. At that time, there was already an attempt on the part of the Swedish government to alleviate the problems of the liberation movement.

On my arrival in Sweden, I did not have any source of income. My approach to SIDA resulted in a scholarship to study the Swedish language. I started by attending classes for foreign students at Wennergren Center in Stockholm. Later I transferred to the university. That gave me a bit of income, but it was not enough. My wife had completed her studies in London and joined me in 1972. I think that my income then was 900 Swedish Kronor per month.

Immediately upon my arrival I realized that I must develop relations with the people at the Foreign Ministry. I also had a very close relationship with the Social Democratic Party, which to a large extent came to my assistance.

TS: How about the solidarity movement? The Africa Groups in Sweden, for example?

BA: What we concluded at Tanga was that our struggle was one of liberation and identity. To be recognized in our own right and to stand up for what we believed was correct. Sweden and the Nordic countries were to be approached in order to help us establish that we wanted to be seen as Namibians. Our right to self-determination should be recognized.

Sweden was not a newcomer to the question of self-determination. Way back in the mid-1960s we had read about people like Alva Myrdal and her work at the UN, where she stood firm for the right to self-determination. There were also colleagues of mine who had visited Sweden before me, like Peter Mueshihange, Andreas Shipanga and Paul Helmuth. And the President of SWAPO had met Olof Palme. However, there was a strong presence of Namibians in Sweden through the SWANU students. They were accepted as legitimate representatives of their country, but their recognition suffered a blow because of the serious work of SWAPO and the OAU criteria of who should be supported or not. Most of the time when I called information meetings on behalf of SWAPO, the SWANU people came in big numbers to distract me from what I was doing, trying to maintain their identity as spokespersons for the people of South West Africa.

OAU was very forceful that liberation movements with a liberated territory should be given priority. The case of Vietnam was well established in Sweden. Now, where do I come in with SWAPO? It would have been easy for me to tell a story and state that we had liberated areas, but I thought that it was not correct and I refrained from it. It became an issue. Most of the support groups, especially the Africa Groups, were very lukewarm on Namibia, because of earlier problems I did not know of. Some people believed that we did not have the seriousness of movements like Guinea-Bissau's PAIGC, Angola's MPLA and Mozambique's FRELIMO, because we did not have liberated territories. They were seen not only as 'ideologically clear' between Moscow and Beijing, but they also met the OAU criteria. I was a 'newcomer' to the politics of the outside world, who 'understood very little about the ideological differences of the Soviet Union and the Chinese and the imperialistic policies of the West. Marxism-Leninism was new to me'. So, it was very difficult. I always found it very difficult to pretend what I was not. The active solidarity groups had a network and in order to work through that network you had to prove you were Marxist-Leninist.

TS: At the beginning of the 1970s, I guess that SWAPO's relations with UNITA were controversial within the solidarity movement?

BA: It is possible. Before my arrival in Zambia in 1967 I was told that there had to be some contact between SWAPO and UNITA. You are right. That is the price we paid. The reaction from the Africa Groups.

However, my strategy was to use the Namibian legal position at the UN and take the resolutions of the United Nations as a way of presenting the legitimacy of the SWAPO struggle to the Swedish public. In order to do that I had to rely on the Swedish UN Association. There were also the people at the Foreign Ministry, like Jan Romare, who had just returned from the United Nations, and Torsten Örn, who later became ambassador to Moscow. They knew the legal aspects of the Namibian case. I thought that by playing the Namibian legal card I could establish credibility and acceptance by those who felt that they were overcrowded with other issues. It worked, because with the UN Association we developed a booklet on Namibia. And with Per Sandén we did a film strip on Namibia. We actually tapped not the mainstream, but the off-stream of the support groups. Those who looked at the UN as an authority, just as OAU was seen as an authority.

I think that SWAPO's position gradually became clear to quite a number of people who had an option between supporting what they saw as 'direct blood-letting activities' and the UN endorsement of the right of the Namibian people to self-determination. It possibly also became clearer to the support groups like the Africa Groups. Gradually, they began to ignore some of the things that were not acceptable to them and started to embrace SWAPO. Well, I should not say that they had rejected SWAPO. They did not. It was only that I, as a person, did not say the things that they expected to hear and then, of course, the UNITA question.

TS: So, the fundamental issue that you raised was the question of the right of small nations to self-determination?

BA: I was convinced that within the context of the ideological tension between the superpowers, Namibia had a legitimate right as stated by the UN. I thought that it was a very strong tool to make a distinction between Namibia and the liberation movements who did not have that kind of qualification. I exploited it to the full and by 1974 SWAPO was receiving close to ten million Swedish Kronor from SIDA. The urgency to supply shelter and food to thousands of Namibians arriving in Zambia and Angola became a priority. That was part of a testimony of our seriousness towards the cause of nationhood. We took responsibility for our people. I persuaded SIDA and the Foreign Ministry to look into the need of not only supplying food, but also means of transport.

There were also the Emmaus groups in Björkå and Stockholm, who were collecting used clothes and useful items for refugees under our care. If they did not have the money for the transportation, SIDA would make it available. The legitimacy of SWAPO's struggle for liberation benefited from the UN resolutions and made my task easy.

TS: Was that also the case in the other Nordic countries?

BA: Yes. In Denmark it was slightly different and slightly difficult. The Paul Hartling government did not want direct contacts with the liberation movements. They distanced themselves by making money available through non-governmental organizations for particular projects. Norway was slightly poorer than Sweden at that time and there was a limitation in terms of their material assistance. The first serious effort by the Norwegians towards the liberation movements was the OAU conference in 1973. There were active anti-apartheid groups in Norway. We also obtained some financial assistance to pay for legal costs for people who were prosecuted in Namibia and did not have the means to defend themselves. I think that the amount was 200,000 US dollars, which was channelled through Mr. Hellberg at the Lutheran World Federation in Geneva. Politically, Norway was not different from Sweden, but they did not have the resources Sweden had in those days. Regarding Finland, there had been a long relationship with Namibia via the churches. The influence of the churches on the Finnish government as to what was good for Namibia was still very strong. But it changed when Kalevi Sorsa became Foreign Minister and, especially, through the work done by the NGOs. Others, like Basil Davidson, were also accepted as authorities on the liberation movements. I think that the option developed for the Finnish government to have advisers not only from the churches, but also from people who had a different message altogether and, of course, OAU. Finland was regarded in those days as less strong financially. Most of their money was channelled through the churches. They gave quite a lot to education. Some Namibians went to study in Finland via the churches. Policywise, they became in time very clear on where to stand. In 1976, I went with a delegation to ask the Finnish government to make Ahtisaari available as UN Commissioner for Namibia. He was ambassador to Tanzania at the time. Kalevi Sorsa assured us that he would talk to Ahtisaari and agreed at once to make him available.

I was also covering Germany and Austria. The Germans were not very easy. Occasionally, they were very forthcoming, but one got the impression that they were swapping resources for influence. It was not very pleasant. I remember a number of times when I had to turn down their assistance.

From the Swedish government's side, I did not get the feeling of any conditionality. Most of the people that I dealt with at the government level were internationalists. They were committed. They stood up against apartheid, participating and formulating the international community's policy against apartheid. Sweden was targeting the 1 per cent of GDP goal of solidarity or assistance to developing countries, which they achieved later. In 1974, Sweden took a decision that of the money received from Sweden at least 40 per cent or so was expected to be spent in Sweden. But this did not apply to the liberation movements. They were exempted from that ruling. With other nations there was always an ocean of conditions. Some countries were even going as far as 90-95 per cent. With Sweden there was no conditionality that I remember. I think that it was based on their experience *'från fattig-Sverige till välfärdsstat'* ('from poverty-Sweden to the welfare state'). That guided Sweden's assistance to the liberation movements and the developing countries.

TS: How about political conditionality? For example, all the Nordic countries were against armed struggle as a means of solving conflicts and would abstain from voting in the UN if such a dimension was involved. Do you feel that they respected your struggle on your conditions?

BA: I did not base our strategy for Namibia on the liberation struggle as such, because I realized that there were some difficulties of acceptability by the opinion makers and the NGOs. My effort was to establish the legitimacy of the Namibian people to use whatever means at their disposal to dislodge the South African illegal occupation. That is why I used the various resolutions of the UN.

There were some cases where the Nordic countries abstained from voting for these resolutions, but I got the impression that the right of the Namibians to use whatever means at their disposal was really recognized. Hence they did not see the contradiction of sometimes abstaining from what they were otherwise supporting. They did not use any persuasion to try and say: 'Look here: Armed struggle is not acceptable to us. It is not good. We are giving you this in order to desist from it.' No! All the support given, both at the political and at the diplomatic level, as well as material assistance, was unconditional.

Hadino Hishongwa
SWAPO—Chief Representative to Scandinavia, West Germany and Austria
Deputy Minister of Labour and Manpower Development
(Windhoek, 15 March 1995)

Tor Sellström: You were the SWAPO representative to the Nordic countries from 1977 to 1983. How do you view the support by the Nordic countries to the liberation struggle in Namibia?

Hadino Hishongwa: The liberation struggle in Southern Africa was a general struggle: a struggle for freedom and independence; a struggle against apartheid and racial discrimination; a struggle against foreign domination and occupation; a struggle for human dignity and respect; a struggle for survival, and a struggle for our culture. It was a struggle that deserved the support of all people of good will. It was a struggle where nobody could stand as a spectator.

The Nordic countries—at the other end of our globe—came in on the side of humanitarian assistance. Though far away from Southern Africa, they came to the assistance of the liberation movements in Southern Africa at a time when we had very few friends and our struggle was not really internationally recognized as a just struggle. Their commitment to the humanitarian side of the struggle attracted other countries which were not necessarily ready, or willing, to sacrifice their economic interests in Southern Africa. It was also important that the Nordic countries—Sweden in particular—sacrificed economically. They evaluated what is more important between saving human lives and making huge profits through investments in a society like apartheid South Africa and illegally occupied Namibia, Rhodesia, Mozambique and Angola. It was really a huge decision, which I think that the Nordic countries could be proud of.

The international community—even those who supported South Africa and Portugal—eventually came to support us. But we say that a friend is someone who comes to your assistance when you are really in need. That is why we have special respect for the understanding of the Nordic countries, led by Sweden, to stand firm despite a lot of criticism. They continued to give humanitarian assistance to support the struggle of the peoples of Southern Africa.

This was the time when we needed assistance to prepare ourselves to take over the reins of power. Should we not have had that assistance, it would have been a much bigger problem. It was also important that some of us—maybe I in particular, when I was a SWAPO representative there—were able to convince the Nordic countries, Sweden in particular, to channel humanitarian assistance *inside* our countries. That broke the chains of isolation of our people. They came to realize and recognize that it was true that our struggle was a just struggle: 'It has attracted the attention and support of other nations. We are not alone in our struggle. We have friends'.

This was an experience because for the first time our people came to realize that the problem was not colour-based. People of a different race and religion recognized your struggle as a just struggle and supported you. That is where the Nordic countries came in, supporting the people in the refugee camps in exile, and likewise inside, preparing our people educationally to take over the reins of power.

TS: You said that the Nordic support eventually attracted other countries to assist. You were also SWAPO's representative to Germany and Austria, two countries with close historical links to Namibia. How were you initially received there? How did the Germans look upon the liberation struggle in Namibia?

HH: The apartheid South African propaganda was as poisonous as that of Nazi-Hitler. It was so dangerous that it for a very long time prevented the Western world from responding to the cry for justice and independence. Our just struggle was termed a Communist attempt to militarily take over strategic areas in Africa, which belonged to the Western world and thus diminish the Western world's sphere of influence. We were forced to fight an isolated struggle. The Western world could not make a proper decision regarding their political, socio-economic, military and strategic interests and the genuine struggle of the oppressed people of Southern Africa. Our struggle for freedom and independence was brought into the Cold War. We became part of a Cold War confrontation, where we were seen as belonging to the Communist front and where South Africa was seen as the legitimate representative of Western interests. They failed to realize the truth of the matter because of the fear of the Communist ghost. They were not able to genuinely analyze what kind of struggle the peoples of Southern Africa were fighting.

However, because of their neutrality, the Nordic countries had the sober mind to think independently, honestly and sincerely and find out what type of struggle this was. After the Second World War, the Nordic countries felt that the world deserved peace and that freedom and independence should not be a privilege of the few and not be based on the colour of the skin of a person. It should be a universal right. That is why—when they came in to support—there were a lot of reactions around the Western world that these neutral countries were supporting a Communist plot.

TS: Did you experience that reaction in Germany, for example?

HH: Yes, there was big resistance in Germany. Germany was not an easy front for me. First of all, I was physically assaulted on many occasions because I was seen to represent Russia and East Germany.

I remember, for example, when our President visited Hamburg university in 1980. There were Sam Nujoma, the German Minister of Foreign Affairs and myself as the SWAPO representative. We were really confronted. But not by ordinary people. These were professors, who literally insulted us with questions like: 'Why did we come to Germany if we were Communists?' We told them that we were not Communists and that Communism started there. Marx and Engels were Germans. They were not Namibians or Africans. So Communism started in Germany, not in Namibia. Even when they addressed our President they said: 'You are *Scheisse* (shit).' I was angry and told the President not to answer. They said: 'Go on! Tell us what is going to happen to the German farms in Namibia. And what are you going to do with the minorities? The Hereros? You are just an Ovambo group'.

I stood up and said: 'Look, this is not a civilized way of discussing. You are professors, but you do not prove to be so in my view. You talk of German farms in Namibia. How did you take your farms from Germany to Namibia? If you still have the ship or the planes that took the farms there, could you kindly mobilize them again to repatriate them to Germany?' I continued: 'We have not come here to be taught how to treat minorities, because Germany has a criminal history in that respect. The Jews here were slaughtered. What advice can we get from you about how to treat minorities? We are not going to accept any advice from you on this issue. But we have told you that our struggle is a genuine struggle that has nothing to do with Communism.' And on the question of the farmers, I added: 'We do not consider them Germans. We consider them Namibians of German origin. If you call them Germans, you are mistaken. Germans live in Germany.'

In Sweden—with Olof Palme, Pierre Schori and other Social Democrats—it was relatively easy. I also have to congratulate the other Swedish political parties, the Centre party, the Left Party and so on. They were good and understanding. But in Germany even the Social Democrats were very hostile. One Member of Parliament came to our President and said that 'it is Germany that will determine whether SWAPO will be in the Namibian government or not.' We pushed him out of our office and said that we are going to liberate ourselves. This was the hostile side, but I also have to give credit to the anti-apartheid movement and the Communist Party of Germany. They really helped a lot. And, later, the Social Democrats. They came to realize. Everybody came to realize that there was nothing that they could do to influence the situation in Namibia unless they supported SWAPO.

Let me give credit to Herr Genscher, the former Foreign Minister of the Federal Republic of Germany. He was really a good man. He was able to meet and discuss with me. First privately and later—I think that it was in 1980-81—we finally discussed officially. His interest was to connect German citizens in Namibia with SWAPO. He realized that the support to DTA and other elements was not to bear fruit. We arranged that a delegation of Germans went from Namibia in 1981. We met in Bonn. It was then that the Foreign Ministry of Germany decided to give us some support, especially for students to study in Germany. I think that Genscher was really generous.

TS: He was from the Liberal Party?

HH: Yes, from the Liberal Party. There was a problem with people from CDU and CSU. All the Josef Straussses. It reminds me of a man in Queensland, Australia. He was the Prime Minister when I and Eddie Funde of ANC of South Africa went there. Queensland is a farming area and this man said that the people must be informed that ANC and SWAPO terrorists were coming to Queensland with foot and mouth disease! When we came to the airport, there were blackouts! It is true! There were blackouts, because we were bringing foot and mouth disease to their cattle!

TS: Some would say that the Nordic countries only supported you half the way. They did not support the armed struggle. How did you look upon that?

HH: We divided our struggle into various sectors. There were the armed liberation struggle; the education sector; the health sector and many others. We did not prescribe to our supporters which one they should support. We felt that they had the right to decide. The Nordic countries genuinely supported the humanitarian side of our struggle, which was not less important than the armed liberation struggle. They complemented each other. We needed to be healthy; we needed to have food; we needed tools to produce our own food; we needed to prepare ourselves as a nation and to educate and train our people. And we were only able to do so if and when we got their support.

We did not use any money from the Nordic countries for the armed liberation struggle. We kept our promise. We had our friends in the Soviet Union, China and the other socialist countries and they were giving us top weaponry, which we used to make South Africa recognize us and our strength. We also got it from Ethiopia and others. We said: 'Let the socialist countries give us the weapons and let the Nordic countries and other Western nations give us humanitarian aid'. That was really how we fought our struggle. And, once more, I have to say that the Nordic countries deserve very great respect. The history of Southern Africa would be incomplete unless we mention the contribution and the involvement of the Nordic countries. The people contributed with material support and with clothes, for example the Africa Groups, Emmaus and Bread and Fishes in Sweden.

In Norway I discovered the town of Elverum as I was going all over the country. I decided to stop at Elverum for two days and got in contact with Dag Hareide. They started to help SWAPO with clothes and other things to be sent to Zambia and Angola. I later called the Secretary General of SWAPO to go there, as well as the President and many others. The people in Elverum made a very respectable historical contribution. We would not do justice to our children—nor to history—if the genuine story is not written. Our children should know who assisted them when their fathers and mothers needed help.

TS: Was it difficult to convince the Nordic aid agencies to also give assistance to the struggle *inside* Namibia?

HH: Yes, it was difficult, because all the people did not have the same political understanding. Due to racial discrimination our people inside Namibia felt that every white person was evil. That is what they had been exposed to. It was therefore important for our people—and for our future—that they would not only *hear* that we were getting support, but *see* that it was true and that the people who supported us did not necessarily belong to our race. It was only when we organized some people to go to Namibia as tourists from the Nordic countries that this changed. We informed them that they could meet so-and-so. We also had very good help from people who went to Namibia as journalists, like Per Sandén. It really started to open up the people.

We knew that this was a good strategic way of making people in SIDA recognize the genuine needs of assistance inside the country. Later they made up their minds. They visited Namibia and realized that it was true. That helped us a lot. We also had people who had been arrested and were taken to court. They could not pay for bail and they could not get employed. As long as they had an association with SWAPO they were considered terrorists. And 'terrorists' were forbidden to be employed in Namibia. They tried to break them. Should we not have had this type of assistance, some people would possibly have become demoralized and not as effective as they were. But it was very difficult in the beginning. We had to prove the situation to Sweden and to the other Nordic countries and they did not accept our words only. So there was a gentlemen's agreement that they should send missions inside the country to see some people.

The Namibian churches played a heroic role. They were not spectators in the struggle for their country and their people. They stood firm. They fought with us. I remember when our priests and bishops went to visit the Archbishop in Uppsala. It was our first audience to tell him what was happening. We took them everywhere, to the Prime Minister, the Foreign Minister and then to all the churches. We travelled with them in all the Nordic countries and also to Germany. In

Germany, I remember one gathering when they were accused of bringing Christians to cooperate with Communists.

At that stage, the Nordic understanding of the nature of the conflict and of the struggle in Southern Africa was crystal clear. They would not be deterred by anyone, even by the big powers. They were determined that as civilized nations they had the right to decide on their own.

Peter Katjavivi
SWAPO—Chief Representative to the United Kingdom and Western Europe—
Secretary of Information and Publicity
Vice-Chancellor of the University of Namibia
(Windhoek, 20 March 1995)

Tor Sellström: In general terms, how would you describe the Nordic support to the liberation struggle in Southern Africa and Namibia?

Peter Katjavivi: The Nordic support was extremely important in a variety of ways. First of all, there was the educational and humanitarian assistance, given on the understanding that there was an obvious need to reinforce the liberation movements, who by themselves were responsible for a number of people but did not have the resources to assist the refugees. Many Namibian women and young children who had fled the country were found in refugee camps, initially in Zambia and later in Angola. I think that the underlying understanding by the Nordic countries was that they made a distinction between humanitarian assistance and the recognition that you might extend to a liberation movement.

I think that they felt that this was an important form of help, which they were ready to give. I recall my particular experience in Norway. In 1969-70, the word 'resistance' was well understood by most people there and they identified with what we were trying to do. They might not agree with the method that we were using, but there was a very strong feeling that we were involved in a resistance, designed to achieve freedom and liberation.

Another important consideration was that we as a party immediately understood that it was important not to simply leave our people in the care of UNHCR. We were not ordinary refugees. We were refugees who were out to prepare ourselves to make a contribution towards the liberation of our country. The idea of being in a refugee camp was not to settle there indefinitely. It was an opportunity to regroup and acquire the necessary skills and competence while we were in exile. It became a training camp, where you acquired skills that might be needed in an independent Namibia. I think that that consideration was well understood by the Nordic countries. We were able to have nurses, who could look after the refugees, to have people with skills in carpentry and in agricultural activities etc. This led to the realization that we needed to create a spirit of self-reliance and not simply be spoon-fed by aid. It helped to build capacity within the movement, by helping its members to help themselves. I think that that is what happened. We were helped to help ourselves.

Let me move to another important area: I think that a number of institutions, organizations, churches and solidarity movements—like the Africa Groups in Sweden and others—played an important role in assisting us to develop ways and means of reaching out to the home base. It was extremely important that we were able to maintain the political initiative inside the country. We were not able to be on the spot, but through the assistance we received—initially from the churches and later from the trade unions and from the youth and solidarity organizations—we were able to develop a mechanism to reinforce and strengthen our lines of communication with the colleagues inside the country. I was in the middle of that, using London as a base.

We were able to provide funds directly from exile into the country. The party was then able to organize itself and its activities inside Namibia. I refer to a number of colleagues who were involved, like our Chairman David Meroro, Aaron Mushimba, Axel Johannes, Nico Bessinger, Daniel Tjongarero etc. I can go on mentioning names, like Reverend Kameeta and Martha Ford. This was done through whatever opportunities we had at the time, including a number of old friends from Sweden, who were linked to the churches and were able to spend time here. At the same time, we maintained links with the party officials and were able to co-ordinate activities and update them on the activities of the movement abroad. Necessary briefings were conducted on that basis. With regard to the funding that we were able to provide it was important that we encouraged our leaders and our colleagues inside the country to develop a culture of sharing those funds as much as possible.

Under those conditions, we were also conscious of the fact that any information could be used against individuals and against the party itself if it happened to land in the wrong hands. We were very anxious that the South African agents did not discover that network we had been able to establish between SWAPO in exile and the SWAPO leadership inside the country.

When the South Africans started the Turnhalle project it was important to counter their policies. An initiative developed within the leadership of SWAPO in Namibia and they consulted with us in exile. The process of constitutional discussions was initiated. The colleagues in Namibia wanted a discussion paper which could be used as a talking point within the country. There were meetings in Windhoek and Rehoboth, in Otjivarongo, Okahandja, Walvis Bay and so on. We were able to organize this through Amnesty International or the International Defence and Aid Fund. We received funds from them and lined up a colleague to go to Namibia. I happened to be in Oslo attending some meetings when our colleague was ready to fly to Namibia with this important document. He came to see me in Oslo. It was just a hand-written piece of paper. I called Hans Beukes to come and join me. I involved him in checking some of the wording of this paper. The original idea was to discuss it in Lusaka with some colleagues, including Moses Garoeb. Eventually, the person flew directly to Namibia.

This is how the discussion paper on Namibia's future constitution started. Eventually, there were a number of versions from the original text to a fourth, fifth and sixth revised version. This is the constitutional framework. It goes back to the 1970s, when we started to engage in this particular exercise discussing the concept of an ombudsman, the independence of the judiciary and so on. These were questions which were touched upon not only by SWAPO in exile, but also shared with our colleagues inside the country.

Again, I want to underline the role which the Nordic countries played in this regard. The funding sources can be traced to Nordic bodies which were actively involved in helping us to be able to achieve all this work. I remember a number of colleagues of mine at the Swedish embassy in Lusaka and at the Swedish embassy in London. It is tremendous when you think about it. These people basically positioned themselves behind you. They were not always visible. Nobody knew about that, but the underlying interest and commitment was just tremendous. That kind of international solidarity and understanding is what helped us to do as much as we did.

We are talking about a particular generation of people, who appeared on the scene at a very special time. There was a sense of good will. At no time did we feel that they were condescending. They were people who were committed to something. They were prepared to reinforce the struggle by working in partnership.

TS: It was then a concerned partnership rather than a paternalistic relationship?
PK: Absolutely. It goes back to the days of the late Olof Palme and what he did for the cause of this country when a number of compatriots arrived in Sweden. The way they were received and Olof Palme's own commitment. Through his activity, the first international conference ever on the question of Namibia was held. It was presided over by Palme in Oxford in 1966. That commitment and support continued for many years. It was from a leadership, a party and a country. It was a country's commitment in many ways. I think that that is a kind of tradition which in many ways has characterized the Nordic support.

In the minutes of the SWAPO Central Committee from the 1970s, the support is recognized. The minutes tell you that at the end of every Central Committee we normally issued a declaration and I cannot recall one single SWAPO Central Committee where we did not indicate our thanks and appreciation to the Nordic countries in terms of the material given and the policy of support to our cause. The unwavering nature of the Nordic support was always applauded and recognized in black and white.

TS: On the other hand, in the Nordic countries there was criticism from the political left. It would say that it was not enough to give humanitarian support. There should also be armed assistance. By not giving armed support to the liberation movements, the governments of the Nordic countries showed their real interests, namely a hidden agenda to make Southern Africa safe for capitalism?

PK: As a national liberation movement we would say that we had our own agenda. We were looking for support from countries in terms of international solidarity and goodwill to the cause of the people of Namibia. We were realistic as to the world we lived in.

I remember my own experience in Oslo. One year I was at a big international conference there. We were from different parts of the world. There were people from the Black Panthers of the USA, who went all over the world campaigning for support. When someone from that party spoke, a houseful came. It was very dramatic. Then I spoke. We had a clear mission in terms of what we were trying to gain. Within the Western world, North America and Europe in general, we were looking to consolidate the solidarity on the basis of the objective conditions which prevailed. We were not there to question whether one should be a socialist or whatever. We accepted the reality of the situation. I did not ask for arms. I asked for concrete support of solidarity, educational support for our young people and other things that I thought were obtainable and more realistic and efficient in support of our cause.

We knew where to go for arms, that was not the problem. The problem was to build a strong solidarity support for the cause. For the liberation struggle we knew where to go. Africa had made that commitment. We were supported by OAU, with the Liberation Committee facilitating the supply of arms. But in terms of what we needed in Western Europe we knew what we were looking for. I think that that is what made a distinction between our liberation struggle and other causes which appeared on the scene, wanting this and that.

TS: What underlined the Nordic commitment was the question of apartheid, illegal occupation and minority rule in Southern Africa. Other liberation movements in the world never received the same response?

PK: I am happy that someone is doing this study. It is a question of doing justice to a long tradition of support to the liberation of the entire Southern African sub-continent. It is a unique experience on the part of the people who were involved in this particular process. I think that it is also a major contribution in terms of the resources and the commitment made by the Nordic governments.

You owe it to the people of the Nordic countries to have it on record, so that future generations can understand that at a given time in history the people of the Nordic world stood up in a remarkable way and provided assistance which was a major source of strength to many of us in the region. Another important thing is that it should be pleasing to our friends in the Nordic world to have assisted a people, or a party like SWAPO, and actually be able to see that what we said at that time was not just propaganda. We meant it.

TS: One question raised by people from the political opposition is that OAU sought one sole and authentic liberation movement. In turn, this would have created an imbalance in the democratic system needed upon independence?

PK: I think that we cannot rewrite our history. The critical issue with regard to the decision of organizing SWAPO as the sole and authentic representative of the people of Namibia is the fact that after several years of struggle and patient persuasion of the South African regime to reason with the UN it became quite clear that you needed to build a strong alternative force.

We were in a situation where SWAPO had to embark upon and intensify the liberation struggle, mobilizing its forces at home and abroad, as well as the international community. We witnessed a situation as during the Second World War in Europe. 'Unite for peace, unite for a common issue, forget our differences'. It was a national resistance struggle to rescue the country from foreign occupation. I think that we all realized that unless we presented a united front we would continue to be under South African slavery. The purpose was to make sure that South Africa understood the seriousness of the commitment we made on behalf of the people of Namibia. It did not necessarily mean that we were not interested in encouraging a multi-party democracy, or pluralism. It was simply for the purpose of carrying out a decisive and unified liberation struggle. What happens afterwards, in an independent Namibia, is entirely a domestic matter. I think that we should be able to make that distinction.

I also think that even among our white compatriots, there were people who were seriously concerned about the possibility of South Africa organizing her own half-solutions or neo-colonial solutions. SWAPO was the only visible force. We did not have the situation that occurred in Zimbabwe or in Angola. Namibia was an easy case, with one movement which was clearly committed and was visible. Everybody could see that for themselves. OAU or the UN had no major problem in deciding. But I would also like to say that many of us did recognize the fact that we were, and are, the authentic representative of the people of Namibia. It became a heavy responsibility. It meant that we should also care for those who were not members of SWAPO. We found that we needed to do something about that. We provided scholarships and support to Namibian students who were not members of SWAPO. We provided them with whatever facilities were under our care. We were also willing to help and unify professional Namibians who could be employed by foreign governments in Africa or elsewhere.

Some of my Namibian compatriots came to me to ask for support, knowing that they talked to a SWAPO person. I never hesitated to say that we will do the best that we can. We had an overall obligation to assist not only members of the party, but everyone.

TS: Do you think that the Nordic countries helped to expand your support internationally? Did the Nordic support help you to erode the resistance shown by other Western countries, like Britain, France, Germany and the United States?

PK: I think that the support was crucial in a variety of ways, because it was expressed at different levels. For instance, within the UN system we had a UN Council for Namibia running an important UN Institute in Lusaka, Zambia. We had a UN Trust Fund, through which a number of our students were funded with scholarships and you had the initial support given to a number of agencies like IDAF in London, Amnesty International and Christian Aid.

These funds were all directed to provide educational and humanitarian support systems. They played an important role. When I went to London to set up the first SWAPO office there in 1968, I was received by the head of IDAF, the late Canon Collins, through whom support was channelled to cover trials in Namibia. Funds were also made available to send observers to a number of major trials. Almost every year you had one, two or three major trials. We were able to enlist the services of lawyers to take on these cases after we had been able to work together, particularly with Sweden, to provide us with the funding.

I think that the support highlighted the concern of the international community over the plight of the Namibian people and the general situation in Southern Africa.

Some of the countries—also those who were not with us and who were not prepared to support us in this way—obviously felt embarrassed. There were individuals in a country like the UK who were embarrassed that their own government did absolutely nothing. It was talked about. In the House of Commons there were comments by the Labour Party and the Liberal Party. In Germany, the same thing. But it did not encourage a favourable climate within those countries for obvious reasons, that is, the strong ties which existed between, for instance, the UK and South Africa. In the particular case of Zimbabwe, at the time of independence they were objecting to the Swedish humanitarian support to the liberation movements. I remember a distinguished personality in the UK saying: 'It is holding things up.' I was a bit amazed by that comment. I thought that they should be thankful that there were people in the West who were supportive of the liberation struggle in our part of the world.

By and large, what the Nordic support meant to us is that it distinguished those societies from the rest of the Western world. It was a lesson to us. It was a pleasant experience to know that there were people who were with us while the going was tough. They did not join us after independence. We had been together and that is something which I think most of us value. Whatever happens in the years to come, the relationship was not built yesterday. It is much deeper and I am confident that it will stand whatever pressures of time.

Charles Kauraisa
SWANU—Student in Sweden and Chairman of SWANU's External Council
Chairman of Rössing Uranium
(Windhoek, 20 March 1995)

Tor Sellström: How did you first come into contact with the Nordic countries?

Charles Kauraisa: I came across the name Herbert Tingsten in Cape Town while reading a review of his book attacking the apartheid system in South Africa in the late 1950s. He was the first Swedish academic to study and reject the system and it made an impression on me. I remembered it later when I met him in Sweden. Soon after that Hans Beukes, the first Namibian student to be offered a scholarship by a Scandinavian country, escaped from South Africa into Botswana to take up studies in Oslo, Norway, in 1959. During my years in South Africa, where I completed my secondary schooling and college education, I was actively involved in the Cape Peninsula Students' Union. My political mentors were I.B. Tabata and Ronnie Britton of the Unity Movement. They were the people who exposed a number of us to the study of Marxism.

TS: The book by Herbert Tingsten, was it *The Problem of South Africa*?

CK: Yes. I read a review of the book in a newspaper in South Africa and I was impressed. Some of my friends also read the review and we discussed it. When one talks about the anti-apartheid movement and its origins in Sweden, one should keep in mind the role played by people like Herbert Tingsten and Sara Lidman, who recognized the immorality of the apartheid system and its implications at an early stage.

I returned home a few days after the Windhoek massacre of 10 December 1959, finding an upsurge of political militancy in the making. Ironically, I received replies to my applications for teaching posts at the two main black secondary schools in Namibia at that time—the Augustineum Secondary School in Okahandja and the Rehoboth Secondary School—from the security branch. I was told that the Education Department would advise me where I was to be posted, but I was not going to be offered either of the positions for which I had applied.

I was practically exiled to Walvis Bay, where I taught for a short period in the Old Location before I left for Sweden. I met Ben Amathila, the present Minister for Information and Broadcasting, there for the first time after he had been expelled from Augustineum. He later became the SWAPO representative in Sweden for many years. At the same time, Uatja Kaukuetu and myself obtained scholarships to study at the universities of Lund and Stockholm, respectively, through the assistance of Joachim Israel. Uatja was a friend of mine. He had also studied in the Cape, but had returned home earlier and was involved in politics. At that point he was the SWANU leader.

We applied for passports, but were refused. We informed Joachim Israel accordingly. He, however, managed to obtain permission for us to enter Sweden without passports provided we could get to some country that we could fly from. He was working closely with Ulla Lindström, who at that time was Minister of International Cooperation and worked with the question of Namibia at the United Nations.

We escaped into Botswana towards the end of 1960, from where we proceeded to Southern Rhodesia and to Northern Rhodesia. The political situation was such that we were forced to continue towards Katanga. We thought that there was a chance of getting out from there, but it was impossible. We returned to Lusaka and then went to Dar es Salaam from where we flew via Nairobi to Sweden. We picked up the necessary documents permitting us entry to Sweden from the Swedish consulate in Nairobi. In Sweden we were soon separated. My colleague went to Lund and I started my studies at the University of Stockholm.

TS: One person who was involved when you and Kaukuetu left from Tanzania was the Swedish missionary Barbro Johansson?

CK: Yes, she was very helpful. She was really influential in Dar es Salaam, highly respected by all the TANU officials and Tanzanians in general. She was very excited by the idea that we were going to study in Sweden. She gave us an excellent briefing on Sweden and Swedish politics, particularly as I was rather concerned about the little I had read about Sweden. The picture I had about Sweden was that it was a monarchy with a state church and all the things that we associated with a reactionary country. She patiently explained everything to us. We remained in Tanzania for almost a whole month. We had close associations with TANU, in the same way that we had had with UNIP in Northern Rhodesia.

The first meeting that I addressed in Sweden was in the Great Church in Stockholm, where I talked about the political situation in Namibia and the apartheid system in general. I also met Herbert Tingsten at a meeting organized by Per Wästberg. Thereafter I concentrated on learning the Swedish language, which was not easy, and stated my university studies. In the meantime, both my colleague and I continued to talk at political meetings and particularly at student meetings throughout the country, informing about the situation in Namibia and the apartheid system in South Africa.

During that time, the political spotlight was on South Africa. The President of ANC, Chief Luthuli, received the Nobel Peace Prize and was permitted to visit Oslo to receive it. It generated a lot of publicity in Sweden. I joined exiled South African artists in Sweden in anti-apartheid meetings and discussions that resulted in the formation of the Swedish anti-apartheid movement. Ronald Segal, who was in exile in Britain, was also invited to Sweden for political discussions. He was the first South African to campaign for economic sanctions against the South African government.

TS: Tingsten was a liberal. The early solidarity in Sweden was thus much broader than the socialist left?

CK: Indeed it was. It really took off as the number of Namibian students increased in Sweden. For the most part we were involved in mobilizing the Swedish opinion against the apartheid system and for the decolonization of Namibia. Amongst the students were Zed Ngavirue, who is presently the Director General of the National Planning Commission, Moses Katjiuongua, who is an opposition member of parliament, and Kaire Mbuende, Secretary General of SADC. At a later stage Ben Amathila joined us as representative of SWAPO.

In the early 1960s, Oliver Tambo of ANC and Fanuel Kozonguizi of SWANU were regular participants at the annual First of May rallies which were held all over Sweden. They addressed those meetings in the name of the South Africa United Front. The close relationship between the nationalist movement and the Social Democrats of Sweden—in particular people like Olof Palme, Ingvar Carlsson and Pierre Schori—can be traced to the early 1960s. I got to know Tage Erlander and Olof Palme through my participation as a speaker in these rallies. Throughout the 1960s and the 1970s, ANC, SWANU and later SWAPO addressed these rallies on a regular basis.

TS: What did the South Africa United Front represent?

CK: The South Africa United Front was formed in London by Oliver Tambo (ANC), Nana Mahomo (PAC) and Fanuel Kozonguizi (SWANU). It was a political front to put over the views of the oppressed people of South Africa and Namibia at that time. Basically, it was these three leaders who were the members of the front. Initially, in

1961-62, we addressed most meetings—even in Sweden—in the name of the South African Front and when Oliver Tambo and Fanuel Kozonguizi came to Sweden to address the First of May rallies they spoke as members of the front.

The anti-apartheid movement in Sweden grew very fast and soon became a broadly based movement supported by almost all the political parties, trade unions and intellectuals. Ben Amathila did an excellent job, particularly in the later years when SWAPO moved to the armed struggle. We supported his endeavours on the basis that a genuine armed struggle should be supported irrespective of our political differences. From time to time, we participated in joint meetings with SWAPO. We never had any animosity or strained working relations between ourselves and Amathila when SWAPO later was recognized as the authentic representative of the people of Namibia.

Besides working with the Social Democratic Party, we lobbied the Scandinavian governments to take a firm position on the question of Namibia at the United Nations. Concerted efforts were made by all of us to convince them to take the lead in sanctions against the South African government and to support the efforts of the United Nations Council for Namibia. In that respect we must mention people like Ronald Segal, who had the foresight to work on the initial question of economic sanctions against South Africa.

The question is always asked how Sweden came to play an important role in Southern Africa. I tend to think that the seed was planted in the early 1950s. As we all know, it was really India which took an early and clear stand on the question of racialism and apartheid in South Africa and they also took the lead on the question of Namibia at the United Nations. When one looks at the records of the countries that supported the first resolution not to incorporate the then South West Africa into South Africa and the whole question of the mandate, you will notice that Sweden also took a clear stand against the South African regime. At a later stage, the first intellectual anti-apartheid writings and debates came to the fore.

TS: With influences also from church people, such as Dean Gunnar Helander?

CK: Yes, exactly. Per Wästberg also played a very important role with his writings. He really influenced the Swedish opinion. I think that it was the intellectuals that tipped the scales in favour of Southern Africa. I must come back to Tingsten. What he said and how it was publicized. Subsequent to that, the peace award to the late Albert Luthuli helped to focus on South Africa.

Unfortunately for South Africa, the South African legation was extremely vocal in Stockholm. They were reacting forcefully in defence of the apartheid system. It forced the debate in Sweden, in which intellectuals and writers took a leading role. The imposition of the apartheid system was to the Swedes—particularly so close after Nazism and the Second World War—totally unacceptable and forced people like Joachim Israel and others to take an uncompromising stand against it. The Swedish public reacted and also started taking a clear position on the issue of apartheid. The Swedish intellectuals described and characterized the apartheid system as legalized racism. Although there were dictators in Latin America and elsewhere, the Swedish public could not accept racism in whatever form and I think that it made it easier for the anti-apartheid movement to dominate the political scene until the emergence of the powerful and fantastic solidarity movement for Vietnam, which engaged us all.

TS: The question of the right of small nations to self-determination was important in this context?

CK: That question was very close to the hearts and minds of the Swedes. It was embodied in Undén's foreign policy of neutrality. Sweden took a strong position on the question of self-determination and the rights of small nations. It made it easy for the Swedish public to support the liberation struggle against colonialism.

TS: Was the anti-colonial struggle in the Portuguese-speaking colonies also important?

CK: Yes, the Angolan situation came to the fore during this time. We had people like Neto, Mondlane and Cabral visiting the Scandinavian countries to campaign for support for their independence struggles. They received substantial humanitarian aid from Sweden. There were also a number of students from the Portuguese-speaking colonies. Some were studying in Lund. It also helped to get the Swedes to support their struggles. Cabral was particularly successful and PAIGC received extensive assistance from Sweden.

TS: How many years were you in Sweden?

CK: I was in Sweden for about twenty years. Although I spent some time elsewhere, I retained my Swedish residency and I consider Sweden my second home. I have a daughter there who is about to complete her studies at the University of Stockholm.

I studied at the Lund University for my first degree, but other than that I lived in Stockholm, where I did all my studies at the University of Stockholm. I went to the United States where I spent a year studying at Princeton University and I returned to Stockholm to complete my post-graduate studies. I was involved in research work and lecturing in political science, international relations and the theory of development.

TS: You were in Sweden when the question of development aid really started to be discussed. Do you feel that there were political conditions attached to the aid from the Western countries?

CK: Yes, it was clear that the Western aid during that period was given with the purpose of trying to get the leaders of the nationalist movement and other people involved not to rely on the support of the so-called Communist countries, the Soviet Union and China in particular. This did not, of course, stop the leaders of the nationalist movement—who basically considered themselves non-aligned—from accepting aid from either the East or the West in order to strengthen the liberation struggle against the colonial powers.

However, Scandinavian aid was slightly different, in particular Swedish aid. Sweden considered itself a neutral country, particularly at the height of the Cold War. There was a genuine anti-imperialist intellectual movement which was developing in leaps and bounds and its success was that aid should be given to the people of the Third World who were involved in struggles to overthrow the yoke of colonialism or were fighting imperialism without any conditions attached to it. The Social Democratic Party, the youth and other radical organizations in Sweden who were participating in the anti-Vietnam movement were strongly opposed to aid with strings attached. They supported the liberation movements from South Africa, Namibia, Zimbabwe, Angola, Guinea-Bissau and Mozambique irrespective of whether their leaders received aid from the Soviet Union or China.

It was a realistic approach on the part of the Scandinavian countries to support the liberation struggle without setting conditions. The Scandinavian aid was purely given on a humanitarian basis. They did not support the armed struggle, but concentrated on areas where they could provide the needed assistance. It was mainly political or diplomatic support and, of course, humanitarian support to refugees and students.

TS: You set up the External Council of SWANU in Sweden?

CK: Yes, in 1965 we set up the External Council of SWANU to assist the SWANU Presidency to become more effective. I served as both the Chairman and as Foreign Affairs Secretary. Zed Ngavirue was also its Chairman for a long time, until his return to Namibia in 1978. At that point, we decided to dissolve the External Council and concentrate on political work within Namibia. The main reason for setting up the External Council was that SWANU had taken a conscious decision that the National Executive should remain within Namibia while the political parties remained unbanned. It somewhat affected the decision making process. For example, with regard to our position on the question of the armed struggle, which affected our relationship with the OAU Liberation Committee.

TS: That was around 1966?

CK: Yes, in 1966-67 and particularly in 1968. Although we had people trained in guerrilla warfare for the purpose of infiltrating the country and eventually commence the armed struggle, the OAU Liberation Committee had a different agenda. They did not share our point of view and wanted us to make a clear statement that SWANU was embarking on armed struggle. This we could not do. Subsequently we had discussions with our colleagues in SWAPO, who embarked on the armed struggle with PLAN, but those discussions led nowhere and

SWANU never took part in the armed struggle.

TS: This seems very confusing. In the case of Sweden, we are talking about a government, which took a principled stand against armed warfare as a means of resolving conflicts. The ruling Social Democratic Party supported SWANU. Then SWAPO launches the armed struggle and the Social Democrats shift their support from SWANU to SWAPO?

CK: There were lots of debates with those who were leading the party at that particular point. We had lots of seminars and discussions until it became clear that the armed struggle was necessitated by the situation and therefore must be supported. The Social Democratic Party was slightly divided. You had a left wing which said that it must be supported, in particular the youth. You also had those who were strongly opposed to it. The labour movement position was that they would like to see support on humanitarian grounds and not support for armed struggle.

TS: You returned to Namibia in 1978?

CK: Yes, in 1978 I returned for a short time together with a number of other SWANU members. It was mainly to test the so-called amnesty declaration which South Africa had given us through the United Nations, whereby we were assured that we would not be arrested if we returned to Namibia. I went back to Sweden after two months and returned finally to Namibia in 1981. It was at the time when the Contact Group made its formal proposals for a settlement after some intense negotiations with all parties concerned. I was very involved in those negotiations. As soon as the plan was accepted and only needed to be implemented, some of us thought that there was no longer any reason for us to remain outside the country. The implementation of the plan only hinged on linkage or non-linkage to the situation in Angola. Unfortunately, our calculation was wrong. South Africa persisted and SWAPO continued with the armed struggle, so the implementation process took longer than some of us anticipated.

TS: Is there anything that you would like to add?

CK: My theory regarding the success of the Namibians who went into exile in Sweden is that we were all politically motivated, either studying or working. Those who completed their studies successfully obtained skills that stood them in good stead. For example, I came from a political and academic career. I was involved in research and lecturing in countries like Finland and Germany while attached to the University of Stockholm. I then joined the private sector in my country.

I joined Rössing towards the end of 1981. It was not easy to leave the political and academic fields. I came back to Namibia for just a short visit and my father who was getting on in years asked me to stay. I was faced with the problem of how to earn a living without compromising my principles of working for institutions which were firmly steeped in the apartheid system. I discussed my problem with John Kirkpatrick, who advised me to join Rössing because he believed that I could contribute to the changes that were taking place in the company. At that point Rössing was committed to becoming a non-racial organization.

However, the other factor that contributed to our success was that we were all certain that we would return to Namibia one day to contribute to the development of our country, whether in politics or industry. We all shared a good relationship, whether members of SWANU or SWAPO or merely students working or living in Sweden. All our friends and party officials—academics and others—with whom we worked for a long time contributed to this. Even when SWAPO was recognized as the authentic representative of the people of Namibia all Namibians in Sweden were treated equally and there was no discrimination against people of other parties. This was not the case in some of the other countries.

Dirk Mudge
National Party—Chairman of the Turnhalle Constitutional Conference
Chairman of the Democratic Turnhalle Alliance
(Kalkfeld, 18 March 1995)

Tor Sellström: You are by far the most influential white political leader in Namibia. In retrospect, how would you describe the involvement by the Nordic countries in Namibia's process towards national independence?

Dirk Mudge: Now that we have solved the problem, it is much easier to give credit to all parties concerned. I must say that the Nordic countries played a very important role. There is no doubt about that. SWAPO played a very important role. It is not easy to admit it, but it is true. South Africa played an important role too, although maybe at a later stage. The South African army played a role, whether we want to admit it or not. The internal parties, all of them, made a contribution. As a result of all that we came up with a solution which I hope can work. I am confident that it can work.

I asked Ahtisaari once whether he really believed that independence would have been a success ten years ago, or for that matter twenty years ago, when the liberation struggle started. I would not want to give an answer, but I think that one can have doubts about that. Maybe the good Lord has a way of allowing things to happen and we all play a role. It is a matter of checks and balances. For instance: Would SWAPO have been allowed to take over by force? If they had just conquered the country, hoisted the flag and taken over the government, would we have had a democracy then?

In many parts of the world, human rights were violated in many ways. Apartheid was one of them. I grew up under that dispensation. Separation and apartheid were more or less a way of life. It was also the case in many other countries in the world. Not only in South Africa or Namibia, but also in the United States of America to a very late stage. Of course, we were never forced to think about the situation. It was nice as long as it lasted. As practised by many people in Namibia, apartheid was not in every way crude. Many of the white farmers cared for their workers. They treated them well, but they were not allowed to sit in the lounge or admitted to the same schools. I am often asked: Why did I change my policy? Why did I turn my back on apartheid, discrimination and minority rule? Well, because I saw what was happening. I have never had a problem with good relations with black people. I think that we in Namibia really never were allowed by the South African government to inform ourselves properly and become aware of the complexity and the seriousness of the situation until about 1972-73. The country was ruled by South Africa. The South Africans fought several court cases. They came here, Pik Botha and his lawyers. They interviewed people, but never the local politicians. We were never really allowed to participate.

At the beginning of the 1970s, Dr. Waldheim came to visit Namibia. He wanted to meet the local executive committee. I was one of them. For the first time we had the opportunity to talk to people from the outside world about the future of the country. I then had a meeting with Dr. Hilgard Muller, who at the time was the Minister of Foreign Affairs of South Africa. I expressed the opinion that the local white people must be involved in the determination of the political future of the country. I was not happy with the fact that South Africa was deciding on policy and our future—fighting the battle in the United Nations and other organizations—while we in Namibia had no role to play. As a result of the meeting, I was invited to visit the United Nations General Assembly in 1973, where I came into contact with the international community for the first time. I then came to the conclusion that South Africa was in a 'no-win' situation, because they had the whole international community against them.

Even before I visited the United Nations, I held my first meeting with a black national leader in 1972, namely Clemens Kapuuo, who at that time was the leader of the group that actually started the resistance against the South African government and never accepted any help from them, nor any form of self-rule. The Hereros never accepted that. So I started to talk to a man who was anti-South Africa, anti-apartheid and who was against the homeland system in every way. I felt that he should be involved. I said that it was no use talking to puppets. We must talk to the people who were critical of the South African government.

Now, coming back to my visit to the United Nations: I sat there and saw how Muller tried to address the General Assembly for days, but he was refused. They wanted to withdraw his credentials. Ultimately, he was allowed, but then all the countries walked out. All the African countries. I suppose also the Nordic countries. I think that it was only the United States and Britain and a few others that remained. When I came back, I asked for an interview with the then Prime Minister, John Vorster. I made it clear to him that there was no way South Africa could solve Namibia's problems. They were arguing about technical and legal points, but they would not accept Namibia's right to self-determination. I insisted that that process should begin immediately. Of course, the Prime Minister wanted to know what the bottom line would be: 'How far are you prepared to go? What concessions are you prepared to make?'

My view has always been that if you negotiate, there is no bottom line. If you really want to come to a solution, you have to go there with an open mind and be prepared to talk and see how far you can get. I have seen people draw lines. Then they move them and draw a new line. It does not work. Anyway, I had problems with my own party colleagues. They were not very enthusiastic about a process involving talks with the black leaders. They said that once you start the process where do you stop? I said that I am prepared to start and that the sky is the limit. This is how we started the Turnhalle conference.

The Turnhalle conference was always labelled a South African sponsored conference, which makes me very sad. It is not true. I had to fight a long and hard battle to get it started. Firstly, with my party colleagues in Namibia and, secondly, with the South African government, who had their own ideas, like: 'Let us first get Ovambo independent, then we can talk. Let us first get the Kavango off, then we can talk. Let us get rid of the majority of the black people and then we can talk.' I opposed all of it and said that if we want to talk we have to involve everybody, and we must do so with an open mind.

After a long struggle Turnhalle started. I was elected chairman. SWAPO was not represented. This was the shortcoming of Turnhalle, no doubt about it. Therefore, it could never have been the final solution. It can only be described as a first step towards a constitutional development in this country. I am the last person to say that the conference could have been the final step.

When we started, I discovered that my white colleagues had a hidden agenda. The Turnhalle conference was based on ethnicity. I do not really want to apologize for that, because even today ethnicity is a major problem in this country. In any case, I found that my colleagues wanted to use some tactics to influence the black delegates—even with money—to accept a system which I knew would not be acceptable in the long run. I blocked it and said: 'I have a feeling that my black colleagues do not understand the implications.' I thus allowed more time to discuss.

In the Turnhalle conference, black people became for the first time ever involved in the political debate. For the first time they heard the word 'constitution'. They knew nothing about constitutions and democracy. They fought against apartheid and they fought for liberation, but liberation ends somewhere and then you come to the next question: How do you live in a liberated country? So, we started to talk about constitutional principles and the results of independence. What do you do after independence? In the conference we had people with different motives and agendas, but I had only one idea and that was that as long as the war continued we must have a role to play. Those of us who did not support war as a solution. To me it was always a question if armed struggle was a solution. On the other hand, if there were no armed struggle, maybe nothing would have happened. I must admit that. That is why I say that I must admit that SWAPO played a role. And that the Nordic countries played a role.

TS: But the Nordic countries never supported the armed struggle?

DM: Well, let us get clarity on that point, because that is very important. Nevertheless, this is where it started. Gradually, there was this friendship growing between me and the black leaders in the country, whom I had never hated, but never lived with either. I had never understood them. I travelled to see Clemens Kapuuo. We were together in the Turnhalle conference and during this process he was assassinated. That was a traumatic experience to me. I think that it was the first time that I stood at the grave of a black friend and cried. Such things influence people and it influenced me.

The decisions taken at the Turnhalle conference motivated the contact group to take action. In our declaration of intent we said that we wanted to lead the country towards independence. I think that the Western Contact Group was afraid that there might be another UDI (Unilateral Declaration of Independence). They rushed to Cape Town, met the South African government and said: 'Please, stop this thing that is going on in Windhoek. Stop the Turnhalle conference and the plans that they are making there. Instead, let us look at an internationally acceptable solution.' That is how the Western Contact Group was formed and how they came up with their proposals, which led to UN Resolution 435 and independence.

I could mention the fights I had with P.W. Botha; the fact that I had to break with my party; the humiliation that we as a family had to suffer—being called traitors by the white population—but it does not matter. In any case, in 1977 I broke away from the National Party and since then DTA fought its own sort of liberation struggle. But we found ourselves in a very awkward position. There was a war going on and there was a liberation movement. I am very friendly when I call them a liberation movement. It is not easy to use that name if you have lost personal friends and relatives killed by them. You would rather call them terrorists. We could not support them. We were the victims. My family, my black friends and my party colleagues were killed. We had to defend ourselves or somebody had to defend us. We thus found ourselves in the company of South Africa. While we were opposed to South Africa politically, we were in the same camp militarily. Because we were on the receiving side of the armed struggle, we were defended by South Africa. It made it very difficult for us. It was more or less an impossible situation.

But we continued and I think that we influenced the ultimate outcome in many ways. One way in which we did so was to prepare the white population. South Africa could not afford to let Namibia become independent if that would lead to internal resistance among the whites, which could spill over to the South African scene. In other words, we had to prepare the ground for UN Resolution 435. And it was much easier to convince the white people than the black people. They said that it was suicide. We still have the same problem. In DTA, the white component is less antagonistic towards SWAPO than the black people. Maybe because we are more experienced.

We played a role. We always felt that this role was not appreciated by the international community, including the Nordic countries. At one stage, they would not even talk to us or meet us. They did not want to be seen in our company. We were labelled South African puppets and that was the end of it. They were not even prepared to argue with us. Whatever we did was seen as a manoeuvre to cheat the black population and delay the independence process.

TS: Did you try to reach the Nordic governments?

DM: Yes, on many occasions when they were here. We also made statements in this regard, for instance, during the period of the interim government. They said that they would not talk to us because they did not recognize the interim government. I am not quarrelling about that, but they could have talked to me in my personal capacity, because I think that I had a contribution to make.

The final process was the elections in 1989. Again we had a problem which alarmed me very much. That was the question of financing our political parties. The opinion all over the world was that there must be democratic elections and that they must be fair and free. How can an election be fair if one party has unlimited funds and the others nothing? It must have been obvious to everybody that we could not get money from anywhere in the world. We were labelled puppets and seen as people opposing liberation and independence. We could not get money from anywhere. I then spoke to the South African government and insisted that they should support us. I said that we cannot have an election without money. It is impossible. It will not be fair and free. They had their doubts. There were major differences within the government, between national intelligence, foreign affairs and the military people.

My position was that Namibia was paving the way for a solution to the Southern African problem. We were going to participate in the first process towards a democratic society. I hold it against the international community that they not only did not support us financially, but even criticized us for accepting financial assistance from South Africa, as if we were bought. I was not bought by anybody and I did not accept any money with strings attached. I said that we will have an election, we will elect a Constitutional Assembly and there we will decide the future of Namibia. I think that everybody will appreciate that I played a role in the Constituent Assembly. Mr. Geingob and others have on many occasions said that they do not think that it would have been possible to write a constitution in four months if it were not for me. I always assisted in finding solutions to the problems.

TS: In relation to the Nordic governments, how did you view these Western representatives who in the United Nations and other international fora opposed Communism and armed struggle, but in Southern Africa supported movements that were close to the Soviet Union and waged war?

DM: That was our problem. We could not understand that. When we heard of countries like the Nordic countries making statements against Communism, it did not make sense to us. How could that be possible? You say that you are opposed to Communism, but you are supporting a movement which in its documents and draft constitution is clearly not in favour of a free market economy and initially said that it was not prepared to talk to anyone in the country. Not being properly informed, we could come to no other conclusion but that the Western countries—in particular the Nordic countries—were one hundred per cent in favour of SWAPO and whatever SWAPO stood for. That was the perception.

TS: Do you think that the Nordic countries influenced SWAPO in a democratic direction?

DM: Yes, in retrospect, if I look at the situation today. Having supported them—and seeing that they for a long time were blamed for supporting the armed struggle and all the killings that went with that—they found themselves in a strong position to influence. That is true and I think that they in fact have done so. Not only the Nordic countries, but also other Western countries.

People sometimes criticize the constitution and say: 'You say that it provides for multi-party democracy and everything, but who is going to control SWAPO? Who is going to make sure that they will not violate the constitution?' I say that our best guarantee is the international community, because it knows that it supported SWAPO. For example, I have taken note of the fact that the Nordic countries have sounded a warning to SWAPO that they cannot expect to receive more aid if they do not look after their affairs and their money. To me that is more or less the best guarantee, even if I had my doubts about the role that the Nordic countries played. I appreciate it very much. This is what we want to hear. SWAPO is now in power, but that is not the important thing. The important thing is that democracy is in place.

TS: In your view, what was it that made the Nordic countries so involved in Namibia and Southern Africa?

DM: Well, we could not always understand why. For example, it was different with the Portuguese. They came to Africa to colonize, exploit and make money. It should now be clear that this was not the motive of the Nordic countries. I saw a Volvo car long ago, but that is all that I know about Swedish products. I think that one must accept that they had no colonial ambitions.

Countries like the United States had problems with black people and the Germans fought a war. They came into contact with the people here and made enemies in many ways. They had a hang-up about race. The Portuguese had the same. And the British.

But the Nordics did not have that problem. There was no racial conflict in their countries. The only way in which the Nordic countries came into contact with black people was through the missionaries. So I understand why the people in that part of the world could not approve of racial discrimination and apartheid.

The Nordic countries were on-lookers who said that the things that are going on are wrong: 'It is terrible. We have to do something about it'. I have some understanding for that. It is the same as when we read about what is happening in Cambodia or Yugoslavia or wherever Christians fight Moslems.

I think that they found themselves in a different situation compared to any other country in the world. They were—and I am not saying this in a nasty way—just on-lookers. They were not involved. They had no direct interests and they did not want to have an interest in making money out of Africa. I think that there is a suspicion among the Namibians that during the process leading to independence all countries played their own cards, always having in mind that after independence they would maybe get a better deal with the Namibian government. They do not have that impression in the case of the Nordic countries. I think that Norway maybe is visible, but I do not know of any presence from Sweden, Finland or Denmark.

Aaron Mushimba
SWAPO—Chief Representative to Angola and to Zambia
Director of Namibia Project Engineers
(Windhoek, 16 March 1995)

Tor Sellström: Did you notice the support given by the Nordic countries to SWAPO when you left Namibia in 1977?

Aaron Mushimba: Yes, immediately when we left the country, entering Zambia. You could see it from the day we were picked up at the Botswana border. The means of transport used, for example. We could not comprehend. 'How come that SWAPO has all these vehicles?' They had new cars and four-by-fours. Getting in to Zambia we started to notice the contributions from SIDA, NORAD and the others. Then you started to think: If I ask what SIDA is, it will seem that I am a little ignorant, coming from inside the country. It took some time to find out who SIDA, NORAD and FINNIDA were. SIDA was more present. You found that the cooking oil, the food, the medicines, all these things, came from SIDA. You also saw the supplies to the places where we used to live. We got weekly rations, but they were good and prized a lot. We then got to know that they were contributions from the Swedish government or the Swedish people. The question then came up: Why Sweden? What interest do they have in giving support to the Namibians? In our history we had never heard about Sweden. Of course, we had heard a bit about people from Finland, who were working in the missions.

From Zambia, I was transferred to Angola. There I became actively involved with SIDA on a day-to-day basis. Carin Norberg was the SIDA representative in Luanda. That is where we used to go. If you wanted something to be paid, you would take the pro forma invoice and go to Carin. It was for food, cars, spare parts and all these things. I thought that it was just one contribution, but we were later informed that we were to have annual negotiations with SIDA. I think that the first meeting that I attended was opened by our President in the Swedish ambassador's house. We then continued every year. In this way, we negotiated an increase of the budget. We would be informed that SIDA had decided to set aside a certain amount for SWAPO in Angola, Zambia and so on.

SIDA's arrangements for the release of the funds were not so complicated as with the others. We had an arrangement whereby a certain portion was deposited into our bank account for administration etc. Every quarter we had to submit a report on how we had used the money. But we did not have to wait for them to go through the report. The next cheque was automatically issued, because the feeling was that since we were in a struggle we had to make sure that things were moving. They should not be delayed. At the same time, we could feel the involvement by the SIDA officials. It was exciting. On a personal level, I developed such a good relationship with Carin. We became like a brother and a sister.

TS: So the aid officials did not apply bureaucratic or political conditions?

AM: No, I did not see that. If there was a condition attached, we would have detected it very early. You could call Carin and say: 'We are supposed to bring the report next week, but we are empty and we have nowhere to go.' She would discuss with the ambassador or call Sweden and you would get the money the next day: 'We have looked into the matter and we will give it to you'.

It was very helpful that this relationship developed. It also developed in the camps. It helped our people to understand who the SIDA people were. You could not step on the toes of somebody from Sweden! Our people felt that they were the beloved ones. They knew that the supplies—what they were eating, the children's clothing and all these things—came from these people. They also knew about the UN, UNICEF and so forth, but the bulk of the supplies were from Sweden. That has always been in the mind of our people.

Coming home to Namibia, we miss that. Namibia is now a free country and we no longer find that sort of relationship. SIDA is with the government and the diplomats are confined to their activities. Some of us who worked with them feel that it is unusual. Of course, we are invited to receptions and the ambassador will receive us, but the warmth of that time has changed into something different. He is now dealing with diplomatic work, which was not there before.

TS: Were there no conditionalities attached to the support? Was it strictly humanitarian?

AM: It was very clear that the support from SIDA was only humanitarian. There was never any military support. They had nothing to do with the military. That was very loud and clear to all of us.

I later moved to Lusaka to take over SWAPO's Zambia office and there I also dealt with SIDA. That is also where I got introduced to NORAD. In Angola there was not much Norwegian support. NORAD was quite different from SIDA. They had ideas regarding which areas they would like to support. SIDA was more general. It was for education, health, food and other things. NORAD would, for instance, say that they would like to support in the transport sector. That is where we then used their money. We used to go to Botswana and buy cars, spare parts and tyres and so on. Of course, we sometimes also got food supplies and other things through NORAD.

I also started to get to know the NORAD people. At that time Mr. Petersen was in the NORAD office in Lusaka. We became good friends and we are still corresponding. He is working on the council in one of the cities in Norway.

SIDA got very much involved in the Nyango settlement. We set it up and built the kindergartens, the hospital and other installations through SIDA. SIDA also paid for the clearing of the fields behind Nyango, where we were to plant millet. Our people later became self-sufficient. People from Sweden came as volunteers, teaching at our school in Nyango. They were complemented by people from the Namibia Association of Elverum in Norway. It became part of my life. The people from Elverum became my friends. We also had to provide security for them, because the struggle had become very tense and the South Africans were trying to do a lot of damage. I remained with the excitement of the general relationship in that camp until I moved to Senegal.

TS: When you were in Zambia, I think that you often went to Botswana to talk to the Herero population? Did you then have any contacts with the Nordic representations there?

AM: Yes, I used to go to Botswana to convince the Hereros not to become hostile to SWAPO, but to play their part in support of the struggle. The SIDA people in Gaborone were very helpful. Inger Jernberg and the ambassador, K. G. Engström. Engström liked to go on safaris in a four-by-four. That was another network of our operations.

In Gaborone, I also used to contact NORAD. The cooperation with the NORAD officials was wonderful. I have never dealt with FINNIDA. It was perhaps handled at another level, but I can vouch for SIDA and NORAD. I have never seen such nice support. It was with open hearts. Everybody can give you assistance, but they can also try to control you. The support from SIDA and NORAD was open-hearted: 'This is what we are supposed to give and this is what you have to do.'

I remember when SIDA came to a meeting in Luanda and a suitcase got lost. Our applications and orders—all that we were supposed to receive—was in that suitcase, including documents for the supply of maize flour to Angola. SIDA then had to fly food from Lusaka. If that had not taken place we would have had a lot of disasters in our camps. They were completely empty. But we had these joint experiences and understanding, like the flying in with the maize flour. That was another demonstration. The relationship also built a personal relationship with the people who were with us. If somebody said that he was from Sweden, you took him as a brother.

Mishake Muyongo
Vice President of the Caprivi African National Union—Vice President of SWAPO—Vice President of the Democratic Turnhalle Alliance
President of the DTA Party
(Windhoek, 17 March 1995)

Tor Sellström: As Vice-President of SWAPO until 1980, you were closely involved in the design of the humanitarian support from the Nordic countries to the liberation movement. How did it start? What were, in your view, the motives and conditions behind it?

Mishake Muyongo: Sweden was the first country to support the people of Namibia, at a time when other countries were refusing. To me it was something else. It was a very big contribution. From then I admired Sweden. I used to have a lot of friends there. The Prime Minister who was assassinated, Olof Palme, was a good friend of mine.

I remember when I was in exile, sitting with the people from Sweden—before dealing with SIDA—and appealing to them to help the liberation struggle. I remember them saying: 'We can only help at the humanitarian level.' The lady who we were dealing with in Lusaka said: 'In your camps, we can only assist as far as food and clothing is concerned, but, please, make sure that the clothing is not military. We do not want to get involved in the fight that you are waging. We only want to look after you, since you have been turned out of your homes.' These words I remember very well. And I remember going back to them, saying: 'I understand. We are not asking for military help, but we have thousands of people in the camps. They have to eat and they need clothing. We also want to organize some school facilities for the children.' They said: 'That we can talk about, but we want access to those camps so that we can go there and satisfy ourselves that what you are telling us is true.'

The only condition that I remember was in that line. Humanitarian, period. They wanted to help the people of Southern Africa who had run away from their homes and who were refugees.

What came into my mind at that time was: What makes the Nordic countries, especially Sweden, so interested in the refugees from South Africa, Namibia or Zimbabwe? I asked this lady in Lusaka: 'Tell me, is it really out of sheer humanitarian concern or is there some political thinking behind it all?' She said: 'Sweden does not export its politics to anybody. We only want to share your burden. If Sweden is in a position to provide food, we will do that, but as you eat it we are not going to say: You must know that there is a socialist government in Sweden'.

It was very clear from the beginning. The support was for the people in exile, who found themselves outside their own country, trying to survive and look after themselves. I remember when we were asked: 'Please, put it in writing how you are going to spend the money'. Before we would get a cheque from

DANIDA, FINNIDA, NORAD or SIDA, we had to put our request in writing. You would first sit down and discuss how you intended to spend the money. You then put it in writing and on that strength they would give you the cheque. But they would also ask: 'Can we have the receipts?'

There was accountability, because the expenses had to be counter-checked by the people who provided the cheques. Of course, somewhere along the line two, three or four cents could disappear, but I was very much helped by the aid officials. They would ask: 'Can you explain what happened?' The SIDA officials used to say in a very calm manner: 'But do you not see that some of the money is not accounted for properly?' In a very nice way. But very fair. There was a very good relationship. Whenever you are dealing with taxpayers' money, accountability is important. They insisted on that. 'Bring the receipts!' Then they balanced up. If there was one dollar or one kwacha missing, they would say: 'What happened? Did you buy sweets?'

Accountability in exile was not very easy. We ran into a lot of problems with the SIDA people. But when I think of it now, I think that they were right. They were telling us that 'one day you are going to run a country, and if you do not look after the resources of your country you are going to run into problems'. They also emphasized the point about military involvement. They did not want one cent to be used for military purposes, whether camouflage uniforms or boots. At one time we wanted boots for the people who worked on our agricultural farm and the SIDA people said: 'If you want gumboots, we can buy them for you. What kind of boots are we talking about?' We brought a catalogue and somebody pointed at boots that could also be used by the military and they said: 'No! Not those ones!'

If the Nordic countries had not come to our rescue at the time I was in SWAPO, I am not sure that our people would have survived. I think that they would have died there, like people from Rwanda are dying now. Even the UN High Commissioner for Refugees was not able to do what the Nordic countries did.

We bought tractors from Sweden and the other Nordic countries. We bought trucks. We could load these trucks—sometimes with 40 tons—and take the assistance to our people. When we said that we wanted to buy trucks or jeeps, they said: 'As long as they are civilian vehicles there is no problem.' But once you started saying: 'It is green in colour', they would say: 'Are you sure that we are talking about the same thing?' I said: 'But we want it for the camps.' They would say: 'Why specifically green? Why should it be green?' But when food was bought or given, they did not mind whether you shared it with the people at the front.

Maybe a criticism that I could make is that when they were helping the people outside to develop a culture of humanitarian sharing—a political culture of understanding the democratic system, even inviting people in exile to Sweden, Norway and the other Nordic countries to see how democracy works—they ignored the people inside Namibia. To me that was a mistake. I am not saying that the same help should have been given to them, but the fact is that they were also oppressed and that they did not have a proper voice. They needed somebody like the Nordics. That is why SIDA's involvement with the present government today is seen as political by the people who were inside, although the assistance is being used for the good of all the Namibians. People say that Sweden and the other Nordic countries only favour SWAPO because they became friends in exile. That feeling is very strong. People also say that the fact that SWAPO is talking of a mixed economy and state participation is because they are taking that from Sweden.

I want to be very honest. People say that Sweden does not hesitate to flash a cheque in front of SWAPO and say: 'Here is a cheque. You can do so-and-so'. And they ask: 'Why cannot the rest of the people—those who were not in exile and who are not SWAPO—benefit and be given that trust?' So the Nordic countries are seen to be a bit biased.

TS: How did you establish which goods and quantities were to be donated by the Nordic countries?

MM: We would have a delegation from SIDA Stockholm sitting with us. They would say: 'Give us your opinion on how you want to spend the money.' Then we would draft a document and on the basis of that we would discuss with them. We stated what we wanted to buy. Food, vehicles, all that. When the things were not available in Zambia, they would say that they could bring the goods from Sweden.

TS: At the United Nations, was it a problem that the Nordic countries could not vote for resolutions making reference to the armed struggle?

MM: During our discussions—and during the visits we were able to make to Stockholm to meet some of the people at the highest level—it became easier to understand Sweden and the other Nordic countries' position as far as the armed struggle was concerned. They used to say that 'other countries can vote with you and support the armed struggle, but what are you going to do if your combatants do not have food?' If your people in uniform are on empty stomachs, do you think that they can fight?' They used to emphasize: 'You must understand our position. It is a question of principle that we do not support the armed struggle, but we do support the humanitarian side of your cause.' So, it was not really a problem for us.

I used to go to the United Nations when I was with SWAPO. Every year I used to go there. We did a lot of lobbying and talked to a number of ambassadors, especially when resolutions like that had to be put across. The ambassadors of the Nordic countries would say to us: 'Listen, we are friends. We believe that what is important is to support you with humanitarian assistance. We leave the armed struggle to you. After all, we cannot liberate you. You have to liberate yourselves. But during the liberation struggle we will make sure that you do not starve and that you do not go naked.'

TS: In the Nordic countries the governments were criticized from the left for not supporting the armed struggle.

MM: Yes, that was very strong. But I liked the stand of Sweden and the other Nordic countries. At the height of the US involvement in Vietnam, the Swedish government took a stand. They criticized USA for getting involved and Sweden was prepared to help the Vietnamese on a humanitarian basis. The standpoint of Sweden was very clear.

TS: One question which perhaps has some relevance for the situation of the political opposition in Namibia and Southern Africa is the question of one 'sole and authentic movement' during the liberation struggle. It has been argued that it constitutes the origin of today's problem of a too strong government party and a too weak political opposition. What is your view on this?

MM: Even in exile it was a problem. There was a lot of debate around this issue. People were saying: 'Why should donor countries, or those who are sympathetic to the liberation struggle, take a position as to whom they should support?' Of course, OAU gave directions that in each country they could only support two liberation movements. These two liberation movements would get funding from OAU. And once you got funding from OAU, you were caught. It was like opening the doors for this particular liberation movement to the outside world. But I think—and I believed so at the time—that OAU had to take its own resources into consideration. They were saying to the different liberation movements: 'Please, not too many of you! When you come here, try to unify for the good of your struggle'. I think that this was the message. In some countries, there were about ten or twelve parties, so the OAU resources would really be stretched.

But I also did not agree with the idea of choosing for the people. The 'sole and authentic' recognition created a lot of problems. So much so that it is still vibrating today. For example, in Namibia the internal parties were not recognized by OAU. They were seen as collaborators. But this was not the case. There were people who chose peaceful means to try and change the system from within instead of taking up arms. I think that they should have been given recognition. I am not saying that they should have been given the same support, but at least some.

Why I have a problem with the concept of a sole and authentic movement is because of the connection it had with the then Soviet Union. The Soviet Union could dictate and say: 'These are the only parties to which we can give arms' and the rest were left out. The other day one of my colleagues in parliament—from SWANU—said: 'You know, we were also in the struggle. But just because the Russians did not support us, we were not recognized by OAU.' Which is a fact. Socialism—as understood by the Soviet Union—was almost dictating the terms of the liberation movements. They were using the pressure of the gun and the pressure of training.

I remember very well that some parties that were aligned to China were not welcome in some of the African countries. Even when OAU was meeting they would keep them in the corridors, while the 'sole and authentic movements' who were aligned with the Soviet Union were allowed. The choice of whom to align with should have been left to the people of these different countries. Not to outsiders. It created interference in the political thinking and well-being of the liberation movements. People started to say: 'Maybe it is better if we become friends with the Russians so that we also become 'sole and authentic'.'

TS: Humanitarian support is a question of human rights' support. There were struggles within the struggle inside SWAPO. One is the Shipanga question—when you yourself lived in Zambia—and the other the so-called spy story in Angola in the 1980s. It is difficult to say to what extent the Nordic countries were knowledgeable about what happened, but do you think that they should have put their foot down in a tougher way?

MM: Certainly! I believe very strongly that the Nordic countries should have said: 'Listen, we are giving you aid for humanitarian purposes. If you start detaining each other you can be sure that we cannot continue'. By so doing they would have driven some sense into some in the leadership of SWAPO.

I know the Shipanga issue very well, because I was then in charge of the SWAPO office in Lusaka. When Shipanga was detained, a lot of my colleagues in SWAPO came to me and said: 'Just hand him over so that we can take him to the front.' 'To the front' meant that you were going to disappear. I said that I did not believe in that: 'If we have a problem with him, why do we not ask the Zambian authorities to keep him. Meanwhile, maybe the UNHCR can negotiate his transfer to another country. If he remains in Zambia, he is going to create problems for us. Let him ask the UNHCR if they can find a place for him'.

I personally asked the Zambian authorities to intervene with Nyerere so that he could take him to Tanzania. When Shipanga was in Tanzania, Sam Nujoma and others went there to say to Nyerere: 'Why do you not release this man? Give him back to us'. Nyerere refused. Even now I respect that decision. Eventually, Shipanga had to be released and went to Europe. But when we had that crisis, Sweden—or the Nordic countries—should have said: 'If this is the way you do your things, then you can forget about our assistance.'

They should have put their feet on the ground, saying: 'Please, we believe in human rights. That is why we are helping you. We do not want you to turn against each other.' It was worse in Angola. Until now we have been asking the Red Cross to give us information about what happened there. I still say to myself: 'I think that the Swedes must help us. They are very much involved with SWAPO. They were helping the people in the different SWAPO camps. Obviously, they should know what happened'. Nobody is able to account for those people. I think that Sweden and the other Nordic countries missed the boat there. They should have helped us. We have over a thousand people unaccounted for. The names are there. Nobody knows where they are. Sweden—being very close to SWAPO in Angola—used to visit some of these camps. Can they not help? Even at this late hour? SWAPO is not going to say that they are bad friends. Not at all. They are friendly to SWAPO. Not because it is SWAPO, but because SWAPO is representing the people of this country.

Festus Naholo
SWAPO—Secretary of Logistics
SWAPO Coordinator and Secretary of Economic Affairs
(Windhoek, 15 March 1995)

Tor Sellström: What contacts did you have with the Nordic countries inside Namibia and when you worked for SWAPO in Angola?

Festus Naholo: Our contacts with the Nordic countries inside Namibia started, I think, around 1974-75. We began to communicate with Ben Amathila, who was then our representative in Stockholm for the Nordic countries. He started to send solidarity workers to us—in particular directly to me—so that was when we started to get involved with people from Scandinavia. We carried out certain underground work to collect information, which was needed for the exposure of the apartheid crimes in Namibia. Taking photos and filming. It was dangerous work and I wondered why these people were taking such risks to get involved with us.

When I came to Luanda in 1978, I was introduced to the Swedish embassy. I established friendships with many people there and we worked together in the interest of our refugees and of the liberation movement. I came to admire that the people from the Nordic countries were vocal. When you met them in international conferences and solidarity meetings, they were outspoken and supported the oppressed peoples.

In Luanda, I acted on behalf of comrade Pohamba. The SWAPO Central Committee had decided to put up a project office and comrade Shikongo was appointed as the first project officer. But there were tough demands and he was taken to Sumbe to become the administrator of the school there. So, I combined the work in the Treasury Department with projects and became involved with SIDA in the planning of a huge project. That was the building of the schools, hospitals, clinics and so on in the Kwanza Sul settlement. We soon realized that there was no construction material in Angola, so it had to come from Sweden. Then we realized that we needed trucks to transport the material from the port to the settlement. As we started to set up the hospitals and clinics, other problems came up. Electricity was needed and water was needed.

By then, Pohamba had arrived in Luanda and I was appointed Secretary of Logistics, working closely with SIDA. At that time, the work was massive and it needed much involvement, because we did not have the experience. Some of the projects were not going well, but it later changed when Berit Rylander and George Dreifaldt came in. They were really wonderful people. The Nordic people have a moderate culture, which you also find here in Namibia. They are wonderful, I must say. They fit in with the Namibians. When we were negotiating different points, we were just exchanging views, teaching each other. That characterized our negotiations. It was a wonderful working relationship.

The contribution made by Sweden and SIDA was immense. Wherever you went in Sweden, everybody was supporting the national liberation struggle or was involved in the effort to eradicate apartheid. In all the Scandinavian countries there was an admirable support. At international conferences you could see how their opinion influenced other countries to understand what apartheid was. The support and solidarity we received from the Nordic countries was important for the liberation movement. It was indeed a factor.

I remember—I think that it was in 1981-82—when the South Africans with support from the USA and Thatcher in Britain turned against the Nordic countries, Sweden in particular. They wanted to stop Volvo. It was difficult for us. We were afraid of not getting trucks from Sweden. By then we were also receiving some Volvos which were a kind of military vehicle. They were very important to get loads into the bush and people into hospitals and clinics. Even the shipping lines were organized not to receive our humanitarian goods, but together with the SIDA officials we worked very hard to find ways to get the food and medical assistance to Angola.

I also remember when sugar to ANC of South Africa was poisoned. They were assisted in the same way. There is no liberation movement—whether FRELIMO, ZANU, ZAPU or MPLA, not to mention SWAPO or ANC—which cannot really commend the work done and the support received from the Nordic countries.

There was work done in the education field. Support to our activities in the education centres and support to our students, who were deployed all over the world—particularly in the English-speaking countries in West Africa—to be trained. Today, we are proud that we have young people who are technicians in various fields, trained through the support of DANIDA, FINNIDA, NORAD or SIDA.

The Namibia Association of Norway and many other anti-apartheid organizations in these countries—as well as churches and cultural groups; everybody—were involved. Some were collecting used clothes to be sent to Africa. It was wonderful. People who were never involved do not realize that they missed something in their lives. It was a time of sacrifices and excitement, but you were satisfied, because what you did felt right. You were convinced. The greatest achievement that we had—all of us—was that we succeeded in crowning ourselves with the end of apartheid. Democracy in South Africa and freedom and independence in Namibia. Unfortunately, we have problems in Angola and in Mozambique, but democracy now seems to be taking root. All those successes are due to our friends.

TS: You got support from the Eastern countries for the military struggle. Apart from the Nordic countries, what was the position of the Western governments?

FN: The West was a great disappointment to all of us. When we grew up, we heard so much good about the Queen of England. We thought that the Queen was the most humanistic person on earth. Then, all of a sudden, we understood. When the struggle started, we did not see the Queen. There was no support. It shocked us all. I remember when Sir Alec Douglas-Home came to Namibia in 1959, pleading that the royal ships—their battleships—should have a base in Simonstown, South Africa. The whole world was against it. He came to Namibia to address us. I thought of 'Long Live the Queen'. This man was saying terrible things against our independence. We thought that he would tell us that there was something good from the Queen. But, instead, he said that they were thinking about Britain.

We were later offered support from all corners, even from people at the extreme, close to fascism. People who vandalized human rights, for example Idi Amin of Uganda. I remember when we went to the OAU Heads of State Summit in Khartoum in 1978. Amin was passing the chairmanship to the President of Sudan. He went to our President to offer him young people to deploy them to fight apartheid in Namibia. Nujoma was quiet. He never responded. How can you respond to that kind of things? We did not want to indulge in such behaviour. We avoided getting involved with certain regimes or organizations, although it was not always easy. Sometimes we really needed the support to further the struggle.

TS: As a church person yourself, how do you look upon the involvement of the Finnish church and mission in Namibia?

FN: The Finnish church has done a lot of good in Namibia. The early education—particularly in the northern parts—was by the Finnish church. Schools, kindergartens, hospitals and clinics. The people who were trained at that time are good civil servants. When the South Africans created the bantustans, they also took over the schools, in particular the lower grades of education. However, the Finns kept one secondary school. It had been the best and I understand that it is still the best.

The Finns have done quite a good job. They furthered education and training. The community profited from their efforts. So did spiritual leaders of immense importance, like bishop Auala, who really was the father of the nation. His voice was accepted throughout the country and internationally. He was a man of peace, reconciliation and righteousness. Bishop Dumeni and many others continue in the same spirit even now. In Swakopmund, there were also Finnish missionaries and I had a very good relationship with them. I also had very good Finnish friends who had been working as doctors, nurses and teachers in the north and who really had been part of the struggle and helped a lot, even treating guerrillas. It was wonderful.

TS: Did you as a liberation movement see any problems with the division in the Nordic countries between the more militant solidarity movements and the governments?

FN: I would say that it was a blessing that so many forces worked for the liberation struggle. For example, there were conferences to which we were invited and where everybody contributed. The fact that there were various ideas—coming from the clergy, the students, the politicians and from other walks of life—was very important for us. We also learnt a lot through such interaction.

TS: In exile, did you feel that the relations between the Nordic countries, SWAPO and the host countries were constructive and based upon common understanding? For example, if you wanted to set up a farm in Zambia, you would seek funding from SIDA, but, in turn, SIDA would seek clearance from the Zambian government?

FN: Of course, we understood that fully. SIDA is a government agency and governments have diplomatic relations. Definitely, SIDA had to act according to the wishes of the host government. But I suppose that they also worked to influence the host countries' attitudes towards the liberation movements. That was quite obvious and we really appreciated it.

TS: So you experienced that the Nordic countries served as your ambassadors vis-à-vis third countries?

FN: Yes, particularly in the international organizations. It is not easy to deal with international organizations. First we looked around to see if there was somebody from the Nordic countries or Southern Africa present. That is how we had to do it. Otherwise we could not get our positions through.

Zedekia Ngavirue
SWANU—Student in Sweden and Chairman of SWANU's External Council
Director General of the National Planning Commission
(Windhoek, 17 March 1995)

Tor Sellström: You lived in Sweden for many years. Who were the first Namibians that went there?

Zedekia Ngavirue: Uatja Kaukuetu is considered as the person that opened the door for Namibians to Sweden. It was his letter to Joachim Israel which started things. He went there together with Charles Kauraisa.

TS: How did you come to Sweden?

ZN: Since I already had these two friends in Sweden, it was easy to contact them. I left Namibia on 21 May 1961. They spoke to the Swedish South Africa Committee. The person who first wrote to me in Dar es Salaam to tell me that they would facilitate my going to Sweden was the late Hans Haste. I believe that his role was that of secretary of the Swedish South Africa Committee. Other members, like Gunnar Helander, Olof Tandberg and Per Wästberg were the most active in the committee at the time.

Initially, I went to the UN to petition. It was at the beginning of 1962 that I was able to go to Sweden. The South Africa Committee facilitated my coming and they were sure that they would find means for me to study, but nothing had yet been arranged. One good day the announcement came that the students at the Sundsvall high school had raised funds to help a victim of apartheid. They had decided to adopt me for a scholarship. I was then in Joachim Israel's home in Bandhagen. It was in the morning and I was in my gown when they came with the news.

TS: I believe that you were already involved in the 1950s with ANC and the South African struggle?

ZN: The Namibian who became directly involved in the sense that he became a member of the ANC Youth League was the late Fanuel Kozonguizi. But from the 1950s, ANC was inspiring all of us. We also used to read the publications of the Communist Party, which was in the Congress Alliance with ANC.

When I went to the Hofmeyr School in Johannesburg at the beginning of 1956, I had a good friend who eventually ended up in Sweden and died there. He introduced me to ANC. We used to visit the Mandelas' home in Orlando very often. That is where I first met people like Walter Sisulu, the late Duma Nokwe and others. I used to go to the ANC rallies in Johannesburg and Kliptown. The famous Freedom Charter was signed in Kliptown in 1955. Then they held another big Kliptown rally in 1956, which I attended. In those years you could not help but be part of that. 1956 was also the year of the Treason Trial, with all the crowds at the synagogue where people were being questioned. It used to capture our attention. I lived in the city of Johannesburg myself.

In those days you really had dedicated men. The road was not at all as clear as it became later on. We had very little support, but people were determined.

TS: When you came to Sweden, you raised the issue of boycott of South African goods. How did the Swedish people respond?

ZN: Very positively. To find even young kids in the north of Sweden, working for a cause so far away was moving. The response was just incredible. What really struck my mind was that when we went to Africa to ask for support we mainly spoke to governments. If you got support from the head of State, that was it. But in democratic societies like Sweden it was not just the political leaders who took a decision. It was the whole nation. We went to schools, trade unions, women organizations and each and every one of them made a commitment. It was not merely a government action. That was one major difference that I recollect from those days.

TS: Was the government pushed by this popular mobilization?

ZN: Yes, and the popular mobilization was for moral and material support. When we had to increase the number of Namibian students in Sweden we would appeal to a trade union for bursaries to get a Namibian to a folk high school. We got that, for example, for Moses Katjiuongua and Godfrey Gaoseb.

TS: Was that through the trade unions?

ZN: Yes. They went to a trade union-sponsored school. We also got, for instance, a place for Mrs. Erika Muundjua. I think that the support came from the women. Equally, when Mrs. Katjiuongua, Rebecka, was stranded in Botswana my wife went to appeal to the women and they helped her with the funds. It was that kind of thing.

TS: This was very early in the formation of an anti-apartheid movement in Sweden, in the wake of the Sharpeville massacre and of the granting of the Nobel Peace Prize to Chief Luthuli. I presume that apartheid South Africa was the main question?

ZN: Yes, very correct. With the South Africa Committee it was apartheid and South Africa, but because of our presence they realized that interrelated to that was the occupation of South West Africa, now Namibia, and that the same apartheid regime prevailed there. It was additional information, which I believe many did not know until we got there.

Well, the people who set the ball rolling were the members of the Swedish South Africa Committee. Then came the political parties, women organizations, trade unions and the many student organizations.

TS: And the churches?

ZN: The churches came in pretty late, I think. I remember that at that time we even questioned the role of the Finnish mission. Then they changed very quickly and started to adopt a very progressive attitude towards the liberation movement. If you look at the missionary reports by the Finnish society in the early 1960s you will see their suspicions about the liberation movement. But we campaigned and got them onto our side.

Already when we were in Sweden, we also had this church organization Birkagården. The nurses under the leadership of Ulla Stolt paid the fare for my wife, adopted her and gave her a scholarship. Ulla Stolt herself was a member of the Swedish South Africa Committee. She mobilized the nurses.

TS: Where in Sweden did you live?

ZN: I lived in Stockholm for my entire stay, but I did my last course in sociology at Uppsala university. The result was that Uppsala gave me my BA. I was also present at the formation of the Scandinavian Institute of African Studies in Uppsala in 1962.

TS: You created a SWANU branch in Sweden?

ZN: Yes, we had a representation there, but we did not only campaign within Sweden. We also went to the other Nordic countries. The major take-off was in 1965, when we persuaded the Social Democratic Party to invite people from SWANU to speak throughout Sweden on May Day. Kozonguizi came to speak, as well as Katjiuongua, Kandjii and others. Kauraisa went to speak with Olof Palme. We were all posted to different places on May Day 1965. The whole idea was to have a kind of joint venture with the Swedish labour movement to give the May Day an international theme. It would also help us to get SWANU people for our own conference. The Social Democratic Party agreed to pay for these people to come from different parts of the world to Stockholm. After that they financed their stay at Saltsjöbaden (Stockholm), where we decided to form a SWANU External Council.

Because of that nation-wide action with people posted in different places, presenting the apartheid question in Southern Africa, 1965 was a major breakthrough. From then on we got started. I do not remember the exact first amount that we received, but I think that it was in the order of 50,000 Swedish Kronor, which was a lot of money in those days. Since SWAPO was not known much at that time, we agreed that it was to be a Namibian fund and it would be split on a fifty-fifty basis between SWANU and SWAPO.

TS: In 1966, the SWANU and SWAPO student bodies also met in Uppsala?

ZN: Yes. We wanted to form an organization for Namibian students and people attended from both parties. I was Chairman of the SWANU External Council. SWANU was then more established in Sweden, but it was a condition and an agreement between us and the Swedish authorities that it was not a political SWANU event. We wanted to get all Namibian students together.

TS: Was this initiative sponsored by the Swedish National Union of Students (SFS)?

ZN: Yes. We invited Olof Palme to open it. Sam Nujoma and I made the opening statements on behalf of our parties.

TS: Later on the Social Democratic Party moved closer to SWAPO than to SWANU?

ZN: Quite frankly, that story I would not be able to tell, because that happened after I had left in 1967. I do not know whether it was a question of representations being inadequate, SWANU not being directly involved in the armed struggle or recognition *per se*. I am not so sure that it was a question of recognition and non-recognition. I do know that SWAPO really was being seen as having the guerrilla fighters, doing the actual fighting. OAU had at that point indicated support for SWAPO and I think that organizations that were sympathetic to the Namibian cause felt that they should follow the guidelines set by the Organization of African Unity.

SWAPO did initially not have that much of a presence in Sweden. It came later. One thing that impressed me was that we linked up with so many organizations and groups. For example, in 1966 or 1967 the Metal Workers Union paid for a jeep to be used in Namibia. They just gave the vehicle to SWANU. A Land Rover.

Hifikepunye Pohamba
SWAPO—Chief Representative to Tanzania—Secretary of Finance and Administration / National Treasurer
Minister of Home Affairs
(Windhoek, 15 March 1995)

Tor Sellström: As SWAPO's Treasurer, you worked closely for many years with the Nordic countries in several countries in Africa. Could you describe this relationship?

Hifikepunye Pohamba: I have been involved in the aid programmes extended to the people of Namibia, particularly in exile, by the Nordic countries and many other organizations and governments of the world. In the early 1970s I started to work with the representatives of SIDA in Dar es Salaam, where I was the SWAPO representative. At the same time, I was also dealing with FINNIDA and NORAD. On a very small scale, I should say. SWAPO then had its headquarters in Lusaka.

Let me first talk about SIDA. And when I talk about SIDA, I talk about the government and the people of Sweden. Through SIDA the people of Sweden have given an enormous financial, material and moral assistance. The people of Sweden and SIDA assisted us politically. At the UN, the representatives of Sweden and of all the countries in the Nordic world supported the liberation of Namibia and SWAPO, which was fighting to liberate this country. They opposed apartheid and imposed sanctions against the apartheid regime, both in South Africa and here. That expression of solidarity with the peoples of Namibia and South Africa was extended to humanitarian assistance to those who ran away from the oppression.

The refugees who left this country—particularly after the collapse of the Portuguese empire in Angola and Mozambique—faced a lot of problems when they came to Zambia. We had no means to give them assistance. Sweden was the first country to decide that the Namibian refugees must be assisted. They gave us money, with which we bought food for the refugees at the Old Farm in Zambia. The food and clothing—including clothing for the babies—was given to us by SIDA.

As time went on, the Swedish government made special budget allocations for the people of Namibia in exile. I do not recall exactly how much it was when it began, but it grew into millions of Swedish Kronor every year. It started with food and was then extended to vehicles. If the food was bought in Lusaka it had to be transported into the camps. We did not have any vehicles, so we said: 'OK, here is the food, but we have no means to take it to the people.' SIDA then made provision for vehicles. Not only that: shelter, schools and hospitals were provided. It even went to the building of garages for our vehicles, which eventually became many. Not only those contributed by SIDA, but also from FINNIDA, NORAD, DANIDA—through WUS Denmark—and from other countries, for example, the Holland Committee on Southern Africa. The assistance that we received was also extended to Namibia itself, through SWAPO.

SIDA's financial contribution to the people of Namibia was divided between Angola, Zambia, Tanzania and Namibia. We had a lot of problems here. People were detained and the families had nowhere to get the means to live. SIDA's assistance increased when the children boycotted the apartheid schools. Our people inside the country then decided to put up their own schools. Gibeon is one of them. The money was channelled into Namibia to assist them. Volunteers also came to our assistance. Some came as teachers and others as medical personnel or as workers. Being responsible for the aid programmes to SWAPO from various countries, I rated it. When I did that, the SIDA assistance was the largest.

We received similar assistance from WUS Denmark, DANIDA and NORAD. NORAD put up a school in Loudima (Congo) and provided the teachers and the funds. WUS Denmark—apart from food and clothing—assisted in putting up housing structures at Kwanza Sul (Angola), where most of the Namibian refugees were accommodated. Ships came from the Nordic countries to Luanda full of building materials with which we put up the houses in the settlements.

Each country contributed what they could. FINNIDA played a very important role. They provided, for example, materials and money, and many young Namibians went to study in Finland. Some have become ministers in independent Namibia. The first person we sent there was Nickey Iyambo, who is now the Minister of Health and Social Services. There are many others in the Namibian government who had their education in Finland. For example, my former Permanent Secretary, Dr. Freda Williams. Dr. Hangala and many others are graduates from Finland. We also had many people who studied in Sweden. I recall an institute in the north at Sandö. We sent people there, especially those who were working in my office, dealing with finance, book-keeping etc. There were also some people who were sent to one of the universities near Finland, Umeå I think. They were trained as teachers. When they had completed their studies they came to teach in the Namibian health centres in exile.

There were also private companies, although they were contracted and paid, but to us it was still assistance. Container Express, for example, put up building structures in our camps. We also had people from Denmark and Norway assisting us. In the Nordic countries you also had organizations such as church aid organizations. I discovered that they were given some kind of subsidies from SIDA and the other government agencies, like NORAD.

In other words, the assistance that we received from the Nordic countries was not only channelled through SIDA, NORAD, DANIDA or FINNIDA. We also received assistance from non-governmental organizations in these countries. When you put all the assistance together, you see that they were the largest donors of humanitarian assistance to the people of Namibia. Of course, they told us: 'We are assisting you on a humanitarian basis and we do not want to give anything that could promote the military struggle'. They made it clear. However, when they gave us food, it went to the camps and the camps were also the reserves of the PLAN cadres. It would therefore not be wrong to say that the people of the Nordic world also assisted PLAN. But they never gave us guns. They fed our people, they educated our people, they clothed our people and they gave shelter to our people, but they never gave us guns.

TS: Did the Nordic countries demand anything in return? Were there any conditions attached to their assistance?

HP: There were no strings attached. There were some countries that assisted us in order to get our support—politically or diplomatically—but the assistance from the Nordic countries did not have any strings attached. It was free humanitarian assistance given to the people of Namibia.

Something that I particularly enjoyed with the people representing SIDA was the non-existence of strict bureaucracy. One person who I worked with and really assisted me is Berit Rylander. That lady was attached to SIDA to work with us. I will not forget how she assisted us. She would come and tell you what you should do. She would go to the camps and assess the situation herself. Then she would come and say: 'This is what you should do.' Another lady who did a lot was the representative of WUS Denmark, Tove Dix. She made a fantastic contribution to me personally when it comes to the administration of the goods and money donated by different organizations. Like Berit, she would go to the camps and assess the situation.

You would perhaps think that the men did not do much. However, we had people like Roland Axelsson, who worked with us for a long time. I started with him in Dar es Salaam and we worked together right through, up until independence. We had individuals like Ola Jämtin and the one we used to call Ongwala. These people made enormous contributions. You would sit with them and they would tell you what to do. I owe them a lot.

Let me talk about the transport assistance. As time went by, we had a lot of vehicles bought with money not only from the Nordic countries, but also from other countries. The problem was that we needed garages where these vehicles could be served. SIDA then agreed to establish garages for us in Lusaka, Luanda and Kwanza Sul. So the fleet of vehicles was serviced by SWAPO with the assistance of SIDA experts. I was very happy to see the head of the garages, who was here recently. He came to visit us.

SIDA also put up bakeries. There was one in Lusaka and one in Nyango in western Zambia, where the Namibian refugees were. Others were put up in Luanda and in Kwanza Sul. These bakeries were of great help, particularly to the children. They could now get bread. Cakes were also made there. I recall Berit Rylander's father, who is a baker himself. He came to Angola to assist us.

This was an enormous assistance, not only from the governments, but from the people of the Nordic countries. That assistance made us go forward. Other countries did assist too. The government of the Netherlands came to our aid. And, as time went by, more assistance came from other countries when they saw the light in the tunnel and that the situation was going to change. But when we talk about real friends, we talk about the people of the Nordic countries. They started to assist us when there was no light in the tunnel at all. There is a proverb in English which says: 'Your friend in need, is your friend indeed'. They are the friends, indeed, of the people of Namibia. They started to assist when the South Africans were saying: 'No independence in Namibia! No freedom in South Africa!' We really have to thank them for what they have done.

Andreas Shipanga
SWAPO—President of SWAPO-Democrats
Former Minister of Economic Affairs, Mining and Sea Fisheries in South West Africa/Namibia
(Windhoek, 20 March 1995)

Tor Sellström: How did you first come into contact with the Nordic countries?
Andreas Shipanga: I think that I will start by saying that the first Swede that I knew of was Charles John Andersson. I read his book about South West Africa. He was right when it comes to the Ovambo traditions and culture. I am a product of the Finnish missionary schools. There were Finns, but there were also—what do you call them: Swedish-Finnish?—Lindström, Eriksson and so on. They were the ones that I came to know during my school years and also during the three years when I was teaching.

After teaching, I ended up in Cape Town in 1958. There we got into the political struggle. One thing that always gave us strength was the Nordic countries' opposition to apartheid. The Nordic countries were really vocal in their condemnation of the evils of apartheid. The only other country in Europe to do this was Holland.

In 1963, I was sent to Congo-Léopoldville as a representative of SWAPO. There I met the Swedish ambassador, a very good gentleman. We had problems in Léopoldville. I had several Namibians under my care, one woman and some young chaps, and there was a civil war going on. I met the Swedish ambassador at an Egyptian embassy reception. He came up to me and said: 'Where are you from?' I said: 'From South West Africa.' From then on he not only provided us with food. He also provided us with accommodation. When Tshombe got back in power a lot of mercenaries returned to Léopoldville. The ambassador then arranged tickets to fly us to Dar es Salaam because of the dangers. That was in September 1964. That is when I came to appreciate the support and sympathy of the Swedish people and government.

I went back to Accra and Cairo. In March 1966, there was a conference on South West Africa in Oxford, England. That is where I met the late Olof Palme and Pierre Schori. They invited me to Sweden. I went to Sweden late that year, in 1966.

TS: It would appear that it was after the Oxford conference that the Swedish Social Democrats shifted their support from SWANU to SWAPO?
AS: I think that it was the first time that they really came across Namibians other than SWANU. I also think that in a sense that was a break-through. When I went to Sweden, I stayed with Zedekia Ngavirue of SWANU. Later I moved to the apartment of Bernt Carlsson. It was not easy. The Social Democratic Party had not really moved away from SWANU. It took some time. I think that it started at that time when the Social Democratic Party through the newspaper *Aftonbladet* campaigned to collect money for SWAPO and SWANU. It was a first concrete break-through for SWAPO in Sweden. Then, of course, followed the Uppsala student conference. It brought a lot of people from SWAPO to Sweden. It was one of the things that we had worked on. SWAPO and SWANU students came from the East and from the West. It was very interesting.

After that I travelled to Norway, Finland and Denmark and visited the anti-apartheid groups there. For many of them it was the first time that they heard somebody from SWAPO. The result was very positive.
TS: Was it positive in all the Nordic countries?
AS: Because of the missionaries, the Finns were not openly supportive of SWAPO. But especially the Finnish Seamen's Union gave us open support. The Finnish missionaries who went to Namibia first came to South Africa, where they attended a Calvinist college in Wellington, near Cape Town. They were supposed to be taught Afrikaans, but they were also introduced to 'the wild man's life' in Africa. With a few exceptions, they were highly conservative, paternalistic and anti-Communist.

Anyway, the Seamen's Union was very good. In Norway it was all systems go. In Denmark there were not too many. They were not very strong.

TS: 1966 was also the year of the first armed confrontation between SWAPO and the South African security forces at Omgulumbashe. Was it not difficult to campaign for support to SWAPO in an environment where there was principled opposition against armed struggle as a means to solve conflicts?

AS: I did not come across anybody who was critical about why we took that decision. I addressed many meetings. In fact, at a meeting in Uppsala I was admonished by some Swedish students who said: 'Shipanga, your people are fighting in Namibia now. You must go and join them! Leave the United Nations!' No, we really did not have any problem, but, of course, we had to explain. The sympathy was with us, because of the verdict of the International Court of Justice which went against Ethiopia and Liberia. People understood. At least those who we could talk to.

TS: Later Sweden started to give official humanitarian support to SWAPO. Do you feel that this really was humanitarian support?

AS: Yes, it was and it really helped, first in Tanzania and then in Zambia. But I must say that some of the aid was abused by the SWAPO leadership. There is no doubt about that. I remember that I talked to the Swedish ambassador in Lusaka about it in 1975. He told me that some leaders wanted to buy Range Rovers with Swedish aid. I said: 'Mr. Ambassador, if you go to the refugee centres there are people who cannot even get bread every day. A Range Rover is too expensive and unnecessary. Why not Landcruisers?' I do not know what happened, but the leaders were fighting to get Range Rovers.

TS: Sweden was the first country to give SWAPO direct support. But Norway also did so at an early stage?

AS: Yes, but with Sweden it was on a much larger scale. No other country gave us that kind of support. There were the Eastern countries, of course. They were supporters, but it was different. Sweden was followed by Norway and Finland, to a lesser extent.

TS: Then—in 1976—your association with SWAPO came to an abrupt and tragic end. You were detained in Zambia. You had worked very closely with the Nordic countries. Did they intervene on your behalf? Did they put pressure on SWAPO, Zambia and Tanzania by diplomatic or other means?

AS: When we were arrested in Zambia—where there was a law on *habeas corpus*—my wife went to the Swedish embassy to ask for political asylum. The ambassador said that it was possible. But, on the whole, people were saying that if you campaign for the release of Shipanga you are giving absolution to South Africa. Then there were other events. Immediately when we were put in prison, SWAPO approached, for example, the Finnish government to appoint Martti Ahtisaari to become the UN Commissioner for Namibia.

At least, Sweden and Norway agreed to receive the colleagues that were in prison with me. Sweden took three or four, Norway about three. That is how we eventually came to Sweden. There were already those colleagues of mine, as well as Kenneth and Ottilie Abrahams and other Namibians.

TS: Upon your release in 1978, you founded SWAPO-Democrats in the Abrahams' house in Spånga outside Stockholm. Did you then have any support base in Sweden?

AS: No, none at all.

TS: Finally, do you think that there was a hidden political agenda behind the Nordic involvement in Namibia and Southern Africa or was it purely humanitarian?

AS: I must emphatically say that is was purely humanitarian. What hidden agenda did Sweden have for Vietnam? It was simple, moral sympathy for the suffering people. That is humanitarian. They were never into colonies in Africa or anything like that. What was there for Sweden? A few Volvos? What else? Nothing! I honestly believe that it was out of simple and pure humanitarian consideration. I am convinced of that.

Andimba Toivo ya Toivo
SWAPO—Secretary General
Minister of Mines and Energy
(Windhoek, 17 March 1995)

Tor Sellström: During your time on Robben Island, did you hear about the Nordic countries supporting the liberation struggle of ANC and SWAPO?
Andimba Toivo ya Toivo: I heard that the Nordic countries were a special group and that they were supporting the liberation movements. In fact, perhaps all the liberation movements that were struggling for freedom and independence had support from the Nordic countries. As well as from the socialist countries, headed by the Soviet Union. I was also amazed to hear that the Kingdom of the Netherlands had assisted the liberation movements. There was even a case when the Queen assisted FRELIMO. There was a row in the Dutch parliament, but the Queen said that she gave of her personal money.

When I came to Angola, I met some friends and had the opportunity to go to Norway and Finland. I skipped Sweden. I think that somebody I wanted to meet was not in town. I went to Sweden in 1985. My immediate contact was Anne-Marie Sundbom. Many Namibians have been in her care. I was told that she was the one who introduced SWAPO to the Swedish government at the time when she was working with the youth movement. She met Peter Mueshihange at a conference and invited him to Sweden. That is how the relationship between Sweden and SWAPO came about in the early 1960s.

TS: So, in general terms, you found the Nordic assistance to SWAPO established when you were released from prison in 1984?
AT: I found a lot of Volvos flooding SWAPO and our camps. All from Sweden. Volvos and Scanias. I fell in love with the Volvos. I am still driving a Volvo now.
TS: Do you think that the support had political conditions attached or was it given on purely humanitarian grounds?
AT: I am sure that it was given on humanitarian grounds, without strings attached.
TS: Sweden was barred from participation in UNTAG, because the South Africans said that Sweden was not neutral, but partial to SWAPO. How did you look upon that?
AT: It was against us, but what could we do? The South Africans wanted it like that, just as they wanted the Cubans out of Angola. The Cuban government said: 'All right, we are prepared to go out provided that Namibia gets independence'. The South Africans had no alternative but to agree to that. More so when they were beaten at Cuito Cuanavale. In the case of barring Sweden from participating in the UN forces, we said, well, there is nothing we can do. If we attain our independence, our friendship with Sweden will continue. That is also what has happened.

Sweden supported our liberation struggle. As far as the question of transport is concerned, we never suffered. Most of our vehicles came from Sweden and we very much appreciate the fact that the Swedish government and people stood by us through thick and thin. Now we are independent and I am happy to say that our relationship continues. Whenever the Swedish people come here they must feel at home. This is their home, and I think that we are trying to do our little bit to pay back what they have done for us. We cannot do much, but the little we can, we shall willingly do.

Ben Ulenga
SWAPO—Secretary General of the Mineworkers Union of Namibia
Deputy Minister of Wildlife, Conservation and Tourism
(Windhoek, 16 March 1995)

Tor Sellström: As a Namibian trade union leader, when did you come into contact with the Nordic countries?
Ben Ulenga: In 1977, I was tried and sentenced to prison. I spent the prison term mostly in South Africa, but I used to hear about what was happening. Very sketchily of course. There was a certain Paul Carlsson, who came to Namibia from Sweden to work with the trade unions. Sometimes he had to disguise himself as a cleric, feigning pastoral work. The title of reverend was attached to his name. However, Carlsson had to leave Namibia in a hurry.
TS: It seems that the South Africans knew all the time what he was doing. He cannot have been very successful?
BU: No, he does not seem to have been.
TS: When did you start to work with the trade unions?
BU: I was captured in the war in 1977. It was close to Etosha, in the area of Tsumeb. But that had nothing to do with trade unions. At the end of 1985, we were released. Especially among some of us who came from prison it was of great concern that there should be greater organization among the working people. That is why we proceeded to persuade some colleagues on the political side to embark on a project to start workers' committees and so on.

Initially, we did not contact anybody. We did not ask for assistance. Very soon it came out that the work was being done and, of course, we linked up with the so-called leadership outside and also with the international trade union movement as far as we could. It did not take long before we were in contact with the trade union movement in Sweden, Norway and Finland.

Only about three or four months after the setting up of the first two unions of the National Union of Namibian Workers (NUNW) I went for a visit to these three countries. In Sweden, I was invited by LO/TCO. It was the first time that we established a direct relationship between the trade unions in Namibia—not from Luanda—and the trade unions in Sweden. That was in February 1987. We had very good meetings with the LO/TCO joint council that dealt with international co-operation. I was working for the Mineworkers Union, but I was also involved with the general trade union organization. What we agreed was, basically, that they were going to give us assistance for the organization of part of the unions and also for mobilization.

Later, we got support from them for the setting up our offices, projects like the *Newsletter*, organizing May Day celebrations, acquiring vehicles and so on. I think that it was not always easy for them to approve assistance that went to certain sections where they actually could not give us the money openly.

Those were very interesting years. In the end, the chairman of the Swedish Mineworkers Union—who at the time was also the President of the Miners International Federation—was thoroughly on the side of the Namibian Mineworkers Union. I was also lucky to link up with a guy called Stig Blomqvist, who was in Zimbabwe. He was a person who was very much down to earth. He understood what was happening. He was the best as far as I am concerned. The President of the National Union of Mineworkers of South Africa, James Motlatsi, and the General Secretary of ANC, Cyril Ramaphosa, worked with him. Actually, they worked out the whole support plan with Blomqvist. He did his own thing with the Swedes and pulled some strings here and there.
TS: Was Blomqvist linked to the other Nordic countries through MIF?
BU: Yes, he was. Blomqvist co-ordinated with the Swedish Mineworkers Union, LO/TCO and, of course, with the people in Brussels, that is with MIF and—although maybe not directly—with the International Confederation of Free Trade Unions (ICFTU). This cooperation continued until independence. There was also another kind of assistance that this group helped us to get.

That was during the strike we had in Tsumeb in 1987. They gave us some money to relieve the situation of the workers and we paid out quite a few thousand Rands to assist them.

TS: When you visited Sweden in 1987 and met LO/TCO, did you encounter any problems regarding international affiliation?

BU: I must say that it was handled very nicely and very diplomatically. It was a problem, because everybody spoke about it. Not necessarily in Sweden. When I was with the officials from SWAPO in London, they really talked about it and said that it might be a problem. We also discussed it with other unions in London. Before coming to Sweden, I had a meeting with the people from MIF and it was a question that was nicely skirted round. You could see that it was quite an obstacle. It was there, but it was never bluntly made a condition of assistance. I have never faced a situation where it was.

We worked together with MIF, which—although an independent and autonomous international—was closely related to ICFTU. They gave us money. We did not have to state that we were not affiliated to the World Federation of Trade Unions (WFTU), although we sometimes talked about it. It was essentially not a problem. There was no conditionality.

TS: Do you have the impression that the people inside Namibia knew about the support that they were receiving from the Nordic countries?

BU: The mineworkers were the people to whom I reported. I reported everything. I did not travel to negotiate something on my own. Especially in the beginning, when I did not know how much the Nordic trade unions could do. I talked to them and then I related to my colleagues how matters were proposed to me, what we had discussed and what the understanding was. As far as that is concerned, the people knew what the involvement of the Nordic trade union movement was.

A very clear example is Stig Blomqvist, who was based in Zimbabwe. He represented the Miners International Federation, but he also very much represented the Swedish LO/TCO. And he was not just a Swedish comrade, trying to assist as a Swede. He was directly representing the trade unions, so it was known that the assistance was from the Nordic countries.

Another example is our relationship with the Norwegian trade union movement. We had direct links. We had people like Dr. Bertelsen, who came to Namibia as a representative of LO/TCO in Norway. She was not just a visitor from Europe or from Scandinavia. She was specifically representing her union body. There was another Bertelsen, an industrial physician, who also came here and did some work on behalf of the Mineworkers Union. The whole thing was sponsored by the trade union movement. There was some co-ordination between the Norwegians and the Swedes. The support was understood at the branch level of the union. Everybody knew. The people in the branch committees knew who was coming, on whose behalf and who was supporting us. If you got into the street, people were aware of the friendly relations, especially between Namibia and Sweden. But maybe they did not really know that there was something called SIDA.

If you go back into the history, looking at the first links between the Nordic countries and Namibia, I think that it is important that the first missionaries from Finland came here more than a hundred years ago. Many people in Namibia actually take these links as far back as that. There were also quite a few Swedes. My teachers were, for example.

There was a Finn, who was detained by the South African security at the time when SWAPO was rounded up at Omgulumbashe during the first military clash in 1966. He was very much involved with Toivo and the other SWAPO people around Ondangwa. He was tortured. I do not know whether he died due to causes having to do with his arrest, but he died about two weeks thereafter. Later, Mikko Ihamäki was the chief representative of the Finnish mission society. He died a few years ago. He was a strong SWAPO supporter and behind the scenes a mover of many things. He hated the South African regime and was kicked out of here. He was picked up one morning. The police came and said: 'The sun must not set while you are here. You must leave today.' It was terrible.

South Africa

Jaya Appalraju
ANC—Student in Sweden
Executive Director of Matla Trust
(Johannesburg, 14 September 1995)

Tor Sellström: When and how did you come to Sweden?
Jaya Appalraju: I came to Lund in April or May 1968. I had made an initial visit in December 1967 on the recommendation and suggestion of the ANC office in London. I had come to London two years before that, in 1966. I finished my university entrance in England with the intention of going to university there. The ANC Chief Representative at the time was Reg September and he and people like MP Naicker, Aziz Pahad and Thabo Mbeki recommended ANC students to look at the Scandinavian countries as a possible place for further study. Since London was just as new to me—although it was English-speaking—I decided to investigate it further and went to Sweden in December 1967, where I decided that I was going to apply for a grant. I got the response in March 1968 and left. It was a small student grant, which paid for my initial travel and the first three months. I was then told that I could apply for various student support grants, which I did. That is how I got to Sweden.
TS: Was this through the Swedish National Union of Students (SFS)?
JA: Yes. That is right.
TS: At that time, were there other ANC students in Lund?
JA: There were other South African students—some of them were ANC—whom I had gone to see. One of them was Billy Modise. Raymond Mokoena from South Africa and Sydney Sekeramayi from Zimbabwe were also there. Rupiah Banda from Zambia had just left. And, of course, there were quite a few Namibians from both SWANU and SWAPO.
It was only when I had gone there to discuss with them that they recommended that I should come. None of the other South Africans who were also recommended to come actually ended up in Scandinavia. They had gone to other countries.
TS: You came to Sweden at a time when the student movement was very active. There was a strong anti-imperialist solidarity movement with Vietnam and Southern Africa. How did you view this?
JA: I think that it was one of the major aspects that convinced me that I should go to Scandinavia, actually. When I initially arrived there—before deciding to apply –, I found that the political climate of support was positive. While that existed in England as well, it tended to be much more complex. The South African issue seemed to be buried amongst everything else and the task of organization was much more difficult there. In Sweden, I found that even though the scales were smaller and you were talking to a much smaller group of people, the possibilities of actually operating and working in that political climate were much more exciting, much more positive. I therefore decided to go there.
TS: Did you find it strange that the Nordic countries, being Western countries and in two cases even NATO members, were involved in struggles that otherwise mainly were supported by the Soviet bloc?
JA: That was extremely strange and, again, a major motivating factor. There was this situation—which was not prevalent in other parts of Europe—where NATO members would openly criticize the position of the United States vis-à-vis Vietnam and there was very little open opposition to our cause. There were hurdles, there were obstacles, but there was no real opposition to the Southern African struggle, given the backdrop of the political climate of the time. Yes, big power politics entered as well, but in spite of that we found that the room for manoeuvre, the room for operating, on the issues of Southern Africa was much greater both at the information and at the political level.
We always raised the issue of Southern Africa, not just South Africa. In fact, it was ANC's position to always raise the issue in the context of Namibia, FRELIMO's struggle in Mozambique, MPLA's struggle in Angola and of ZAPU-ZANU in Zimbabwe. We always raised it in that context. One of the is-

sues that we debated very strongly within the solidarity organizations was, firstly, whether that was the best strategy and whether one could define the Southern African region as subject to sub-imperialism. Secondly, whether one should actually project the image of Southern Africa at that time as a weaker link of imperialism and look at Mozambique and Angola in that light. Our position was always that we should do that and that the struggles were intimately linked. I found the atmosphere very exciting. We also had to compete with other issues around the world very strongly. But in the Scandinavian countries there was a sense of general camaraderie and support.

TS: Did you also visit the other Nordic countries?

JA: Yes, I went to Denmark, Norway and Finland. And, of course, to various parts of Sweden. At the time, there was not an organized ANC presence in Sweden. There were individuals who were doing ANC work with the solidarity movements.

TS: Was Sweden covered under the London office?

JA: Yes, people used to come over from London from time to time, but there was no really serious representation. That was a problem.

TS: Were there ANC students in the other Nordic countries?

JA: There were a few, like Freddy Reddy in Norway. I cannot recall all the names, but there were a few people. In Denmark as well. But in all these countries there was no officially recognized ANC representation as such. That was an internal issue that we had to face by organizing ourselves and by bringing in leaders from London and elsewhere. We reported as much as we could on the projects and the support that we had and argued that more attention ought to be paid to the Nordic countries. A lot of intensive work was done at that stage.

TS: I guess that you mainly worked with the Africa Group in Lund?

JA: Yes, the Africa Group was the most consistent support group. They had very little resources to assist the various campaigns, but would advise us on what to do, where to go etc. They would arrange meetings at various places, in clubs, schools, organizations of various types, trade union groups and so forth. It was very rewarding when I look back at it now. But we were also craving for some kind of recognition from the state and the government and had great difficulty in carving out an identity for ourselves at the same time as we were working under the umbrella of the existing Swedish solidarity organizations, which had a very clear identity. Sometimes this worked against us and sometimes it was in our favour. So, while the Africa Groups were very supportive, at times we had to distance ourselves from their positions.

TS: That could not have been easy. The Africa Groups were critical about the government and at the same time the government was more progressive than other governments?

JA: Precisely! The Social Democrats were just as supportive, but perhaps they were not as informed as the Africa Groups on the Southern African situation.

TS: Thabo Mbeki has said that the crucial element in the Nordic involvement with the liberation movements in Southern Africa was that they in the 1970s recognized the liberation movements as governments-in-waiting, so to speak. Until then they had rather been seen as resistance movements.

JA: Yes, I agree. Things happened very quickly from 1968 in terms of ANC recognition and support. It was surprising. We did not get that kind of recognition anywhere else. Elsewhere we worked only with the support groups, in the United States, Europe and so forth.

TS: When did you leave Sweden?

JA: Well, I left Sweden at different points and came back. I finished my studies in 1973/74 and went for further training in England. I came back to Sweden and finally left in 1980 for Tanzania. That was on the suggestion and organization of the late Thomas Nkobi, who used to come to Sweden at the time. He was developing various projects and was closely involved with the Scandinavian countries in Tanzania. Nkobi found my skills relevant to project planning, but, again, we were very restrained with resources and he quite simply asked me to apply for jobs in Tanzania from where I could also assist with the Solomon Mahlangu Freedom College and later with the Dakawa project. I did so and went to Tanzania under a UN hat.

TS: The planning of the ANC settlements was to a large extent done in cooperation with Norway?

JA: That is right. I worked mainly with Dennis Oswald and a little bit with Spencer Hodgson. Dennis was the first ANC Director of Construction and Projects. Later on I was involved with the planning of Dakawa, while working with the Tanzanian government in the Ministry of Planning, Housing and Urban Development.

TS: I know that O.R. Tambo requested that you should be transferred to Zimbabwe and work in the Ministry of Local Government there. In Harare you became very involved with what was called the PASA project—planning for a post-apartheid South Africa—with a number of activities taking place between the home front and the exiled leadership.

JA: Yes, the move from Tanzania after three and a half years was instigated, as you say, by Oliver Tambo. The intensity, the content and the style of the liberation movement were rapidly changing. We had now moved into Zimbabwe, which in 1980 had gained independence. However, there were serious constraints in the support of the Frontline States to the liberation movement, so Oliver Tambo considered my function and role as a technical person ideal. I could operate in a supportive role for ANC and also be a fully-fledged civil servant in my own right, rather than—as was suggested by another department of ANC—joining the Treasury. He opposed that and suggested that I move to Zimbabwe, which I did. We had a very slim and very small outfit there in the beginning. It reminded me of my first years in Sweden. There were so few of us to undertake such a big task. It was a very intensive period.

TS: Which year did you arrive?

JA: In July 1984. Zimbabwe was then going through its own period of adjustment. The lessons I learnt in Zimbabwe were very useful when the discussions on the PASA project were taking some concrete form from 1987. I was always behind various ANC departments. There were a few of us in different fields pushing ANC for resources and to put some manpower behind the planning and thinking about a post-apartheid situation now that Zimbabwe had changed. Although the objective circumstances did not allow us to rationalize when this would take place, the momentum put pressure on ANC to start to think about what should be done—assuming there was a change in South Africa—,given the scale and complexity of the issues the Southern African states had faced up to that time.

Tambo raised this issue very strongly in various informal gatherings and when we learnt that support had been obtained from the Scandinavian governments towards this project we were all very excited. As I had worked very closely with the host government in Zimbabwe they obviously depended on me for quite a lot of inputs in terms of formulating some aspects of it. I spent a lot of resources and time on the PASA project. We insisted that it had to be done not by ANC alone, but in collaboration with groups inside the country. They were in the front-line, facing the issues from a day-to-day basis, fighting for rents, water etc., and we had to translate this into some sort of long-term demands. We worked under very difficult circumstances with activists on the ground from all over the country. I was very much involved in the logistics of getting key people out to advise us on what was going on in various sectors. For us outside South Africa this was an important learning period.

TS: This was to a large extent done with Nordic, mainly Swedish, funding, but the Zimbabwean contribution was also very important?

JA: Yes, it was broadly supported by the Zimbabwe government. They sanctioned the project. For example, we had to get people into Zimbabwe on bantustan passports and so forth. We had to explain to them what it was all about and that we had to get so-and-so into the country over a weekend or a couple of days to hold intensive workshops or all-night sessions. The Zimbabwe government was very supportive in that respect. The University of Zimbabwe, the Cold Comfort Farm Trust and various institutions assisted us in making that possible.

There were also difficulties, because one needed consultations with all kinds of people, such as legal groups, medical groups, groups on rural and urban development, health, education, land etc. Often people would come from some remote part of South Africa, speaking different languages that we had not heard of. That was, I think, the foundation of the democratic process in this country. In some respects, the post-apartheid discussion that we are in at the moment was started in that consultative process. No policy goes through parliament without being pretty well canvassed and ANC has established this consultative policy-making process as a principle for its political work

TS: Zimbabwe was then an important meeting point between the ANC leadership that to a large extent had been outside South Africa for perhaps twenty years and a new upsurge of democratic movements inside the country?

JA: Oh, yes. Zimbabwe was crucial and whenever possible we involved and interacted with the Zimbabweans. For them it was quite an interesting dynamic as well, because, largely, their policy-making did not involve this kind of process. There was political consultation through the party and the development committees and so forth, but such large-scale, broad and horizontal consultation did actually not take place. So it was a learning experience also for them and they acknowledged that. Given the structure of government in Zimbabwe and their own political process towards independence, it was different, but they interacted tremendously with us, assisted us and facilitated the process.

TS: It was not until 1985 or so that the ANC was allowed to have an office in Harare and only two years later Zimbabwe was already an important meeting-ground for the future of South Africa?

JA: Yes, but we always had a very slim and low-profile office. We worked in terms of committees. There were groups of people outside the formal ANC representation who were doing a lot of the work, whether it was in education or health or keeping the various departments afloat, as well as working on the PASA project, which was a major initiative.

The Harare Declaration, which this thinking sort of led up to, was a landmark for the way in which the process unfolded after that. We did not really know where the process was leading to ourselves, but it was intensive and it grew. It was a groundswell and after a while it was not clandestine any more. Businessmen would come out and declare that they were consulting with ANC. We would agree on a lot of issues and disagree on others, and for the first time the media were giving us a lot of legitimate coverage.

In these consultative discussions on the post-apartheid project, Swedish involvement and Swedish thinking was always sought after, whether it was on the question of constitutional development or in education. We always made sure that somebody had actually researched what was Swedish policy, or Scandinavian policy, towards the various issues of women, welfare, macro-economic growth and so forth. Besides financial resources, I think that inputs from the Scandinavian governments in terms of their own historical experience always featured in our discussions.

TS: Do you then think that Nordic policies have had any influence on the thinking of ANC regarding the future of South Africa?

JA: I was very much involved in the economic strategy meetings. From the Bommersvik PASA meeting in 1987, our economists really started to look much more closely at the history of Swedish policy-making, comparing and critically assessing the impact on both the economy and the politics of Sweden. It definitely had and still has a major influence, I think. We hope that this is reinforced, because now the field has been opened so considerably and there are so many other views that have come in and to some extent have diverted us from our initial ideas of where we should be going. I think that we are now going through a moment of resignation from this tremendous amount of input, discussion and debate about what should be done, for instance with the South African economy.

TS: Do you think that there was a political hidden agenda behind the Swedish or Nordic support to ANC?

JA: Even if there was I do not think that we ever felt it. There were no strings attached to the support which we received. In fact, we were extremely free in the way we used the support and we understood very well that we were to deal with an extremely complex capitalist economy in South Africa. Nobody was going to convince us that we were going to have to prepare for an essentially planned economy. We had to deal with the realities of that complex and monopolized situation.

Even if there had been an agenda, it would not have been relevant under our circumstances, because we had to look very carefully at the objective realities. It would have been totally unrealistic to think that we could have intervened in a drastic way to change things in South Africa without the danger of the economy really reacting negatively against our own objectives. No, we did not feel either then or now that there was a hidden agenda. It is true that the issue was raised very much by the left in Sweden at the time, but we were also very naive about this kind of thing. However, with the hindsight of experience you can now say that we did not feel it. It did not show itself at all, which was very different from a lot of other countries.

Alex Boraine
Progressive Federal Party—Director of the Institute for a Democratic Alternative in South Africa
Vice-Chairperson of the Truth and Reconciliation Commission
(Cape Town, 12 September 1995)

Tor Sellström: As founder and director of the Institute for a Democratic Alternative in South Africa (IDASA), you have been a recipient of Nordic anti-apartheid support. What was the background to the support?

Alex Boraine: Let me start with the time when I was a member of parliament. I was there from 1974 to 1986. One of the laws at that time was that a political party could not receive financial assistance from abroad. Any support that we received as an opposition party was in the nature of encouragement, solidarity, invitations to speak at a conference or whatever. That was through the Liberal International and as a result we worked much more closely with the German foundations than with the Nordic countries.

I think that the Nordics were extremely suspicious of white liberals. At that time, my impression was that the Nordic people only saw the possibility of ANC overthrowing the regime. It was fairly simplistic. There was a feeling that they did not want to assist anybody inside South Africa. Only those outside were the heroes. The people in exile. I can well understand how they reached that conclusion, but I think that it was unfortunate, because it meant that a lot of people who were trying to undermine apartheid from inside—much closer and in some ways under more difficult conditions—were discouraged from trying to get assistance.

TS: Considering that it was around the liberal centre, at least in Sweden, that the anti-apartheid opinion originally began that appears contradictory.

AB: Right. That is why I think that it in some ways was a fairly simplistic line to take. The ambiguities and contradictions inside South Africa and the South African struggle were not as evident as I thought that they might have seemed. I think that one of the reasons for that is that very few people from the Nordic countries actually came to South Africa during that particular period of time. It was almost impossible for them to come. They were kept out. They were not given visas. Funny enough, Denmark for example, refused to send an embassy official. Norway was actually acting for Denmark. Now, how you analyze your strategy without being on the spot defeats me. I tried to make that point as strongly as I could and I was very delighted when, finally, Peter Brückner from Denmark came to South Africa as its ambassador. He did a superb job in a very short space of time. He began to asses where people were really making a difference and needed encouragement.

I only really started to visit the Nordic countries when I left parliament. Before that we had visitors, for example, from the Liberal Party of Sweden. A number of them came and a number of them were very forthright. I remember one particular evening when they said that the best thing that Sweden could do was to provide arms to ANC, which shocked a lot of my colleagues. It was said by a member of parliament, who later became a minister in Sweden.

TS: From the Liberal Party?

AB: Yes. He has since changed his mind. We criticized him quite strongly, but agreed with the strong rejection of apartheid. Not the manner of support.

It was also very difficult to support the Nordic commitment publicly, because the government misused that to such an extent. It used isolated illustrations of how hostile the Nordic countries were. How they wanted to overrun the country and what about the Communists, etc. That sort of things.

TS: There was an editorial in *The Citizen* saying 'Sweden go to Hell!'.

AB: Yes, it worked up feelings very strongly. It made it difficult for an opposition party which was forced to deal with white politics. At the time, there were no blacks in parliament. No black constituencies in a sense. Saying that we must end apartheid, you had to be extremely wise and sensitive about what you could and what you could not do. However, when I left parliament in 1986 it freed me to take a much more open stance. That is also why I left. I felt that the constrictions of the official party system made it very difficult to take a really tough stand. I also thought that it was necessary for some whites who had the status, the protection and the opportunity to sacrifice that, break away and be with those who were saying the same things, but who were very strongly punished and sometimes tortured, jailed, driven out or underground. IDASA was just an idea. We had no money; no staff and no programme. It was our discussions with black leaders outside and inside South Africa that made us feel that we needed to start some vehicle for democracy. So we called it the Institute for a Democratic Alternative in South Africa.

TS: I understand that the first person you talked to about IDASA was the Norwegian consul Bjarne Lindstrøm?

AB: Yes. He had just arrived. He could not understand why somebody would just walk out of parliament. You normally resign, lose an election or retire, but you do not walk out. He met me at a function and said: 'I am intrigued. Could we not meet sometime?' I said: 'Sure.'

TS: Was this in Cape Town?

AB: It was in Cape Town. He was based here. I had lunch with him and I told him more or less what I have been telling you. He said: 'How on earth are you going to get this going?' I said: 'I have not the slightest idea, but if it is right, it will work. I am going to pursue this.' The first thing that I really wanted to do—this was a week after I walked out of parliament—was to try to travel around the country and consult the blacks. He then said: 'Well, let me give you some money to enable you to do that.' It was ten thousand Rands, I remember it well. It was very awkward, because I was very sensitive about how to look after other people's money. I really could not put it into my account. I had no organization. I went to my bank manager and opened another account with that amount of money. My colleague van Zyl Slabbert and I—both of us—had to sign every cheque. So, then we travelled and we listened and we consulted. We started the institute and I reported back to Bjarne Lindstrøm. He said: 'Well, what I think you should do is to visit Denmark, Finland, Norway and Sweden.' I said: 'That is fine, but it is a long way. I have no guarantee that they will help.'

TS: You had no connections in the Nordic countries?

AB: No connections at all. The only ones that I had met were fairly hostile, as I said. Even lukewarm towards so-called white liberals. But I could really understand that. Lindstrøm said: 'I will send a message ahead and we will buy you two plane tickets to go there. You can visit the four countries in six days.' I must say that the reception was not entirely warm. There were some, particularly in Sweden, who did not believe that we had met ANC. But we had. I had actually gone to Lusaka and I had met Thabo Mbeki. I said to him: 'You must understand that if we are going to get support from people who normally have been supporting you, there will be those who will say: Are you going to take money away from us? I will ask for additional funding so that no one suffers. Secondly, Thabo, you must tell me whether you think that there is any point in internal opposition or whether it is only external?' He said: 'That is nonsense. The two must work together. If they ask us, we will tell them to support you. But if we think that you are not doing what is right, then we will tell them to stop supporting you.'

So we went to the Nordic countries and met the Foreign Ministers. It was at that level for about half an hour. Very nice. But the real discussions took place with officials from the ministries, SIDA, DanChurchAid and the trade unions. They were very tough. They had declared boycotts and felt perhaps that what we were saying was that sanctions did not work and that we therefore should do something else. I said: 'No, both external and internal pressures.'

TS: Did you also go to Finland?

AB: Yes, I went to Finland as well. After some delay, which is inevitable—they had to consult, talk to each other, talk to ANC and that sort of thing—they gave us an initial grant for one year, which was enough to start one office, for some travel, some workshops and a major conference on democracy, which we held in Port Elizabeth. Even the comrades from the townships came. Then we started the work. And because we were able, I think, to deliver and because more and more people started to get interested and supported what we were doing, the Nordic countries renewed the amount of money. In fact, they gave more.

TS: Who gave you this financial support?

AB: Denmark, Sweden, Norway and a much smaller amount from Finland, which is understandable. What I am very thrilled about is that as a direct result of our initiative, the Nordic countries were forced to ask some very tough questions, such as: 'Should there not be a more multiple strategy, and if so, who should we assist?' Well, there were the trade unions, the churches and organizations like IDASA. More and more, we developed the idea and in 1987 we went to Senegal and met the ANC top leadership, led by Thabo Mbeki. That was supported by the Nordic countries. Not only by them, but principally by them. Funny enough, the Swiss government also supported the initiative. They actually paid for the hotel. They told their ambassador to pay the account for ANC and for the people who came from inside South Africa. That was a great help.

The South African government's reaction to the Dakar meeting was very strong. They threatened to close us down and to take away our passports. We had all sorts of death threats. All kinds of stupid things took place. P.W. Botha made a speech for more than an hour in parliament, criticizing us. It, however, helped us enormously in terms of the outside world. They thought that we must be doing something right if P.W. Botha hated us. So the assistance grew. We started to hold workshops and seminars all over the country on a variety of issues. We also started to send teams outside. A women's conference was, for example, held in Harare with women from ANC. There were meetings with lawyers and meetings with young people. We also had a very fascinating meeting at Victoria Falls with artists, poets and writers from ANC and cultural organizations in South Africa. We tried to discuss the transformation of South Africa at every possible level. It seemed to work quite well.

We also had to ask some tough questions about the role of the Soviet Union, because they were working closely with ANC. We had a conference in Germany with people from Moscow. Top people from the Moscow State University, scholars and politically active people, plus ANC and us from inside South Africa. That was also funded very generously by the Nordic countries. Every year I went back and met the Nordic Foreign Ministers, SIDA and the Liberal Party. The Swedish government decided that they would not give us money directly, but through a partner. They chose the Liberal Party. Denmark chose DanChurchAid as their partner and Norway the Church of Norway. So we began to meet not only people in government—in the ministries or in the trade unions—but quite ordinary people in the NGOs, which was great. It started to cement relationships beyond a cheque, which I was pleased about.

Then the Nordic countries—particularly Norway in this instance—tried very hard to arrange a meeting between key people in South Africa and key people in ANC to start the process of negotiations. That did not quite work out, but it certainly contributed a great deal to the eventual breakthrough. Two ministers in de Klerk's government have told me that without the work of IDASA, de Klerk could never have made his famous speech in 1990. Whether that is true or not, history will tell.

Our major support came from the Nordic countries. IDASA is still getting very substantial support as is the institute that I have started since I left IDASA, the Institute for Justice in Transition, which deals very much with the Truth and Reconciliation Commission. I have received fairly substantial support from Sweden, Denmark and Norway.

One of the things that I am doing is to document human rights' violations that have taken place in South Africa since 1960, going through evidence that has been kept by lawyers for human rights, the church, in the cupboard or under the bed, affidavits, reports on inquests, press-cuttings etc. I am trying to pull all that together, which is a huge job. Sweden has given me the financial assistance to make that possible. That is going to be a huge help to the Truth Commission. I have got skilled volunteers from four different areas, the Eastern Cape, Kwazulu-Natal, Gauteng and the Western Cape. So there are four groups and I have found some money for workers, computers and so on. It has worked very well, indeed. I have held seminars all over South Africa on the Truth Commission, printed pamphlets, organized major conferences and published two books, all of which has been supported in one way or the other by the Nordic countries. So they not only played a very useful and substantial role in the actual liberation process, but even for the consolidation of democracy, dealing with the legacy of the past, which is so vast in this country. In every area of life they continue to assist and my assessment is that they are not stopping their help now that South Africa is supposed to be a free, democratic country. They are saying: 'How can we help it to develop and grow into a really stable society?'

TS: When you had your first contacts with the Nordic countries they were quite lukewarm. They were not interested in supporting white liberals inside South Africa. In retrospect, do you think that the position of the Nordic countries was exclusively in favour of ANC?

AB: I do think that there were those who in their political analysis at one stage gave too much credence to the armed struggle as a possibility for overthrowing the state. I could never see it happening. In fact, I do not think that ANC ever thought that either. There was really never an armed struggle in that sense, as in Zimbabwe or in Namibia. But, having put themselves in that position, I think that there were those in the Nordic countries who personally came very close to ANC and that they were very influential in determining policy. They felt that support to anyone else would be to weaken ANC and to dull the sharp edge of the armed struggle. There were others who, historically, simply did not have any contacts and did not think it possible to do anything very significant here, except perhaps to give some sort of ambulance help.

But people began to debate the issue and we began to explain. We were always interviewed on television and by the newspapers and people started to ask questions. They were very receptive. I think that there were many who always had been receptive, but there was a dominant block that took one particular stand. I remember how I just in personal contacts sensed quite a strong resentment. They felt that we were like National Party whites, except that we were more humane. We had been in parliament, which blacks could not. We were privileged. I said: 'All I ask you to do is to think strategically. You do not have to like us. You do not have to agree with everything we say or do. But think strategically: How can we best combine to get rid of apartheid?' I think that there were a lot of people who started to think.

Once the decision was made to give assistance to those inside the country, they were very anxious to get more projects. I think that they thought that we were accountable. We sent reports every three months. We sent audited accounts on a regular basis. I think that there was a feeling that 'we can trust these people; they are delivering'. And ANC supported the efforts. There was a synergy.

TS: And the South African Council of Churches?

AB: Oh yes, it was very supportive as well. Beyers Naudé, who happened to be an old friend of mine, actually sent a letter of support. And when Mr. Mandela was released, he called me to come and see him. He knew what was happening and said: 'Is there anything that I can do to help, because IDASA must continue with its work.' I said: 'Well, it would be very helpful.' Because some people were then saying that the actual work was over and that perhaps we should be dealing on a government-to-government basis. I agree that there ought to be government-to-government cooperation, but I also think that civil society is very important. There is no guarantee that a government will remain just, accountable, responsible and not abuse its power. It happens everywhere. You need civil society for checks and balances. So Nelson Mandela wrote a letter. Well, he did not write the letter. He said: 'You write it. I will sign it.' I wrote a modest letter and he signed it. When I next visited the Nordic countries they said: 'Do you not think that your role is over?' I said: 'Perhaps, but you should read this letter.' They read it and immediately said: 'Well, if Mandela says that we should support you, then, of course, we must.' So I have felt that the interest has been sustained and actually grown.

TS: Do you think that the Nordic countries have had an influence on ANC when it comes to the political course taken in government?

AB: No doubt. I have no doubt about that. In terms of economics, the whole question of democracy, accountability, the gentle use of power rather than sweeping away everything and demanding total power. I sense that the Nordic countries have possibly been the strongest influence on ANC in making it less of a far left party and more left of centre. I think that it is tremendous. My personal view is that it has been extremely helpful. There is an openness which was not discernible in the early days. I think that the hold of the Communist Party, which was very strong and remains influential, is not nearly as strong as it used to be. There are other forces at work. There is more pragmatism. What can work? How can we create jobs? How can we listen to other people? How can we get the best for our country?

It is remarkable, actually, if you think of the long years and the dreadful suffering under apartheid. We have had a miracle, where people are not looking for revenge, but really to heal the country. We have a long way to go and there are a lot of big problems, inefficiency and inexperience. But that is the legacy of apartheid. That is what it has given to this country. It is going to take a generation to overcome. At the moment, there are fairly major breakdowns, but I do not know how anyone could expect anything else. I am not worried about it. It is a natural, inevitable development and I hope that the Nordic countries will continue to support the ANC-led government, because I think that it deserves it. I think that it would be extremely good for Southern Africa to have not a super power in the region, but a country that is stable, democratic, consistent and which is not going down the tube as lots of countries in Africa have done.

Roelof ('Pik') Botha
National Party—Minister of Foreign Affairs
Minister of Mineral and Energy Affairs
(Cape Town, 12 September 1995)

Tor Sellström: You served as a young diplomat at the South African Embassy in Stockholm from June 1956 until January 1960. How did you see the relations between South Africa and the Nordic countries, particularly Sweden, in those days?

Pik Botha: For a young South African foreign service official it was a very sudden introduction into a very critical world. A very critical world. The Swedish media at the time were very critical and even hostile towards the South African government.

TS: Already in 1956?

PB: Very much so. There was—I even remember it till the present day—a Swedish missionary in South Africa, a man called Gunnar Helander. You will find quite a number of his articles in *Dagens Nyheter* and *Expressen*. Particularly those two papers. Professor Tingsten was the editor of *Dagens Nyheter* and Dr. Harrie was the editor of *Expressen*. I even remember the names till the present moment. That was forty years ago, so you can conclude that their attitude and the Swedish media's attitude towards South Africa must have caused a stir in my soul, a turbulence in my own thinking.

On the one hand, many reports were exaggerated and distorted. On the other, the reports did challenge the moral basis of the policies of the South African government. After several very severe editorials and articles, published by *Dagens Nyheter* as well as *Expressen*, I asked to see professor Tingsten. He received me in his office and I objected to his editorials and their non-factual basis. The factual basis of many of the articles was inadequate. Exaggerations. If they talked about infant mortality, they would double the figures. That kind of statistics. That, of course, did not detract from the fact that the policies of the government were fundamentally immoral.

I went to see him, and, as a young man, I explained to him that: 'Yes, at the present stage there are many laws and aspects of the South African government's policies which cannot be defended. On the other hand, how would you facilitate change? How would you, as a responsible editor, facilitate change? If you are really concerned about those matters, as you profess to be, then I want to challenge you and ask you: Do you think that you are going about it in the right way? You would be better off if you checked your facts first of all, because if facts are wrong in a newspaper report people tend to reject the impact of the article due to the factual inadequacies contained in it. You achieve more by being factual and correct.' He then said to me: 'Look, you whites have been the minority in South Africa since your history started.' He had a very good grasp of our history. He had studied it, obviously.

TS: He had visited South Africa. In 1954, just before you came to Sweden, he published a book called *The Problem of South Africa*.

PB: Yes. Then he said to me: 'Mr Botha, what is your vision? What is your view? You are a minority, but what about the future? Can you give me your view? If I am wrong in my basic presumptions, how do you see your future?' I explained to him that nothing in life was static and that I foresaw changes, saying: 'Yes, we cannot continue by denying blacks political rights.' That is when he said: 'What do you mean? Are you going to give them political rights?' I said: 'There are various ways to do so.' He said: 'Please explain that to me.'

I then said to him: 'Look, South Africa is a large country. If you look at the whole of Southern Africa, once upon a time the whole region was known as British South Africa, with Botswana, Rhodesia, Northern Rhodesia, Nyasaland, Swaziland, Lesotho, all of it. Britain wanted to govern it with individual administrations and governors, but it was one country. Already there was this pattern of Botswana, Swaziland, Lesotho, Southern Rhodesia, Northern Rhodesia, Malawi—which was known as Nyasaland—having proceeded on what you could call at least a separate statehood.' He then said to me: 'In other words, you say that you could do the same in South Africa?' I said yes. And he said 'Do you mean that the Zulus then would become completely independent?' I said yes. He said: 'The Tswana people?' I said yes. 'And the Xhosas?' I said yes. And he said: 'Mr Botha, if you tell me today that that is the official policy of your country, I will write an editorial tomorrow to support it.'

This was in 1957 and at that stage it was not government policy. It only became government policy long after that, in the 1960s, when Dr. Verwoerd pronounced it. But then it was too late. It was too late, because the immoral aspects of apartheid overwhelmed any merit that there might have been in the concept of complete independence for the various communities. That killed it. If it was not for that you could have had a development similar to the one in Swaziland, Lesotho or Botswana. There was no apartheid there. It did therefore not bear that stigma. It had credibility. Our plan lacked credibility and legitimacy because of apartheid. That wrecked it. It is interesting, looking back today, that Tingsten was prepared to defend it, because to him that would have provided a moral basis: statehood, full independence, a black prime minister in Zululand with a black cabinet, black judges, equality before the law, all that he stood for. One person, one vote, full democracy. And in what would remain of South Africa also, full democracy, even if the whites were in a majority. But, of course, he had me in a corner, because it was not government policy. I said: 'No, I am afraid that I cannot say that this is the government's policy, because it is not. But one day it will become the government's policy.' And it did, but too late. The positive elements were discounted. This was the problem.

I think that this summarizes to me—looking back at my whole career—the development of my own concepts over the years. In other words, looking back at my tenure of service in Sweden there was, on the one hand, harsh, certainly acrimonious and hostile, publicity on the South African government's policies. Partly exaggerated and distorted. On the other hand—and quite apart from the inaccuracies of what was published—I had to account to myself for the moral basis of the policies. I think that I must be fair and say that that early experience in my life, exposing me to this harsh environment of criticism, woke me up to the realities of the situation. Both the moral and economic implications of laws like the pass laws, the Immorality Act and so forth.

If you serve in a country like Sweden and the headlines come out one day about a Norwegian or Danish sailor who has been arrested in Durban because he spent the night with a black woman, well... In my time, an incident occurred which I never will forget. There came from South Africa a group of coloured entertainers, musicians. They had a mixed repertoire of dancing, singing, a band playing etc. Very joyful people as they are known to be here in the Cape. They were called *The Golden City Dixies*. One of them developed appendicitis and had to go to a Swedish hospital. After the operation he was visited by a Swedish doctor who showed him a Swedish newspaper which had as its headline some riots in Durban. I think that it was mainly between Zulus and Indians. It was with a racial connotation and described the police action against the rioters. The Swedish doctor told this South African coloured musician: 'Look here, you say that you come from South Africa. The country is going down the drain. It is finished.' This coloured person could not understand Swedish and the doctor gave him an interpretation which bordered on the perception that a civil war had started in South Africa.

The man got frightened and eventually asked for asylum in Sweden, which brought about a split in the group. Up to that point they had been very happy. They had had a very good first performance. They did well in Britain, where they had been before. With all respect, I think that the mere fact that here was a group of coloured persons who sang, who were joyful, who travelled with South African passports, to a large extent repudiated the exaggerations which appeared in the Swedish media. And I think that some of our friends in the Swedish media could not stomach this and had a hand in fomenting trouble. I had to fly to Gothenburg, where they were stranded. After the negative reporting of the Swedish media, the group attracted no more audiences. The show was killed by the media. They had hired a huge circus type of tent which would have provided, I think, for five or six thousand people. All the costs went up and they were left as stranded South African citizens. I addressed them in the tent and advised them to return to their country. At first they were hesitant and wanted an assurance from me that things were calm and that they could return with safety, which I gave them.

Years later, I returned to South Africa. They gave a performance one evening, either in Pretoria or Johannesburg. They invited me and treated me as a special guest. I am mentioning this to indicate how loaded the atmosphere was in Sweden. Strangely, with our Swedish neighbours, that was never the case.

TS: With Norway, Finland and Denmark?
PB: No, I mean where I lived in Stockholm. I naturally had Swedish neighbours and friends. When I visited Stockholm in 1993 with Mr. Mandela and Mr. de Klerk for the Nobel Prize, I took an hour or two off. It was in December. I went to the place where we stayed. One of my daughters was born there, in Stockholm.
TS: In what area of Stockholm did you live?
PB: It was Äppelvägen 25 in Stocksund. I had great difficulties finding it because of the snow. Unfortunately, I did not find the way I used to drive. It was Ringvägen, a round string, but we took the wrong one and had to do it two or three times. Then I suddenly saw the house. It is still there. I knocked on the door. A man opened and the Swedish security person who was with me explained who I was. The man said: 'Yes, all right, but you must give me a little time to get dressed.' It was early in the morning on a Sunday. Next door was our neighbour, Stig Nelin and his wife Margit. We knocked on the door and a lady opened the window. Suddenly I saw

her face. It was Margit. I recognized her and she recognized me and said that I must just allow her to put on a dress or something. She then invited me in.

Stig was a captain. He was transferred to the north of Sweden in connection with military training or something for a year or two. At that time, we lived in their house. That same house. There we were again. I had pictures taken with her and me standing together at the place where I had lived. Then she said to me that there were two Ström brothers, twins, living across the street. One of them was now very old, not very well any more, and he would love to see me. I walked over to the Ströms', knocked on his door and before he opened he looked through the door. He immediately saw me and we embraced each other. This, I think, indicates to you what the personal relationship was with my family, myself and our Swedish friends, Swedish business people. They were in the major companies then, LM Ericsson, SKF and others, and we had good relations with them all along. In many respects, we placed handsome orders for Swedish products at the time. We exported oranges to Sweden and red wine, which sold very well.

TS: Did you also cover the other Nordic countries from Sweden?

PB: No, only Sweden. Finland to some extent.

TS: When you mention Helander, Tingsten and Harrie, you are talking of people who came from the church or a liberal, non-socialist, political background. Tingsten was a prominent opponent of the Social Democratic Party.

PB: Yes, he was. I know.

TS: They were very instrumental in the formation of the anti-apartheid opinion in Sweden. How did you later explain the fact that Sweden and the Nordic countries supported liberation movements that were assisted by the East bloc?

PB: Looking back, I personally believe that it always was an obsession for the government of Sweden and elements like Tingsten and others. However, not to side with the Soviet Union. No, definitely not. They were offering equally harsh, if not worse, criticism of Soviet policies.

TS: This was after the invasion of Hungary?

PB: Exactly. Ironically, I took into my home a Hungarian family that had fled from Hungary. A man called Ralf Teleki. He was a very well known portrait painter, an artist. We took him and his wife and daughter into our home in Stockholm. The Swedish government had a relief programme. They also requested foreign embassies and missions, or made it possible for them, to take families. Which we did. He later started to sell enough works to be able to hire his own place. I think it was in Lidingö, where Millesgården is. I wanted nothing from him, but he insisted on painting me. I still have the painting, which was painted in Stig Nelin's home.

TS: How could the Swedish opinion become so aligned with Soviet-backed policies in Southern Africa?

PB: No, it never was. The Swedish opinion was not aligned with anything that happened in the Soviet Union. Definitely not. But they coincided, because Sweden and the other Nordic countries—to a lesser extent Norway, Denmark and Finland; Sweden was really in the vanguard, I would say—had this obsession not to have racism ever again, knowing what it had caused the world. Secondly, I think that a basic philosophy of justice and fairness prevailed. Racial discrimination, allocation of rights and duties, responsibilities, on the basis of membership in a group, class, race or religion was anathema. It was not only race, I repeat, but allocation of rights and privileges on the basis of group membership. Already then Sweden was in the vanguard of freedom for women.

TS: How could it be explained? Was it because of a Germanic, egalitarian spirit?

PB: It was there. Any preference in governmental laws and actions based on visions concerning membership in a religious, racial or sexual group, was anathema. Concerned media and others always saw this as a crusade, as something that they had to fight. Irrespective of where it occurred, they were against it. They therefore sided with the organizations that were on the ground, opposed to it, and professed that they were representing the majority of the people who were seeking freedom. I think that that was what was behind it. It was a very strong and emotional, yet intellectual, assault.

I remember colleagues from Spain and Portugal—particularly the Mediterranean and South American countries, even Egypt—who very often found this typical Swedish position offensive when it came to their own countries. Franco was still there. Salazar was still there and Italy was recovering. Regarding France—it was just before de Gaulle rose to power—I praised myself that I as a young diplomat wrote a report to my government predicting that de Gaulle would take over one day as the President of France and reform it. Later on, it did happen. Years later, I returned and perused some of the files of those days. I saw my own reports and smiled. A senior official at the Department had written on them: 'Rubbish! A lot of rubbish!' But it was accurate!

At the time I also made a study of the Lapps. Some of them even came to see me. They brought facts and figures on their treatment, which I found unacceptable.

TS: I think that the South African government raised this question in the United Nations?

PB: Yes, we did.

TS: Sweden had a close relationship with the liberation movements that are now governments in Southern Africa. In retrospect, do you think that what you term as an emotional and intellectual stand had any influence on these movements?

PB: That is very difficult for me to judge. There are no angels this side of the grave, but I cannot escape from either the suspicion or the assumption that the Nordic governments despite the basis on which they gave aid—that it should not be of a military nature—knew that some of it did go for military purposes.

TS: Napoleon said that armies march with their stomachs?

PB: Correct. Secondly, I do feel that because of the emotional side insufficient control was exercised over the destiny of the money and the funds. The major question for the Nordic countries now will be: What now? Will they retain the same standards that they applied vis-à-vis the apartheid regime? Will they keep on applying them? That is going to be a major challenge to the Nordic countries.

TS: Do you think that there was a hidden agenda behind the support, in the sense of fomenting economic interests in a majority ruled Southern Africa?

PB: Not in my opinion. I am not aware of any evidence to that effect. As we say, the proof is in the eating of the pudding. I am not aware of any undue pressure after the 1994 election—or even before—from any of the Nordic countries, coming here saying: 'Look, we helped you. Now we want certain favours for our industry or for our exports.' No, I am not aware of that.

TS: It was, of course, difficult for you to have direct contacts with the Nordic countries. However, did you see the potential of the Nordic countries as brokers for a negotiated settlement?

PB: Well, Martti Ahtisaari is a Finn. I would say that he played a decisively important role. There is no question about it. I hope that history will accord him the credit that is due to him. I think of the years and years that he was waiting for a movement on the Namibia issue and how things went wrong, time and time again. But he displayed a reasonable and balanced attitude. The two of us eventually got on very well together. We developed a personal relationship, which again proved to me—as so many other events in my life—what can be achieved if we move away from stern agendas and minutes, preconceived judgements and ideas, and just retain an open mind towards one another. It was mainly as a result of that informal, yes, trust in each other's personal integrity. That is of great importance, even if you differ. It sometimes enabled him to telephone me on the most sensitive matters, which I would then take to my government and cabinet and push through, because I believed what he told me. Even if what he told me was unacceptable to some of my colleagues. This was very important.

I believe that Southern Africa owes that man a debt, because you must not forget that it was the fact that we eventually succeeded in concluding the agreements—in the end of 1988—in the terms of which the Cuban troops would be withdrawn, that opened the way for Namibia's independence. He himself saw what no other observers—including the Swedes, with all respect—had not yet analyzed properly, namely the impact and the influence that it would have on events here. That was the forerunner. I accompanied Mr. de Klerk, who had then just become President of the country, to Namibia's independence celebrations, where he made a speech which was applauded as much as that of Mr. Sam

Nujoma. There we met for the first time the Soviet Foreign Minister Shevardnadze, who is now President of Georgia. We became good friends. The Swedish Foreign Minister, Sten Andersson, was there too.

TS: You met him there for the first time?

PB: Yes, for the first time. Tall, rather typically Swedish. We had a very open, fruitful and useful discussion with him, pushing from our side. We said: 'Look, things have changed irrevocably.' It was not that he was doubtful, but he explained to us that what they would do would depend on how irrevocable or irreversible the change was in South Africa. Mandela had just been released. He said: 'Yes, the world is now prepared to look at you with new eyes. But we will be waiting for the element of irreversibility.' We tried to convince him and said: 'Look, if the government of the day should now endeavour to turn back, it is finished. Our own supporters would ditch us'. He then said: 'Look, for so many years the public opinion has been almost petrified against you. It will take some time', indicating that he would assist as far as possible in bringing about that change. But he urged us to produce more evidence of irreversibility.

It is interesting that we eventually, in the referendum held here—albeit amongst whites, who were then our voters—asked the white electorate to agree to the irreversibility of what we were doing. That, I think, was really the final break for the whole world on the question of acceptance. They accepted our integrity and credibility on the issue of irreversibility of change.

In Namibia we also met the Nigerian president, Babangida, who later invited us to Nigeria. We met the President of Egypt, Mubarak. We met a host of statesmen. The reception given on our side that evening was attended by 40 per cent more guests than we invited. They just stormed in. It was overwhelming!

Historically speaking, that lowered tensions throughout Southern Africa. But I still had to defend the agreements against the white Conservative Party. They thought that I had signed away the future of South Africa and that Cuban troops would fight on the Orange River. But I did not mind. It was not the first time in my life that I had to stand alone for what I believed in and I knew that it was the right thing. I knew that we had to get rid of Namibia in order to resolve the problem here. Just as I knew that we had to get rid of the situation in Rhodesia if we were to make headway on Namibia. Those were my priorities: Rhodesia, Namibia, South Africa. You could not do it the other way around. I managed the Rhodesian situation and the Namibian situation without incurring sanctions. We never got sanctions on Namibia and/or Rhodesia. We got them on apartheid in South Africa, which was not my function. My function was Namibia and Rhodesia.

I mention this not to underestimate the importance of the whole Namibian independence situation—as well as the withdrawal of the Cuban troops—on events in this country. It made it easier for persons in my position and, I think, for Mr. de Klerk to move faster, to release the political prisoners, to remove acts and laws which were in existence and still formed the pillars of apartheid, like the Group Areas Act and acts of that nature, and to open the way for negotiations. The Namibian events played in my opinion a major role in paving the way for what later happened here. Ahtisaari played a pivotal role in that situation, for which I respect him. I do not think that the world has yet awarded him the respect and the gratitude that he deserves. It is a pity.

TS: But if you read books like the one by Chester Crocker, *High Noon in Southern Africa*, you find the whole process described as an American exercise?

PB: Yes. Except if you read Cyrus Vance's book *Hard Choices*. He gave more credit to me in some of his remarks. And there are some other books from a European perspective. But Chester Crocker really tried to steal the show. A very American approach. But his facts are also not at all accurate, which surprised me. You would expect a man like that to have archives and notes that he could consult. I hope that God will give me the time and strength to write my own book, because then I would certainly reveal what really happened in the negotiations.

TS: Looking back, how do you in general terms view your three years in Sweden?

PB: Having lived in Sweden I think that I came to know the Swedish psyche quite well. Also the problems experienced by the Nordic countries historically, with Norway and Denmark invaded in the war and Finland devastated by the Soviet Union. I had as a young man the privilege and advantage of long discussions with one or two Finnish generals, who really went through that war and who told me what happened on the ground, how their people and soldiers died, and of the devastation. I detected that there was still a measure of slight antagonism between Finland and Sweden.

TS: Yes, of course. Sweden colonized Finland.

PB: Yes, but also from the Norwegian and Danish sides I at times detected some hard feelings, because of the perception that Sweden stayed neutral in the war to make economic and financial gain out of it. At the same time I had Swedish friends who could give their side of the picture, believing—as they explained to me—that if Sweden had also been invaded, the hardship might have been quantifiably greater for everybody concerned, which is a concept I personally understand. It is easy to jump to conclusions for emotional reasons. It is a different matter to sit back and judge a situation, clinically, in its overall implications.

At Uppsala you have the mounds of the Vikings. I was always there, very interested in Swedish history. Very much so. For me, coming from Africa to the snow and seeing the northern lights was just an experience out of the world. In those years, you also had the beginning of the European group, which started, I think, with just six countries. I knew of the very serious debate in Sweden as to the future of Europe, seeing a possible threat to its own economic situation. How it would connect with this new thing that was arising. It was a university for me to be exposed to these debates. I owe a lot to the very intelligent analyses that appeared in Swedish magazines, newspapers and conferences on these issues. It was from that point of view a very rewarding period in my life. It equipped me, I believe, to make judgements and assessments on the basis of a clinical analysis of facts and realities. This I owe to Sweden. There is no question in my mind about it. It was just the Swedish attitude towards South Africa... I was a young man. It was my first posting abroad. I was not a member of any political party.

TS: It was much later that you entered politics?

PB: I only joined the National Party in 1970, after I had resigned from my position in Foreign Affairs. I had then been a member of the Department for eighteen years and I got 4,000 Rand in pension. That was at the time when the split occurred in the National Party. The constituency where I stood, north of Pretoria, was one of the strongholds of the then HNP of Mr. Marais. People said: 'You have been in Foreign Affairs. You know about international matters, diplomats and black children attending white schools. You must come now'. That is how I actually entered politics. I had by then already been appointed ambassador to the United Nations. Four years later, I was again appointed ambassador. It was a political appointment. Dr. Bouteflika from Algeria was the President of the General Assembly and they rejected my credentials. They gave me three minutes to address the General Assembly. That was in 1974, and that was the last time a South African representative addressed the General Assembly for twenty years, until 1994. It was a long walk up that aisle to the rostrum. A long walk.

TS: On balance, did the Nordic countries play a constructive role for change in South Africa?

PB: I think that Sweden and the Nordic countries have played a quiet role in bringing about change in South Africa. It will require research to point out and to put on record what it entails. But it was never really in an aggressive style. That is why I say that there is, from my point of view, this important question: What now? I was privileged to accompany Mr. de Klerk to the Nobel Prize ceremonies at the end of 1993. I think that the Peace Prize was one of the most prophetic decisions ever taken, because it came at a critical moment during the negotiations here. That day I happened to be in Maputo, where also the UN Secretary General Boutros Boutros-Ghali was mediating between President Chissano on the one hand and Dhlakama, the leader of RENAMO, on the other. During a press conference, one of my staff members in Maputo brought me a note which said that they had received a signal from Pretoria that Norway had decided

that the two of them would be awarded the Nobel Peace Prize.
TS: Did it impact on the FRELIMO-RENAMO talks?
PB: Yes! President Chissano immediately congratulated me and also Dhlakama. It was a prophetic decision. It came at a critical time. It almost conveyed to both these leaders and to their followers that the world will reward you if you follow a certain line. It was not put that way, but that was the deep, more profound implication. I discussed it with Norwegian and Swedish friends when I went there, and they did not contradict me. I said to them that this must have been a very difficult decision, because they did not know how things would turn out here. The negotiations went up and down, bouncing on the road. Inkatha withdrew and then ANC withdrew. There were suspicions. Massacres occurring. Those were very difficult circumstances, with suspicion ripe and one party accusing the other of bad faith through acrimonious exchanges in public. As a matter of fact, the media reported that they did not expect much to come out of it. The doom prophets predicted that South Africa might be plunged into a blood bath. It was only after the elections that we eventually received acclaim. From the whole world for that matter.

What impressed me from Sweden and the Nordic countries was the way in which they eventually also reacted to the elections. Not singling out just one party, but sort of praising, supporting and expressing their appreciation also to Mr. de Klerk. Not holding the past against anyone, saying: 'That is now gone. There is a new future for you, and we would like to nurture that and assist you in walking that road.' I am very much aware of that important role.

To summarize: the impact of the Namibian situation together with the impact of the decision to award the Nobel Peace Prize stand out in my memory as the two major events which certainly and decisively had an important influence in this country and held at bay, in my opinion, the radicals. It held at bay those who would say: 'To hell with de Klerk! We are going on our own now.' There was a world that said: 'No, despite the past here is a leader who did it. We can support that.' That made an indelible impression.

Gora Ebrahim
PAC—Secretary of Foreign Affairs
Member of the National Assembly
(Harare, 22 July 1995)

Tor Sellström: When did you, in your capacity as a leader of PAC, have your first contacts with the Nordic countries?
Gora Ebrahim: The Pan Africanist Congress (PAC) was founded in 1959 and we were only eleven months old when we were banned as a political party in April 1960. Immediately after that we established the South Africa United Front outside South Africa with the African National Congress (ANC) and the South African Indian Congress. We had a joint representation abroad until 1963. That paved the way for our contacts, because our ANC colleagues had already established them. As a result of the joint representation, we were also in a position to contact the Nordic countries.

Our official contacts, principally with the NGOs, started around 1965-66, in particular with the International University Exchange Fund (IUEF). It was part of the Nordic support move. We benefited greatly from the Nordic countries, who were the principal donors of the International Defence and Aid Fund (IDAF). That was an important element particularly for us, because from 1963 until 1967 we had about 110 of our people executed by the apartheid regime. Our present Secretary for Political Affairs, Johnson Mlambo, was sentenced to twenty years on Robben Island, but he did not receive the kind of assistance that was required to defend him. At that time, IDAF was not very clear about what aspects of the defence they would support. Would they support what we considered legitimate armed struggle or would they support a non-violent struggle?

When the Organization of African Unity (OAU) was established in Addis Ababa in 1963, one of the very important decisions taken was to create the Co-ordinating Committee for the Liberation of Africa, the Liberation Committee, which recognized national liberation movements from the different parts of Africa that were still not independent. Altogether there were something between 16 or 17 organizations that were recognized in the non-independent parts of Africa. In South Africa, just as in Zimbabwe and in Namibia, you had more than one political organization recognized by OAU. I must say that in the case of Zimbabwe, in particular, and in South Africa OAU continued to the very end to support the two liberation movements that they had recognized. There was, of course, as far as Angola was concerned, and also Namibia, a process of de-recognition by OAU, but in the case of Zimbabwe and South Africa the original position was maintained to the very end.

We were recognized as a national liberation movement by the Organization of African Unity, by the United Nations—particularly by the Special Committee Against Apartheid—the Non-Aligned Movement and the World Council of Churches. IUEF recognized PAC and gave us scholarships. We were also to some degree beneficiaries of the assistance from IDAF. This, of course, paved the way for our contacts with the Nordic countries, because they were involved, particularly in IUEF and IDAF. The United Nations also set up a scholarship fund in which the Nordic countries played a very important role. In fact, they chaired the meetings most of the time. So, in that regard I would say that we also were direct beneficiaries and had contacts with them. But one of the things that surprised us very much is that whilst the Nordic countries had taken what we considered to be a very progressive step towards opposing apartheid, together with the Western countries they never participated in the work of the Special Committee Against Apartheid at the United Nations. They remained outside, only supporting that aspect which had to do with education.

If you look at the developments from our point of view, we had very good relations with IUEF and also with the Nordic countries. We had an office in Sweden. Count Pietersen was our representative at the time. Actually, the relations were with Norway and Sweden. We just had an official contact with Denmark and some contacts with Finland. I remember in 1982, when the late Nyati Pokela came out of the country and became Chairman of PAC. I was at the UN at the time, representing PAC, and I arranged a visit to Sweden, Norway, Denmark and Finland. He paid a visit to all these countries. We got a lot of very consistent humanitarian assistance from Denmark. We also succeeded in getting some assistance from Finland.

TS: Was the assistance from Denmark channelled through the World University Service and DanChurchAid?

GE: Yes, it came through there. Not directly from the government. The Nordic governments had different policies. Some of them said that their parliament did not allow direct assistance. It had to go through an NGO and therefore we were asked to contact the NGOs. In other cases it was direct, in Norway in particular.

We received humanitarian assistance, particularly for our people in Tanzania, for example, for the development of our settlement in Bagamoyo, north of Dar es Salaam. We had quite a lot of assistance in that regard. Now, what happened was that PAC was involved in the 1976 Soweto uprising and there was a trial—known as the Bethal 18 Secret Trial—in which Zephania Mothopeng was the accused Number One. 1976 was important in the sense that it reflected the opposition inside the country even at the level of the youth and the students, besides the political parties and the trade union movement. It also led to political isolation of the apartheid regime. One of the outcomes was that it lost its seat in the United Nations.

The South African government started its dirty tricks at that particular period and sent out a person by the name of Craig Williamson. I met him on two occasions abroad. He specifically campaigned against PAC. The three lines of action that he took were that a) to some he was saying that we did not exist in the country, b) to others that we were a racist organization and c) that we were a terrorist organization. Those were the kinds of things he was putting across. Of course, he joined ANC and the

South African Communist Party and eventually IEUF began to take a position against PAC because of the influence of Craig Williamson. As a result, we found that we were no longer getting any assistance. But it did not stop with IUEF. It also influenced Sweden. Sweden took a decision against PAC based on the recommendations of Craig Williamson. That was the end of any assistance from Sweden.

Of course, we were accused of racism on the grounds that we said that he was a spy. We had our own information. Eventually, it was clear that he was, in fact, a double agent, and as a result you find what happened to Lars-Gunnar Eriksson. The consequences were grave. Having taken that decision, Sweden unfortunately did not reverse it after it was clear what Craig Williamson had done. To the very end, we received no assistance whatsoever from Sweden.

TS: Do you think that this was a Swedish decision or was it influenced by ANC?

GE: Well, I would say that the fact that ANC was prepared to use a man like Craig Williamson to fight against PAC meant that to them Sweden was an important ally. But I would have thought that the principle that Sweden was supporting was compromised, because the Social Democratic Party demanded that there must be multi-party democracy. Why did they then support only one political party? Secondly, at that particular stage I do not think that there was any justification for excluding PAC, politically or otherwise.

I think that the correct position for Sweden would have been the position adopted by Norway, namely to continue to support those liberation movements that were recognized by OAU and the Non-Aligned Movement, but more importantly the United Nations. Sweden did not take that position. Norway continued to take that decision as a government and continued to give us support. I remember that in 1992 we went with a delegation to Norway where assistance of about 200,000 US Dollars was promised. But there was an incident that occurred in 1992, known as the King Williamstown attack on a golf course. The Norwegians then decided to suspend all assistance to us. We went into the election campaign without any assistance from any source.

TS: You have been the PAC Secretary for International Affairs since 1969. How did you view the Nordic group of countries in the bipolar world?

GE: In PAC we believed that the internal struggle was the decisive factor. Then there was the question of international support, which from our perspective had two dimensions. There were those who were prepared to put pressure on the apartheid regime and there were others who were prepared to materially support us to wage the struggle.

We viewed the Nordic countries as important allies in the question of putting pressure on the apartheid regime, as opposed to making it possible for us to physically wage the struggle. That assistance came from OAU and other countries. Not from the Nordic countries. That was the role they played.

In the international campaign to politically isolate the apartheid regime and to apply sanctions against it, the Nordic countries were in the forefront. We could always count on them in international fora.

For instance, I was one of those who together with comrade Thabo Mbeki of ANC negotiated what came to be known in 1989 as the Consensus Declaration of the United Nations against South Africa. The Nordic countries played a very important role. Particularly Norway on the question of the oil embargo. I would say that from the point of view of humanitarian assistance to the liberation movements to the question of politically isolating South Africa and starting the sanctions campaign, the Nordic countries played a very important role.

TS: Do you think that the support extended to you, and more substantially to ANC, was given without strings attached or were there hidden agendas behind the support?

GE: Well, it will be very difficult to say. You cannot say that there was a common Nordic position on that question. I believe that Sweden had its own agenda. I think that the position of Norway was more to support the struggle, without necessarily saying what you must do and what you must not do. We never had that kind of problem with them, but from Sweden we certainly had conditions. As I said, decisions were taken against PAC.

I think that they were wrongly influenced and I am surprised that a country like Sweden could allow itself to be influenced in that way. It would have been very simple to say: 'We are supporting the liberation struggle and the liberation struggle is in fact spearheaded on the continent by OAU.' That is, to support those that OAU supported, which Sweden never did. Norway did.

TS: Over the years, ANC and Sweden became very close. Do you think that the so-called Swedish model influenced ANC?

GE: Well, when you talk about ANC you are not talking about a political party. You are talking about a front organization made up of very different political tendencies. The problem we have in South Africa at the moment is that we have ended minority rule and we have a democratic dispensation. Now, ANC itself is a front of different, very clearly defined political tendencies and it is also operating in another front in the Government of National Unity, so it is very complicated.

If you are asking whether ANC is a Social Democratic organization, I would say that within ANC there are Social Democrats, but I would not say that ANC is a Social Democratic organization. That is our view.

Secondly, I would also say that there is an influence from the experience of the liberation struggle. At least three political parties in South Africa, ANC, PAC and to some degree the Black Consciousness Movement, developed what we call an internal wing and an external wing. Their experiences were very different. The ANC wing that was internally based is predominant at the moment. Therefore, you find that these were not people who were directly involved. In my view, the policy that Mandela is pursuing emerges basically out of the negotiations that he had over a number of years. That is the major influence. I would have thought that if Oliver Tambo had succeeded, there would perhaps have been much more influence. He was really a Social Democrat.

TS: You did not get much support from Sweden, but you must have had relations with the Swedish NGO community and the solidarity movement?

GE: No, unfortunately they followed the government policy, particularly SIDA. There were some small organizations that we were able to contact, but we never received any substantial assistance from them.

We would not have minded if the Swedish government had taken a position not to support PAC. But we feel very strongly about it at this particular moment. We are disappointed. We had all negotiated and we were going for an election. At that crucial moment, the Swedish government made a very substantial donation to ANC for election purposes. Naturally, that influenced the election result and we regard that as gross interference.

TS: Is there anything that you would like to add?

GE: Let me briefly say that the concept of the 'sole and authentic' liberation movement came from an organization that was created in the Cold War period known as the Afro-Asian Solidarity Organization, largely run by the Soviet Union. It was that organization that took the decision on 'authentic organizations'. In Zimbabwe, ZAPU was regarded as the 'authentic' one and in our case it was ANC. It is very interesting that in Namibia the original 'authentic organization' was SWANU. It was only subsequently that they changed and supported SWAPO. Of course, in the Portuguese territories it was clear that FRELIMO, MPLA and PAIGC were the organizations on the ground.

But I am prepared to say that it did not adversely affect the OAU decisions, because we received equal treatment. However, it did affect some countries that were aligned with the Soviet Union in one way or the other. Algeria, to give an example. After the independence of Mozambique they pursued that position. But countries like Tanzania committed themselves to the OAU position and supported both ZANU and PAC to the full.

Gerald Giose
National Liberation Front/Yu Chi Chan Club—ANC/Umkhonto we Sizwe
(Cape Town, 6 December 1995)

Tor Sellström: How did you come into contact with the Nordic countries?

Gerald Giose: My interest in the Nordic countries dates back to the Second World War. Our own anti-racist struggle was a mirror image of the Second World War struggle against racism. It was therefore encouraging to note that the Nordic countries carried on the tradition of opposing racism, which was established during that war.

The support which the government of Sweden in particular, and the Nordic countries in general, gave to our struggle in such international fora as the United Nations General Assembly and Security Council was a cause for inspiration and appreciation. Indeed, in a memorandum which I submitted to our Department of Defence, motivating my application for a proper ranking in the new South African National Defence Force, I made a reference to Sweden. I directed this memorandum to our Minister of Defence, comrade Joe Modise, requesting an urgent personal audience to defend my submission in rebuttal of being downgraded to the rank of a mere major in the South African National Defence Force. As part of my motivation I stated that: 'I successfully interacted with the government of a major European country via its ambassador to South Africa in 1962-1964. That country's government became one of our major European Frontline States. It was not a member of our socialist bloc allies. Our President, Oliver Reginald Tambo, received medical care in that country. Shortly after his release, the Umkhonto we Sizwe High Command and the ANC National Executive Committee accompanied Rolihlahla Nelson Mandela, our State President, to an appropriate official reception in that fraternal anti-apartheid state, Sweden.'

TS: Were you a founding member of Umkhonto we Sizwe?

GG: Yes, I am a founding member, as you will note from this letter of certification from the ANC Military Chief of Staff Office, dated 28 July 1995, stating: 'This is to certify that Gumbilomzamo Gerald Giose de Guise, also known as—*nom de guerre*—Mr White, joined Umkhonto we Sizwe on 16 December 1961 and has served this military force in various capacities to date'. The name, my signature and identity number. Signed by the Chief of Staff and underlined by the motto of the African National Congress: 'The people shall govern'.

TS: How come that you got in contact with the Swedish ambassador?

GG: The international support that we were receiving for the anti-apartheid struggle during that period brought to our attention the role which was played by Sweden and the other Nordic countries. I was specifically mandated to make contact with the Swedish government in order to, first of all, thank the people and the government for this brotherly support.

TS: Who mandated you?

GG: Dr. Kenny Abrahams, who subsequently was accommodated in Sweden when he was forced to flee from Southern Africa. For us who remained here under arrest, it was a great encouragement to learn that the Swedish government had given him political refuge.

TS: Abrahams was from Namibia. Was he involved in the setting up of the Yu Chi Chan Club?

GG: Yes, that is correct. Andreas Shipanga joined it later. When we formed the Yu Chi Chan Club, the name was chosen for security reasons. The organization was in reality the National Liberation Front. We had commenced preparations for the armed struggle against apartheid as early as in 1959, whereas the Umkhonto we Sizwe operations were launched on 16 December 1961.

TS: When Umkhonto we Sizwe was launched, were you a member of ANC?

GG: I was born into the African National Congress and the Communist Party. There was this situation in Southern Africa where a majority of the leadership of the liberation struggle were priests. My father was a priest in the Methodist Church, initially until 1928, but because of racial segregation he then joined the African Methodist Episcopal Church. Like most priests, my father accepted the apostles' creed of the Christian Church as the theoretical basis for the practical Communist Manifesto, both of which enunciate the principles of equality and justice. Not merely in theory, but in practice. Not only politically, but also economically.

In our home, my father made us memorise and recite the Lord's Prayer—Our Father in Heaven—and then the Communist Manifesto. He cited the example of Christ ministering to the multitudes. When the multitudes were hungry, Christ did not theorise on life hereafter, but paid attention to the economic needs of the people. He said: 'Come, because you are hungry. Take out whatever you have and let us share'. My father always cited this as an example of socialism. In later years, when I was able to be informed of the social principles of the Swedish government, I could therefore identify with the correct philosophical policies of the welfare state.

Those who formed the National Liberation Front came from different backgrounds. Dr. Kenny Abrahams was a medically qualified doctor. I was a qualified school teacher, whose father had been a Church minister and one of the founders of the Communist Party of South Africa. He was also one of the early people who developed the African National Congress. I remember when my mother and father used to discuss the possible future roles of Nelson Mandela and Oliver Tambo. Although we as children were not permitted to intervene and take part in the discussions of our parents, that was my fundamental education. When I began to practise my profession as a school teacher it was only logical that I should become involved in the struggle for liberation, particularly of the youth.

When we decided to call our organization the National Liberation Front it was in order to consolidate all the elements in South Africa who were struggling against racism. Dr. Neville Alexander, Dr. Kenny Abrahams, Reverend Don John Davis—who was also a Church minister, a top ranking member of both the Communist Party and of the African National Congress and who served ten years together with comrade Nelson Mandela on Robben Island from 1964 to 1974—and myself had decided that we must launch the armed struggle.

Particularly in the Western Cape, the majority of the working class population—which was classified as coloured in terms of the apartheid racial laws, and Afrikaans-speaking—was isolated from the other population and language groups in South Africa. As this separation had resulted in their non-identification with the other oppressed groups, we decided to speak a language which they understood. At the same time, we decided to approach their hearts and minds in a manner that would not imply that we were attempting to make them appendages to, or by force integrating them with, the other groups, whose language was not part of their upbringing. As Mao Tse Tung has stated, social leadership must speak the language of the people. Bringing forth this reason, we mobilized a significant part of the population into the National Liberation Front. At that time, this population was identifying as their role models comrades Fidel Castro and Ernesto 'Che' Guevara of the Cuban 26 of July Movement, as well as the Algerians Ben Bella and Boumedienne. They were often identical in appearance and pigmentation and seen as examples of a successful 'coloured' rebellion and revolt against racism. Incidentally, at the same time comrade Reggie September, who had been a high school teacher, had for the same reasons decided to mobilize this group within the Coloured Peoples' Congress.

The success of this tactic was proved in the international leadership, built up by people like Dr. Kenny Abrahams and comrade Dulcie September, who as ANC Chief Representative in the 1980s was assassinated in Paris by agents of apartheid. She and I served in the High Command of the National Liberation Front. She was one of the leading members.

Now, while we had formed the National Liberation Front in order to mobilize the Afrikaans-speaking people classified coloured, our motive was to consolidate all the anti-apartheid elements into one liberation movement, which to me from the outset was the Congress movement.

TS: Abrahams asked you to befriend the Swedish ambassador. How did you contact him?

GG: I made the contact at the embassy, which was here in the centre of Cape Town.

TS: Was he understanding to your cause?

GG: Yes. His name was Dr. Bratt. He was very understanding, possibly because of the seriousness of the situation at that time and because he represented the Swedish government and the Swedish people's sympathetic policy. When I explained our situation to Dr. Bratt, he listened attentively and pledged support by the Swedish government to our cause. I also pledged, of course, the normal confidentiality which was essential during those years. I should state that Sweden was regarded, and indeed was, the Frontline State of our liberation movement in Europe, as distinct from the socialist bloc of countries.

TS: So you had established a contact with Dr. Bratt. Then the police started to make life difficult for you?

GG: That is correct. To the extent that in August 1963 I went to Dr. Bratt and requested political asylum, which he very kindly agreed to and invited me to his official residence off Brommersvlei Road, Constantia, outside Cape Town. I stayed there until the end of January 1964.

TS: And then you left with a Swedish ship?

GG: That is correct. Dr. Bratt had given me the schedule of the Swedish ships, as they would be leaving. There was the *Sunnaren*, the *Hallaren* and others, but the one which was due to leave was the *Sunnaren*. I was given instructions how to get on board the ship. I was disguised as one of the stevedores who had been loading bunkers onto the *Sunnaren*. If I remember it correctly, it was at the East Pier, which now has been converted as part of the Waterfront.

TS: Was Dr. Bratt knowledgeable about all this and how you should get on board the ship?

GG: Yes, he was knowledgeable. The advice from Dr. Bratt was to wait until we were outside South Africa's territorial waters and then I should report to the captain.

TS: What was the name of the captain?

GG: I was subsequently told by the security police that it was a captain Nilsson.

TS: How did you know that you were on international waters?

GG: I had a compass with which I observed the direction and on the third day, when we were outside South Africa's territorial waters, I went to the captain. He wanted to know whether I had any money for the passage to Sweden. I did not want to divulge Dr. Bratt's involvement in these arrangements and I told him that I had no money, but that I would be willing to sign an I.O.U., that is a credit note, which would be honoured by the international office of ANC. He said that he could not accept a credit note. He wanted five hundred Rands in cash. I told him that I did not have five hundred Rands. He then asked me whether I had three hundred Rands. I said no. I did not have three hundred Rands. He further asked me how much money I had. I said that I had absolutely no money. One of the reasons for not having taken any money aboard was that should I be detected before the *Sunnaren* left the port of Cape Town, being in possession of a large quantity of money would be compromising.

While the captain was asking me, I noticed a white person standing half behind him. The captain was not aware of this person and when he saw him, he said to me. 'Look, you have no authority to be on my boat.' At that time this person asked me: 'Who are you? How did you get onto this boat.' I did not reply to his questions. Then the captain addressed this person and said that 'this is a stowaway who has just reported to me'. The white man then said that I must be taken to port and handed over to the authorities in Walvis Bay.

TS: Was this white man Swedish?

GG: No, he was not Swedish. I subsequently learned that he was an agent of a shipping company in Cape Town and that he was on his way to Walvis Bay.

TS: Do you know his name?

GG: No, I do not know his name.

TS: Was he South African?

GG: He was South African. I could distinguish his pronunciation of the English language.

TS: Did the captain or this South African man contact the South African authorities?

GG: Yes, they did. That is how they went about it. The captain called two Swedish sailors to take me to a small room where I was to be detained. The room was about 1,5m x 2m. I was kept locked up there. Some meat was brought to me. I particularly remember meatballs, very salty, but I accepted this as a standard diet for seamen on long voyages. The following morning, the door was opened and I was called out. I saw three burly white people. I was used to the appearance of members of the security police. These were white policemen. The captain handed me over to them.

TS: Was this in Walvis Bay?

GG: Yes, this was in the harbour, around 1 February 1964.

TS: What happened then?

GG: A Major Coetzee came to Walvis Bay. He was accompanied by two other members of the security police. They had their semi-automatic rifles wrapped in brown paper. We left Walvis Bay via Usakos and Omaruru, then East and South to Windhoek. This was by car. As we were moving to Windhoek, Major Coetzee stopped along the way and told me: 'Look, if you escape now we are sure that you will survive. We are giving you that opportunity'. I immediately recognised this as a ploy and remained seated in the car. He laughed and said to the driver that they must continue. We reached Windhoek at twelve o'clock. It was very hot. I was not given any food or water. I was kept there overnight and very early the following morning I was given maizemeal porridge. Then Major Coetzee told me that I was being taken to Windhoek airport. The aeroplane left at eight o'clock that morning of 3 February 1964 and we reached Cape Town at approximately twelve.

As we left the plane, a cloak was put over my head and I was taken to Belleville police station. In the late afternoon, I was interrogated by the security police. Major Coetzee was one of them. He wanted to know who had arranged for me to be on board the *Sunnaren*.

TS: Had they identified you by now?

GG: Yes, by that time they had identified me. They had been searching for me those months when I was at the Swedish residence, not knowing that I was there. This is the first time that I divulge to someone from Sweden the circumstances and the fraternal role which the Swedish ambassador, Dr. Bratt, played.

TS: On the *Sunnaren*, did you not say to the captain that you were protected by the United Nations?

GG: Yes, I did. In fact, I first cited the anti-apartheid resolutions of the United Nations which had been supported by the government of Sweden and I told the captain that I was claiming protection.

TS: What did he say?

GG: He said that the United Nations had no jurisdiction on his boat. I then asked for protection in the name of His Majesty King Gustaf of Sweden. He asked what King Gustaf had to do with me being a stowaway. I pointed out that King Gustaf was the head of the Swedish people, who were supporting our anti-apartheid struggle. But the captain said that he was not interested in bringing King Gustaf into the situation. I then said that he must kindly make contact with the Swedish embassy in South Africa and check whether my name appeared on the register of members of ANC. I told him that I was a school teacher. The South African man said that I should not bring the Swedish embassy into this.

TS: You did not want to divulge the name of the ambassador?

GG: That is correct. Later the white man said: 'You pretend to be so knowledgeable about the Swedish government. Can you tell us who the Swedish ambassador in South Africa is?' I said that 'if you look in the official diary where the name of all embassies and ambassadors are entered you will see that Dr. Bratt is the representative of the Swedish government in South Africa'. But I did not divulge that Dr. Bratt had arranged for me to be on that boat.

TS: Was this unfortunate story ever published in the newspapers?

GG: I was in custody and I had no access to newspapers, but my mother and my wife told me that the matter had been brought up in the United Nations. The matter of a captain of a Swedish boat handing me over to the apartheid regime.

TS: Were you then sentenced?

GG: No, I was not sentenced. The security police interrogated me at Bellville police station. Then the assistant Attorney General said that because they knew that my father was a Church minister and that I was misled by Communist terrorists into opposing the civilized government of South Africa they were going to give me an opportunity to save my life. The alternative would be to face charges under the terms of the Sabotage Act, which carried a minimum sentence of five years and as a maximum the death penalty.

They said that 3 February 1964 had been the last day of the trial of Dulcie September, Dr. Neville Alexander, Reverend Don John Davis and other members of the High Command of the National Liberation Front and that they were giving me the opportunity to become a state witness against them. I did not reply. It was four o'clock in the morning. They had been interrogating me ever since I was taken from the airport, but I did not divulge any information to them. By four o'clock in the morning I shut my eyes, but I was hearing what they were saying: 'He is exhausted now. But at seven o'clock we must come and fetch him so that he can go and testify'.

I was taken to the Cape Town Supreme Court and again they said to me: 'You are fortunate that you are not in the dock, being one of the accused with Dulcie September, Neville Alexander, Don John Davis and the others'.

TS: You refused to testify?
GG: Yes, I refused to testify.
TS: What happened then? Did they lock you up?
GG: Yes. I was taken to Caledon Square police station on Buitenkant Street. It was very hot. I was not given any food or water. About six o'clock in the evening I was called out of the cell and given coffee. It was very sweet. Being thirsty, I drank the coffee. Hardly half an hour afterwards I began to feel tingling sensations all over my body and my mind became very light. I began to scream uncontrollably. When the ladies were walking down Buitenkant Street, the sound of the stiletto heels on the stone pavement sounded like pistol shots in my head. That is how light-headed I had become. And when the police vehicles were turning out of Buitenkant Street it sounded like machine-gun shots being fired into my head.
TS: They had drugged you?
GG: Yes, that is correct. Then three very tall and heavily built white men came into the cell. They said to me: 'You are mad. We are going to show you.' They began assaulting me.
TS: How old were you?
GG: I was 31 years of age. I was then taken to the Roeland Street jail and there I was kept with the ordinary criminals. At that time, Dr. Neville Alexander and Reverend Don John Davis were kept in a separate section for political prisoners. The common law prisoners were instructed to assault me. When my mother complained, I was transferred to the section where people condemned to death used to be kept. I was kept in a cell without any bedding. There was only a little hessian carpet on the floor. Every day the water was thrown into the cell. I was kept there until April 1964 and when I complained to the doctor he prescribed certain medications, but it was never given to me. When I repeatedly went to complain, I was transferred to the medical section, where the convicts were given permission to smoke dagga. The atmosphere was so thick that I opened the window and then the chief warder accused me of attempting to escape.

My weight had dropped from 70 to 40 kilos. I was then taken to the mental institution at Valkenberg Hospital. The chief warder said that it was obvious that I was mentally disturbed. When I came there, I was injected with a so-called truth drug. The male nurse injected me. I remember that while I was under the influence of the drug the first question which was asked was why I refused to cooperate with the police. I clearly remember replying: 'Because I was not indoctrinated by the security police'. The next question was: 'Why did you refuse to testify against Dr. Neville Alexander and the other accused?' I again replied: 'Because I was not indoctrinated by the security police'.

On 17 June 1965, I was suddenly told that I had to go to the Supreme Court in a case against a person charged with murder. This was someone classified African who could not speak English or Afrikaans. Because it was discovered in Valkenberg Mental Hospital that I could speak these languages, as well as Xhosa, I was requested to act as interpreter. I refused, saying that I could not accept that a mental patient could be called to be part of the process of justice.

The prosecutor called Dr. Simmons, the superintendent of Valkenberg Mental Hospital, to testify. These were his words: 'Mr. Giose is as normal as I am. A month after his admission, he had recovered completely. His condition had exclusively been due to the conditions under which he had been held. If I had had any jurisdiction over Mr. Giose, I would have had him released within a month of his arrival at Valkenberg Mental Hospital. However, the security police had given the information that Mr. Giose was facing charges of sabotage for which the minimum sentence is five years and their instruction was that he did not fall under the jurisdiction of the superintendent of the mental hospital, but under the jurisdiction of the State President of South Africa, and that he must be detained for a minimum period of five years'. He further stated that Mr. Giose 'is a brilliant linguist and that he has been of invaluable assistance to the psychiatrist in communicating with the patients'. The presiding judge then said: 'We have heard the testimony of Dr. Simmons that you are absolutely normal. Dr. Simmons would have released you, but the security police gave instructions that you must be detained as a mental patient. So, you will now co-operate'. Again I refused. I was taken back to Valkenberg Hospital.

TS: How long were you eventually kept there?

GG: I was kept there until 31 January 1968. I then escaped and wrote letters publicizing the injustice under which I had been held. I demanded either to be released or to be brought to trial. I also said that I was going to return, and I did so. Fifteen minutes after I had returned, the security police came and took me back to Caledon Square, where they interrogated me for fifteen days. Finally they said: 'You are fortunate that all your comrades—Dulcie September, who was in Kroonstad serving a five year prison sentence; Dr. Neville Alexander; all of them—have refused to testify against you'. For that reason I was going to be released.

TS: You never went into exile?

GG: No, I never went into exile.

TS: So, after this gruesome experience you were active here in the Western Cape?

GG: Yes, I continued being active in the underground struggle.

TS: And today you are a Lieutenant-Colonel in the new South African National Defence Force?

GG: That is correct. We were thirteen officers who had applied for integration. The other officers had been trained in the Odessa military academy in the Soviet Union, in Yugoslavia, in Czechoslovakia and in the German Democratic Republic. I was the only one who successfully went through all three pre-selection boards.

TS: Congratulations! Finally, you said that you are considering the creation of a South African-Scandinavian friendship association? With your experience, how is it possible to think in those terms?

GG: Well, the Scandinavian countries stand out as role models for socio-economic development. They are also the countries which consistently supported us, while countries like the United States, Britain, France, West Germany and Italy were voting against the United Nations resolutions. In addition to political solidarity, the industrial, technological and social policies of the Scandinavian countries have proved to be examples worthy of being seriously studied. If I may quote from the Communist Manifesto: 'Workers of the world unite!' I see unity between our workers in South Africa and the workers in Scandinavia, despite some differences, such as language and historical and cultural differences.

John Gomomo
Federation of South African Trade Unions—ANC—South African Communist Party
President of the Congress of South African Trade Unions
(Stockholm, 6 September 1996)

Tor Sellström: As a young industrial worker in the Eastern Cape, were you aware of the support extended by the Nordic countries to the anti-apartheid struggle in South Africa?

John Gomomo: Yes, I was aware of the involvement by the Nordic countries in our liberation struggle. I was aware of the fact that ANC had built a very strong link with Sweden and that there was an anti-apartheid movement which was close to ANC and to SACTU.

In the trade union movement, we also became close to the Nordic anti-apartheid groups. Whenever we visited Sweden or any other Nordic country we would not go back to South Africa without meeting them to brief them about the developments at home and talk to them about our expectations. We did have some COSATU-affiliated unions that received money from the Nordic countries through SACTU, but we also had direct links with the Nordic trade unions. For example, I am from the National Union of Metalworkers of South Africa, NUMSA, and there are longstanding relations between NUMSA and the Swedish Metalworkers Union. Also, the South African National Union of Mineworkers, NUM, have longstanding relations with the Swedes, as well as the clothing and textile and the transport workers' unions.

When we established COSATU in 1985, we took a resolution that we should not affiliate to any international trade union centre. At that time, there were some who said that we should affiliate to WFTU and others who said that we should affiliate to ICFTU, but we felt that in order to keep our federation united we should not do that. Although we were not affiliated to ICFTU, we had already established close, direct relations with the trade unions in Sweden, Finland, Norway, Denmark and the Netherlands. Our main financial support came from these five countries. But we were under pressure from ICFTU, saying that we were undermining them. Since the trade unions in all these five countries were affiliates of ICFTU, why did they not channel their money to ICFTU and from there to the South African unions? However, we thought that it would put us under serious controls and we did not want that to happen. We thus established bilateral relations and within this relationship we met every year—either abroad or in South Africa—to discuss the budgets for the following year, how we were to run the federation and so on.

The Nordic unions have done super work for us in South Africa and we still maintain that relationship. For example, two weeks ago three delegates from COSATU spent two days in each of these five countries to discuss our future co-operation. We feel that Sweden and the other Nordic countries have played a very important role in helping us to fight for our freedom. This will be enshrined in the history books of our country. However, now is the time to strengthen that link. They helped us morally and financially in the past, but to enable us to get out of the present transition period in South Africa we now need them even more.

The South African trade union movement is suffering from brain-drain, especially in COSATU. We have lost about eighty-eight leaders, excluding administrators, who have left for positions in government and in non-governmental organizations. Some of the good union leaders left with their administrators and a big gap was created between the leadership and the rank-and-file. Political developments are so fast in South Africa. We need education and, in general, lack the capacity to carry us through the transition period. That is why we need the support of the Nordic unions even more than before.

TS: The question of international affiliation must have been a problem. For example, the ICFTU-affiliated Swedish LO/TCO did not recognize the WFTU-affiliated SACTU and the situation was the same in the other Nordic countries. You solved this problem by establishing direct links between the South African and the Nordic unions?

JG: In March 1995, COSATU had an international policy conference. It was an important conference, because after the 1994 democratic elections we thought that we should look into these matters. We had seen that some of the WFTU-affiliated unions were joining ICFTU. Where were we going? We had a long debate and spent about six hours on this question without coming to a real conclusion, because some of our affiliates—especially the smaller unions—felt threatened that they were going to be pulled by the nose by the bigger unions to join ICFTU. But we were not divided half-and-half. Those who held that position were very few and if we had taken a vote we could have voted for joining ICFTU. However, it has never been the policy of our federation to take such a decision by vote. We would rather discuss, reach consensus and come to a conclusion. So, we decided not to affiliate, but rather to extend links to all international unions, speak to them and get to know even the independent federations to see who could help us to take our struggle forward.

Last month we were invited to the ICFTU conference. I lead the COSATU delegation and managed to bring along all the affiliates that I believe are the ones that are feeling threatened by joining. What was interesting at that conference was that I was able to speak to the international secretariats of their union counterparts, asking them to speak to the South African unions and build up a relationship. After that our unions felt different, telling me that 'we cannot be isolated'. I said that I did not want to push them and that 'next year in September there will be a new COSATU congress, where the question of international affiliation also will be an item on the agenda. There you can take it up.'

TS: In the mid-1970s, you worked at the Volkswagen factory in Uitenhage. Two Swedish-owned companies—SKF Ball Bearings and Volvo/Lawson Motors—were also based there. How were the conditions at these companies regarding trade union rights, salaries etc.? How was the behaviour of the management?

JG: In those days, the behaviour of the management at the Swedish-owned companies was no better than that at any of the South African companies. The attitude of the management was clearly the attitude of the government of the day. But, after the visit by the LO/TCO delegation in 1975 we managed to have an exchange between the Swedish trade unions and the workers in South Africa, which was helpful.

Our approach in those days was that if there was a delegation from Sweden or from any other country coming to South Africa, we would invite all shop stewards from the various sectors to come and talk to the delegation and the delegation would respond. I think that the first visit by LO/TCO helped a lot. It even helped shop stewards from other companies to know the inside of SKF and to get a good response from the trade union delegation from Sweden as to how they saw things. After the visit, they went back to talk to their respective managements, saying that they must change things and that they must allow the constitution of free trade unions and so on.

Following that visit we sent a delegation from South Africa to Sweden. I was very new in the trade unions, but I went with the delegation. We flew to Sweden. This was in 1979 and it was my first visit. We came to a hall and the secretary said to me: 'Before we open this door you must know that there are many people inside'. I said: 'What are they here for?' 'They want to know about South Africa from you'. I said: 'But I have never talked to an international audience before. What should I say?'. She said: 'I do not know. Let us open the door'. We opened the door. There was a big gathering inside and I started to explain our situation. People were frowning and you could see them asking themselves: 'Is it real what he is talking about? Is it true? Can they really be treated that way?' Well, that helped a lot to build a relationship of solidarity. Later, we sent some shop stewards from SKF South Africa to Sweden to meet the Swedish metalworkers and learn about the company. That broadened their minds and strengthened them to come back to South Africa and speak to the management, challenging them on issues that they believed were unjust.

We went as far as to establish what we called 'multinational shop stewards' solidarity' with German and Swedish companies. They met every second year. The South African shop stewards sent reports to their colleagues in Germany and Sweden about what was happening in the country. Sometimes they would go to Sweden, or people from Sweden would go to South Africa to meet the shop stewards that worked in German and Swedish companies there. We also extended that to American companies in the engineering sector.

TS: Did you encounter the same understanding from the Swedish trade unions regarding sanctions against South Africa?

JG: Well, I must say that of all the countries that supported South Africa by imposing sanctions, Sweden was number one. They even suffered a lot in that process. To give an example: the German companies in South Africa wanted to bypass sanctions and improve their machinery. In return, we then formulated fourteen points, demanding that the German companies that were operating in South Africa should not abide by the apartheid laws. For example, if any of their workers were detained, the companies must ensure that they were kept on the pay-roll until they were being charged. Eventually, that forced the German companies to allow the formation of shop steward councils, taking part in the struggle to pressurize the government.

At the same time, the Swedish companies were also complaining that they—because of sanctions—could not improve their machinery. They were still using their old machines. So, they asked for a code of conduct from ANC and the trade unions in South Africa. It was a hell of a struggle. We had to travel from South Africa to Lusaka to meet ANC and SACTU. Some agreed and some did not agree, but in the end they would not establish such a code. At the time of the unbanning of ANC and SACP in 1990, we were still battling. If you looked at the machines at the SKF factory they were all old, because the company could not replace them. The Swedes suffered from that. But they stuck to their guns. I praise the Swedes for all what they have done. Others tried to manoeuvre, but the Swedes did not.

TS: Swedish trade union support to South Africa was mainly oriented towards organization, education and legal aid. In your opinion, what aspects of the support were particularly important for the building of the South African trade union movement?

JG: The Swedes pushed the players in the country to agree that there should be paid time for the training of shop stewards and workers. If the trade union wanted to take out some shop stewards for training—for example, twice or four times a year—that should be paid by the company. That set a precedent and allowed us to push other companies to follow suit, which was great. Their sanctions' campaign was also really outstanding. I do not need to comment further on that.

Another important point regarded the so-called human resources structure, which was key to the running of the plants. A manager in this structure was the key person to us in South Africa, because he was dealing with labour and nothing else. He could either take the road of Sweden or the road of South Africa. When the shop stewards at a Swedish company raised the problem with us we contacted the Swedes about the attitude of that person. The Swedes immediately intervened and said: 'Either you toe the line or you get out and we put somebody else there.' This matter was even discussed in Sweden. We sent the chairperson of the shop stewards to go and discuss it. The person in question was changed and they brought in a new manager.

TS: Due to the prevailing circumstances, the assistance was extended in a covert manner. Do you think that the South African workers knew that they were supported by the trade unions in Sweden and the other Nordic countries? Could you inform them about the support?

JG: If we had mentioned the details of the support in a general trade union meeting it would have leaked to the security of the government. Even if I had come to Sweden to collect money I would not have taken it with me, because I would have been searched like hell at the airport upon arrival in South Africa. Instead, we would say: 'Can you please send the money through the Swedish embassy. We will change it into South African currency and put it into our account.'

But what we did was the following: when we were giving our financial reports to the members, we would go to the screen and say: 'This is the yearly contribution from the workers and this is the expenditure. This is what is left over and this is the money that we have spent.' Now, the question would then come up: 'Where do you get the money from?' We would say: 'We get it from our counterparts'—the international trade unions—but we would not go into details. We would say that we got the money from our counterparts in the Nordic countries, supporting our struggle. Now, any worker had the right to come to our office and get the details, but we could not divulge them in public. That was how we used to do it. So, the workers knew that we were getting money from the Nordic countries.

TS: Did you experience that the support was given with political conditions attached to it? If so, what were the conditions?

JG: The labour movement in South Africa was very divided in those days. There were some who said that it was clear that the money came from political organizations to influence our members, arguing that if you are receiving funds you are going to be influenced in this or that direction. But in all our contacts with the Swedes and the Germans it was made clear that they could not interfere with our politics. What they wanted, however, was accountability. Even if it was stipulated what the money was going to be used for, you had to report back what you had done with it. But they would not say to us that we had to go in this or that direction. There was no such condition attached.

Rica Hodgson
Congress of Democrats—ANC—International Defence and Aid Fund—
Solomon Mahlangu Freedom College
Secretary to Walter Sisulu at the ANC Head Office
(Johannesburg, 19 September 1995)

Tor Sellström: You worked with the programme to support dependants of political prisoners inside South Africa at the International Defence and Aid Fund in London for many years. When did you start at IDAF?
Rica Hodgson: I started in the beginning of 1964, after I had escaped from South Africa. I had worked for the Treason Trial Defence Fund in South Africa and for the first Defence and Aid Fund that was started here in 1961. I was the secretary of that fund from 1961 to 1963.
TS: IDAF was one of the first organizations to benefit from support from the Nordic countries?
RH: That is correct.
TS: How do you see this support in retrospect?
RH: When I started, it was the British Defence and Aid Fund. It was not yet international and my job was mainly to raise money. At that stage, we were not so involved in the channelling of money to South Africa and we had not yet worked out a modus operandi. That came later, when we started the international. It was in 1964, I believe, that we became an international organization. Then I had two functions. I raised money for the British side of the fund and I had to find ways and means to send the money, surreptitiously, to the families in South Africa. The first organization I remember giving us money was from Sweden. I think it was SIDA. Well, there were two organizations, SIDA and *Rädda Barnen* (Save the Children), but I think that SIDA was the first one.

When we started we were great amateurs. We were not professional at all. Our post was intercepted somewhere along the line. Knowing what we know today of what happened here with the Special Branch and the security police in other countries, I realize that there was somebody tampering with it in the post office in Britain. But I did not know then how it was happening or where it was happening. The first thing that I realized was that we needed to find a safe letterbox so that the mail should not come to the Defence and Aid Fund as such. We had a poky little office at the time, just up the road from Amen Court, and we decided that my records were not safe in that place. Canon Collins lived in Amen Court, in one of those beautiful old homes. To begin with, they gave me what used to be the children's nursery right at the top of the house, with one of those lovely old cabinets with a chest of drawers. Those drawers always stuck and my files were in there. I was usually on my knees, getting out the files.

Of course, people wanted proof of what we were doing and we did not keep books as such. The only proof we had were the letters that came back from the people in South Africa. We got them put onto tape. We filed them and kept every original letter. The letters we had written and the letters people had written back to us. In the beginning we were not prepared to show anybody anything. The first people we showed them to were SIDA, *Rädda Barnen* and the United Nations. Those were the three organizations that we gave access to our records. I think that later we may also have done so to a Norwegian organization, but those three used to come every now and again and they would ask for proof. I then had the basement office in Canon Collins' house with my three very dedicated typists. The donors would come in, we would pull out a drawer and I would take out the letter stacks. They would read the letters from South Africa. Certainly the Swedes. I think that the others came in later, the Danes and the Norwegians. I do not remember the Finns giving us support on that level.

The welfare work was getting so big that we could not find enough people to work as correspondents. I did not know enough people in England to do the work and we were not using South Africans for obvious reasons. So we started to spread the work. Anna-Lena Wästberg was one of the early people to take on a sector. I never really asked her how she did it in Sweden. Whether she engaged other people to do it. Then we got people to do it in Norway. Kari Storhaug, Abdul Minty's wife. She was wonderful, adorable. She engaged a large amount of people. I went to Holland to set up a religious group. I think that they might have been Catholics. We had groups all over the world. In Ireland, Kader Asmal's wife did the whole set-up. I think that we had somebody in Denmark later, but Kari and Anna-Lena were the first two. They worked through the central fund. We sent them the money to send out to the individuals. They wrote the letters and forwarded the money. That was the involvement.

Of course, Gunnar Helander was wonderful. I am sure that he as a single person did more in Sweden to raise the whole issue about South Africa than anybody else. He was a great friend of Canon Collins. He came religiously to all our conferences and made a wonderful input.

TS: 'Pik' Botha has mentioned Gunnar Helander as one of the hostile activists in Sweden.

RH: I am sure! At a later stage Lars-Gunnar Eriksson started to come in with Craig Williamson. But Phyllis Altman and I knew. I just knew from early days that Williamson was a spy and I tried to warn some of the ANC people that he was. Phyllis and I did not trust him. In fact, somewhere he says that there were a couple of people that he could not get past and that was us two in the Defence and Aid Fund.

TS: Per Wästberg just published a book where he mentions how Williamson tried to penetrate IDAF, but never succeeded.

RH: So did Eriksson! I did not trust Eriksson to tell you the truth. I may have been wrong, but I did not trust him and Williamson. They were trying to get in on the trials and Canon Collins arranged a meeting with them. At that stage, I think that Canon Collins maybe saw Lars-Gunnar Eriksson as taking over from him, because he knew that he was not going to last that much longer. He was getting old and I think that he saw Lars-Gunnar as a possible successor. He was trying to build him up at one late conference of ours. He was going to have this meeting and Williamson was to come. Phyllis Altman, who was dealing with the trials, simply said: 'If Williamson is there, I am not going to be there'. So that was it. We never had Williamson at any of our meetings. Eriksson did come to some of our conferences, and, of course, he knew about our work. That worried me, but at least he never had any proof of what we were doing and that was our strong point. Also the South Africans knew, but they did not know any of how it was done, so they could not prove anything.

TS: Did IDAF give direct support to the liberation movements?

RH: Yes, Canon Collins, certainly. The Treasurer General of ANC, Thomas Nkobi, would come and see him, but that was not my part. If they wanted money for dependants in South Africa they had to give me the names and addresses. He also gave assistance to individuals in exile.

TS: When did you leave the Fund?

RH: I left for the SOMAFCO settlement at Mazimbu, Tanzania, at the end of 1980. Of course, the work continued. I did manage to get a very good woman to take it over. But before I left, I did a tour of the whole of Canada and set up the Canadian end of the fund. We never had a Defence and Aid Fund there before. When I came back from East Africa to London in 1986, I attended the Defence and Aid Fund conference. We had just got a million dollars from the Canadian government so I was very happy. That was my swan song at IDAF.

In 1978 I also did a tour for the Defence and Aid Fund. It was the Year of the Child, and I was charged by Canon Collins to go and visit the refugee camps in Africa and meet representatives of ZANU, ZAPU, SWAPO, ANC and PAC. I went to Zambia, Tanzania, Mozambique and Angola. When I came back I produced a little booklet on it.

Joe Slovo was in Mozambique at the time. I remember going over to have a swim. He lived somewhere where there was a swimming pool and there was a young man with long, golden hair. Everybody was really friendly with that man and I said: 'Who is that, Joe?' Joe said: 'That, my dear Rica, is the SIDA representative and without SIDA we would all be starving.' That stayed in my mind as something very important.

TS: Did you not see it as quite odd that the Nordic countries, two of them being NATO members, were giving support to the same liberation movements that were supported by the socialist bloc?

RH: Well, I could see different political reasons why we were being helped. The Defence and Aid Fund never got any money from the socialist countries, for example. Not at all. Holland became quite a big contributor later. But if we now come to the ANC settlement at Mazimbu, Tanzania, there was a different kind of aid. Foodwise, I guess that there were times when we really would have starved if we had not had food from the Soviet Union and the GDR. Our ANC representative collected food in Austria and Germany, but the Russians certainly were the backbone for our food. There were many times when we did not have anything to eat except the food from Russia.

But without the Scandinavians we would not have had SOMAFCO. In every way. The first person that I met there was Lars Larsen, our architect. He was from DanChurchAid in Denmark. What a wonderful guy! He was the first man to build for us. Spencer Hodgson came in 1979, but Lars was already there. Then we had a succession of Nordic volunteers. The Swedish volunteers were mainly teachers, like Knut Bergknut and his wife. Fantastic! And the children! Knut's little girl, I remember, spoke English, Zulu, Swedish and Kiswahili. Lars' child too spoke Kiswahili perfectly. I remember very well the last woman who came from Finland to run the library and Lars' brother who came to do farm work. We also had a lovely Danish guy who ran our furniture factory. Without the input from the Scandinavian volunteers we would have been hard hit. Of course, moneywise as well. We survived on money mainly from Scandinavia.

TS: Did you feel that there was some sort of hidden agenda behind the support from the Nordic countries?

RH: I never thought about it like that. I had known them for so long, already from IDAF. No, I did not think so. I thought it was humanitarian. But other people did. Lots of people did. I believe that nobody does anything out of pure humanitarian reasons. They also look to the future. I believe that the socialist countries were the same. They would want to continue trade and things like that. I think that it applies to all countries, but I think that the Scandinavians started earlier with the humanitarian support than anybody else. The Russians were giving guns and that is a different story.

Another thing that I remember very well is those marvellous clothing parcels we used to get from Sweden. I think that I still have a skirt that I got through them. We used to look for cotton materials and there was some very good stuff amongst all that. What was not suitable for us we would send to areas where they needed it for the winter, like in Botswana. I believe that some of it even went into South Africa. The labels were removed from the clothing before it was sent there.

TS: There were several organizations in Sweden that collected clothes.

RH: Yes, I remember that one was Bread and Fishes and another was Emmaus. I always had to write the thank-you-letters, because I was also the secretary to both Mohammed Tikly and Tim Maseko, the directors of the Solomon Mahlangu Freedom College.

Lindiwe Mabuza
ANC—Chief Representative to Sweden and the Nordic countries
Ambassador of South Africa to Germany
(Bonn, 14 March 1996)

Tor Sellström: You came to Sweden in 1979 as ANC Chief Representative to the Nordic countries. How did you find the anti-apartheid movement in the Nordic area at that time?
Lindiwe Mabuza: I did not want to leave Africa. I had lived in the United States from 1964 until the beginning of 1977 and I just wanted to be part of what was happening on the African continent. I then realized that the decision of the ANC National Executive Committee to send me out had been well considered. I would let many people down by not accepting it. But I did not understand what I was going into. I was just afraid. There was apprehension about going to—first of all—a white world. I had lived under apartheid and racism in South Africa and in the United States. What was now going to happen? But, fortunately, so much had been done prior to my coming to Sweden by other people from South Africa that I found a very receptive and accepting climate. A climate that was conducive to do more, and my responsibility was to see how much we could tap of that.

I remember the parting words I got from President Oliver Tambo when I was going to Sweden. He was aware—everybody was aware—that I was nervous about this new exploration. He said: 'Sweden stands as a brilliant landmark in the history of our struggle'.
TS: I think that he had already been there in 1962?
LM: The first time, I think, was when he left South Africa in 1960. He went straight to Denmark, at the invitation of the Social Democratic Party. I remember him telling me what a fantastic experience it was. Arriving in Copenhagen, the streets were paved with Danes with the Danish flag to welcome him. At that time, there was also a meeting of either the Socialist International or the Swedish Social Democratic Party in the southern part of Sweden. So from Denmark he went there.

I was fortunate, because he said to me: 'You are going to friends. Do not be afraid'. I remember that. Later, when we talked about it, he would say: 'If the apartheid regime and its allies knew the extent of the Swedish engagement with us in the struggle, there would be problems for that country'.

The anti-apartheid movement was already there. Billy Modise and others had been there before me and there had been countless students from South Africa who were using their time in Sweden to inform about apartheid. The anti-apartheid movement was there, but I think that by the time I left—at the end of 1987—it was a phenomenal organization, with structures and networks. When I arrived, you had the Africa Groups of Sweden and the beginnings of the Isolate South Africa Committee (ISAK). I think that at the time it had about five member organizations. The Social Democratic Party, the youth wing of the Social Democratic Party, VPK and APK. I cannot remember the fifth one. But, by the time I left I think that you counted the organizations in Sweden that were *not* part of the Isolate South Africa Committee.
TS: How would you explain that Sweden at an early stage recognized and supported ANC, but was quite late when it came to the imposition of sanctions.
LM: In terms of declared policy, I think that all the Nordic countries by 1978 had taken an anti-apartheid and pro-sanctions position. However, the non-implementation of this was not because of a lack of political will. I think that it was due to dynamics in the society. The decision to support ANC was popular and accepted by all the political parties and the government. But when it came to imposition of sanctions, there was division within Sweden.

Political parties have their constituencies and whereas the Social Democratic Party, VPK and APK—who were not in government—were eager, you also had to deal with the position of the Centre Party, the Liberal Party and the Moderate Party, who, while supporting us politically, were not about to sacrifice their allegiance to the companies that were investing in South Africa. We understood that. We had to work to convince them and I think that the People's Parliament Against Apartheid in 1986 was most decisive in bringing all the groups which were for isolation of South Africa to the same position. But it took a long time, even with our fervent supporters within these organizations. I think that it was due to the contradictions within the Swedish society, as there were contradictions within so many others. It took twenty years in the United States. Sweden was not an exception in that.

We counted on various levels in the society to help us pursue our objectives. The political parties in and out of government. The trade unions were a formidable component of the anti-apartheid movement. There was not a decision for sanctions for a long time, partly because people believed that by imposing sanctions you actually made the victim a sufferer. We had to deal with all the arguments where our own positions were not accepted and our reasoning was questioned. It was an educational process all the way, until you got to a position where the trade union movement itself was divided. For us, the division meant that there was a movement forward, because where there had been only one position before there were now those who said that the trade union movement was for sanctions. Then you knew that progress was being made.

The churches had the same problem. It was much easier with the youth organizations of the political parties, as well as with youth organizations of the civic society and the church youth organizations. Once they understood, they were not ambiguous about the need for sanctions. When the school pupils' organizations decided that sanctions was the way, they were ready to go and fight Esselte: 'If you do not accept our position there will be no paper, nothing from your company in our schools in Sweden!' They posed the question in such a way that there was a choice. You choose apartheid or you choose the Swedish schools. It was a development. It took time to get to positions like that.

TS: As the representative of a liberation movement you were visiting different political camps. You were talking to the government one day and to the trade unions and the opposition parties the other. Were you acknowledged by the different milieus in the Nordic societies?

LM: It was unbelievable how we were recognized. This might sound a little bit presumptuous and arrogant, but we were better treated and recognized than some of the real, accredited ambassadors in all the Nordic countries. Our leadership met with all levels of leadership in all the Nordic countries. Members of the National Executive Committee would have serious discussions with Olof Palme as well as with the leadership of the Centre Party when they led the coalition government. They would also be talking to the leadership of the churches, the archbishops, because they were an important constituency.

A precedent had been set when the Social Democratic Party was the governing body in Sweden. It became part of the political culture. Anybody who would have gone against that would have looked so absurdly right-wing that it would have had negative consequences for them. It was very important that understanding became a rule when the Social Democrats were in government. Of course, it also had to do with the Swedish attitude of seeking consensus rather than confrontation on some international questions.

TS: The non-socialist government actually increased the support to the liberation movements in 1976. There was this precedent?

LM: Yes, part of that precedent was that they always had discussions with the liberation movements and evaluated the needs in accordance with the time. It was normal that the support would increase. If it had remained the same, there would have been criticism against the government. They had no option but to go forward. We were experiencing an increase of people into ANC and our needs were growing. Our ways of solving those needs were also developing. We needed more resources and there was always an adequate response to our calls for assistance.

TS: Nordic support to ANC was strictly civilian. How did you experience that the military side of the struggle was kept out of the debate?

LM: I do no think that it was kept out of the debate. How do you fight apartheid? I think that a decision had been made by the Nordic governments in which areas to participate in the struggle against apartheid and in which areas, for historical reasons, they would not participate. But it was very much part of the debate. Every time Oliver Tambo or Thabo Mbeki came, we would tell the Swedish authorities what was happening in the armed struggle. Not to involve them, but so that they should understand where we were. This was a partnership among equals and friends. As a liberation movement, we also took the position that each country should assist us in accordance with its objective positions. And here the situation was such that supporting the liberation struggle by infusing assistance to the military would have killed our positions and would have undermined those governments.

We were always talking and debating with church people about why we took up arms: 'Jesus Christ whipped people out of the temple and there are just wars'. We had to talk with the trade unions. I remember mobilizing in different schools and it was always a question that came up. Talking to whatever structure it was always a question. But the reality is this: We did not have to lambaste the governments of Scandinavia for not helping us to buy arms, because they were fulfilling a very important role even for our military objectives. If you have soldiers who cannot brush their teeth in the morning; who cannot wash; who cannot have breakfast, lunch or supper; who cannot have clean clothes; then you have a mutiny on your hands. So we think that the Nordic countries contributed enormously even to the development of our armed struggle in that they assisted the soldier to live and to carry out his or her objectives.

We understood. I do not think that there is any ANC leader who questioned why the Swedish government did not help us to purchase arms. For the mobilisation of Europe we also needed to remove the argument that the Swedes were helping ANC militarily. We needed to remove arguments that were obstacles to the mobilisation of other governments. The Nordic governments had to keep their hands clean, but we knew that there was a significant contribution to the military. We had the Home Front allocation, people in Swaziland and people in Botswana. They were in transit to join ANC; to go to military camps; to go to schools; to be professionals, or to be professional soldiers. They had to be catered for. There were many ways in which the military was being assisted.

TS: But at the same time there were political forces in the Nordic countries who criticized the governments for not giving armed support to ANC?

LM: Yes, but as they did that we never responded. Of course, we said that it would be nice, but that there were other ways of assisting. It is also true that no Swedish government prevented Swedish political parties or nationals from making contributions towards the military struggle. Every day we had contributions coming in to the ANC fund without any tags attached. Individuals and organizations were saying 'use the money as you see fit'. If we decided to buy guns or whatever the military wanted—which we did by the way—no government actually stopped the unmarked contributions, and it was assumed that if they were unmarked, ANC reserved the right to use them as it saw fit. These contributions came from all sectors of the Nordic societies: from political parties, trade unions and trade unionists, church organizations or church individuals. They were there and without any conditions. I know, because we also had to make certain procurements in the Nordic countries related to the military, using these funds.

TS: Some countries would not support ANC or SWAPO with transport means because it was said that a truck can be civilian by day, but military by night. Did you experience the same limitations with the Nordic governments?

LM: As far as I remember, absolutely not. There was no debate or argument on that. We had annual negotiations where we allocated funds to different ANC departments. If a department needed transport means, those responsible for the negotiations with ANC would accept ANC's judgement on what was needed and where it was to be purchased. For example, we could order Japanese vehicles, because it would be cheaper, and send them to Mazimbu, Tanzania. The assistance was not tied to Nordic procurement. There was an allocation. Now, how do you stretch it to meet the needs of a growing population over a longer period of time? With the assistance of experts within the Nordic governments, we could say that rice from Indonesia and oil from country X would be the best. I think that what was fundamental was the respect for the judgement made by ANC and that the credentials of the people negotiating on behalf of the liberation movement were accepted.

TS: If we look at the composition of the ANC delegations to the annual talks, you would be represented by politicians at a very high level—people like Thomas Nkobi, Thabo Mbeki—and on the Nordic side there would be aid officials. Was that contradictory to you?

LM: No. It would be wrong to say that they were only aid officials. They were implementors of political decisions. They were playing a political role across the table from our politicians and could not split themselves from that responsibility. There was absolutely no problem with that, because the aid officials were accountable to the political decision makers. In fact, as agents of Swedish foreign policy we found in them a readiness to understand the political dynamics so well and they would communicate that. They actually ensured that we were properly represented when it came to communicating our positions. You had to trust them to be able to do that, which I suppose also was the reason why certain people were put in certain countries and not everybody in an embassy was handling things relating to the liberation movements. It needed a certain judgement, a quick ability to change with the dynamics and to be sensitive all the time.

I would think that probably they, more than we, would have had certain problems. Perhaps a resistance to go in accordance with what we may have wanted, but, again, it was their responsibility to say to us and to their government: 'We think that this position would have this kind of implication'. No, they were not just robots and agents. They were very much co-participants. Their word carried much weight and the politicians that they were discussing with had to respect that.

TS: Many of these aid officials were women. Do you think that it affected the aid allocations? Did they promote women's interests on the ANC side as well?

LM: They promoted all the interests presented by the various ANC departments, but because they came from a region of the world where women's emancipation and equality questions were paramount they promoted that. Their presence also guaranteed that ANC women's questions would be given the same weight as, for example, what the department of education required. It would be taken into account as much. But it went beyond that. As women, they also knew the women's organizations in their respective countries that could get access to SIDA, NORAD, FINNIDA or DANIDA funds in order to augment the already on-going assistance. So that assistance could come in a multi-pronged way. They were themselves understanding of where we needed to go as women within the liberation movement. Without being conscious of it, they assisted us in strengthening the organizational capacity of the ANC women's organization, helping it to become viable.

TS: I remember that there once was a comment from a male representative of another liberation movement who said that 'you know, in the Nordic countries they delegate these important political issues to women without clout'. But later that very same person changed his position completely, because he found what you have just said.

LM: Because he was a man. He came with a certain perspective, a certain prejudiced position.

When I entered the Nordic area, the SIDA desk officials were women. It was not because a women was coming to represent ANC, but that was the responsibility given to them. Birgitta Berggren was then the responsible official at SIDA. It was very important for me that it was a woman. From her I could find out things that I probably would not easily have found out from men, because you hit a certain level of communication that does not easily exist with men. We learned to confide in each other.

TS: The same was probably the case with the Africa Groups?

LM: Yes, absolutely. The women were really the channels of communication, the organisms of delivery in all spheres. I am not saying that the men did not play their role, but it was just a phenomenal thing. From the day I started to work with the Africa Groups until the day I left Sweden, Lena Johansson was responsible for liberation movement activities. We saw the expansion and conspired. 'Conspired' is a nice word to use in that we sat down and planned our strategy. We had succeeded with this. How far do we now take the cultural dimension? What should be the different phases of that? She could say: 'If we are going to the women's front, then minister so-and-so is somebody we should be talking to'. She was in a position to know who were most effective as proponents of women's positions in the Nordic countries.

But I also have to say, in all honesty, that the Scandinavian men were not behind in that. When I saw the development of the support—which really was phenomenal—I came to the conclusion that it had to with the upbringing of the Scandinavian children. There was a culture of intolerance for ugliness, unfair play and war, and an instinctive desire that came out of a people's culture for fairness, equality, freedom and peace. It came from men and women from the time they were young.

Let me give an example. I went to a school, I think that it was in Sundsvall, when we were fundraising for the ANC school in Mazimbu. We were just supposed to work with high schools, but one of the teachers asked if I could also talk to the smaller children, because they had a message for me. I went there and on their own the smaller children started fund-raising! I was going there to mobilize the big children, but the smaller ones said: 'We won't wait for that!' Then I went to a class to talk to them about South Africa and about children of their age under apartheid. When I finished—I was speaking in English and the teacher was translating—the teacher said: 'Ask Lindiwe questions if you have some' and many hands went up. The first question was from a little girl—these kids were eight years old—and her face was really going red: 'I just want to ask this question: How can people be so wicked?'

TS: Do you think that the programmes of co-operation between ANC and the Nordic countries reflected your needs?

LM: Yes, of course. After all, SIDA, NORAD, FINNIDA and DANIDA, had annual meetings amongst themselves and I would think that on their agenda was also the assistance to liberation movements so that there could be a co-ordinated Nordic approach. The difference, of course, was the size, the amount and the direction. But what was not given by country X was given by another country.

We started with a limited view of what we were doing and that was reflected in the amounts and in the negotiations themselves. But our perspective of what ought to be accommodated grew as we had more people coming out of South Africa to go into schools. We then decided that it could not be an end to send them to foreign countries to finish high school, but that we should build our own school. So education had to come in as a part. At the same time, the school had to be provided with a clinic, so you would also have the health sector coming in. We were forming the departments as we were having increased assistance. The Nordic countries were actually helping us to form the nuclei of the future ministries. It comes out of that. The assistance had to go in accordance with the needs. Some ANC departments got a bigger chunk, because their work was increasing. Their accounting methods were also improved. The responsibility was on us to make sure that to get more assistance everything was legitimate and quantifiable.

TS: Could the annual negotiations between ANC and SIDA be described as negotiations between equal partners, where the agenda was set by both parties?

LM: The agenda belonged to both parties. ANC people from the regions of Southern Africa had to come to Lusaka and so did the Swedish counterparts. Everybody contributed to the agenda. I know that SIDA had to be sure that the reporting from the Home Front was accurate. We also needed SIDA's reports, because we had to have a panoramic view of the entire contribution. It was a negotiation between equal partners. I would also be consulted and so were the other chief representatives of ANC.

TS: Do you not think that there were strings attached to the support?

LM: I think that it really would be the height of naïvety to say that there are no strings attached in a contribution. If somebody helps somebody else to be free it is a reflection of the desire of peace for themselves as well. That is a string. I do not believe in altruism. There was also a very real and human desire that should these people be free, it would guarantee peace between South Africa and Sweden or Norway, because we would have established firm bonds of friendship for generations. It was an investment in peace and in freedom for a people, but in unity with other peoples and other countries. I think that that was the kind of string attached to the support.

TS: As a poet and a cultural worker you were actively promoting a cultural boycott of South Africa, which perhaps sometimes was more difficult than the economic isolation campaign as you were dependent on cultural outflows from South Africa. How did you experience the Nordic anti-apartheid movement in the cultural field?

LM: When I left Lusaka to work in Scandinavia, one of the things that I discussed with Oliver Tambo was that I had just started the development of a cultural approach which would eventually lead to the formation of a cultural department. We had a cultural committee, which I was heading, and I was excited about that. We had started it in 1977. His response was: 'Perhaps being the Chief Representative in Sweden gives you more power to do what we have been talking about'. He gave me the authority to continue from that base. Now, one has to constantly bear in mind that in every area, whether it was culture, health, education or politics, for us there was the question of economic engagement in South Africa. There were two sides to one coin, the isolation of apartheid and support to those who were fighting apartheid, and if you had that as a basis there was absolutely no confusion. Even in the area of culture you had to isolate everything that promoted apartheid. You would not have the *Drakensberg's Boys Choir* coming to Sweden, but you certainly would have Miriam Makeba, *Buwa!* or the Gothenburg gala, because all contributed to the isolation of apartheid. Any time people who were not representing apartheid were on stage, that in itself was an attack, but it was also in support of the victims. So, there was never a contradiction.

That also meant that you had to be very vigilant, checking who was doing what, which Swedish performer was going to Sun City and so on. You had to be awake to all these developments, reading the papers, listening. Finally, the artists themselves would call the Africa Groups or the ANC office and say: 'I have this offer. What should I do?' It became very easy in a sense. I think that it was more difficult with economic sanctions.

Sweden, Denmark, Norway and Finland all assisted us in having that enormous cultural manifestation in Gaborone in 1982, where we were able to bring out of South Africa about 800 cultural workers and from around the world about 200 others. There, for the first time, we were able as South African artists to declare that we were going to be active in the cultural boycott. It was the consolidation of a position that was already established, but we were also going to assist the marginalized artists in South Africa through the establishment of a trust fund.

Isolation meant just that, isolation of the reactionary apartheid instruments of oppression and repression and upholding the principle of the right of the people to struggle and to resist. It was manifested in their writings and that is why we did not oppose André Brink's or Nadine Gordimer's works coming into the Nordic countries and that is why SIDA promoted a competition among female short story writers in Southern Africa. ANC participated in that and won. But, all of this supposed daily work, where you reached out to different artistic or cultural expressions in the Nordic countries. Once you had succeeded in doing that, it became easy. Thus, after all the years developing these various structures it would just explode in the cultural gala for ANC in Gothenburg in November 1985.

Similarly, after years and years of mobilizing in the schools, you would have explosions of support for the SOMAFCO school, such as the teachers' organisation establishing a teachers' block and the Swedish students establishing a laboratory. Apartheid denied science to the black children, but the Swedish pupils said that the first thing that we must build was a science block. There were all the time answers to the bankrupt philosophy of apartheid. In every sphere, including the cultural field through *Buwa!* and the efforts by South African mega artists like Letta Mbulu and Caiphus Semenya, who said: 'Let us get the professionals together and see if we cannot as one voice say that we also are part of this mainstream assaulting the walls of apartheid'.

With Swedish funds we also had cooperation between ANC and Zimbabwean artists, that is, artists of a liberation movement and artists of a free country. They came to Sweden under the auspices of ANC, the Africa Groups and the Zimbabwean embassy. It was a recognition of ANC as a government in waiting. There was no alternative to ANC. What the regime and its allies were doing was always to try to push an alternative. But the hard work of the people of Scandinavia and of the ANC offices in Scandinavia meant that we created a climate that was impenetrable by any voice that was contrary to ours.

TS: But in Zimbabwe—and partly also in Norway—there were alternative voices trying to compete with you. I am thinking of PAC.

LM: We never questioned any government for recognizing PAC. We just had to deal with our own position. We were doing a function and doing it seriously, putting everything into that. The best brains of South Africa were going into that. The energy of South Africa was going into that. The ethics, the convictions and the commitments were going into that. We were not compromising our positions through corruption. It was very important that the leadership was most credible. They had to sacrifice a lot to maintain their credibility. They had to be seen in the eyes of the donor community as good and dependable allies, as very committed people and not just as people mouthing words of commitment. People who were ready to give and actually gave their lives and their time completely and totally to that commitment. It was in the performance of the liberation movements that other countries judged who they wanted to help.

When I arrived in Scandinavia, the allocation for ANC and PAC from Norway was around four million Norwegian Kroner. We were treated as equal. But we were not equal! They later corrected their position and by 1987—when I was getting ready to leave—I think that the allocation to ANC had reached some 45 million Norwegian Kroner. So, people were able to judge by our performance. I know that even within some of the Nordic governments there were voices that said: 'You cannot put all your eggs in one basket'. Well, they put their eggs in different baskets and the eggs broke when the baskets fell, except the ANC basket.

TS: Do you feel that the importance of culture, sports etc. as weapons in the anti-apartheid struggle was duly recognized at the political level in the Nordic countries?

LM: I think so, without any qualifications. One of the first things that I did following the dictum of President Oliver Tambo was to use my position to push this. In that way, I was able to convince the Nordic countries to bring *Amandla* there. By that time, *Amandla* was not even formed! It was a notion. Once they said yes, I painted the concept that it was an ANC cultural group that would perform on stage and win the people in Scandinavia. When that was accepted by the Africa Groups, *Fellesrådet* in Norway, the Africa Committee in Finland and the Danish solidarity movement, we built *Amandla*.

We built this cultural ensemble from our base in Angola, which was associated with the military. This shows the dynamics. When we built that group we said: 'Where do we find the people who are sufficiently disciplined and organized?' We went to the military camps, where the culture of South Africa continued to thrive. The culture of liberation. The soldiers were writing liberation songs and liberation poems, motivating their military perspective through culture. *Amandla* was organized there, but to form *Amandla* we needed to start from zero. They did not have any instruments. They did not have uniforms and we did not have the money to bring them to Europe. Once the four Nordic countries said yes, we went to Holland, because there was a strong anti-apartheid movement there. We also went to Germany. It was these six countries. I started in 1979, but in 1980 we were already able to bring *Amandla*. The second tour was in 1983. By 1983 they were nearly professional.

What happened was that the creativity of our soldiers came out. They created the script. They were able to explain the formation of ANC and what had happened in the different phases of our struggle. This was the best bullet we had, because where you did not convince people with your political argument *Amandla* did that in two hours. It was graphic. It was for everybody to hear and see. It was for people to end up saying 'I am stupid if I do not understand this'. It was happening in Scandinavia, but it was also happening in South Africa, where they were hearing about the achievement. The people in South Africa were inspired by the liberation movement outside. And we were inspired by their efforts, for example when the play *Woza Albert* became an international success.

TS: The political leadership in the Nordic countries understood the importance of this?

LM: They appreciated it more than we can tell, because it was not the bullet. We were strengthening their hand when it came to dealing with other countries. Because the Nordic governments acted on our behalf within the international community at various fora. They did not have to defend us. They would just explain why they were doing things in a certain way, which in itself offered the best defence for what we were doing and why they were assisting us.

TS: So they broadened your international contacts and opened up diplomatic space for ANC?

LM: Of course! Also in the Nordic countries. *Amandla* was seen by ambassadors from other countries and they were sending reports to their own governments: 'Here are the Swedes at it again. This time it is on the cultural front'. Which government was to say that Sweden was doing something wrong by assisting us in that way?

Culture was a weapon in the struggle, but it was more than that. Culture was the best way of talking about the soul of the people, the feelings of the people. The irrepressible desire for freedom and the infectious hope for liberation. Through culture we were injecting our sensitivities into the audience. Whoever was part of that felt that their decision to support us was correct.

TS: Over the years there has been a close relationship between South Africa and the Nordic countries in the cultural field. For example, in the late 1950s there was the defection of the band *The Golden City Dixies* from Cape Town in Sweden.

LM: Yes. Peter Radise was one of those and there were others. I cannot remember all the names, but I do remember how in the late 1950s—I remember it as if it was yesterday; reading the newspapers—Swedish artists went to meet Miriam Makeba at the airport. They had created Miriam Makeba hats and welcomed her, because she was an artist who represented the politics that they supported. It was always there.

TS: You were close to both Oliver Tambo and Olof Palme. How would you describe the relationship between the South African and the Swedish leader?

LM: The picture that comes to my mind is the opening of the Swedish People's Parliament Against Apartheid, where both Olof Palme and Oliver Tambo were the key spokespersons. There Palme said: 'If the world decides today that apartheid goes, apartheid would go'. He had taken his position. It was brave for a political leader to say that the responsibility was with the world. He was endorsing the principles of the People's Parliament Against Apartheid, which was that the people of Sweden had decided that sanctions was the way to go. He agreed. A week later, he was killed. We have no doubt, absolutely no doubt, that he played a leading role in Scandinavia, within the Social Democratic movement in Scandinavia and within the Socialist International.

We have to say that the most phenomenal thing about the Nordic support is that it came from all parties. However, the ruling parties had for a long time been the Social Democratic parties. They broke the ground. I think that the relations between Oliver Tambo and Olof Palme determined how far and how. I have never known two leaders from two parts of the world being so much like brothers in the struggle. Look at the pictures from that day! Look at the way they are looking at each other! As ANC chief representative I have been in meetings with the two and privileged to hear secrets being exchanged: 'Which front should we try to deal with? Which country could then be approached? How, as a liberation movement, should you be going about this?' I know.

I also know of the presentations at the United Nations to influence other countries.

They would sometimes say: 'Oh, those Swedish do-gooders', but it was because it was pricking their conscience. They would try to undermine Sweden, but it did not work. Instead, their own people were to follow. The American public rose up against Congress and Congress overrode a presidential veto. The Nordics had been doing that. It had grown within the United Nations, the international church community, the international labour movement and the entire democratic world.

It was one thing to get support from Brezhnev and the Communist parties in the world. We did get that, without any strings, and it was highly appreciated. But it was a different thing to get support from a member of the international community that was not Communist and that believed in the things that Reagan also believed in and who had the power—because of the successes in Angola, Mozambique and Zimbabwe—to know that we could win in South Africa as well. The significance of Olof Palme was also that he sometimes—when we were not able to deal with a sensitive situation—because of his own credibility as co-participant in the struggle could say what we could not say. I have the example of a meeting held in Arusha, Tanzania, with the Frontline States over the question of the Nkomati Accord between Mozambique and South Africa. We had made our statement and President Nyerere had said that ANC should have been more firm. Our approach was that South Africa was interested in a Constellation of States and that the Nkomati Accord meant that Mozambique was participating in that. Palme just said to the late President Machel of Mozambique: 'How could you?'

What Palme was saying was that the Swedish assistance was about restoring Mozambique's dignity. Now they were on their knees. The accord had nothing to do with what Sweden had been assisting, that is, the liberation of Mozambique so that they could be able to stand on their own. In other words, where he could have been interpreted as arrogant, negative and too critical of a brother or a sister, Palme could assert a principle without fear of being attacked as a racist, a white Swede, who was interfering in African affairs. He was seen as a partner in the enterprise of liberation.

Tambo was most privileged to have met Palme just before his assassination. Two weeks later he was back to bury his friend and brother. The Delmas prisoners in South Africa then sent a statement of condolence through Birgitta Karlström Dorph at the Swedish legation in Pretoria. We were sitting there with the new Prime Minister, Ingvar Carlsson, when he pulled it out of his inside pocket and said: 'Mr President, we are so moved and proud of our relationship with you. See what your people have done on this occasion'. He read the statement. They had all signed it. I think that that tells you in nutshell.

Reddy Mampane (aka 'Reddy Mazimba')
ANC—Chief Representative to Tanzania and to Zimbabwe
National Director of the African Development Corporation
(Johannesburg, 17 September 1995)

Tor Sellström: When and why did you leave South Africa?
Reddy Mampane: I came to ANC in 1959, when I was working in a hotel in Pretoria. Umkhonto we Sizwe (MK) was formed in 1961 and I became a MK member in December 1962. I took part in some reconnaissance of the places to be sabotaged, specifically the synagogue where Mandela was sentenced to five years imprisonment in November 1962. My unit went and sabotaged it, but I did not take part in that operation.

In December 1962, when we were planning to sabotage the synagogue, the person who was responsible for taking ANC people out of the country—together with Joe Modise, the present Minister of Defence—came to collect me. He said: 'Look, you are going!' So I left on 7 January 1963. We were supposed to go for training and then come back and continue the armed struggle. From

South Africa we went to Tanganyika and from Tanganyika to train in Algeria for eight months. When we were about to finish the training, we were told that the MK High Command had been arrested and, therefore, that we could not go back home. What should we do and where should we go? We first went back to Tanganyika, but it soon became clear that we really could not go to South Africa. The whole machinery which was supposed to receive us was completely destroyed. Many people had been arrested, some had been killed, some driven into exile and others had gone underground. There was nothing left. Then, in January 1964—immediately after New Year's Day—we left for the Soviet Union for further military training and political education.

TS: Did you go with Chris Hani in the group that went to Odessa?

RM: Yes, to attend the Odessa Military Academy. Joe Modise was our Commander and Moses Mabhida, the former Secretary General of the South African Communist Party, our National Commissar. People like Chris Hani and others were in our group in Odessa. We finished in October 1964 and went back to Tanzania.

TS: Did you meet Che Guevara there?

RM: No, I met Che Guevara when we were training in Algeria. We also saw the Algerian President, who came to our camp. Che Guevara also went there. We were training in a small town not very far from the border with Morocco.

TS: When did you come into contact with the Nordic countries for the first time?

RM: If I remember correctly, it was when I was in Dar es Salaam. I was the administrative secretary at the ANC office. I started as an administrative secretary in 1973. My task was to deal with applications for travel documents for the ANC people leaving Tanzania and to organize their visas from the embassies concerned. I also had to apply for air tickets for the ANC people. We worked with an airline which belonged to a Tanzanian. I had an account with him. I applied for return or single tickets and at the end of the month the ANC Treasury would pay him. These were my activities, besides the normal administrative work in the office, filing and that kind of thing.

Through my activities, I came into contact with the embassies of the Scandinavian countries. In the Swedish embassy, I later became very close to Anna Runeborg. She was the person who was dealing with me directly all the time.

In 1976, I was promoted to ANC Chief Representative in Tanzania. At that time, we had a lot of young people coming to Dar es Salaam as a result of the Soweto uprising. I would go to the airport and divide them. Those who went for military training on one side and those who went for academic studies on the other. The accommodation was also separate. The military people had two places where they stayed and the students were put up in guest houses or hotels in town. That activity made me be more in contact with Anna Runeborg. Thomas Nkobi, our Treasurer General, gave me instructions to organize charter flights to fly our MK personnel out of Tanzania to Angola. I would then go to Anna and say: 'Anna, here is my problem'. She was helpful all the time. She was a fantastic person.

At that time, there was a war in the Shaba province of Zaire. From Dar es Salaam to Luanda you had to fly over the Shaba province. But we decided that the flight must go from Dar es Salaam to Ndola, Zambia. We would go down there and from Ndola we would continue to Angola to avoid the Shaba province. That added to the price, but SIDA covered the costs. Everything, the flights and everything.

TS: When did you finally leave Tanzania?

RM: I left in 1982.

TS: So you were in Tanzania during the construction of the Solomon Mahlangu Freedom College, SOMAFCO? How did SOMAFCO come about?

RM: Yes. In fact, the Solomon Mahlangu Freedom College came into being as follows: We had a problem with a lot of South African children in Dar es Salaam. Dar es Salaam was the capital and the Tanzanian authorities became sensitive about the fact that there were children all over the place. You know how young people behave. We therefore had to find a place for them and that was my responsibility as Chief Representative. We transported the children from Dar es Salaam to a place near to Morogoro, where ANC had a plot. However, that place was adjacent to a military base of the Tanzanian defence force. It did not take very long before it became a serious problem. The Tanzanian military got so excited by seeing these children from Soweto. They opened the gates and the children would go there at weekends to see films etc., interfering with security and the normal administrative work.

Together with a comrade of mine I then went to the Tanzanian Regional Commissioner in Morogoro, Anna Abdallah, and told her that we needed a bigger place for our children. Anna delegated it to some of her colleagues and they took us to Mazimbu. Mazimbu was an old sisal estate with some dilapidated houses. There was no other place. We realized that this was the place and that we must do something about it. I sent a report to the ANC Headquarters in Lusaka, informing them that the Tanzanian government had given us a place in Mazimbu. It was funny. My ANC name was Reddy Mazimba and the place was Mazimbu. After that, many people wanted to address me as Mazimbu.

ANC replied that it was very important that we built a school at that place. Now, there was no water and no electricity. Just bush. And some old houses without doors or windows. People could not live there. The leadership in Lusaka then called Dennis Oswald, who had just finished his studies in architecture in the German Democratic Republic. When he came to Tanzania I showed him the place and said: 'Dennis, do something!' He studied those vacant old houses, called the students to clean the place, renovated the houses and, finally, we moved the students into those very same old houses. Nicely renovated, with doors and windows and so forth. But there was no electricity, so we used candles. And no water. There was a truck which would transport water for cooking, washing and drinking in drums from Morogoro. Life was very difficult for the first group of students at Mazimbu. But that is how SOMAFCO came into being.

TS: Did you get any support from the Nordic countries for SOMAFCO at that early stage?
RM: Yes, there was a Danish fellow—Lars Larsen from DanChurchAid—who was working for the Tanzanian government, building a school in Morogoro. He had already finished his contract when Dennis said to me: 'I wonder if he can come and work for ANC?' I went to the Tanzanian Ministry of Home Affairs, but they said that it was not possible. He had been sent to work under the Tanzanian government and once his contract was over he must go back to Denmark. I said: 'But we need him to build our school'. After some time, the Tanzanian government normalized all the papers and said to me: 'Now, he is working for ANC!' It was the first case where a person who had been working in Tanzania came to work for ANC.

Lars did the first drawings of the buildings at Mazimbu with Dennis. We laid the first foundation on 8 January 1979, which, of course, also was the date on which ANC was founded in 1912. We invited people from Dar es Salaam—diplomats and whoever wanted to come—and had a big meeting.
TS: How could you be confident that the Nordic aid workers were not going to run away with all your plans to the enemy? Did you feel that close to them?
RM: My experience from working with them in Dar es Salaam was that I could trust them. If people said that they were from a Scandinavian country—Norway, Sweden or Denmark—I saw them as part and parcel of our big detachment in the struggle, occupying different trenches to uproot apartheid in our country. That was how I looked at them. Of course, I had to say to myself: 'If one of them turns to the enemy, it will be a problem'. But I addressed myself to people who I trusted. And I must say that those people did their very best. They did a fantastic job.

Mazimbu was named the Solomon Mahlangu Freedom College—SOMAFCO for short—after an MK member who was trained and infiltrated into South Africa to carry out MK activities. He was captured and hanged by the South African regime. The school was named as a tribute to his contribution to the struggle of our people. It was very close to our hearts.

People from the different Scandinavian countries participated directly in the building of Mazimbu, through training, working in agriculture, house-building, teaching and in the medical field. Our medicines came from Scandinavia, as well as clothing and food for the people. I think that 99 per cent of the food-stuff that we bought came from Scandinavia. SIDA, in particular, shouldered the burden. We even built a hospital with two operating theatres. It was built with money and expertise from the Scandinavian countries. The Tanzanian people had never experienced that kind of thing. They could not understand why we had so much confidence in the Scandinavians, who were white!

You must understand that ANC also had problems with some African states, Tanzania in particular. They were saying: 'You people say that you are fighting against a white regime, but you have white people in your ranks. And now you allow whites from other countries to come and help you'. They saw PAC people as the true freedom fighters, because PAC maintained that black is black and did not welcome any whites.

The Tanzanians were very close to PAC for a long time. In fact, we were all chucked out of Tanzania in 1970. ANC was expelled from the country! The background was a coup attempt, organized by the former Tanzanian Foreign Minister Oscar Kambona, who tried to overthrow Nyerere. In the trial, the PAC leader Potlako Leballo was the key witness of the Tanzanian government and he said that ANC was responsible for part of that attempted coup! We were expelled! Out of Tanzania! In fact, the Tanzanian government wanted us to go to a refugee camp, but our leadership refused, saying that we were not refugees, but freedom fighters. ANC leaders like J. B. Marks, Moses Kotane, Oliver Tambo and others said: 'No!' Then they went to the Soviet Union and the Soviets came to Tanzania to pick us all up. We were taken to various parts of the Soviet Union while the leadership tried to negotiate a solution to the problem.

When I became the ANC Chief Representative in 1976, our relationship with Tanzania was not yet good at all. But then we had this influx of people from the Scandinavian countries, coming to help not PAC, but ANC.
TS: Did that have any influence over the Tanzanian government?
RM: Yes, it had an influence. They realized that ANC could and did work. PAC could not deliver. There was quite a number of them. A lot of money was given to PAC, but there were no results.

When people from Europe came to help ANC we had to get permits for them through the Prime Minister's Office. Eventually, we established a routine between ourselves, looking into the security aspects of the visitors. I was responsible for that, because the Tanzanians did not know them. The first people who went to Mazimbu were from the Holland Committee on Southern Africa. They went there with their cameras and everything. They were the first people to photograph the place. At that time, we had not yet put this routine in place. I had just told the Tanzanians that I had people going to Mazimbu. However, Mazimbu is adjacent to military installations and when the Tanzanians saw them taking photographs they arrested them and confiscated their cameras. I was phoned from Morogoro: 'Hey Reddy! There is something wrong here. People are arrested!' I contacted the Prime Minister's Office and said: 'My colleagues are arrested! I told you that they were going there'. Then they phoned Morogoro to release our visitors, give them back their cameras and not spoil their photos. We had to explain that those photos were very important. They were taken to raise funds to build SOMAFCO.

One person who from the beginning understood the importance of Mazimbu was Anna Abdallah. She took a very active part in seeing to it that Mazimbu was built. She planted a tree of friendship there. It is a big tree today. At one time she led a Tanzanian delegation to the Nordic countries, including Finland. Wherever she went, she placed Mazimbu on the world map. She really became an ambassador for ANC, telling people about Mazimbu, what we needed there, why it was important to the liberation struggle in South Africa and how important it was to the Tanzanian people. From time to time, she would just take a car, come to Mazimbu and spend the afternoon there.

After some time, the ANC leadership in Lusaka said that Mazimbu was supposed to be an educational institution and that ANC people who had no connection with education should not be there. They told me: 'Ask the Tanzanian government to give us another area where we can settle this people'. I went to the Ministry of Home Affairs. I had very good relations with them. I forwarded the request and they understood, saying that we must go to Morogoro to meet Anna Abdallah. She listened and said: 'Well, there is an area in Dakawa. There are a lot of fields there which are not utilized'. They were old farms which had belonged to some Indians years back. They had all left Tanzania for Canada and so forth. The farms were not used. Of course, the Masai were using that area to graze their herds.

We drove there and visited the police station of that area. The lieutenant was an agriculturist by profession. We explained what we were looking for and he said: 'Fine, let us go!' He took us to an area not very far from where he lived. He said: 'You can take this area if you like it'. A big piece of land. Very big. He just said: 'This is somewhere to move around. You can take it'. He gave us the maps and we went back to mama Abdallah. She was very happy.

I consulted Dennis Oswald and we went with the administration of Mazimbu to have a look at the place. After that, we took some *umgwenya* there, MK people who left South Africa for training in the 1960s. Like myself. We call ourselves *umgwenya*, that is, veterans of the Luthuli detachment from the Wankie Operation. We assembled some of them, collected torches, food and so on and pitched up our tents in the area, demarcating the place. That is how Dakawa came into being. It was called the Dakawa settlement area.

Later on, people from Mazimbu would go to Dakawa and take part in the agricultural activities. Mazimbu had a big farm, which was managed by Niels from Denmark. We had cattle, goats and so forth. Mazimbu was beautiful and Dakawa also became beautiful.

Mazimbu, in particular, drew people from all over the world. It was important for ANC. We would encourage international people to go there, look at it and see what ANC and its friends—the Scandinavian and other countries who were supporting our struggle—could do under normal circumstances. But, in the beginning we also had problems, because the South African government had recruited a lot of young children as spies and infiltrated them among the students and also within MK. In Mazimbu itself, there was a lot of enemy agents. I took part in arresting them, to the extent that when my Volvo came to Mazimbu people would say: 'Now, who is going to be picked up?' We had to arrest a lot of them.

TS: Were any Scandinavians involved in any funny business there?

RM: No, not at all. In Mazimbu, we then organised a Directorate and developed an administrative policy for the settlement, because it was not only a school. We had a crèche, where expecting young mothers stayed, nurseries, pre-schools and primary, secondary and adult education. There was also a garment factory, a sewing factory and a welding factory, as well as a very big carpentry, all with sophisticated machines.

TS: You produced your own furniture?

RM: Yes, beautiful furniture for the school. Doors, tables, chairs, you name it. We also had a farm with all the necessary equipment. It was a very big place, with pigs, cows, goats and chickens. We had to set up a proper management structure to run the operations. It was also responsible for Dakawa.

TS: When the first SIDA allocation to the ANC was given in 1973, Thomas Nkobi wrote a letter of acknowledgement. Thanking Sweden for the contribution, he said that the ANC had a policy of becoming self-sufficient in exile and that they were going to set up their own farms.

RM: Yes, that is exactly what happened. Mazimbu and Dakawa made the ANC self-sufficient. We also had a big farm in Lusaka, which was supplying our community in Zambia. ANC was really a government in exile.

TS: The development plan for Dakawa was a ten-year plan, financed and drawn up by Norway. Those were the real dark days of the struggle. You had to plan for a long exile?

RM: During those days it was very difficult to visualize when one would be back in South Africa. There were no signs at all. The horizon was just dark. The regime was more and more intransigent, more and more brutal. I think that most of us were saying that: 'Well, we have to make conditions better for ourselves here in exile'. And that that is how people came to be self-sufficient.

TS: Did you then go to Zambia?

RM: In 1981, when I was still the ANC Chief Representative in Tanzania, I was sent together with other colleagues for training in security and intelligence in Moscow. When we came back, I was appointed Head of ANC's Security Division and transferred to our headquarters in Lusaka.

I was posted as ANC Chief Representative to Zimbabwe in 1985. In the beginning, I had difficulties there. The ZANU government was looking at ANC as people who were still conniving with ZAPU. The background was that ANC had been close to ZAPU and that PAC was close to ZANU. In 1967, we formed an alliance with ZAPU and fought in Rhodesia with them. Our aim was to use Rhodesia to cross into South Africa, but in Rhodesia we had to fight when we were confronted. That is the reason why we could not use Botswana, where we would not have fought if the Botswana police had confronted us.

Now, if they saw me with ZAPU people, they would think that I was up to something, but I said: 'These are my colleagues. We know each other. I cannot run away when I see them. As ANC we are dealing with the ZANU government'.

In 1985, there was a serious problem in Matabeleland, so it was very difficult. The Zimbabweans preferred PAC. There was no rally or meeting that I organized without having to invite PAC. They made it into a rule: if I organized a rally, I must also invite PAC. One of their aims was to bring PAC to the people and only ANC could do that. One day I spoke to the ZANU leader Didymus Mutasa about the relationship between ZANU and ANC. I said to him: 'It is important that our relationship is cemented. To do that we have to come together, have a meeting and discuss'. He agreed and the Secretariat of ZANU agreed. I then informed our leadership in Lusaka. They also agreed and the meeting took place in Harare. Our delegation was led by O. R. Tambo. After that meeting, the relationship with ZANU became excellent.

TS: Did you know that the government of Sweden and SIDA constantly were discussing the question of an ANC representation in Harare with the Zimbabwean government and with ZANU?

RM: Yes, that is why I was sent to Harare. I remember it very well. It was part of the endeavour to help us to do away with apartheid. In fact, the Zimbabweans did not want SIDA to give us aid without also assisting PAC. But SIDA said: 'It is our right to decide which side we wish to support'. The Scandinavian countries did a lot. They knew their political line and they knew who to support.

After that first meeting between ANC and ZANU, another meeting took place between Joe Modise, our Army Commander, and Rex Nhongo, the Commander of the Zimbabwean armed forces, to discuss how Zimbabwe could assist us to cross the border into South Africa. A decision was taken that one of the bedrooms in my house should be turned into an armoury. A truck would leave Lusaka full of weapons and drive to Harare and I would tell the Zimbabweans that it was coming. There would not be any search. It would get into my yard and off-load all kinds of weapons and explosives into the bedroom. My house was guarded by the Zimbabwean para-military around the clock. It was used like that, because the Zimbabweans said that nobody would expect to find weapons in the Chief Representative's house.

TS: In the 1980s, about one third of the Swedish support to ANC went to the Home Front. Do you think that it was important for the reorganization of the struggle inside South Africa?

RM: I have no doubt that the SIDA support which was channelled to the Home Front had a tremendous impact on the reorganization of the internal structures. In order to create an underground machinery, we had to get cadres into the country, organize the people and set up good communications. To do this, we needed funds and the money which was channelled by Sweden represented, I think, the bulk of the resources which assisted ANC to be able to operate. It supported people who were doing ANC political work inside the country.

TS: 'Pik' Botha has implied that the Swedish support was not only humanitarian, but also military. Did ANC receive any military support from the Nordic countries?

RM: I know very well that the Nordic countries did not give ANC weapons. They did not. They gave us humanitarian assistance, including food, medicines and so forth, but also funds to make it possible to travel, to go into the country and to organize the machinery there. But no weapons. That I know for a fact, because I was dealing with that, especially when I was in Zimbabwe as the ANC Chief Representative.

However, the South African regime tried to imply that the Nordic countries were giving ANC weapons. For example, when our office in Harare was bombed a very interesting thing happened. This was on 19 May 1986, at one o'clock in the morning, and the very same day *The Citizen* in Johannesburg wrote that Reddy Mazimba—they said 'Jan Mampane, who is known as 'Reddy Mazimba', the Chief Representative of ANC, responsible for the mines that broke the legs of whites in Northern Transvaal'—was dead! They took that to the Swedish legation in Pretoria, which transmitted it to the Swedish embassy in Harare. The ambassador called me and said: 'Do you see how they talk about us down there?' This was a way of saying that 'Sweden gives ANC weapons'. But the Scandinavian countries made it very clear that their money could not buy weapons. It was for humanitarian use. No weapons!

TS: Do you think that there were conditions tied to the Nordic assistance or was it given without strings attached?

RM: Well, as far as I know there were no strings attached. There was a commitment by the Scandinavian people to assist our people, who were ready to sacrifice their lives to eradicate apartheid in South Africa. The Nordic countries believed that apartheid had no place on our planet and they really demonstrated it, not only in words, but practically. If there had been strings attached, today they would be saying: 'OK, we gave you aid, so now you have to give us this'. But there is no such thing. They were always willing to support. They made the struggle of the people of South Africa their own struggle. So, there were no strings attached whatsoever.

TS: Were the responsible DANIDA, FINNIDA, NORAD and SIDA officials well informed about your real needs? Did you have a constructive dialogue with them?

RM: Yes, they were very well informed about our needs and about the situation of our struggle. I think that there was transparency between ourselves and the leaders of the Scandinavian countries. They became part and parcel of ourselves and in that way they were able to give us assistance. They knew exactly where A met B.

TS: You mentioned the bombing of the ANC office in Harare in 1986. What happened?

RM: We always used to get some information that BOSS was coming to raid us and took precautions. That day, at eight o'clock in the evening, we got the same information. Alfred Nzo, our Secretary General and presently Minister of Foreign Affairs, was in Harare and I explained the situation to him. We went around to all our residences and told the people to get out of the houses. Some of them went to sleep at the police station and so forth. Nzo had a flat in town and I stayed with him. At one o'clock, we heard an explosion. We were not far from the office. We woke up without an office! We then drove to Ashdown Park, where the house was also finished.

In this situation, who was on our side? Who was on the side of the South African liberation movement, ANC? The Scandinavian countries—SIDA, in particular, the Norwegian People's Aid, NORAD and others. The Lutheran World Federation in Harare even made space at their office to let us operate from there.

Other countries were not there. They were on the side of the regime. Countries like the United States, Britain and so on, oiling apartheid to continue murdering our people. They made a lot of money through apartheid at the expense of the lives of our people.

TS: Did you see what the German Chancellor Helmuth Kohl said to the South African Parliament in Cape Town last week? He said that even in the darkest days, German companies were here to help the oppressed?

RM: It is very bad. It is criminal, in fact. People like this—who were oiling the apartheid regime to continue the oppression of our people—now come and tell us that they are proud that they were busting the sanctions' policy. They did not care about our people. Sanctions was our weapon against apartheid and they did not care about that. Now they come here and boast. It is very bad. It really worries me.

Trevor Manuel
Western Cape Regional Secretary of the United Democratic Front—ANC
Minister of Trade, Industry and Tourism
(Cape Town, 8 September 1995)

Tor Sellström: You were one of the leading persons in the setting up of the United Democratic Front (UDF) in the Cape in August 1983. Subsequently, the Nordic countries channelled support to UDF. Did you have any personal contacts with the Nordic countries before the launch of UDF?

Trevor Manuel: No, I did not. I was working in civic organizations on a full-time basis from 1981, but we had very little access to resources. For campaigns, we used to go around the townships, but also to the churches. I later came to understand that we then also used facilities that were extended by the Nordic countries. On the Cape Flats, the Lutheran Centre in Belgravia was, for example, a meeting point which was very widely used. But I did not immediately understand the connection. Not until later. Even the launch of UDF was done through Johannesburg contacts and through the dispatch of an individual to Botswana for an ANC hook-up to get some hard cash that we could use. No, we were kept removed from contacts. It was probably not until 1984 that I strengthened contacts with Birgitta Karlström Dorph at the Swedish legation. They worked very closely with us.

I certainly was involved in putting together the UDF budget for 1985, which requested the princely sum of 455,000 Rands. I came from a tradition of much lower budgets, but I think that there was a turning point with the intensification of the activities. Very early in 1985 we realized that even the resources of the budget that I had spent so many nights putting together were just gone. I do not know whether it would even have carried us until the ANC conference in mid-1985, because by then you had had the shootings in Uitenhage and a number of other events.

During that period, I became intensely aware of the general support from the Nordic countries. We had people like Allan Boesak who were based in Cape Town. They could do the running. I did not even have a passport.

TS: And you were detained on a number of occasions?

TM: Yes, from 1985 I was repeatedly detained, so I participated in those discussions for only a fairly short period.

TS: Without previous contacts with the Nordic countries, was it strange to you that these Western countries—two of them being members of NATO—supported UDF?

TM: No, it was not strange. I think that the tradition of Nordic Social Democracy gave a very strong moral image to the support. You must also bear in mind that many of the conduits were the Nordic churches. They were involved outside the Swedish legation itself. It was also a time when the churches here were raising the same issues. No, it was not strange at all.

In those days we had a very strongly bipolar world and we came from a fairly strong anti-imperialist tradition. But, needless to say, being inside the country there was no contact with any Warsaw Pact country. The Nordic countries presented themselves as a fairly safe route. These were the channels used for the resources, as well as the World Council of Churches.

TS: Do you think that the Swedish and Nordic support to UDF was extended without strings attached or was it part of an ideological package?

TM: I think that there may have been some part of the latter. In 1984, UDF won a Swedish prize and extensive offers were made for people to spend time in Sweden and in the other Nordic countries, going there for training and for an examination of the way in which Social Democracy functions. This was debated in UDF in the early days. There was some suspicion about elements in the Nordic countries, such as the general improvement in living standards, the role of the trade unions and the change from what we narrowly understood as a necessary, very militant position by the trade unions. Almost an emasculation of a tradition.

Looking back, I can say that the issues that were then strongly in focus in South

Africa were issues related to the question of ownership of the means of production. Our view was that the general improvements and the general conduct of Social Democracy—capitalism with a good face—had numbed the sense of the workers about the question of who should own the means of production. You must imagine the context of this debate. They were not big public debates, but amongst us there were at the time certainly debates about whether the Nordic support was not a very careful plan to have us focus on reform rather than on revolution.

TS: Did you find that projects were imposed on you or did you yourselves design the projects for which you received financial support?

TM: I think that in the early period the support was primarily for political activities. Budgetary support. Towards the latter part of the 1980s you actually saw a shift to projects, and I think that on all sides there was a turning point which I still find a bit disconcerting. During the State of Emergency, survival became imperative to the kind of fund-raising that we had done in the early 1980s. The demands were also much greater. In the early 1980s we were far more frugal.

Some of these points may sound contradictory. Here I am: a minister, nicely dressed, sitting in Trade and Commerce and talking about ownership of the means of production. But, historically, these were then the issues. We spent a fair amount of time in prison debating with some concern the ease with which money had suddenly become available.

In the early period, a lot was done from resources collected from the workers. We were earning 350 Rands a month in UDF when they were still earning 125 Rands in the Food and Canning Workers Union here in the Western Cape. There were set rules in the movement. We stood at the gate and collected dues from the workers on Friday, because the bosses would not give us any supportive facilities. You kept the money collected until you paid it over, either on Saturday morning or the following Monday. If indeed you used a penny, the General Secretary had the executive mandate to call in the police and hand you over for theft. It hardened the organizers. There was a frugality about the involvement, with people of a very strong character. High calibre activists. There was a commitment that certainly had no relation to any pecuniary advantage for those involved. Good organizers were also lost, because when the third week of the month came and there was no food in the house some would take the money collected and buy some food. Thus, they could not pay the money over on Monday morning and they would have to go.

However, in the circumstances where there was an underground operation—I am not talking about the military underground, but of the conditions imposed by the State of Emergency—all financial accounting went out through the window, and I think that there was a measure of corruption. Whether this was per force of circumstance or by design remains a moot point, but there was just too much money around. I also think that a great deal of personal enrichment took place.

At that time, the European Union (EU) started its twin-track strategy and we had the establishment of the Kagiso Trust with project financing in South Africa. Again we had a series of debates, this time about the power of Thatcher in shaping the twin-track strategy of the EU. And once again money was made available without sufficient financial controls. I think that you saw this during the height of the State of Emergency, particularly in 1986.

When we launched UDF, activists who had a track record went out. We were involved in the cooking of the meals. We hired mattresses and people slept in schools, church halls, mosques or whatever space we could find to accommodate them. But at the COSATU launch in Durban in 1985 people stayed in hotels. For me that was a big shift.

I also recall when we prepared what was called the first anti-apartheid conference. It was scheduled for September 1988 and was to be held in Cape Town. I was fresh out of jail and was asked by the UDF people to be involved. COSATU, then a very young organization, was also involved. Our dates coincided with the short September university vacation, so I went to see directors of institutions that had hostels to find out whether we could use the student residences. Having made the initial contacts, I discovered, however, that COSATU had moved somebody down to Cape Town, located in the

COSATU regional office, and that this individual already had found hotels and made block bookings. It was a shock to my system, because I think that what came with it was a style of organizing that we would never be able to sustain on our own. But, you said 'anti-apartheid conference. Fine, do a quick project and get it through to the donors'. And when it was funded you went ahead.

When the conference eventually took place in Johannesburg at the end of 1989—it was called Conference for a Democratic Future— we all stayed in hotels. In the early period of UDF we stayed in houses even for executive meetings, but when we came out of jail there was a shift to hotels and a shift from driving to flying. There were all those kinds of things. Sure, it may have happened in different ways, but I think that we were spoilt in a way that it was virtually impossible to retreat from.

TS: I guess that this probably was difficult to do much about from the side of the donors, apart from the fact that the amounts involved grew very big from the mid-1980s onwards.

TM: Well, I can understand the pressure on people with bleeding hearts, sitting in frosty Nordic countries, when you said: 'This is what the conference will cost. This is the cost of the flights and this is the cost of the hotels etc.' Nobody there was going to say 'Don't fly. Drive! Don't stay in hotels. Go and sleep on the floor!'.

Now, did we need all these conferences? Perhaps we did. Perhaps we needed to take the struggle through these kinds of processes. Perhaps they were important in preparation for what by the late 1980s was to become part of the ANC agenda. The central issue at that Conference for a Democratic Future was how to generate support for a negotiated settlement. Perhaps we needed the fights with AZAPO on these issues. Hindsight is always very important. Would we have done things differently? Your guess is as good as mine, but I think that these activities assisted in building a depth of support.

TS: Do you think that the people in the Western Cape were knowledgeable about the Nordic countries' involvement and support?

TM: I think that there was only a very small group of people that was. I do not remember anybody asking where the money came from, and I do not remember anybody ever being willing—if asked—to indicate the source of the money. That may have been a major difference between exile and the situation inside South Africa. In exile you knew. Inside the country, there was a pretty tight circle. The source of support was seen as covert and we would not do anything to jeopardise it.

TS: And there was, of course, legislation against it?

TM: Yes, so I do not think that the message of support really got through to the people.

TS: I am asking this because of the contradictory dimension of the relationship. In the Nordic countries practically everybody was involved in some kind of support, through the solidarity movements, the trade unions, the churches or otherwise. The result is that you have a strong legacy of solidarity with a people that in itself is not that aware of the involvement. That would make it more difficult to build a popularly based relationship between, for example, Sweden and the new South Africa?

TM: I think that there are certain things that one became aware of during that period. There were contacts. One of the individuals who repeatedly came through was a man from Sweden called Magnus Walan. I do not remember when I first met Magnus, but it would have been before my long stint in jail. It was probably with the Swedish priest Per Svensson at the Lutheran Centre in Belgravia in early 1985 or something like that. He communicated, for example, that there were annual days of solidarity with South Africa when school children went out and collected money.

Those were wonderful stories that we used to illustrate the deep morality of our struggle and how important information was kept away from us through the control of the media by the apartheid regime. But we would not make a speech about it. It would be too light. If indeed there were visitors, we would say: 'These are our friends from Sweden. They are coming to look at what we are doing here because of a, b, c or d. And this is what is happening back in their country.' Whether that made any impression on the general consciousness, I cannot vouch for at all.

Now, coming back to the questions of means and ownership, which are very meaningful to me: two weeks ago I spoke to a small rural organization located in Namaqualand and with little networks all over the Cape. The nice thing is that even their headquarters are in a place called Saron, not in a city. I shared a few insights with them. One was communicated to me by an Italian woman who visited from Mozambique when I was running ERIP, the Education, Resource and Information Project, where we had a small press for the printing of community pamphlets. We were sitting in my office and she really chided me, saying: 'Look at all the white space on the paper.' Then she told me a story about Mozambique and how RENAMO with apartheid support had destroyed not only the paper mills, but even the tree nurseries that provided the raw material. She explained that in the department in which she was teaching at the Eduardo Mondlane University in Maputo they only got two reams of paper and how the students had learnt to write in small print and use every space of the paper available. They had also started a programme of recycling.

That was one story that I told. The other was a story of a church. Terror Lekota and I were trying to get UDF going in the northern Free State in early 1985, but we could not find a venue. There was a vigilante group called the A-Team which was taking out young activists. However, the pastor of a traditional African Zion Apostolic Church gave his church to us for a Sunday, provided that we were out by evening. He would suspend his services during the day so that we could use the facilities.

I am making a point about ownership. I would draw these two examples together and say: How does an organization function when the tap can be closed off? Particularly now, when it is easier for donors to deal bilaterally with the government? Because no government—no matter how good—is going to say that 'we will forego this money. We are not going to use it. Give it to some NGO.'

I was making this point already when I was moving from being a regional organizer here in the Western Cape to sort of a higher profile national representative. In the beginning of 1989, soon after I came out of jail—I was still banned, but I went there in defiance—I addressed the Kagiso Trust and I spoke about the need for austerity programmes, which was also published in a report. Well, again I say that I must be living the complete contradiction, but I think that in the debate on funding the shift I talked about was an important change.

I was heading a SADC meeting the other day and there was a debate about a forestry programme, meant to have been located in Malawi. It is an important programme. Malawi got up to object: 'Why did Zimbabwe take this project away from them? Why is it now in Zimbabwe?' And the Zimbabweans said: 'In all honesty, we did not know that this project used to be located in, or was taken out of, Malawi and brought to Zimbabwe. The Danes who are involved in the project came with it to us.' In the context, Zimbabwe had the good grace to say no: 'Thanks for raising it. The project will now go back to Malawi.' To me it just told that entire story again.

Another example: for good, sound reasons we kept a very flat structure in ANC and the lowest paid people were earning 2,200 Rands a month. Those were the people that we sought to bring over into the police force. They would have been security guards at the ANC headquarters at Shell House in Johannesburg and so on. But it is almost impossible to take them in, because the starting rate in the police force is only about 850 Rands a month. That is a problem. In SADC we have chosen a 'softer option'. The Executive Secretary is getting 10,000 US Dollars a month, tax-free, which is not bad by any standards. If you are a Mozambican minister, you could kill to get a position like that. But, having been there, what are you going to do thereafter?

We have got the same thing here. There are salaries set for the President, the Deputy Presidents, the Ministers and Deputy Ministers, the ordinary parliamentarians etc., which are largely shaped by what existed in the past. Even though we have made salary cuts—driven by us—the gap is still very big, but people won't give up. It is very seductive.

Thabo Mbeki
ANC—Director of Information, Secretary of Presidential Affairs and of International Affairs
First Executive Deputy President of South Africa
(Cape Town, 8 September 1995)

Tor Sellström: Next to the late President Oliver Tambo, you have had closer contacts with the Nordic governments than anybody else in the ANC leadership. How would you describe the relations between Sweden, the Nordic countries and ANC during the liberation struggle?

Thabo Mbeki: I think that, first of all, the principal input would have been made by Sweden in terms of the definition of the relationship, its purposes and its wider contextualisation. For instance, if you take the question of the legitimacy of the liberation struggle, including the armed struggle. In the eyes of the Western world that was an important question during the 1960s and the 1970s.

What was a liberation struggle? It was a protest movement against oppression and denial of civil rights and all that. As such it must, quite legitimately, be supported. All must join to protest against the abuses. Secondly, it was a welfare cause. The situation against which you are protesting produces victims, so you also extend welfare to them, through scholarships or whatever. Now, the particular role of Sweden—presumably of the Social Democratic Party more broadly, but I think particularly of Olof Palme as it also relates to the war in Vietnam—was to say that the people have got the right and the duty to rebel against oppression and that the concept of emancipation of a people cannot be reduced to a protest movement, but concerns the right to self-determination of small nations. That is something which is legitimate, which is necessary and which must be supported.

There is a second element to this, which is that as part of the recognition of that right to self-determination you support the people who are engaged in the struggle. You do not define what they should be. You might have a debate about what is happening in Vietnam, where some would say that the people were led by Communists and so on. But Olof Palme would say: 'Sure, I do not like Communists, but once you have said that you recognize the notion of peoples' right to self-determination you also recognise the right of the people to decide what they think.' That made a contribution also in terms of the representation of the South African struggle. Solidarity was no longer merely a protest against apartheid, but support for a struggle for liberation.

TS: Olof Palme's view was very much to try to break up the bipolar world by supporting oppressed peoples, colonized peoples, the people under apartheid, within a non-aligned movement.

TM: Sure. That is the point that I am making. There was an input from Sweden and the rest of the Nordic countries, which said that there was a protest movement, so 'let us protest against the abuses of the system in South Africa and extend welfare assistance'. But at a certain point it changed. This is how I see it. It changed with the rising to the surface of the notion of the right of peoples to self-determination and therefore their right and duty to fight and to assert that right. As well as the duty of Sweden to support the struggle without seeking to define what the people should be. For instance, if they were fighting for self-determination and independence from the Portuguese, the people might decide to have a normal multi-party democratic system after independence. That is fine. Or they might decide to have a dictatorship of the proletariat. That is also fine: 'It is your sovereign right to decide that. It is consistent with our opposition to continued Portuguese colonialism. Of course, we will disagree with you. We do not think that it is the right system, but it is your right to decide.'

Those are two important elements. I think that that is what really defined the nature of the interaction between ANC and Sweden, maybe from the mid-1970s onwards. I would not be an authority on the political processes within Sweden, but, as I say, there began to emerge a movement away from protests against apartheid and the concept that ANC was a protest movement to say that we need to remove the system and get rid of it.

Now, once you take the position that here is a system which needs to be removed and that it is the right and duty of the people of South Africa to remove it—as well as our duty to support them—the exercise of that right to self-determination cannot merely stop at 'We support them in the struggle to remove the system of apartheid.' You go further to say, 'but we must respect their sovereign right to define themselves.' It may be that some of them are ugly, but you cannot turn your back and say that you will not deal with them because they are ugly. It is part of their right to self-determination to be ugly. Or they may decide to take up arms. I might myself be a pacifist and say: 'I do not like this thing.' But once I have said that you have a sovereign right to define who you are, if I want to support you I cannot say: 'I will support you on condition that you construct yourself in the image that I would like.'

This was important from the ANC point of view. The material, humanitarian assistance was very important, but it was that political stance that was critical to the people inside the country and to the people outside the country. For instance, when the issue of the legitimacy of the South African regime arose, with a whole range of implications, somebody like Olof Palme would say that 'the reason why I support the right of the people of South Africa to fight for their own liberation is that I do not believe that the South African regime is legitimate. We are not protesting against bad things done by an entity which otherwise is legitimate.' Once you had gone beyond that to say: 'We do not recognize the legitimacy of this government and the system that it is defending; let us rise against it and get rid of it', the position of the ANC inside the country and elsewhere radically changed, *even* in terms of the armed struggle.

For decades a big point of attack against ANC was the whole issue of the armed struggle. However, once you start from the basis of the right of peoples to self-determination it ceases to be a challenge. I think that this really was the critical contribution of Sweden. In the first instance because it was a Western country. There was no problem on the African continent with regard to the right to self-determination and the struggle for independence. Well, in the non-aligned movement in general. But when you got to the Western world, there was a solid view: 'Yes, indeed, we must protest against apartheid and develop a movement for civil rights. Indeed, we must extend such support as we can to help the victims of apartheid. But in terms of *changing* the situation in South Africa, well, let us persuade the government to change'. When you said that it cannot be persuaded to change, so let us organize mass demonstrations in the streets, back would come the response that 'you are making this people more stubborn. The more you challenge them, the more they will defend themselves, so do not do that. We are talking to them'. Then you take up arms and you are called a terrorist...

You had a Western world which was stuck in a particular position. When you said: 'I would like to talk to the British government about South Africa, about sanctions, about all sorts of things,' they would say: 'Why must we meet you? If you want to come and discuss scholarships for some of your people who are refugees or maybe for some of your young people inside South Africa, sure, let us meet.' When you said: 'No, let us meet to discuss sanctions against apartheid in South Africa', they would say: 'No, that is not the way to move the South African government. The way to move the South African government is to engage them. We do not want sanctions, because with sanctions they will put their backs up'. So, the particular approach by Sweden was a critical contribution in my perception.

TS: Did it create space for you to work towards other Western governments?

TM: The position of Sweden created more space than the African or non-aligned position. It created space for ANC to be able to deal with the rest of the Western world. And not just the Western world, but even with regard to the Eastern world and the relationship of ANC with those countries. For instance, the first time the President of the ANC met the General Secretary of the Communist Party of the Soviet Union was when Gorbatjov became General Secretary. Before that, the highest official of the Communist

Party that received ANC would be the Secretary for International Affairs of the Central Committee. Again, I think, because of their own understanding. They called you a liberation movement, but they had a conception of that liberation movement as an opposition party. The notion that you could defeat a government that represented a system and have it replaced by the liberation movement might have been there theoretically. But in practice it was different, whereas Oliver Tambo could go to Sweden and be met by the Prime Minister who understood that he represented a system that must replace the one in power.

TS: Already in 1962, I think, Oliver Tambo met the Prime Minister of Sweden.

TM: Yes, there was an old connection. My sense of this is that the relationship originated in a particular theoretical and philosophical political position. Then you got the humanitarian assistance. In reality, the humanitarian assistance translated as: 'OK, here you are—a government-in-waiting as it were—with different portfolios. You have a health portfolio, an education portfolio, a defence portfolio, an intelligence portfolio and so on. We recognize your right to have all those things. However, our own political constraints tie us to support you in regard to the following five portfolios. You had better take care of the other five.'

TS: Which would also be the case with assistance to Zambia, Mozambique, Zimbabwe or any independent country.

TM: Yes, with any country. Then they would say: 'As your sovereign right you have decided to embark on armed struggle. We cannot either give or sell you arms, or finance your purchase of weapons, but if you decide to get your weapons in the Soviet Union that is not a condition for a continued relationship and assistance from Sweden. That is your own business.' What I am saying is that even the humanitarian assistance occurred in that particular context. You might have had some humanitarian assistance during this period from a country like Great Britain, who might say that 'there are twenty scholarships available for your people and we are ready to give them to you', but that was of a different kind.

TS: In Southern Africa, there was at times a complicated relationship between the independent states, ANC and the Nordic countries. For example, it took many years to establish an ANC office in Harare. How did you see the ANC relationship with the Nordic countries in this context?

TM: Again, the starting point was the emancipation of the people. A complication might arise between ANC and the government of Zimbabwe, with whom Sweden wanted to maintain the best of relations. But you could not sacrifice the objective of the emancipation of the people of South Africa simply to maintain good relations with the country hosting ANC, so we had to find a formula around this. It derives from the starting point. If your starting point had been different and Sweden, for instance, had wanted to create a sphere of influence and become important to these countries with regard to Social Democracy and the struggle against Communism or something, then, of course, if complications had appeared between ANC and Zimbabwe it would have said: 'Look, we cannot afford to lose our influence on Zimbabwe, so cool down ANC! We will talk again after six months.' But that is a different starting point. I do not think that the popular movement which developed against apartheid in Sweden was predicated on protest.

TS: Oliver Tambo always insisted upon continued Nordic support to the BLS countries. At the same time one seriously doubted the effects of the assistance to these countries, particularly when it came to their independence vis-à-vis South Africa?

TM: Yes, that is true. Now, part of ANC's capacity to do things and part of the weight that was attached to ANC derived from the weight that it was given by other countries. The Nordic countries were important with regard to more than development assistance in the region of Southern Africa. Also by the nature of their relations, where a Zambia, a Zimbabwe or a Tanzania would not feel threatened or as junior partners, as they would feel vis-à-vis the United States. You had a particular set of relations between the Nordic countries and the countries of Southern Africa. The manner in which ANC was treated by the Nordic countries—not as a welfare and protest movement, but in the way that we are describing, where you would have annual, bilateral negotiations with the ANC as you would have with the Zambian government, for example, and where ANC enjoyed a sort of official status—impacted upon the way that the countries of the region would approach ANC. They would not want to handle ANC in a manner that could upset the allies of ANC, which also happened to be their own allies. It mediated the relationships.

Billy Modise
ANC—Student and Chief Representative to Sweden
High Commissioner of South Africa to Canada
(Johannesburg, 15 September 1995)

Tor Sellström: What circumstances led you to Sweden?
Billy Modise: I had joined ANC in 1955 and I became a student leader at Fort Hare University. The main fight as far as the students were concerned was against the introduction of the Extension of the University Education Bill, which was to legalize apartheid at the universities. Until 1959, the universities could theoretically, accept students of all colours, but in practice they did not. Now they wanted to legalize apartheid through that act and we fought it. At the end of the day, I was a wanted man. I was also elected to the National Executive of NUSAS, the National Union of South African Students. In 1960, they asked me to attend an international student conference in Switzerland, which I declined. I knew that I would be arrested if I went to apply for a passport. But both ANC and my family said: 'Look, it is a matter of time before the police will pick you up, so leave the country. Try to see if you can get a scholarship.'

The Lund University Students Union in Sweden offered me a scholarship for medicine and the British Students Union paid for my ticket from Accra, Ghana, to London. ANC arranged that I would be on their only chartered flight to lift South African ANC refugees from the then Bechuanaland to Accra. But when I got to Bechuanaland my contact had gone, and I missed that lift. So I hitchhiked to Tanzania and later got on a plane to London.
TS: In Tanzania you met the Swedish missionary Barbro Johansson?
BM: I met Barbro Johansson and she was very helpful, because the ticket from the British Students Union was still lying in Ghana and I was in Tanzania, Tanganyika at that time. I was not going to West Africa, so I had the ticket transferred to Dar es Salaam.
TS: This was in 1960?
BM: Yes. At that time Barbro was a member of parliament for TANU. A very strong and dynamic woman. She said: 'I can top up your ticket to allow you to get to Sweden. I will lend you the money. One day you will repay me.' I am still in the process of paying her... She will not tell me how much it is.

I then came to Sweden and got to Lund. Anna Wieslander was in charge of the foreign students. She met me in Copenhagen. But I never settled down to medicine. I was with two Liberian girls who are now doctors, and every time I was supposed to go to class I was busy politicizing Sweden. In the end, the student union and the professor said: 'Look, you have got a choice. If you want to do medicine, you stay here and study. If you want to do politics for South Africa, look for another subject area.' I thought, well, I cannot give up South Africa for medicine, so I gave up medicine and ended up in sociology.
TS: If you had continued with medicine you would perhaps not have represented President Mandela as High Commissioner to Canada today?
BM: I do not know. You never know what happens in life.
TS: Among the students in Lund there was also a group of Namibians. I am thinking of those who came very early, such as Uatja Kaukuetu.
BM: Yes, they were SWANU. Their leader, Kozonguizi, who lived in London, was a colleague of mine at Fort Hare. That is where he really was politicized. He became a member of the ANC Youth League. In Lund at the time, we had SWANU and ZAPU. We coor-

dinated and we supported one another. We planned together. With SWANU there was a common enemy, South Africa, so we had quite a lot in common.

TS: When you came to Sweden in 1960, how did the Swedish people look upon South Africa and the struggle against apartheid?

BM: When I got to Sweden, the problem of South Africa was distant in a sense. People did not understand what was happening, except for a few politicians and perhaps a few scholars and businessmen. For the ordinary man it was just a distant problem. That made it very difficult. Some of the things that we were asking the Swedes to do they would not contemplate, because they had not done it in the past.

We asked for sanctions. I remember when the former Prime Minister Tage Erlander used to come down to Lund for his annual visit to his *alma mater*. He said that according to Swedish law and practice you could not declare economic sanctions against a country unless you were at war with that country. Sweden was not at war with South Africa in the legal sense, so they could not apply sanctions by the government. But if we were able to persuade the ordinary Swedish consumer not to buy South African products, there was no problem. Hence, that was a big challenge to us. We must talk to almost every Swede and say 'Don't buy! Don't buy from South Africa! Don't export! Don't export to South Africa!' But we could not stop the goods from entering Sweden. I addressed the students. My base was in the student structures. I travelled to Gothenburg, Stockholm, Lund, talking to high schools. All over Skåne, informing them about the situation in South Africa.

TS: Did you also visit the other Nordic countries?

BM: Yes. I went to Denmark, because Denmark was my neighbour. It was easier there. I went to Århus and to Copenhagen. I also went to Norway. I attended the 1961 Nobel Peace Prize ceremony for the late Chief Luthuli. We had a few South African ANC students in Oslo and we worked with them. Finland is the only country that I did not go to until very late.

In 1961, I was almost the only South African who was active in Sweden. The other students were really not into politics. I do not blame them, because they paid attention to their studies. I was irresponsible and paid attention to politics. It was clear that I could not do the work alone, so I started working on the Swedes, proposing to form a committee that would spread among the Swedes themselves. That is how we started the South Africa Committee in Lund, with people like Lars-Erik Johansson and Ulf Agrell. We also started a publication and addressed meetings.

I remember addressing the Social Democratic women in Malmö. Johansson was translating for me. I kept referring to Jesus Christ, thinking that I was talking to elderly women. But he did not translate the Jesus Christ part and when we went back to Lund he said: 'Look, do not waste your time referring to Jesus Christ. Some of these people probably do not go to church. Just make your point, but do not refer to any religion.' Also, many of these women had not really met a black person. After I finished speaking they asked me to sign autographs. I could feel the pressure as I was signing and the next thing was that they pushed their hands onto me to feel me and to touch this funny hair.

The committee developed to cover the whole of Southern Africa. We had SWAPO, SWANU, ZANU, ZAPU, FRELIMO etc. and it picked up very strongly throughout Sweden. There were demonstrations all over. We would write pamphlets and posters. We lobbied the parliament very strongly. Also the trade unions and separate members of LO. Although I was a student, I was more of a foot soldier in politics.

TS: There were a number of personalities in the liberal camp that raised the issue of apartheid. I am thinking of Herbert Tingsten and Gunnar Helander. Could it explain the broadness of the solidarity movement?

BM: I think that no one person can claim to have politicized Sweden regarding South Africa. One could single out myself and a few others, but on the ground there were the students in the South Africa Committee. Then you had Per Wästberg, who had just been kicked out of South Africa, and Helander, the church minister. In fact, those two gave stature to what the students were doing, because they were accepted Swedish personalities in their own right. They added weight to what we were doing against apartheid. It added dignity, if you can say so. There was also Sara Lidman, a very powerful lady.

Without what you call the liberal centre I think that our work would have been more difficult, perhaps even slower. They came in when we needed muscle on television. One of them would be there when we needed a good, powerful speaker. When we needed a lobbyist who could reach the echelons of power in the Swedish government they were there. They were very helpful, subsequently joined by people like Pierre Schori, who brought in the Social Democratic youth.

There was a receptiveness on the part of a number of structures. It was not a one person performance. It could never have been. Apart from us from outside, you already had, I think, a democratic basis in Sweden that could understand what we were saying. Much more than in the United States, for example. The wind of change, as somebody called it, had not yet properly hit the United States in spite of the fact that they had done away with slavery on paper. But Sweden was ready to understand, because, I think, of the social mindset of the society.

TS: There was a strong egalitarian credo in the Nordic countries?

BM: Right. I think that that was it. The other possible explanation is that, in fact, they had not been a colonial power in the traditional sense of the word and, hence, had not created this seemingly insoluble problem of the colonial master always remaining the colonial master, even in his mindset. They were able to relate much easier and much more readily to people from developing countries, almost without any active racism or negative prejudice. That made relations much easier. That made them a little more receptive to what we were saying. They could empathize much easier than the former colonial powers. The fight in Sweden was not as tough as the fight in Britain or France, even if in the end the heart of the anti-apartheid movement in the world was in London. But still, it was a real fight.

What could have been a problem was racism. I made a distinction between negative racism and positive racism. Negative racism is when I am denied an opportunity on the basis of race. In Sweden the problem was not that. The problem was that I was treated preferentially because of race. At the end of the day that is still racism, because they are not treating me as an equal. They are treating me as a pampered little child. You saw it on the ground. I would go and bash at whites and everybody would agree with me. Then you would have the Swedes saying exactly the same thing and you had a heated argument: *'Va' fan! Det kan inte vara sant!'* ('What the hell! It cannot be true!')

When I got to Sweden that was the problem. The reason was that there were no black people in the country. People did not know how to behave to blacks. Many times in the small towns I would walk around and the children would be asking me: *'Varför är du så smutsig?'* ('Why are you so dirty?'). They did not know a human being who naturally was like this. If hands were like these, in their eyes it meant that the father had been working with oil. He was dirty. It was not racialistic. It was just that I was dirty.

TS: I guess that in those days the only contacts with blacks were with American jazz and gospel singers?

BM: Yes, and sailors. Places like Stockholm, Gothenburg and Malmö had seen blacks, but, if you went inland very few blacks had walked there. Let me also say that there were institutions that took the question of racism and apartheid into their fold. You had schools that started to bring in teachers that were taking up the topic of racism. I guess that some of those teachers probably might have seen some of the problems that were to confront Sweden with regard to migrant workers from the South, gypsies and Lapps. But this question had not yet become too problematic in the society. Now, South Africa was a good example of where things can go wrong along the racial line. 'So why don't we discuss that to sensitize the children? If we look closely at home, we might find that we also do have some phenomena that are related to the problem that South Africa has got.'

You had schools like Nässjö Folkhögskola, where I went to learn my Swedish and which Yolisa, my wife, also attended later. It became very involved. The folk high school movement was very helpful because it was composed of mature students. They had been out on the ground and suffered, perhaps not racially, but they knew what class discrimination was. They could not understand why people were kept out only because they were black or did not have education and so forth. So they were amenable to thinking about the problems that we raised.

TS: The churches, I suppose, also came in to support you?

BM: Definitely, yes. Very much so. In Uppsala, particularly. In Stockholm and then in Lund and Malmö the churches were also very active. As in Jönköping. Anders Johansson, who later became editor at *Dagens Nyheter*, joined this work whilst he was at the Jönköping high school. He was the student leader there and he brought me there several times. It is a very, very religious area.

TS: You lived in Sweden until 1976, when you took up a post as Assistant Director of the United Nations Institute for Namibia in Lusaka, Zambia. You returned as the ANC Chief Representative towards the end of the 1980s. How did you then find Sweden compared to what you had experienced some twenty-five years earlier?

BM: Sweden refined my politics. I probably imbibed some of the philosophical positions that Sweden as a society took, because I lived there for sixteen years. Sweden is a non-violent country and that probably rubbed off onto me even if I supported the armed liberation struggle. I never apologized for supporting that, but, basically, at the bottom of me there was that non-violent position. Sweden had taken the position of supporting ANC. ANC was in the armed struggle and Sweden as a country was non-violent. Many people never understood that and found it contradictory. Yet, I do not think that it was.

Sweden also contributed to my professional career. I did a lot of work as a sociologist there. I did research with people and started the development studies programme at Lund University. I took students, including Jaya Appalraju, to East Africa for research purposes and so forth. Sweden also gave me a chance—even before SIDA was established—to talk to the so-called experts when they were sent abroad for technical aid work or for the United Nations on the issues of developing countries, racism, etc. The fact that they would ask me—a black student—to come and discuss with them meant that Sweden recognized that they needed a certain experience which they did not have. They wanted to listen to outsiders. That attitude internationalized the Swedish political vision of the world. They never said: 'We know.' The trouble with colonial powers is that they always know better than other people. Sweden, on the other hand, was always ready to say: 'Can we learn from you?'. You could see on environmental issues, on human rights' issues, all around, that Sweden always was interacting with the world in order to do certain things.

By and large, the receptiveness of the Swedish political system and mindset was a plus and a strength. Sweden was very engaged and involved in world issues, which was unique. Already at the end of the 1960s, Sweden had made its mark internationally on Third World issues. Sweden did not just support any developing country. The selection was politically motivated. They were able to look for social democracy. The Swedish philosophy was social democracy and, hence, support to Vietnam, Cuba, TANU in Tanganyika, ZAPU or UNIP in Zambia was not a problem for Sweden, whereas it was a problem in other donor countries.

Now, when I went back in 1988 as the ANC representative, I was frankly shocked to find that Sweden had become an ordinary developed country, whose youth and people were just focusing on a better house, a better car and better clothing. The political activity was really very much lower than when I left in 1976. I do not know what happened in the meantime. It could have been the state of the economy. In the 1980s, Sweden was struggling. It was feeling the pinch of the worldwide recession and inflation and people were saying: 'Hey, first my job before I can engage in correcting the wrongs of the society.' The university system had also changed somewhat. I think that it was in the late 1960s that the debate came that you should stop studying for the sake of studying. There were people who were studying for ten years, one course a year. They became unemployable. I do not remember the exact period when industry was brought closer to the universities, but at the time we fought that, because we feared that capital wanted to take over and run the universities. I think that this influence led people to focus more on their careers at a time when they should be philosophical dreamers.

The last time you can afford to dream and almost live your dreams is when you are still a student. Once you start working that is the end, because your hours, your positions and your behaviour are controlled by your employer, directly or indirectly. As a student you can afford to dream and think beyond reality. Every society wants dreamers who can try to project what that society is going to be beyond the present. The only people who can do that in a society are the students. When you lose the students and they start to behave like adults while they are still at the university—already calculating that 'I am going to have two children and a Volvo; I cannot risk or do that etc.'—it means that you are not getting that necessary injection into the thinking of the society. For me, that was a very drastic change. I spent almost two years in Sweden as ANC Chief Representative without getting an invitation from the universities.

TS: Perhaps you could say that Sweden had been normalized and that the whole relationship with ANC to a large extent had become bureaucratized?

BM: More bureaucratic, that is true. Very much so. However, in spite of that bureaucracy, Sweden continued to support the liberation struggle and ANC. The Social Democrats had become weaker as a political structure and they now had to be seen to handle public funds in a responsible manner. I am not saying that they were irresponsible before, but people were now questioning ANC because the Americans and the British were regarding ANC as terrorists and all that. So you would get the opposition to the Social Democrats saying 'We want to know how we support ANC.'

Let me be fair to everybody. On balance, you can say that all in Sweden supported the liberation struggle. Where the parties might have been differing was on how the support should be channelled and on the accounting of that support. The government of the Social Democrats used to give straightforward support and understood why receipts in a township perhaps had not been kept. The controls that normally any lender of money exercises were not set that strongly. But they controlled. However, as time went on the whole process became bureaucratized. They had to check how every Krona was used. At times this interfered with the political work, because it was in fact true that many of the activities were funded in a manner where there were no receipts. It just had to be based on trust.

The bottom line is that the struggle was ours, as ANC, but Sweden was very central in that struggle. They took it onto themselves much more than a normal government would do. Secondly, because its leadership at all levels spent time discussing the struggle with our leaders, the Tambos of this world, Sweden was in its own way able to influence them how they should handle things. In the minds of our leaders, Sweden helped to confirm that the basis of the struggle was to create democracy. The interaction between Sweden and ANC strengthened the democratic urge of the ANC leadership. Finally, Sweden played a significant role in terms of racism in South Africa, because by totally identifying with ANC and the struggle, it enabled ANC to say that 'not all whites are racists. We have this country which is lily white and it has supported us up to the hilt, so do not generalize and say that all whites are racists.' I think that it helped to mellow whatever racism we might have had. That is the argument we also used with the Slovos of this world. It is important that we had whites who were seen alongside us in the struggle, because today we are able to say that there is no need to take revenge.

Kay Moonsamy
ANC—Treasury Department—Treasurer General of the South African Congress of Trade Unions
Treasurer General of the South African Communist Party
(Johannesburg, 14 September 1995)

Tor Sellström: In exile, you were involved with humanitarian assistance from the Nordic countries for a long time. When did you leave South Africa?

Kay Moonsamy: I was in the Treason Trial of 1956, which ended in 1961. I left the country after a trial for participating in banned organizations which went on for several months. Finally, by decision of the movement I had to leave the country. I left, to be exact, on 29 June 1965. I went into exile in Bechuanaland, now Botswana. Those were what we refer to as 'the dark days'. It was two years after the Rivonia arrests in 1963 and the sentencing of our illustrious leader comrade Nelson Mandela and his colleagues in 1964. They were sentenced to life imprisonment and that was, I think, the darkest period in our history in so far as the leadership and the struggle was concerned. From 1962, the Sabotage Act, the Ninety Days Law, the Terrorism Act, in fact the most vicious, wicked and savage laws were passed to smash and destroy ANC, the Communist Party and the entire democratic movement in our country. But, of course, history has proved that the reactionary forces and the apartheid system failed to do that.

Well, my going into exile—like so many of the members of ANC and the party—led me to Bechuanaland. I remained there for more than three years. It was only after that that I was asked to proceed to Zambia. I used to get frantic calls from the late comrade Thomas Nkobi, who said that they needed someone to go to the ANC headquarters in Morogoro, Tanzania. The Treasurer General at that time was comrade Moses Kotane. When he fell ill, the position was taken over by comrade J.B. Marks and because of pressure of work and so on he wanted someone to assist him in his office. That is how I first made my way to Zambia in 1968. At that period we were preparing for the Morogoro Conference of 1969, so I went at a very interesting time. After a short while in Zambia, working with comrade TG (Thomas Nkobi), who was the ANC Chief Representative there, we proceeded to Tanzania. We all travelled with the Lusaka delegation. We travelled by road. The road from Zambia to Tanzania used to be called the hell-run. It took us about four or five days. We arrived on 25 April 1969, during the opening of the Morogoro Conference. We entered the hall as the late comrade O.R. Tambo was addressing the conference. That was the beginning of my stay in Tanzania, in Morogoro, working with comrade J.B. Marks.

TS: When you came to Tanzania did you have any previous contacts with the Nordic countries?

KM: No, I personally did not have any contacts. But I think that my contacts, at least with Sweden, should go back to 1972-73 by virtue of my position assisting comrade Thomas Nkobi and also in Tanzania comrade J.B. Marks. Comrade Marks passed away in 1972 and then comrade Thomas Nkobi became the Acting Treasurer General. I used to commute between Tanzania and Zambia, and I had my first dealings with SIDA in Lusaka. They began to give us aid, a very small amount at first. I know that comrade Treasurer General quite often used to refer to this. He always used to take us back to 1973, saying that there was something like 150,000 Swedish Kronor given to ANC by SIDA.

TS: That is correct. That was the first allocation.

KM: It was a very small one, but, nevertheless, it was the beginning of the massive all round aid that was given by the Swedish government, SIDA and the people of Sweden. And, of course, when you talk about Sweden you talk about the Nordic countries. But I think that one can say, without casting any reflection on any of the other countries, that Sweden played a pivotal role as far as aid was concerned, not only to our movement, but to the liberation movement as a whole. When you look at this in a broader context, the Nordic countries played a gigantic role.

TS: How did you view this when you got the first support from the Nordic countries? Did you then see it as genuine support or as support with a hidden agenda?

KM: No, none whatsoever. The support from the Nordic countries—especially from Sweden—was in our view support given to the people of South Africa who were struggling to overthrow the most savage system in modern history, that is, apartheid. The relationship was one of openness, one of fully appreciating our struggle, although it was both peaceful and non-peaceful. In fact, we started from the peaceful and went to the non-peaceful, because of the changed conditions in our country.

The Nordic countries have a history of fighting against racism and stood up in the United Nations and in other world and international fora condemning apartheid. Not merely condemning, but giving us full support. It was not only the governments—and now we are talking about Sweden—but the people of these countries themselves, the anti-apartheid groups, the Africa Groups, that gave us moral, political, diplomatic, financial and material support. I think that it has been proven that the support was one of commitment. In my relations with all those that I came into contact with, I always preferred the Nordic countries, because we worked so closely and their support was genuine, with no hidden agenda. The basis of their support was to liberate our country. The testimony is that from a mere 150,000 it ran into hundreds of millions of Swedish Kronor over the long period that we received support.

Not only in the field of humanitarian assistance. It went beyond that. The humanitarian assistance covered food, clothing, shelter, upkeep and the running of ANC offices throughout the world, but, much more, it also included a component which was simply called the Home Front. That is when one could say, yes, here is a country and a people who support our cause, because the millions that were given to the component called Home Front were given without any strings attached whatsoever. It was budgetary support. That is important, because those funds did a lot. It was under the heading humanitarian assistance, but the Home Front allocation was for underground activities, for organizers, meetings, publication of leaflets, pamphlets and so on. That is, to move the struggle forward.

TS: Was that unique to the SIDA assistance or did other Nordic countries also support Home Front activities?

KM: No, SIDA was the only one that had this Home Front item very clearly. The allocations from DANIDA, FINNIDA and NORAD were mainly for external support for projects in the settlements in Morogoro and Mazimbu. Unlike SIDA, which very distinctly had this Home Front component. Not that the others did not support the struggle of ANC that was taken inside the country, but the SIDA component was very clear. In fact, it was the first item on the agenda at the negotiations with SIDA, dealing with publications and activities in South Africa. But SIDA did much more than that. What about the various organizations inside the country? They used to make requests to ANC and some organizations used to make direct appeals to the Swedish government although some were afraid to ask because of the confidence that was built between our two organizations and peoples.

TS: The Swedish government did not want to end up in a situation where they were supporting activities inside that would go against the thrust of the support to ANC?

KM: That is right. SIDA was concerned about that and its concern was justified, because for SIDA ANC was the major liberation movement, without excluding others. It was an organization proven, first of all by its policy and programme of non-racialism and, secondly, of being in the forefront of the struggle.

TS: Within the Nordic countries there was often criticism of the governments by the solidarity movements. You had relations with both the broad base of the Nordic societies and with the governments. Did that constitute a problem for you?

KM: Well, as I stated earlier, we went from a peaceful form of struggle, non-violence, to the launching of the armed struggle in 1961 with the formation of Umkhonto we Sizwe. We entered a radically new era in the struggle. There were countries that did not see that clearly, but they softened and said: 'Well, we will give you humanitarian support.' That was their right.

In Sweden, the Africa Groups were very strong. But I do not think that there was anything that undermined our struggle and I cannot recall when the Nordic countries, especially SIDA, said: 'You cannot do this or you cannot do that!'

TS: There were no conditions attached to the aid?

KM: There was no condition whatsoever. Now, if you look at the Western world, especially the United Kingdom, Australia, Canada, France, West Germany and so on, the people took a different position to the governments. The people supported totally the stand of the people of South Africa to overthrow the apartheid system. They supported the armed struggle. They supported the Isolate South Africa Campaign, economic sanctions and so on. The people took an anti-apartheid position, but the governments of those countries took a different stand. After a period, they also had to change. We, therefore, make a distinction between the people of a country and the government. Even in Sweden, the Africa Groups were more radical on some of the issues and tried to push the government, saying 'please give more so that we can end the savage apartheid system'.

TS: Did you read Helmuth Kohl's speech to the South African parliament last Monday? He said that the German companies supported you even in the darkest days of the struggle by maintaining their businesses in South Africa, assisting discriminated population groups.

KM: Well, everybody knows that we were critical of the United Kingdom, the United States of America, France and the Federal Republic of Germany, because they were the sanction busters. The whole world knows that. Of course, when the situation was changing in our country—when we went towards negotiations and after the lifting of the ban on ANC—these countries saw the writing on the wall and began supporting, in the main, ANC and, generally, the struggle against apartheid and for the negotiation process. But one must be very clear and make a distinction between the government and the people of those countries.

TS: You mentioned the annual consultations between ANC and SIDA. Did you also have annual consultations with DANIDA, FINNIDA and NORAD?

KM: Yes, with all the Nordic countries, but the most intensive was with SIDA. I would say that the second was with NORAD, because of their involvement in Mazimbu. Also FINNIDA. We had annual consultations to look into our budgetary requirements and so on. But there was much more than the annual meetings. There used to be many meetings even before the annual consultations took place, to discuss new programmes, to review the progress that we were making, to see how they could assist us, increasing the support etc.

All this also bears testimony to ANC's commitment. In spite of our weaknesses—we are not saying that we are perfect—the Nordic countries and all those who were supporting us recognized the leadership of ANC, its ability to implement projects and to account to its donors. I think that it is very significant. I was in it and I know that from a mere 150,000 the support ran into hundreds of millions of Swedish Kronor. That in itself is an indication of the confidence that these countries had in our organization. I think that we carried out our obligations to the best of our ability, in spite of our weaknesses. We were an underground movement. We did not have many trained people. Our main aim was to train people and send them into the country. That was the important thing, because that was the key to liberation in the shortest possible time.

TS: The Nordic countries would in this respect treat ANC as a sovereign country. There would be the same procedures for annual consultations, budgetary follow-ups etc., as with, for example, Zambia, Zimbabwe or Angola. As the representative of the ANC Treasury, do you think that there were sufficient financial controls?

KM: Again, a clear indication of their confidence in ANC was to deal with us as a government.

Yes, we had reporting mechanisms, not only financial, but through quarterly statements and progress reports on what had been done in a particular field. I know that there were certain critical areas. When SIDA said: 'We are not very happy. Not that there has been embezzlement, but we need to know more', we went back to the various

ANC departments and held departmental meetings. We found cases where the department was slow in reporting or when it was not utilising the funds rapidly. I think that these things were dealt with very frankly. What is important is that there was an agreement which was very clear on what the two parties had to do, how the accounting was to be done, how the reporting was to be presented, the audited financial statements etc. And, again, it is significant that SIDA did not want any statement apart from a report as far as the item called Home Front was concerned. It shows the confidence which the Swedish government, SIDA and the people had in our movement.

TS: I think that it is important to record that people like Thomas Nkobi, Kay Moonsamy and Roland Axelsson, worked very closely and actually held the whole thing together. And that the officials in the Procurement Division at SIDA, Stockholm, which normally would be seen as a technical unit, were involved in the shipment of considerable amounts of food and humanitarian goods to Angola, for example.

KM: Indeed. It was a great tragedy when we lost our outstanding comrade Treasurer General, Thomas Nkobi, soon after the birth of the new South Africa. Our relationship was based on a very genuine friendship and commitment. He always used to refer to the Nordic countries, especially to our colleagues in SIDA, and the manner in which they used to approach our problems with a view of always finding a solution to assist and not to create difficulties for us. I think that it was very important. I have very fond, and I would say revolutionary, memories of my association with all the SIDA representatives, right from the Director General, Carl Tham, to Roland Axelsson, Jan Cedergren, Johan Brisman, Anders Möllander, Lena Johansson, Birgitta Sevefjord, Ingalill Colbro and many others.

Although the Nordic countries geographically are not Frontline States like Zambia, Tanzania and Zimbabwe, politically, diplomatically, morally and in giving us financial and material assistance they were right in the frontline. We really cherish this long friendship. With the new South Africa, I think that the relationship is quite different. There will be a state-to-state relationship. There will be relations between different organizations and we look forward to closer cooperation in all fields, economically, culturally, in the sports field, in every way, so that the countries come closer. We have entered a special period after 340 years of colonial rule and 45 years of the worst form of apartheid to transform our country. And we can say that we look with confidence to the future. The transition process is taking place and with the support of the international community we will be able to transform our country into a strong, viable, democratic, united, non-racial and non-sexist South Africa.

TS: The Swedish government supported SACTU within the SIDA allocation to ANC. Did other Nordic countries support SACTU in a similar fashion?

KM: No, not as far as I can recall. It was only SIDA that found a formula to assist.

TS: But at one stage it was said from the Swedish side that SACTU was a trade union organization and therefore could not receive official support under the ANC umbrella. SACTU should seek contacts directly with the Swedish LO/TCO.

KM: Yes. Again we have to thank SIDA and the many officials who tried to set up meetings with LO/TCO. We did succeed and we had more than one meeting. I participated in the meetings and we even drew up an agreement of intent. Let us be very clear: They were very supportive of ANC, SACTU and the struggle against apartheid, but their problem was that SACTU was an affiliate of WFTU, that is, the World Federation of Trade Unions. They were members of ICFTU and therefore felt that they were not in a position to assist. That did not in any way sour our relationship, because through their own channels they gave support to ANC in the struggle. I think that it was important. But, unfortunately, we could not cement this in a more tangible way.

TS: Later, LO/TCO channelled a lot of support to COSATU and to the unions inside the country.

KM: Yes, that is true. During the struggle against apartheid I recall that we started discussions on how the new South Africa would relate to our genuine friends who supported us in the very critical period. We used to assure our colleagues in the Nordic countries that the new South Africa under ANC would have the closest relationship with them, in the diplomatic field, in the cultural field, in the sports field, in the economic field and so on. I think that it is very vital for us and that it is important because of the past. The new South Africa needs to have this very active interrelationship to build a strong, better and prosperous nation.

The Nordic countries were our staunch and committed supporters, while some of the big Western powers were obstructing our struggle. Of course, they have now changed. ANC would like to have the closest all round relationship with every country, but we have our principles. Sometimes expedience gives way to principle, but we have to be the torchbearers of democracy, freedom and equality, because such an approach will ensure that we build a better South Africa.

We want this relationship. I thought that I should say this. I think very strongly on this question. There are some, for instance in the Western countries, who think that they were in the forefront. I want to say very emphatically that they were not. On the contrary, they were obstructing our struggle. The countries who were in the forefront were the Nordic countries and Africa, in spite of all her problems. Of course, apartheid was responsible for them. I think that it is important to state that SIDA also used to assist the Southern African countries. If it were not for the Frontline States, our struggle would probably have taken a little longer. In spite of their economic problems, they gave us much more than shelter. For that we are most grateful, just as we are very grateful to the Nordic countries and to all those who supported the struggle against apartheid.

James Motlatsi
National Union of Mineworkers—ANC
President of the National Union of Mineworkers
(Johannesburg, 25 April 1996)

Tor Sellström: When did you first come into contact with the Nordic countries?

James Motlatsi: My first contact with the Nordic countries was in August 1983. I and Cyril Ramaphosa flew to Harare, Zimbabwe, where we met Stig Blomqvist from Sweden, who was a regional educator for the Miners International Federation (MIF). We had a meeting overnight and he contacted Anders Stendalen of the Swedish Mineworkers Union by telephone the very same day. In the morning he told us that there was a possibility of getting financial assistance from Sweden and that we should draw up project proposals. We then worked on three projects, namely a health and safety project, an education project and a legal project, and left them with Stig Blomqvist.

In 1984 I attended the Miners International Federation conference, which was held in Luxembourg. There I had a discussion with Jan-Erik Norling, who was working for the Swedish LO/TCO. We continued our discussion about how best they could assist us. Immediately after that they approved financial assistance for the three projects. They also said that they would try to approach other Nordic countries, namely Norway and Denmark. Finland did not really play a role. The countries which played a role were three: Sweden, Norway and Denmark. They assisted us. Later, they were joined by the Netherlands on those three projects.

TS: What did the education project consist of?

JM: We developed what we called the E-plan, the education plan, drew up education material for study circles and took it to quite a number of shop stewards.

The E-plan worked like this: We took it to the union leaders and the leaders identified the activists. Then we took it to the activists. After educating the activists, they went to the hostels, where they ran courses in the rooms when the workers had the time. It was an informal education. We realised that unless we moved in that direction we would not be able to educate the masses. Blacks were not allowed to be organized under a trade union and precisely because most of the mine workers were illiterate it was not as easy as one could have thought. But through this assistance and the plans of mass education we succeeded in recruiting thousands and thousands of miners between 1982 and the 1987 national strike.

The other projects helped us as well. For instance, in 1983 we had the Hlobane disaster, where we were assisted by Sweden. They did not only give us some money, but via MIF they also made it possible for international experts to come to South Africa to argue our case. That in itself assisted the mobilization, because the workers could now see and realize that MIF was an organization which was protecting our interests, not only when we were still alive, but even when there was an accident. We also had the Kinross disaster in 1986 and again Sweden and the Nordic countries played an important role, not only through financial assistance, but also by identifying the experts who could come to South Africa, paid by the Miners International Federation.

We are organizing a volatile industry, but if one looks at the strike of 1987, we managed to command more than 300,000 workers for 21 days without really having a conflict amongst them due to the education and the assistance from the Nordic countries. And the assistance has continued. After the general elections in 1994, quite a number of non-governmental organizations ceased to get financial assistance from overseas, but we managed to discuss with Sweden and have a down-scaling of the assistance, rather than drop it in one go. At the same time, I think that we as an organization used the money for the purposes it was donated. Even today, LO/TCO send their own auditors to us and I am proud to tell you that they have left South Africa happy with the manner in which we have used the donors' money. I am willing to allow any auditor from any organization and from any country to come and audit our books.

TS: I guess that you received support from Sweden and the other Nordic countries through various sources?

JM: I know that the money we received from LO/TCO was coming from SIDA, but we have also had a good relationship with the Swedish miners. We were not treated like friends, but like brothers. Our relationship with the Swedish miners went beyond a normal friendship. For example, sometimes when we had problems here there used to be a telephone call between either myself or Cyril with Anders Stendalen or Jan-Erik Norling, saying: 'Look, this is the problem we are having. Is it possible for you to organise X amount of money?' Then that amount of money would reach us within two or three months. That is why I am saying that our relationship really went beyond friendship and up to brotherhood.

TS: Did you personally visit Sweden?

JM: Yes, from 1985 I think that I visited every year, maybe once or twice or sometimes even three times.

TS: Also Norway and Denmark?

JM: I think that I have been in Norway once and in Denmark about four times.

TS: When you started around 1983 the world was still very divided between East and West. How did you view the Nordic countries in this context?

JM: Well, before that time one was not really exposed to the international community, except through the media. When we went there for the first time, it was strange to me. It took time to understand the position of the Nordic countries between the East and the West. I was unable to find out exactly where they were standing. ANC was getting quite a lot of material support from the East, but it was also getting quite a lot of financial assistance from the Nordic countries. Lindiwe Mabuza, now ambassador of South Africa to Germany, used to be the ANC representative in Sweden. Always when we were there, she would entertain us and we would have quite a number of discussions about the assistance they were getting from Sweden.

If you look at the labour movement, I think that quite a number of COSATU affiliates were getting very little assistance from the West. The Western country which really tried to assist us—although not as much as one would have thought—was Germany, through the Miners International Federation. As NUM we did not receive anything but token assistance from Britain. Immediately after the formation of NUM, I thought that Britain would assist us. Why I thought of Britain I cannot tell. Maybe it was because of its historical colonial links with the

African states. But when I was in Britain in 1984, trying to mobilize assistance, I spent 16 days there and I came back with a negative answer. From the United States we really did get some assistance, but not very much. Canada assisted us as well, but more or less in the same way as the United States.

The countries where we really received the bulk of our assistance were the Nordic countries. Second were Germany and the Netherlands and third Canada and the United States. From all other countries it was just token assistance. But during the strike of 1987 we received money from almost all corners. I must be honest there. We were assisted from individuals, up to organizations. I still recall that after the strike we visited Denmark and one of the newspapers there, *Politiken*, raised money for us. I think that we received about one quarter or half a million Rands. What was amazing was that even cripples donated money to assist us and within two or three days the newspaper managed to collect that amount.

TS: The question of SACTU and its international affiliation had always been a controversial issue in connection with Swedish or Nordic assistance to the South African trade union movement. Was it also a problem for you?

JM: Well, it was not a problem in the beginning, but in 1987, before the strike, we visited Sweden and during that visit we were on a tour with Sven Fockstedt from TCO. He wanted to make it an issue, asking about our thinking of SACTU and what our association with SACTU was. This was because SACTU was affiliated to WFTU. We said that we could not dictate terms to SACTU, that we had a relationship with SACTU and that we believed that SACTU was a legitimate federation which was forced underground because of political oppression. He was so arrogant about SACTU and in such a manner that he and Cyril had hot debates and arguments. He wanted us to distance ourselves from SACTU, but we said that 'we cannot do that. If you give SACTU financial assistance that is up to you. We are not going to dictate the terms, but we would appreciate your support. If you are going to stop it, it is also up to you. But we would be disappointed.'

Other trade unionists accepted that. I do not recall one day when SACTU became an issue in our meetings with Jan-Erik Norling from LO/TCO or Stig Blomqvist from MIF. Jan-Erik Norling is the man who really played an important role. I was told by other sources that one of the reasons why he ultimately had to leave LO/TCO was that he decided to defy them and allocate more money to us. We felt sorry for him and invited him to our congress. Stig Blomqvist, as well, was really a driving force. Stig is my personal friend. I cannot go to Sweden without seeing him.

TS: Apart from this discussion on SACTU, did you experience that there were any political conditions attached to the support that you received from Sweden or the other Nordic countries?

JM: No, no. We did not really encounter any political conditions whatsoever.

However, they were very clear that we should not use the money for purposes that we had not requested it for. In 1988, we were desperate. We did not have any money. We had an overdraft on our general account and had to transfer money from the projects to cover that overdraft, the idea being that when we had the money we would pay it back. It created a problem, however. We had a meeting in Denmark where they said that they could not understand why we should transfer money between the accounts. We explained that we had an overdraft. It was after the general strike and the management was penalizing us. They would send cheques late, sometimes after three months. As we were not protected by law we could not do anything whatsoever.

TS: But that was a problem of accounting. It had nothing to do with political conditions?

JM: Yes. We did not experience any political conditions.

TS: Did your members know that they got support from the Nordic trade union movement?

JM: Yes, when Stig Blomqvist managed to get a visa to South Africa in 1986 or 1987 he addressed a meeting at Western Deep Levels which about 15 000 workers attended. We explained that 'this is Stig who is assisting us with money' and so forth. Do you know what they said to him? They said: 'Thank you very much for what you have done for

us, but we do not want money, we want guns!'
TS: Did they see him as a representative of Sweden or of MIF? Did they know that he was Swedish?
JM: Yes they knew. We were affiliated to MIF, but we wanted to make sure that our members knew that we were getting money from Sweden. We introduced Stig Blomqvist to quite a number of branches and said: 'Stig is a representative of the Miners International Federation. However, he is Swedish. He comes from Sweden, from where we are getting our financial assistance.'
TS: I understand that you and Cyril Ramaphosa also were instrumental in designing projects for the Namibian miners?
JM: Yes, when we started to organize the miners we also went to Namibia. When Ben Ulenga was released from prison and they started to organize themselves, we assisted them. We then talked to Stig and said: 'Here is another country, Namibia. Can you visit it?' That is how we facilitated the meeting between Ben Ulenga and Stig Blomqvist.
TS: How would you assess the importance of the Nordic assistance to the struggle for national liberation in South Africa?
JM: The importance of the assistance that we received from the Nordic countries for national liberation lies in the fact that we succeeded in mobilizing the rank and file through education and that we were able to sustain quite a number of painful strikes, sit-ins and dismissals without demoralizing those who were still working. That was very important. It was also very important in that we were able to interact with the entire world. Our network of communications went beyond our boundaries, because through the education assistance we were able to extend friendship with sister unions all over the world. That also made a proper communication possible between the liberation movement, namely ANC, and the mass democratic movement inside the country. It made it possible to have public and underground meetings, so I would say that the Nordic countries played an important role. Indeed, we are where we are today because of the role that they played.

Even today we are able to sustain growth because of them. The labour movement in Mozambique, Zimbabwe or Namibia is weak. But we have learned that it is important to keep labour autonomous from the political party. Rather than going the way which Namibia went when NUNW affiliated to SWAPO, we took another approach. We opted for an alliance with ANC, an alliance in which we will remain autonomous and which will be reviewed time and again.

We are an independent and autonomous organization. We take independent decisions. For instance, this morning the Assistant General Secretary of COSATU was questioned by the Gauteng Premier about our decision to call a general strike on 30 April 1996. He said that COSATU should suspend its action, but the Assistant General Secretary said: 'Nonsense! Who do you think you are to tell us to suspend? It is only the National Executive Committee of COSATU which can take that decision.' We are not married to the party. No ways! We are keeping our autonomy and that in itself is very important, not only for today, but even for the future of the labour movement in this country.

Sankie Mthembi-Mahanyele (aka 'Rebecca Matlou')
ANC—Administrative officer at the ANC mission to Sweden and the Nordic countries—Deputy Secretary of International Affairs
Minister of Housing
(Cape Town, 7 September 1995)

Tor Sellström: In your experience, how would you describe the relationship between ANC and the Nordic countries?
Sankie M. Mahanyele: The experience of contact with the Nordic countries was very fulfilling for a member of the liberation movement, especially for those of us who had direct contacts, either with the governments or the solidarity groups. I did a lot of work on culture and women's issues when I was

still in Lusaka, trying to establish what support we could get from the Nordic countries. We had clothes collected for cadres in the residences of ANC all across Africa. Some of the clothes also went to the soldiers in the camps. We were maintained in that way.

I was fortunate to go to Sweden for a year and a half, although it was for health reasons. I was able to work in the ANC office, so I could actually go and see the places and the people who were collecting clothes for us, Bread and Fishes, for example. I was in contact with *Rädda Barnen* (Save the Children) as well. Their responsibility was to take care of the children's needs with clothes. On the medical and nutrition levels, I remember that a course was put together which was tailored for those who were going to take care of our children. The Swedes were involved in that through the UN structures in Zambia and Tanzania. It was an introduction on how to take care of an infant when you do not have all the resources. I know, because immediately after that I benefited from the same experience when my daughter was born with lots of allergies. I had to get the knowledge from people who had gone through that course.

This was very important, because within ANC women were expected to play an equal role to men as members of the liberation movement. You were not to be discriminated against because you were a mother. We were expected to participate fully and have an input towards the liberation of our people. We needed child care facilities to be able to keep our children while we were at work. Otherwise most of us would never have had the opportunity of going to school, taking part in the process of running ANC offices or being part of the military structures. You would have had to look for somebody to take care of the child. But we had established support institutions to take care of that aspect. It was very important. At times it also assisted us to cater for casualties, such as unplanned pregnancies, where a young mother still wanted to pursue her schooling. There would be a centre where the children were taken care of, like Mazimbu, and maybe a family would take responsibility as godparents for that individual child.

It was an atmosphere where we encouraged continuity of progress and ambition. It was very important and we are appreciative of that experience. We also did a lot of work around women's programmes. I was in the ANC women's section for many years, on the executive and in the council of the Women's League. We did a lot of work with Nordic NGOs, like teaching women skills in Tanzania.

TS: Was this through the Africa Groups?
SM-M: Yes.
TS: And through the women's branches of some Swedish political parties?
SM-M: Yes. It was a whole effort by the Swedish society, from the different occupational groups. If it was women, you would get that from the women's desk at SIDA. If it was youth, from the youth section, and so forth. We received a lot of support, financial and non-financial, and that enabled us to push on with the struggle. I was editor of the ANC women's journal, *Voice of Women*, for some time and I remember that our publication was funded at some stage by SIDA. It enabled us to produce and distribute the bulletin, both internationally and internally through our underground structures. That was supported by SIDA. Through this support, we were also able to be part of the cultural world. For example, through SIDA we produced what was called *Malibongwe— Poetry is Their Weapon*, which was a collection of anthologies from women who had the talent for writing. I remember Lindiwe Mabuza and myself collecting the writings from our comrades in the camps and from all over the world where we knew that some of our people were writers. That was very important at the time, because we felt that all aspects of life that are part and parcel of a social being and activity should be encouraged.

When you are a member of a liberation movement you do not stop being an individual, a person, or part of a community or society. All these aspects had to be encouraged, so that at the end of the day you would emerge as a person with feelings, a person who respects human rights and confirms human dignity.

We felt for those who were artists and as encouragement we produced *Malibongwe— Poetry is Their Weapon*. Just after I left Sweden, we also collected short stories from our women to enter a continental competition organized by SIDA women's section for female fiction writers in Africa. I was happy to read the manuscripts of those who entered the competition. I sent in two stories and was lucky to be nominated and honoured with a prize.

TS: And Baleka Kgotsisile?

SM-M: Yes, she also participated. I am happy to say that the final copy of the collection adopted the title of my story, *One Never Knows*. It was an inspiration. The second part of the collected stories appeared in an anthology called *Whispering Land*, a very enriching collection, where women give their opinion and thinking about different social issues in life. That we also produced with SIDA.

While I was in the ANC office in Stockholm, I was asked to coordinate the *Amandla* visits. *Amandla* was the ANC cultural group, which was part of our cultural package: we were engaged in poetry, in fiction and graphic art itself. We also had a music and dance group, the *Amandla Cultural Ensemble*. When I was there, I coordinated their tour of the Scandinavian countries together with the ANC Chief Representative at that time, Lindiwe Mabuza, who is now our ambassador to Germany. It was amazing how the crowds came out to really, practically, support our struggle. Also to be exposed to the kind of solidarity and emotion that was expressed through the support of the musical ensemble. It was a very exciting time!

TS: Did you visit all the Nordic countries?

SM-M: Yes, I did.

TS: Would you say that the involvement of the Nordic societies in arts and culture constituted some sort of cement when it came to the political stand on Southern Africa. Did arts and culture involve the Nordic societies more closely for your cause?

SM-M: It did play a very important role. The *Amandla* ensemble also generated funds for ANC. In addition, it informed the people of the Scandinavian countries of the kind of culture we practise in South Africa. If you listen to their records, you will find that they sing about lost friends, loved ones, the struggle in South Africa and about solidarity. It covered a whole range of themes. It was also very important to show the people who were supporting us that we were there to promote all aspects of our life, not just the military, armed struggle, as some people wanted to believe. At that time, anybody who was a member of the liberation movement was referred to as a terrorist or a soldier. But not everybody was a soldier. Being a soldier is a specialized, professional form of training and experience. We needed to expose people to the different activities that we were engaged in as members of the liberation movement.

Those in the Scandinavian countries who were inclined to the arts felt that here was something that they could associate with and contribute to directly. Something that they understood. It opened a whole world of communication and contacts between the Scandinavian countries and ANC and both parties held and maintained that relationship and partnership jealously. But that was not all. Around this cultural activity we also hosted graphic artists and photography artists against apartheid at the cultural institute close to our old office in Stockholm. We could therefore present a comprehensive picture of our culture in South Africa. We also managed to bring in Ndebele art, for example, and some artists that we could invite from South Africa at the time. It was very exciting and fulfilling.

We saw the solidarity movement as a force which encouraged and motivated the government to do more. The role played by the government and that played by the NGOs could not be disputed. Governments have limitations. They are members of international bodies like the UN and bound by resolutions of those bodies. They function within certain limitations. But where they could not assist us, the solidarity movement could. The governments did not stop them, because they believed in what was being done for the liberation of our people. It was a commitment which was appreciated and commended by our people.

TS: The very first government supported project by Sweden in South Africa was the arts' workshop at Rorke's Drift in Natal at the beginning of the 1960s. Culture in a broader sense, performing arts, poetry and writing, goes like a common theme through the Nordic countries' involvement with Southern Africa?

SM-M: True. Also, the majority of the projects in our settlements in Tanzania were funded by the Scandinavian countries. Through them, we had a piggery, a tanning factory—where people could make belts and shoes—a carpentry section, farming and so on. Throughout the years, our people were kept active by these projects, learning skills and moral values. If you instil a sense of labour and responsibility in a people, you also have possibilities of instilling moral and value standards.

These projects kept our people engaged and occupied. Many wondered how ANC in exile could be so stable and not have major crises around its membership. It is because, day in and day out, our people were occupied. Nobody was allowed to go idle. If you were not at school, you were running a project. If you were not running a project, you were studying. You were at school or in the offices. The Scandinavian countries helped us to deal with the nagging presence of time. The whole period of some twenty years in exile went past without one feeling burdened by it, because it was a period of action, where you always had something to do. You were not left hopeless and nostalgic by exile. We were helped to concretize our hope and were given strength to do what we believed in. You never had to sit and look at the problematic aspects of exile. There were, actually, productive, positive issues that you could immediately relate to. The armed struggle progressed well, although of course, with expected hiccups here and there. You did not have to be perpetually subjected to depressed feelings of disappointment because people you knew had moved into the country and had been killed or arrested. The support maintained a balance in our lives which was a very important factor. Exile is not easy. Some of the people in exile who were not part of the revolutionary stream had nothing to sustain them. Exile does tend to eat the spirit inside and challenge your mental stability. But for us in ANC, there was a basis to keep us stable. The future, the hope for freedom sustained us. Our vision was kept alive.

The Scandinavian countries were very consistent, which is something that has to be commended. There is no point in getting assistance for a year or two and then it stops. Without continuity you cannot plan, but because we had friends in the Nordic countries we could plan ahead and they could contribute within their respective capacity. For example, all students in the Nordic countries were asked one day a year to go out and collect money, pens and paper for our students at the Solomon Mahlangu Freedom College in Tanzania. That was Operation Day's Work. Through that contact with our children who were in exile all over Africa, there developed a pen-pal relationship. They made friends who could write to them, send them cards and so on. The mental stability, growth and all that goes with this was critical in our environment. Everybody was encouraged to do something. I also remember very well that some of the teachers at our school were expatriates from the Scandinavian countries and Holland.

TS: You participated in a tour with the late President Oliver Tambo, Thabo Mbeki and Thomas Nkobi to the Nordic countries in 1980. Did you notice any differences between the governments in the Nordic countries?

SM-M: The Social Democratic governments were dominating at that time. Of course, the position on South Africa depended on who was in the driving seat at a particular time. I remember very well when we went to Denmark during that trip. We tried to convince the Ministry of Foreign Affairs that they should observe the economic boycott against South Africa and stop their importation of South African coal. But they said: 'We need South African coal, because it is very special for our industry'. We tried to argue that 'it won't be for long. If you stop the importation of coal, the South African regime is going to feel the pressure, and when they feel the pressure you will be shortening the time frame in terms of getting them to the negotiating table'. They did not understand us, but we appreciated the little bit that they could do, because at that time it was tough for the liberation movement. We had to try to convince and influence people to support the boycott. But now and then there were countries—through the private sector or some elements in government—busting the sanctions. We continuously had to lobby and mobilize the forces for democracy.

I think that we did very well, especially in the Scandinavian countries. At the end of the day, the larger part of our support against apartheid came from that region. It was followed by some countries outside the Nordic region, especially anti-apartheid groups in Europe and the Americas. They were very strong in those countries where the governments did not understand our point of view. Through the anti-apartheid movements, the people supported us. There was that kind of balance. But in the Scandinavian countries we had the support of both the governments and the society. This actually gave us strength and confidence.

TS: Do you feel that the Nordic support was given with political conditions, or was it without strings attached?

SM-M: There were no political conditions. But when it comes to accounting, there was a special requirement. They could not give us money for the armed struggle. They would give us money for social needs and we would have to find the means to deal with the other aspects of our struggle, in this case armed struggle.

TS: In your dialogue with the Nordic governments, did they comment on the fact that you received support for the armed struggle from the socialist countries?

SM-M: The issue would be discussed now and then. I remember one of the meetings where I was present The argument by Sweden was that they were neutral during the World War. They would like to abide by that principle and not support the armed struggle. We made sure that they supported other needs of the liberation movement. We were fortunate that the Eastern countries understood both the political and the military aspect of our struggle and beefed us up in terms of the armed struggle. We managed to do as much as we did because they were there for us. At that time, they were very stable and we enjoyed their support immensely.

TS: Did you never have the impression that the Nordic countries made it a condition that you should side with the Western world?

SM-M: No, we did not feel that. They never put those kinds of pressures on us. Not at all. It was discussed very openly. They maintained their position and they did whatever they could at the humanitarian level. They never tried to say that 'we think that you should follow this or the other camp'. The warm camp or the cold camp. They did not do that. They just said: 'We are going to support the liberation of the people of South Africa. We believe that they are fighting a just cause. We are against apartheid and any form of injustice and we are going to support them.' That is, for example, the reason why some of our students were accepted for studies. We have many people who qualified in the Scandinavian countries.

TS: Norway and Denmark were members of NATO. How did you look upon that?

SM-M: On the question of South Africa they formed part of the Scandinavian bloc. They believed in us and we really appreciated that. After the unbanning of ANC, we were also lucky to receive some diplomatic training in Norway. A group of us went there to be exposed to foreign affairs' issues, because at that time we were running ANC missions all over the world. We were taken for a special course, funded by the Nordic countries, but led by the Norwegian government. It was in 1992 or 1993, just before I came back.

We were now operating at a different level, because we were getting into things like Norwegian trade, foreign policy options of Norway, NATO and the future vision of Norway towards the European continent. We were engaging at a different level. We were dealing with policy issues. It was not just humanitarian assistance, but a package of how to move forward, getting exposure to how governments work and run their business. We had done a similar course at the European Union, but there was something specific that we received from Norway, namely aspects of communication. It was because of our close friendship with that country.

Indres Naidoo
ANC—Umkhonto we Sizwe—South African Communist Party
ANC Senator
(Cape Town, 7 December 1995)

Tor Sellström: Did you have any contacts with the Nordic countries before the formation of Umkhonto we Sizwe?

Indres Naidoo: No. Before that our contacts with foreign countries were minimal. We were involved in the struggle in South Africa. I come from a family that has been actively involved in the struggle from the latter part of the last century. My grandfather went to prison fourteen times. My grandmother gave birth in prison and my father was a very active person. He had contacts with the Scandinavian countries, particularly during and after the Second World War. Exactly what nature of contact it was, I am in no position to say. My mother had been an activist all her life. She died two years ago. My brothers and sisters, all of us, were active as youth leaders in the 1950s and the 1960s.

At the time when Umkhonto we Sizwe (MK) was formed, there was a lot of uncertainty about what was happening. However, one thing was quite clear to all of us, namely that becoming a member of Umkhonto meant tremendous risks. It meant that you could be arrested. Up to that time, we always believed that we were two or three steps ahead of the security branch and the police. We underestimated them. We felt that they would never be able to catch us. We had heard that a group of South African police had been sent to France for training, but we never took this matter very seriously. Little did we realize that they were going to France to train as a specialized force in torture methods and how to extract information. Little did we realize that on their return to South Africa they would form the Anti-sabotage Group, headed by the infamous Swanepoel himself.

When we were forming our MK group we discussed the possibilities of running away from the police in case we were being looked for. One of the things we always said was that we must choose countries that were friendly towards us. Here, of course, the Scandinavian countries were on top of the list. They were countries where we possibly could go to the embassies and ask for asylum. But I must tell you that it was merely talk. There was nothing concrete about it. This was the position of Umkhonto we Sizwe in the beginning.

TS: You were then arrested and sent to Robben Island?

IN: Yes, in 1963. We were four in our unit. However, the Regional Command of MK instructed us to drop one of the four and get another person into the unit, who we understood as being quite an expert in the use of explosives and that had access to dynamite. He should be quite useful to us. However, he turned out to be a police agent. Little did we realize that he was working directly with the police, who for that matter gave him a whole case of dynamite. A hundred sticks, which he sold to us. On that particular campaign we used four sticks, leaving the remaining 96 in the box. We were arrested on the scene of our act in April 1963. He was with us, but when we were arrested he had disappeared. The police denied any knowledge of him. He was never brought to court. They claimed that there was no such person and that the three of us were solely responsible. The fact that they did not bring him to bear witness against us weakened the case quite a bit. If he had come, we would have got a much heavier sentence than we did.

TS: But you got a heavy enough sentence, ten years?

IN: Yes, we got ten years in spite of that. You must bear in mind that we were among the very first Umkhonto cadres to be arrested. The judge wanted to set an example to other Umkhonto people through a heavy sentence. In the process of being arrested I was shot. In fact, I have the distinction of being the first Umkhonto person to be shot by the enemy.

We ended up on Robben Island. We spent the next ten years on that awful island, being tortured under very difficult conditions. We had to try to bring about changes. The Scandinavian countries played a great role in our campaigns. We would hear about it from our comrades who were arrested in Zimbabwe, trying to infiltrate the country.

TS: Was that the Luthuli detachment?

IN: That is right, the Luthuli detachment in particular. They would tell us of the support that we were receiving from the socialist countries, particularly the Soviet Union and East Germany, and from the West. We would hear of the support that we were getting from the Scandinavian countries. That was very encouraging.

I personally believe that there were a number of factors that kept us going for the ten years. The first was the unity that we as ANC people had on the Island. We came from different walks of life. I came from the Transvaal Indian Youth Congress and the South African Indian Congress. We had people from the Coloured Peoples' Organisation, from the African National Congress Youth League, from SACTU—the South African Congress of Trade Unions—and people who were arrested and charged for being members of the South African Communist Party. In spite of all this, we were united. When we arrived on the Island, we were only 35 ANC people. When I say ANC, I include the whole lot from the Congress Alliance, including the Communist Party. PAC numbered over a thousand.

Before coming to the Island—in transit between Johannesburg and Cape Town—we spent six months in Leeukop Prison. It was quite obvious that they did not know what to do with us. We were the first non-Africans and they were not too sure whether to dump us on the Island with the rest, or what. So they kept us at Leeukop Prison on the outskirts of Johannesburg. Not far from the famous Rivonia. In fact, during the Rivonia raid a black warder came up to us in Leeukop Prison and said: 'A number of your comrades have been arrested not far from here, in Rivonia, and among them are Walter Sisulu and Nelson Mandela.' Of course, we could not understand this. What nonsense was he talking? Mandela had already been sentenced. He was supposed to be on the Island, serving five years imprisonment and now they said that he had been arrested in Rivonia. Subsequently we learned that it was true. Mandela had been brought from the Island and tried as well.

During the opening of the trial in Pretoria we were still at Leeukop Prison. This was the period when many poor people from the Pretoria area and from the Eastern and the Western Cape started to flood the Island. But when we got to the Island we found a situation where the PAC prisoners were very hostile towards us. Very hostile.

The Prison Department was cruel, barbaric, to all of us. In particular to the three young Indians. They would look for us and ask: *Waar's die koelies?* (Where are the coolies?) and pick on us. Being dark in complexion and having no hair whatsoever—it was completely shaved off—I was a bit difficult to recognize. But the comrade who was lighter in complexion and wore glasses was clearly identified and picked on every time, beaten to a pulp. But as a result of the opposition to the cruelty of the warders and because of PAC's attitude towards us—a total non-collaboration attitude: we were nobody; they had nothing to do with us; they would serve their sentences as PAC and not collaborate with us—the 35 of us became united as one. Our comrades were very good. If we smuggled one cigarette, we would all share it. Whenever we were able to smuggle tobacco to the Island we would share it. With PAC it did not happen. We developed a comradeship which stuck to the very end.

By 1965, the situation had changed completely. ANC now numbered almost a thousand while PAC had been reduced to about 500 or so. But we maintained that comradely spirit of always sharing whatever we had. All that you were able to buy was toothpaste, a toothbrush and soap. Nothing else. The few who had money would buy the toothpaste and soap and we would share it amongst all of us. There was that united effort. Of course, we very often tried to bring PAC into our campaigns for better conditions. One of the first things that we did was to refuse to use the word *baas*. We felt that the warders were demanding the word just to belittle us and therefore we were not prepared to use it. But the PAC prisoners were divided on the issue. Many of the militant PAC chaps would refuse to use the word *baas*, but there were others who did. Their attitude was that they had come to jail to serve, suffer and sacrifice. Not to make conditions easy.

Another thing that we campaigned against right from the beginning was the *tausa*. *Tausa* was when a prisoner must strip stark naked. He must then jump into the air as high as possible, and while in the air he must make a complete 180 degree turn, open his mouth, click his mouth and spread his legs and arms wide. All in the air. The purpose behind the whole thing was that if the prisoner had any article concealed in his body it would drop out. When you landed, you were supposed to completely bow to the warder, so that he could see everything. We found it humiliating, degrading and refused to *tausa*. ANC immediately went on a campaign against it. It was not organized. It was just a natural campaign. We tried to bring PAC in, but we failed miserably. When our numbers increased, we decided to act on our own and go into campaigns. The very first hunger strike on Robben Island was started by ANC. PAC were left standing. About fifteen PAC people, among them some of the top leaders, refused to participate in the strike, saying that it was a Communist plot. Anything that they could not explain was a Communist plot. This was a Communist plot to mislead the PAC freedom fighters and the fourteen or fifteen of them refused to take part. Others, of course, followed naturally and the strike went on for five days. It was quite successful.

It is very strange that everything that PAC found unacceptable was called a Communist plot. For example, they maintained that the Freedom Charter was drafted in Moscow and presented to ANC in South Africa and that it was a Communist document. This was said in lectures given by PAC people on the Island.

Unity was something very good to us. Of course, in the mid-1960s we were joined by comrades in exile. They found this society of ours and fell right into it. They would also tell us what was happening outside the Island.

TS: Do you know if any Nordic country through its diplomatic representation in Cape Town visited the Island or in other ways tried to look into the conditions there?
IN: No, not that I know.
TS: The only visits you had in those days were from the International Red Cross?
IN: That is right.

TS: Quarterly visits or something like that?
IN: It was half-yearly! Later they became quarterly and then even more frequent. We had a few other visits. One by Helen Suzman. We also had visits from some cabinet ministers and a visit by an Australian right-wing journalist. But I cannot recall that there ever was a visit from the Scandinavian countries.
TS: In his biography, Nelson Mandela mentions that he had visits by an International Red Cross representative who was Swedish and who was not very sympathetic at all.
IN: I would not know that. But talking about visits from the Nordic countries, I must tell you one little story before I go any further. In 1960, there was a very attractive Swedish journalist who came to Johannesburg to report on the Treason Trial. Her name was Sara Lidman. We used to meet her quite often. She was very attractive. I think that she was reporting for a left-wing newspaper in Sweden. She was arrested in Johannesburg under the Immorality Act with one of the treason accused by the name of Peter Nthite. What happened was that Peter went to her flat in Hillbrow, Johannesburg, where they were sitting talking about the trial. The immorality squad burst into the place and arrested them. Immediately, the Swedish government protested and demanded their release. They released her and put her onto the next plane back to Sweden. Of course, now they could not charge Peter. However, they wanted to. He was an ANC Youth League leader and a treason accused. It would have been big publicity for them if he had been arrested under the Immorality Act.
TS: Was he African?
IN: He was African. A married man with children, arrested under the so-called Immorality Act! Now that she had been put on a plane and flown out they could not charge him. They had to have the co-accused to charge him. They had to acquit him.
TS: She is a very famous author. When she came back to Sweden she was instrumental in the development of the solidarity movement with South and Southern Africa.
IN: The reason why I have given you an outline of the prison conditions and how we fought them is to show you one of the reasons why they started improving. But this was not the only reason. The second impor-

tant reason was the constant struggle that the people in the country put up on our behalf. Our people demanded that we should be unconditionally released and that we be recognized as political prisoners. That we should be given treatment as political prisoners. This campaign was very strong throughout the country, in Johannesburg, Durban, Cape Town and the Eastern Cape. The third, very important aspect was the international solidarity.

I remember very clearly that in 1963 about half a dozen or a dozen people would stand in the cold weather outside South Africa House in London, demonstrating and demanding our release. I remember quite clearly that in Paris, outside the South African embassy, anything between ten and twenty would stand, and I remember that even in Stockholm you would find a handful of people coming together, demanding our release. But what is important is that this handful grew as the years went by. This was absolutely fantastic. In the 1980s, we were now talking of tens of thousands—no longer a handful—in Stockholm, Copenhagen, Paris, Bonn or London. In 1988, I was involved in the Free Mandela 70th Birthday Campaign. I took part in the walk from Glasgow to London and 250,000 people gathered in London on Mandela's birthday. Compare that with 1963, when we had anything between 20 and 30. This had a tremendous impact on bringing about change. Here, of course, Sara Lidman and others who took a prominent part in educating the people of Sweden and the other Scandinavian countries of the horrors of apartheid played a very important role.

On the Island we constantly had new arrivals. The irony, of course, was that we were very happy to see new prisoners coming in! Our comrade was coming with a 25-year sentence, and we were happy that he came to join us! Because he was coming with news of what was happening in our country and what was happening externally. We learned more and more of how the Scandinavian countries had given not only moral support to the liberation movement, but also financial, material support.

When I came out of prison in 1973, one of the first names that really struck me was Olof Palme. I think that he already was the Prime Minister of Sweden and his name was on the lips of every person as one of the champions. I do not know why, but he actually chose South Africa—and in particular ANC—as an important issue. He gave us tremendous support.

TS: How do you view this? You were supported by the socialist countries, led by the Soviet Union and the GDR, but also by the Nordic countries.

IN: Well, in Britain we had anti-colonial forces in a very big way. People like Bertrand Russel and John Collins. Britain was a mighty colonial power—'East to West, North to South, the sun never sets on the British Empire'—and these people took a leading role in the anti-colonial struggle. In France we also had people who were involved in the anti-colonial struggle. I viewed Olof Palme as one of these people. This is how I looked upon it and I found that his contribution to our struggle came from an anti-colonial background.

TS: Fundamental to Olof Palme's vision and politics, as well as to the Social Democratic movement in a broad sense, was the right of small nations to self-determination. I think that this, to a large extent, explains the involvement with countries such as Cuba and Vietnam, but also with the independence struggles in the Portuguese colonies, in Namibia and, of course, the struggle against white minority rule in Rhodesia and South Africa.

IN: What is baffling is that they chose the so-called authentic liberation movements. In South Africa, we had ANC and PAC and for that matter also the Unity Movement; in Namibia, we had SWAPO and SWANU; in Zimbabwe, we had ZAPU and ZANU; in Angola we had three, FNLA, UNITA and MPLA. In Mozambique, we had COREMO and FRELIMO. Yet, they chose FRELIMO in Mozambique, ZAPU in Zimbabwe, SWAPO in Namibia, MPLA in Angola and ANC here. These organizations had close links. They worked together. They exchanged information and, in fact, it has been recorded that ANC people fought in Angola, in Zimbabwe and in Mozambique. These were the authentic liberation movements. Sweden, in particular, supported the so-called authentic struggles. I cannot explain it.

TS: Could it be the result of the close personal relationship between some of the Nordic leaders, particularly Olof Palme, and people like Mondlane, Tambo, Neto, Nkomo and Nujoma?

IN: I think that a more important aspect was the integrity of not only the leadership, but the movements as a whole. Subsequently, of course, we had the situation in Zimbabwe where ZAPU and ZANU came together to form the Patriotic Front. Sweden and the Scandinavian countries continued to give support to the Patriotic Front. I think that they were quite realistic in their outlook. They found that these were definitely genuine movements. They were not only talking, but they were actively involved.

It was difficult for PAC to state what it was doing in the country. I remember clearly—it must have been in 1977 or 1978—when I was involved in a discussion with SIDA in Maputo. PAC had applied to Sweden for assistance and SIDA was considering whether they should grant that. They sent out word to all the missions in Southern Africa to give their opinions. I was invited, amongst others, to the Swedish embassy in Maputo and said: 'Look, if you want to support PAC, that is your business. However, I will tell you what ANC is doing in the country, what our programme is and what we have done.' I was fresh out of the country and able to give a good account of what was happening in South Africa. I also went on to show that there was no record of what PAC was doing. After giving our side of the story, the Swedish mission in Mozambique was quite convinced that they were going to turn the application down.

TS: I think that one important factor was this, namely who actually was delivering the goods. The other important factor was that PAC appeared to be exclusively African. I think that it was a combination of practical and egalitarian policies. When did you leave South Africa?

IN: I got into exile in 1977, not long after the Soweto uprising. My ANC underground unit was recruiting young people and sending them out of the country. We were all ex-Robben Islanders, so we were very careful how we worked. After the Soweto uprising, the number of people that had to leave South Africa increased tremendously. In fact, it threw the whole underground into a bit of a chaos and we had to do things unplanned. We were sending young people out by the dozens, because they were being looked for by the police.

On New Year's Eve 1976, I was on my way to see comrade Joe Gqabi when I was stopped by somebody who asked where I was going. I said that I was going to see Joe and the person said: 'Don't go. He has just been detained'. This worried me a great deal. He was the leader of our group and he had the keys to our underground office, which was under my name. I came home later that day, just before I had to be indoors. This was in Johannesburg. I found a young lady sitting waiting for me and she said: 'You know, I have been sitting waiting for you for the last three hours. I have been told to tell you to leave the country immediately!' Of course, I was in a panic. It was New Year's Eve and, in fact, we were having a gathering at home, which I was not supposed to be attending because I was under house arrest. I kept quiet about the whole thing. People came home that evening and enjoyed New Year's Eve in my house. I did not say a word to anybody. New Year's Day I also kept quiet, but the day after I revealed to my family that I had to leave the country and that ANC would be taking me out. I was taken via Swaziland to Mozambique.

I then went around all over Europe and was finally based in Maputo. I developed a very good relationship with the various solidarity movements that were set up in Mozambique. Mozambique was a dynamic area. A lot of people came to Mozambique seeking the challenge to build a new society, a society that we all had been talking about. From Canada we had CUSO sending people. From England we had MAGIC. Mostly professional people, teachers, agricultural workers, experts on water etc. In Sweden we had the Africa Groups, recruiting young people to come and work. From Denmark we had people from WUS and other organizations and from Norway people from the solidarity movement. Then, of course, we had people from the socialist countries. Large numbers from the GDR, Hungary, the Soviet Union and Cuba, coming to help.

TS: There were also many from Latin America, from Chile and Uruguay, that came via the Nordic countries?

IN: There were lots of Chileans. Most of them were refugees and a lot of them were based in the Nordic countries, in Sweden in particular. There was also a very large number of Brazilians. However, in the beginning we found that the only people who were properly organized were the Africa Groups' people. They came as a group and they used to meet us as a group. We made contact with them immediately and they gave us both moral and material support. I must emphasize that the moral support was absolutely excellent. We would organize a demonstration and find them there with their banners. So what did we do? We decided to get all the other groups organized as well. MAGIC was not difficult. CUSO was not difficult either.

The Chileans were very well organized in Maputo, although there were different factions. There was the Communist Party of Chile, MIR and a few other groups. But in Mozambique there was no difference. They worked as a Chilean solidarity group. Of course, the GDR and Cuba were not a problem. We had all these groups that would give us support.

SIDA, on the other hand, would give us large sums of money. Our numbers fluctuated from hundreds to thousands. There was a time in the late 1970s when the number of people fleeing the country was incredible. We could at any given time have 200 people just coming in and we had to look after these people. Here SIDA played an important role. We would inform SIDA and say that we had so many refugees coming in and that we would need support. SIDA's funds were controlled from the ANC Head Office in Lusaka and Lusaka would allocate the money to us. But we would also go directly to the SIDA office in Maputo and explain our needs. They would then help us to bring in more money and more material.

There was SIDA, NORAD, DANIDA and FINNIDA. All of them were officially involved with ANC. But then there were the solidarity people. On the May Day demonstrations they were all there. They would come *en bloc* to our meetings. I also remember when the Matola raid took place in January 1981 and thirteen of our comrades were shot dead. SIDA, NORAD, FINNIDA and others gave us material support, but the solidarity groups came to us and said: 'What do you want us to do?'

I must tell you that very often our people would use the Africa Groups' people to go to South Africa on quick missions via Swaziland. I would think that there might have been some SIDA people too who would have done that, but they were more official. They had diplomatic status. This was very useful to us. If I ever wanted something in Swaziland and I wanted it urgently, I would not hesitate to go to somebody from the Africa Groups and say: 'Please, go to Swaziland and do this or that for me'.

There was a case in point where we had to send a person to South Africa to do certain work. A Swedish woman got into her car and went to South Africa. They were instructed not to go there, but she went to South Africa, did the job, came back and phoned me. Of course, we had a code. I went and met her in Julius Nyerere Avenue, got into her car and while we were talking I noticed that we were followed. I told her to turn and she drove towards the beach, but I noticed that we were still being followed. I then said to her: 'Listen, we are being followed. I do not know who is following us, but we are being followed and we got to lose our tail'. She was fantastic. She drove up the hill from the beach. I think that they used to call it 'Lover's Walk' or 'Lover's Hill'. She drove up to Karl Marx Street, pulled into the bushes and waited until the car passed us. We waited some time and off we went. These were little things which helped a great deal.

TS: Did you work with other Nordic organizations in Mozambique?

IN: Yes, there was also a Danish group. In fact, the person who was in charge of the Danish group for a long time was Alpheus Mangezi's wife, Nadja Mangezi. Through her a lot of work was done. Then there was another group that was very idealistic. They put up tents and brought along their little kids to live in the tents with them.

TS: Danish Aid People to People, DAPP?

IN: Yes, People to People. We had good relations, but, of course, we found it difficult to work with them. They were very idealistic. In fact, they would criticize ANC for having all the cars that we had. But, all the same, their support was unending. I appreciated it and the farms that they put up, the dams that they were building and so forth.

TS: Do you feel that the official support from the Nordic countries was given with political conditions attached to it?

IN: After the Nkomati Accord our official numbers were drastically dropped to ten families. We came down from ten thousand to maybe twenty people. We then faced a problem with SIDA. We had to inform SIDA and they said: 'Well, we are cutting your allocation by 80 per cent'. Of course, we had to tell SIDA that many of our people had gone underground and that they were in more need than before. How were we to look after them? I was among the ten that had to see SIDA about this. SIDAs agreement was to give purely humanitarian assistance. No support to the armed struggle. Working with SIDA, I very often spoke about MK and I made no bones about the fact that we were involved with the armed struggle. The SIDA people listened to us and it was quite obvious that we were taking some of the money for MK activities. But, what they did not see and what they did not talk about we kept quiet about. Now, all of a sudden, the allocation was to be cut by 80 per cent. How were we going to manage?

We had sent hundreds and hundreds of people out of the country, but who did we send out? We sent out old men, women and children. We were not sending out names, we were sending out numbers to Tanzania and other places. The others had all gone into hiding, like 'Guebuza' Nyanda, who is now Chief of Staff in the South African National Defence Force. Jacob Zuma and myself went to see SIDA and put our cards on the table. We said: 'Yes, it is true that we officially are only ten ANC families in Mozambique, but we also have lots of children. We got to look after them'. They said: 'OK, give us the names. No problem'. We then said: 'We also have others that you do not see, but we cannot give you their names'. We put it to them and, of course, it was a problem. We also said that the flow of refugees continued, although it had come down quite a bit, and that we had to look after these people as well. After some debate on the issue they said: 'OK, just give us a list of names, meaningless names, and we will accept it'. Which they did.

So, we managed to convince the SIDA people. We did not, in so many words, say that we had underground people. It was accepted and they continued to give us the full funding.

TS: Well, within the SIDA budget to the ANC there was an allocation for so-called home front activities. It was also granted on trust. When it came to reporting, the only requirement was a political statement.

IN: That is right. I know about it. Of that, probably 50 per cent went directly to the armed struggle. Anyway, it was interesting that the SIDA officials in Maputo accepted our argument. We never told them about our underground people.

Something similar happened with the Mozambicans. The Mozambican Minister of Security, Jacinto Veloso, called all of us and said: 'Well, you know your status now. You are diplomats'. He spoke in Portuguese, giving us the official line. After that he dismissed the translators. We were having drinks and he said: 'When I was in exile in Tanzania, the government said that we must stop carrying arms! But we still carried our arms and we got to Mozambique. What they did not see did not hurt them'. That is all he said. He did not say anything else. I will never forget that.

I must tell you of another incident. In about 1985 we went to get our allocation from SIDA, but the SIDA officials said that there was something wrong. 'You guys are getting money from somewhere else, because the ANC account has a quarter of a million dollars. How did you get that? Until you tell us who has given you the money we are not going to give you the allocation'. We said: 'Nonsense, there is no quarter of a million dollars!' Then we went to check and discovered that there was a quarter of a million dollars! Bobby Pillay had just taken over the treasury and I said to him: 'Bobby, go and check. How come that we have a quarter of a million. Who has given us this money?' SIDA insisted that they wanted to know who else was supporting us, but Bobby said that this particular account was only for SIDA, nobody else. Eventually, I went to the bank and they let me see a quarter of a million'. There was no explanation how this money had got there.

We then had a meeting and said: 'There is this quarter of a million, but we do not know where it comes from'. We decided not to use the money. How were we to account for it? But since we were not getting any money from SIDA we were forced to. We met again and said: 'OK, let us use it, but very carefully. Let us not overspend!' We started to use the money, being very worried. Somebody was Father Christmas, giving us money. I went back to the bank and said: 'Please, let us check this money'. The woman who was the manager of the bank sat with us the whole day until they finally found the mistake. One extra nought! The bank had added an extra nought by mistake! So we said: 'Now, what do we do?' Knowing nothing about finance matters, I simply said: 'Listen, we now have a big overdraft, but you must not charge us interest on that. After all, it is your fault, not ours'. She was in a bit of a mess. Eventually we agreed that they would give us a year of grace to settle the amount. We then went to SIDA to explain the whole story.

TS: After Mozambique, you were invited to Sweden?

IN: That is right. In 1987, ANC was celebrating its 75th anniversary and at the same time the Swedish ABF (Workers' Education Association) was celebrating its 75th anniversary. On a very cold January evening they had an open air ANC meeting in Stockholm, where the Swedish Foreign Minister read out a letter from the Prime Minister. He offered scholarships to come to Sweden and study local government administration. I was in the first ANC group that was chosen to go to Sweden. By this time I had already left Mozambique.

Let me tell you why I left Mozambique: I survived the Nkomati Accord and was one of the ten ANC people that remained in Maputo. On Christmas Day 1986, P.W. Botha wrote to President Chissano and said that there were six terrorists in Mozambique who were responsible for 90 per cent of all terror activities in South Africa. He named them as Jacob Zuma, Susan Rabkin, Bobby Pillay, Mohamed Timol, Keith Mokoape and Indres Naidoo. He then went on to say that if they were not removed from Mozambique, he could not be held responsible for what would happen to them. At the same time, he threatened to block the port of Maputo and disrupt the Beira Corridor project.

Chissano called our President and had long discussions with him. The Mozambicans did not insist that we leave, but it was quite clear that they would like us to go. It was too dangerous for all concerned. Tambo agreed, but we insisted that we were going to see in the New Year in Mozambique and that we were going to see the 1987 anniversary of ANC there. We did so and then all six of us left.

I got to Zambia and while I was there, I was appointed to go to Sweden. It was chaotic. Only two of us were on the plane instead of nine. There was chaos between ANC and the Swedish embassy in Lusaka. The two of us landed in Stockholm and a week later the others joined us. The Social Democratic Party was having a congress in Stockholm and Prime Minister Carlsson invited us to have lunch with him, all of us. But, unfortunately, because only two of us had arrived they had to cancel that. However, there was a big welcome for us. We also went to attend the Social Democratic Party congress. I looked around and the first thing that struck me was all the red banners and the letters SAP. I started to laugh and said: 'Oh God, SAP—South African Police—everywhere'. But I realized that SAP was short for the Swedish Social Democratic Party.

When the others pitched up we were taken to the LO school at Brunnsvik, where we spent two weeks studying the theory of local administration, the civil structures of Sweden, the laws, the police force etc. It was a very exciting course. I enjoyed it very much. The Swedes seemed to have prepared it very well, the materials were there and the living conditions were absolutely fantastic. The school was really top class. I travelled quite often to Stockholm, because each time there was some meeting I would be asked to go there. After we had completed the course, we were then allocated to different areas to see the local government structures in operation.

Fortunately, or unfortunately, I was not paired up. We were nine and as a result I was alone. The people who were in charge of me drove me all the way to Sundsvall, where they rented a flat for me. A fully furnished flat, right in the centre of town. I got a daily allowance for food, but I never ate at home. The only thing that I ever had at home was breakfast, because I was out at lunchtime. I went to factories. I went to schools. I went to government offices, and I used to have my lunch there.

TS: Was it the local ABF office that set up the programme for you in Sundsvall?

IN: Yes, the local ABF. The agreement between ANC and ABF was that we should spend time with all political parties, the Social Democrats, the Communists or Left Party, the Liberal Party and the Centre Party, and that agreement was kept. I was very busy. I sat in at meetings of the local council and they took me along to show me how the local administration worked. I spent two days with the police force. I went on the road with the police and I stayed at the police station. I spoke to the prisoners. I also spent some time with young people who had a club which was controlled by the police. It was a very good way of keeping the kids off the streets. A lot of them were dropouts, but they controlled them and kept them together, which was very exciting.

I then spent two days with the Centre Party. I was taken to a farm and it was very impressive. On the farm there were a husband and wife and two adult sons and a daughter. Just the five of them controlled the entire farm. It was a dairy farm and they had fields of alfalfa. They worked very hard. They were up at five in the morning, milking the cows, collecting the eggs and so forth. It was the first time in my life that I stayed on a farm and saw it in operation. I am a city man. Smelling the cow dung it was very exciting!!

TS: What was your impression of people's knowledge about apartheid and the South African struggle?

IN: Well, it was good. I addressed a number of schools and colleges in Sundsvall. I was very impressed by the way they would question me, especially the young kids. They would challenge me: 'Look, you cannot tell me that blacks were not allowed into certain buildings?' It was difficult to explain it to them. They would not believe it. When I told them that blacks had never represented South Africa in sports and so forth, they would question me. Generally, I think that most of the adults had quite a good knowledge of what apartheid was. But I was also challenged, sometimes to the extreme.

One thing that I will never forget was when I was travelling from Stockholm to Sundsvall by train. There were only two of us in a compartment, myself and a young man. He introduced himself and I introduced myself and we started to talk. As we went on our night journey, I realized more and more that this chap was a right-winger. I then became a bit concerned. I was with a right-winger and he was digging into my background. I was avoiding certain questions. It was at the time when a Russian spy had escaped from a Swedish prison and they could not find him anywhere. They put up roadblocks and the seas were being searched. This guy was challenging this. 'How did this spy escape? It is definitely the government's work. The government and the Communists are responsible. Moscow is responsible'. He was attacking Moscow, left, right and centre. I just shrugged and kept quiet, saying yes, yes. He insisted that Russian submarines were violating the Swedish waters and he was absolutely certain that this chap was in one of the submarines! Of course, he went on to talk about terrorism. But I kept my cool and did not let out who I was. This was the only time something like that happened during my six months in Sweden.

Beyers Naudé
Director of the Christian Institute of Southern Africa—South African Council of Churches
Director of the Ecumenical Advice Bureau
(Johannesburg, 15 September 1995)

Tor Sellström: When did you first come into contact with the Nordic countries?

Beyers Naudé: Well, you will be surprised at my answer. The first time that I came into contact with the Nordic countries and churches was in 1953, when I was still on the other side of the struggle for liberation, a devoted Nationalist.

TS: And a member of the Afrikaner Broederbond?

BN: Yes, a member of the Broederbond. I was a young minister of the white Dutch Reformed Church, sent on a study tour for church youth work. There were two of us, Dr. Willem Strauss and myself. The World Council of Churches organized our study tour. It included visits to Denmark, Norway and Sweden on forms of church youth work, to which we were introduced and on which we had discussions. The first time that I returned was after I had accepted to work in the Christian Institute.

TS: Which was in 1963?

BN: It started in 1963. I cannot recollect exactly what year my first visit was, but through the work in the Christian Institute I became more and more acquainted with the Church of Sweden Mission. I was constantly visiting Uppsala and I also attended the World Council Conference there in 1968. I also visited Norway and Denmark. That is the basic background. In the course of my work in the Christian Institute I had several visits undertaken to Sweden, Norway and Denmark. Once also to Finland, a number of years ago.

TS: The World Council of Churches' synod in Uppsala in 1968 led to the launch of the Programme to Combat Racism the year after?

BN: Yes, it was launched in 1969, but the decision was taken in 1968.

TS: 1969 was an interesting year. It was also the year when Henry Kissinger concluded that there would be no black rule in Southern Africa. It was the year of the Lusaka Manifesto and it was the year when the Swedish parliament paved the way for direct official humanitarian assistance to national liberation movements, which led to the support to ANC from 1973. In those days, how did you in this context view the Nordic countries?

BN: Well, let me start by saying that as far as support to the liberation movements was concerned, I had in principle no problem with that. In the Christian Institute and through a growing and more meaningful contact with the black community in South Africa—especially the black Christian community, but also the Black Consciousness Movement with Steve Biko, and many others—it became more and more clear to me personally, and to a number of us, that, firstly, we had to legitimize the liberation movement in South Africa. Secondly, although we might disagree with the armed struggle, we had to approve in principle that they had the right to liberate themselves. There was no problem with that. My problem was the question of the armed struggle. Not with the decision of individuals to participate in armed struggle if they believed that they had done all other things to prevent that. My problem was to what degree the church had the right to support the armed struggle.

Throughout history, the churches in the world have always held two main views in this regard. The pacifist view and the view of those who would say that you must first try all the peaceful means and only if they fail are you allowed to participate. To me it was a very difficult decision, because in my heart I am basically a pacifist. I seek solutions by peaceful means. It was a very deep and painful struggle for me. Also to eventually say to myself: I have no problem in supporting the goals, the aims and the objectives of ANC, including the Freedom Charter. As a Christian, I believed that the Freedom Charter reflected the values of justice and peace of the gospel much clearer than any other document that we had in South Africa. My problem was whether I had the right to support the armed struggle as such. I could not bring myself to that. I could understand why many others did, but for myself I made a distinction. I said that blacks in South Africa with so much less opportunity for being involved in peaceful protests would certainly be entitled to give themselves to the armed struggle, but I, as a white, still had the opportunity to present pressures and viewpoints, for instance on sanctions and other actions, much better than by joining the armed struggle.

TS: On this point, your position coincided with the position of the Nordic countries. For example, when resolutions came up in the United Nations calling for support to the liberation movements, the Nordic countries would vote for these resolutions as long as they were not advocating armed struggle as a means of solving the conflict. If so, they would abstain.

BN: Yes, that is correct. Let me say that the principled approach of the Nordic countries helped me very much. I had to consider, for instance, the example of somebody like Bonhoeffer, who eventually came to the point where he said: 'I know that I am participating in sin if I try to kill Hitler, but it is the lesser of two evils. Therefore, knowing that I am guilty, I am still committed to do that, because I have no other option.'

In my case, I always asked myself: Is there no way in which—through the application of all other peaceful means—the countries of the world who are really committed to non-violent change can more effectively bring about a transformation? Through those means, rather than with weapons, nuclear bombs and everything else? Looking back today, I would say that the world eventually will be forced to come to the conclusion that there is no way in which we in the long run can solve problems through armed struggles, because the more you take them up, the more vicious, devastating and eventually suicidal they become. But it needs, I would say, the wisdom of experience to hopefully bring us to that view.

TS: In a recently published book on the World Council of Churches there is a description on how the different ecumenical movements embraced the Programme to Combat Racism. I was a bit surprised to read that the Nordic churches were quite slow in the implementation of the programme. Is that also your view?

BN: That is true. I think that it relates to the fact that in the Nordic churches the pietistic, evangelistic movement has always played, and is still playing, a very strong role. The danger of pietism is always to be non-political, non-controversial and to withdraw from any political debate and discussion. I think that it needed a whole transformation in the thinking, a new set of mind, on the part of the Nordic churches and their members to realize that social justice based on the gospel may need a much more active participation in politics. Not necessarily in party politics, but in the whole political struggle of a nation for liberation. To me it seems to be one of the major reasons why there was this hesitancy. I would not say unwillingness, but confusion and over-caution.

Is it not also true that the propaganda which came from the West—from South Africa and from the United States and others—in a certain sense always presented the liberation movement as Communist, terrorist and anti-Christ? It was on the basis of that totally distorted conception and impression that many of the sincere, devout pietistic Christians in the Nordic countries felt that they dared not give any support of any kind, not even humanitarian support, to the liberation movement.

TS: Does that mean that you were mainly receiving support through the government structures in the Nordic countries? I am thinking of the support to the South African Council of Churches and the Christian Institute?

BN: No, that was forthcoming through the churches. As far as that was concerned, it was not seen to be part of the support for the liberation movement as such. It was seen as humanitarian support for the victims of apartheid. That distinction is basic and very important.

TS: You could perhaps say that the churches in the Nordic countries would view the liberation movements as resistance movements, while the political structures would see them as liberation movements?

BN: Yes, that is a very important point to be made.

TS: You were probably the most central person inside South Africa when it came to the channelling of Nordic humanitarian support to a number of structures and organizations. How did you view the cooperation with the Nordic countries? How did you liaise with them?

BN: Well, I could not meet the Nordic governments. My passport had already been withdrawn in 1972, long before my banning. I could not leave South Africa. I simply had to learn how to regularly communicate the needs of the people and the organizations. Secondly, how to respond to requests coming from them and convey them to the Nordic governments. And, thirdly, how to set up contacts from the other side.

This was done in various ways. Firstly, through constant letters which were written confidentially and sent out. Naturally, never by mail. And we never talked over the phone, because I knew that my telephone was tapped. I knew that anything that I would send probably would be intercepted. So you simply had to use your wisdom to find ways and means to convey the messages and do it as confidentially as possible. Secondly, by arranging visits which had to be undertaken by representatives from the other side and also set aside adequate time for in-depth discussions of their needs. The way in which I did that was that I constantly gathered as much information as I could. I could never meet socially with more than one person at a time. I therefore had to break my banning order from time to time to meet secretly with more than one person, because in the African culture—and that is a very good principle—anyone with an order to corroborate his or her statement would insist that somebody else should be present. I had no problem with that. In this way it was possible to, first of all, gather the information—I deliberately went out of my way in order to seek and find such information—secondly, to communicate it confidentially and, thirdly, to make myself available at *any* moment. Sometimes it was in the middle of the night. Sometimes it was early in the morning. At a moment's notice, in order to meet somebody somewhere.

TS: You also met with representatives from the Nordic legations in South Africa?

BN: Oh, yes! For instance, for a long period I regularly met with Birgitta Karlström Dorph from the Swedish legation. I had long and meaningful discussions with her. I reported to her in full about what was happening. I heard which information she and the legation needed, gathered the information and then, at a given point, reported back to her.

Apart from many other qualifications, Birgitta had the gift of winning the trust of the black community through her person and through her commitment. She was the kind of person who blacks, intuitively, after a certain period would know that they could trust and open their hearts and minds to. Whenever Birgitta promised anything she kept her word. When she could not, she was very clear to say: 'I cannot promise anything, but I will see what I can do.' Among those who came to know her personally in South Africa there is a deep and lasting respect for her person and her commitment.

TS: Would you say that the Swedish and Nordic officials were personally more involved or committed than other diplomatic representatives?

BN: Yes, I would immediately say that as far as the Swedish representatives were concerned. I am thinking of Birgitta, Cecilia Höglund and others. There was no doubt that they were deeply committed. As far as certain of the other countries were concerned, I think that the general feeling was that they did this because it was their professional responsibility. But they did not always emanate the spirit of commitment which came from the Nordic countries. I am here thinking of Sweden, but I also want to refer to Denmark and Norway. For instance, somebody like Trond Bakkevig from the Norwegian church and the real, intimate trust which he developed. I think that they gave a very clear impression to the community that here you had representatives of governments of three countries which were committed in a deeper sense than may have been the case with others. Without my knowledge, there may have been one or two other embassies who also had that commitment. But I think that the black community in South Africa—struggling for liberation—had the impression that the deepest commitment came from the representatives of the Nordic countries.

TS: At the same time, I understand that those who were knowledgeable about the Nordic support were the direct recipients and not so much the broader community of beneficiaries?

BN: I think that the reason for that was the tremendous repression. It was not unwillingness to convey the information, but the fear that the security police, the phone-tapping and everything else would jeopardize the support. But now it should be brought much more into the open.

TS: In your opinion, was the Nordic support to the liberation process in South Africa given without strings attached or was it extended with a view to influencing the future South Africa in a particular political direction?

BN: I personally believe that it was done to influence South Africa. Not in a specific political direction, but to realize that the values of democracy, peace and justice which the Nordic countries had experienced—and which had given them so much of both freedom and commitment—for the sake of countries such as South and Southern Africa should be discussed and debated. But I never saw that as political manipulation with a view, for instance, to financial gain or anything of that kind.

TS: Nor to prepare the terrain for investments?

BN: No, I never saw it as such. I personally also do not believe that it was the motivation. I think that it was different, for instance, with the United Kingdom, the United States and Germany, where our impression was that this was not done from a political view, but specifically with the view to further influence financial developments which would benefit the economy, the trade and the finances of those countries. But I do not believe that it was the impression with any of us regarding the Nordic countries.

TS: This week, Chancellor Kohl addressed the South African parliament in Cape Town. He said that the German companies stayed in this country—even during the darkest period—to give employment to the most downtrodden.

BN: Well, first of all, his statement is not correct. If you ask any of the black communities who were involved with the majority of the German companies, including Volkswagen, Mercedes-Benz and others, that was never the impression that the workers had about the motivation of the German companies' staying and operating here. In fact, in many respects it was seen to be the opposite. Whoever informed Chancellor Kohl about that did not give him the full information.

TS: You channelled great amounts of solidarity funds from the Nordic countries. Did you experience any problems with accountability and financial controls?

BN: I cannot speak for any of the other parties and organizations which were supported. I can only reply to what I myself experienced and the way I saw it. Perhaps I should emphasize that for the sake of accountability—I should say, for the sake of always being able to account to myself that what I was doing could reflect integrity—I always tried my very best, even when it was not requested, to report on the way in which support was given to individual persons in different parts of the country. There were instances where for the sake of security and the safety of the persons concerned I could not give their names, but I always explained that. For me it was taken for granted that whenever I could I should report as fully as possible. Not because it was required—there was a large measure of flexibility—but because I felt that it was important that I should never at any stage create the impression that either I, or a few friends or others, were benefiting from those grants.

There was never any pressure, but, certainly, a flexible, regular reporting was required in so far as it was possible. I tried to do that to the best of my ability and I never felt that it was not supported in that way.

TS: Is there anything you would like to add to characterize the relationship with the Nordic countries?

BN: Yes, I would. It is of vital importance that the human communication at all levels of our societies—our thoughts on the building of a responsible, free and democratic movement in South Africa—should be maintained and strengthened. I believe that there are historical values of democracy, justice and peaceful resolution of conflicts which the Nordic countries have developed in the course of a number of years and which we desperately need. So, for the sake of South Africa, my plea is: Please maintain and strengthen those contacts. Secondly, I would wish to say that there is to my mind a very substantial contribution which also South Africa can make to the insight and the understanding of the liberation struggle in general, of the human struggle for freedom and democracy, to the Nordic countries. I think that both societies should be open to that regular communication. Thirdly, I would wish to say that, if unattended, the tremendous gap between wealth and affluence in the Northern countries and the poverty and destitution in the Southern world will create major problems. For the sake of the world, the global economy and economic justice it is of vital importance that countries like the Nordic countries and South and Southern Africa remain in constant contact to communicate, discuss, debate and dialogue on these issues. Not in the first place for the sake of South Africa or for the sake of the Nordic countries, but for the sake of the global commu-

nity. This seems to be the task that lies ahead of all of us.
TS: That is a much more difficult task.
BN: True, in the past it was easy to clearly indicate that apartheid was the enemy. We all opposed apartheid, regardless of our political affiliation. The task ahead is much more difficult, no doubt about it. But in the long run it is going to be much more meaningful and productive, if we have the wisdom to understand how to do it.

May I end by saying that I personally wish to express my deep and lasting gratitude for the enrichment of my own life through my personal friendship with the Nordic countries, through the commitment that they made to justice and peace and through the way in which they helped me to understand much more what it meant to make that contribution.

Barney Pityana
President of the South African Students Organisation—Black Consciousness Movement—ANC—Director of the Programme to Combat Racism of the World Council of Churches
Chairman of the South African Human Rights Commission
(Uppsala, 23 January 1997)

Tor Sellström: As a young student activist at Lovedale and at the University College of Fort Hare in the 1960s, were you aware of the Nordic support to the anti-apartheid cause in South Africa?
Barney Pityana: No, I was not. In those days, I was very much involved in the Student Christian Movement (SCM) and the University Christian Movement (UCM), of which I was an officer. However, I do think that SCM and the Anglican Students Federation had visitors from Sweden coming to address us, but I cannot remember their names. So, there were links between the Student Christian Movement and Sweden.

I was expelled from Fort Hare in 1968. I was regional director of the University Christian Movement and president of the Anglican Students Federation before I joined the South African Students Organisation (SASO). While I was with UCM, I became aware of the World University Service (WUS), partly because at that time I also participated in the work of the National Union of South African Students (NUSAS). From 1968, I knew of the financial support to NUSAS from the Nordic countries. Of course, in my early days I was not unaware of Dag Hammarskjöld during the Congo crisis.
TS: There were refugee students in Sweden who had been expelled from Fort Hare at the time of the Extension of the University Edu-

cation Act in 1959. One of them was Billy Modise, who is now South Africa's High Commissioner to Canada. They may have been in contact with their *alma mater*?
BP: I am sure that there were those links, but for me it was a gradual realization as I got involved and moved into the leadership. That was also when I became aware of the support structures that were needed to carry out our work.
TS: In her contribution to the book *Bounds of Possibility: The Legacy of Steve Biko and Black Consciousness*—which is co-edited by you—Mamphela Ramphele describes how there was a reluctance on the part of funding agencies to support black initiatives in South Africa during the period from 1970 to 1977, with the exceptions of the International University Exchange Fund (IUEF) and WUS. Both IUEF and WUS were to a high degree funded by the Nordic countries. What projects were supported by these organizations?
BP: We started SASO with really nothing but commitment. However, we recognized very early on that we were going to need some funding support. Our initial access to financial support was through Beyers Naudé and the Christian Institute, who connected us with various people and also gave us small amounts. The second channel at the time—we were in Durban then—was UCM. Many of us in the Black Consciousness

Movement (BCM) had been involved in UCM and through them we began to receive support from the United Methodist Church in the United States. Through UCM we also linked up with WUS. Via the Christian Institute and UCM, our initial support was thus very much from the churches.

The Nordic support increased quite quickly as we developed projects. The University of Natal Medical School had an exchange programme with a university in Sweden. They used to have two students going to Sweden for a term or something like that. In 1969 or 1970, two students—Aubrey Mokoape and a colleague—went there and they were the ones who made the first major approaches for funds. I think that it was through them that we made the first contacts with IUEF. Before that IUEF was not a major funding source, as far as I remember.

However, I think that Mamphela Ramphele is right, because in those days the funding was never substantial. We were never trusted, in spite of the fact that we had clear programmes. In fact, NUSAS was getting more support from the same sources than we did. But NUSAS was developing projects in reaction to us. Also, they were always limited to scholarships and things like that, while we started projects that, for example, involved students going to the communities to run clinics and have winter schools. NUSAS did not have that, but we did and we carried them out with very little funding support. I think that the reason why the donors were so reluctant was that they were not used to blacks establishing their own organizations. Whatever they might say, there was a racist element. It was a struggle for us, although we were convinced that we had a claim.

Having said that, our first breakthrough came when Ben Khoapa and Steve Biko managed to break out of Spro-cas (Special Project on Christianity in an Apartheid Society) to establish the Black Community Programmes, or BCP. Major funding was now coming to a body that was black. So, when Steve Biko was banished to King William's Town, he was able—as part of the Black Community Programmes—to establish all the projects that were based there, including the clinic and the study programmes. The funding for this came from the Nordic countries through IUEF and WUS.

TS: Lars-Gunnar Eriksson, the Director of IUEF, was a Swedish Social Democrat. However, while the Swedish Social Democratic government had extended direct official humanitarian assistance to the ANC since 1973, Eriksson and IUEF were allegedly looking for a 'third force' in South Africa. Would it be fair to say that the support given by IUEF to the Black Consciousness Movement was motivated by anti-ANC considerations?

BP: I think that the situation was a lot more nuanced than that. Even before Craig Williamson came onto the scene I think that Lars-Gunnar Eriksson recognized that there was a very new and very significant political movement represented by SASO and Black Consciousness (BC) inside South Africa. His main interest was to recognize that movement and then to support and nurture it. What happened subsequently—prematurely, I think—was that large numbers of BC people left South Africa in the wake of the 1973 upheavals, that is, after Turfloop, and that they began to develop material needs in exile. In the process, people like Harry Nengwekhulu—the first senior BC person who left South Africa—became close to IUEF. He experienced the need to get resources in order to provide scholarships and cater for a growing number of BC people outside South Africa. According to him, in order to get that support many of the traditional donor agencies required that the people belonged to ANC. Bearing in mind the arrogance of the BC people in those days, it was very difficult for most of them to contemplate that. But Lars-Gunnar Eriksson and IUEF gave them support. I do not think that he did so because he was seeking to form a 'third force', but simply because somebody like Harry Nengwekhulu approached him for that.

In addition, Lars-Gunnar Eriksson hired Craig Williamson with the support of ANC and against opposition from us and from the South African Council of Churches. We told him that Williamson was not a person to be trusted. There was a lot of controversy around that. In fact, Williamson was according to Eriksson in those days clearly supported by ANC. So, it could not be that Lars-Gunnar Eriksson was in favour of the formation of a 'third force'. Craig Williamson's emergence at IUEF had the support of ANC and one of the first things that he did when he got there was trying to stop the support for BCM and concentrate IUEF's support on ANC.

I do not think that Lars-Gunnar was thinking in terms of a 'third force', but there was on his part a recognition of BCM as a new political movement in South Africa. From talking to him I know that he felt that too many refused to acknowledge that. His insight was that BCM was a political force that had to be taken into account.

TS: That kind of hesitancy on behalf of the donors could perhaps also be noticed when the United Democratic Front (UDF) was created in 1983?

BP: That is right, but after the exposure of Craig Williamson and the collapse of IUEF it became increasingly important for the donors to make sure that any position that they took on South Africa had the support of ANC. Informally, ANC was in that way able to indicate what could and what could not be supported.

When I left South Africa in 1978—in the wake of the murder of Steve Biko—there was a very clear sense that it was important for us to start negotiations with ANC about the political scene outside South Africa. Within BC there were people who were taking all kinds of positions. One group was becoming close to the Nigerians, also training people there. Others were moving to Libya and even to Palestine. And there was a lot of conflict among the BC people in Botswana. By 1978, it had become very clear that the situation was untidy. And, indeed, Steve Biko would have come out of South Africa to try to bring some order into the situation and encourage people to have a creative relationship with ANC. That would have been the main objective of the talks.

I was never convinced that it was necessary to have both a BCM and the traditional liberation movements. When I came out, I told everybody very clearly that that never was the intention of BC. BC had a role inside South Africa at the time, but I was never convinced that I was going to come out of South Africa and become BCM. But I also recognized that if we were going to move ahead, it was important that we could take as many people with us as possible. So, in faithfulness to what the people in South Africa wanted we organized meetings with ANC. These meetings were financially supported by Lars-Gunnar Eriksson. However, we did not get his support for a BC conference that took place in London and that we felt was necessary. When there was concern on behalf of some people that there was going to be a 'third force', IUEF did not support that.

We had a very useful meeting with ANC in Lusaka, which for me determined that there really was no need to form a separate organization. But it was necessary to hold this national meeting in London in 1980 to report on our discussions with ANC. I then discovered that things had gone so far—largely because of the relations between BC people and ANC people and others—that it never was going to be possible to keep anything like a united, cohesive position and, secondly, it had also become very clear that the idea of having a common position as BC was not going to operate.

TS: In an interview with Craig Williamson in 1996, he said that the background to Steve Biko's arrest and death in September 1977 was that Biko was preparing to leave South Africa to meet Oliver Tambo and that this meeting was being organized "by the Swedes" through IUEF. Would this be correct?

BP: On his initiative, Steve Biko planned to clandestinely meet ANC abroad. And to come back. He had no intention of permanently leaving the country. I am aware that IUEF was to make it possible. Harry Nengwekhulu was part of it and he would have found some means of support from them. I do not know how advanced the plans were at the time of Steve's arrest. It had nothing to do with that. It was due to the fact that he had breached his banning orders.

It is true that there were definite plans for Steve Biko to meet with ANC. There were various reasons for that. One was the fact that growing numbers of BC people were leaving the country and many of them were seeking military training. Secondly, especially the situation among the BC people in Botswana was very bad. There were lots of factions and it was necessary that those who really did want to get involved in armed combat could be trusted. Steve would have explored the possibility of BCM engaging in open political struggle internally in South Africa and of letting those who wanted to be involved in armed struggle do so through ANC. Essentially, that is what he was going to explore. It was to bring some sort of discipline into what had been happening in exile.

TS: In exile, you joined ANC and subsequently became the director of the Programme to Combat Racism (PCR) of the World Council of Churches, based in Geneva, Switzerland. In a recently published book, it is said that the Nordic churches were quite slow in implementing the PCR recommendations. Is that also your opinion?

BP: Well, I was the third director of PCR and by that time there was very strong support from the Nordic churches. However, there was also a very strong movement for the isolation of South Africa and it is true that some Nordic churches—certainly in Norway—were not supportive of this. For example, Norway did not believe in the actions we took against Shell, which was a major campaign. They did not support that at all, but supported instead a process which we did not support, namely that of channelling funds to groups within South Africa. Like ANC, we believed that it undermined the isolation of South Africa.

However, the Special Fund to Combat Racism, which was our main fund, in fact relied a great deal on Nordic and German support. The support from the churches in Sweden and Norway was considerable, while the support from Germany did not officially come from the churches, but rather from groups who were raising funds informally. It is also true that the funds of the Nordic aid agencies came from their governments and we were aware that they were distributing public funds that they knew were going towards the support of ANC and other liberation movements. During my time as director, the Special Fund increased dramatically because the consciousness of the need to combat racism all over the world also increased. But the major part of that fund was contributed because of South Africa. The money was, however, not necessarily spent on South Africa.

In brief, I would say that we did receive funding from the Nordic countries and that—in the formal sense—some Nordic churches were ambivalent about supporting the Special Fund.

TS: You were also closely involved with the ANC Department of Religious Affairs and Inter-Faith Chaplaincy, which from the beginning was almost fully funded by the Lutheran World Federation (LWF). In turn, LWF was strongly supported by the Nordic churches. In the light of the fact that the membership of ANC represented a very wide religious spectrum, did this Lutheran link constitute a problem?

BP: No, not at all. Around 1983–1984, ANC had come to recognize the very important role played by the churches in South Africa. ANC was beginning to have a very direct sense of that from the cadres that came out of South Africa into the camps. The sense of religion had become very evident. ANC had also come to recognize that there was a need for some kind of pastoral care among its cadres. Especially, this was clearly understood by President O.R. Tambo and to some extent by people like Thabo Mbeki.

The international campaign against South Africa could not continue without the involvement of the churches. The churches were critical. By 1983, when UDF was formed, religious communities were also involved in the struggle inside South Africa. The products of that—the people who were going to ANC—were for the first time clearly people who were aware of their religion. That is why it was necessary to have a Department of Religious Affairs. But I do not think that it ever really achieved its potential. It was seen as a way in which ANC could have religious people within the movement and bring their zeal for liberation and their religious commitment together. ANC was not asking people to give up their religion in order to become committed cadres.

The other aspect was the chaplaincy, that is, the means of caring for people in the camps or in the general refugee situation in which the ANC cadres were living. It was also to be a forum where links between the churches in South Africa and ANC could take place. That did not happen as well as it could have. There was an interest from religious people in South Africa in the work of ANC and people did—in a clandestine manner—continue to meet and focus on what

ANC was doing about religious issues, but those formal links with the churches were not sufficiently established.

Walter Sisulu
ANC—Secretary General
Former ANC Deputy President—Senior adviser to the President of South Africa
(Johannesburg, 15 September 1995)

Tor Sellström: Did the ANC leadership have any contacts with the Nordic countries before the Nobel Peace Prize was given to the late Chief Luthuli in 1961?
Walter Sisulu: No, I think that the first contacts with the Nordic countries were with Chief Luthuli.
TS: When he went to Norway, did he travel alone or was he accompanied by other ANC leaders?
WS: Unfortunately, he was not accompanied by any leading person. He was accompanied by his secretary and, of course, by his wife.
TS: So the involvement by the Nordic countries started when you were on Robben Island?
WS: Indeed so. That is the time when it became shaped according to our desire.

Now, on the question of Chief Luthuli: We had not, I must confess, by that time attached such an importance to the Nobel Prize itself. But from that time on we began to analyze it and realize its significance.
TS: In the Nordic countries it was very significant. It came after the Sharpeville massacre and when you took the decision to launch the armed struggle.
WS: Yes, it came at a time when a drastic change was taking place.
TS: The good relations between the Nordic countries and ANC were, of course, to a large extent the work of the late Oliver Tambo?
WS: Yes, indeed so.
TS: He came to Sweden in 1961.
WS: Yes, I think in 1961.
TS: When you were on Robben Island, did you get any information about the Nordic support?
WS: Yes, we were quite well informed. Although we were not allowed newspapers, we were able to get information. We knew of the role of the Nordics.

TS: How did you view this? You had these Western countries in the North that supported the same liberation movements in Southern Africa as the Soviet Union did.
WS: Well, this was an eye opener. We had never before thought of them in that way. We began to look at them and realized what a tremendous advance we were making, having good relations with the Nordic countries. Its importance was beyond our understanding.
TS: Do you think that it assisted you to create political space?
WS: No doubt. It was a tremendous move to have such a relationship. O.R. Tambo did great work, particularly in that field. He was able to analyze the situation. He was a diplomat and a politician.
TS: I think that Thabo Mbeki was very much working along the same lines as O.R. Tambo?
WS: Yes. After all, he is a product of O.R. Tambo.
TS: I have read that the late Olof Palme, the Swedish Prime Minister, corresponded with you and Nelson Mandela when you were on Robben Island. Is that possible?
WS: I cannot remember that. They would not have handed them over. You see, the letters were kept and when the relationship changed, Mandela was perhaps able to read them. I do not think that they would have allowed it during the early times.
TS: When you were released, you went to Sweden to see O.R. Tambo. Coming there, how did you assess the Nordic countries and the relationship that he had built over the years?
WS: It was fantastic! Amazing! Just to cope with that relationship and to consolidate and improve it. It was our task. It had a tremendous impact on me. The information of the part that they had played.

TS: At that time Sweden had a conservative government?
WS: Yes, but the right and the left were able to work together.
TS: One reason for that is that very early on it was not only the political left, but also the church and the liberal centre that were involved.
WS: My understanding was that that was able to bring the right to realize. It seems that without the left they had known very little.
TS: There followed an intense process leading up to the elections in which the Nordic countries supported ANC. Do you think that it had any significant impact?
WS: It had a tremendous impact! The Nordic countries have got one aspect which perhaps now we understand. From the point of view of humanity, I think that they are among the greatest. I think that the part they have played in international politics is beyond understanding.
TS: The Nordic countries are very modern, but also very traditional, with a strong tradition of egalitarian policies and democratic principles.
WS: Yes, I think that that helped to shape the relationship and for us to understand what kind of society we were dealing with.
TS: The relationship will now continue.
WS: It must grow! It must be intensified! We just cannot afford to lose it, to allow it to cool down. It must continue on a high level, because we are not only dealing with a particular struggle. We now have a fiddle and we have a role to play on the international arena. We have to see to it that good friends such as we have had are maintained. And that we together will work out a new programme, a new era, a new approach. The Nordic countries are indispensable to us in that situation.
TS: I believe that it is also important for the Nordic countries to have allies that think in similar terms.

WS: Yes, I agree with that fully.
TS: It is part of the reason why the Nordic countries supported ANC, SWAPO, MPLA, FRELIMO and ZANU/ZAPU, namely the question of small nations' right to self-determination.
WS: It is very important. We will never be able to fully grasp this relationship. I have no words to express it, but the feeling in me is the feeling of greatness and of the function that awaits both the Nordic countries and ourselves. In the same way that we have worked together, I have no doubt that we will be able to take this a step further. I lack words to say how we should consolidate this relationship, how it should be taken further. We need each other. We have a greater job to do and this time not for a particular country, but on a global basis.
TS: Yes, but this struggle is even more difficult.
WS: Yes, more difficult, because it involves by and large the question of non-racialism. We now have to lead other countries in this direction. We have difficulties in getting people to understand it at home and yet it is the greatest task that we must work for. The first stage without the second is not worth it.

I am very much attached to and feel very sentimental about the relationship that has been built with the Nordic countries. I happen to have been to Sweden and Norway. I came into contact with the people of those countries and my respect for them grew beyond what words can explain.
TS: Did you hear the children sing in Xhosa and Zulu?
WS: Yes! I came back and said that they sing Nkosi Sikelele better than we do! I emphasised this to Oliver Tambo because he himself was a musician. I listened to it in Norway and in Sweden. They were very good.

Garth Strachan
ANC—Umkhonto we Sizwe—South African Communist Party—Director of the Education, Resource and Information Project / Voter Education and Election Training Unit
Responsible for fundraising at the South African Communist Party
(Cape Town, 10 September 1995)

Tor Sellström: You went into exile around 1975. What made you leave South Africa?
Garth Strachan: I ran away from the army. I had been politically involved in the student movement, but in 1974 I was called up to go to Angola. I had been on the run from the army for about a year, but in June 1974 the military police caught up with me. I served a four week refresher course and then I was due to go to Namibia and Angola. However, since I had a passport I just left the country. It was more of a self-imposed exile, plus the fact that Brigid, who later was to become my wife, had left South Africa. So, it was two things, to run away from the army and to join her. It was only at that point that I became involved with ANC.
TS: Before leaving South Africa, did you not have any contacts with Nordic support to the liberation struggle?
GS: No, none whatsoever.
TS: In exile, you started to work with the International Defence and Aid Fund (IDAF) in London?
GS: Yes, I got a job at IDAF's research and publications department. That was in 1976-77. At the end of 1977 and in 1978 I worked for the Anti-Apartheid Movement (AAM) in Britain. In both places I came into contact with Nordic support. Obviously, at IDAF there was a whole host of programmes, such as support for legal fees of people who were detained and charged as well as support for publications. As far as I know, that was supported by the Nordic countries.
TS: IDAF was, of course, one of the main sources of information on the situation in Southern Africa.
GS: Yes, but also AAM got Nordic support. I remember that it was very difficult, because it was support for an organization in another country. I very much recall that the Anti-Apartheid Movement through some sophisticated methods was given money for international campaigns against apartheid.

TS: How did the South Africans in AAM and IDAF view the support by the Nordic governments to the national liberation movements in Southern Africa?
GS: Although it has become popular not to admit this now, at the time—at least in the circles where I moved and up to the mid or late 1980s—the reality was that in ANC—well, there was a much more sophisticated political analysis on the part of some individuals—there was a kind of pro-Soviet hysteria. Although the support from the Nordic countries was obviously gratefully received, at an ideological level I think that there is no doubt that there was a strong sense—a kind of analysis, if you like—that the Social Democratic movement (a) was homogeneous, (b) that there was no common left within the Social Democratic movement, and (c) that the support for the liberation movements from the Nordic countries and from the Social Democratic movement as a whole very often was characterized as imperialist and sometimes even as American support, channelled through those countries which were most amenable to give support to ANC and other liberation movements. It was characterized as imperialism, keeping the door open here, if you like.

I think that there was a very unsophisticated, undialectic and unidimensional understanding of the Nordic support for the liberation movements. For me, it says a lot about the Nordic countries—and it says a lot about the Social Democratic parties in those countries who in a sense drove that support—that despite that unnuanced, unsophisticated characterization of their support within the liberation movements, they (a) continued to support them and (b) that the support was genuinely disinterested. To the best of my knowledge, there was never any effort, either in the form of literature or in the form of personal contacts or interventions, which aimed at turning around the misconception in the ranks of the liberation movement. And that characterization was not just in ANC. Certainly, in ZAPU I know that it was there and also in SWAPO, although I do not know about it in detail. I think that the analysis was very unsophisticated and incorrect.

TS: That view was to a large extent also held by the non-governmental left in the Nordic countries. The criticism mainly boiled down to the fact that the Nordic governments would not support the armed struggle.

GS: I did not realize it then, but by the late 1980s we began to look at the situation in a slightly more nuanced way. The reality was that the Nordic support was for prisoners, their dependants, the trials and the mass movements inside the country and therefore, as we well know, very often also for the internal underground structures. They were very closely linked to the mass movements—which in a sense provided a fertile environment for the underground structures to operate—and to the external movement in so many, many different ways. The only form of support that to the best of my knowledge was not given was literally the military hardware itself. But without all these other elements, the armed struggle would not have been possible anyway. As ANC itself always said, the political and the mass struggle as well as the international struggle—especially the mass struggle—was more important, and in some ways—as ANC also often said—the armed struggle was really to mobilize mass support. So, looking back one does not see any problem.

TS: SIDA also supported ANC in Angola. In the camps, were you aware that part of the support was coming from SIDA?

GS: Yes, we were. I was in Angola in 1979-80, part of 1981 and part of 1983. The conditions were not as bad as they had been, let us say in 1977, but there were very long periods of time when the conditions were *extremely* bad. I remember someone saying that even Robben Island had been easier than the camps. So, the conditions were very bad and I think that it was well known, at least in my experience, that the support was coming from friendly countries. The food was from the Soviet Union and some of the East bloc countries. But we were always told that the financial support for the food that was being purchased, as well as for the clothes and the soap and all those things was from Holland and Sweden.

TS: I think that you got meat and other products from ANC's agricultural farms in Zambia, which in turn were supported by SIDA?

GS: I remember that from time to time, probably from bad management, but also from a host of other factors, there would be very bad crises in the camps in Angola. On at least three occasions I remember that big Boeing 707s were chartered to take food from Harare to Angola. On two of the occasions, I was working in Zambia and I was involved in the arrangements. On the third occasion I was in Angola. We got relief food from Harare which was particularly poor in quality and became known as 'Mugabe'.

Another observation that I would like to make here is that the fact that the MK people very often did not know where the money was coming from had a negative component to it, but it also had a positive side. The ANC Treasurer General's office was remarkably good at keeping quiet about the lines of supply, especially on Rands, and we had millions of Rands passing through our hands for the struggle inside the country, for example, for MK soldiers moving into South Africa. It was an incredibly tightly kept secret. I am simply saying that there was a negative, but also a positive element: keeping quiet about the exact sources of some of the funds in those particular circumstances.

TS: Later on you went for training in the Soviet Union. How was the Swedish or Nordic support seen from that perspective?

GS: Well, I was on record as far back as in 1985 saying that although ANC suggested and put out in all its propaganda material and communications that the political struggle was more important than the military struggle, in reality it paid lip service to that. Notwithstanding the need for armed propaganda, my own view is that very serious strategic errors were made with regard to the underground struggle because of an overemphasis of the armed struggle.

Obviously, one can go into a great deal of debate and detail on that matter. The reason why I think that it is important is that it played itself out at the political level. What was seen to be—and what was said to be—most important was the military training and the supply of military weapons. What was also said was: 'Yes, Swedish, or Nordic, support is in general terms important, but at the end of the day they do not want to see the complete defeat of apartheid. Otherwise they would have supported the armed struggle.' I came to the conclusion as far back as in 1985 that this was a fundamental error. There was an error in the strategy of ANC, which led, in a sense, to a fundamental error of understanding the relationship between ANC and other countries.

I am not saying that everybody in ANC had that position. I am sure that there might have been some who did not. But that was a general understanding and it was profoundly incorrect. Given the particular historical moment, it was also part and parcel of a very profound failure to understand the dynamics within the international Social Democratic movement. ANC's and SACP's understanding and analysis of that was very much that of the Soviet Communist Party. It was more or less the same, which was very wrong. I think that it was particularly damaging to ANC, because it failed to see that the anti-imperialist struggle went beyond the Cold War dynamic. And that, I think, was a very poor understanding of the need to develop close political ties with Social Democracy, especially the left Social Democracy. Not just in Europe, but also in other parts of the world. I think that it was a very unfortunate product of a very close relationship between, in particular, SACP and the Soviet Union. As much as people say that this was not the case, I think that my experience in ANC suggests that it was very strong and entrenched.

TS: When Thabo Mbeki characterized the contribution by the Nordic countries to the liberation process in Southern Africa, he emphasized that Sweden particularly—and he singled out Olof Palme's contribution—recognized the liberation movements not as resistance movements, but as governments-in-waiting.

GS: Absolutely. There is not much one can add to that other than possibly to make one very obvious point: I suppose that one can take nothing away from the contributions made by the Soviet Union, Nigeria or any of the East bloc countries. They were massive contributions. However, in a sense, they were contributions from the governments and the ruling parties, which did not necessarily have either the blessing or the knowledge of the populations of those countries. I was personally often very surprised. Maybe it is not a good yardstick, but when you came across ordinary people in the then Soviet Union they were not necessarily in agreement with the support for the liberation movements. And—sometimes quite alarmingly—there were massive problems with racism directed to ANC and black people in the Soviet Union.

I think that the Nordic support to the liberation movements in a sense was something that one can hold up almost as a model of solidarity. It was disinterested, because of the reasons that I have already given. Secondly, it appeared to have the voluntary agreement and support of large sections of the population. Perhaps it is being too wise, with the benefit of hindsight, but, as people say, it is better to be wise too late than never to be wise at all. I think that that support really was a model of disinterested international solidarity. Its weakness, though, was that perhaps precisely because of the nature of the struggle—that is, armed, underground, etc—a corresponding popular knowledge and linkage between the people in Sweden and the other countries and those who were the recipients of the support was not possible.

The challenge for me as a South African is to be able to say to other South Africans that we received XYZ during this period. It is not that we owe a debt, because I do not believe in that kind of relationship. The money was not given in order to secure a debt. But we should learn from those experiences and extend a hand of friendship to the people of the Nordic countries, especially given our history. That is for me real international solidarity. It would be a great pity if the tremendous support from the people of the Nordic countries ended now. Not that it is ending, but the challenge to make it more popular and deeper should be taken up.

TS: You were also involved with the channelling of funds to the forward areas in Southern Africa and to the Home Front. Lots of funds allocated by SIDA to ANC were destined for the Home Front. Were they channelled to South Africa with your knowledge?

GS: Many of the internal non-governmental organizations and mass movements very often had a link to the underground or to the external ANC. A lot of the project proposals—a very large amount of them; I would not know the precise proportion which were destined to receive funding from the Nordic countries or Holland—passed through our hands. I was the administrative secretary to, first, the ANC Revolutionary Council and later to the Politico-Military Council in Zambia.

ANC did not jettison or sabotage project proposals or support applications from organizations which did not hold the same ideological or political view as ANC. There was a line of communication, to the best of my knowledge, between ANC and the Nordic representatives. Information was exchanged. When an NGO was being set up as a front, it was possible for ANC to say: 'We cannot interfere with your support for the internal mass struggle and the democratic movement, but this information might assist you in taking an informed decision.' There was that kind of dynamic. Certainly, in my position—and I am not saying that it was a widely held view; in fact, it was not a widely held view because of the nature of the struggle itself and the nature of secrecy—I was very much aware of the fact that the overwhelming majority of the internal organizations simply would not have been able to survive were it not for the external support from governments and NGOs, specifically from the Nordic countries.

TS: During the 1980s, millions of Rands were allocated by SIDA to the Home Front. The reporting requirements on this part of the cooperation were based on trust. In a sense, ANC was here on the same side as the donor. Do you think that there were problems with the accounting of the funds for the Home Front to ANC and then by ANC to SIDA?

GS: I think that there were, but I think that it will be very difficult to say how much corruption there was. I also think that a culture of dependency probably was engendered. But one has to ask the question: Was there any alternative? I do not think that there was. The only alternative was not to supply the money. Of course, you take all the steps you can to negate and stop corruption. In a way, it took a great deal of courage to provide money and support, knowing full well that the lines of accountability were not strong and therefore open to abuse. It meant that Sweden was supporting the struggle while knowing that there would be some corruption.

TS: There was the case of the infiltration of the South African agent Craig Williamson into the International University Exchange Fund (IUEF), which was strongly supported by the Nordic countries. The IUEF affair must have had an impact on ANC's trust and confidence when it comes to Nordic support?

GS: I do not think that it had any impact. The South African government made a big song-and-dance act out of it and it was in the headlines of the South African newspapers for a few days. To the best of my knowledge, not a single arrest followed upon the return of Craig Williamson to Pretoria and I think that I would have known. Of course, he came across sensitive information about money and lines of supply and he probably gave a lot of political intelligence on ANC, but my impression was that the damage was not altogether that serious.

I am not saying this with the benefit of hindsight. It was certainly the understanding of the people who worked with him on a very close basis. The key people were Mac Maharaj and to some extent Aziz Pahad and Jacob Zuma. Maharaj was my immediate boss at exactly that time and he did not trust Williamson as far as I could see. I personally feel that serious damage was not done. Neither did it in my view have a serious impact on the perception of the people of the Nordic countries. Williamson was seen as a South African who had gone to work for IUEF with the blessing of ANC. Maybe I am wrong, but this is how I see it.

TS: Before the 1994 elections, you became the director of an important organization for voter education in South Africa. What was the background to VEETU, the Voter Education and Election Training Unit?

GS: I was the director of ERIP, the Education, Resource and Information Project, which had been established by Murray Michell, Trevor Manuel and Cheryl Carolus in about 1984. In those days, it did a host of semi-clandestine, sometimes clandestine, support activities for the struggle in the form of research, training and provision of free services for media, such as videos etc. When I became director of ERIP in 1992, we were asked by the Centre for Development Studies to do voter education for the forthcoming elections. We agreed to do it, but in meetings with people from the Swedish Olof Palme International Center—specifically delegations led by Bo Toresson—we put forward the idea that as much as voter education was important, unless you provided elections training support you would never level the playing field in South Africa. Because you were asking a sector of the democratic movement with no experience of elections whatsoever to compete on an equal footing with the National Party, which at that time had the monopoly of the media, both electronic and printed, and a huge, highly sophisticated and experienced election machine. Toresson and his colleagues not only quickly came to see the logic of what we were saying, but also very swiftly linked up with ANC.

To cut a long story short, VEETU was then established as a subsection of ERIP. It was a consortium of four big training NGOs in Cape Town, Durban, East London and Johannesburg. ERIP was the recipient of the funding support from Sweden and managed the national process, both in terms of financial management and in terms of design of the training, specifically together with ANC. It was a very big project. I think that forty thousand people were trained for the elections. They were trained in elections management, media, security, communications, canvassing and speech making, public relations, fund-raising, financial management, administration etc.

TS: The trainees were not only from the ANC?

GS: No, there was an agreement with the Swedes that we would train all the political parties which hitherto had not participated in an election. That meant ANC, PAC and the Inkhata Freedom Party (IFP) which only joined the process three or four weeks before the elections took place. However, in spite of repeated written and face to face requests to provide IFP with training, they never agreed to that. But we also trained the trade unions, NACTU and COSATU, the civics—not just SANCO, but even small civic organizations—CONTRALESA and fifty different women's organisations.

It was a massive project. It would never have been possible without the Olof Palme International Center. It was not just the financial support. During the seven months before the elections, I cannot recall a period longer than two weeks when somebody from the Olof Palme International Center was not here to give advice, support and, in a sense, knowledge and experience of elections in Sweden and other countries. In a way, I think that the massive effort of some twelve million Rands was seen by the Swedish people as a sort of natural culmination of a long process of support for the coming to fruition of democracy. It was the final contribution that should be made, although there was obviously a good understanding that the struggle for development was only just beginning with the coming into existence of formal democracy.

It also had a massive international impact. People from VEETU travelled to Russia, Ukraine, Tanzania, Vietnam, Palestine and other countries, basically to provide people in those countries with an understanding and a framework of what VEETU did to prepare for the South African elections. So, it had a much wider impact than South Africa itself. Two books have already been published on the subject of VEETU.

TS: Was the Olof Palme International Center the main funder of VEETU?

GS: There was also support from Denmark, Holland and from NGOs in the USA, such as the Mott Foundation. The Italians had promised money, but it was not forthcoming. There were governments that categorically refused to give money. The British, the Americans and the Germans. I met their ambassadors on a number of occasions. What was remarkable for me was that it in a sense characterized the Swedish and the Nordic ability to come to terms with the real issues of the liberation struggle in a way that other countries were not able to do. They were able to see that just doing voters' education did not level the playing fields at all. You had to provide elections' management training. You had to train people to be able to contest an election in order to be able to fight it on an equal footing.

I left VEETU four months before the elections. I then worked with ANC for the campaign in the Western Cape. Here there was Swedish Social Democratic Party support. That was invaluable in terms of advice, guidance and for gaining a strategic understanding of an election process. It was absolutely invaluable. What I recall as being most important was the meetings with the ANC leadership—Nelson Mandela, Walter Sisulu and others—but also with the regional leadership. The biggest problem for ANC before the election was a lack of understanding of what an election is. The politicians thought that they could lead the election, but there was no understanding of the management component. I think that the Swedish Social Democrats went a very long way in assisting ANC to reach a proper understanding of what an election is, of its component parts, its political parts, its management parts. ANC could have made very serious mistakes, but the potential for those mistakes was very much minimized by the support from Sweden.

Craig Williamson
National Party—Military intelligence officer and commander of foreign operations—Deputy Director of the International University Exchange Fund—Member of the President's Council
Executive Outcomes
(Pretoria, 23 April 1996)

Tor Sellström: In your personal view and that of the structures for which you worked in South Africa, why did Sweden and the other Nordic countries become so involved in Southern Africa?
Craig Williamson: That is a question which we tried to answer for a long time. I think that the best answer that I can give you—and the best analysis that we came to over the years—is that it related to the Nordic, particularly the Swedish, brand of Social Democracy. It was different to the Marxist-Leninist brand and also to the socialism of the British Labour Party and parties like that.

Throughout my involvement with different organizations, I noticed and reported on political tensions which existed within various structures, especially aid agencies, governments and organizations such as SIDA, but in particular within the non-governmental organizations that they were supporting. I worked with people who identified political forces in various areas of the world and who tried to take them under their wing. In other words, a non-governmental organization would try to become involved with a political group, say in Latin America or Africa, the leaders of which they believed to be salvageable. It was almost a religious thing. You must develop and nurture the political leaders and organizations who were following a political course which you, the aid donor, felt was correct. Rather than have these people becoming hard-line Marxist-Leninists, it was better to raise some support in the international arena and give them assistance.

At that time, a lot of the liberation organizations were complaining that the only people who gave them assistance were the East bloc countries and that the West was, in fact, guilty of being in complicity with apartheid and with the regimes in Latin America. I think that there were political forces in the West who agreed that the conservative political organizations in the West were in complicity with apartheid and with the Latin American dictators and so on, but felt that they should not be. At the same time, they also did not think that they should be supporting Moscow's foreign policy objectives in whichever region.
TS: It appears contradictory that the Nordic countries—who were clearly anti-Communist—supported the same movements in Southern Africa that were backed by the Soviet Union.
CW: I think that one of the key elements of the South African security forces' war

against ANC and the other liberation movements at that time was to paint them as part of the international Soviet view of things and to discourage anti-Soviet countries and organizations to support them. One of the biggest problems, or hindrances, to that policy was, in fact, the Swedes and the Nordic countries. Later on even the Canadians and the Dutch. Those were the most stubborn Western countries who continued to support ANC. What South Africa would have liked was that everybody should take a black and white, or a white and red, colour view of things, which Sweden never did.

TS: Would it in this context be correct to say that Olof Palme played an important role?

CW: Yes, that is where Olof Palme came in as, I suppose, one of the ideologues of that view. Palme and the people around him were a third force in this type of political situation and they saw it as a very important role. Therefore, they supported, or they were open to support, people who phrased their requests in a way that they found attractive. But that is not unusual. I think that it happens in any funding activity. When people come with a funding request they will obviously design it to get the best possible response from the person who makes the decision.

TS: Olof Palme and his colleagues had old personal relations with many liberation leaders from Southern Africa. Do you think that personal relationship made it easier for the Social Democratic forces in the Nordic countries to see beyond the East-West divide?

CW: Yes, I think so, because I had a similar experience. Getting to know various leaders personally, you get to know more about their personal political world view than if you just read their writings or the official magazine of the movement. Those who had a chance to meet these people personally, to go to university with them or become close political friends with them, understood that none of them, or very few of them, actually were Communists. That the type of socialism that they were thinking about, and probably wished to promote, was a type of socialism which fitted with the ideological view of the Nordic leaders, or people who became leaders in the Nordic countries.

TS: Was that contradictory to you? You were working for forces that wanted you to paint the world white-red?

CW: Oh, no! I always used to say that 'I have spent ten years looking for a black Communist and I have not found one yet'. Everybody would laugh. People might call me a racist, but there were actually very few blacks in the Communist Party who were ideologues. The ideological driving force in the Communist Party was mainly eurocentric. But that did not mean that it was not useful for us—for political purposes—to paint the whole organization red. And a lot of politicians, of course, believed that. I still think that some National Party politicians believe that if we could just split the Communists away from the other black guys, then we would not have any problems. Even in 1990-91, when I finally got out of the National Party, that was the belief. Even during CODESA it was still the belief. But I think that there were more accurate views in the security forces and the intelligence community.

TS: You worked with the International University Exchange Fund (IUEF) for a long time. IUEF was accused of supporting a so-called third force in South Africa. How true would this be? Was it something that the Nordic Social Democratic parties promoted?

CW: I think that the way Lars-Gunnar Eriksson and his friends in the Swedish Social Democratic Party saw it—putting it very simplistically—was that there is a liberation struggle in South Africa which is a just struggle, but the black political groupings have a problem, because they are dominated by ANC, which in turn is dominated by the Communist Party, which is controlled by the Soviets. They did not only get that view from their own personal experience of the situation. They also heard that view expressed very loudly by certain black South African politicians, particularly by PAC people and, of course, after 1976 very vocally by Black Consciousness Movement people, who refused to join ANC. They did so for two reasons. One, because they said it was ineffective. It had not done anything. Two, because basically it was an organization ideologically dominated by whites and the Soviets. The Swedes were seeking a way to assist this new, younger generation of thinkers in the South African liberation struggle, and they tried to avoid being dictated to by ANC and others in determining who should be assisted. Obviously, ANC would only assist people who were in their camp.

The Swedes took an independent view and started to say 'We must give support to Harry Nengwekhulu, Barney Pityana—who, of course, later went very strongly into ANC—and these types of people'. A Christian, non-Marxist group of people. But socialist. There was definitely substance to this, because I saw the personal memoranda written between Lars-Gunnar Eriksson and Pierre Schori and these people, where he would give them some views on what was going on. They would sometimes write back to him and he would even draft questions to be asked in parliament, or replies. That was definitely their belief.

I think that NGO's were used to do and say things and promote policies which the Swedish government and the other Nordic governments could not officially do. They had to officially tell Oliver Tambo: 'Oliver, we are a hundred per cent behind you and we like you very much. You know, we do not like Joe Slovo too much, but we understand.' But, in reality, they did not want ANC to be allowed to push the emerging black leaders into obscurity. If you do not give a flower water, it dies. I think that it was the view. Give these flowers some water and do it through IUEF. And IUEF had a clever way of saying that the aid was humanitarian. 'We have to give aid to all refugees, to all people' and so forth. So, it was a defendable policy.

TS: Is it your impression that Denmark and Norway—being members of NATO—were less in favour of ANC than Sweden?

CW: I always got the impression that Denmark was the least interested. I think that they went along because it was an emotional thing. It was right. I did not ever get the idea in Denmark that there was a strong ideological involvement. The youth movements and others that we worked with in Denmark were very much less political than in Norway. In Norway, there was a conflict between different political forces in the youth movements. We used to go there with the South African programme, or other programmes, to give credibility as part of a political battle within those organizations. It was more political. For example, when I in 1978 manipulated IUEF into accepting ANC as the sole liberation movement in South Africa, the Swedes accepted it, but in Norway people were very angry. In Denmark, Poul Brandrup and them said: 'What you guys do, you do.' They did not have a very strong political approach. They were doing something that they believed was correct. Anybody who was against apartheid—as long as they were not throwing bombs—should really be given some assistance.

TS: There was never any direct support by IUEF to Inkatha?

CW: No. There was only some very small support to Inkatha. Buthelezi came to Geneva and met with Eriksson several times. There was a guy there, an old trade-unionist, who was meant to be Buthelezi's sort of representative, but when Musa Myeni came to Geneva they gave him some support, in terms of a scholarship and this type of thing. But they would never assist the organization as such. Buthelezi tried to get support from IUEF, but he never succeeded. Lars-Gunnar blocked it because of the 'puppet-of-apartheid' thing. He could not justify such support. I think that he was given the advice that Inkatha should not be supported. In fact, I know that he discussed it with ANC in Maputo. With Joe Nhanhla, who told him not to. At times he was confused. He came to me and said: 'Buthelezi is a good friend of Tambo. They have met in London. Would it not be useful to support him?' But Joe Nhanhla and ANC said no. And, of course, the instructions I got were also no. I mean from the ANC-Communist Party side, not from our government.

TS: Reading between the lines, it seems that the interest of the South African security establishment was that you should get to ANC through IUEF. Was that the objective?

CW: Yes, but not as simplistic as that. It was to understand the whole dynamic behind the anti-apartheid support internationally. We had to sabotage it. We were much more worried in the mid-1970s about the Black Consciousness Movement than about ANC. That is why we started to sabotage IUEF's support for BCM. It was like a double-edged sword. It was also to get me more popular with ANC, obviously. I was doing something that they believed in. 'Even if this man has a dubious background, he is doing something which we want him to do. He is effective.' So, if somebody went and said this or that about me, ANC would say: 'Hey, just leave him alone. He is working under discipline and he is doing his job'. That was good for me.

We wanted to cut the funding support to the Black Consciousness Movement. For two reasons. Number one, they were a problem internally. Politically, that was where the problem was, not with ANC. Number two, it was part of the whole process of trying to have a very clear black and red situation. But here we had a difficult situation. It was not so easy for 'Pik' Botha or his people to go to a foreign minister overseas and explain that the BCM guys were also red. We could not give them the proper ammunition. And you start to sound less credible if you say that anybody who opposes you is a Communist. Then people would say: 'We have heard that type of story before'.

Sweden and the Nordic countries were also supporting the World University Service and there were a lot of ideological problems with that, because WUS started to support—in fact, more and more—the Black Consciousness Movement. They had a much more religious approach, more of the centre, maybe. This became a political problem, because one had not only to try and stop the support from IUEF, but also to make sure that funding did not go into WUS, because that could defeat our goal.

TS: That must have been uncomfortable for you? At the same time as IUEF was trying to broaden the support, you wanted it to be narrowed down to ANC?

CW: Yes, it was very difficult because of that. I had to narrow it down to ANC, but without being illogical. If I suddenly would have said to Lars-Gunnar that we must support this or that ANC initiative, he would immediately have thought that I was a Communist. He would have thought that this is a SACP guy. Which is what people like Buthelezi and people from ZANU told him. They were not so worried about me being a spy for South Africa. They were worried that I was a white South African Communist. So, on the one hand he had to tell people: 'He is not a Communist'. And on the other: 'He is not working for the South Africans either'. It was a bit tricky. If I had just said: 'Look, ANC is *the* liberation movement', he would not have gone for it.

It took a bit of time. Of course, the only reason it worked was that the Black Consciousness Movement started to have some problems of its own from 1976-78. They broke up into fractions. The Gaborone office was asking one thing, the London people another and then Lusaka was saying something else. Some people were talking to ANC and some were not. For IUEF, a non-governmental organization having to justify money and expenses to donors, it became a bit tricky. But, using that confusion, I was able to move the political decision to recognize ANC. And, of course, during that same period ANC got its act together. After 1976, they got a wake-up call and realized that they had better get the organization to do what it was supposed to be doing. They started to look better and at the IUEF conference in 1978 I was able to get the policy through.

TS: Who was then Lars-Gunnar Eriksson? You have described him as an anti-Communist. Many have asked if he was working for Swedish, or Nordic, interests or for South Africa?

CW: He was a fanatical Social Democrat. Fanatical. Lars-Gunnar Eriksson liked to play. He loved intrigue and he created intrigue, but he really disliked Communists. That is why we found him useful.

TS: Even before you joined IUEF, the financial management of the organization had been strongly criticized. You have stated that you managed to divert funds through Lichtenstein to your structures in South Africa. Daisy Farm has been mentioned. Could you comment on this?

CW: First of all, I would say that Lars-Gunnar's problem was that he was not a good manager in terms of technical things. He was a politician. He was very good at getting to know people, to understand what they wanted, the political structures and so on, but he did not care about the actual figures and the financial management, making sure that this account and that account were balanced. Money was money. If he had something that he needed money for, he would spend it and worry about trying to justify which account it came from afterwards. I suppose that you can get away with that if at least—after you spend the money—you find a way to account for it. If not, it becomes administratively impossible to start unravelling the mess. And it became a complete mess.

TS: Which was handy for you?

CW: Yes. He then created a slush-fund. At first, he had a less structured slush-fund, but at a certain stage he realized that he had to have a proper one. So he created this thing in Vaduz, Liechtenstein, called Southern Futures. He then used to report to the donors: 'Look, on certain confidential projects all I can tell you is that when the money leaves IUEF's account, you have to accept that for auditing purposes it has been spent'. He would take the money out of IUEF and put it into Southern Futures Vaduz and, of course, he could then do what he liked with Southern Futures Vaduz. This does not mean that he stole the money or spent it on his chalet in France. He was well paid. He had a good salary. He could afford a good life. But if he had gone to SIDA and said: 'The ILO conference is on in Geneva. All the liberation guys are there and I am going to take them to a night-club and this and that', they would have had a heart-attack if the money was coming out of IUEF. So it would come out of Southern Futures Vaduz.

Some of these guys, for example Sam Nujoma, would come to town and say: 'Lars-Gunnar, I need money'. Lars-Gunnar would say: 'How much?' 'Well, 20,000 Francs'. Lars-Gunnar would then give him 20,000 Francs, which would come out of the slush-fund. Every time Joshua Nkomo came to town he got money. He stayed at the Intercontinental Hotel, which was an expensive business.

Lars-Gunnar was playing a political game. So, what we did was just the same. IUEF was supposed to have a leadership training programme for white students in South Africa. The money had to be spent, because if it was not spent there would not be any more grants given. Sometimes there was pressure. Lars-Gunnar would say: 'We have got money for this white student programme. Are we not going to spend it? What am I going to tell the donors if it does not exist?' That is how it was done. It was a leadership training programme, but, unfortunately, it was a leadership training programme for the security forces, not for the anti-apartheid forces. At one stage we ran an internal structure here which was financed by IUEF. People even came from Denmark and other countries and were shown the programme. They went to the farm and were very happy.

TS: To Daisy Farm?

CW: Yes. Poul Brandrup from Denmark lived on the farm for a while. He was told that this was the secret place we had for training of anti-apartheid activists. They all said: 'Oh, wonderful! This is in the heart of apartheid, just twenty kilometres from Pretoria. They have got a farm where they are training the opposition'. They believed the romance of the thing.

TS: One wonders how the Nordic governments could continue increasing the allocations to IUEF?

CW: I think that they were doing it deliberately. I mean, we believed that. For example, I gave cash to ANC. We were supposed to be supporting this or that programme, but I would go to the bank in Geneva with Swiss Francs and buy Rands at a discounted rate. I would get about twenty or thirty per cent more Rands and then go to Lusaka and give ANC Rands. Thomas Nkobi would give us a written account of the money, with a big ANC stamp on it. 'Thank you very much!' I mean, what did I write in my reports to the South African government? Sweden and the other donors could not give money to ANC for political and military purposes, but they gave it to IUEF, who then played some games and it went there anyway.

I know that people in Sweden knew that he was giving out cash. Sitting late at night, having some schnapps and coffee, he would say: 'This is politics. This is the real world. We do not all live on refugee scholarships and little farms that make handicrafts. These people are fighting a liberation struggle. They have to pay hotel bills and so on'. He often used to have that argument. The donors would say: 'Yes, but you know that we do not have funds for that'. But he found a way to create the funds. Air-tickets were one of the biggest slush-fund activities. The guys would phone from Lusaka and say: 'We have to send so and so many delegates somewhere. We need air-tickets'. He would then buy the tickets, although there was no project that could buy them.

TS: Who were the most critical among the donors?

CW: I think that he was less scared of the Swedes, because he had more political influence with SIDA. He was more scared of the Danes. They were very pernickety. The Canadians were another problem, because Paul Ladouceur was actually on the IUEF board and he was a real auditor. But Southern Futures Vaduz was unbreakable. The recipients also played ball. It was not that the money was disappearing into Southern Futures Vaduz. The recipients would tell the donor that they got the money. ANC would give them a piece of paper saying: 'We have received the money'. So the donor left it there. Especially for the internal programmes it was understood, for security reasons. Between the recipient and himself, Lars-Gunnar could make any arrangement.

TS: IUEF also tried to serve as some sort of fund-raiser for the SOMAFCO settlement in Tanzania and you tried to work with IDAF in London. Do I see you behind these initiatives? If you were pushing the ANC line?

CW: Yes, the Solomon Mahlango Freedom College. ANC, Lars-Gunnar and everybody saw that as a prestige project. IDAF was a different thing. Lars-Gunnar was convinced that it was run by the Communists and he wanted to take over its function. But he also had people who came to the office complaining about IDAF.

People can say what they like about IDAF, but the fact at the end of the day is that IDAF for a long time supported who they felt like supporting. There was a strong South African Communist Party influence there. IUEF paid lawyers for people on trial, because IDAF just could not get the bureaucracy together and Lars-Gunnar never believed that it was purely because of funding or bureaucracy. He said: 'These guys have got problems. They have been arrested. They are on trial and they need lawyers to be paid'. Often we paid. IDAF would then get angry and refund IUEF, which we usually would accept, because we had used money from some other programme. IUEF did not have the money to pay for trials.

Lars-Gunnar and Canon Collins had a reasonable relationship, but his relationship with the rest of them was very antagonistic. He planned to take over IDAF. He thought that he could do it when Collins went. This was not only a personal ambition. It was political. He did not like IDAF.

TS: So this was nothing that you had to push?

CW: No. I helped him, obviously, because the more trouble we could cause for IDAF the better. But I had a difficulty there, because I could not be too openly anti-IDAF since I was supposed to be on the ANC side.

TS: In the Swedish media, both Pierre Schori and Mats Hellström have been asked to comment upon IUEF, Lars-Gunnar Eriksson and yourself, but they have declined to do so. Why do you think that they have never talked about this. Is it because they were very close to Eriksson?

CW: I do not know. I think that they were good friends. Lars-Gunnar was a guy who at the end of the day was doing what a lot of people wanted him to do. He was tripped up.

TS: Coming back to South Africa, you have admitted to planning the actions against Ruth First in Maputo and Jeanette Schoon in Lubango in Angola. Do you know of any plans directed against SIDA people in the Frontline States that were assisting ANC or other liberation movements?

CW: I revealed the actions against Ruth First and Jeanette Schoon because I realized what was going on, but when we did our cross-border operations we tried to avoid to have any international people hit due to the political problems involved.

TS: The SIDA people were also diplomatic personnel. It would probably have been difficult for you to do anything against them?

CW: They would not have done anything against SIDA people. At one stage—when the Rhodesians bombed Lusaka and we had given information to them of where to strike—there was a German aid worker killed and everybody was very upset. No. They did not even go for the Soviets, so they would not have gone for the Swedes.

TS: I also asked UNITA this question. They once kidnapped—and actually killed—Swedish aid workers. But they said that it had been a political error.

CW: Yes, it can be carried out by a unit who does it because they think it is the right thing, but it is not the organization as such who thinks so.

TS: Do you know who were behind the bombing of the ANC office in Stockholm?
CW: I actually did not even know that it was bombed.
TS: Did you have any agents in Sweden or in the other Nordic countries?
CW: Our involvement there was not very good. I would say that the first time that we really got a lot of information was when I was operating there. They would obviously have had some people there, but I do not think that there was anything particular. I really think that South Africa was not—how should I put it—obsessed with the Nordic countries. It was more of a political problem. I mean, the support was not in the same context as the Soviet support. I think that they wanted to deal with it more on a political level. The Nordic countries were left very much to the foreign affairs people.
TS: It has also been alleged that your intelligence in IUEF led to the assassination of Steve Biko.
CW: Well, the reality of that was that Steve Biko was coming out of the country to meet with Oliver Tambo. It was set up by the Swedes and by Lars-Gunnar. I reported that it was going to happen, but I do not know if the fact that they then beat him up and killed him was based on that. I actually do not believe that the people who arrested him would have known that intelligence. It would never have been revealed to them. They would never have told them: 'Look, we have got information that Biko is going to see Tambo'.
TS: Was it not the same structure?
CW: It was the same structure, but they would never have told them, because it would have been too sensitive. They may have told them that Biko is up to something. 'Detain him or question him!' I do not even know. But the reality is that Biko's detention and then death was at the time when he was secretly going to leave the country to meet Tambo. It was all funded by Swedish money through IUEF. That was bad news.
TS: There are also some people who have mentioned your name in connection with the Palme assassination.
CW: It is fantasy.
TS: Is it plausible to talk about a South African link to the Palme assassination?

CW: I do not think that anybody here hated Olof Palme. If they were going to kill a head of state, hell, there are a lot of people before Olof Palme that would have been on the list. I really do not understand why Olof Palme. If they were prepared to do such a thing, I think that there would have been quite a few other targets. One day I saw a newspaper article which said that the murder was done by *Koevoet* under my command and that we had camped in the forests outside Stockholm in winter. Some journalist asked me and I said: 'Yes, we actually went overland from Africa with *casspirs*, all the way from Johannesburg. We drove in *casspirs* to Sweden. We did the operation and nobody saw us. Then he said: 'You are joking!' I said: 'Well, please, do me a favour'. They said that it was *Koevoet* people. I said that 'we were trained in desert warfare and now you tell me that we went and camped in the forests outside Stockholm in the middle of winter. That nobody saw us, that we crept into the city and killed the Prime Minister and left. And that nobody found one trace. That is really quite good'. Now there is some lunatic here in Pretoria who keeps telling the Swedes that I was the commander and that he bought the gun. He is a madman. He wants money.
TS: Is there anything you would like to add?
CW: Well, if you go through the IUEF files of the Latin American programmes, you will find that there is a parallel. For example, Eden Pastora, Comandante Zero in Nicaragua, was getting money from IUEF and that was because he was an anti-Communist. They were playing exactly the same role with the Contras. Chile, Argentina and Nicaragua were IUEF's main programmes. I do not know the names, but all of it was designed to support the Social Democratic elements of these groups. That is why IUEF always had the reputation among the left of being CIA. The old ISC was set up by the intelligence agencies and IUEF came out of ISC. When ISC collapsed, Lars-Gunnar, Schori and them kept it alive as an independent organization. It always did the same thing. It always supported anybody who was Social Democratic, but not Marxist. I do not think that you will find one contradiction there.

TS: In retrospect, would you then say that the role of the Nordic countries was constructive for Southern Africa?

CW: Well, I think that the Nordic influence has been very strong. As I flippantly said—a bit cynically maybe—we looked for black Communism and we failed to find it. I do not know whether *ubuntu*— the traditional element amongst the African people, which some people equate with Communism—has got more in common with Social Democracy than with Marxism-Leninism. But I think that Lars-Gunnar and those people clearly saw that it could be nurtured and developed.

Obviously, I think that the success here has been greater than in other places. The quality of leadership in Namibia since liberation has not been the same as we have here. In Zimbabwe the same. Here, I think that the basic thinking of ANC probably has benefited a lot from the Nordic influence. But, at the end of the day we all know that if it was not for other historical forces—which brought about the time of Gorbachev—we would probably not be sitting talking here. By this time, we would probably be in quite a nice fighting situation.

Zimbabwe

Canaan Banana
Co-leader of the African National Council—ZANU—President of Zimbabwe
Professor at the University of Zimbabwe
(Harare, 3 June 1996)

Carl Fredrik Hallencreutz: From your perspective, how would you explain the involvement by the Nordic countries in the liberation struggle in Zimbabwe and Southern Africa?
Canaan Banana: I think that the involvement of the Nordic countries was very central and crucial to the advancement of our struggle for freedom in the region. We were operating at the time of the Cold War and while the socialist countries appeared to be ready to assist the liberation movements in Southern Africa, the bulk of the Western countries—including the United States of America—dismissed us as terrorists, merely repeating the language of Ian Smith. It was a great disappointment.

The Nordic countries were viewed by the nationalist forces in particular and the people of Zimbabwe generally as a very welcome neutral force that did not have any perceived interests to protect, while both the Western and the Eastern powers were busy supporting one group against the other for reasons of ideology and so-called spheres of interests. However, we felt that the Nordic countries came in purely on humanitarian grounds and it is against that background that their involvement became very crucial and also lent a certain amount of legitimacy to the freedom struggle.
CFH: What would you then suggest as possible factors that made the early involvement by the Nordic countries possible?
CB: I believe that the missionary work played an important role and that missionaries—although they were also divided between a progressive and a conservative element—were concerned about the plight of the majority of the black people of this country. From time to time they submitted written reports to their home missions. Others wrote to magazines to give the Swedish people a picture of the situation that was prevailing in our country. Also, do not forget that they had begun a trans-Atlantic voyage and that a few Africans who got scholarships from the mission centres were beginning to study in Europe. They became a kind of ally through which the church and the people of Sweden generally would be introduced and exposed to the nature of our struggle. I really believe that the role that the church played through its missions and through the witness of people who got assistance to study in the Nordic countries was important.
CFH: As a Methodist minister, did you have any contacts with Swedish missionaries?
CB: Well, we used to meet within the context of various church councils. In the Rhodesian Christian Council there were missionaries from Sweden that I got in touch with and during my studies at the Epworth Theological College we also had tutors—missionaries—who came from Sweden. I think that a good number of them understood the dynamics of the struggle, although I must hasten to say that many of them also tended to distance themselves from the politics of the country. However, they did not necessarily support the status quo. In this, what was true of the Swedish church was also true of many other churches.

We have to distinguish between what I call the official position of the church and the non-official. The official was represented by the leadership defending the status quo and the non-official position was represented by individual missionaries who were non-conformist with regard to the proclaimed policy of their home churches and who went out of their way to try and understand the dynamics of the African struggle for freedom. Some of them identified with that struggle.

My real active contact with the Church of Sweden Mission in Zimbabwe was, however, really through the indigenous priests. I used to join forces with a number of them when we were mobilizing material support for the freedom fighters, particularly those who were operating in the Mberengwa area.
CFH: You were, of course, active in the Council of Churches in Bulawayo. Did you then work with the Church of Sweden Mission?

CB: Yes, very much so. When I was chairman of the Bulawayo Council of Churches, the Church of Sweden was part of the council. We also joined forces when we addressed the problems of school leavers and the drift of blacks from the rural areas. We established centres where community schools took place in church halls and the Church of Sweden was very co-operative. I was also invited a number of times to preach in the Swedish churches.

CFH: The African National Council (ANC) was formed in December 1971 and you became one of its leaders, together with Bishop Muzorewa. From the ANC point of view, how would you assess the role played by the Church of Swedish Mission?

CB: Well, at that particular time the churches were very careful not to be seen by the secular government to be linked with the liberation forces outside. That was the case with all churches and as far as ANC was concerned, we did not make a clear distinction between the operations and activities of individual churches as such. The church was seen by ANC to be a little bit lukewarm, although ANC itself had its leadership from the church. A lot of church people participated and ANC got support from most of the major churches in Zimbabwe. I have no reason to believe that the Church of Sweden Mission was different. I think that they also saw ANC as an organization that filled an important vacuum in the absence of the detained nationalist leaders, but as far as the internal forces were concerned there was not very much pronounced, open support for the struggle by the Church of Sweden.

Of course, the Nordic countries were extending assistance to the liberation movements outside the country and I think that it was done in a manner that would not endanger anybody here in Zimbabwe. It was a very difficult period and a lot of the activities that were carried out inside the country were done so quietly.

CFH: Did ANC have any direct or official links with the Nordic governments?

CB: Not that I know of, but you must appreciate that the ANC period was very short and that soon after its formation I left Zimbabwe for studies in the United States. Whether there were any formal contacts established during my absence I would not know. And soon after my return to Zimbabwe I was detained.

CFH: Sweden decided at an early stage to support both ZANU and ZAPU. Did you see that as a problem?

CB: No, I would want to interpret that as an act of tremendous maturity. They were supporting the cause of African freedom regardless of the ideological persuasions of the various nationalist forces. I think that a great amount of respect should be given, because if anybody wants to dictate to any people—let alone to the people of Zimbabwe—what philosophy, doctrine, policy or system they should embrace, they would be insulting the integrity of that people. Co-operation and support, yes, but on our terms.

I think that this was the problem that we found with a number of Western organizations who said: 'Yes, we are ready to give you support on condition that you renounce your links with certain countries and that you commit yourselves to so-called free enterprise and democratic traditions'. We felt that those were matters that were best left to the people of Zimbabwe. It was their democratic and sole prerogative to decide their own policy. So, the fact that the Nordic countries supported the cause of Zimbabwe's freedom without regard to the future ideological and political system was a mark of great maturity and something that the Nordic countries must take a lot of credit for.

CFH: The assistance to ZANU and ZAPU was for humanitarian purposes only and there were strict rules on reporting and auditing. Do you remember if there were any complaints regarding the utilization of the support?

CB: No. If there were complaints they would have been communicated directly to the leadership concerned, maybe behind closed doors. And the fact that I at that time was not part of the leadership of the liberation movement meant that I was not privileged to that kind of information.

CFH: You were detained from 1975, but released to attend the Geneva conference at the end of 1976. Did you have any contacts with government representatives from the Nordic countries during the conference?

CB: Not personally, but I would not be sure whether or not contacts were established because my period in Geneva was somewhat divided. I went to Geneva in the Muzorewa delegation and then moved to ZANU and the Patriotic Front. I was among the top eight who were negotiating in Geneva. I do not recall any Swedes coming to meet us as a negotiating team, but that is not to say that contacts were not established, because there were spokesmen on foreign matters from both ZANU and ZAPU in the Patriotic Front delegation.

CFH: Did anyone from the Nordic countries recognize your move from ANC to ZANU? Did they approach you about it?

CB: No, I was not approached.

CFH: After the internal settlement in 1978, there were discussions in some Nordic circles about possible support to Bishop Muzorewa. Did you have any information about that?

CB: Not at all. All of that period I was in prison and they made sure that there was a very heavy censorship. I never received any newspapers and the only radio information that we were being exposed to was the very official Rhodesian broadcasts. We were not even allowed to listen to the Africa service of the BBC.

CFH: When the Lancaster House Agreement was signed in December 1979, did you then discuss the future of Zimbabwe with representatives of the Nordic churches?

CB: Yes, very much so. I remember a meeting that we held at Bishop Shiri's office in Bulawayo with a visiting delegation from the Lutheran World Federation. They were very concerned and wanted to know what to expect. We had a very frank discussion and I advised them that it would be beneficial for the church to seek an audience with the new leadership that was likely to emerge after the elections, that is Robert Mugabe and Joshua Nkomo. They expressed their concerns, hopes and expectations and wondered very much about the future of the church in a new, free and independent Zimbabwe. On my part, I had, of course, no fears whatsoever and I assured them that although I was an individual, I was going to do what I could to ensure that the church had its place in the new Zimbabwe.

I think that everybody was concerned about the so-called links with the East and that when the Patriotic Front won the elections, the churches were perhaps going to be closed down. I did not foresee that taking place, so I tried to assure the churches that they did not have to fear the new government, that this was an irrelevant fear and that the true fear was their own fear. They could redeem themselves by doing the right thing and be liberated from the old paternalistic approach, recognizing that the African people had the sole right to define their own agenda. I was merely stating the fundamental principle of respecting people to determine their own destiny, so that the interests of the people would be paramount in determining the decisions that were going to be made in Zimbabwe by the new government, but also by the churches. I urged the churches to take advantage of the change, move in the direction of reconciliation and participate in the programmes of reconstruction, because if the people saw the churches working actively, no one would attack them. If so, the people would rise and defend the churches.

The Lutheran World Federation responded positively and to a great extent by mobilizing material support at independence. They drilled a number of boreholes in Southern Matabeleland and continued their education programmes. They were ready to participate at independence, but whether or not they did enough prior to independence is a question that history, and history alone, will be able to answer.

CFH: You were appointed the first President of the Republic of Zimbabwe in April 1980. In that position, were you able to maintain your contacts with the Church of Sweden Mission?

CB: Well, not really. However, I did meet with individual Swedish missionary leaders and with the local leadership, who discussed things in a general manner. We also met within the context of the Zimbabwe Christian Council at the time when Bishop Shiri was the President of the Council. Problems emerged when information reached us that there were individuals within the council who wanted to sabotage the programmes of development and we felt that some investigations had to be carried out. Bishop Shiri led various delegations to discuss the problem that had arisen between the council and the government at the time. I got the impression that Bishop Shiri himself was very genuine in wanting to seek some kind of accommodation, but initially the council itself was a little bit worried about what Sweden perceived as interference in church matters by the government. It was only when they realized that we were serious that they began to sit down to talk to us in earnest.

The problem was centred around the General Secretary, who did not understand the challenges of the new situation and as government we felt that he had to go. He belonged to the old order. He belonged to Zimbabwe/Rhodesia and wanted to frustrate the efforts of the new government. The churches understood the allegations—in fact, the information had come from the Christian Council itself—but it became a matter of principle. There were churches which said: 'Look, as a matter of principle we cannot be told by the government what we should do!'. However, as a government it was our responsibility to ensure the security of the state and to ensure that the programmes of reconstruction and development were implemented, particularly at a time when international assistance was most needed.

CFH: Finally, as a statesman, you very much opened up a theological perspective on liberation and development and you have continued this endeavour as a scholar. In this context, have you also kept in close contact with Sweden and the other Nordic countries?

CB: Yes. Since my retirement from active politics, I have made numerous visits to Sweden—to Uppsala in particular—where I have had close contacts with you, Professor Hallencreutz, and the Nordic Africa Institute, who have organized various seminars where I have presented papers and participated in discussions. They have had a very active interest in the social, historical and theological connections between Sweden and Zimbabwe. However, what was once a hive of activity in Uppsala now seems to be going towards a natural death. Perhaps we need some resources from Sweden to enable us to reflect. Before independence, we were reflecting and critically looking at the powers that we were dealing with, but now it is not very easy for us to do that. I think that joint efforts with well-meaning people from the Nordic countries and other parts of the world could help us to redefine our own agenda and see to what extent we can build a society that is truly democratic and in harmony, socially, mentally and in all aspects of life.

Dumiso Dabengwa
ZAPU / ZIPRA—Head of Military Intelligence
Minister of Home Affairs
(Harare, 27 July 1995)

Tor Sellström: You led negotiations with Sweden on behalf of ZAPU in Lusaka in the late 1970s regarding humanitarian support. Did you also participate in similar discussions with other Nordic countries?

Dumiso Dabengwa: No, it was mainly with Sweden. I had discussions with SIDA. We were looking for support at that time, particularly for the refugee population that had come through to Zambia. I was then in command of the ZIPRA forces, and whilst we were bringing our own recruits from inside Zimbabwe we had a problem with young people who decided to leave school. They wanted to join the liberation struggle. But we realized that they were too young to be involved, so, instead, we organized schools for them. We had two camps which were responsible for these young people, J. Z. Moyo Camp and Victory Camp. A boys' camp and a girls' camp. We put them into classes. They were studying, and it was mainly for this purpose that I led the ZAPU delegation, requesting assistance for the young people who we were not going to use in the military.

TS: The Swedish relationship with ZAPU goes back a long way. Even in the 1960s, support was channelled through Christian Care and IDAF to families like the Chinamano family and others who were imprisoned in Rhodesia.

DD: Yes, that is correct.

TS: When did you have your first contacts with the Nordic countries?

DD: My first contact with the Nordic countries was in Zambia, at the beginning of the 1970s.

TS: I think that the first protocol between ZAPU and SIDA was signed in 1973?

DD: Yes, that is correct.

TS: How did you view the support from the Nordic countries?

DD: Well, we had very good relations with the Nordic countries. We were, for instance, part of the Helsinki World Peace Council. That is, to a very large extent, how we got in touch with the Nordic countries. After that it spread to Sweden, where we had a representative. He was based in Sweden, serving all the Nordic countries. We had good relations right from the beginning, as I say, through the Peace Council.

We were very clear that we accepted assistance from anyone. Whoever gave us assistance. It does not necessarily mean that we got that assistance because we shared the same ideological concepts. What was important for us was if people were willing to give us assistance to get rid of the oppression in our country.

TS: As long as it was without strings attached?

DD: Yes, as long as it was without strings attached. The Nordic peoples gave us assistance and recognized our plight and our struggle and that was what was important. We did not need to have to subscribe to their ideologies. It was not received in return for anything.

TS: It could look contradictory that member countries of NATO like Denmark and Norway joined forces with neutral Sweden in giving humanitarian support to the liberation movements that followed a socialist path. You did not see that as a problem?

DD: No, we did not have a problem with that. We were very genuine and frank and said to them that we accepted aid from the socialist countries, but that that did not necessarily mean that Zimbabwe eventually would subscribe to their policies. The main thing was to get rid of the oppression in our country, to fight the Smith regime.

TS: Was it not strange to your supporters in the East?

DD: No, I think that they also appreciated and understood that we had to get support from whatever country sympathized with our liberation struggle. Never did they try to say: 'Look, these countries are part of NATO and therefore you should not get any assistance from them. If you go to them, we will cut off your assistance.' That was never the case. Instead, they appreciated it and actually encouraged us to get in touch with as many countries as possible that wanted to assist the struggle.

TS: Did you ever visit the Nordic countries yourself?

DD: I did not visit the Nordic countries until independence. The furthest I went was Leningrad. I was able to look across the sea and see Finland.

TS: Was the support you got from the Nordic countries only of a humanitarian or civilian character?

DD: Yes, it was. It was strictly civilian.

TS: I have just read your contribution to the book edited by Terence Ranger and Ngwabi Bhebe, *Soldiers in Zimbabwe's Liberation War*, where you discuss the situation in 1977-78. ZAPU was then to create semi-liberated areas inside Zimbabwe and there was a need for another kind of armament and trained personnel to administer these areas. The timing of this coincides with strong criticism that Joshua Nkomo made of Swedish support at the beginning of 1978. Within the friendly relationship, he criticized Sweden for not supplying arms and training to ZAPU. In retrospect, should this be seen in the light of your decisions regarding the warfare in Rhodesia?

DD: Yes, I think that comrade Nkomo was making that criticism in the light of the heavy pressures that we were getting in the combat areas inside the country and the fact that we were moving to a new stage after the Smith regime had proved to be completely intransigent in any negotiations. The only thing that Nkomo could turn to was: 'Look, there is no other way. The only way that we can get rid of the Smith regime is through military efforts.' I think that he did not realize the fact that the countries who were aligned to NATO probably saw that the efforts that we were making—particularly as we were supported by the socialist countries—were efforts which would destroy their own base in Africa, and as such they could not come in and give military support. We did realize at a certain stage that most of the so-called

Western countries who supported our liberation struggle did so purely on a humanitarian basis, rather than anything else. They accepted that the Smith regime was wrong. It was racial and they did not share anything with it. But when you put the question: 'What do you expect us to do?', no one would support the military struggle. To us it showed only one thing: that the Western countries felt that they had their kith and kin in Rhodesia, who they did not want to be harmed. That is the reason why they would not give us any military support.

TS: In the case of the Nordic countries, is it not more relevant to talk about non-military support? There was a lot of support given to the refugee camps and soldiers also march on their stomachs?

DD: I do realize that, but the support was meant for the civilian population, even though some of it filtered into the military. When it was given, it was on the understanding that it was for the civilian population.

TS: At the United Nations, the Nordic countries would support your cause, but they would not vote for resolutions referring to the armed struggle?

DD: That is right, yes.

TS: In spite of these differences could you develop a good relationship with the Nordic governments?

DD: Yes, we did develop good relations. We understood their problems. Our explanation—or our justification—was that as part of NATO they found it difficult to come out in the open and support our military efforts towards liberation. All they would do was to say: 'Look, we are supporting the civilian population. We want to make sure that those people do not suffer, but we will certainly not support the armed intervention promoted by the liberation struggle.' We understood them as people who wanted to play safe and still remain in NATO. Not burn their fingers with NATO. On the other hand, they felt that they needed to assist. They appreciated the operation that we were undertaking, but they were not brave enough to come out and say: 'Yes, your armed effort is also justified.'

TS: Sweden was a neutral country and the late Prime Minister Olof Palme was probably quite understanding of the question of armed struggle in Southern Africa. He often discussed it with people that were close to him, like Oliver Tambo and others.

DD: I know that, but on the other hand Sweden could not come out openly and say: 'We support.' We felt that Sweden at heart supported the armed struggle, but they could not burn their fingers by coming out in the open and saying: 'Now we are going to give full support to the armed struggle.'

TS: Did you meet Olof Palme when he was in Zambia?

DD: No, unfortunately I did not. Actually, when he came to Zambia I was out in the bush.

TS: SIDA also contributed to ZAPU's farms in Zambia. What happened to those farms at independence?

DD: We gave all the farms back to the Zambians. These are the farms that were used for the schools. As a matter of fact, the J. Z. Moyo Camp, where the young boys stayed, was bombed by the Rhodesians, so we did not develop any infrastructure there. We gave that farm back to the Zambians. At Victory Camp, where the girls were, we had developed some infrastructure. That one was given to SWAPO, and I think that when SWAPO finally left we decided to give it back to the Zambians.

TS: Victory Camp was also bombed?

DD: Yes, but there was only slight damage.

TS: In that connection Sweden supplied a mobile field hospital.

DD: Yes, they did.

TS: That was probably the closest you came to military cooperation with Sweden?

DD: Absolutely. But it was very useful.

TS: You later moved it to Solwezi?

DD: Yes, we moved it to Solwezi, where we had a big camp to which we intended to move all our refugees.

TS: Is there anything that you think one should particularly look into when it comes to ZAPU's relations with the Nordic countries during the struggle?

DD: Not really. I think that we to a very large extent felt at ease with the Nordic countries in all our relations. We got the impression that they were, as I said, people who at heart supported our liberation struggle, but on the other hand found themselves in an embarrassing situation, where—because of their membership in NATO—they could not come out openly to support it. We tended to be accommodating in our understanding and in our dealings with the Nordic countries.

TS: In this respect, did you draw upon the experiences of other liberation movements? I am particularly thinking of ANC and SWAPO, who had close relations with the Nordic countries from the early 1960s?

DD: Yes. We actually drew our lessons from them. We got to understand that we could only go to a certain limit with the Nordic countries and that we could not stretch it any further than that.

TS: Do you know if at any stage ZAPU discussed the question of Swedish or Nordic support to projects inside Rhodesia under your direction?

DD: Yes, this was when comrade Nkomo made that statement in 1978. One of his main thrusts was to get that kind of support, because that was the time when we were looking at the creation of liberated zones. Obviously, we were going to require an infrastructure when we created such zones. We would have to take over the schools. We would have to take over all the social functions of the Rhodesian government in those areas. It was for this kind of support that he to a very large extent was appealing. While the Nordic countries probably were not able to supply the arms as such, they must be able to support the liberated zones inside the country, the administrative effort that we intended to make there.

TS: In the case of ANC and SWAPO, a lot of support went inside Namibia and, particularly, to South Africa.

DD: I suppose that it happened as a result of the lessons learnt from the Zimbabwean liberation struggle. Because of the developed infrastructure in Zimbabwe no one ever believed that we could have liberated areas as such. And yet, in practical terms, what we were talking about was really areas where we thought that we were able to move, more or less without being molested by the Rhodesians. They would, of course, come in and still continue to bomb and so forth. Probably try to launch a military offensive against our forces there. But these areas were liberated in a sense, and this was what was being disputed. It was argued that the infrastructure was too developed to have liberated areas. To that we said: 'Look, a guerrilla's tactic is that once he has established himself, he is able to get the acceptance of the population in that area. We consider that a liberated zone. The dispute of whether he actually can control and defend that area, without the enemy forcing him out, is neither there, nor here. What should be recognized is that he has been accepted by the population. He works with the population. He has an influence over the population. And therefore he needs to be assisted, also in helping the population in that area.'

This was disputed. Many did not understand this. The OAU Liberation Committee itself did not want to understand. They talked about 'liberated areas' in Zimbabwe in inverted commas. This is the reason why our effort was to bring in big military units that would actually be able to physically protect those liberated areas, as against leaving only the guerrilla movement there. Because as the guerrillas were coming in, consolidating the support of the people and then moving forward to the offensive, the enemy forces would eventually come back into the areas where the guerrillas had initially established themselves. They would harass the population and carry out a lot of torture and murder of the people there, because they had supported the guerrilla forces. What we said was that we wanted these people protected. This is why, when it came to Namibia and South Africa, they had learnt the lesson. I think that the lesson went down very well after our experiences in Zimbabwe.

TS: You mentioned the OAU. I have noted that both ZANU and ZAPU did not want funds to be channelled from Sweden through the OAU Liberation Committee, but preferred direct, bilateral contacts.

DD: Yes, because we wanted to make a difference. The Nordic countries were channelling funds mainly for the civilian population and we did not want the OAU to mix those funds with the funds that were meant for the liberation struggle.

TS: So it was not because of distrust vis-à-vis the OAU?

DD: No, there was no question of distrust. It was mainly to make sure that the funds were not mixed up. The liberation funds should come through the OAU and the humanitarian funds for the civilian population should come directly.

Kumbirai Kangai
ZANU—Secretary of Transport and Social Welfare
Minister of Lands and Water Resources
(Harare, 19 July 1995)

Tor Sellström: When did you first enter into contact with the Nordic countries?
Kumbirai Kangai: It was in the mid-1960s. In fact, after the formation of ZANU in 1963 we got to know that there were friends in Sweden, but I had not met anybody. However, before I left the country in 1965 I met some friends from Sweden. I was struck by their openness and friendliness, which was quite different from the colonialists we had here. Then I went to the United States for many years, where I never had any contact.

Upon completion of my studies, I went to work full-time for the party at our office in Dar es Salaam. There I got in touch with the staff in the Swedish embassy. Then I came down to Lusaka, where we established a relationship in which every year there would be a discussion between Sweden and ZANU. We actually signed a protocol and in that document the Swedes would indicate how much was going to be given to ZANU. By the way, at that time it was all called humanitarian assistance. On a number of occasions I was part of the ZANU delegation led by comrade Chitepo to those discussions. ZANU also acquired a farm not far from Lusaka which the Swedes paid for. That is when we really started to rehabilitate our refugees, carrying out quite a number of activities.

We had those meetings on a yearly basis, and each year the grant to our organization increased. When we got to Mozambique—and I was in charge of transport—the Swedes introduced the Scania truck and each time we would get three or four new trucks. It really made a tremendous impact on our people as far as the Swedish and the Nordic peoples are concerned. I am singling out Sweden. This is not to say that the other Nordic countries have not assisted, but as far as ZANU is concerned, Sweden was the driving force when it comes to humanitarian assistance.

TS: Why do you think that Sweden developed a strong commitment to ZANU at an early stage? Was it through the influence of the churches in Zimbabwe? Was it the political leadership in Sweden?
KK: I think that it was a combination of these factors, and also due to the position that our party adopted. We were straightforward. We were a non-racial organization, fighting the oppression of the majority by a minority. We wanted to establish a democratic society and I think that it went down very well with the principles that we shared with the people of Sweden.

TS: The first protocol between ZANU and SIDA was signed in 1973. That was the first protocol SIDA signed with any liberation movement. There must have been a solid mutual foundation of trust?
KK: Exactly. There was really a mutual understanding between the two of us. Each time I visited Sweden, or I had a Swedish delegation in my office, you would feel like you were speaking to another comrade in the organization. That was really the feeling.

TS: Sweden and the other Nordic countries mainly supported what was called 'the authentic six' liberation movements. ZANU was not in this group.
KK: NORAD focused on 'the authentic six'. Later on, when we formed the Patriotic Front, we also got some assistance from them. That is when NORAD actually started to assist us. But when you talk of the assistance from the Nordic countries, as far as ZANU is concerned, the major support came from Sweden.

There is another aspect to Sweden's involvement. It is the international posture which it gave ZANU. I will give an example. In 1978, after we had signed our protocol, there was money set aside for the procurement of vehicles. I was sent to Europe to look for transport, Land Rovers, lorries and things like that. The British had actually outlawed any sale of Land Rovers to Mozambique. I got to the UK and posed as somebody from West Africa. I went to Southampton, where they assemble Land Rovers. I talked to the management there. I introduced myself as a businessman from West

Africa who wanted to buy Land Rovers and they said: 'How are you going to pay?' I said: 'I have a bank in Sweden. I will just tell it to transfer the money to your account.' I tell you, I was given VIP treatment by those people! I said: 'Fine, let us look at the cost of the vehicles.' It was, I think, four Land Rovers, one ambulance and one fast vehicle, a Range Rover. I got the price and I said 'OK, fine.' I got on the train, went back to London, called Mozambique to inform comrade Mugabe what I had got and then called SIDA to simply say: 'Can you transfer X amount of money to account number so-and-so in London?' Everything just went smoothly. When I got back to Southampton, these British people checked their account and saw that the money had been transferred. I tell you! I packed my vehicles and shipped them to Maputo.

You can see the type of relationship we had. To simply call from London and say: 'My name is Kumbirai Kangai from the sector for transport and welfare of ZANU. Can I speak to so-and-so? We are buying one, two, three, four vehicles at this price. The total price is so-and-so much. Can you transfer the money from SIDA to account so-and-so in the UK?' And it was done! I do not know if today, government-to-government, people have that kind of trust. Who can act so expeditiously on an amount such as that, involving thousands of pounds?

TS: In 1980, just before the elections, Lord Carrington turned to the Swedish government and said: 'We are having problems with Mr. Mugabe and ZANU. Mr. Mugabe is in clear breach of the understanding which he signed in Lancaster House and there is every reason to fear that any undertaking which you have been given regarding the use of Swedish funds will be disregarded.' The Swedish government—which at the time was non-socialist—replied: 'Regarding your doubts about Mr. Mugabe's will and capability to keep agreements, we would only say that our experience is different from yours. Development cooperation between Sweden and ZANU has always been founded on mutual respect and conscientious observance of concluded agreements.'

KK: That is good. Excellent! It says a lot. The transaction I told you about was very typical and very simple. There was that kind of honesty.

TS: Do you feel that there were political conditions attached to the Nordic support or was it given without any strings?

KK: It was aid without *any* strings. What we did when we met was to brief them about our operations, describe the situation and maybe go over our objectives. Then we would move into business. They understood that we were a group of people with objectives and that these objectives furthered international peace and cooperation. We made it quite clear. When we looked at our situation, it looked like a conflict between blacks and whites. But that was not the motivating factor for us to take up arms. We wanted to establish a democratic country. Once the Nordic people understood that, they really came to our support.

When you moved in other circles you would say: 'I am just coming from Sweden. I had a meeting with the SIDA people to request humanitarian assistance for our refugees.' The result was that the Dutch started to come in and a number of other countries would follow. They would see what the Nordic countries were doing, saying: 'I think that there must be a reason why these people are assisting this group.'

TS: It broadened your diplomatic field?

KK: It added impetus to really increase our international support.

TS: Did you co-ordinate policy with the Nordic countries at the level of international organizations, like at the United Nations?

KK: Yes, we did. In fact, it was quite common that comrades in the Nordic countries came to us and said: 'Do you hear what these countries are saying in the UN? This is the position they are taking.' Or when we were going to a meeting, they would say: 'Look, you may be confronted with this issue. This is the position that has been adopted by country X.'

TS: So there was not just co-ordination with the Nordic aid organizations, but also with the Ministries for Foreign Affairs?

KK: Oh, yes! Of course! In fact, whenever I visited Sweden, I had meetings at the Ministry for Foreign Affairs, SIDA and with all the officials that were involved. For us it was really support from the country.

TS: Including the solidarity movement and the NGOs?

KK: Yes. When I was in Sweden I never went to sleep. I moved from group to group. I would spend each night with comrades, discussing various aspects of our struggle, looking at various models throughout the world and also seeing how we could improve our operations. It was really a pleasure!

TS: At government level, the Nordic countries could not support you on the question of the armed struggle?

KK: That we understood. It never became an issue. What we did was simply say: 'Look, we understand your position. We want diplomatic, political, financial and material support. We can assure you that the material support is for our refugees and for the welfare of our people, in the movement and outside the country.'

TS: From the Swedish side the support to ZANU started in 1969. Later on ZAPU also received support, but there was never any assistance from Sweden to FROLIZI or to UANC. But there was some support from Norway to Muzorewa, I think?

KK: Yes, we heard that the bishop had some support from NORAD.

TS: In the case of Sweden, it was both ZANU and ZAPU. Was that a problem?

KK: It was not a problem for us, although we would have liked all the support to come to us. Particularly in the 1970s, our position was that the democratic forces in Zimbabwe should find a common ground. That would be the best way to defeat the enemy. Hence the number of organizations formed to try and create a front between us and ZAPU. That is really important.

TS: After the assassination of Herbert Chitepo, the Zambian government detained you and de facto banned ZANU?

KK: Yes! It banned ZANU.

TS: But you kept your contacts with the Swedish embassy during this difficult period?

KK: Yes. Anders Bjurner had arrived to Lusaka and I had just started to work with him when that happened. All of a sudden things happened, and I was detained. I managed to send a note to Bjurner, introducing one of our comrades. I said to this comrade: 'Please, take this to the Swedish embassy. Give it to Bjurner and simply say that we have some women and children who are at place so-and-so. They need medical attention and welfare assistance.' They received that assistance right through the time when we were in detention.

TS: The Swedes also came to visit you in the prison in Kabwe?

KK: Yes, they came to visit us. They also assisted us when Tongogara, Chimurenga and Sadat were charged with the murder of Chitepo. When we heard that they were charged, comrade Muzenda arranged through Bjurner for a lawyer to defend them. But eventually there was no case. In fact, the lawyer did not have much work.

TS: I know that the Swedish section of Amnesty International also intervened. It was initiated by a church person with experience from the Mberengwa area.

KK: Right.

TS: It is quite interesting, because Sweden had, of course, at the same time very good relations with Zambia?

KK: Yes, but they maintained the relations with ZANU in spite of our differences with the Zambian government.

TS: Did you later renew the relationship with Sweden from the Mozambican side?

KK: Yes. It went very well. When comrade Mugabe came out of detention, we briefed him and said: 'Look, this is what we have done. We have established a relationship with Sweden where we every year discuss our needs and sign a protocol.' Then we continued from Mozambique.

What the solidarity groups perhaps do not realize is the relief caused by the bales of clothes which they shipped. In 1977, the Chimoio refugee camp was attacked. I happened to be in Maputo when the attack took place, but I immediately rushed back to the camp. The little hut where I was staying was burnt. Everything was burnt, my medical books and equipment, stethoscopes and blood pressure cuffs. Everything was destroyed. I remained with the pair of trousers that I had. It was raining very heavily. You just had to stand by a tree. All night. I immediately went to Beira. I looked around and saw some bales of clothes which had arrived from Sweden. I quickly took them, rushed back to the camp and distributed the clothes to the people, including women and children.

I tell you, it was a big relief! I am mentioning this to illustrate what actually happens to a person in the bush who has no alternative. He has no money to buy anything. And all of a sudden somebody comes and says: 'Hey! Here is another pair!'
TS: The collection of clothes was also important in the Nordic countries. It was a way to mobilize people.
KK: Yes, but when somebody gives away a pair of trousers, I do not think that it brings to mind the significance to somebody who is in a remote area in the bush, completely destitute.
TS: In the case of Sweden, it was Emmaus, Bread and Fishes and the Africa Groups that primarily collected clothes.

KK: Yes. They were very good.
TS: Independent Zimbabwe became a host to the liberation movements from Namibia and South Africa. All the Nordic countries supported SWAPO and ANC. Norway also supported PAC. As a government, did you see that as a problem?
KK: That was never a problem for us. In fact, it was a pleasure to assist our comrades. All we did was to say to them: 'Due to the fact that we are very close to South Africa and that we still do not trust some of the people in our own security units, we would like to make sure that you move cautiously, but feel free.' We facilitated their movements.

Didymus Mutasa
ZANU—Deputy Secretary of Finance
ZANU-PF Administrative Secretary
(Harare, 25 July 1995)

Tor Sellström: When did you first come into contact with Sweden or any other Nordic country?
Didymus Mutasa: I started my serious political involvement in 1963. At that time, there were quite a number of Swedish missionaries in Rhodesia who had come to work with the American Methodist Church, for instance in our area. We used to go to meetings organized by different churches.

There was a meeting at Waddilove in 1957 or 1958. I do not remember the exact date. The missionaries insisted that they did not want to have separate accommodation from the African delegates and that they did not want to eat different food from the African delegates. They said that they were the same people as the Africans, and if Africans were invited to the conference they should be treated in the same way. So they packed their bags and slept with us in the same dormitories. They opened our eyes to the fact that, really, the white people that we had in Rhodesia were not different from others. They were people of the same class, and sometimes even people of a very much lower class, who—certainly when they settled in Africa—however, pretended to enjoy a status which was higher than their class. Instead of looking at themselves as workers, they wanted to become masters. I think that that problem was set out in my mind through our involvement with the missionaries, and particularly with the missionaries from Sweden.

TS: Did you also meet missionaries from the other Nordic countries?
DM: No, unfortunately. I only met missionaries from Sweden, but during the later period of our involvement in the liberation struggle we met all sorts of people. We visited Sweden and got support from a group called Emmaus Björkå. They were young Swedish people, full of enthusiasm, hoping that their work—collecting bits and pieces of clothes—would help the Zimbabwean refugees in Mozambique. They lived a very simple kind of life, which we enjoyed. Like a community. We were sent there from the bush. And there we were in Sweden, experiencing a bit of bush life!
TS: When was that?
DM: That was in 1976. There were three of us who left Mozambique and were told to go to Emmaus Björkå. We went around collecting some clothes, packed them and sent them to Mozambique. Then we went to another little group in Stockholm. We also worked

with them, going from one office to another. We were a scruffy little liberation movement and not very many important people wanted to see us. But those youngsters were very keen. They would telephone around and say: 'Why do you not want to see this people? Why do you not want to know what their wishes and their demands are?' And then, occasionally, they were told: 'You know, we give quite a lot through SIDA. Why do you not go and see SIDA?' So we went to SIDA and talked to them, which I believe people like Herbert Chitepo, President Mugabe and comrade Simon Muzenda had already done. So we were updating SIDA on our needs. Back in Mozambique, the SIDA representative in Maputo came to see us and said: 'I understand that you have been to my country. I am sorry that you did not tell me before you went, but what are your needs?' We then sat down and discussed with him.

TS: With Jan Cedergren?

DM: Yes, Cedergren. He would sit down with us and very generously give us the things we asked for. I think that SIDA also paid for the freight of the clothes from Emmaus Björkå. They also supplied us with the food that we needed—tinned food particularly, beans, meat, milk—partly for the children and partly for us. When we started working with SIDA, the budget for ZANU was in the region of two million Swedish Kronor. We then had people who were running away from Rhodesia and we went to Cedergren and said: 'Now, this is a problem.' He said: 'Fine, I can raise your budget to about 8 million.' We thought that this was tremendous. It was a lot of money. He said: 'Well, as long as you can account for it and as long as you can give me a list of the things that you need, I will buy some of the things and give you the money to buy the other things. But you must definitely account for it.' It was our responsibility together with the late Ernest Kadungure to provide that information to Cedergren.

After that we did not find it really necessary to make long journeys to Sweden and the other Nordic countries any more, because SIDA was right in our midst. The man was absolutely sympathetic to our cause. It was the same sort of experience as I explained about the Swedish missionaries. Here was a Swedish man, who—because he trusted us and we trusted him—actually was walking with us more than just one mile. You asked him to go one mile and he came two miles with us. That was absolutely good for us. By the time we left Mozambique, I think that the Swedish assistance to ZANU-PF alone was somewhere in the region of 16 million Swedish Kronor.

TS: Yes, it was. Then you got an extra allocation for the repatriation of the refugees of 5 million.

DM: Exactly. That is true.

TS: How did you view this? Sweden was a Western country. You were a liberation movement which had adopted Marxism-Leninism as the guiding principle and you were using armed warfare to get rid of the colonialists.

DM: Well, all Western governments were clear on one question. They could not give us arms, but they could give us food and after they had taken that stand there were a few who did that, like Sweden, Belgium to some extent, Norway again to some extent and Holland to quite a great extent. In Holland it was not the government, but non-governmental organizations, as in Denmark. Those countries gave us clothes, food and many of the things that we wanted, but not arms. But we understood why, because the racist regime that we were fighting against was to a great extent white and many of the people who came to settle in Rhodesia were not from England. Some had come from Italy, some from Holland and others from all over Europe. It was very difficult for these governments to give us arms to fight against their own people. But they did not mind giving us food, because I think that in their own argument we had to exist.

But the Swedish government went a little further in that their support was much greater than the others. In fact, at one time it was greater than all the other Western governments put together. We explained that as due to the understanding of the Prime Minister, Olof Palme. He himself was a socialist. Although he wanted change through non-violent means, I think that he understood our cause when we explained that we were really getting enough arms from China and that we were not fighting a conventional war which needed huge supplies of arms, but just a few guns to protect ourselves. Our mission was not really to go and kill people, but to protect them. In the course of the events, we might find it necessary to kill the enemy, but that was not the objective. The objective was to change his way of thinking and let him see that what was going on in Rhodesia was wrong.

TS: Do you feel that there were political conditions attached to the Swedish and Nordic support? Was there a hidden agenda attached to it?

DM: None whatsoever, but I do not know whether this is just a feeling which I developed from my own experience with the Swedish people. When I was in detention, I was adopted by a Swedish group of Amnesty International. A young fellow called Peter Malmström used to write to me all the time. He also used to write to Ian Smith almost every month, asking him to release me or try me. That experience gave us an understanding of the Swedish people, which was very different from others. We could see that they were absolutely concerned about us and would like our situation to change. When we found that extending to the Swedish government, we realized that they must have the same heart because with Amnesty International and the schools that were involved in sending letters and clothes, adopting children or detainees and their families, it was tremendous, absolutely tremendous. It could not come from any other group of people, except those that had the correct heart.

TS: Did you or your family members receive support through Christian Care or IDAF?

DM: Yes. My family received assistance from Christian Care here in Zimbabwe. My children were educated through Christian Care and all my legal fees were paid by IDAF. The man who was instrumental in the setting up of these funds was Guy Clutton-Brock, who was a very close friend of mine. Right at the beginning—when I was still a 'free' man in Zimbabwe—I was also involved in setting them up. I never knew that I myself would be a beneficiary!

TS: There were a lot of Swedish funds via Christian Care and IDAF?

DM: Indeed.

TS: I know that some families were supported, like the Chinamano family. Others got scholarships, among them President Mugabe. I think that he studied law and economics at the University of London with that funding?

DM: Yes, that is very true. Through Reverend Collins at IDAF. His wife is still running that fund. Yes, I am aware of that.

TS: Coming back to the assistance to the refugee camps and for the running of the ZANU office in Mozambique, do you think that the principles of accountability were both sufficient and flexible?

DM: Oh, yes. They were simple and convenient. Cedergren was in Maputo and rather than us going to Swaziland to buy vehicles or whatever we needed, on occasions we would ask him to do it for us. He actually used the money, showed us the receipts and said: 'This is the amount of money that I am subtracting from the budget that we have put together.' The accountability was, as far as I am concerned, absolutely perfect.

TS: There was, of course, the alternative to channel the SIDA funds through the OAU Liberation Committee, but in the case of Zimbabwe both ZANU and ZAPU explicitly wanted the funds directly. Was it because you had a modus operandi with the local Nordic aid offices?

DM: We had already established good contacts with SIDA and the other Nordic countries. We had to a great extent also experienced the bureaucracy within the OAU. They would say that we must wait for the summit meeting of the Heads of States, which then would take quite a long time to decide whether it was necessary for us to pursue the liberation struggle. In the meanwhile, we would be sitting under the sun, waiting and hoping that the assistance would arrive. Why should assistance from Emmaus Björkå, first of all, sit in Stockholm for three or four months before it was sent to Dar es Salaam, where it would remain for another three or four months before finding its way to the OAU man, Hashim Mbita, who then, ceremoniously, would bring it to our President? It would take about eight months to get the money and the struggle would be delayed or slowed down for that length of time. So, we felt, well, why do we not get the money directly?

When we got the money directly, we also became more enthusiastic. You could then say to the youngsters: 'Go inside the country. You can take this amount of food, and when you need it you can use it.' And when there were areas within the country that needed food, they could actually come and get some from us. During the later stages of the struggle, the liberated areas inside the country needed food. And sometimes the food was brought from Mozambique.

TS: Did the Nordic countries support ZANU and the Patriotic Front diplomatically? When you met in diplomatic fora, did you consult with them?

DM: Yes, we did. To a great extent. Most of our time was taken up by explaining the activities of the British government, because it was the main actor vis-à-vis the regime in Rhodesia. It was to a great extent the stumbling block, being a colonial power which did not accept that situation, at the same time stopping the international community from having anything to do with Rhodesia. We found that it was necessary to explain the situation to our friends and we believe that they in turn quietly approached the British and said: 'Why are things happening that way?'

There were many fronts in the war. Within the country we had to make our people understand what was going on and within the liberation movement itself all of us had to understand the purpose of the war. We also found that our friends needed people who could work with them almost on a full time basis. Our external relations office in Maputo was very busy, collecting newspaper cuttings and giving out information to the people that assisted us.

TS: You invited both Emmaus Björkå and SIDA to the independence celebrations in 1980?

DM: Yes. By the time of independence, we had made quite a number of friends. As the saying goes, success breeds more success. The small beginnings in Sweden were noticed by people in Holland and the Holland Committee on Southern Africa started to work with us as well. In Germany, there were about four groups that helped us. The Communist Party of West Germany worked very hard. A group of enthusiastic youngsters went around with us from one town to another, collecting funds. I think that at one time we must have raised somewhere in the region of two million US Dollars, with which we bought Scania trucks to transport food and other materials. These people sent out their information material in the German language, which also could be read in Switzerland. The German part of Switzerland then started to be interested and to organize assistance for us.

There was a proliferation of these solidarity groups. The only country where they did not appear was Britain. I do not know why. Aid organizations like War on Want, Christian Aid and others actually gave us assistance, but the organized solidarity groups were not to be found.

TS: How about Finland?

DM: For some reason unknown to us, Finland was more connected to ZAPU than to us. The Social Democratic Party in Germany was also giving more assistance to ZAPU than to us. But we did not mind. We felt that it really was for the same cause. We were very pleased that assistance was forthcoming and that it was going to people who needed it and made use of it.

TS: In the case of the Swedish government, the same amount was given to ZANU and ZAPU. How did you look upon that?

DM: I used to joke with Cedergren and say: 'I do not think that there are as many refugees in Zambia as there are in Mozambique.' And he would say: 'Yes, I know, but this is the decision by my government.'

TS: You could live with that?

DM: Oh, yes! We knew that the Swedish government gave 32 million Kronor to the liberation movements. That was a lot of money. We were most grateful for the 16 million that ZANU received, although it did not come as cash, but as material support. Otherwise we would have been inundated with people that we could not have fed and the Mozambican government, which helped us, would have absolutely found it difficult to carry on. Some of the economic problems the Mozambican government was facing were due to the support of our war effort. They were bombed and their infrastructure was destroyed by the Smith regime.

TS: After independence, you hosted SWAPO, ANC and PAC. In the case of the Nordic countries, SWAPO and ANC—but partly also PAC—were recipients of official support in Zimbabwe. Did you view this as a problem?

DM: No, we viewed it as a duty, a duty which earlier had been carried out by Tanzania and Mozambique throughout our own liberation struggle. We had been received by FRELIMO. They hosted us and in turn we felt duty-bound to host the other liberation movements. We were very pleased to have them here. We did not have much trouble from them as liberation movements. They had a purpose. They were really keen to work hard for the benefit of their countries. We were, in a way, proud that we were able to give them sanctuary.

TS: You yourself worked hard through the Cold Comfort Farm and other organizations to link the South African liberation movements with the democratic forces inside South Africa?

DM: That is very true. We did that, and again thanks to the help that we received from Sweden. We were able to get people from South Africa to experience Zimbabwean life after independence. We used to say to our South African friends: 'Our boundary is the Limpopo. When you go beyond the Limpopo, you must realize that you are going beyond apartheid and when you return we hope that you will keep it that way and start to influence people who will not be able to cross the Limpopo, but nonetheless should leave apartheid behind.' It was important for them. We had some South African farmers who came here and lived with fellow Zimbabwean farmers, sharing the peace and quietness and the development that these communities of farmers were experiencing. We brought in students. The students' programme went on a little longer, because it involved not only students from South Africa, but from Southern Africa. We had students from Tanzania, Mozambique, Malawi, Zambia and Namibia. It was very interesting to watch these youngsters discussing and thinking about the future.

But the funniest meeting that we organized was with a group of women from South Africa. They came to the airport in Harare and as they were waiting in the hall, the white South African women thought that the black South African women were their Zimbabwean hosts. We then drove them to Cold Comfort Farm and said: 'Well, ladies, you may not realize this, but we have brought you here together because we think that it is necessary for you to live in your own country in this way.' One woman raised her hand and said: 'What do you mean? Are you saying that these ladies are from South Africa?' We said: 'Yes.' And she said: 'Fancy, we have come all the way from South Africa to meet here in Zimbabwe. Why can we not do this in our own country?' We found that absolutely important. Indeed, we think that it was crucial.

When we met with the white South African women we said: 'You know, it is your children who are being involved in the war and they are being killed. What are they dying for? It is not that the South Africans are poor and have to fight for food. South Africa is one of the richest countries in the world. So what is your son fighting for?' Those who had grown-up children in the war started to shake. We found it necessary, because when they went back home they decided: 'We have had enough. We cannot let our children suffer. We cannot let this war go on.' It was very important for us to undertake that programme.

TS: Did Sweden or the other Nordic countries support these programmes?

DM: Yes, tremendously. I think that we got the biggest assistance from SIDA. We ought to talk to them now to let us do a programme for rural development. That is our next struggle.

Abel Muzorewa
Leader of the African National Council and UANC—Prime Minister of Zimbabwe-Rhodesia
Bishop of the United Methodist Church of Zimbabwe
(Harare, 26 November 1996)

Carl Fredrik Hallencreutz: Could you say something about your early contacts with the Nordic countries?
Abel Muzorewa: Well, the first white person that I ever met, so to speak, was the Swedish nurse Sister Ellen Björklund. She was the midwife when I was born, so the first white person that I ever met was that woman. I probably would have been just sand or mud—nothing—if she had not been there, because I was born a premature baby and in those days, with all due respect to my African ancestors, people did not know what to do with a premature baby, except to just put it in a pot and throw it away. But because she was there, I was saved. That was my very dramatic first contact with Scandinavia, or specifically with Sweden. Sister Björklund is buried at Old Umtali and whenever I go to the cemetery I clean up the grave and put flowers on it, because she means a lot to me.

When I grew up, there was also a female Swedish nurse, Sister Ruth Hansson. She was a good friend of my parents and the last person that my wife worked for before she got married to me. I used to go to her house to see my wife-to-be. As far as I am concerned, that is my most important connection to Scandinavia, although it is personal.
CFH: I think that you met Sister Ruth when you were in Sweden?
AM: Right. I had to go and see her, up in the mountains.
CFH: Did you have any contacts with Norwegian Methodists at that time?
AM: Well, that was much later, when I became a preacher and, above all, when I became a bishop. That is when I used to go to Scandinavia to tell the people about the missionary work and so forth. Unfortunately, I do not remember the places I went to, but I visited Norway about three times and Sweden about the same, I think. I also went to Denmark and to Finland.
CFH: When you were at college, did you have any contacts with Sweden then?

AM: No, I studied all the time. But there was another important contact before I became a bishop. The first white home to which I was invited to actually spend two nights was the Swedish home of Lennart Blomquist and his family. That was at Mutambara. I had been invited for a meeting on the mission station. It was very important for me. I consider the context and the attitudes of our time racially and that was the first time that I actually stayed in a white home as a guest. Later on we had, of course, all these missionaries from Scandinavia, nurses, preachers, educators and so forth.
CFH: If we turn to the more political dimension of your life, in your opinion, which factors could explain the Nordic involvement in Southern Africa?
AM: I am sincere when I say that I am very grateful and very impressed by what the Scandinavian countries have done, not just for Zimbabwe, but in Southern Africa as a whole. It is quite obvious that they have been much involved in the liberation struggle in this part of the world. I have tried to think what the reasons could be. I know that they are not former colonizers, so it would not be like in the cases of Britain or France.

As a Christian myself, I want to believe that their involvement was motivated by Christian hearts and that it came from the church influence that they had, first of all, because they believed in freedom themselves and they as Christians wanted to share with others. But they did not only share their beliefs. They also shared their sons and daughters, who came to Zimbabwe as preachers, ministers of religion, nurses and educators. These people came as missionaries and I believe that the Scandinavian countries, so to speak, later continued to be missionaries in the social, political and economic life in this part of the world. But I do believe that it emanated from their Christian experience and that they wanted to share. They wanted to share not just part of the life here, but the total life, which meets with my theme from the time of liberation that we wanted to preach a total gospel for the total person. I think that it was what the Scandinavian countries practised and continue to practise.

CFH: You were in contact with Scandinavia as a Methodist bishop before you became involved in politics. How did these contacts develop when you later led ANC and UANC?

AM: Well, first of all, we had the confidence in Scandinavia which I had experienced through the church. I also knew what they were doing for other countries that had become independent before us, like Tanzania. So, we felt very confident that we could go to Sweden and feel welcome as people who were struggling for our liberation. We went there a number of times, asking for help. We wanted UANC to be recognized as a party parallel to the other liberation movements.

CFH: So it was a matter of establishing UANC as a liberation movement?

AM: That is right.

CFH: Would it have been the same with Norway and Denmark?

AM: Yes. We actually went to beg for money wherever we could get it. We wanted money for some of our young men and women who wanted to go to school. As we were struggling, we had to prepare our people and have trained personnel. We were begging for money for scholarships. You may find it difficult to believe, but I could point out a number of men and women in the present government administration who we trained when we were not yet in government. A lot of people who we sent to the Ranche House College.

We had to have money and we went to countries like Sweden to beg for money, also to maintain our external offices and to get all the material help we could find, clothes and so forth, for our dispersed people. To make a long story short, we went to ask for recognition, for money and to mobilize Scandinavia to fight against UDI, so that it would not succeed. Those were the reasons why we went there.

CFH: You had a Swedish ANC representative in Sweden, Erling Söderström, the son of a teacher at the United Theological College. Did you have many representatives like that?

AM: Yes, in each Nordic country we tried to have somebody. We also had one in Norway and one in Denmark.

CFH: I suppose that you must have been disappointed with the attitude of the Nordic countries to the internal settlement?

AM: Unfortunately, as we were trying to fight the oppressors here, there was a big competition going on regarding who was going to be the king. Some countries that were liberated before us, like Tanzania and Zambia, did not support us, but tried to be the king-makers. Here I had a problem in that Nyerere, Kaunda and Machel were already acquainted with other people, such as Nkomo. I think that they had made up their minds and wanted to support those people. I also think that they believed that the most effective way was the armed struggle, because otherwise they would have chosen to support me instead of the others. Have you read my book, by the way?

CFH: Yes, indeed. Did you know that it was translated into Swedish?

AM: I read that, but I thought that it was banned or something.

CFH: No, it was published in 1980.

AM: OK. I also think that we were not understood. I tried to do what Mandela did. I did not believe that we should continue to throw guns at each other, destroying ourselves—black and white—our properties and so forth. We could talk with the enemy and, in spite of all the criticism against us, I went to talk with Smith and he granted us what we had been calling for during all these years, namely 'one person-one vote'. That was the first concession and I want to believe that it was the internal settlement that shortened the bloodbath and the armed struggle in Zimbabwe.

We could have gone on, saying: 'I am strong. I am going to go on'. Mugabe would then have said the same thing. We had a lot of resources. Really, if I had not cared about the bloodshed, we could have gone on. We could have engaged South Africa and other people, mercenaries, but we stopped the bloodshed through negotiation. I am quite aware that it was not favoured by many people, but we could have gone on until such a time when we would have been recognized, in the same way that people carry out bloody coups and just go on until they are recognized.

CFH: Is there anything that you would like to add?

AM: Well, with all my heart, soul and mind, I am grateful to the Christian, democratic and general spirit that the Scandinavian countries demonstrated in supporting the liberation struggle in this part of the world, and here we are talking of Zimbabwe in particular. The only question that I have at this point is that the Mugabe government—which they supported and continue to support—now is known as one of the worst and most corrupt governments around. There is corruption, mismanagement of funds and deprivation of the freedoms of speech, assembly, association and so on.

I do not understand why the Scandinavian countries are still supporting that kind of government. I would have thought that they—as the people of integrity that they are—should be open and frank with Mugabe and say: 'Friend, we do not believe that we should continue to give our money to Zimbabwe to be used in the way that you are using it'. I think that they have got a holy power and a right to tell Mugabe: 'Stop one, two, three, because we do not believe in what you are doing and we do not support that kind of thing'. It is shocking for me to realize that the Scandinavian countries are still supporting Mugabe in spite of the mismanagement of their monies. I do not understand it.

John Nkomo
ZAPU—Secretary of Administration
Minister of Local Government and Rural Development
(Harare, 21 July 1995)

Tor Sellström: You led a ZAPU delegation to talks with Sweden in 1979. Was that your first contact with the Nordic countries?

John Nkomo: No, that was not my first contact. Over the years of our struggle—before the Lancaster House Conference in 1979—I worked very closely with the Nordic countries, particularly with SIDA in terms of the annual review of the assistance that we were getting from Sweden. It was, of course, humanitarian assistance, not military. As our numbers began to grow in the camps in Zambia it was very convenient to ask Sweden to assist us with the logistics, such as food, transportation and any other assistance that would enable us to handle the thousands of refugees that had come there.

We were always under attack and at times we would have everything destroyed. But we understood why Sweden could not go beyond humanitarian assistance. There was the Cold War divide between the East and the West and we understood that the Nordic countries had taken a neutral position. The ideological thrust coming from the East had a bearing on us. It created a situation that gave us the impetus to get going and we tended to develop a much firmer leaning to the East than to the West. In the West, we only had contacts with solidarity groups that were collecting clothes and other items. People who were disseminating our propaganda. But in the East, and in the Eastern-inclined countries, we were actually getting arms. In between, you had the Nordic countries. We really appreciated their assistance, because it enabled us to move around.

TS: Did you not find that strange, with Denmark and Norway being members of NATO?

JN: Well, there was not so much involvement by Denmark and Norway. They were not very supportive of the liberation struggle as such. They supported on humanitarian grounds. I recall that ZAPU once used the services of a Danish airline, ferrying refugees from Botswana across to Zambia because the camps in Botswana could not accommodate any more people. That exercise only stopped when the Rhodesians threatened to shoot down the plane. Of course, the cargo—which was supposed to be refugees—was also a potential army for our war. The Danes were members of NATO. They were not dealing in arms, but assisting on humanitarian grounds. It was different with Sweden, which is why we also had a

ZAPU mission there. From Sweden it was easy to reach all sides, even the Soviet bloc. Preferably we would, of course, have liked the majority of the countries to be on our side.

TS: The first ZAPU mission in Sweden was, I think, headed by Dr. Makhurane, who was based at the University of Uppsala?

JN: Yes, and later on we had people like Canaan Moyo and Isaac Nyathi, who is now an MP here.

TS: Nyathi was heading the ZAPU research department in Lusaka, which also received support from SAREC, the Swedish Agency for Research Cooperation with Developing Countries?

JN: Yes, that was very important for us. Also the training aspect was very important. Although we were fighting a war, we wanted to make sure that we would be ready to take over the administration in Zimbabwe. So, we spread our wings to cover as much as we could.

TS: What do you think made the Nordic societies, and Sweden in particular, involved with ZAPU and ZANU? Did it partly have to do with old links through the missions?

JN: I think that what encouraged Sweden to really come out in full force was the exodus of the population in Mberengwa and Gwanda, which is predominantly Lutheran. What they did later on was to try and provide as much comfort as possible to the people that they regarded as part of their community. However, I think that Sweden also had a much wider focus. They were really looking at the future, preparing for a time when Zimbabwe would be independent. It was important for them that their support programmes were implemented. It had nothing to do with our struggle. They were implementing them in the districts that we mentioned, Mberengwa and Gwanda, through the involvement with the missions there.

TS: I think that Edward Ndlovu, ZAPU's General Secretary at the beginning of the 1970s came from that area?

JN: Yes, he had that background.

TS: And on the ZANU side, people like Richard Hove also had a background in the Church of Sweden Mission schools?

JN: Yes, Richard Hove comes from the Mnene mission in Mberengwa. There was that influence.

As I said, I think that Sweden was looking at the future and how they could expand their involvement in this part of the world. They saw that the resolution of our problem had the potential for a more stable environment. That is why they cooperated with both ZANU and ZAPU. Theirs was not an ideological influence, as opposed to those countries that supported the two parties separately. You had the Soviet Union supporting ZAPU and China supporting ZANU. Their support was based on an ideological orientation. For Sweden, it was more of a social, or humanitarian, approach than an ideological approach.

TS: Do you think that the late Swedish Prime Minister, Olof Palme, played a part in this?

JN: He played a very important part in this. I also think that his orientation was more supportive of the liberation struggle, although he could not give us arms. But his orientation was more in support of the liberation struggle.

TS: In international fora, such as the United Nations, did you feel that you had support from the Nordic group?

JN: Yes, the Nordic countries always played a sort of catalytic role. Their support was not based on any ideology, be it socialism or capitalism. It was a mixture of both, which was useful for the purpose. They were very supportive of our diplomatic efforts. There they could not be accused of being militarily involved. That was a role they could play without risking any condemnation. The other countries, particularly in the West, felt that they could scale down their diplomatic support. The Nordic countries did not do so, because I think that they also were convinced that our struggle was just.

Had it been today, I am sure that we would not have had any problems, because now there is so much emphasis on democracy and human rights. And here was a situation where human rights were being down-trodden. Democracy in Rhodesia was based on qualifications. You had to qualify to enjoy democratic rights.

TS: I think that the Nordic involvement to a large extent was a question of human rights.

JN: Yes, and that is what we enjoyed, because we knew that although they would not give us arms, they were giving us diplomatic support. And the struggle was multi-pronged.

TS: On the other hand, in the United Nations the Nordic countries could not support resolutions advocating armed struggle. Did you understand that position?

JN: Obviously, there were times when we were disappointed, but we felt that this was not an issue to be pushed, because we knew that they were with us in the diplomatic field. We appreciated their position. If they had taken another stand, we would probably have lost diplomatic leverage. We understood that. And, as I said, they continued to support us and that support encouraged us to move forward. They had a rather important role to play. It was not by choice that we went military. When our initial diplomatic approach failed, it had to be militarily supported. But we were always convinced that it was not the military that was important. It was diplomacy. The military effort was simply a tool to pressurize the others to come to the table and talk. That is how we went to Geneva in 1976, to Malta in 1977, to Dar es Salaam in 1977 and to Lancaster House in 1979. It was because we used the military struggle to pressurize the other party to come to the talks.

TS: Sweden gave equal amounts of humanitarian assistance to ZAPU and ZANU. You had a relationship based on trust with SIDA and your colleagues in ZANU—with whom you were competing for resources—also had this relationship of trust. Was that difficult?

JN: We had a project department, headed by Edward Ndlovu, which was intimately involved with the Swedish embassy in Lusaka. There were other supporting agencies with SIDA in Zambia with whom we discussed our problems. We were not making any comparison with what was going on with ZANU in Mozambique. Later, we became the Patriotic Front. We were then able to send joint missions to make life easier for those who were supporting us. As to the amounts of support given to the individual movements, there was no jealousy at all. We would, of course, have preferred to get more, but since the Nordic countries, or Sweden specifically, were in support of the Zimbabwean struggle, it was only right to accept that we should share whatever there was. You say that 'beggars may not be choosers'.

TS: The closest to any military involvement by Sweden was, I guess, when the Swedish Air Force delivered a mobile field hospital after the Rhodesian attacks on the ZAPU camps in Zambia in 1978?

JN: Yes, I received that hospital at the Lusaka International Airport, with the jeeps and so on.

TS: There were rumours that the Rhodesians might sabotage the operation?

JN: Yes. In a war, there are military casualties, but the camps that were attacked were refugee camps. Our argument with those who wanted to accuse us—or accuse Sweden for supporting us—was that the poor children there were not suffering by choice. They should look at the situation as a symptom of something wrong. What was wrong was inside Rhodesia. Those who supported the casualties of this violence were doing it on humanitarian grounds. What we had to deal with was to correct the situation inside the country, and that became our diplomatic message.

Zambia had to suffer for accommodating us and we had to sacrifice so much, trying to put a situation right. You could say that you can do that by talking, but we tried to talk. We went to Geneva, but it failed. We went to Malta, it failed again. Certainly, there had to be other methods. To those who were saying that we should talk, we said that they must put pressure on Smith. I recall when Kissinger was running around. In October 1976, I was in Botswana when suddenly we were told that they had cornered Smith with Vorster and that we were going for talks. We felt that maybe it would bring about a solution, but once Smith said 'not interested', we said: 'That is it.' I also recall the Victoria Falls meeting in 1975. I was heading the secretariat on the bridge. I was responsible for assuring that half of the train was on this side and half on that side! They said: 'Fine, that is an effort!' Kaunda was staking his reputation and credibility as a political leader by saying: 'Right, I am going to join Vorster. I am getting the two parties to meet.' All those efforts. If we had gone for the military, we would have said: 'No talks!' But we knew that those who were supporting us could not let Smith win the game by saying: 'Look, they just do not want to talk.'

The Swedish assistance at the time when our camps were being bombed and children were dying was a humanitarian act. But we had to carry out a night operation in order to avoid detection or even destruction of the mobile clinic.

TS: Later on you moved that clinic to the ZAPU camp in Solwezi?

JN: Yes, we moved it to Solwezi, because life had become very difficult there with malaria and so on. It was very useful as it had its own generators. It was really a fully-fledged hospital. Fully equipped, which was very useful. These are some of the things that a lot of people do not know.

TS: What happened with the clinic?

JN: We took it home to Zimbabwe, but as time went on it failed. After independence there was more focus on what was readily available, which is a pity. Some of our equipment was, of course, donated to Zambia. They had sacrificed so much.

TS: What happened with your farm outside Lusaka?

JN: We handed it over to Zambia. In fact, we had taken it over from FRELIMO. When FRELIMO left we took over the farm and when we left I think that initially SWAPO was going to take it over, but eventually it was sold to a fellow who used to be a minister in Kaunda's time. When I later went to Zambia to arrange for the fencing of the mass graves, he had already put up the fence himself.

Sydney Sekeramayi
ZANU—Student in Sweden—Deputy Secretary of Health Minister of State for National Security
(Harare, 27 July 1995)

Tor Sellström: You were a student in Sweden in the 1960s. You were also the ZANU representative there. How did you end up in Sweden?

Sydney Sekeramayi: I actually came to Sweden in June 1964 from Czechoslovakia. I had gone to Czechoslovakia after I had been expelled from school in Rhodesia. The party—then NDP and later ZAPU—organized scholarships for me and four others to go and study in Czechoslovakia, and when we had a few problems there we left. At that time, Rupiah Banda, who was the International Secretary of the Zambia Students' Union, facilitated my coming to Sweden. He established a contact between myself and NIB—later SIDA—which resulted in a scholarship to study in Sweden. That is how I came to Lund. But first I had to complete my secondary education, which I did at *Grännaskolan*. Then I came to the University of Lund, where I first studied genetics before I got into the medical school.

Billy Modise, who is now the South African High Commissioner to Canada, was already in Lund, studying sociology. And, of course, Rupiah Banda, the former Zambian Foreign Minister.

TS: Were you appointed representative for ZANU while studying in Lund?

SS: Yes. Well, I got to Lund when the split between ZANU and ZAPU had already occurred. I supported the ZANU side. When I got to Lund, I was interacting with Rupiah Banda and with Modise. We all felt that it was necessary to mobilize support to ZANU and ZAPU for purposes of invigorating the struggle. There were other Zimbabweans who I discovered a little later on. One was Claude Chokwenda, who was also a very active member of ZANU. Finally we had in Sweden about five students from Zimbabwe and we all happened to support ZANU. We started to get into contact with the groups in Sweden which were supporting the liberation struggle in general in Southern Africa. By then none of the countries was yet free. Ourselves from Zimbabwe, with our colleagues from South Africa, Namibia, Angola and Mozambique, all of us formed a group that was spearheading the support, asking the Swedish organizations to support the liberation struggle in Southern Africa. This was in the early 1960s. The armed struggle had not yet taken off, so we were more concerned with mobilizing material support, especially to those people who were in prison or in detention.

TS: I think that one of the first Swedish solidarity committees for Southern Africa was

the one in Lund, which was called the South Africa Committee?
SS: Yes, and which then had persons like Ulf Agrell, who was very active. We also had Per Garthon and others who were very supportive of our struggle.
TS: That means that you were in Sweden when the Båstad demonstrations took place against the Davis Cup tennis match between Sweden and Rhodesia?
SS: Yes, I was in Båstad at that time. The Africa group in Lund was very active. Båstad is near Lund, so we went there, but I was very careful about one thing. I did not want to do anything that would lead me into a situation of conflict, especially with the police. I felt that if the activities that we were promoting in support of the struggle turned into a confrontation with the Swedish police, it would not create a good impression. So when we were organizing the demonstrations against the tennis match all of us were saying: 'Whatever happens, we should avoid confrontation with the Swedish police'. Sweden is basically a peaceful country and any kind of violent action would not be positively interpreted. We were very careful about that.
TS: Sten Andersson, who later became Minister for Foreign Affairs, was brought to court because he was demonstrating on a First of May under the slogan 'Verwoerd commits murder on African soil'. It was seen as defamation of a Head of State.
SS: Yes, at that time Sweden was extremely peaceful. Any violent action, or even statement, was not taken very well, so we were to operate within those guidelines.
TS: In what circles did you find support in those days? The student movement, of course?
SS: Well, we had the student movement, which was very strongly supporting us. The National Union of Students (SFS) in Sweden and the students in Denmark, Norway and Finland, all of them, held the position that they must support the liberation struggle in Southern Africa. In my case, that also facilitated contacts between me and the Zimbabwean students who were in England. We would meet during the summer, reprogramme ourselves and see in which areas we could give maximum support in terms of ordinary dissemination of information and propaganda and in terms of collecting material things, like clothes and some money where it was possible. I remember—I think that it was in 1967 or 1968—when the party in Lusaka was having problems with their office machinery. We collected money for a Gestetner machine and sent it there. It was a humble beginning which was building up slowly.
TS: The very first request by ZANU to SIDA came in 1969. From then on you received official assistance from Sweden?
SS: Yes, we had a bilateral relationship.
TS: When you were the ZANU representative in Sweden, did you also represent the organization in the other Nordic countries?
SS: Yes, in the whole of Scandinavia. I had become Secretary General of the Zimbabwe Students' Union in Europe, which was really the students' wing of ZANU. I was co-ordinating all the student activities in the Scandinavian countries and with the larger group that was in the United Kingdom. That was one side. On the political side, I was de facto the party representative. When people like the late Herbert Chitepo and Richard Hove were going to Sweden, I was the person who facilitated their coming there to present our case. I remember when the late Chitepo came. We were able to organize meetings for him in Lund. It was also possible to take him to Stockholm. His presentation of our situation was very well received and in terms of support for us it was quite a reinforcement.
TS: Was that in 1972?
SS: Yes, about 1972.
TS: When he came in October 1972 he really surprised the officials at SIDA, because he said: 'We are going to start the armed struggle in Rhodesia and this will result in refugees pouring into Zambia. So we would like to discuss with you how we can help these refugees.' Here was a representative from an anti-imperialist liberation movement, waging armed struggle, openly telling a Western country about its military plans!
SS: Yes. He was very clear that if you take the history of the Scandinavian countries we could not discuss military support, but we should be honest: 'Let us tell them that we are going to wage an armed struggle. Where we will get the arms from is none of their business, but from the moral and political

point of view we want them to support us.' When he talked about launching the armed struggle in Rhodesia, it was really part of a policy that there were certain people whom you could tell the truth, because it would not help if you hid the truth from them. They would later find out and think that you were not quite honest in the presentation of your case. So we agreed: 'Tell them that the struggle is on the way and that we expect non-military support from our Scandinavian supporters.'

TS: It shows a large degree of trust between ZANU and SIDA?

SS: Yes.

TS: Perhaps it helped that you had quite a strong support base in the Swedish church due to the old relations with the mission stations?

SS: With the mission stations, yes. And later with Emmaus Björkå. That was the organization which really got into the homes of the Swedish people, especially appealing for clothes, which we would sort out and send over. But after I got to Mozambique in 1977 and as things were beginning to unfold, I really became very scared of the situation when we were sending clothes, because in 1978 the Rhodesians were beginning to poison clothes. Imagine if they had poisoned the clothes that we were sending at that time! We were sending them to people who were in prison, who were in detention, to our leaders. It would have been a really terrible situation. I thought about it and said: 'Oh, help me God if anything happens!' The Rhodesians would just have been very happy. They would have poisoned the clothes and accused the Scandinavians of sending poisoned clothes.

TS: This technique of poisoning clothes was invented here in Harare?

SS: Yes, at the Chikurubi prison. Quite a few white guys at the university were involved, but they all left the country. Years later, I realized that this could have happened, but thank God it did not happen.

TS: Did ZANU also get support from the other Nordic countries?

SS: Yes, particularly from the Social Democratic Party in Denmark. In Sweden we had Sten Andersson and in Denmark we had Steen Christiansen, the secretary of the Social Democratic Party. He was very strong in supporting us and it led the Danish government, whichever coalition there was, to also support us. On a social note, Steen Christiansen was the best man when the now Foreign Affairs Minister Mudenge had his wedding, so they were very good friends right from that time. We had those contacts. In Finland it was the same. Obviously, in terms of geography Finland was a little further away, but anything that was done by the Social Democratic Party or the Liberal Party in Sweden was emulated in Finland. They would do the same. Whatever appeals we made through Pierre Schori and other leaders of the Swedish Social Democratic Party were disseminated to their friends in the other Scandinavian countries, and their support would come.

TS: You represented a party which was outside of what has been called 'the authentic six'. Did you feel ill treated or in a lesser position vis-à-vis the other African liberation movements—ANC, SWAPO, ZAPU, PAIGC, MPLA and FRELIMO—at the Nordic government level?

SS: I think that at the government level there was no real difference. I am not excluding the others, but if you take the Swedish Social Democrats and the Centre Party then, whether under Thorbjörn Fälldin or earlier. Alex Chikwanda from Zambia, later Minister of Finance and also Agriculture under Kaunda, was in Sweden and he was a very good friend of Thorbjörn Fälldin's. We had been able to make a presentation of ourselves which at the government level did not distinguish between us and 'the authentic six'.

But clearly, if there was a meeting organized by what you might call the pro-Soviet organizations of that time, we would get there and sometimes be humiliated to the extent that even if you had been sent a ticket you would be told that there was a mistake somewhere. You were not expected to attend the meeting. We would accept the situation and go back, but it also made us more committed to support the party. We were able to tell where we did not have any support and we also knew where we had support. We told our leadership in Lusaka and in Dar es Salaam in very clear terms that whatever assistance we were able to mobilize in Scandinavia was from these sectors, but from those other sectors we did not expect very much. We had no illusions. If a meeting was organized by those who called themselves 'the authentic six', we would not make lots of efforts to be present. But if we got there, we would make our position very clear. It slowly began to have an impact.

If you take an organization like SWAPO, they knew the situation on the ground, how we worked, fighting as hard as anybody else. If you take FRELIMO, in the end they also knew and became our hosts. A change began to develop which was taking into account the objective situation of the fight for the liberation of Zimbabwe, a situation which was no longer dictated by the ideological cul-de-sac of the so-called 'authentic six'. We were beginning to be accepted as much as our colleagues in ZAPU. But, obviously, there were others who did not want us at all. At the height of the Sino-Soviet dispute, the Soviet Union and all the allies of the Soviet Union would not hear of us. Sometimes that would be unpleasant.

TS: You lived in Sweden and you knew of the strong anti-Communism that, for example, Olof Palme represented. At the same time, Palme was very supportive of movements like ANC of South Africa, which allegedly was influenced by Communists. How do you explain that?

SS: When you read Palme's book *Politik är att vilja* ('Politics Is Dedication'), I think that it to some extent explains the ideological conflict between the East and the West. But I think that he was also able to identify the fact that our situation required the type of action that we were taking and, probably, that the support that we were getting from the Soviet bloc was very coincidental, rather than deliberate. If you take Palme, having spoken to people like Mondlane, Chitepo and others, he could understand what they were saying. I think that they were able to impress on him that 'the issue at home is not an ideological issue between Communism and capitalism. It is one of liberation. If we are able to liberate ourselves, we will be able to make up our own minds about the best ideological position to take'. In terms of bloc support there might have been some ideological contradiction, but in terms of national liberation—which Palme was supporting, for example in Vietnam, Cuba and elsewhere—I do not think that there was.

TS: Did you co-ordinate or consult with the Nordic governments in international fora like the United Nations?

SS: Yes, if you take the Nordic countries, you had, for example, also the Socialist International, where we were very active. That is one platform where we were given a status which enabled our leadership to communicate with the leaders of all the Scandinavian countries. And at the UN and in other international fora we would brief the Scandinavian countries very well, because we knew that they would eloquently put our position across. You had a position where the British—as much as they were opposed to UDI—tended to be protective of the Rhodesian regime. But I think that the Scandinavian spokesmen really put it in the correct moral context: 'This issue should be looked into for what it is. Others have stood and fought for their liberation and it is in that same light that the Zimbabwean struggle should be looked at. It should not be looked at in the ideological or in the racial sense, but in the sense that there is what has been accepted by the UN, namely the principle of self-determination'. That is what was at stake.

TS: Do you think that the Nordic countries played a role in broadening your diplomatic field of action?

SS: Yes, very much so. For example, with the Labour Parties in the lead in the Nordic countries, we would be invited to the congresses of the Swedish Labour Party, the Danish Labour Party, the Norwegian Labour Party and the Finnish Labour Party. Other representatives of independent countries—or those in the liberation struggle—also attended these congresses, so we had a platform where we would be able to spread our own message to a much larger audience.

TS: You were also working in Sweden as a medical doctor?

SS: Well, I did my internship and when I finished it was a question of what next? I discussed it with my leadership. I had been sent out of the country by the party. I remained in the party as part and parcel of the struggle and I felt that it was quite natural that when I had qualified as a medical doctor I should come back. Since we were not yet independent, the only country that was close to us was Zambia and I decided to go and work there. I left Sweden in 1975.

TS: So you were in Zambia when Chitepo was assassinated?

SS: No, that occurred when I was still in Sweden. I was working in Ängelholm. When the news came I was actually in theatre, doing surgery. One of the young doctors, who knew my political affiliation and activities, came to me and said: 'I hear from the news that your Chairman Chitepo has been killed. Do you know anything about it?' That was the first time, so I removed my gloves and gown, listened to the news and phoned my friends.

TS: Sweden maintained contacts with ZANU through that crisis. That is interesting, because Sweden also gave a lot of support to Zambia, but Zambia banned ZANU?

SS: Yes, Zambia put the ZANU leadership in prison. It was a difficult time. When I went to Zambia in about September 1975, the tension was still there. You could not speak very freely as a member or a leader of ZANU at that time. But I was working in the hospital, so I was not in the real limelight. The leadership was in prison and we were trying to see how best we could keep the organization together. It was a difficult time.

TS: Kaunda has later said that it was not until he left government that he found out that one of his own ministers was working against ZANU.

SS: Well, I think that of all the Zambian ministers who were anti-ZANU, the hardest was the former Minister of Home Affairs, Aaron Milner. He was extremely anti-ZANU.

If I look at our situation after independence, I would say that when I was Minister of Health, a lot was done by Sweden in the health sector. To me it was like a continuation of where I had left. When I returned to Sweden as a Minister of Health, I went to SIDA and met all the friends. Despite the various problems that we have, sometimes you wish that we could have the kind of balance that Swedish politics struck, which centres on the goal of uplifting the generality of the people. Of all the things that I studied in Sweden, what still strikes me when I talk with my friends is the way in which Sweden was able to organize itself and really make sure that the generality of the people, from the peasant farmers—who are now very few in Sweden—to the white and blue collar workers and the obviously affluent ones, progressed with avoidance of conflict. The position that 'this is our country: Whatever we do, we do it together'. Where you do not have a very antagonistic relationship between, for example, capital and labour. I remember the old leader of the trade union movement, Arne Geijer. When he and the big guns from industry spoke you saw a convergence: 'In the Swedish national interest, this is what we must do.'

I sometimes find that lacking here. You do not have the convergence of 'let us move together in the national interest of Zimbabwe.' You have the kind of situation where some people tend to say: *Your* government, as if it is not *their* government. It is that kind of orientation which I often wish that we would be able to build. It cannot be an event. I think that it is a process that one should consciously try to build up. We may not be able to achieve it ourselves, but I think that for our children and grandchildren we should lay a foundation where the common interest is paramount and all the other things can be set aside. Let the central common interest guide us in what we do. That is one thing that I did not learn in the textbooks, but after eleven years in Sweden and having studied Swedish politics very much in my spare time. I find that the main issue that I raise when I am resting and talking with friends is: 'We should be able to do this and also develop a work ethic where, if work begins at eight, people get into the factory at a quarter to eight, and if work finishes at five, people get out of the factory at a quarter past five.' That type of attitude is one of the few things that you learn by staying in a country. You cannot impact it on anybody. You cannot say: 'Do this!' That type of culture begins when you absorb it after eleven years. I came to Sweden when I was very young and at a very active time. When my children ask me which countries are the best, I say Zimbabwe and Sweden.

TS: Did you feel that there was a political agenda hidden behind the Nordic support to ZANU? Did the Nordic countries try to influence you in any direction?

SS: No, that was not really there.

TS: Was it purely humanitarian?
SS: It was purely humanitarian. Well, one must obviously be human. If I am assisting you, it is natural that after some time you begin to appreciate the assistance that I give you. From that appreciation you also begin to be a little curious about what it is that makes it possible for me to assist you. I think that it is only a natural development. ZANU was not very ideological in its outlook, East or West. I think that you will find that ZANU has tried to follow a middle course.

When we came in we did not nationalize. People often say that the constitution stopped us from doing so. But constitutions are written. If you do not want to follow it, you tear it up and write a new one. I think that a social democratic tendency in a positive way influenced a lot of what we were doing in the beginning. How much of that is Swedish influence on my part, or on the part of others, one does not know. But the end product has tended to be something along those lines.

Ndabaningi Sithole
President of ZANU, Chairman of the Zimbabwe Liberation Council and President of ZANU-Sithole
President of ZANU-Ndonga
(Harare, 25 July 1995)

Tor Sellström: There was an early involvement by the Nordic countries in the liberation struggle in Zimbabwe. How can you explain that? Did it start with the missions?
Ndabaningi Sithole: Well, to begin with it was an involvement by the missions. Sweden had a very big mission in this country at Mnene. Incidentally, my first child was born at that mission. When the struggle started, somehow the good-hearted people at Mnene sympathized with the African nationalist cause and we were able to send some of our fellows to Sweden. My own son, for instance, got into a family there. They looked after him. My daughter also got there through a Swedish family. But it is not only my family that benefited from being kept by Swedish families during the struggle, but other families as well. They benefited a great deal.
TS: I know that family members of nationalist leaders received support from Sweden through organizations like Christian Aid and the International Defence and Aid Fund. So, you think that the missionary influence was important?
NS: It was very important, indeed. The missionary involvement is always very important. That is my view, which I held as way back as in the 1950s when I first wrote on African nationalism and said that the African liberation movements would have been much poorer without the missionary influence. Practically all the leaders of the African movements in this country—and elsewhere in Africa—went through mission schools. Take Mugabe himself, the President of Zimbabwe. He went to a Roman Catholic mission school. Take Nkomo. He schooled through the Methodist church. And I studied through the United Church of Christ.
TS: Did you have this connection in mind when you appointed the first ZANU representatives to the Nordic countries?
NS: Yes, that is right.
TS: Was this because you had contacts with the Nordic people?
NS: Yes, we already had contacts with them. We always admired the Nordic people and wanted our promising young people to go there.
TS: Later you sent ZANU members to Sweden on scholarships, like Sydney Sekeramayi?
NS: Yes.
TS: You were waging an anti-colonial, anti-imperialist liberation struggle in which you eventually were forced to take up arms. Was it not strange that the Nordic countries supported you?
NS: No, there was nothing strange about that as far as we were concerned. Westerners are able to distinguish between personalities and causes. We were not fighting white people as such. We were fighting imperialism, which in this country was represented

by Britain, and we knew that Sweden was not in support of imperialism. They just wanted the people here to be free and we took advantage of this. We did not appeal to them for weapons of war. We appealed to them for medicines, clothing, food, footwear and blankets and they came out with their very best. They helped us in that way. But as far as the military side is concerned, we never even made an effort, because we knew that their policy was for peace.

But we told them that we were waging a war. We did not hide it. We said that there is a war because people are not listening to what we are saying. If we fight they will probably listen much better, and, in fact, then they did listen! For a long time we told the whites here—and in Britain and elsewhere—that they had to give in to the demands of the majority.

TS: When did you have your first contacts with the Nordic countries? Was it through the church?

NS: Yes, with the church. I was trained at Dadaya mission, two or three hundred miles away from the Mnene mission. Mnene mission was Lutheran and Dadaya was of the United Church of Christ, but we used to have inter-sports relations and a good number of my friends came from Mnene. Even at this stage, when I go to Mnene I am treated as though I belong to that part of the world.

TS: Later on you also visited Sweden?

NS: Yes, I did. In 1977, after I had been released from jail. That is when I visited Mrs. Ingrid Lilja, who was looking after my daughter. Actually, Mrs. Lilja was my daughter's second mother. I stayed with them.

TS: You were released before the Geneva talks in 1976. After the talks, the Swedish government decided to support ZANU and ZAPU. Were you not disappointed that your formation, ZANU-Sithole, did not receive any support?

NS: Well, naturally I was disappointed. But I could see the point, because Kaunda was on the side of Mugabe and Nkomo. The same with Nyerere, for one reason or another. They gave their whole-hearted support to Nkomo, Mugabe and so on. But what was most important to me was the question of majority rule. If their support would cause us to get majority rule that was all that mattered as far as I was concerned. Even when we lost the first elections here in Zimbabwe I said—when the journalists asked me if I was not disappointed—that 'naturally, as a party leader I am disappointed, but as a nationalist leader I am very happy, because we got our principle of majority rule'.

TS: Did you get any support from any other Nordic country?

NS: No, only from Sweden.

TS: How about Finland?

NS: No, I cannot remember that. But most of the time I was inside, in jail.

TS: Denmark or Norway?

NS: Well, I visited Denmark and I met the Prime Minister of that time. And Norway. In the 1970s we received some material support. Not military support.

TS: Was this Nordic support given with conditions attached to it?

NS: No, with Sweden we did not detect that. They just helped for humanitarian reasons, really. More than anything else. I think that humanitarianism is something that we detected all the time in our dealings with the Swedes.

TS: What about accountability? Were the Swedes strict on that?

NS: Well, I would say that at that time the problem did not seem to arise. But as corruption in the nationalist movement began to raise its head, they were very particular on that. Things given should be used for the purpose for which they were given.

TS: In the Cold War situation that prevailed at the time, were you supported by the Nordic countries at the United Nations and in other international fora?

NS: Yes, you could trust them almost absolutely.

TS: So you worked with them?

NS: Yes. They were sympathetic to our cause.

TS: Is it your opinion that the Nordic countries actually meant something for the liberation struggle in Zimbabwe?

NS: Oh yes! Not only for the liberation struggle at that time, but their values were so impressive that up to this day we still want to emulate their views on peace, tolerance, co-operation, helpfulness and so on. If we can get more Nordic sympathy even now, we would be most grateful.

Josiah Tungamirai
ZANU/ZANLA—Political Commissar
Former Air Marshal
(Harare, 7 June 1996)

Carl Fredrik Hallencreutz: In your strategic role in the armed liberation struggle, when did you first come across the Nordic countries?

Josiah Tungamirai: The first time that I heard that Sweden was helping us was in 1971, during our training at the Mgagao camp in Tanzania. At that time, we were only recruits and we did not know much about where the liberation movement was getting its support from, with the exception of the OAU Liberation Committee, which, I think, then was the basic supplier of ammunition and humanitarian aid.

Later on, as we went on with our training and political education—adopting a socialist ideology—we were told by our instructors that the people who supported us were from the East, but also from some European countries. When we asked how we could get support from the capitalist countries, we were told that there were some progressive people in these countries who saw our struggle as a just cause and that they were there to help us from a humanitarian point of view. From the East we got training grounds, ammunition, military uniforms and all the military hardware. At times they also gave us some humanitarian assistance, but—as I said—we were told that it mostly came from progressive people within the capitalist countries. For example, the Americans gave us some clothing and from Britain we also got some clothing. However, the bulk of our clothes, food and transport came from the Nordic countries, especially from Denmark, Norway and Sweden.

CFH: Before you came to Tanzania, did you have any contacts with or information about the Nordic countries?

JT: No. I come from the Masvingo area, but, unfortunately, I did not know much about the outside world. From 1965—after UDI—Rhodesia was closed by sanctions and we had very little literature about what was happening outside our borders. Even radio communication and news media were very restricted, so I did not know much about the Nordic countries. Of course, I knew from geography classes in school that there was a Denmark, a Norway and a Sweden, but not much about them.

CFH: You did not have any contacts with the Swedish missions in Mberengwa?

JT: No. In my district the missionaries were from the Dutch Reformed Church and the Roman Catholic Church. The Catholics were mostly Bethlehem Fathers from Switzerland and Germany.

CFH: In your view, what was the motive behind the Nordic support to the liberation struggle?

JT: I think that they just saw the Zimbabweans as being oppressed. I did not detect anything strange. They did not teach us their ideology and they did not tell us how good Sweden was, how good Denmark was or how good Norway was. They were simply there to give assistance to refugees from an oppressive country. That is how I very clearly understood it. That was different from our Eastern friends. They put in the guns and the ammunition and helped us with our uniforms, which was very important and vital for the liberation struggle, but besides that they also taught us their ideology. You could see that it was because of the Cold War. They had had no chance in the past—during the colonial days—to colonize us, but there was now a chance to do that by helping us with the liberation struggle.

CFH: Did you notice any difference between Sweden, being a neutral country, and Denmark and Norway, who were part of NATO?

JT: I would not know. I was part of the military structures and our role was to receive what the party leadership brought us and distribute the goods to different camps. The people who would know better where our goods came from are people like Kumbirai Kangai, who was directly involved with that.

CFH: Sweden supported both the so-called 'authentic six' and ZANU, trying to adopt a non-partial attitude. How did you see the policy in that regard?

JT: Well, I think that the people in Sweden who supplied us with humanitarian assistance were very clever. The 'authentic six' was not a creation of the six liberation movements. It was a creation of the Soviet Union, but when Sweden started its support, they supported both the six and ZANU. I think that what they really had in mind was not the question of what party the people belonged to, but what pushed them out of Zimbabwe and into exile. They supported us as exiled people from Zimbabwe who were fighting for our liberation.

CFH: From Tanzania, did you move straight to Mozambique or did you pass via Zambia?

JT: For some time I was in Zambia, but not for long. It was only a stepping stone to move into Zimbabwe. In May 1972, we were taken from Tanzania in a group of fifteen to reinforce a group of forty-five. The group leader was the now retired General Mujuru (Rex Nhongo) and I was his deputy, leading a group of fifteen fighters. Originally, we were supposed to come through Botswana as a sabotage group. Most of us had done what we called military engineering in sabotage. But when we reached Zambia, it was changed. The group of forty-five had already settled in Mozambique and it was calling for reinforcements. At that time we were ferrying war material from Zambia to Zimbabwe, but when the group asked for reinforcements the idea of sending us via Botswana was changed into sending us through Mozambique instead.

CFH: When you started operating from Mozambique, what sort of contacts did you then have with the Nordic countries?

JT: The only contact that I had with the Nordic countries was through the humanitarian goods which were delivered to us by the party leadership. There was no direct contact. Through the Department of Transport and Welfare, the ZANU leadership looked for food, clothing and so forth, because our numbers were swelling. But it was our leadership that handled these questions and it was based in Lusaka from 1965 to 1974. General Mujuru and myself were considered pure military people. We had not yet entered politics, as we later did. We were also still very low in the command structures. We were not even members of the High Command, but just ordinary general staff members.

CFH: Did you experience any changes in the Nordic policy as the war went on?

JT: I think that they maintained their policy of supplying the Zimbabwean refugees with food. In my mind, I do not think that they said: 'We should support the people who fight'. They said: 'We are supporting the refugees'. I also think that that is why they managed to support us, because I do not think that they would have been able to continue if they had said that they were going to support the liberation movement straight out.

What I saw changing were the quantities of the supplies. They were increasing as our numbers were increasing. After the détente exercise—which almost brought the struggle to a standstill in 1974-75—and after the release of the leadership from the Zambian prisons and the reinforcement by the leadership from home, we established ourselves very well in Maputo and there was a big increase in supplies from the Nordic countries.

CFH: From a military perspective, how would you assess the effect of the Nordic support?

JT: First and foremost, in the years from 1977 to 1979, the numbers of homeless from Zimbabwe increased greatly and at the end of the day we had over 40,000 refugees in Mozambique. At that time, we faced three major problems, namely, food, clothing and medicine. And here the Nordic countries helped us tremendously. Why do I say that it was a very big help? Because at that stage we were no longer recruiting from home, but from the refugee camps and if the refugees had not been fed, if they had not been clothed and if they had had no medical care, then our source of recruitment would have dried up, meaning that they would have died. Before 1977—when the leadership had not yet taken a grip of the refugee situation—a lot of this was taking place. We then had some camps which recorded an average of over twenty people dying each day due to lack of food. That is when the Nordic countries came in full force, giving us food, medicines and clothing. And that is also why the ZANU leadership never went to Sweden, Denmark or Norway saying: 'Could you give us some guns?' or 'Could you give us some ammunition?' We only got clothing, but as much as we wanted. We also got some medicines and food.

The importance of this assistance went even further. For example, in what we called the North-East—which is now Mashonaland Centre and part of Mashonaland East—there were areas where we had fought the war and everybody had gone into the bush. The cultivation of the land had come to a standstill, so we had to take food from Mozambique into Zimbabwe to feed the ordinary people, the poor, the masses. We fed them and clothed them with the supplies that we had got from external sources like Sweden, Norway and Denmark.

CFH: Did you tell the soldiers and the local people where the humanitarian assistance came from?

JT: Yes.

CFH: Did you also discuss the difference between the Nordic support and the support you got from the East?

JT: Yes, we told them. Besides telling them, we also kept the labels and people would read and ask: 'You say that Norway is a capitalist country and that Sweden is a capitalist country. Why then is this medicine coming from Norway and this medicine from Sweden?' People would ask such questions. It educated the people in the rural areas where we were operating. We had to sit down and explain to them and—since we had adopted a socialist line—we would say that 'we do not agree with their government line, but it is true that there are progressive people within their governments and they are the ones who are asking their governments to help us with humanitarian goods. We are getting our guns, ammunition and weapons from China, the Soviet Union, Czechoslovakia, Poland, Hungary and so forth. They are helping us to liberate ourselves. So, the West is giving us medicines, transport, food and clothing, while the East is giving us arms and ammunition'. We had to explain that, because the people could not understand. They asked us if we were getting these goods from the Mozambican government and we said that Mozambique had given us shelter, but that the clothing mostly came from countries overseas.

CFH: After the Lancaster House Agreement, how did you see the Nordic support?

JT: Actually, I cannot comment much on that, because after the Lancaster House Agreement there was a total demarcation between the armed forces and the party and we were concentrating on the armed forces. We were preparing the integration of the armed forces into one force.

CFH: After independence, you became a Major-General and then Air Marshal, forming part of the leadership of the Zimbabwean National Defence Force. Of course, Zimbabwe also became involved in the continued regional liberation struggle. Did you during this period have any contacts with the Nordic countries?

JT: No, I did not. After independence I concentrated on the defence force and it did not deal directly with what was happening in the government. Also, we did not see what Mozambique had experienced. We received some refugees in Zimbabwe and they were handled by the Ministry of Social Welfare, but their numbers were comparatively small. By the time we got our independence, there were moves towards a democratic change in Southern Africa and there was no major flow of refugees from South Africa or Namibia into Zimbabwe. There was very little of that and we never had major refugee camps, except for the camps for people coming from Mozambique because of the civil strife in that country. We had more refugees from Mozambique than from Namibia and South Africa.

CFH: On the basis of the relationship with the Nordic countries during the liberation struggle, what role would you like to see them play in Zimbabwe today?

JT: Well, what I expected on our part after independence was to call upon the countries—both from the East and the West—who supported us during the course of our armed liberation struggle to come to Zimbabwe and say to them: 'Look, here we are with our independence which you have supported in so many ways. We want to sustain it. Please, come and invest, so that you can see the fruits of what you have supported'. On the part of the countries which supported us, I also think that it would be wise to come and say: 'Look, we have established an embassy. You are now independent and we are no longer supporting you as a liberation movement. We are supporting you as an independent country and the support we are pushing for is in the form of investments'.

I am very worried by the fact that after independence you could see Germany, the United States and Britain entering in full force. They are now playing major roles compared to the countries which supported us until independence. I am very worried about that. They were on the opposite side years ago and now they are on our side, while the countries that supported us from day one are not seen to be in the forefront, helping us to build our economy and to establish ourselves as an independent state.

Zambia, OAU and the Soviet Union

Kenneth Kaunda
President of Zambia
President of the United National Independence Party
(Lusaka, 15 July 1995)

Tor Sellström: I would like to clarify that the objective of the interview is to discuss the involvement of all the Nordic countries in the liberation struggle in Southern Africa.
Kenneth Kaunda: Well, it was Olof Palme who led the Nordic countries in this process. It was his contribution which aroused the interest and the feelings of the other Nordic countries. They also made very wonderful contributions, there is no doubt about that. But I am merely being factual when I say that it all started with Sweden.
TS: You went to England as a young man in 1957 and met the Labour Party and others there. Did you at that time have any contacts with a Nordic country or organization?
KK: No, not at that time. We were very insular in those days. We were more or less locked out. We had no contacts with the outside world. For example, in 1954 a few colleagues and myself wanted to organize a Pan-African Congress for this region. We invited some people from the neighbouring countries, but even they were banned. Only one man from the United Nations, a Burmese, managed to attend. We were very insular. It was not our choice. It was the way the colonial masters wanted it to be. When I visited England it was the first time that I went outside the region.
TS: Were your first contacts with the Nordic countries made then after Zambia's independence in 1964?
KK: No, it was a little earlier. In fact, I visited Sweden in 1962 as a guest of the late Olof Palme's party. I was very well received, indeed. I felt very much at home.
TS: Perhaps you visited with Oliver Tambo, who also went to Sweden in 1962?
KK: No, he must have gone on his own. That was the first time that I went to Sweden, but my first contacts with the Swedish people were, I think, at a World Assembly of Youth (WAY) conference in Dar es Salaam. I met Swedes there and I kept my contacts with them until 1962.
TS: The Nordic involvement with Zambia started in response to an appeal by the United Nations to assist Lesotho, Botswana, Swaziland and Zambia?
KK: Yes. That is how we organized scholarships for some of our students. For example, Alex Chikwanda, who was in my government for a long time, studied in Sweden. Rupiah Banda came under the same scheme. I organized those scholarships.
TS: I know that Rupiah Banda studied at the University of Lund together with Billy Modise, who is now South Africa's ambassador to Canada. They had a little band, called 'Billy and Banda'.
KK: I did not know that!
TS: They were also among the founders of the Swedish solidarity movement. In 1969, the Swedish parliament decided that it was legitimate to give direct support to the liberation movements. The other Nordic governments followed later. How did you view the Nordic position?
KK: Well, first and foremost, let me say that I am sure that I express the view held by many leaders of this region. Firstly, because of the time when the assistance was given; secondly, the way in which it was given; thirdly, the type of aid that it was; and, fourthly, the impact it had on us, made us all realize that the Nordic countries had something special to contribute. Not only to Southern Africa, but to the struggling masses and to God's people the world over. They were very human. They did not grant aid to us because they expected something in return. They granted aid to us because they knew that fellow human beings needed that aid, almost saying to themselves that 'if we were in that position and they were in ours, we know that they would do the same thing to us'. So, really—and in many ways—at the time of our struggle for independence in Zambia and in the neighbouring countries the impact of that aid was such that even if we had had—I am not saying that we did— but even if we had had some anti-white feelings, that aid would have changed our minds.
TS: Did you not feel that there were strings attached to the aid? Any hidden agendas?

KK: This is exactly what I am saying. The aid had no strings attached. This is what I am talking about. It was: 'Our fellow human being needs assistance. We will give it to him as best we know how.' Really, it helped a lot to make us what we are. That contribution was very important.

TS: Did you feel that the Nordic countries had different outlooks depending on their international alliances? Sweden was neutral, Finland had a 'special relationship' to the Soviet Union and Denmark and Norway were members of NATO?

KK: Well, when we became independent we started off as truly non-aligned and we saw something similar in Sweden on these issues. Non-alignment did not mean that we were saying to anyone that we are holier than thou. When they made a mistake, we said to the West that according to us they had made a mistake. And if they did something right, we praised them equally strongly. The same goes for the East. If they did something good, we praised them. But if they did something wrong, we condemned them.

To make this properly understood, let me give you an example on Zambia's behalf of what we did in two clear cases: when the Americans were bombing the Vietnamese people, using napalm bombs and things of that nature, I spoke about it on behalf of Zambia several times in public, condemning the action. I remember that I twice spoke about it in parliament, dealing with foreign policy matters. I was condemning it. But when the Americans stopped bombing the Vietnamese and it ended, we became friends again. There was nothing more for me to condemn. Then, some day in 1968 the Soviet Union invaded Czechoslovakia. I remember that I was at the border with Tanzania when this happened. I was listening to a broadcast from BBC and I heard that the Soviet Union had invaded. That same morning I addressed a huge mass rally. I condemned the Soviet Union and I made it clear to the rest of the world, and to them as well, that if they were going to withdraw their aid to us because of my condemnation, they were free to do so.

Now, coming back to Sweden, I remember that it was under Olof Palme that the young men and women in America who did not want to go to Vietnam found a place there.

TS: In the case of Sweden, Olof Palme marched with the North Vietnamese ambassador and condemned the American bombings to the extent that the United States withdrew its ambassador. On the question of Czechoslovakia, Palme condemned the invasion and talked about the new Czech government as 'the cattle of the dictatorship'. Your positions were very similar?

KK: Very similar, indeed. I gave these examples, because I know where Olof Palme stood on these issues. He received these students when they refused to go to Vietnam and they were persecuted by the American government. They ran away and found solace in Sweden. We had a very similar stance on these issues.

TS: You also supported liberation movements that received material and military assistance from the Communist bloc. Here some would argue objectively that you, Palme and other Nordic leaders were supporting the East in an East-West confrontation?

KK: Those who did not know the leaders of the liberation movements might have thought that way. But for those of us who knew them it was different. They were pushed against the wall and they had to get arms from the Soviet Union or the People's Republic of China simply because they had to fight. You can refer to the Lusaka Manifesto on Southern Africa, where we—the Heads of States of this region—made it clear that the liberation movements that could attain independence through non-violent methods should do so. But we had no moral or political right in the situation prevailing at the time to say that if they could not attain independence through peaceful means: 'Do not fight!'. We had no right at all. We urged them: 'If you can negotiate peacefully, please, by all means, do so. But if you cannot, we will support the means you decide to use.' And this is what happened.

It did not mean that we were siding with the Soviet Union or the People's Republic of China. If the West had given them arms, the liberation movements would have been very happy to receive them. They did not have a choice in this matter. They had to go to the countries where they could receive this aid, like the Eastern European countries and the People's Republic of China, who supported them and backed them very strongly and fully.

We knew that the situation was not easy. When it comes to the Portuguese colonies, I myself met with political leaders on several occasions. I met settlers from Angola and Mozambique. I wrote to them and my argument was: 'Look, your countries have been under Portuguese rule for centuries. There is no way that you will lose if you hand over power peacefully, because culturally they will be tied to you. They are just part and parcel of you now, so you are losing nothing. You have everything to gain by handing over power to the majority of the people.' But they continued to behave as if Angola, Mozambique and the other colonies were truly provinces of Portugal. That is how the liberation movements embarked upon the armed struggle.

Similarly, when we were dissolving the Federation of Rhodesia and Nyasaland, we did not dissolve it because we were against larger units, but because it was a second South Africa being imposed on us. We objected to it and we fought against it. When we were ending the Federation, I said to the last Governor: 'Please, let me meet the leaders of the white minority groups, the Prime Minister and the Deputy Prime Minister'. Guess who was the Deputy Prime Minister? Ian Douglas Smith! I said to them: 'Gentlemen, when we become independent, we will recognize you as white nationalists in Rhodesia. But we are conscious of the fact that the indigenous nationalists, the black nationalists, are by far the majority and that you will have trouble with them. So, please, if you ever need our services to try and be bridge-builders, we will be quite happy to assist.' The Prime Minister then said: 'Mr. Kaunda, if we did not know that you are serious and sincere, we would have told you to mind your own business.' Well, I was minding my own business until Ian Smith landed at State House here in Lusaka with his army and his choppers, coming to ask for assistance.

That was at a time when it was taboo for African nationalist leaders to meet those people. But because my conscience was clear, I met them. That is how I met the late Vorster, Botha and finally de Klerk. It was to show that if they would negotiate we had nothing against them at all. We were not anti-white as such. This is the point I made earlier, and which the Nordic people strengthened so much in us.

TS: At the time of independence, you—and also President Nkrumah of Ghana—tried to establish diplomatic relations with South Africa as a means not to be subdued or to open up space?

KK: Yes, I said to them: 'If you can look after my ambassador in the same way that you look after white ambassadors, we can establish relations.' But they could not.

TS: When it comes to the different liberation movements, the Nordic countries supported MPLA in Angola, FRELIMO in Mozambique, ANC in South Africa, SWAPO in Namibia and both ZANU and ZAPU in Zimbabwe. Also here your position was very similar?

KK: Yes, exactly the same. That is clear. That is also how we worked. In the case of South Africa, in the beginning we recognized both ANC and PAC and allowed them here. But what happened was that PAC had a camp for their cadres in Livingstone and that they decided to kill some of their members, suspecting that they were sell-outs or South African agents, reporting them to the South African authorities. I came to hear about it and said to PAC: 'Please, do not do that. On this soil of Zambia, I am the only one who is constitutionally allowed to take life. I do not like it, but the law says that I should do that when the High Court has found somebody guilty and has so decided. So, do not do that.' However, they were going to kill them, so I gave instructions to the Zambian army to get into their camp and save the lives of those people. Fortunately, we did it without loss of life. I then said that they could not work from here, because they were defying my orders and there was no way that we could have two governments in the country.

They were sent to Tanzania. But when I became chairman of the Frontline States and also chairman of the Organization of African Unity (OAU), I had to welcome them back. Because in that capacity I had to receive all the movements that were recognized by the OAU. That is how PAC came back to Zambia after many years.

TS: The Nordic countries supported the liberation movements in Zambia through humanitarian assistance. I presume that it was with your knowledge and approval?

KK: Yes, we accepted it, indeed. We were very happy to do so. We knew what kind of aid they were giving and how it was given. It was given without strings. It was aid given because certain fellow human beings were in great need.

TS: Was it strictly civilian?

KK: Yes, strictly civilian. I might add that if the Nordic countries for any reason had given them armed support, we would not have had any objections at all. Not with the Nordic countries.

TS: In 1972, the ZANU leader Herbert Chitepo came to SIDA in Stockholm and said: 'We are about to launch the armed struggle and the result will inevitably be retaliation by the settler regime and refugees pouring into Zambia. So, can you please assist us in Zambia?' It was quite amazing. Here you had a representative from a liberation movement coming to a Western country and exposing their military plans. I guess that it says a lot about the trust between the parties involved?

KK: Exactly. That is very true. That was supposed to be top secret information, but in Sweden he talked freely because of that trust.

TS: It eventually led SIDA to purchase a farm for ZANU here in Zambia. Later SIDA financed the purchase of farms for ANC and SWAPO. Did you, in this context, feel that there was undue interference by the Nordic countries in the affairs of Zambia?

KK: Certainly not. Without hesitation, none at all. At least none that I know of or that my colleagues who were dealing with these matters knew of. Nothing at all.

TS: Because at some stage, Zambia and the Nordic countries could come on different courses? I am, particularly, thinking of the Angolan issue in 1974-75.

KK: Exactly. The background was that we had kept UNITA away from Zambia, but after the coup in Portugal I sent my Minister of Foreign Affairs—guess who? Vernon Mwaanga!—to speak to his African colleagues. They met in Cameroon. I said that now that there is a change in Portugal, let Africa open up to all the Angolan liberation movements. Let them be accepted by OAU. If we do not do that, there will be all sorts of internal problems in the future. That was in 1974. Indeed, Mwaanga spoke to his colleagues and the Foreign Ministers accepted that position and passed a resolution which in turn was accepted by several Heads of State. After that, in 1974-75, things began to happen very fast. The Heads of State of this region met in Kananga and we agreed that if Agostinho Neto were to become President we would support him. We would also support Savimbi becoming Minister of Defence and we would support de Andrade.

Zambia was later detailed to try and bring the Angolans together. We met all the factions here, at a farm. Reuben Kamanga was my representative. He had been in Cairo and to most other centres when we were struggling for our independence and he knew most of the Angolan leaders. They met for fifteen days. And failed! The following day, I asked to see my brother, the late Neto. I loved that man. He was a Marxist-Leninist and I am a Christian, but we were very good friends. We met for sixteen hours at State House. No breaks for lunch, only tea and scones. I tried to persuade my brother and said: 'Look, you are an organizer. Please, bring all the parties together. It must be possible to do that, because for the time being you need a coalition government.' But I believe that he was under pressure from the Soviet Union. We could not accept that at all. I stuck to my approach. That is when I made a statement saying that it was like letting a tiger's cubs into Angola. It would bring no peace at all. I referred to the Soviet Union and Cuba. Again, Fidel Castro is a very good personal friend of mine, but I attacked the Soviet Union and I attacked him too. Because of the fear I had that it would bring problems to Angola.

And, indeed, what followed was very sad. We were forced to have an OAU Heads of State summit meeting. Julius Nyerere and myself had vowed never to go to a summit under the chairmanship of Idi Amin, who was then the chairman. We refused to recognize him. But this time we were forced to go to the summit. And, unfortunately, of the 46 countries that voted, 23 were for and 23 were against. It was very sad. It was a lost case. As I said to President dos Santos when he came here for a state visit: 'One does not settle scores. It is not right. I told you so.' But that is what I discussed with my brother Neto.

TS: Did you have any consultations—informal or otherwise—with Olof Palme? He was very much involved in some sort of diplomatic exchange between Neto, Castro and Kissinger in the beginning of 1976.

KK: No. I did not know about that, but it shows the point I was making earlier. Even a man like Kissinger recognized that only somebody like Palme could talk to Neto about their differences. He had to fall back on someone who had defied him during the Vietnamese war. That's interesting.

TS: After the assassination of Herbert Chitepo in 1975, you detained a number of ZANU people while Sweden gave humanitarian assistance to ZANU. Did that create any friction between you and Sweden?

KK: No, certainly not. We suspected that the assassination was an inside job. At the funeral of the late Chitepo I said that my government would do everything possible to find out who had done this, arrest them and bring them to a court of law. We set up a Special International Commission. What I did not know then—I only came to know about it much, much later; in fact, after I had left government—was that one of my own ministers actually had been persecuting ZANU, because he was a supporter of ZAPU. I did not know that at all. A researcher in Zimbabwe found out about it. Well, my minister was not supporting ZAPU as such. He was an agent of Ian Smith's, informing on ZANU. He was given instructions to disorganize ZANU within Zambia. My colleagues on the ZANU side unfortunately believed that he was acting like that on my instructions. So they were hostile for a long time. I did not understand why, because I thought that I was giving equal support to all the liberation movements. That is until I left government and the researcher was told by one of Ian Smith's former agents that this is what had happened: 'Kaunda did not know about it.' This researcher—David Martin—was a strong ZANU supporter. He had earlier published a book against me, but now he apologized.

TS: There was also the so-called Shipanga affair in SWAPO in Zambia in 1976. It involved three parties that were very close to the Nordic countries, namely SWAPO, Zambia and Tanzania. Was there any pressure by the Nordic countries, demanding that the detained SWAPO leaders should be duly processed or that they should not have been detained at all?

KK: No, not that I know of. It was a very difficult thing for us. Very difficult, indeed. We really tried as humanely as possible to maintain law and order and to do things as established by law. On the other hand, our commitment to the cause of independence and freedom of the peoples of Southern Africa was such that there were certain things that we had to do. For example, accepting to launch the armed struggle from here was not easy at all. By the same token, it was not easy for me to defy a matter that was before the High Court and give instructions to fly somebody who was going to appear in the High Court of Zambia out of the country in our own plane. It was not easy at all. But when we weighed the two, it was quite clear where our duty lay. So I had to order that Shipanga and the others be taken to Tanzania. But as far as I remember we had no pressure at all from the Nordic countries.

TS: I guess that it was a difficult issue for all the parties involved?

KK: Yes, for all of us. For the Nordic countries and for ourselves, both in Zambia and in Tanzania.

TS: Later, when Shipanga was released, he went to Sweden, where he formed SWAPO-Democrats. That was perhaps symbolic?

KK: Yes, and in a way helpful to us!

TS: Did you normally consult with the Nordic countries at the United Nations and in other international fora?

KK: Yes, indeed, on Southern Africa. Certainly, there were standing instructions that my ambassadors should consult with the Nordic governments and—if we needed support—that they should seek that from them.

TS: One problem was perhaps that the Nordic countries as a matter of principle could not vote for resolutions containing calls for armed struggle?

KK: Yes, certainly, but we understood that very well. There was no problem with that. Not at all.

TS: With regard to economic and development issues, the Nordic countries at an early stage formulated the so-called Oslo Plan to co-ordinate their policies and from 1984 they met with the Foreign Ministers of the Frontline States on a regular basis. The Finnish Prime Minister Kalevi Sorsa also took an initiative to broaden the Nordic assistance to SADCC and from 1986-87 all the Nordic countries applied economic sanctions against South Africa. There developed what one could call a region-to-region cooperation?

KK: That is true. We appreciated that. It strengthened us a lot. We quarrelled publicly with the big powers of the West on the issue of sanctions against South Africa. Here we were, small countries that were suffering, paying a high price, only supported by countries like the Nordic countries and the People's Republic of China. The big powers continued to pay lip service to the struggle against apartheid. It used to pain us a lot and that is how some of us were said to be anti-West. But we were not. We were just anti-wrong. I gave the examples of the Americans bombing the Vietnamese and the USSR invading Czechoslovakia. These were matters of principle for us. Whenever we thought that something was wrong, we condemned it publicly. This did not place us on good terms with the Western countries, especially not with my 'dancing partner' Margaret Thatcher!

I remember when we were at a Commonwealth meeting in the Bahamas, where I was detailed to move a motion of sanctions against South Africa. Margaret Thatcher opposed it. We adjourned and met again after tea. I said: 'Margaret, you are worshipping Mammon, not God.' You could have heard a pin drop! There was silence amongst the Heads of State and Government. But, it was nothing personal. I was just arguing the point of sanctions. At another meeting in Canada, I said: 'Margaret, you do not know Africa at all. It is important that you listen to the people who know these things'. I was not trying to make her look stupid or something like that. Not at all. I was just thinking of the sacrifices we made.

TS: I remember reading that when you hosted the 1979 Commonwealth Conference in Lusaka—where you were to discuss the Rhodesia question—she demanded that the leaders of ZANU and ZAPU should not welcome the Queen at the airport?

KK: Yes. First she did not want Queen Elizabeth to come here at all. She said that it was too dangerous. All she tried to do was to sabotage the summit. She even went to Australia to try to win Prime Minister Malcolm Fraser over to her side. She could not. But because she trusted him, we made him the chairman of an internal meeting that we held here in Lusaka with her and her Foreign Minister, Lord Carrington. She tried to sabotage, but everything went well in the end.

TS: Finally, it has been argued that support to one sole and 'authentic' liberation movement in the countries under colonial or apartheid rule was detrimental to the development of a democratic society after independence. How do you look upon that?

KK: I think that during the struggle it was important for us to support one strong movement, although in Zimbabwe the Nordic countries and ourselves in the Frontline States supported both ZANU and ZAPU. In South Africa as well. Now, I think that the situation changes after independence. I would have thought that, in terms of support, governments should support the peoples, but political parties should support the parties which think like they do. In that way you strengthen various voices towards the build-up of a democracy and we need a strong opposition.

Salim Ahmed Salim
Minister of Foreign Affairs and Prime Minister of Tanzania
Secretary General of the Organization of African Unity
(Copenhagen, 16 November 1995)

Tor Sellström: You were the chairman of the United Nations Decolonization Committee from 1972, also chairing the UN Security Council Committee on Sanctions against Rhodesia. In those capacities you must have worked closely with the Nordic countries?

Salim Ahmed Salim: My contacts with Swedish and Nordic representatives started in the early 1970s, when I went to New York and to the United Nations. We worked very closely with the Nordic countries on issues relating to African problems, especially in the decolonization area. We respected the Nordic position, even if we sometimes did not agree with them.

I can give one classic example, which I think is important. In 1972, we sent a team to the liberated areas of Guinea-Bissau. It was a very difficult exercise, because the Portuguese government was totally opposed to the idea. They continued to stick to the myth that there was nothing like liberated areas. Besides, they held the myth that Portugal was pluri-continental and that all the Portuguese colonies were part of Portugal. In order to defy that myth and give legitimacy to the liberation movements, we decided to send a team into the liberated areas. Among those who went in that team was a Swedish national, a junior officer in the Swedish UN mission. We had three people in the team. There was an Ecuadorian and, I think, a Tunisian. As a result of the mission, we had a dramatic breakthrough in the international understanding in terms of greater legitimacy to the liberation movements vis-à-vis the United Nations. We could now call for recognition of the liberation movements as observers in the Fourth Committee. Before that they were simply considered petitioners.

TS: Was the team sent as a United Nations mission by the Decolonization Committee?

SAS: Yes, under the Decolonization Committee, but in a subterranean manner. Due to the Portuguese, we could not announce that they were going there. We had to be very careful about their security. But it was a United Nations mission and immediately after the return we had a meeting of the whole Committee of 24 in Conakry, Guinea, to welcome the mission back. In fact, the meeting was a camouflage, because otherwise there would have been a concentration on the mission to the liberated areas. We said that we had a meeting of the Committee of 24, but at the same time we had this team.

What happened after that? We went to the Fourth Committee and it decided to invite the liberation movements as observers. But then we had something which I say is important. Amílcar Cabral, the leader of PAIGC, came to New York and we were trying to get him to address the UN General Assembly. In those days it was inconceivable for a representative of a liberation movement to address the General Assembly, but we had the necessary support. However, the Nordic countries had reservations. I remember the ambassador of Sweden and the other Nordic ambassadors telling me: 'Look, we are not happy with this. Legally, it gives us problems if representatives of the liberation movements address the General Assembly. It has not been done before and it causes a lot of problems.' So I went to Amílcar Cabral and said: 'Mr. Secretary General, if you want to address the General Assembly we have the votes. We have the necessary support of the African countries, of the Asian countries and of a number of the Latin American countries. But I want you to know that the Nordic countries are very unhappy about it. What do we do?' Cabral then said: 'Look, the Nordic countries are our friends. They have supported us through thick and thin and we do not want to embarrass them. I will not address the General Assembly.' He did not address the General Assembly in that session. And he was killed in January 1973.

There was so much respect for the position of the Nordic countries. There was no question of doubting their integrity or their sincerity towards the liberation movements. If any other country or combination of countries had said no, we would have pushed the matter to the General Assembly and received the necessary votes. Of course, subsequently it became quite common for the liberation movements to address the General Assembly. SWAPO did so and ANC did so, but in 1972—having obtained observer status in the Fourth Committee—we could not get Cabral to speak in the General Assembly.

TS: I guess that another problem was that the Nordic countries as a matter of principle could not vote in favour of resolutions that made reference to the armed struggle?

SAS: Occasionally we had to insist on the formulation of armed struggle, but to get maximum possible support we sometimes used the term 'all possible means'. That was something which everybody could interpret the way they wanted. Sweden and the other Nordic countries could say: 'We do not include the armed struggle', and we would say: 'The armed struggle is not excluded.'

TS: But, de facto, the Nordic countries supported movements that waged an armed struggle?

SAS: Well, let me say one thing which perhaps is more fundamental. I also remember saying it to the late Prime Minister of Sweden, Olof Palme. I knew him very well. We used to serve together in the Independent Commission on International Security. One day we were informally discussing the Southern African situation and I said to him: 'Look, the role of the Nordic countries goes beyond the practical assistance that you provide to the liberation movements. It is what it means in the context of the North-South divide.' The struggle in Southern Africa was basically against white rule—whether in the case of Zimbabwe, then Rhodesia, in the Portuguese colonies, in Namibia or in South Africa—but I think that the contribution by countries like the Nordic countries made it impossible for the African countries to see it in terms of colour. The issue was not simply colour, because here were the Nordic countries—as white as they could be—, who were the most active supporters of the struggle. So I said to Palme: 'It is more than what you provide. It is the symbolism involved in the commitment which the Nordic countries have made to the struggle against colonialism and racialism, against apartheid, in Southern Africa.'

TS: Do you then think that the Nordic countries served as some sort of bridge-builders between the East and the West? They supported the same so-called 'authentic six' liberation movements that were supported by the East bloc, while at the same time forming part of the West?

SAS: Yes, absolutely. Also as a moderating factor. By virtue of their situation, the Nordic countries were quite conscious of the concerns and reservations of the Western countries, who did not share their attitude towards the struggle. The Nordic countries were much more vigorous and much more supportive in a very serious manner. The support was not only political and diplomatic, but also tangible, through financial and other assistance to the liberation movements. They did act as bridge-builders, promoting understanding not only between East and West, but also between North and South.

For the entire period that I was the chairman of the United Nations Committee on Decolonization I had very good relations with all the Nordic ambassadors, many of whom became my personal friends. I was very conscious of and very sensitive to what they had to say. At no time did I ever question their sincerity to the struggle. When we differed on the methods, one had always to appreciate their points of view, because we knew that the Nordic countries' position was to support the liberation movements in a practical manner. We sometimes had to hold back. That was also the only way in which I could understand Cabral's position. Amílcar Cabral was one of those luminaries—a giant among people—and he did not hesitate when I said: 'We have the votes, but we have the problem of our friends in the Nordic countries. What do we do?' He said: 'OK, I do not have to speak to the General Assembly.' That shows something. It shows the respect which he had for the Nordic countries, and, of course, those of us who were supporting him and the struggle shared that respect.

TS: Tanzania was the decisive meeting place between the Nordic countries and the liberation movements. In the case of Sweden, support was channelled to PAIGC, MPLA, FRELIMO, ZANU, ZAPU, SWAPO and ANC. With the exception of ZANU, they were 'the authentic six' that were close to the Eastern European countries. Tanzania followed the broader OAU recognition principle. How can you explain that Sweden decided to support these movements?

SAS: Well, in the case of FRELIMO it was obvious. It was not controversial. At the initial stage of the Angolan struggle, the Tanzanian government was supporting MPLA. It was also accommodating FNLA and UNITA by virtue of being the headquarters of the OAU Liberation Committee. But, over a period of time Tanzania became more and more identified with MPLA. In the case of South Africa, we always considered ANC as the strongest movement. But I should in all frankness say that there was a belief throughout many African countries—not only in Tanzania—that PAC had bona fide support.

I had long arguments on this question with Johnny Makatini, who was a brilliant South African leader. He used to tell me: 'Look

Salim, you people are wasting our time. The only authentic national movement in South Africa is the African National Congress. You are the only ones who support PAC.' We used to have endless debates. But we did not find it difficult to understand the Swedish position, especially by virtue of the policy of ANC. ANC always followed a more inclusive policy. The policy of PAC was for some time depicted as a more radical Africanist position. So for us it was very easy to comprehend why Sweden would be more supportive of ANC. In addition, ANC did its homework. It did tremendous work in the Nordic countries.

TS: It is still interesting that Palme and Nyerere—who were very close—partly disagreed on the question of which movements to support?

SAS: Actually, it was not a contention. Over a period of years—especially from the 1970s—Tanzania's support for PAC became more pro forma by virtue of its obligation as headquarters of the OAU Liberation Committee. This was contrary to the early days, when there was a belief that maybe PAC was more dynamic. It was for the armed struggle when ANC was not and all that. But when Umkhonto we Sizwe started to operate things became clear. Another thing that really turned the Tanzanian government's position regarding South Africa was that the ANC trainees in Tanzania did not remain there. They were moving into South Africa. Most of the PAC trainees remained as armchair revolutionaries. That was, of course, a difficult situation.

TS: Tanzania received lots of South African refugees. After the Soweto uprising in 1976, there was a Regional Commissioner in Morogoro who facilitated the setting up of the ANC Solomon Mahlango Freedom College, SOMAFCO.

SAS: Yes, that was Anna Abdallah, who is now a Minister of State in the Prime Minister's Office.

TS: SOMAFCO became a focal point for international solidarity. Those who could not assist the struggle inside South Africa could at least give humanitarian support to the school, and thus to ANC?

SAS: It was a modern school in every sense of the word. I have on several occasions visited it. It was a pride for ANC, but it was also a pride for the Nordic countries, who actively supported the school.

TS: When you agreed to this kind of huge project of the liberation movements in exile, did you never have second thoughts regarding the buildup of 'statelets within the state'?

SAS: Not really. You also have to understand the policy of Tanzania, particularly the personal contribution of President Nyerere to the struggle. He was a leader who really identified himself completely and without the slightest reservation with the struggle in Southern Africa. He saw it as an extension of Tanzania's own struggle. At no point did he hesitate to give everything that the country could give in support. In fact, this is one of the points where Nyerere was criticized by some of his opponents. They would say that he paid too much attention to foreign policy—especially to the liberation struggle—at the expense of the affairs of the country.

TS: Palme would receive the same criticism in Sweden.

SAS: Exactly. In addition, the liberation movements—especially ANC and FRELIMO; despite the fact that we had the assassination of Mondlane and so on—were serious. They had an internal discipline and they respected the sovereignty of Tanzania. At no point was there any fear that you would create a ministate within the state. Most important was that the Tanzanians themselves identified with the struggle. This was crucial, because it was not solely a question of Nyerere or the government. It was a sense of identification of the people of Tanzania with the struggle. The people felt very strongly that this was their own struggle, whether it was the question of Mozambique, Rhodesia, Namibia or South Africa. It was then easier for the government to assume policies and do things which in other circumstances would have created problems.

TS: Can one also say that about the local population in the Morogoro area regarding the ANC presence in the settlements of Mazimbu and Dakawa?

SAS: Absolutely. I remember visiting those areas in different capacities, as chairman of the UN Committee of 24, as Minister of Foreign Affairs, as Prime Minister and as Minister of Defence. Every time I found sympathy and pride among the people of Morogoro. I never noticed any element of resentment or jealousy on the part of the local population.

TS: In spite of the tragic accident that happened to your predecessor as Prime Minister, the late Mr. Sokoine, who died in a car crash outside the ANC settlement?

SAS: Absolutely. It involved an ANC cadre. It shows the extent of the political commitment and the maturity of the ordinary Tanzanian to the struggle of South Africa. A thing like that could easily have clouded people's judgement. It could have brought about emotions and anti-ANC feelings, but nothing of that sort happened. It was just considered as one of those unfortunate accidents that do take place. There was no stigmatization, either of the man himself or of the movement from which he came.

TS: Were you fully informed about the Nordic support to the liberation movements in Tanzania? Did you at any point see this as interference in your internal affairs?

SAS: I am perhaps the wrong person to ask, because I was so involved and I so much valued the contribution of the Nordic countries that I am almost biased. I think that the contribution made a major difference in the struggle in Mozambique, Zimbabwe, Angola and certainly and most surely in South Africa.

One of my most pleasant memories is from 1987, I believe. At that time, I was Deputy Prime Minister and Minister of Defence. Oliver Tambo, the President General of the African National Congress, and people like Alfred Nzo and Thabo Mbeki organized an anti-apartheid conference in Arusha. I co-chaired the conference with Lisbet Palme. It was a really moving experience. What was remarkable was the sense of identification with Sweden and the Nordic countries, especially with Lisbet by virtue of Olof's contribution. People remembered the contribution he made. For example, the important statement in Stockholm just before his death.

For me, it has always been pleasant memories. Firstly, because the support was real. It was genuine, with no strings attached whatsoever. Secondly, it was support which made a difference at the practical level of the struggle. It also made a difference at the political and diplomatic level, and I was a witness to both. As permanent representative of Tanzania to the United Nations and chairman of the UN Decolonization Committee for ten years I know what it meant. Also as the representative of my country to the Security Council. There were times when I served there with Mr. Rydbeck, who used to be the ambassador of Sweden. I know what it meant when we were dealing with the problems of South Africa or Angola. It was remarkable to be able to talk the same language between myself from an African country and the Swedish, Danish or Norwegian representatives.

When I was the chairman of the Committee of 24, we went to Botswana. I had a Norwegian with me, Tom Vraalsen, who is now, I think, ambassador in London. He was one of my vice-chairmen. This was in 1976, after the independence of Mozambique. We were preparing for a conference in support of the struggle in Zimbabwe and Namibia. We went to Lusaka and from there to Gaborone. We had to negotiate our way, because the plane had to make sure that it did not go through Rhodesian or Namibian air space. Somehow we reached Gaborone, where we stayed at the Gaborone Sun. Like any UN mission, we had people of all colours. We had a Japanese, a Jamaican lady who was very black, a Yugoslav, an Indian and Tom Vraalsen. We had a UN. We got to the Gaborone Sun. At that time apartheid was in its prime and the hall was full of white South Africans. We got there and Vraalsen decided to dance cheek-to-cheek with this lady from Jamaica. You should have seen the people in that hotel, looking flabbergasted, offended or both! But we enjoyed it! It is terrible, but we liked it and Vraalsen said: 'Look at this disaster. Look at the honky dancing with a nigger.' There was such an unbelievable spirit of camaraderie. I think that even for the South Africans it was an occasion—stiff as they were—because they were also people who waited for things to change.

I recall some of these events that really made us part of the same family. We felt alike, as friends fighting for the same cause, struggling for the same issues. If we disagreed, we would disagree on tactics, but, basically, the strategic objective was the same. I have really very pleasant memories of the Nordic support, which I believe was *very* important for the struggle against colonialism and racialism. It came at a time when it was not fashionable. At the end of the struggle, everybody wanted to be identified. Everybody wanted to join and say that they had supported the struggle. But in the early days it was not fashionable. In those days, the Nordic countries were, in fact, committing something next to sacrilege. But we had their support and I must add that it did not matter who the government in power was, whether in Sweden, Denmark, Finland or Norway.

They were our allies. We always say that the only traditional allies of the struggle in Southern Africa were the Nordic countries.

When we talk in terms of 'traditional', we think of people who were supporting the struggle when it was in its infancy, who were critical when it comes to criticism and who did not have any particular vested interests in the classic, narrow sense of the words. Their vested interest was humanitarian. Seeing the injustices and rectifying the wrongs that were going on. The Nordic countries made a monumental contribution also in terms of race relations. People simply did not know how to hate. How can you hate when you have allies whose skin and colours are like your oppressors'? The question of colour became irrelevant. What was relevant was the nature of the struggle.

Vladimir Shubin
Head of the Africa Section of the International Department of the Communist Party of the Soviet Union
Senior Research Fellow at the Centre for Southern African Studies, University of the Western Cape
(Cape Town, 12 September 1995)

1. On how the Nordic support to the Southern African liberation movements was viewed in Moscow:

"I do not think that there was any negative opinion about that. I remember a discussion I had with the ANC Treasurer General, Thomas Nkobi, in the mid-1980s. He said that the Soviet Union had been very correct when it in the 1960s recommended ANC to work for more financial support in the West."

2. On why Sweden supported the liberation movements:

"Sweden and some other countries should be given credit for having the foresight to know that changes were inevitable and that their contribution—or investment, if we use a word which I do not like very much—in the liberation process would be paid back one way or another. But that might not have been the decisive factor, because the humanitarian traditions in Sweden are very strong and there was pressure from the grassroots, from political organizations, churches and, in general, liberal, humanitarian personalities. However, the direct support to the liberation movements was very small in the beginning. The policy could have been introduced by the Social Democratic leaders to diffuse internal pressures from the more radical solidarity movements. There was an element of that. In Russian, you would say that it served as a lightning conductor. There was a combination of factors, humanitarian, political and economic.

I am a bit sceptical to the assistance in the beginning. The amounts given were very small as far as ANC, SWAPO, ZAPU and ZANU are concerned. Of course, MPLA, FRELIMO and PAIGC used to get sizeable amounts and after the Portuguese revolution the situation changed with regard to Zimbabwe, Namibia and even South Africa.

When Olof Palme became vice-president of the Socialist International in, I think, 1976, there was a certain breakthrough. The Socialist International sent a mission to Southern Africa, but that was to a large extent Palme's own project.

It is interesting to note that the policy of Sweden did not change when there was a change in government. In 1976, when the Social Democrats lost the elections for the first time in many years, there was no decrease in the assistance to the liberation movements. In fact, during the years that the so-called bourgeois coalition was ruling, the assistance increased. Maybe the support was not so much social democratic policy, but a kind of national policy. Here, of course, the question is what was behind it. Economic interests, general feelings in Sweden or what?

This was also the case in Norway. When Norway hosted the 1973 OAU/UN conference, the Labour Party was not in power. But the bourgeois government went to the conference as if nothing had happened. It is rather interesting".

3. On Nordic support to the so-called 'authentic six' and ZANU:

"All these movements were the leading organizations at that time. Maybe with the exception of Angola, where FNLA tried to become the leader. They signed this unfortunate agreement with MPLA in December 1972 which nobody remembers any more and which became one of the problems between the Soviet Union and MPLA at that time. FNLA claimed to be stronger than MPLA, but it was very much discredited.

I think that pragmatism guided Sweden and the other Nordic countries. They were also well informed, because they were quite close to the liberation movements, at least from the mid-1970s. The 'authentic six' were stronger and cleaner, if you could use these words. For example, COREMO in Mozambique was nothing and PAC had an unfortunate history of stealing and killing in exile. But I know that Sweden had some contacts with PAC, although it did not result in anything. Some support would go to PAC through the United Nations, but Sweden did not give them any direct support."

4. On the role of the Nordic countries:

"By and large, I think that the Nordic countries played a very constructive role, both politically and in a broader sense. Politically, because they served as a kind of bridge between the Southern African liberation movements and the West in general. I have also seen in the ANC archives that ANC at one stage wanted to concentrate on the smaller countries when the big Western countries were playing a bad role in South Africa. In the late 1980s, big groups of ANC people came to study in Sweden within the PASA project, Post-Apartheid South Africa. Big money was apparently involved in this project. It was very prominent at some stage, but it seems that it then just faded and disappeared."

5. On the Nordic countries and Communism in the liberation movements:

"I was present at the 1984 Socialist International meeting in Arusha, Tanzania, which was organized by a Preparatory Committee headed by Professor Ki-Zerbo from Burkina Faso. It was a bit funny. We did not hide from the Social Democrats, but when people came to the meeting the organizers were openly telling ANC members that they were worried about the influence of Communists and the Soviet Union. They were saying this to South African Communists! It was a bit stupid. They were open about their negative agenda. They did not just say that they wanted to increase their support, but also that they wanted to diminish the Communist influence. That was a bit primitive. If they wanted to influence things, they should at least have known who they were talking to."

6. On the 1973 OAU/UN conference in Oslo:

"The Oslo conference was a bit of a breakthrough, but even the Scandinavian governments down-played it. Firstly, there was a lot of talk about the name and scope of the conference. It was a 'conference of experts to support victims of colonialism and apartheid', but we said that we were not there as only so-called experts, but as supporters of the liberation movements. They then tried as much as possible to portray us all as non-governmental representatives, although it was a conference of the United Nations and the OAU. Secondly, in Oslo one could see the difference in attitude of the Norwegian hosts—maybe also of the Swedes—towards the liberation movements from the Portuguese colonies and the other movements. In spite of his status, Oliver Tambo—who was the highest representative—was not given suitable treatment compared with the Portuguese anti-colonial movements. SWAPO was led by Shipanga and ZANU by Chitepo. I do not remember who was there from ZAPU, but it was not a high-ranking representative."

7. On the International University Exchange Fund (IUEF):

"I think that one must highlight the role of IUEF. I used to know Lars-Gunnar Eriksson. I was rather friendly with him in the 1970s. We met in Moscow. He was a very interesting fellow. Of course, IUEF was very much discredited by the Craig Williamson affair, but you should not close the whole issue of IUEF because of that. IUEF played a very important role, although controversial. For example, it was stated in the press—I do not know if it was correct or not—that there was some secret funding through IUEF to dissidents of ANC, but by and large it played a very important role. At some stage, the bulk of the Nordic assistance to the liberation movements was going through IUEF and not directly from the governments. A lot was done by IUEF in the early 1970s. I am sure that the Nordic assistance through IUEF then was bigger than the direct support, which was rather limited.

IUEF played a particular role, because they could send people inside South Africa to have a look. For example, they were a major channel of support to the South African Students Organisation and the Black Consciousness Movement. I remember that Lars-Gunnar Eriksson told me about it and I said to him that it was about time that we also contacted them. He then said—boasting a bit, but still—'OK, give me two weeks and I will organize it in Nairobi'. Or, 'give me three days and I will organize it in Botswana'. He was serious."

8. On IUEF, MPLA and the Soviet Union:

"The information that Lars-Gunnar Eriksson gave me on Angola was very important. It was at his place in Geneva, towards the end of August or at the beginning of September 1974. I was in Geneva to attend an OAU/UN conference on colonialism.

The background was the agreement between Neto and Roberto in December 1972, which almost nobody mentions in the literature and through which Neto was to be second to Roberto. It was a mistake and became a problem for us at that time. I was present when Neto came to the Soviet Union after the agreement and he tried to explain the needs for it. Our people were not convinced and the assistance was suspended. Not stopped in the full sense, because there were still MPLA students in the Soviet Union and the military supplies continued. It would have been rather difficult to also give political support to FNLA. The agreement immediately lowered the prestige of MPLA.

The IUEF people were almost the only ones who were present at the 1974 MPLA Congress and at the Inter-Regional Conference. It was important. At the congress, it was officially said that they had elected Daniel Chipenda as MPLA President, but they then had this conference inside Angola where they over-ruled that decision. It was very controversial. Lars-Gunnar Eriksson told me about this and about the importance of support to MPLA. The IUEF position was very good. They absolutely supported Neto, which was very important. It helped our people in Moscow to better understand the situation, so credit must go to IUEF and to Lars-Gunnar Eriksson."

Sweden

Ernst Michanek, Director General of SIDA and chairman of the Consultative Committee on Humanitarian Assistance, Stockholm, 1966. (Photo: Pressens Bild)

Roland Axelsson
SIDA—Regional coordinator of Swedish humanitarian assistance to Southern Africa
Private consultant
(Stockholm, 31 October 1996)

Tor Sellström: When did you start working for SIDA?
Roland Axelsson: I started to work for NIB (Swedish Agency for International Assistance) in 1962. I had then graduated with a masters in business administration from the Gothenburg School of Economics and I had worked for two years at the Swedish National Audit Bureau (RRV).
TS: You went to Africa very early. When and where did you get involved with Swedish humanitarian assistance to the Southern African liberation movements?
RA: I first spent six years in Ethiopia and there I had very little contact with any liberation movement. But in 1972, I came to Tanzania as an administrator at the Swedish embassy and I almost immediately came in contact with FRELIMO, ANC and SWAPO. I was not a programme officer at that time. It was people such as Anders Möllander who dealt with the liberation movements, but as I paid all the money to them I got to know them quite well. Those I especially remember from that time are Hifikepunye Pohamba, who was the Chief Representative of SWAPO, Thomas Nkobi, who was the Treasurer General of ANC— at that time living in Morogoro—and my old friend Kay Moonsamy. So, it is now over twenty years since we met. In FRELIMO it was Janet Mondlane, who was the head of the Mozambique Institute. With ZANU, ZAPU and MPLA I had very little contact.
TS: That means that you were involved with Swedish support to ANC from the very beginning. The first allocation was given in 1973.
RA: Yes. In the beginning the amounts were very small. I bought some office furniture and a lot of vegetables for the ANC office in Morogoro and the South African refugees there.
TS: From then on you worked very closely with all the Southern African liberation movements. These movements waged an armed struggle and received military support from the Soviet Union or China. How did you experience this in your day to day relations? Did you feel that the movements were striving for a Communist cause or that they were nationalist in outlook?
RA: Let me talk about ANC and SWAPO only, as they were of a greater concern to me. I did not speak Portuguese, so I had very little contact with FRELIMO in that respect.

I understood quite well that weapons were necessary in the liberation struggle and also that Sweden could not supply those weapons. The Soviet Union could and did. That was fully acceptable. I strongly believed that the Soviet Union could never influence the thousands of students who were granted scholarships for studies in Moscow and other places. On the contrary, many of the students there became in fact anti-Communist. Some individuals within ANC and SWAPO were, of course, Communists—at least they said so—but they were hardly Stalinists. The majority of the people I got to know worked hard for the liberation of their countries, to get rid of colonialism and introduce democracy. I would say that they have also managed now, to a great extent at least.
TS: You mentioned Kay Moonsamy. He is today the Treasurer General of the South African Communist Party.
RA: Yes, he was a Communist, but he was shocked when he learnt about the real situation in Moscow. If he had known what was going on during the Stalinist era, I do not think that he would have been a Communist. My friend Thomas Nkobi also used to read the monthly magazine issued by the South African Communist Party, so I once asked him: 'Are you a Communist?' And he said: ' No, I am not. I could never be'.
TS: From the point of view of accounting, financial openness and transparency, how would you describe SIDA's relationship—and your relationship—with SWAPO and ANC? Did you get access to the necessary information and documentation?
RA: Well, financial openness and transparency were, of course, delicate questions. SIDA wanted to know as much as possible

about how the donor funds were used, but ANC and SWAPO could not accept external audit. We had to stick to internal audit and what I could get out of various documents. I was very much trusted and allowed to study the respective systems of financial management. Neither ANC nor SWAPO accepted at that time that any other SIDA official should look through their books, so I was privileged. I am talking about the end of the 1970s and the beginning of the 1980s.

TS: In general terms, is it then your view that the payment and accounting procedures were satisfactory?

RA: Yes, absolutely. We had an agreed system, whereby the movements got advance payments and then submitted their settlements of accounts with vouchers. Everything had to be shown in one or another way. If they had spent the money correctly, we stamped the documents. We had a rubber stamp 'Financed by SIDA'. Every single little receipt was stamped, not only by me in Lusaka, but also by my colleagues in Ethiopia, Kenya, Tanzania and the other countries. It applied to all funds, except the home front allocations.

TS: All receipts were stamped so that they could not be used twice?

RA: Exactly. Because they also had to submit receipts to the Norwegian embassy and Norway did not request that they should be stamped. I was afraid that they would bring the same receipts to the Norwegians.

TS: Some people have alleged that SIDA's humanitarian assistance either was misappropriated by the leaders of the movements or used for military purposes. How would you comment upon these allegations? Were the financial control mechanisms comparable to those governing Swedish development assistance to independent countries or were they less strict?

RA: There were, as everywhere in life, small pockets of misuse and mismanagement. It happened, for instance, in Lesotho. A person called Kanalelo got a small amount of funds which he was to distribute among the ANC families in the country. But he stole the money, left the country and established a small enterprise in Zimbabwe instead. But he was not an ANC leader. He was an outsider who used the liberation movement. The leaders who I got to know were honest, to the best of my knowledge.

No funds were used for military purposes. It happened, however, that funds were used to feed military people. They had to live too. Except for the home front allocation, the financial control was in my opinion better and stricter than the control exercised concerning aid to independent countries. In those countries—like Zambia or Tanzania—it was the national audit bureau which audited everything. At that time, they had not yet started to get help from the Swedish national audit bureau and the audit was not very good.

TS: But in the case of international NGOs—where SIDA did not have the direct responsibility—we know of at least one case where there was mismanagement of funds and even political infiltration, namely the IUEF. In your view, how could this happen? Why did SIDA and the other donors not monitor IUEF more closely?

RA: Well, that is difficult to know exactly, but probably because Sweden placed an administratively incompetent person as director of IUEF. As auditor at SIDA, I tried in 1976-77 to make an audit of IUEF, but I was stopped by our government. Stig Abelin and I wanted to do that, but we were not allowed to.

TS: In 1984, you moved to Lusaka, Zambia, and served there until 1991 as SIDA's regional coordinator of humanitarian assistance to SWAPO and ANC in Southern Africa and Uganda, Ethiopia and Madagascar. During these years, the South African regime constantly attacked the liberation movements in the Frontline States and Lesotho and Swaziland. Offices were bombed and representatives were killed. Yet, you managed all the time to get the humanitarian assistance through. How did you work?

RA: Funds were disbursed to ANC and SWAPO by the Swedish embassies in most countries, Ethiopia, Kenya, Tanzania, Zambia, Mozambique, Angola, Zimbabwe and Botswana. The money was normally paid by cheque, but in Botswana it was in cash. In Lesotho, Swaziland, Uganda and Madagascar, various methods had to be used. In Swaziland and Lesotho, I created fake organizations and managed to open local bank accounts in the name of those organizations. 'SIDA Housing Project' in Swaziland, for example. In Swaziland, we also used Ephesus House. It was a branch office of the defunct IUEF which lived on after the dissolution of IUEF. I used that office as a cover until it was bombed by the South African security forces.

ANC and SWAPO supported me. Thomas Nkobi, Hifikepunye Pohamba and all their co-workers supported me one hundred per cent. They trusted me, but it was, of course, in their interest that their people were fed and that the money was correctly spent.

TS: In some countries I understand that you also administered Norwegian humanitarian assistance. Was there an agreement on this cooperation between Norway and Sweden?

RA: No, I never administered Norwegian funds. Being a SIDA coordinator, I however, cooperated very closely with the Norwegian embassies and consulates, especially in Lusaka, Harare and Gaborone. As I travelled much more in the region than my Norwegian colleagues, I sometimes acted on their behalf. I did so especially in Mozambique, but also in other countries, Botswana, for instance. But there was no written agreement between Sweden and Norway. It was a verbal agreement between me and the Norwegians.

TS: How would you describe the difference, if any, between Swedish and Norwegian humanitarian support to ANC?

RA: The assistance was very similar, but Norway had no budget item called 'Home Front'. They were also more eager than Sweden to support big agricultural and infrastructural projects, like Dakawa in Tanzania. SIDA preferred smaller agricultural farms, such as Alpha and Chongela in Zambia and Mazimbu in Tanzania.

TS: Norway paid for the planning of the ANC settlement at Dakawa?

RA: Yes. All the roads and the water and sewage systems were paid for by Norway. They used the non-governmental organization *Norsk Folkehjelp* to do the job.

TS: How about the ANC farms in Angola? Josef Jonsson went there to make some kind of feasibility study for SIDA. Was any Swedish assistance given directly to these farms?

RA: Yes, we purchased quite a lot of equipment that was sent to the ANC farm in Malanje. Josef Jonsson was there, overseeing the arrival of the equipment. But after a few months, the ANC people had to leave. The area was not secure. Some people were killed and others were frightened. So, the Swedish assistance was unfortunately of very little use.

TS: Being responsible for considerable amounts of money and travelling around in what de facto in the 1980s was a war zone in Southern Africa, you must have been closely monitored by the apartheid regime?

RA: Well, I always suspected that I was observed, but very little happened. They were always very kind to me at Jan Smuts airport in Johannesburg. They asked me: 'Why don't you get a temporary visa to go to Johannesburg and spend the day there instead of sitting here?' Sometimes I had to wait for ten to fifteen hours at the airport, so every time I said: 'Yes, please'. I waited and waited, and in about half an hour they always came back and said: 'Sorry, we can't grant you a visa'. They were nice and did their best, but I was listed as a terrorist sympathizer. Such people were not let into the country, of course.

A very unpleasant thing once happened in Mbabane, Swaziland. I was driving from my hotel to see a Swedish priest who lived just outside Mbabane. It was in the evening. Around seven, I think. It was dark anyhow. Just when I passed the city centre, a small pick-up truck hit me head on at full speed. I fortunately survived without a broken leg. But the car was completely wrecked. It had to go to the scrap-yard. I was lucky. I still cannot believe that it was an accident. It was done on purpose.

TS: Do you know of similar incidents against other SIDA officials involved with support to ANC and SWAPO in the Frontline States? I think that there was an incident in Lesotho, where the brakes of a car were tampered with?

RA: That is true. It concerned a lady employed by the Swedish Ministry for Foreign Affairs. It was bad. The South African security service was very alert in Lesotho. Once I was together with the Swedish ambassador. Going to the airport, we were followed by the South African police. We knew that, because they had ten minutes earlier tried to persuade the ambassador's driver to tell them about Swedish assistance to ANC. But nothing happened. We were just observed the whole time until we left.

TS: The authorities in Botswana, Lesotho and Swaziland must have been interested in Sweden's support to the liberation movements. Did they ever question you or create obstacles to your work?

RA: No, I cannot say that they did. They never questioned me, but I never sought any contact with them either. But I remember that my colleagues in Maseru and Gaborone sometimes were harassed. We always tried to be careful. For instance, in Gaborone we never met ANC in the Swedish embassy. We had to arrange some other place where we could meet. We knew that the embassy was always watched. And we never used diplomatic cars. We always used other cars, both to and from such meetings.

TS: At a certain stage in the late 1980s, I think that it became impossible to continue the payments to ANC in Lesotho and Swaziland. Was the decision to freeze the payments taken by SIDA or by ANC?

RA: In the case of Lesotho, I had to convince Thomas Nkobi that it was necessary. He agreed and then, of course, SIDA Stockholm also agreed. It was too dangerous to work there any longer. The South Africans had infiltrated everywhere. We could not get the money to the families who needed the support. And we could not find a reliable person to assist us. But in Swaziland we never stopped the assistance completely. SIDA wanted to stop it several times, but I managed to convince them that it should go on.

TS: You mentioned the budget item 'Home Front', which was included in the Swedish allocation to ANC. For this activity, Sweden did not request a comprehensive financial audit, but only a descriptive report. As an accountant, were you satisfied that the assistance to the 'Home Front' was used for humanitarian, civilian and not military purposes? It was used in South Africa, where you could not go.

RA: Absolutely. In our agreement on financial procedures we said that receipts regarding home front activities should not necessarily be delivered to SIDA if it implied any risk to ANC. Each year we got what I would call half financial statements. We got statements, but they were not so detailed. However, all the material that ANC bought for the money, like small cars, duplicating machines, simple office equipment and so on were listed, even if there was no detailed purchase price for each item. We could anyhow estimate how much they would have paid. These items were obtained to distribute political leaflets within South Africa. South Africa is a big country, so they needed a lot of cars and so on.

TS: So, it was mainly for organization, information and political work inside South Africa?

RA: Yes, for political work inside the country. Not for making bombs and other things. Absolutely not. I do not know who became the registered owners of the vehicles, for example. It was definitely not ANC. It must have been someone else. But the home front aid was humanitarian in the political sense of the word.

TS: After the unbanning of ANC, you were invited by Thomas Nkobi to assist him with the setting up of ANC's financial administration in South Africa. How would you describe your relationship with the late Treasurer General of ANC?

RA: Thomas Nkobi was a great and honest man. He was a person of great importance to the liberation struggle and he was a unique friend of mine. We treated each other like brothers in an open and frank manner. I had known him for twenty years, and when I met him at our last meeting on 26 April 1994 I told him as a joke to buy a new hat: 'You have to buy a new hat before you will be appointed Minister of Finance in the new South Africa'. But he replied: 'No, I will keep my old hat, because I will never qualify for that governmental position'. He was a very honest man.

TS: Looking back over all these years, how would you assess the role played by Sweden and the other Nordic countries in and for the struggle for national independence and democracy in Southern Africa?

RA: The Swedish and Nordic role was quite essential. Without our assistance in the form of daily necessities, health care and so on, both ANC and SWAPO would have been faced with enormous problems, which most probably would have delayed the liberation considerably. Of course, liberation would have come anyhow, sooner or later, but it would have taken more time, with more suffering for many people. There were no alternatives. No other countries in the world were willing to assist in the way that Sweden and Norway did.

TS: Many SWAPO and ANC leaders have fond memories of the cooperation with SIDA in general and with you in particular. You participated very closely in an important historic process in Southern Africa. What has it meant for you on a personal level?

RA: I would say that I got many friends. I felt personally involved in one of the greatest—and for humanity most important—events in our lifetime, the liberation of Southern Africa. I was proud of being in a position to do something and not only watch what was going on. I am still closely following the developments in Southern Africa. It was a great time for me.

TS: Is there anything that you would like to add?

RA: Well, maybe I could mention the airlifts of thousands of South African refugees who had found a temporary retreat in Swaziland, Lesotho and Botswana, but had to leave those countries rather quickly and be moved to Zambia and Tanzania. The airlifts were arranged by UNHCR, but SIDA was heavily involved, especially in the financing of those airlifts on many occasions.

Another important event took place in 1978, after the terrible Kassinga massacre of Namibian refugees in Angola. I remember how we chartered a British airplane in Lusaka to fly foodstuffs to Luanda as emergency assistance. We procured mealie-meal to fill five airplanes, but when we were about to load the lorries we had rented from Zambia National Milling, the Zambian Minister of Agriculture gave contra-orders, saying that we could not export maize flour: 'You have to find something else to send to Angola'. Elisabeth Michanek of SIDA, the Vice-President of SWAPO at that time, Mishake Muyongo, and I then had to run around in the market places in Lusaka to buy other foodstuffs. We found beans, rice, wheat etc. We needed quite a lot to fill five DC 8 aircraft, but we managed. I personally accompanied one of the flights to Luanda. It was very interesting. When we arrived at Luanda airport, Angolan military planes were already parked there. Everything was re-loaded into these military aircraft, which then flew the food to Kassinga and the surviving Namibian refugees.

Birgitta Berggren
SIDA—Secretary to the Consultative Committee on Humanitarian Assistance—Head of SIDA's section for Southern Africa
Secretary General of the Swedish NGO Foundation for Human Rights
(Stockholm, 27 March 1996)

Tor Sellström: You have been involved with Swedish humanitarian support to Southern Africa in various capacities—as programme officer with SIDA, as secretary to the Consultative Committee on Humanitarian Assistance, as head of the Southern Africa section at SIDA and as head of the SIDA office in Zimbabwe. When did you first start to work directly with the national liberation movements?

Birgitta Berggren: That was in Dar es Salaam in 1976. It was at the time of the Soweto uprisings, when new life came into the South African struggle. It was very interesting to follow, since the information in Tanzania about events in Southern Africa was amazingly good. Of course, all the liberation movements were supported by the Tanzanians, so you could easily meet all the people there. People who later returned to Zimbabwe, Namibia and South Africa.

What I most clearly remember from Dar es Salaam is that each quarter we would have the local ANC representatives coming to leave reports and get new funds for the sustenance of their people in Tanzania. Thomas Nkobi and a fellow from SACTU, George Monare, would come to the Swedish embassy. Monare was a big fellow. They would be dressed up in suits, ties and be wearing South African hats, and the girl in the reception would call me and say: 'The uncles have arrived'. I would go out to see the 'uncles' and we would sit down and talk. So, it was in Dar es Salaam that I had my first contacts with the liberation movements. Also with people like Eli Weinberg, for instance. He had just arrived together with his wife Violet. We listened to them, because they were of the older generation. They could tell the whole story of the struggle. It was very interesting to meet all these people.

After Soweto—around 1978—people started to leave South Africa in big numbers. When they were released from jail, they were so restricted in their movements that they eventually opted for exile and often for military training. When you followed the struggle, you understood even more how important the camps in southern Tanzania were.

TS: Before that you had already been involved with Swedish humanitarian support to the victims of apartheid in the form of legal aid, scholarships to students etc.?

BB: Yes, with refugee students in Sweden. But I just knew that they were refugees. I was actually not involved in the party picture in the way that I became in Tanzania. That was a different thing, much closer to reality .

TS: Going back, in 1969 the Swedish parliament cleared the way for direct official support to the liberation movements in Southern Africa. In your view, what would be the main motives behind the decision to give direct support to the liberation movements?

BB: I think that it was a sign of confidence and trust. The Swedish government wanted to show that these were movements that they supported politically. There were several aspects to it, but the most important was, of course, the political one.

TS: The Swedish support was prepared by a Consultative Committee on Humanitarian Assistance, where you served as secretary from 1978 to 1980. What were the main functions of the committee? How would you assess its role?

BB: The committee had existed for quite some time when I came into the picture. Very clear routines had been established. There were representatives from the major parties in parliament, the trade unions and various non-governmental groups. The important thing was that the issues discussed—which at times were quite sensitive from a political point of view—were properly anchored in a broad spectrum of the Swedish society. The main function of the committee was, I would say, to discuss in a forum that was knowledgeable. Many of the committee members had been involved in African and Latin American questions, matters of human rights abuse and political support to resistance groups or liberation movements. It was a very qualified forum for debate. The Ministry for Foreign Affairs was, of course, represented with qualified people. Since you had to find reliable channels for the Swedish support and you had to protect the recipients, it was very important that the deliberations were confidential, that people were loyal and that they felt that this was something that they should not go to the press with. Even if you did not agree—or maybe had objections to some of the decisions taken—you should be absolutely loyal, because we had to protect those who were receiving the support.

TS: Were there dissenting voices in the committee regarding the support to the liberation movements?

BB: No, not really. No one said: 'I am not going along. I want the minutes to say that I was not part of the decision'. I cannot remember that that ever happened.

TS: From the beginning of the 1970s, Swedish official support was channelled through SIDA to a number of Southern African liberation movements that later assumed power in their respective countries. However, direct assistance was never extended to competing movements, such as PAC and Inkatha of South Africa and UANC of Zimbabwe. Did the committee at any point discuss possible Swedish support to these movements?

BB: Not all the time, but regularly there would be requests from PAC, Inkatha or UANC for support and at times it was discussed. As regards PAC, the main attitude was that they received or had the possibilities of receiving considerable support from the United Nations. Having worked in Dar es Salaam, I also knew that PAC was very torn by internal struggles and even killings. Already in Tanzania I knew that they could not make use of the funds which were available to them through the UN system. They were not organized enough. It was a rather tragic picture that PAC presented in Dar es Salaam.

As for Inkatha, they did receive Swedish support. The motive was that they wanted to increase their ethnic image and promote ethnic cohesion among the Zulus. So the support was actually given to strengthen Inkatha as a Zulu organization. It was channelled to the newspaper *The Nation*, but also to training programmes or education material on the Zulu culture and nation.

I had a very strong feeling that this was to strengthen the position of Gatsha Buthelezi. That was very much the impression I got. I was very critical of the fact that a decision was taken to support Inkatha. Even then it was obvious that Buthelezi and the Inkatha movement were receiving support from CIA. I could not understand why we should be involved. At the secretariat, we were really harassed by people—especially in Holland—who insisted that we should support Inkatha. They just went on and on.

TS: Whose initiative was it to support Inkatha?

BB: I think that it was due to direct contacts between Buthelezi and the Swedish government and SIDA.

TS: Was any Swedish support similarly extended in favour of UANC of Zimbabwe?

BB: No. We got requests from UANC, but it was obvious that Muzorewa was not a real force. You cannot call him a quisling, but he was being used as a tool for Ian Smith. It was so obvious that there was no question of supporting him. Norway was very actively involved, but we never were. In 1977-78, when I was working in Dar es Salaam, Muzorewa once came to the embassy, but no one wanted to receive him. I remember meeting him while he just stood there waiting, hoping for an appointment. He was a rather pathetic figure even then.

TS: Over the years, there were growing allocations to Swedish humanitarian support in Southern Africa. You must have faced a problem in identifying NGOs that were willing and able to channel funds to the different recipients, particularly as confidentiality was important. How did you select and involve such NGOs? Would it be fair to say that the official support through SIDA actively contributed to a broadening of the involvement of the Swedish society in the liberation process in Southern Africa?

BB: Yes, very much so. One has to remember that regarding the question of apartheid and the situation in Southern Africa there was not much debate whether Sweden should support the struggle or not. People were generally supportive. When various requests were channelled to us—in very different ways, to say the least—we tried to look for the group, party, organization or institution that could take an interest in that very activity and identify itself with the project. For instance, if it concerned training of girls or women, we would look for a women's group in Sweden which could be especially interested, either in a political party context or as an ordinary NGO. We tried to use our imagination. We worked very hard to find people who could take such an interest that they really would work with great solidarity. I would say that the absolute majority—maybe 98-99 per cent—of those who agreed to work with the various projects did so in a fantastic way. There were hardly any leaks to the media. Neither would you hear from someone that they knew about the activities. It was kept very confidential by such a great number of people that I am still surprised that it worked so well. It was like a collective secret.

TS: Did SIDA have sufficient administrative resources for the rapidly growing Swedish humanitarian support to Southern Africa?

BB: Well, I think that there was a lot of overtime, which was never acknowledged. As the workload grew—and it did so very rapidly in the 1980s—there were problems when it came to financial administration. I remember that I in the end refused to make any payments, because we did not have the structure to follow-up all the transactions. I felt that it was overstretched. At times, you had to make a lot of noise. It was mainly because the decision makers were not fully aware of the very rapid increase of the workload. As the support was confidential, the workload was made even heavier. It was at times cumbersome to handle the material. It was more time-consuming than SIDA's ordinary assistance.

TS: In Sweden, there was a very strong solidarity movement with Southern Africa around the Africa Groups in Sweden and later the Isolate South Africa Committee. The solidarity movement was often critical of the government. You were sitting in the middle, being a government official and cooperating with the solidarity movement. How did you experience this?

BB: Returning from Tanzania in 1978 to work with the Consultative Committee on Humanitarian Assistance, I found that there was no cooperation at all, or at least very little. The atmosphere was rather antagonistic, which I thought was unnecessary. We definitely needed to cooperate, because the work was growing very fast. All the good forces had to cooperate to do a good job.

I took several initiatives to improve our relations with the voluntary groups. We started to cooperate, making use of each other's capacities in a complementary fashion. For instance, we would invite lecturers from the Catholic Institute for International Relations in London, which was the best source of information on Rhodesia/Zimbabwe. We would pay for the trip and the solidarity groups would then arrange a lecturing tour of Sweden. We did this on several occasions. When it came to the Swedish scene, the solidarity groups had a network and SIDA could more easily raise the necessary funds. There were no big costs involved, but it was important that we had this cooperation. It had very good effects on the Swedish knowledge of what was going on. One example is the support from SIDA to the organizations that collected clothes which they sent to the refugees in Southern Africa. We increased that cooperation by paying for their freight costs. We really worked hard on that kind of practical cooperation. I think that it worked out very well in the end.

TS: Many of the NGO channels SIDA used were non-Swedish, particularly UK- and Holland-based organizations. Was this a problem vis-à-vis their governments? Did they view this as interference by the Swedish government?

BB: If you look at some of the organizations in London, for instance IDAF and Africa Educational Trust, they were rather international, but happened to be in Britain. In the case of IDAF, it was connected to a person, but it could as well have been a person in another country. It was not looked upon as a very British organization. But there were others, like Shirebu, the research organization in Holland that looked at the shipping of oil to South Africa. That affected the Dutch in a different way than the Africa Educational Trust would affect the British.

Our support to Shirebu started through a phone call I had from the Swedish embassy in the Hague. Rolf Ekéus called and said: 'I have such a good project here and I think it is very important. Do you happen to have 70,000 Swedish Kronor, which we could use to support a research organization which just has been established?' It was a very small amount, but it had a tremendous impact. The facts which Shirebu presented and gave publicity to were absolutely devastating. The shipping companies contacted the Ministry for Foreign Affairs and parliamentarians in Sweden in order to stop the support from SIDA.

TS: I guess that the Norwegian shipowners—a very strong lobby—were not very happy?

BB: No, they were among those who tried to influence the decision, but we continued to support Shirebu for many years.

TS: The British or Dutch government never presented any official complaint to the Swedish government?

BB: I do not know. I do not remember hearing anything to that effect. They might have talked to people at the Swedish embassy in London or the Hague, but I never saw any such report. It was a different matter when Zimbabwe was about to become independent. Then, of course, the British were very difficult when it came to the support we were providing to ZAPU and ZANU. But that was quite another matter.

TS: When it comes to the Africa Educational Trust, 95 per cent of the funds were from the Nordic countries. Sweden alone stood for about 60 per cent.

BB: I am not surprised. They were good. They really assisted on a basic level when it comes to education.

TS: The direct support to the liberation movements was administered by SIDA. while the political relations were the responsibility of the Ministry for Foreign Affairs. You worked for SIDA, but you were also the secretary to the Consultative Committee on Humanitarian Assistance where you had a direct dialogue with the ministry. Did you experience the division between SIDA and the Ministry for Foreign Affairs as a problem?

BB: No, I thought that the cooperation was excellent. Working at SIDA's headquarters in Stockholm, I would always receive the latest reports and I would always be kept in the picture. It made the handling of these at times very difficult requests so much easier. We had a very good cooperation, full of confidence. We had to show that SIDA had the necessary security regulations in place and that we were in a position to keep everything confidential. I think that it worked very well. The only time that I felt that there was a collision was in the context of the independence of Zimbabwe, over the issue of Swedish support during the election process.

TS: Many of the SIDA officials involved with the support to the liberation movements were women. As a woman yourself, how did you experience this?

BB: As a donor representative, I never had any problems in that respect. However, when a Swedish delegation was sent to the independence celebrations in Zimbabwe it included twelve members, but not a single woman. I asked the Ministry for Foreign Affairs why this was so. Afterwards I also heard that when Mugabe met the delegation, he looked at them and said: 'I thought that I was going to meet a delegation representing the Swedish society, but I cannot see a single woman'. I thought that it was ridiculous. When it came to the hard work and all the overtime, then it was alright with women. But when it came to sitting on a podium and receiving thanks, then there were only men. That was a poor show.

TS: Over the years, the Swedish cooperation with the liberation movements changed. A wide spectrum of activities were included, such as education, health, agricultural projects, etc. What consequences did this broadening of the support have?

BB: Yes, the Swedish support to the liberation movements eventually became very similar to SIDA's regular country programmes. The content changed. There was much more of sectoral policies in the support to each movement. The fact that we changed the model in 1983-84 was important in the long run. The quality of the support improved. It also encouraged the liberation movements to appoint people who were knowledgeable in certain sectors. They had to start planning, discussing strategies and policy matters. I think that it was positive. I am very pleased when I think of how we discussed and pushed this idea.

TS: Considerable amounts of money were channelled through SIDA to the liberation movements. In retrospect, are you satisfied with the accounting and reporting procedures? Were the funds used in accordance with the agreements?

BB: On the whole, I would say that the procedures were satisfactory. It would have been desirable to have a more adequate reporting system, but it was difficult under the circumstances. We made the requirements concerning reporting and auditing as realistic as possible. It was not easy, especially in the refugee camps. I also think that in some cases—for instance, at the ANC office in London and the ZANU office in Stockholm—the resident representatives were not exactly cautious. Some of them did not care too much about accounting, but that was discovered very soon. When you saw them driving around in their Volvos, you knew that something was not really the way it should have been. We did what we could. We appointed people who looked into these matters. In the latter part of the 1980s, we took all kinds of precautions so as not to neglect these aspects. We had, for example, special missions going to Southern Africa to look at certain aspects of the programmes. I am sure that there were things that were not discovered, but I cannot see how that could have been avoided really. I think that we did our very best and that we can have a good conscience in that respect.

TS: In the case of IUEF, there was both infiltration by South Africa and mismanagement of funds. You were one of those who very early raised a warning flag regarding both issues. What made the infiltration and mismanagement possible?

BB: I think that there were a number of reasons why this could happen. It was mainly a question of an 'old-boys-network'. Political decisions were not followed up by good management and there were certain personal weaknesses. The South Africans had been looking for a possibility to infiltrate somewhere. They looked for that all the time since the activities that were supported from outside were causing them great problems. In the case of IUEF, Craig Williamson was simply a very competent agent. He made use of people's weaknesses and of the structure of management. It was easy for him to manipulate and since there was this loyalty between old friends and politicians, it was difficult to bring about a change. As a plain civil servant, they would accuse you of disloyalty to the cause or whatever, which, of course, was rubbish.

It was impossible to get any response from those who took the decisions. It took too long and then the damage was already done. It was terrible. I am convinced that it led to the death of a number of people.

TS: Would it be fair to say that the Swedish government and SIDA made this possible by constantly increasing the allocations to an organization that could not handle that amount of funds?

BB: I do not think that the amounts were enormous, but they were certainly too big for IUEF's structure and competence.

TS: SIDA officials in Southern Africa who handled Swedish support to the liberation movements were, of course, exposed to the interests of the regimes in Portugal, Rhodesia and South Africa. Were there any threats against SIDA's officials? Did you have to take any particular precautions in this respect?

BB: There would be warnings now and then, coming through US security units or other channels. People would then change their habits and take another way to the office, for example. Working with these questions, you were generally on the alert. Of course, there were problems at times, but nothing really serious as far as I can remember. When SIDA people travelled via South Africa and the luggage passed through Jan Smuts airport in Johannesburg it was very likely that it was checked. It also happened that letters in a suitcase were torn and put back. It was part of the situation. I do not think that one took it that seriously. You had to expect it and be very cautious, never leaving any documents in your hotelroom and always carrying what was important in your hand-luggage. That was a normal precaution. It was not all that dramatic, really.

TS: In some cases, there were instances of human rights abuse and internal struggles within the liberation movements. In the case of SWAPO, there was the Shipanga affair in the 1970s and the so-called spy drama in Angola in the 1980s. There were similar developments in the ANC camps in Angola. As you recollect it, how did the Swedish government react? Was SIDA informed about these situations?

BB: No, not really. It would also have been difficult to judge from outside what actually happened. In most cases you could not do that, because it might as well be a case of infiltration. If you look at the events in Zimbabwe after independence, only ten years later you could see how much of that actually was caused by deliberate actions by South Africa. At the time, some said that it could be the case, but no one had direct evidence to that effect. The same applies to the camps in Angola in the 1980s. How could you judge from outside?

We did discuss it. We raised some questions, but I do not remember that it influenced our attitude very much. It was a problem and we understood that such problems would appear. It was, however, very difficult even to ask pertinent questions to get better knowledge of the problems. We would at the same time more or less regularly get information from groups in Germany, accusing the liberation movements of being Marxists, Leninists, oppressors etc. You could not really say that it was all that true. It was difficult to know the true picture.

Tore Bergman
Church of Sweden Mission, Zimbabwe—Member of the Consultative Committee on Humanitarian Assistance
(Uppsala, 10 February 1997)

Tor Sellström: I understand that you went to Rhodesia as early as 1953 and that you worked there with the Church of Sweden Mission (CSM) for a very long period, or until 1970. Why did you go to Rhodesia?

Tore Bergman: Well, I was born in Rhodesia. My father was a missionary. He came out as an agriculturalist, first to Natal, South Africa, but in the 1920s he moved to Rhodesia to develop the mission farm at Mnene in the Mberengwa district. I attended school in Bulawayo up to secondary education. Eventually, I came back to Sweden and stayed there for my teacher's diploma. When I had completed my training as a teacher, it was natural to go back to Rhodesia. I had the qualifications to teach at the secondary school level. There were no secondary schools in Mberengwa at that time, but it was part of the mission plan to start such schools. I very much felt an urge to go back for that purpose.

During my first year, in 1953, I worked at the teachers' training school at Musume, because the plans for a new secondary school had not yet got off the ground. But in 1954 we started a secondary school at the same place where the teachers' training school was. We just had one class at that time. Eventually, we moved to Mnene for a few years until we finally got new buildings designed for the purpose at Chegato in the middle of the Mberengwa district. I stayed at Chegato until 1966. At the same time, I assisted with the establishment of another three secondary schools, the Musume and the Masase secondary schools in Mberengwa and the Manama secondary school. In 1966, I became the education secretary for the Lutheran church, which meant that I had to move from Chegato to Gwanda. I regretted that very much, but I was then responsible for the co-ordination of the educational system that the church was running in the Mberengwa-Gwanda-Mtetengwe areas. It involved four secondary schools and about 160 primary schools going up to grade seven. All in all, there were 700 teachers and 24,000 pupils. There were also close contacts between the Lutheran church school system and the government education authorities in Salisbury (Harare) and I took part in some of the meetings.

We lived at Gwanda until 1970, when we decided to go back to Sweden. I left that part of my career and since then I have not been back in education. Coming back to Sweden, I became the Africa secretary of the Church of Sweden Mission in Uppsala.

TS: Several of the early nationalist leaders in Rhodesia were also church leaders, such as Sithole and Muzorewa. Did you personally know any of them before UDI?

TB: No. I had heard Sithole addressing a missionary conference in Marondera, but I did not know him personally. Muzorewa came from the American Methodist mission and worked in the early 1960s as secretary for the Student Christian Movement. He travelled around to the various secondary schools to encourage the formation of Student Christian Movement groups. As such, I had him as a guest at Chegato for a night or two. But apart from that, I did not meet either him or any of the others.

TS: In the 1950s, Rhodesia was very little known in Sweden outside the churches. This started to change with the publication of Per Wästberg's book *Forbidden Territory* and Sithole's *African Nationalism*, which both appeared in 1960. Then, in June 1962, a number of prominent Swedes were behind a Rhodesia campaign in support of Kenneth Kaunda's UNIP party in Northern Rhodesia. Do you remember how the campaign was seen by the government in Salisbury?

TB: No. I do not even remember having heard of that campaign in Rhodesia. What I do remember is that I met Per and Anna-Lena Wästberg when they visited the mission area at the end of the 1950s. I believe that he was an exchange student with Rotary International. There were some Letters to the Editor in the papers concerning his general attitude towards the farmers and the farm workers.

They did not like the way in which he fraternized with the local employees.

TS: The Zimbabwean historian Ngwabi Bhebe has written about the Swedish missionaries in Zimbabwe. He emphasizes the preaching of the Lutheran doctrine of the two kingdoms and how the CSM missionaries frowned upon local church employees who a participated in nationalist politics. That was regarded as rebellion against the secular rulers. In your view, is it a fair assessment of the general attitude of the CSM missionaries towards nationalist politics in Rhodesia until the mid-1970s?

TB: I think that you cannot generalize. Among the Swedish missionaries there was a rainbow of different attitudes and opinions in this regard. The general opinion among the missionaries was that we should not involve ourselves in party politics, and therefore not take sides for ZANU, ZAPU or any particular political movement. On the other hand, we saw what was happening in Rhodesia. Particularly after the breakup of the Federation in 1963, we noticed a steady worsening of the government's attitudes towards the African population. More and more of us saw this development as making it increasingly difficult for the Africans to participate in the democratic development of the country.

We lived right out in the bush, far away from the larger urban centres, and we were not restricted by any racial attitudes. We felt that we could live in a natural way with the local population and with the local church leaders. The goal that we had in mind as far as our social work was concerned—educational, medical and other types of work—was to prepare the way for the Africans to actively participate for the benefit of the country. In cases where we came face to face with the effects of the legislation—where it affected somebody that we knew—we tended more openly to take sides.

I was personally affected by an incident at Chegato secondary school. I had a student there by the name of Byron Hove. He was from the area. He had received a degree from the university in Salisbury and wanted to come back to teach at Chegato. I accepted him as a teacher. However, he had been involved in some student demonstrations in Salisbury and after only three weeks the police came and picked him up on the orders of the Minister of Law and Order. I was not even able to speak to him or accompany him to his house. The police searched his house and carried him away. I came face to face with the situation. He had not done anything. He had done his work as a teacher in an exemplary manner and I felt that he was a good teacher, but I lost him. Incidents of that kind became more and more common during the 1960s. We therefore tended to sympathize with the nationalist movement, although we did not speak out officially and openly about the situation, as maybe we should have done.

TS: It appears that the church at an early stage was important for the future relations between the Zimbabwean nationalist movements and Sweden. For example, in an interview with Ndabaningi Sithole he said in July 1995 that ZANU consciously appointed persons with a personal knowledge of CSM as representatives to Sweden. In general terms, how do you see CSM as a bridge-builder between the Zimbabwean nationalist movements and Sweden?

TB: I first and foremost see it as a personal relationship between individuals. Between missionaries who had been working in Rhodesia and individuals who had passed through the CSM schools and hospitals. We could mention a number of people in key positions in Zimbabwe who come from this area and through the education and the contacts they received were trained for this role. The first Zimbabwean ambassador to Sweden, Sifas Zhou, had been both a pupil and a teacher in the CSM/Lutheran church schools.

TS: In December 1965—immediately after UDI—the Swedish government allocated an amount of 150,000 Swedish Kronor in favour of family members of political prisoners in Rhodesia, such as the Nkomo, Chinamano and Sithole families. The support was channelled by SIDA via Christian Care and the International Defence and Aid Fund (IDAF). Did CSM also assist the family members of these political prisoners?

TB: I did not know of any humanitarian support by the Swedish government to the nationalist movement until later, in the 1970s. As far as assistance to family members of political prisoners is concerned CSM did not provide any funds directly to particular family members. In the 1970s, we channelled support through Christian Care and the Lutheran World Federation. It was Christian Care that had the contacts with the families. Individual missionaries also supported children of political prisoners with school fees and so on. It was very common among missionaries to support children for various reasons.

In the case of CSM, there was, however, a direct involvement with the political prisoners around 1977-78. A number of pastors and other church members had been imprisoned for political activities. Four of them were held at the Wha Wha detention camp outside Gweru. One of our missionaries, Hugo Söderström, was in contact with the imprisoned pastors. Their families requested that they should be released from detention and come to Sweden. The request was eventually approved by the authorities, so the four families were brought to Sweden, living with different congregations in various parts of Sweden. Some of them continued their studies in the UK and in the US, returning to Zimbabwe after independence. I visited some of them at Wha Wha in the 1970s.

TS: Did they have any political affiliation?

TB: Yes. One was outspokenly ZAPU. Another was probably also ZAPU. I am not quite so sure whether the other two closely identified themselves with any of the parties. However, when I visited them at Wha Wha they explained that there were different ways of greeting one another. The ZANU greeting was a clenched fist and the ZAPU greeting an open hand. When I left the detention camp, they were looking at me through the barbed wire. They waved at me in their different ways, but I did not know how to respond so I waved with one hand clenched and the other open! They just laughed!

TS: In 1969, the Swedish parliament paved the way for direct official Swedish humanitarian support to the liberation movements in Southern Africa. These movements waged armed struggles and received support from the Communist countries. How would you explain that Sweden took the decision to assist them? How did the Church of Sweden look upon this?

TB: If I had to explain the Swedish government's support for the liberation movements, I would say that armed force was used against the peoples of Southern Africa by the respective regimes and if armed force is used—resulting in deaths, detentions and torture—it would also be legitimate for the liberation movements to take up arms. As far as the church was concerned, we could, however, not involve ourselves in a kind of support which would result in the purchase of arms. The Church of Sweden Mission had some problems in that regard. In 1969, the World Council of Churches started a special fund called the Programme to Combat Racism. The fund was intended for humanitarian aid to the liberation movements. The Church of Sweden Mission was very quick in providing limited funds to the programme, but we also received very heavy criticism from certain quarters in Sweden because of that. It resulted in a loss of contributions towards the general work of the Church of Sweden and the Church of Sweden Mission was branded by some people as pro-Communist and as a movement propagating armed violence.

On the question of official Swedish support to the liberation movements, I also remember Joshua Nkomo saying that he was rather upset about the assistance ZAPU received from SIDA and Sweden. They were not allowed to decide for themselves what the support was to be used for.

TS: In the case of Zimbabwe, official Swedish support was already extended to ZANU from 1969, while the support to ZAPU only started in 1973. One gets the impression that ZANU had a broader support base in Sweden than ZAPU. Would you agree with that?

TB: Yes, I think that I agree with that. I think that the main reason was that ZANU had developed a network of personal contacts in Sweden. I know that Sally Mugabe had contacts with a number of popular movements and groups in Sweden and that Robert Mugabe himself also had contacts in Sweden before we had any relations with him. For example, with Bread and Fishes in Västerås, where he was received as a friend, and with Emmaus Björkå.

TS: Bishop Muzorewa and his UANC never received any official Swedish support, although some people in the Swedish church advocated that. In particular, church circles in Norway supported Muzorewa. Did CSM ever channel support to UANC?

TB: No, we did not channel any support to UANC. UANC was first formed as a movement, and not as a party. Muzorewa's contacts were mainly through the Swedish Methodist church via the American Methodists. When he came to Sweden, he was a guest of the Swedish Methodists, but we did not have any contacts with him.

TS: Why do you think that the Swedish government never supported Muzorewa?

TB: I think that he was regarded by both ZANU and ZAPU as something of an upstart and that he could not be relied upon. When Muzorewa launched UANC it was not seen by the liberation movements as the answer to the problems in Rhodesia.

TS: When you came to Uppsala in 1970, you started to serve as Africa secretary of CSM. During the second half of the 1970s, you became closely involved with humanitarian assistance to ZANU and ZAPU. I understand that you were in direct contact with both Robert Mugabe and Joshua Nkomo. Could you describe the background to your involvement with ZANU and ZAPU?

TB: In March 1976, I received a circular letter written by Guy Clutton-Brock in Britain, requesting support for ZANU in Mozambique. I wrote back to him and asked for further details. Clutton-Brock was in contact with Didymus Mutasa and they recommended that I write directly to Mugabe in Mozambique, which I did. I explained who I was, told him about my connections with Zimbabwe and asked for details with regard to possible support. I got a reply from him in which he outlined the situation in the camps, saying that he had asked his colleague Edgar Tekere to present it in a more detailed way. Very soon afterwards, I received a letter from Tekere with a comprehensive and detailed list of all their requirements. It rather overwhelmed me. I had not quite thought in those terms. I should also add that due to the criticism we received for providing funds to the Programme to Combat Racism and CSM's contacts with armed movements, I wrote in my personal capacity. The correspondence was never registered with the Church of Sweden Mission. Anyhow, I wrote back to say that I would explore the possibilities of support in Sweden. Unfortunately, not much came of it at that time. I consulted with various people, but I was unable to find sources of support.

However, possibly as a consequence of this contact, a ZANU delegation came to Sweden in September 1976. It included Didymus Mutasa, Chiwara, who was then the ZANU representative in the UK, and Mrs. Tekere, who was in charge of the ZANU women's affairs in London. We had discussions with them in Uppsala. Shortly thereafter—in January 1977—the pupils at the Manama secondary school were kidnapped by ZAPU. They crossed the border into Botswana and were eventually taken to Zambia. During my visits to Zimbabwe as CSM's Africa secretary and through correspondence, I was in contact with the parents of some of these children, who expressed concern over what had happened to them and how they were being cared for. Addressing meetings in Sweden, I tried to question the attitude among some church people that those who had left Zimbabwe for political reasons and taken refuge in other countries were being called terrorists, as was then the term. Why should the act of crossing the border change our attitude to them? Whether this had any effect, I do not know. But that was my reaction.

I tried to advocate support for those who had crossed the border. Within the Church of Sweden Mission board, it was accepted, and as far as ZANU was concerned—where we knew that school children had been crossing the border after the independence of Mozambique—we received information that the Christian Council of Mozambique through their general secretary, Reverend Mahlalela, had a concern for the refugees. We therefore contacted him, asking if he or his staff could find out what the situation of the children was and whether we could support them, providing some kind of humanitarian assistance. At the time, I felt that it was not possible to channel any funds through the liberation movements. We had to find other channels. We started to support the Christian Council of Mozambique to enable them to administer assistance to the camps. At about the same time, the Lutheran World Federation established an office in Maputo, also providing support to the camps. And later in 1977, Mugabe himself, finally, came with a delegation to Uppsala. That is how the contacts were established with ZANU.

In the case of ZAPU, it was the Manama exodus that initiated our contacts. Tord Harlin of CSM visited Zambia in March-April 1977. The purpose was to explore the possibilities of establishing a contact. Harlin had been the headmaster of the Manama school in the 1960s and he knew quite a lot of the ZAPU people in Zambia. Through the contacts that Harlin made with ZAPU, I was then able to enter into correspondence with the ZAPU office in Lusaka. On one of my trips to Southern Africa, I visited Zambia in March 1978 to see what the situation was. I had contacts with John Nkomo, who was ZAPU's administrative secretary. Everything was very secret. I just told them that I would be at certain hotels at certain times and suddenly John Nkomo appeared. I was taken to the ZAPU headquarters in Lusaka, where I had about an hour's interview with Joshua Nkomo and his staff. He explained the situation to me and I asked him about the possibility of channelling funds. It was on this occasion that he criticized the Swedish government for being too particular about its funding.

I did not expect more than this interview with him, but Nkomo said that he would take me back to the hotel and that we later would go to some of the refugee camps. It was very exciting! I had not expected that at all. I think that it showed some confidence in the Church of Sweden Mission. He then came with a whole convoy of cars. There were two of us, myself and a youth leader from Sigtuna, who accompanied me on this tour. We first drove to Victory Camp, where there were some 3,000–5,000 girls. Joshua Nkomo took me around the camp, showing me the facilities and explaining their needs. From Victory Camp we went to another camp, where they kept young mothers with babies. In both places, I was given the opportunity to say a few words to the refugees, explaining who I was. At Victory Camp, Nkomo called out all the girls on parade. It was quite impressive. We then had further discussions regarding the possibility of channelling funds to ZAPU. It was subsequently done through the Church of Sweden Aid. CSM also sent some funds to ZAPU through the Lutheran World Federation.

TS: Finally, turning to South Africa, official Swedish assistance was from the beginning of the 1970s extended to ANC. Over the years, there were close contacts between Gatsha Buthelezi and the Church of Sweden Mission in Zululand. Did CSM ever channel any support to Inkatha?

TB: Well, not directly to Buthelezi's Inkatha, but to programmes administered through certain movements in Natal which were linked to Zululand. There was, for example, an ecumenical centre in Pietermaritzburg which was running agricultural projects in Natal. At this ecumenical centre there were also a number of practical courses for young people who needed further clerical and administrative training, women in particular. The Church of Sweden Mission channelled some funds from SIDA to this centre on the recommendation of and through our contacts with Chief Buthelezi. But CSM never gave any direct support to Inkatha. We held the view that Buthelezi to begin with stood for a positive movement in South Africa in that he refused to declare Kwa-Zulu independent. After the formation of Inkatha, his intentions were, however, not as clear as in the beginning.

Stig Blomqvist
LO/TCO—Miners International Federation—Regional adviser in Southern Africa (Bro, 29 January 1997)

Tor Sellström: You have had a long and important involvement in trade union matters in the whole world. What is the background to your involvement? When did you go to Southern Africa?

Stig Blomqvist: Well, the background is that when I was working for the International Transport Workers Federation, John Näslund and Anders Stendalen of the Swedish Mineworkers Union asked me in 1981 if I was willing to start an international education project. Peter Tait, the former general secretary of the Miners International Federation (MIF) had agreed with

Stendalen on that. Tait came to Stockholm and we had a chat. I did not speak very good English in those days. Maybe not now either, but in those days it was terrible. A mix of seaman's English and cockney. However, Anders Stendalen persuaded me to jump into the boat. It was the most difficult boat that I have ever boarded, but it was interesting.

It started as a six month project, through which I was supposed to introduce a new system for trade union education in the Third World, at a very basic level. It was largely inspired by the Swedish study circle activities. I soon found myself sitting in London to start the work, but MIF had nothing to fall back on. There was no policy, nor history of education. I thought that there was something, but there was nothing to build on. What I had to do first of all was to get a platform to work from. It was not very easy. I was also clever enough to begin in the most difficult part of the world, Latin America, a continent full of rotten trade unions. Not trade unions for the workers, anyway.

I started in Colombia, but I learnt very quickly that it was a difficult country, full of corruption, drug cartels and corrupt trade unions. There was not one union that was not corrupt. But I was lucky, because the union stopped the project and instead I went to Peru. Peru was interesting. There was no corruption, but lots of political intrigues. I worked in a small mine up in the Andes, about four to five thousand metres above sea-level. It was owned by the Japanese. Very isolated. There was only one road and it was guarded by the police, the guardia civil. The miners' lives were in the hands of the damned company. One day, the police started to attack me and a union leader, but the miners came from everywhere. They stoned the guardia civil to release us. The next day, when we were planning the education activities in the union hall, hell broke loose. The police opened fire against the miners about 500 metres from where we were. There was blood all over the place. One person was killed and others had bullets in their legs, arms and upper bodies.

That was my experience from the trade unions in Latin America. After that, I went to Guyana and in 1983 from there to Zimbabwe, in the centre of the mining activities in Africa. I knew that I could live decently there and also go home to Sweden sometimes. I also knew that there were lots of contract workers down there.

TS: Were you employed by MIF?
SB: No, I have never been employed by MIF. I have been on loan from the Swedish Mineworkers Union. I am a Swedish miner and I will die as such.
TS: Your base was in Harare. But from where did the funds for your projects come?
SB: From the beginning, the project was funded by LO/TCO through SIDA. It was completely financed from Sweden.

Now, soon after my arrival in Harare, I got involved with one of the most important unions in Africa, well, in the whole world outside Europe. One day I was approached by a man called Cyril Ramaphosa. He called me from Johannesburg and said that he was the General Secretary of a newly formed National Union of Mineworkers (NUM). He asked me if I was willing to get the union moving through education activities. He was himself a very well educated fellow. He had been chosen to set up a union and really get something going in South Africa. I then met Ramaphosa and a fellow called James Motlatsi at the airport in Harare. I first took them to the trade union office in town and introduced them to Geoffrey Mutandare, the chairman of the Mineworkers Union of Zimbabwe. Mutandare was joking and said: 'We must have a party for our friends from South Africa'. But Cyril said: 'No. We have not come here for a party. We have come here for work'. That showed me what kind of man he was. That was enough for me.

We then went to my house, and I told them about the low cost education which I had been introducing in the unions. Ramaphosa said: 'It sounds good'. In those days, James Motlatsi was not saying one word. He was just sitting there. But Cyril presented his plans and wrote down the layout on a paper. He showed his capacity. How he can form ideas into an almost perfect layout. Because it was he who did that, not I.

We designed the whole structure of NUM's education activity that night. It is still there today. So it was not a bad job. Cyril was very interesting. He could easily get my ideas on a paper. That was not my strong side. He also worked out a preliminary budget for one year. I then phoned the former director of the LO/TCO Council of International Trade Union Cooperation, Jan-Erik Norling. It was late in the evening. I said to him: 'Can you get the money?' And Norling said: 'You can go ahead with the planning. I will get the money'. He took a risk that nobody else in Sweden in those days would have taken.

Norling was the one who saved the face of the Swedish trade union movement's international involvement, I would say. He had the brains to analyse the situation very quickly and take a high risk. He struggled through the Swedish bureaucracy to get the money, as he had promised. There were not many who supported him in those days, but later on—when NUM and South Africa became star projects—then there was a different tone.

That was the beginning. At the time, NUM had 40,000 members. Then, slowly, things started to develop in South Africa. In the beginning, NUM was working from one room, where Ramaphosa and Motlatsi were also sleeping. As a team, they were perfect. As I said, Motlatsi was not talking, but in the mines he was talking a lot. He is the best agitator I know. Talking to mass meetings. He is better than Cyril even.

TS: So the first support to the National Union of Mineworkers of South Africa was from Sweden. How about the United States and other Western countries? Were they not involved in the trade union movement?

SB: Cyril told me that he had been running around the world, to the Americans, to the Germans, everybody, trying to get assistance. But they did not get anything practical which was useful to them. What they got was peanuts. Nothing to start a mass movement with. And that is what we are talking about, the start of a mass movement. NUM started as a union for blacks. That was the only way to mobilize the black mineworkers. Today, everybody is allowed into the union. Anyway, when the activity started to develop, the money required was also starting to be enormous. I then got Norway and Denmark involved. They are my neighbours and I was able to talk to them. Later, the support also involved Holland. The bulk of the money was always from Sweden, but the other countries helped a lot.

In 1986 or 1987, I was invited to the mineworkers' congress and I got a visa to South Africa for the first time. It gave me the opportunity to meet the miners who I had been trying to support for so long. It was unusual to do a project when you never had been to the country! Anyway, the South African mineworkers showed me their appreciation in many ways. They carried me on their shoulders around the congress hall, for example.

TS: Where was this?

SB: That was outside Johannesburg, in Soweto. I also went with Motlatsi to the mines. In those days, he was talking. The silence was over. I was one of them. Motlatsi was the first President of NUM. He started as a contract worker from Lesotho. I have seen his mines, his bed and the steel cabinet where he kept his clothes. We visited the gold mine Western Deep Levels, where there was a mass meeting of about 15,000 people. I addressed the miners there. They greeted me, but said: 'Can you give us guns?' That was the most important. They were revolutionary minded, but I explained: 'I am sorry, I cannot do that. The Swedish people do not believe in a violent change of society. We believe in peaceful methods, including strikes, but not in violence'. And they accepted that.

TS: Were you the only foreign representative at the NUM congress?

SB: I think that there was somebody from England, but I was the only mineworker. Naturally, there were also some political people invited, because ANC was involved in the development of the trade union movement in South Africa. Without the trade union movement, ANC would be nothing.

TS: The project that you developed, was it the so-called E-plan?

SB: Well, E-plan simply stood for education plan. But it was confusing to the police. They did not know what the E-plan was. The whole system in South Africa was built on the cell-system, the communist-inspired system, and the Swedish study circle activity. We started cells which could operate in a country where nothing was allowed and that is how South Africa is free today. That is the whole thing. It also worked in the closed hostels.

TS: You were also closely involved with the Mineworkers Union of Namibia (MUN). How did that begin?

SB: It began the first time I was in South Africa, really. There were two representatives of the Mineworkers Union of Namibia at the NUM congress. We talked a lot and agreed that I should come over to discuss education activities.

I went there and when I arrived in Windhoek, I was met by one of my oldest friends, Ben Ulenga. He was a very interesting fellow. He was a former guerrilla commander in Namibia who had spent nine years on Robben Island. He told me about this, how it was and how he kept his mind clear. He is very sharp. We began a long friendship.

In Namibia, we also agreed to use education to try to get the union on its feet. The background of MUN was really that it was Cyril Ramaphosa who formed it among the contract workers from Namibia. When they formed the mineworkers' union in Namibia, they signed over the membership. However, Ben Ulenga, Cyril Ramaphosa and I agreed that NUM of South Africa should take their brothers and sisters of Namibia under their wings and assist them in whatever way they wanted.

TS: Did you ever have any contacts with SACTU in South Africa?
SB: No.
TS: Was that because SACTU was a member of the World Federation of Trade Unions (WFTU)?
SB: No. MIF often discussed what to do about the involvement of WFTU, but I said: 'Don't worry about that. Worry about what you yourself do or not do'. The dictator-style of a trade union is nothing that the Third World buys. No way.
TS: Was the LO/TCO council in Sweden worried that you were supporting trade unions in South Africa and Namibia that were controlled by Communists?
SB: I do not know. They did not say so. If they were, they kept it for themselves.
TS: Did you ever visit any Swedish companies in South Africa or Namibia?
SB: No, because my way to operate was to keep away from Swedish activities in the country where I was. I did not even visit the embassy.
TS: In general terms, what do you think that the role of the Swedish trade union movement was for South Africa and Namibia compared with that of the big Western powers?
SB: The big Western powers did nothing for the development of the movement in South Africa. That is my judgement. It was only the Nordic countries and Holland. They should have full credit for that. Nobody else, especially not the Germans. They have not done anything, other than invite people for seminars where they tried to brainwash them. Against that background, what is happening today is very worrying. MIF has been hijacked by the Americans and the Germans. I fought against it and I almost lost my health. I was fighting, because I saw that the Americans and the Germans wanted to control others with their money. Everything they assisted was connected to their own countries. They used the trade union movement for political purposes, which has been described very well by the Latin American expert Åke Wedin. He says that the Americans and the Germans are trying to control the trade unions in the Third World. I agree with him completely.

Pär Granstedt
Centre Party—Association of Western European Parliamentarians Against Apartheid
African European Institute
(Stockholm, 3 June 1996)

Tor Sellström: How did your involvement with Southern Africa begin?
Pär Granstedt: As a matter of fact, my entire political involvement started with South Africa. It was when I was at secondary school in Södertälje in the early 1960s. My first political act, I would say, was to sell anti-apartheid badges in the school-yard. Out of that grew a political interest in Third World issues and in issues related to justice

between the North and the South. I later joined the Centre Party Youth League. So, my South African involvement is older than my involvement in the Centre Party.

TS: Were you then a member of a solidarity organization?

PG: I was not a member of any structured organization. I think that it was the National Council of Swedish Youth (SUL) that distributed these badges. People were approached in the schools to sell them.

TS: Was that part of the 1963 SUL boycott campaign?

PG: Yes, it was.

TS: In the 1960s, the Centre Party—particularly the Youth League—advocated support to the national liberation movements in Southern Africa. These movements waged armed struggles and they were supported by the Communist countries. How would you explain that a Swedish non-socialist party took this position?

PG: I think that it is important to understand that the Centre Party—although a bourgeois or non-socialist party—is based on the underprivileged segments of society. When founded, it was in itself a kind of liberation movement for the smallholders in Sweden and interest in questions related to social justice have therefore always been fundamental to the Centre Party. It was natural for the party to side with the underprivileged in the Third World. I think that that is the main ideological reason. In fact, in most Third World countries the social movements have been based on small farmers with a similar socio-economic base as the Centre Party.

TS: Was it not controversial that the liberation movements were supported by the Communist countries?

PG: It was to a degree, although it was part of a more general controversy in the 1960s. The Centre Party Youth League was to some extent part of the Left wave in Sweden. Of course, more conservative groups within the party were rather opposed to that, but much less when it came to the situation in Southern Africa. It was more politically correct to support the liberation movements there. Apartheid was considered so horrendous and memories from the Nazi period made action against racism generally accepted.

TS: At that time, the Centre Party also strongly advocated Swedish support to Zambia. Do you think that Kenneth Kaunda played a role for the involvement of the Centre Party in favour of the liberation movements in Southern Africa?

PG: I have no memories of my own from that process. I was not involved in the Centre Party at that time. But, I imagine that he did play a role. It is obvious that a number of individuals were important for this process, both Swedes who created an awareness about what was happening in Southern Africa and people from Southern Africa visiting Sweden.

TS: In the early 1960s, it seems that liberal intellectuals and people from the churches were the most active in the formation of the Swedish solidarity opinion with Southern Africa, while the organized labour movement joined much later. Would you agree with this?

PG: Yes, in a way I believe that it is a true picture of what happened. I once studied the debate about development aid in the Swedish parliament and I found the same pattern. The Liberal Party and the Centre Party were pushing very hard for increased aid, while the Social Democrats were a bit more careful. One of the reasons, I think, was simply that the Social Democratic Party was in government and therefore felt that they had to be careful not to spend too much government money. They also had to consider the reactions in other countries, especially in the West. At the same time, the youth and women's leagues within the Social Democratic movement have always been much more progressive than the party itself.

TS: Do you think that the early contacts established with leaders such as Oliver Tambo, Eduardo Mondlane and others helped the Swedish politicians to understand the nationalist core of the struggle in Southern Africa, beyond the East-West divide?

PG: I think that that is very true. It was evident from the Swedish debate that most people realized that the liberation movements were not part of the Eastern bloc. The problem was that their main source of support happened to be the Communist countries. We saw it very much as our task to see to it that they also had other supporters, to make them less dependent on the East and more interested in becoming part of the free world in the future. A general opinion in the Centre Party and the Liberal Party—and also among Social Democrats—was that we had a responsibility to try to move the movements towards the West, with more liberal views on democracy and the economy. Looking at the situation today, it proved very successful.

TS: In 1969, the Swedish parliament paved the way for direct official humanitarian support to the Southern African liberation movements. Some movements that were recognized by the OAU were, however, never supported by Sweden. This was, for example, the case with PAC of South Africa and FNLA of Angola. What were the reasons behind this position?

PG: Although I was not active in the parliament during that period, my impression is that we doubted the base of certain movements. Our feeling was that they did not have a really strong base at home and that they were not representative of the peoples in their countries. That is mainly why we did not support them.

TS: Has the Centre Party given direct assistance to any liberation movement in Southern Africa?

PG: There has been some support to the youth leagues of both SWAPO and ANC. Our women's league has also given support to the SWAPO women.

TS: You have been a member of SIDA's board, the parliamentary standing Committee on Foreign Affairs and the Advisory Council on Foreign Affairs. Were you satisfied that the Swedish support to the liberation movements was used for the humanitarian purposes stated and not for the armed struggle?

PG: I think that we had sufficient control that our support was not used for buying arms or directly financing armed operations. But, of course, it was in a way support for the armed struggle. I do not think that we wanted to prevent that. Giving humanitarian aid to a liberation movement involved in armed struggle was in a way support for that struggle. But, we were satisfied that it was not directly used for arms or military operations.

TS: How did the other Western countries look upon the Swedish involvement with the Southern African liberation movements?

PG: I did not encounter any really strong reactions against our involvement. It was not at all as the Swedish support to FNL in Vietnam, which really provoked strong reactions, especially in the United States. The case of Southern Africa was less controversial as everybody was against apartheid.

TS: You never experienced any pressure from the British or the Americans?

PG: No. The discussions in which I was involved with the British concerned economic sanctions against South Africa, where we were on the offensive, asking them why they did not do anything.

TS: In 1976, after a long period of Social Democratic rule, a non-socialist coalition government took over, led by the Centre leader Thorbjörn Fälldin. Many expected that it would change Sweden's policy on Southern Africa. Instead, the official support to the liberation movements increased and as the first Western country Sweden legislated against investments in South Africa. How would you explain this?

PG: Well, it was rather logical, knowing the position of the Centre and Liberal parties. What is important to note is that there was only limited influence on foreign policy by the Moderate Party at that time. Both the Prime Minister and the Foreign Minister were from the Centre Party and the Minister for Development Aid from the Liberal Party. In fact, the Moderate Party was very much an outsider in this field. They were not as strong in that coalition as in later non-socialist governments.

TS: Humanitarian assistance is, of course, support for human rights and in this respect there were instances of abuse within the liberation movements. Do you recall if these problems were discussed by the SIDA board or the Foreign Affairs Committee and if they were taken up with the leadership of the liberation movements?

PG: Yes, they were definitely discussed. Not as a reason to stop the support, but rather as an embarrassment as it weakened their case. Of course, it did have a negative political impact. I suppose that it was taken up in the official contacts between Sweden and the liberation movements. I was not involved in that, but on the youth side I remember, for instance, participating in discussions with representatives of SWAPO on these questions. It definitely did play a role. We were eager to point out how much it hurt the case of the liberation movements and how counter-productive it was for the struggle.

TS: Since its foundation, you have been closely involved with the Association of Western European Parliamentarians Against Apartheid, which was the original name, and you are still the treasurer of AWEPA. In the Swedish parliament, did AWEPA have members from all the parties?

PG: All the traditional parliamentary parties have been, and still are, represented in AWEPA. Even very prominent Moderate MPs such as Carl Bildt, who later became Prime Minister, and Margaretha af Ugglas, who became Minister for Foreign Affairs, were members of AWEPA. In fact, the first member from the Moderate Party was Carl Bildt and Margaretha af Ugglas was also among the first. AWEPA has always had a broad political base. The only political party that was never represented in AWEPA was New Democracy during its short period in the Swedish parliament. I think that it was our fault as much as theirs. We never asked them. We did not consider that their ideology was in tune with AWEPA's.

TS: Looking back, what would in your view constitute the most important contribution by Sweden to the process of national liberation in Southern Africa?

PG: I think that it was very important that we, as a Western democracy, played an active role. It would have been disastrous if the liberation movements had been seen to have friends only among authoritarian Communist parties and countries in Eastern Europe. That was very important. Another factor was, of course, that we in the long run managed to persuade other Western countries to support the process towards democracy, maybe not so often the liberation struggle as such, but through sanctions. In the end, there was a kind of international consensus to force the apartheid regime to give up. I think that it played an important role for the rather peaceful transition that we have witnessed.

TS: Would a similar Swedish active involvement be possible today?

PG: Yes, I think that it would be possible. Of course, in the present situation the Swedish priority would be to try to get the EU member countries to do the same as we do. But I am sure that we would also be prepared to work unilaterally if necessary. It is interesting to look at Denmark, which was almost as active as Sweden. Denmark was a member of both EU and NATO, but played a very constructive role. The EU membership might put some restraints on our freedom of action, but at the same time it also adds more tools to our palette of possible actions.

TS: Is there anything that you would like to add?

PG: Yes, I think that it is important to stress the role of the neighbouring countries—not least Zambia—for the liberation struggle, what they have done and what sufferings they had to undergo. I think, in fact, that the support we gave to the Frontline States was about as important as the support we gave directly to the liberation movements. These countries took many risks and sacrificed many economic possibilities in favour of the regional struggle.

Birger Hagård
Moderate Party
(Stockholm, 9 October 1996)

Tor Sellström: As a scholar, conservative politician and member of parliament, you have had a long involvement in international affairs. In your view, how could the broad and active Swedish opinion on Southern Africa be explained?

Birger Hagård: There are, of course, many different background factors. I think that one explanation is that the Cold War was intensified in the 1950s. Also, it may be that the Swedes had a bad conscience, in some way. Sweden was rather prosperous and many people thought that we should try to help other parts of the world that were not so well off. It has also been said—maybe with some truth—by Gustav Sundbärg, one of the Swedish authorities at the beginning of this century, that the further away a country is situated, the more interesting it becomes in Sweden. If a country is very distant from Sweden, people may be interested, because they do not know anything at all about it. Of course, there was also an irritation—well, more than an irritation, a frustration—when you saw the developments in the region, especially in the Union of South Africa and the hardening of the apartheid system. That was very strange to a Swede or to a European, particularly after what we had experienced during the Second World War and the Nazi persecutions.

TS: The former South African Minister of Foreign Affairs, 'Pik' Botha, served at the South African legation in Stockholm from 1956 to 1960. In an interview, he said that he found the climate in Sweden very hostile towards his country and that the main opinion makers against South Africa were liberals, such as Ivar Harrie and Herbert Tingsten, but also the churches.

BH: Yes, that is true.

TS: How did your own involvement with Southern Africa begin? Was it with the Congo crisis in 1960 or with your tenure as chairman of the Swedish Conservative Youth League (HUF) from 1963 to 1965?

BH: I think that it was during the Congo crisis. Maybe I should stress that I have always been a very firm anti-Communist. I was very much engaged when the Russians occupied the Baltic countries. From my childhood and my youth, I remember the Baltic refugees coming to Sweden. I had a lot of friends among them and, of course, they could never forgive the Russians for the occupation. I became a very firm anti-Communist and I have been a very firm anti-Communist all my life. At the time of the Congo crisis, I was the vice-chairman of the Baltic Committee. Professor Birger Nerman, who had had a chair in Dorpat, Estonia, was the chairman. His brother, Ture Nerman, was also very strongly engaged in our work. When the United Nations' troops—including the Swedes—attacked Moise Tshombe in Katanga, there was formed a Katanga Committee in Sweden, with Gillis Hammar, Birger and Ture Nerman and many others. People who were not in the same political camp as I was. They were more liberal. Anyway, we found that we had much in common and we considered this attack on Tshombe very unfair.

I was also very much influenced by a book by Torsten Gihl, who was a Swedish expert in international law. At that time he was a professor in Uppsala. He wrote a book in which he really accused the United Nations because of their behaviour and I must admit that it had a lot of influence on me and my thoughts. Another basic thing was that being a firm anti-Communist, I have always been Western oriented and in this case that meant that we together criticized what the UN and, of course, the Swedish government did. That, I think, was my first interest in Southern Africa.

TS: On 1 March 1963, when you were in the HUF leadership, the National Council of Swedish Youth (SUL) launched a consumer boycott against South African goods. The conservative youth also participated in this campaign.

BH: Yes, we participated, but I do not think that we were very active.

TS: And in 1974, the conservative Moderate Youth League (MUF) launched a project under the heading "support the struggle against racism in Southern Africa", where it asked for financial contributions in favour of "the organizations that strive for freedom and democracy". How was this viewed by the mother party, the Moderate Party?

BH: Well, to be quite frank, I do not know. After my chairmanship of the young conservatives between 1963 and 1965, I went back to university and was working there as a lecturer at the same time as I was preparing my dissertation. In 1967, I was appointed university lecturer in Linköping and moved to Östergötland. I settled in Vadstena and very soon—in 1970–1971—I became involved in local politics. Thus, between 1965–1966 and 1982 I did not have so much to do with national politics. Especially not in the inner circles.

TS: In 1969, the Swedish parliament paved the way for direct official Swedish support to national liberation movements in Southern Africa. These movements professed a socialist ideology, waged armed struggle and were assisted by the Soviet Union and/or China. Against the background of traditional Swedish policies of neutrality and peaceful solution of conflicts, how would you explain the stand taken by the Swedish parliament and the Social Democratic government?

BH: Well, there was the general radicalisation and the 1968 events. You also had people like Olof Palme, Pierre Schori and others involved in the socialist camp here in Sweden. It is not a secret that we in the opposite camp did not like them very much, precisely because of their socialist—or Communist—sympathies. I think that the general radicalisation might be one explanation.

TS: The Swedish government had set up an advisory committee on refugee—later, humanitarian—assistance, chaired by the Director General of SIDA. It did not have a parliamentary composition, although the ambition was to have different political opinions represented there. How did you look upon the committee?

BH: I wonder if there were many that knew about it. It was only later that I became aware that the committee existed. Of course, I very much dislike and disapprove of the fact that there was such a committee, without any parliamentary control.

TS: It was an important body when it comes to official Swedish support to the Southern African liberation movements?

BH: Yes, in the way that all the millions went to ANC, for instance.

TS: After a long reign of Social Democratic rule, in 1976 the Moderate Party entered a coalition government with the Centre Party and the Liberal Party. Not only did this non-socialist government maintain official Swedish assistance to the liberation movements in Southern Africa, but it increased the assistance and—furthermore—introduced the first Swedish boycott legislation against South Africa and Namibia in 1979. How would you explain this?

BH: It is very difficult to believe that there was any enthusiasm about it in the conservative camp, but maybe it could be said that this, after all, was a minor question. There were difficulties in the co-operation between the non-socialist partners and this question had no priority within the Moderate Party, I think. If the Centre Party, which had the Ministry of Foreign Affairs under Karin Söder, was interested in doing something like that, I am quite sure that Gösta Bohman, the leader of the Moderate Party, said 'OK, go ahead. We will not fight you on this point'.

TS: Carl Bildt, the former conservative Prime Minister, was a member of the Association of Western European Parliamentarians Against Apartheid, AWEPAA, based in Holland. Were you also a member of AWEPAA?

BH: No, I was not. I was not at all active in international politics at that time.

TS: Did you know that Carl Bildt was a member of AWEPAA?

BH: No, I did not even know what AWEPAA was. But I can understand it to some extent. As I said, there had never been any sympathy for apartheid as such. On the contrary.

TS: Considerable amounts of Swedish funds were over the years channelled to the liberation movements in Southern Africa. Are you satisfied that SIDA exercised sufficient control over these funds and that they were used in accordance with agreements, that is, for humanitarian, non-military purposes?

BH: No. As I said, I think that there should have been parliamentary control.

TS: Your involvement in Southern Africa has primarily concerned Angola, where you at quite an early stage advocated humanitarian support for UNITA in Angola. How did you come into contact with UNITA? Did you meet Jonas Savimbi when he visited Sweden in 1967?

BH: No, I did not meet Jonas Savimbi in 1967. Not at all. I think that my first contact with UNITA must have taken place in 1984 and, if I remember it correctly, my first parliamentary motion on this question was submitted in January 1985. The first contact was through Luís Antunes, the UNITA representative in Sweden. I do not remember who took the initiative. I think that it was Antunes. I had talked to a lot of friends about the situation in Angola and somebody who knew Antunes introduced him to me. And, of course, I became more and more interested in what was going on. Especially in 1984, when there was this massive support from Russia and all the Cubans were going there. Angola could be regarded as a Communist country, or at least a country in which the Russians and the Communists were very much interested. I got a lot of material from Antunes and I also started reading the French magazine *Jeune Afrique*. It all developed from there. I found that something had to be done and wrote my motion in January 1985.

TS: So, from your point of view, what was important was the East-West dimension?

BH: Yes, indeed it was.

TS: UNITA had close contacts with RENAMO in Mozambique. Why did you not also advocate humanitarian support to RENAMO?

BH: Well, the main reason was that we did not have enough information on what was going on in Mozambique. There were many different opinions. Was RENAMO a terrorist organization or was it not? I could not get the information that I wanted. That was the main reason for not writing about RENAMO. If you are not sure about something, do not write about it!

TS: From January 1985, you wrote several parliamentary motions against Swedish assistance to the People's Republic of Angola. Your motions were never signed by the leadership of the Moderate Party, but would later enjoy the support of more than twenty conservative MPs. Would it be fair to say that your position on Angola was not fully endorsed by the party or that you were 'the first mover' of a broad party opinion?

BH: Well, you may say that I was 'the first mover'. I never asked the party leadership for any support at all. I just tried to introduce the question to the Swedish public. It was very interesting, because there was some kind of a conflict between me and Carl Bildt. He said that the motion was okey, but that I could not have so many co-signatories because it almost became a party motion. But I think that there was a majority for my position in the conservative parliamentary group. Many colleagues came to me and asked if they could have their names on the motion. I could not deny them that. That was the reason why there were so many names on a motion like this, which was very unique.

TS: In September 1987, three Swedish aid workers were kidnapped by UNITA in Angola. One of them was shot dead and the other two were taken hostage. About one month before this incident, you and your fellow conservative MP Göran Allmér launched a campaign in support of UNITA, called Swedish Angola Help (*Svenska Angola-hjälpen*). In several press interviews you continued to express support for UNITA, in spite of methods which some described as terrorist. In view of the attack on the Swedish aid workers, how would you explain your position?

BH: Of course, it came as a shock to us when we heard what had happened. But what was truth and what was propaganda? That was very difficult to say. You could say that this was some kind of terrorist attack, but on the other hand it was the same kind of methods that the MPLA was using all the time. There was a civil war situation in Angola and the three Swedes must have been quite aware of the dangers. It happened, but that did not change our views.

TS: In an interview with UNITA's former Secretary General, N'Zau Puna, he said that it was a mistake to kidnap the Swedes, because at that time they were building up support for UNITA in Sweden. I guess that he was thinking of the Swedish Angola Help and your work in parliament. Do you agree with his assessment?

BH: Of course, it was a mistake. The kidnapping did not support the cause at all. But I do not know if it meant that much, because so much was happening in Angola at the time. It is very difficult to judge. Anyway, it was not good.

TS: Towards the end of the 1980s, a Swedish support group for UNITA was formed, called the Swedish Angola Groups (*Svenska Angola-grupperna*). It published the bulletin *Angola-Rapport*, and you were appointed Honorary President. What political parties or milieus supported the Angola Groups? Do they still exist?

BH: No, they do not exist. As a matter of fact, you cannot say that they have existed as an organization. There were only a few meetings and I think that I was present at one of them. That was when I was appointed Honorary President. Tommy Hansson was rather active and among the conservative youth there was heavy support.

TS: According to *Angola-Rapport*, in April 1989 you visited UNITA's headquarters in Jamba, where you met Jonas Savimbi. Was this your only visit to Angola?

BH: Yes, that was my only visit.

TS: How did you find UNITA's organization and Savimbi's leadership?

BH: I was very impressed by what I found in Jamba, above all concerning education and discipline. Of course, Jamba was a primitive place, but it seemed very well organized both from a military and a civilian point of view. Dr. Savimbi was rather impressive and there were other UNITA members that I found very interesting. I do not remember their names, but one of them was, I think, head of their interrogation service or something like that. He was a very intelligent man. But there was also a conflict, because there were rumours that one of the leaders had been shot by Savimbi and his followers. As a matter of fact, we met him too, but he was later shot. I do not remember his name.

TS: How did the UNITA leadership look upon Sweden? Did they see Sweden as backing the Communist side?

BH: Yes, more or less.

TS: Did other Swedish politicians visit Jamba?

BH: No, I was the only one as far as I remember.

TS: In September 1992, presidential and parliamentary elections were held in Angola. They were declared free and fair by the United Nations and other international observers, but UNITA did not recognize the outcome, broke the cease-fire and relaunched the military campaign against the MPLA government. How did you look upon these developments?

BH: Well, firstly, I doubt if the elections really could be called free and fair. I received reports that mentioned a lot of incidents. I cannot say that they were absolutely true, but I know how very difficult it is to observe these matters. Angola is a vast country and they used these mobile polling stations. Anyhow, it can be doubted how free the elections really were.

After the elections, UNITA was attacked in Luanda. Many of the leaders were killed by MPLA. One of them was a General Mango, who had visited Sweden some years before. I found him a very interesting man. He was killed at that time. One of the Christian Democrats that I had met was also attacked. She was of Portuguese origin. She was held for at least three months in very bad conditions before she could return to Portugal. So, I think that this was a rather bad event.

TS: If we extend the horizon to the whole of Southern Africa, including South Africa, both socialist and non-socialist politicians have characterized the long period of Swedish humanitarian assistance to the liberation movements as one of the most positive and constructive components of Swedish contemporary foreign policy. Would you agree?

BH: I doubt it very much. As I said, we had no parliamentary control over what happened. Maybe it made Sweden a popular country with ANC, but definitely not with the Inkatha movement and most definitely not among the white South Africans. Instead, I found that they really hated Sweden.

TS: Very little has been written about this chapter in Swedish foreign policy, partly because it was treated confidentially.

BH: Yes, but I also think that the secrecy was preserved. Outside the political circles I do not know of many who knew what happened. If we had taken up this support from a constitutional point of view, I am not quite sure that it would have been accepted, due to the lack of parliamentary control. I am also not quite sure that it was ever discussed in the Council on Foreign Affairs. If we had known that 900 million Swedish Kronor was given by Sweden as direct support to ANC, I think that we would have launched heavy attacks on the government.

Of course, you could say that the support to ANC has been good for Sweden in a short perspective and in the context of the Mandela government in South Africa. But what will happen after Mandela? I do not know. My first and only visit to South Africa was in 1992. I met people from all sides, from ANC, Inkatha, the Nationalist Party and the Liberal Party, as well as representatives from the education sector, industry and so on. I found the opinions very divided.

TS: Finally, do you know of any protests against Sweden by other Western countries due to the support to the Southern African liberation movements?

BH: No, but they cannot have been very happy about it.

Sven Hamrell
Scandinavian Institute of African Studies—Swedish South Africa Committee—Member of the Consultative Committee on Humanitarian Assistance—Director of the Dag Hammarskjöld Foundation
Senior Adviser to the Dag Hammarskjöld Foundation
(Uppsala, 10 April 1996)

Tor Sellström: You have been involved with Africa and African issues for well over forty years. How did it begin?

Sven Hamrell: My involvement in Africa and African issues derives from my early studies in the USA, at Bowdoin College and at the Graduate Faculty of Political and Social Science at the New School for Social Research in New York, where I had an opportunity to meet with quite a number of leading American liberals and African-American scholars, who became friends of mine. I took an interest in African affairs already in the late 1940s, not least in developments in Southern Africa, particularly South Africa, which was then in the limelight and much discussed in America.

TS: When you were in the United States, Gunnar Myrdal's famous book on the race question, *An American Dilemma*, was already published?

SH: Yes, Myrdal was well known in America at the time and I was courteously treated as a compatriot of his.

TS: When you came back to Sweden there was no organized opinion in favour of liberation in South or Southern Africa. But it slowly grew during the 1950s?

SH: Yes. There were two people who were extremely important in forming public opinion, especially on the South African issue. One was Herbert Tingsten with his book *The Problem of South Africa*. Tingsten was considered one of the best political journalists in Europe. He spoke with great authority and his book had a tremendous impact, not only in Sweden but also in other European countries and in South Africa. Another person who was very important and influential was Ivar Harrie, who also travelled in South Africa and published a number of articles that were rather good, especially those that dealt with the intellectual life of the Boers. And, of course, Alan Paton had been in Scandinavia. His *Cry, My Beloved Country* was actually partly written in Norway. Harrie, Tingsten and Paton were liberals and it meant that the Liberal Party became a very influential force in this respect. Then there were others, like Gunnar Helander, the dean of the cathedral in Västerås. He was already influential in church circles. There were also those who were not liberals. I would not be surprised if Joachim Israel, the sociologist, was active in the early 1950s. He later played an important role in these matters.

TS: Israel was a founding member of the Swedish South Africa Committee?

SH: Yes. I also believe that there was an international organization that played a very important, but often neglected, role. That was the Congress for Cultural Freedom. It was an international organization, founded in Berlin. They had a librarian by the name of Jørgen Schleimann as Scandinavian secretary. He was a very influential man in the late 1950s and the early 1960s. The Congress for Cultural Freedom issued a number of publications, such as *Encounter* in England and *Der Monat* in Germany. There was also an Italian publication and in Sweden they had a journal called *Kulturkontakt*. All sorts of people wrote in *Kulturkontakt*. Per Wästberg wrote about Rhodesia and Anders Ehnmark about meetings with African leaders. Alan Paton also wrote there and so on. One of the editors was Bengt Alexandersson.

TS: Of course, Per Wästberg was another very influential person, but of a younger generation?

SH: Yes. He went on a Rotary scholarship to Rhodesia. It must have been in 1958. He came back in 1959. In those days, he was more of a Liberal than a Social Democrat.

TS: Would it be fair to say that it was mainly Liberals that were behind the anti-apartheid opinion in Sweden before 1960?

SH: I would say that up to 1960 it was mainly liberal forces. Then Jørgen Schleimann and the Congress for Cultural

Freedom came into the picture. It was mainly made up of Social Democrats. An important person in the Congress for Cultural Freedom was the South African journalist Colin Legum. There was a conference organized by Schleimann for librarians from Africa and Scandinavia that had important results. After that, there was a big socialist conference in Dakar, which was followed by a conference of historians in Accra. I was invited to that conference. It was the beginning of the movement for African socialism.

There we heard Mamadou Dia and Léopold Senghor speak. But the person that I met there for the first time was Joseph Ki-Zerbo from Upper Volta, now Burkina Faso. He is today the leader of the Social Democratic Party in Burkina-Faso and came to play a very important role in the Socialist International as chairman of its South Africa committee. Our friendship started already then.

TS: In 1962, you and your colleague Anders Ehnmark published a book called *Africans on Africa*, with contributions by several African leaders. What was the background to the book?

SH: Mário de Andrade and Marcelino dos Santos were already well known to Anders Ehnmark, because he had met them in Paris. Kenneth Kaunda had been to Uppsala before Zambia became independent. He laid a wreath on the grave of Dag Hammarskjöld. I accompanied him there. And, of course, we knew Ronald Segal. He was a friend of ours.

What made it possible to produce this book was that Anders Ehnmark was sort of a cultural editor of the newspaper *Expressen*. He could commission articles, pay for them and then edit them. They were published in *Expressen*, but then expanded into this book. We had the resources of the newspaper, although they did not understand that they were also being used for a different, but good purpose. It was a deliberate strategy on our part. We used *Expressen* in order to gather material for the book.

TS: At the time, you were, of course, already the editor of *Verdandi-Debatt*.

SH: Yes, I was the founder editor of *Verdandi-Debatt*. What is perhaps interesting is that *Africans on Africa* was not the only book published by *Verdandi-Debatt* in the early 1960s. Anders Ehnmark and Per Wästberg also did a book on Angola and Mozambique. And we translated two books by Colin Legum. One was his famous book on Pan-Africanism and the other was his and his wife Margaret's book about South Africa. They had a big impact.

TS: Was that because they were used in study circles?

SH: They were used in study circles and they were reviewed, not only in *Dagens Nyheter* and *Svenska Dagbladet*, but in all sorts of local papers. This was followed up a bit later with a seminar. I had then become the editor of the Scandinavian Institute for African Studies in Uppsala and we were looking for subjects for our international seminars. Our first seminar dealt with the Soviet bloc, China and Africa. It was held, I think, in 1963 and we published the proceedings in a book in 1964. We had very good participants at the seminar, like Colin Legum, David Morison, Walter Laqueur, Franz Ansprenger and Richard Lowenthal. They were experts on international Communism and, of course, also on Africa. Especially Colin Legum, who showed that one strain of Pan-Africanism—the one represented by George Padmore—was a good alternative to Soviet Communism. As a Social Democrat, he advised us in the Nordic countries to support similar policies and efforts in the African countries. In the end, that would make for a good, balanced development, he thought.

TS: Did Colin Legum have good contacts with the Swedish Social Democratic movement?

SH: Yes, he developed very good contacts, but I would say that it started with us. We introduced Legum to the movement through Verdandi and his contributions to our seminars. He was the Commonwealth correspondent of *The Observer* in those days, which was an important position. If you read the books by Pierre Schori for instance, you can see the enormous importance attached to him. It is rare that a journalist is given such an importance by policymakers.

TS: As early as 1961, together with Per Wästberg, Joachim Israel, Gunnar Helander and others, you founded the Swedish South Africa Committee. How did it work? What issues did you raise?

SH: Well, it was a kind of advocacy organization. But, of course, in a way it may have contributed to all sorts of things, for example to the establishment of the Consultative Committee on Humanitarian Assistance. We also began to approach the trade union movement and the Social Democrats. Joachim Israel was instrumental in that.

The South Africa Committee later led to the establishment of a South West Africa Committee, around 1966 I think. I was also active in the South West Africa Committee together with Tom Nässbjer. We did something most unusual. We managed to engage the social democratic evening paper *Aftonbladet* in a campaign and collected about one hundred thousand Swedish kronor, which was quite a bit of money in those days. We had a friend at *Aftonbladet*, who helped us. That was Gunnar Fredriksson, who later became the editor-in-chief. He was also a contributor to *Verdandi-Debatt*, although not on African affairs. In the beginning, Tom Nässbjer was actually given an office in the Social Democratic Party headquarters in Stockholm and then he was moved to *Aftonbladet*, where he had a room while the campaign was running.

When we had collected the hundred thousand Kronor, there was a bit of a controversy about how it should be used. Should it be handed over to SWANU or to SWAPO? There was a bit of a fight about that. In the end, it was decided that SWAPO should get fifty thousand and SWANU fifty thousand. This laid a very good foundation for the future cooperation between what is now Namibia and Sweden. Since quite a lot of money came from the Swedish trade union movement, it also meant that the Social Democrats became more actively involved in the Southern African issues. It contributed to a process where the initiative, so to speak, moved from the Liberals to the Social Democrats.

Important in this context was, in addition, the establishment of the Consultative Committee on Refugee—later, Humanitarian—Assistance, where I was a member from the very beginning. I remember meeting Anders Thunborg at Stockholm airport in 1964. He came to me, saying: 'Now we have one million Kronor for South African refugees'. Thunborg was then the international secretary of the Social Democratic Party. The committee was set up to discuss the utilization of these funds.

TS: Thunborg was also a member of the South Africa Committee?

SH: Yes. That is how advocacy works. But I think that he must have talked to Olof Palme about this. Palme, it should be remembered, took a very sincere interest in African developments. In 1960, I wrote an article in *Dagens Nyheter* about the atrocities in the Congo at the time of King Leopold. It was an account of a famous book by the Swedish missionary E. V. Sjöblom, *I Palmernas Skugga (In the Shadow of the Palms)*, published at the turn of the century. A few days after my article appeared, I received an envelope which contained E. D. Morel's book *Red Rubber*, the famous book revealing the conditions around the exploitation of rubber in the Congo. It was a gift from Morel to Olof Palme's grandfather. Palme felt that my article was so good that he sent me the book.

TS: How did you view the role of the Consultative Committee on Humanitarian Assistance?

SH: Well, when Ernst Michanek was the chairman, we felt that we were taking decisions, but it might be that he was doing that. Then there was another Director General of SIDA, Anders Forsse. He behaved differently. We thought that we did not take any decisions. He took them. It was a different style.

In the beginning, the committee was intended to primarily help refugees from South Africa. We were in contact with a very good Norwegian doctor by the name of Cato Aall, who was head of the refugee operations in Zambia. He used to drive down to Botswana in a Landrover, get the refugees over to the Botswana side and then drive them up to Zambia, where they were taken care of by the International Refugee Council of Zambia.

In 1966, I felt that the Scandinavian Institute of African Studies should organize a seminar on refugee problems in Africa and that the proceedings should serve as a guide to the committee and to the Swedish government. Here again you find the name of Margaret Legum, Colin Legum's very able wife. The book was the first study by a number of competent persons on the African refugee problem. It was followed by a huge conference in Addis Ababa in 1967 on the legal, economic and social aspects of the African refugee problem, organized together with the UNHCR, the OAU and the ECA. At the time, it was one of the biggest conferences on refugees ever organized. It drew up plans for the handling of refugee matters in Africa. This was a very important contribution, but it also shows that in the early period the activities were more strictly humanitarian. Of course, the idea was to help the liberation movements, but they came more into focus later.

At this conference, John Eldridge represented the African American Institute. What should be remembered is that there was a strong American influence in those days, generally in a liberal direction. It is difficult to say what grew out of the commitment of individuals in Sweden and Scandinavia and what may have been, so to speak, stimulated from the USA.

TS: Looking at the membership of the Consultative Committee on Humanitarian Assistance over the years, you find that there were representatives from various political currents in Sweden. However, there were no representatives from the then Swedish Communist Party?

SH: Not that I can remember. It is interesting that there were always representatives of the Moderate Party. Some of them were a bit out of touch, but they had no problem. The Communists were kept on the side-line. However, it is very difficult to assess to what extent the committee was a political instrument.

TS: During your long period as a member of the committee, did you experience that there was consistent opposition to the Swedish support to Southern African liberation movements from any quarter?

SH: No, I would not say that I could note that. I was rather surprised, actually, that there was so little opposition.

TS: In the beginning, the Swedish support was purely humanitarian. But there were also links to the liberation movements. One obvious link was the Mozambique Institute in Tanzania, which was run by FRELIMO. You received the FRELIMO leader Eduardo Mondlane and his wife Janet in Uppsala in 1964?

SH: Yes, Mondlane came to Sweden every year until he was killed in 1969. He and his wife were extremely nice. Eduardo was, of course, also a very good scholar. A very impressive man.

TS: In 1969, the Swedish parliament paved the way for direct support to the liberation movements in the Portuguese colonies and in Rhodesia, South West Africa and South Africa. These movements waged armed struggles and were also close to the Soviet Union. Was this contradictory to you?

SH: In my case, I would say that it was natural, because I always believed that Pan-Africanism of the Padmore variety would win in the end. You took a bit of a risk here, but it was actually in favour of a democratic cause and I think that we did the right thing. I think that we assisted the liberation movements in making the right choice.

TS: Would it be fair to say that the very early and close relations between many of the African leaders—such as Eduardo Mondlane, Oliver Tambo and Amílcar Cabral—and the political milieus in Sweden made it easier for Swedish politicians to see beyond the ideological surface?

SH: Yes, I think so. Swedish politicians understood that Mondlane, Tambo or Cabral were no simple-minded Communists, because they were not. They were African nationalists.

TS: There was never any official support by Sweden to FNLA of Angola, UANC of Zimbabwe or Inkatha of South Africa. How would you explain that?

SH: Well, it is in a way surprising, because if I remember it correctly, there were people in the Liberal Party who were in favour of Holden Roberto and FNLA. But I did not think that that was such a good idea. Muzorewa had, of course, supporters in the church, but support for UANC somehow did not materialize either. I was against Buthelezi, because I knew that he had some strange connections. But there were people who really spoke in favour of him. He even came to the Hammarskjöld Foundation and had sandwiches once. However, we had been advised against him by friends in South Africa. I do not think that Inkatha was discussed much in the Consultative Committee on Humanitarian Assistance and I was personally against supporting it.

TS: Considerable amounts of public Swedish funds were over the years channelled to the liberation movements in Southern Africa. Did the committee exercise any control over the funds or was it delegated to SIDA?
SH: It was largely delegated to SIDA, but I remember, for instance, that Per Wästberg really tried to look into this matter to make sure that money allocated for humanitarian purposes was not used for purchases of arms. I was personally suspicious of the way that the International University Exchange Fund (IUEF) used some of the money. I had been a member of the board of IUEF and I felt that things could be kept in better order. I requested that the Secretariat of the Consultative Committee on Humanitarian Assistance should go through the accounts of IUEF to make sure that every Krona was used for the right purpose. However, this did not take place. But I was on record as doing that.
TS: Humanitarian support is support for human rights in general. Some of the liberation movements were at different stages rocked by internal strife and there were cases of human rights' abuses. Did you discuss these matters in the committee? Did you know about them at the time?
SH: Well, I sort of heard about them, but they were not, as I recollect, discussed in the committee. Similarly, the IUEF affair was never properly reported to the committee. I think that it was a mistake. The report on the IUEF should have been made available to every member of the committee, but it was not done. That was not correct.

TS: Do you think that the IUEF affair tarnished Sweden's relations with ANC?
SH: No, not particularly. I think that they had so many other things to care about and I also think that they felt partly guilty themselves, because they had, so to speak, to a degree endorsed Craig Williamson and given him some legitimacy.
TS: How would you assess Olof Palme's role in and for Sweden's involvement with the struggle for national liberation in Southern Africa?
SH: I have always felt that I was working in his tradition, both at the Scandinavian Institute of African Studies and at the Hammarskjöld Foundation. Palme was a towering figure. Wherever I go in Africa, his name is mentioned with enormous gratitude for what he stood for. Everybody wants to pay tribute to him. Rightly so, I think. It is also very significant that the last major speech that he gave—a week before he was killed—was addressed to the Swedish People's Parliament Against Apartheid. We published it in *Development Dialogue* and it is still read with admiration by many Africans.
TS: Looking back over all these years, what would in your view constitute the most important contribution by Sweden to the process of national liberation in Southern Africa?
SH: That is a very big question. Of course, one must emphasize that if the Consultative Committee on Humanitarian Assistance had not existed and if the Swedish government had not allocated the funds, you would not have had the developments that you have had in South Africa.

Gunnar Helander
Church of Sweden Mission, South Africa—Founder of the Swedish Fund for the Victims of Racial Oppression in South Africa—Chairman of the Swedish South Africa Committee—Member of the Consultative Committee on Humanitarian Assistance—Vice Chairman of the International Defence and Aid Fund
(Västerås, 12 February 1996)

Tor Sellström: When and in what capacity did you go to South Africa?
Gunnar Helander: I volunteered in the mission, because I was a bachelor and I had no debts. I could go anywhere. I reported to the Swedish mission that I was willing to go anywhere and it was their decision that I should go to South Africa. They had a mission station there which was unoccupied and it was too bad, really, for a family. Emtulwa was the name of the place. It is not far from Pietermaritzburg. I said, all right, they

could send me there. It was a terrible place. No telephone, no road, no post, no running water. You had nothing, except six green mambas living in the house. It had been unoccupied for ten years when I arrived there in 1938.

Not far from me lived an Indian who I had met in England. We were very good friends. We had studied a term together. He was in the room next to mine at a college in Birmingham. We were together all the time. We studied and played tennis together. He later became a professor in Durban. Now, when we tried to meet in South Africa—he lived about sixty kilometres from my place—everything was against our wish to be together. We could not go to a café together. We could not sit on the same bench in a park. He was a highly educated man. He was rich, too. His father was a businessman. A top fellow in every respect. He could not even go to a café with me because of apartheid. That made me furious about the apartheid laws. As an Indian he was a non-European and thus deprived of full citizenship.

I then started to look for resistance and found very little. I spoke to my fellow missionaries. They were sad about the way people were treated, but some of them thought that it was enough if we gave them schools and hospitals and taught them to be good and so on, but not necessarily extended franchise, because perhaps they were not ripe for it yet! I also contacted ANC. Luthuli was not yet President of ANC, but he was one of the important leaders in the movement. Some of the missionaries at the Natal Missionary Conference in Durban in 1941 then decided to elect him our chairman. We had these ecumenical conferences once a year. All the white missionaries, Catholics, Protestants and everybody. We decided on policy matters regarding schools and so on. At that time, perhaps 95 per cent of the schools for Africans were missionary schools.

TS: So you were like an African Department of Education when you met at this annual conference?

GH: Yes, that was the main thing. I was on an advisory board which regularly met in Pietermaritzburg with the Education Department. We missionaries were grantees for the schools. The service came through us. Luthuli was engaged in the church even then.

In the 1930s, he had attended the International Missionary Conference in Tambaram, India. He was a delegate for South Africa together with the Archbishop of Cape Town and others. He was highly respected as a hereditary chief and also as a church leader. He was a Methodist. He was also trained as a teacher, but at the time of the missionary conference he was doing a chief's work. He was of royal origin and, of course, he opposed apartheid. It evoked some interest that he was elected chairman for all the white missionaries and we were criticized for it.

That was in 1941 and it was the first contact. We met him as a church leader, but he was also an ANC leader. We had contacts with ANC now and then. I was on the board of the Institute of Race Relations together with Luthuli. It was a sort of government board where people of different churches and other institutions met to discuss race questions. They did not listen to us, but it was a forum where we could complain even if nothing happened. I also tried to write to the Swedish newspapers, but they did not believe that an ally of Britain which was fighting against Nazi-Germany could be racist. My articles were sent back.

TS: Did you write to the Swedish Church or to the Swedish newspapers?

GH: I wrote to the newspapers, but it was noticed by the church. I had one article published in some smaller paper. They noticed it and warned me that I was spoiling the cause of the mission if I angered the South African authorities. I should shut up!

TS: When was this?

GH: Somewhere around 1941.

TS: Was that warning from the Church of Sweden Mission?

GH: It was from the Mission Director, yes. He said that I did not understand the black people. The white people who lived in South Africa knew the natives and I should listen to them!

TS: How about your Norwegian brothers in the missionary field?

GH: They were very much politically involved for England during the war against Germany for natural reasons. They thought of Norway and the occupation and had so much interest in what happened there that it was difficult to make them think of anything but the liberation of Norway.

I was transferred to Johannesburg in 1950 and there I found many Jews who were very liberal. They were not Nazis for obvious reasons. Some had fled from Germany. One of them, Dr Simon, was the chairman of the Humanistic League in Johannesburg. That was the group I could deal with and speak freely to.

TS: Having taken a stand against apartheid, I guess that you were subjected to the interest of the South African authorities?

GH: Yes. In 1944, I took over a mission farm called Oscarsberg. A big one, ten kilometres long with a lot of people living there. People loved to move there, because they were free when they came to us. They could have any occupation they wanted. Otherwise, their only choice was to work for farmers, mostly Boers living nearby. They were very ill-treated, underpaid and sometimes flogged by their masters. When I came there, I took in quite a lot of people and my Boer neighbours were furious. They came in a big gathering to the magistrate. His name was Campbell, an Englishman. They said that I was a Communist. I was a dangerous fellow, trying to incite the natives to rebellion and what not. I should be expelled from the country. Campbell promised to investigate the question. It so happened that Campbell did not like the Boers at all. He was very British and he and I played chess together. So, he arrived at our mission station and said: 'I need to investigate: Are you a Communist, a terrible, dangerous revolutionary?'—'No.'—'Well, I thought so. Let us play chess.' He saved me that time, but later on it was touch and go that I was expelled.

At Emtulwa there were mostly German farmers. They were slightly more decent to the natives. I married a German girl. She had never shaken hands or had a meal with a native before, but now she had to do that. We did not marry for political, but only for natural reasons. But she turned like that and said: 'It is all wrong what we have been learning in the schools; that the natives are stupid and uncultured and all that.' We had a black neighbour, a priest, whom we mixed with. He came to have meals with us now and then. She became quite changed, was caught onto my side and got her relatives against her. It was a difficult situation. Not terribly difficult, but, anyway, we did not talk politics with them.

TS: If you look at the Swedish Church and the mission there must have been a contradiction when it comes to politics. On the one hand, you had a strong pietistic tradition in the church. On the other, the mission was established by an Act of Parliament. It was part of the state and most of the missionaries were academics?

GH: Well, we did not have much of pietism in the Church of Sweden Mission in South Africa. It was more obvious among the free churches. They had a more outspoken line: 'Stop polygamy; stop the natives from drinking beer; teach them to say hallelujah. And teach them to be obedient to the white man and thankful for the good white cabinet we have'. We did not have that outspoken line in the Swedish mission, but more of a careful line. Doubts about the natives' ability to rule themselves.

TS: Paternalism?

GH: Yes, paternalism. You can have pets and treat them very well. Like you do with dogs. But you do not want a dog to vote. There were other missionaries, like professor Åke Holmberg. He was a teacher at Umpumulo Teachers' College and he was wholly and fully against apartheid. And Magnus Danell. He even let one native boy live like a child in the house. So there was a cleft in the mission, but one could not oppose very openly. The newspapers would not publish anything against apartheid, not much anyway. It would have been possible to get something into *The Star* in Johannesburg, but one had to be careful. There was a new law that said that if a missionary opposed the government, it would be possible to confiscate the church, the school and the buildings where he was working. That law came in 1952. One had to be a bit careful. Also, I could not buy a bit of land to build a school or a clinic if I openly opposed apartheid when I spoke to my white neighbours. I had to listen. I was furious, but I had to listen to their nonsense until I signed the contract to buy the land or whatever it was.

TS: Is this the reason why you chose to express your opposition to apartheid through writings in the form of novels?

GH: Well, the first was a book for teaching students in theology. That was in Zulu. My first novel was in 1949, *Zulu Meets the White Man*, where I expressed my opinion. Then the Swedish newspapers gradually came to accept my articles. I wrote regularly in *Göteborgs Handels- och Sjöfartstidning* in Gothenburg. That was observed by Herbert Tingsten, who came down to South Africa. He wrote to the mission that they should ask me to receive him and give him all the information he wanted. He came in 1953 and wrote about the mission and about apartheid. Great articles. He praised the mission, although he was an atheist. Ivar Harrie had done that already in 1949 and that changed the opinion in Sweden.

TS: You were then declared *persona non grata* by the South African government?

GH: Yes, but they did not want to arrest me, because I was a Swedish citizen. They knew that I was well known in Sweden and they did not want publicity. At one time I met Piet Mairing, Chief Information Officer in the Malan government, and he said in his Boer English: 'Mr Helander, this is a free country and you are of course allowed to express any views you want to, but we are getting tired of you and your criticism. We do not like your books'. I said: 'Well, Sir, I only try to speak the truth and tell people what I see.'—'Yes, but you are so negative. We do not like you and I warn you. We are not going to tolerate this any more'.

In 1956, I went home on holiday. I took a chance, because one had to get a return visa from the legation in Stockholm. But they did not want an open conflict. I also wrote in English newspapers sometimes and my books had been published in English during the 1950s. In 1957, I applied for a visa to go back to South Africa. It was refused, so I had to stay. I then worked for the anti-apartheid movement in Sweden almost every day.

TS: In South Africa, were you in contact with church people involved in anti-apartheid activities or support to the black community, like Trevor Huddleston?

GH: Oh, yes. Trevor and I were very good friends. He stayed not far from the place where I lived in Sophiatown. He built the first swimming-pool for black people in South Africa. The white people had swimming pools all over the place. The Anglican Church and the Church of Sweden are very much alike. We had much in common. There were protests when they destroyed Sophiatown and took it away from the natives. Tingsten and I had been to see Dr A.B. Xuma, who lived there. He was one of the ANC leaders. I met him several times and I took Tingsten to meet him in Sophiatown. He had quite a fine villa, which was confiscated. He was chased out. He stayed only a hundred yards from my place in Doornfontein. He did not live there, but he had his clinic there.

TS: So when Tingsten was in South Africa he actually met leaders from ANC?

GH: Yes, he met Xuma at least. I do not know if he met anybody else. I do not think so.

TS: When you came back to Sweden in 1956, how did you find the Swedish opinion compared to when you left?

GH: It had changed very much. People phoned me from everywhere, asking me to come and speak about apartheid. Folk high schools, university clubs, churches and so on. Social Democratic and Liberal organizations asked me to come and speak. I gave a tremendous lot of speeches, sometimes two a day.

TS: At that time, 'Pik' Botha served in the South African legation in Stockholm. In an interview, he said that it was a very sudden introduction to a critical and hostile world. He mentioned yourself, Harrie and Tingsten as opinion makers around South Africa and apartheid. Did you have any contacts with 'Pik' Botha when he was in Sweden? Was he active in the debate?

GH: No, no. But there was another. I think that his name actually was Malan. He was senior. They wrote articles. There was one paper which was on their side, *Nordvästra Skånes Tidningar*, which almost daily persecuted me in its editorials.

TS: Who wrote these articles? Journalists?

GH: Yes, local journalists, but they could also use articles from the South African legation. Actually, the legation spread stencilled papers in my congregation in Karlskoga. I was a vicar in Karlskoga from 1958, when I could not go back to South Africa. They got the addresses through the telephone directory. They sent out a lot of papers saying that I was a Communist. I was employed by the Soviet Union to undermine the white Christian civilisation in South Africa, and so on. They tried to make life difficult for me, but I sent the papers to the Ministry for Foreign Affairs and they spoke to the South African government. The ministry gave them a good telling off and they stopped it. I do not think that anybody believed them in Karlskoga, but they did their best.

TS: When the South Africans raised the question of the Sami in Norway and Sweden in the United Nations, one of the newspapers that they were quoting was *Nordvästra Skånes Tidningar*.

GH: Oh, yes. That is right. They were on their side. And *Missionsbaneret* or whatever it was called. I think that it was a weekly, published by the Holiness Union Mission. They also wrote articles. Not so crude, but anyway. They were on the South African side.

TS: After you had been in Sweden some years, Chief Luthuli was awarded the Nobel Peace Prize. I understand that you were involved in that?

GH: Yes, I had thought of it and found it a jolly good idea. My friend Olof Tandberg, the Foreign Secretary in the Royal Swedish Academy of Sciences, and I spoke about what we could do for South Africa. He had been to South Africa a short time, but the authorities stopped him from working there. He said: 'I think that Luthuli should have the Nobel Peace Prize'. I said that it was a brilliant idea and asked if I could speak on the radio. They let me do so. I also wrote articles, first in *Handelstidningen* and later in other newspapers, and I gave speeches. I also wrote to Evert Svensson, a member of parliament, because we had to have a MP to put a formal proposal to the Norwegian Nobel Committee. Svensson was a Social Democrat and a member of *Broderskapsrörelsen* (The Brotherhood Movement).

TS: You were also one of the founders of the South Africa Committee in 1961?

GH: Yes, and I proposed that Joachim Israel should be the chairman. I became the chairman after him. But we had also formed another committee in 1959. That was the Defence and Aid Committee in Sweden. I was the chairman and Per Wästberg and Eyvind Johnson, who in 1974 was awarded the Nobel Prize in Literature together with Harry Martinsson, were founding members. At first we were only three. All three of us had to sign the remittances to the Defence and Aid Fund in London. In the beginning, it received small donations through church and street collections and things like that. Later SIDA started to send money. We then enlarged the committee and ambassador Ernst Michanek, Anna-Lena Wästberg and Olof Tandberg were included in the Swedish Defence and Aid Committee.

I was also vice-chairman of the International Defence and Aid Fund in London for many years. Sweden gave as much as all other countries put together to IDAF.

TS: How many IDAF correspondents did you then have in Sweden?

GH: We had at least five or six in Sweden at that time. Also in Norway, where we had Kari Storhaug and her husband. Anna-Lena Wästberg and several others were in Sweden. We tried to keep it as secret as possible and would not tell each other about those things unnecessarily. We kept it secret. It was very confidential. But, of course, we had our enemies, such as Lars-Gunnar Eriksson, a Swedish fellow. He was a traitor. He worked for the South African racist government, in their interest, and for Craig Williamson, who was a spy for the secret service in South Africa. Eriksson tried to get things out of me. He phoned me and said that he was interested in Defence and Aid, that he had many contacts and that he wanted to know how we sent the money out. I said: 'I know nothing. Nothing!' But he said: 'I want to get in touch with Canon Collins. We could work very nicely together. We also have some money that we could send through you.' I said: 'We do not do anything. We know nothing!'

TS: What could they contribute?

GH: Well, they said that they had many contacts, that they knew people in South Africa and that they had their sources of money. The Social Democratic Party in Sweden sent them money. So did the Swedish students' organizations. They used Lars-Gunnar Eriksson as a channel. I am sure that monies went to the other side, to the South African secret service or whatever. They tried to get into IDAF, but they never managed. Then there was a burglary in London. The South African secret service was seen there. Those who were from South Africa recognized them. The Defence and Aid office was broken into, but they did not find any papers, because they were hidden at another place. I know that they got hold of one fellow who squealed about something, so one of our agents in South Africa was arrested when he was going to the family of a black prisoner. He was jailed. I do not know his name, but I know that there was one who they caught. Otherwise they did not catch us down there. But they did terrible things. Ruth First, who was one of our workers, was killed by a letter bomb in Maputo.

TS: When you started campaigning in Sweden, in what sectors did the solidarity for South Africa find support?

GH: Well, it was among the students, of course. We held many demonstrations. We travelled and talked in Jönköping, Sundsvall and what not. Of course, the political organizations, Social Democrats, Liberals and also the Centre Party were very much on our side. Many clergymen were also on our side. Perhaps the audiences were not always on my side, but most of them were and when they heard about how the natives were treated they were horrified and made donations. The Church of Sweden made official collections for the Defence and Aid Fund.

TS: For your Swedish Defence and Aid Committee or IDAF?

GH: Both. All the money that we got went through us to London. We did not use any money. We worked through IDAF. When SIDA came in, it was useless to stand on the street corners and collect a hundred Kronor a day. We only had to tell SIDA: 'We need another million, or ten'. What we worked for was a boycott against South Africa. To make the Swedish government boycott South Africa.

TS: You were very critical of the non-action by the Swedish government. You wrote in *Örebrokuriren* in 1966 and talked about South Africa as our 'ideological lap-dog', an ideological little pet that you could feel sorry for, but that you did not do anything for in practical terms. There was a Social Democratic government in Sweden at that time. Do you think that there was a generation gap between people like Palme and Schori and the old guard under Prime Minister Erlander?

GH: I knew Erlander very well. I was not a member of any political party, but at a demonstration in Örebro in 1965 Erlander and I marched together with Oliver Tambo, who was giving a speech which I should translate. I had lunch with Erlander. He was very friendly and understanding. Palme was quite different: 'We shall not postpone; we shall not be the last ones; we should go out fully.' Yes, there was a change of generations. Erlander was friendly and understanding, but he was not fiery.

TS: Your criticism in that article was very heavy against the government of the day.

GH: Yes. I thought that they did not do anything about the boycott.

TS: What do you think made Palme involved in Southern Africa?

GH: Well, he was very radical in every respect. As soon as he saw that something in his opinion was wrong, he did something about it. He called them names, you know. He was like that. In every respect. Cuba, Vietnam etc. I did not always agree with him, but he caught on to the African issue straight away.

TS: In the early 1960s, the first refugees from South West Africa and South Africa came to Sweden, people like Zed Ngavirue and Billy Modise. There were also the first visits by Oliver Tambo. Did you involve these people in your work?

GH: Well, I met Oliver Tambo, of course, and Billy Modise. I met Tambo every time I went to London. I went there twice a year. Tambo was also in Sweden quite often. When he fell ill he was taken to Ersta Hospital in Stockholm. We were quite friendly. We went hand in hand in the South African way. It sounds funny in Sweden. You might suspect something wrong, but the South Africans do that!

TS: In December 1961, ANC launched the armed struggle together with the South African Communist Party. This introduced two new dimensions, the armed struggle and a closer alliance with the Communist Party. How did you look upon this?

GH: I had no objection. I admired Luthuli and his line had been 'violence under no circumstances'. That is why he could be nominated for the Nobel Peace Prize. That was the main thing. But later he said: 'I have been knocking on a closed door for year after year. I could not use violence myself, but I cannot any longer condemn those who advocate the use of violence. I agreed with that. You had to defend yourself. The whites used violence all the time and I think that it was right to use violence to defend yourself. It did not horrify me at all. I very much remember that Mandela never advocated violence against persons. It was only sabotage against buildings and railways and things like that.

Of course, I disapprove of Communism, but I had known many Communists in South Africa and they were not Stalinists. They were like the Swedish Communists. You could have them in furnished rooms, but I could not possibly vote for them. I asked Luthuli and he said: 'I would ally with the devil himself if that could help.' I also said so to Malan at the South African legation in Stockholm. I said that 'I am against Communism altogether, but it is a bit better than your form of racism'. He probably used that against me. I think that Communism in South Africa is not of the dangerous type.

TS: You were leading the solidarity movement and at a certain point ANC launched the armed struggle within a closer alliance with the Communist Party. Did that affect the solidarity work and the response by the people in Sweden?

GH: Not at all. Of course, it was used by our opponents. They said: 'What about the Communists?' I said that 'they are a minority and they will not dominate. ANC is not a political party. It is a movement with one single goal, namely to eliminate racism. They would use anybody, even Communists. But the Communists that I have seen in South Africa are not violent'. I cannot imagine old Alfred Nzo, for instance, sending people to concentration camps or anything like that. Or Joe Slovo. No, I did not worry about that.

TS: In 1969, the Swedish Parliament paved the way for direct official Swedish support to the liberation movements in the Portuguese territories, Rhodesia, South West Africa and South Africa. In the case of South Africa, the support was from the beginning of the 1970s channelled by SIDA to ANC. Why did Sweden not support PAC too?

GH: I found PAC a bit racist, black racist. They did not want to have any white members, really. ANC was absolutely neutral when it came to colour. Indian, white or black. Of course, 95 per cent of the members were blacks, but still. PAC was not neutral. If we strove for a South Africa as Luthuli and Mandela wanted it—where all people would work together irrespective of colour—I did not think that PAC was the thing to support.

TS: PAC was strongly anti-Communist. Swedish policies were also anti-Communist and very critical of the Soviet Union, which supported ANC. Still, Sweden put all its eggs in the ANC basket. Why was not part of the support given to PAC?

GH: In the Defence and Aid Fund we did not like PAC very much. Canon Collins did not like it and I did not, because they had made some expressions of a racist character. I did not think that it was the right thing to work for.

I was against Communism, but apartheid was so big for me. It was bigger than anything else and anybody who fought against it was my ally. I had no reason to look for faults in those who fought against apartheid. And I thought for myself that when it comes to a free election, the Communists will be very unimportant in South Africa. We have a strong leadership. Those at the top were never Communists. Luthuli was not, nor was Oliver Tambo or Mandela. Joe Slovo was nearest to the top, but the main stream was democratic or social democratic. The fact that they had some Communists in ANC was not enough to condemn it.

I have five children and I suppose that they look left or right. One daughter was very engaged in the Cabora Bassa question. She still votes Communist, although she is church-going and a capitalist. It is an old habit. It does not worry me, really. I could not possibly vote for racism, but I can, theoretically, understand the Communist idea. That people should own everything and so on. Theoretically, it is not against Christianity. Obviously, the way in which it formed Eastern Europe is terrible, but theoretically it is not wrong.

TS: In South Africa it is quite common that people are both Communist and Christian?

GH: Oh, yes.

TS: All the Southern African liberation movements that Sweden supported were close to the Soviet Union and they all waged an armed struggle. Did you discuss that in the Consultative Committee on Humanitarian Assistance?

GH: No, we did not. We were not scared about that. I think that all of us were so dominated by the question of quenching apartheid. That was so important that we did not care who our ally was.

TS: Another question that comes to mind is, of course, the question of Inkhata and Gatsha Buthelezi. He had a close relationship with the Church of Sweden Mission, did he not?

GH: Yes. I know Buthelezi very well. He stayed with me here in Västerås. He is a scoundrel. But Ernst Michanek believed in Buthelezi. He thought that it was possible to talk to Buthelezi and Buthelezi put pressure on him. Buthelezi said that he was a good Christian, which he is not, indeed. Anyway, Michanek thought that we should arrange a meeting between Tambo and Buthelezi so that they perhaps could be reconciled and stop this strife in South Africa. He phoned me and said that this must be done secretly. 'We cannot do it in Stockholm. We want somewhere out in the country, a quiet place. What about your home?' I then lived in the dean's house. We had 600 m^2, so I said: 'OK. Certainly, Buthelezi and his ministers can stay with us'. He was here for a few days, perhaps a week.

TS: Do you remember what year that was?

GH: It must have been around 1978. He came with three of his ministers. A journalist leaked it to the radio. Then Oliver Tambo did not dare to come, because he would be considered a traitor if he met Buthelezi on friendly terms. So, he left.

Buthelezi felt that he had some sort of obligation to my wife and myself, so in 1991 when I for the first time in 35 years was allowed back to South Africa he invited me and my wife to come and stay with him for a couple of days as his guests, not in his home, but in a hotel of which he was a director in Ulundi. We had lunch with de Klerk and the Zulu king and two of the Zulu king's wives. This was when the Zulu parliament opened. De Klerk was speaking there. I met him and King Zwelithini, who is a silly young boy. He can tell left from right, but that is all he can do.

I had met Buthelezi on some other occasion in Sweden and I understood that it was impossible to trust that fellow. He is hungry for power. You cannot trust his word. He is as sly as a fox. He wants all the money he can get from Pretoria and he would want to be a real king. I do not like him. I do not trust him at all.

TS: When he was with you here in Västerås, how did he look upon Sweden's involvement in Southern Africa?

GH: We did not speak much about that, really. I did not know him well enough to suspect that he was not on our side. I thought that it was obvious that a black man should like our involvement against apartheid. He did not speak much about that. He probably avoided it. I heard about his traitorous movements afterwards. He advocated that there should be no boycott against South Africa and so on. No, we did not speak about that. I speak Zulu and we had a lot of fun, talking about old habits, Zululand and what not.

TS: When you were on the Consultative Committee on Humanitarian Assistance, at some stage you also participated in official negotiations between Sweden and ANC. Were you satisfied with the way in which the Swedish funds were utilized?

GH: I do not know how the ANC money was used, although, of course, I read the reports about the schools in Tanzania, the Zambian farms and so on. However, I am satisfied that the money that went through IDAF was used very, very well. We had some small conflicts with Collins. He was a bit too generous to people who had fled from South Africa, also supporting them in England. Otherwise, I am definitely sure that the money was used very well.

TS: Are you also satisfied that the Swedish support was used for humanitarian, civilian purposes and not for the military struggle?

GH: I have not heard of any incidents where it was used for military purposes. I do not think so. I really do not think that it was used for anything like that. I am almost sure.

TS: Humanitarian support is also support for human rights. In the liberation movements there were instances of internal strife and abuse. I am thinking of the so-called Shipanga affair in SWAPO in Zambia in the late 1970s and also of both ANC and SWAPO in Angola in the 1980s. Do you know if the Swedish government discussed this? Did the Consultative Committee on Humanitarian Assistance recommend that this should be discussed with Tambo and Nujoma?

GH: I heard that Nujoma—who I also met—and Tambo, all the leaders, were against this and had strongly criticized those who had done these things. That was enough for us. Of course, you always have such garbage in every movement, but it was not so serious that it was necessary to take it up with the government.

TS: Do you know of any pressures by the USA, Great Britain or others on Sweden to stop the support to the liberation movements?

GH: I do not know of any pressures, but I know that all that we did in the Defence and Aid Fund was strongly opposed by the British government. We did not ever get a penny from them. They were against all that we did. Of course, now they try to take some credit for what they did not do. The US government too. They were more sympathetic in the USA, but not enough. We were quite unique, but I was really amused when I saw that the former conservative Minister for Foreign Affairs, Margaretha af Ugglas, went to South Africa and took credit for things she had opposed the whole time. She was on the SIDA board, but voted against everything that had anything to do with South Africa.

TS: In terms of political currents, would it then be fair to say that it was Liberals and Social Democrats that carried the solidarity movement in Sweden?

GH: Yes, there is no doubt about that.

TS: And the Centre Party?

GH: They were very sympathetic.

TS: As well as the Communist Party?

GH: Yes, of course. But we never dealt with them in Sweden. We never had anything to do with the Communists. We had to draw the line somewhere.

TS: So, those who were opposed were in the Moderate Party?

GH: Yes, and, of course, the industrial leaders.

Carl-Henrik ('C.H.') Hermansson
Chairman of the Swedish Communist Party and of the Left Party Communists
(Stockholm, 22 November 1996)

Tor Sellström: You were the chief editor of *Ny Dag*—the official newspaper of the Swedish Communist Party—from 1959 to 1964, that is, when the question of apartheid South Africa became a political issue in Sweden. At the time, most voices against apartheid were raised from the liberal camp, while both the Communist and the Social Democratic Parties played a less active role. How would you explain this?

Carl-Henrik ('C.H.') Hermansson: Internationally, the apartheid problem had been taken up rather early by the World Peace Council and also by the Communist parties. I remember that the Moscow Declaration from 1960 mentioned the struggle against apartheid as one important problem. In Sweden, however, it is right that it was mostly liberal opinion makers who raised the problem. I think that it had to do with the rather big influence of the free churches on the Swedish liberal movement. It was composed of two parts, one influenced by the free churches and the other by political liberals. Some of the people writing about apartheid, like David Wirmark and Gunnar Helander, belonged to the free church tradition.

There were many international problems during these years, many oppressed peoples and many liberation movements. The question arose which problem we should take up and try to make visible to the Swedish people, and around which it was possible to have a mass movement. I think that other problems were in the fore front for us during these years. There was, of course, the war in Vietnam, but also the democratic movement against the military junta in Greece and, later, the struggle in Chile, to take some examples. Also in Africa there were many important problems. We had long discussions in the party around which position to take on Eritrea. We supported the movements in the former French colonies—especially in Algeria—for their liberation, and so on. We were a small party, and it was not possible to take up all the problems in our general propaganda and action plan.

We also had a sort of division of labour between the party and our youth movement.

They raised some problems and the party others. During these years, we supported the World Peace Council. We worked very actively in the Swedish Peace Committee, which formed part of the World Peace Council, and in that forum we took up many questions. They spoke for us in many cases.

If you go to the parliamentary work, we were a very small group. We had very few people working for us. For example, only one secretary for all the things that we had to take up. For some years we only had four members of parliament. They should also carry out general propaganda for the party, attend meetings around the country, and so on. We also had the practice that we should not take up the same proposals every year, so some years important proposals were left out. That must be borne in mind when one looks at the party proposals and motions made in different years.

I must also confess that our knowledge of the problems was not as great as it should have been. We had no possibilities of sending journalists to different countries. When I was chief editor of *Ny Dag*, we sent for the first time a journalist to Africa. It was Sture Källberg, who now is a rather well known author. But we could only give him a couple of hundred Swedish Kronor. However, he managed on that and wrote a lot of articles for the paper. That was the first time that we had the possibility to go to Africa and get firsthand information on what was going on.

TS: The influence of the churches appears to have been important. The first anti-apartheid voices in the Social Democratic movement were also from people close to the Brotherhood Movement, that is the Christian Social Democrats?

CHH: That is right. Through Swedish missionaries in Africa they had knowledge of the problems, which was very important.

I think that the reasons why leaders like Oliver Tambo and Eduardo Mondlane turned to Sweden for international support had to do with the religious tradition of the free churches. Of course, it also had to do with the position of Sweden as a non-aligned country. At the time of the Cold War—when the blocs were standing against each other—it was a channel available to them. That was probably the main reason why they contacted Swedish political groups.

TS: You became chairman of the Communist Party in 1964 and soon embarked upon an independent course vis-à-vis Moscow, reorganizing the party as the Left Party Communists in 1967. In your book *The Road of the Left*—published in 1965—you stressed non-traditional Communist issues, such as the question of poverty in the Third World. Did Third World issues play a major role in the process leading to the subsequent break with the Communist Party of the Soviet Union (CPSU)?

CHH: At that moment—in 1964-67—the international position of the Soviet Union did not play a decisive role. It was the question of independence that was decisive for us. But later it did play a role, because we very soon found that the CPSU played a rather egoistic role in many international questions. We were therefore careful not to mechanically take the same stand as the Soviet Union and the CPSU on international questions.

TS: But it seems that the questions of exploitation, oppression and poverty in the Third World had a significant influence on your own thinking?

CHH: Yes, they really did. In that respect, there was also a break with the official positions of the CPSU. In the Moscow Declaration of 1960, the struggle against apartheid was mentioned, but we did not think that it was taken up in the right way. It was rather seen as a power game and not approached from the position of the millions of people who suffered from starvation and oppression.

TS: When did the Swedish Communist Party/Left Party Communists establish direct bilateral relations with the South African Communist Party (SACP)? Many leading SACP members visited Sweden from the early 1960s, but it would appear that they did so under the ANC umbrella and not as party members?

CHH: I think that the first time we had bilateral contacts with the South African Communist Party was as late as in 1966, during an international conference on Namibia in Oxford in which Olof Palme also took part. Our party secretary, Urban Karlsson, was at the conference and there he met Ruth First. Before that we had no bilateral contacts.

There were contacts at the World Peace Council, but that was not at the party level. In the 1950s, I was myself a representative of our party in the World Peace Council. I visited the headquarters in Prague. There were people from South Africa, but we had no formal bilateral relations.

I think that the reason why the SACP members who visited Sweden did not make direct contacts with us was that they wanted to have a broad political platform. They came here as representatives of ANC, not as representatives of the party. For ANC it was, of course, most important to have contacts with the ruling party. They also knew our position, so that was not a problem.

TS: From the mid-1960s, official Swedish humanitarian support to Southern Africa was extended on the advice of a Consultative Committee on Humanitarian Assistance, chaired by the Director General of SIDA and composed of both officials and members of political parties and non-governmental organizations. The Left Party Communists was never represented on the committee. How did you look upon that? How would you describe your relations with SIDA?

CHH: Well, during these years, the policy of the government was to keep our party outside such structures. I do not even remember if we knew of the existence of the committee. But our relations with SIDA were very good. Different Director Generals from SIDA came to our parliamentary group to speak about their positions and proposals. In that way, we also had the opportunity of giving them our views, but we did not know of this committee. If we had known about it, we would perhaps have demanded to be represented there.

TS: As leader of the Left Party Communists, you introduced parliamentary motions in favour of unconditional official Swedish assistance to the CONCP alliance between 1968 and 1972. Why did you advocate support to CONCP and not to the individual member organizations, that is, PAIGC of Guinea-Bissau, MPLA of Angola and FRELIMO of Mozambique?

CHH: I do not remember exactly, but we probably thought that it was more neutral to support the CONCP co-ordinating body and not get involved with the individual movements. It was also a question of the possible support you could mobilize in the Swedish parliament. Perhaps we assessed that it was easier to raise support for CONCP than directly to the liberation movements.

It was very important for us that the support should be unconditional. It should be given to the liberation movements without any restrictions. In our opinion, they should, for example, have the possibility of buying arms—all that they needed in their struggle—with the Swedish assistance. The support given by Sweden was not always unconditional.

TS: In the 1960s, did the Communist Party/Left Party Communists carry out its own support activities for the national liberation movements in Southern Africa or did you give preference to the work within the broader solidarity movement?

CHH: Our youth movement had already taken part in campaigns before the famous tennis match against Rhodesia in 1968, with the demonstrations in Båstad. There was a match against South Africa in the early 1960s against which it made propaganda, for example. Some of our support to the liberation movements was given in that form.

There was a very broad youth movement in Sweden during these years and our youth participated in the anti-apartheid campaigns by the National Council of Swedish Youth (SUL). We gave priority to the broader solidarity work and later on many of our members took an active part in the Africa Groups and the Isolate South Africa Committee (ISAK).

TS: You were, however, active yourself at an early stage. In January 1965 you signed a parliamentary motion demanding economic sanctions against South Africa. The Communist Party was thus together with the Centre Party the first to raise this demand.

CHH: Yes, that was during my first year as leader of our parliamentary group. Sanctions had been demanded by the Swedish youth movement since 1963, so we did not wake up so late after all.

TS: No, you did not. But why did the Swedish labour movement in general wake up late regarding sanctions?

CHH: I think that the reason why it took so long was the influence of Swedish capital in South Africa. Many of the big Swedish companies had subsidiaries in South Africa and they carried out an intense propaganda against sanctions, pointing out possible loss of work opportunities in Sweden. It probably made the Social Democratic Party—especially the trade union congress—cautious in these matters.

In those days, the chairman of the Swedish Trade Union Confederation (LO), Arne Geijer, was also the head of the social democratic ICFTU, the International Confederation of Free Trade Unions. That was important. The American trade unions were very strong within ICFTU and Geijer was more or less a victim of their interests. That could explain the position of the Swedish trade unions.

TS: In this respect, do you think that Olof Palme made a difference within the Social Democratic movement?
CHH: Yes. There was a change in policy and opinion of the Social Democratic Party when Palme became Prime Minister. It was very clear.

TS: Palme made several of his most radical statements at congresses of the Christian Social Democratic Brotherhood Movement, such as the speech on Vietnam in Gävle in 1965 and the demand for sanctions against South Africa in Skövde in 1976. Do you think that he did so for tactical reasons within the wider social democratic movement?
CHH: Yes, because there he had support at once. It would have been much more difficult for him to get support at the party or trade union congresses. The Brotherhood Movement always took a very progressive stand on international problems. But, still, there was the problem of the international interests of Sweden's finance capital, which one must bear in mind to understand the whole picture.

Lena Hjelm-Wallén
Social Democratic Party—Minister of Education and of International Development Cooperation
Minister for Foreign Affairs
(Stockholm, 14 January 1997)

Tor Sellström: When did you come into contact with Africa for the first time?
Lena Hjelm-Wallén: It was during my years in Uppsala, between 1962 and 1965, when I studied social sciences at the university. Through the Social Democratic student association Laboremus I met a lot of people with a big commitment for Africa and the end of colonialism. In Uppsala, I also met people from Africa for the first time. In Sala, the small town where I was born, there were not many Africans.
TS: Did you meet Eduardo and Janet Mondlane then? They visited Uppsala in 1964.
LHW: Many people came to Uppsala and I think that the Mondlanes were among them. After my years in Uppsala, I was active in the Social Democratic Youth League (SSU), and in 1967 I went to Tanzania on a study visit with twelve others from SSU.
TS: Did you go there with Ingvar Carlsson?

LHW: No, he had been there before. It was not just the leadership of SSU, but people from different districts and the head office.
TS: Were you then a SSU leader in the province of Västmanland?
LHW: No, I was a rather ordinary member. During the visit to Tanzania we met Julius Nyerere. It was something special to go to the rural areas, meet the people in the villages and also the Tanzanian leaders, not least Nyerere.

We went to Tanzania as a follow-up of SSU's Tanganyika Action. We had collected money for the TANU Youth League. I will never forget the meetings in the rural areas, where the people thanked us. I remember an old man. Of course, he spoke Swahili so I had to ask what he said. He said that 'these young people from up there somewhere have collected money, but they are rather poor, so they had to find other means. They therefore went to hospitals to give blood'. In his rhetoric, he said: 'They gave their blood for us'. That, of course, received a lot of applause.

I was also involved in the solidarity movement with Mozambique. When I was nominated to become a member of parliament in 1968, I was very young and not well known. I was then attacked by the trade unions in Västmanland for wanting to stop ASEA from the Cabora Bassa project. It came to a vote and I won, but I could have lost my parliamentary seat due to my involvement with Africa. It was an interesting start.

TS: In the early days of the Swedish anti-apartheid movement, many liberal intellectuals and church people were actively involved. Some say that the anti-apartheid opinion really started in the liberal centre and not in the wider labour movement. Do you think that it is a correct description?

LHW: To describe it correctly, I would say that it did not start in any particular movement at all, but with individuals. Some of them were members of the churches or established organizations and there were many who can be described as liberals. But rather early you also had people such as Ernst Michanek, so it would not be correct to say that there were just Liberals or church people. There were also Social Democrats and people from the trade unions. But it started with individuals much more than organizations. They came later, in the 1960s. However, debate is one thing and how you form an opinion another. In the 1950s, we had boycott actions. My mother, for example, was a member of the Social Democratic women's organization which participated in consumer boycotts. That was a broader concept. There you had the Social Democratic Party and the wider labour movement involved.

TS: How would you assess Olof Palme's early role in connection with the liberation process in Southern Africa?

LHW: I think that he enlightened a lot of people as he at a very early stage saw what was important. He saw the future. In the middle of the 1950s, he was study secretary of SSU and in that capacity he met a lot of people. He went to different meetings, trying to get people interested in not just our own history and future, but also international matters, so, of course, he meant a lot. Within SSU, he gave much inspiration.

TS: Sweden supported liberation movements that waged an armed struggle and were also assisted by the Soviet Union or China. How would you explain that there was a broad parliamentary majority for such a policy?

LHW: In the first place, we wanted to live up to one of the goals of Sweden's development policy, namely the principle of national self-determination. It was based on a unanimous decision in the Swedish parliament and the liberation struggle was about that. Secondly, we never gave direct support to the armed struggle. As we were so clear about that, we were never asked by the liberation movements to do so. In addition, it was easy for them to get weapons from others.

Sometimes you have to avoid relations with organizations or persons that have contacts with, or are allied to, forces that you do not like, but that was not a major problem in this connection. We were a neutral country and could cooperate with both sides. Of course, at times there were discussions in Sweden. We were now and then accused of coming too close to what the Communists wanted, but that was rather an internal Swedish debate and never very big. The support for the liberation movements in Southern Africa was much broader than the Social Democratic Party. We had support for this policy deep within the non-socialist parties and in the solidarity movement.

TS: Do you think that the early contacts established with visiting Southern African leaders like Mondlane, Tambo and others made it easier to see their nationalist visions?

LHW: In general, I think that all personal contacts are very important, not least when you have to work across such big geographical distances and you do not know so much about the countries and the areas. It then becomes very important to be able to trust the leaders of the organizations involved. It has really been fantastic to see how the liberation movements in Southern Africa fostered outstanding leaders all the time. They were tremendous people and it made it easier for us to trust them and their organizations.

There were many moments when we had a special closeness to ANC and SWAPO. One example which I personally remember very well is when we had Oliver Tambo at the Ersta clinic outside Stockholm during his illness. I remember what it was like to be there, just sitting with him, holding his hand. He was lonely at Ersta and we tried to visit him as much as possible. Not many governments were so close to a leader of a liberation movement. To see Mandela and Tambo meet in Sweden after Mandela's release is, of course, also a beautiful and fantastic memory.

TS: When the Social Democratic Party lost the elections in 1976, many expected a great change in Sweden's policies towards the Southern African liberation movements. But it did not take place. The humanitarian support was maintained or increased and a first Swedish sanctions' law against South Africa was introduced. How can this be explained?

LHW: The Swedish solidarity movement with Southern Africa was much bigger than the Social Democratic Party. We welcomed that. Among the bourgeois parties, the Moderate Party opposed our policy now and then, but there was not much opposition from the Liberal and the Centre parties. When the Liberal and the Centre parties heard about the fears from our African friends, they were very eager to show that there should be no change. I think that they did a good job. They knew that if they had changed the policy, they would have had a real problem with the public opinion and, of course, in parliament. So, they continued our policy and the Moderate Party had to give up their plans to change it.

Another thing that played a role here was the way the Swedish support was administered. It was, of course, done by the government, but also by SIDA. You could argue whether such political matters should be handled by an official board, but in Sweden we did that and in the long run I think that it was very good. The change of government, for example, did not therefore play such an important role. We also had the Consultative Committee on Humanitarian Assistance, where all the time different parties were represented and informed, as well as experts and a lot of people who were engaged in Southern African issues. They strengthened each other and when the Liberal and Centre parties entered into the government, they already knew a lot about the Swedish support and it was easy for them to continue our policy, which was also the strategy we had from the beginning.

TS: Did you experience any strong domestic Swedish opposition to the support to the liberation movements in Southern Africa?

LHW: There were some journalists and conservative people that brought it up now and then. In parliament, there were also discussions with the Moderate Party from time to time, but it was not really a problem, because the public opinion was so solid.

TS: Sweden gave direct support to ANC from as early as 1973, but it took quite some time before sanctions were imposed against South Africa. Was it external factors—such as the position taken by the UN Security Council—or domestic factors—such as opposition by Swedish export interests and sometimes also the trade unions—that were the most important here?

LHW: We were very formal and strict on this point. It was the Security Council decision that we waited for. When it was taken, it was rather easy for us to take the same decision, although at that time we also had a debate. A lot of business people and also trade unionists were not positive to our action.

TS: You mentioned the advantages of delegating the administration of the humanitarian support to SIDA. Did you also experience problems with it? It was a highly political support, often carried out by junior aid officials.

LHW: The administration was carried out by SIDA, but there was always a lot of political guidance from the government. The SIDA leadership knew exactly what our policies were. In the field, we furthermore always had a lot of experienced diplomats together with the younger SIDA staff. I think that it was a good combination of experienced diplomats and those with a keen commitment. A good mix, I would say. When we worked with organizations such as IDAF, we knew that Per Wästberg was involved. Ernst Michanek was, of course, there all the time. They were people who we believed in and trusted totally. There was a network of people who trusted each other. I think that that was the most important. We tried to avoid making party politics out of the support.

TS: Were you also satisfied that the administrative routines regarding reporting and accounting of funds were appropriate and that SIDA had sufficient control over the funds?
LHW: We knew that the support must be kept secret. As we could not be open about it—there could not be an open discussion in the media about the channels and so forth—it was very important that the administration was based on trust. It was not just that SIDA handled the money in a correct way, but our partners had also to be trusted. It was a question of mutual interest. The liberation movements knew that even small doubts could destroy very much. Against this background, our partners were very strict, doing all that they could to satisfy our need to know who handled what. I think that there was mutual trust and interest between the donor and the recipients. But, of course, there were also problems as we know from the Craig Williamson affair in IUEF.
TS: Do you think that the Williamson affair affected Sweden's relationship with ANC?
LHW: No, not so much. It was a rather isolated incident, but I must confess that I did not know much about it at the time.
TS: There are always internal problems and divisions in any liberation movement and in the 1980s, for example, there was the so-called detainee issue in the SWAPO camps in Angola. Did you raise this issue with SWAPO or with the Angolan government?
LHW: Yes, in the late 1980s I raised it directly with SWAPO. I remember a discussion I had with Sam Nujoma. But we never discussed it with the Angolan government.
TS: The Swedish support to the liberation movements was often viewed with suspicion by the Western powers. Apart from general criticism, do you recall any pressures against Sweden in this connection?
LHW: They were questioning and perhaps suspicious, but not directly critical. Indirectly now and then, but we did not suffer from that.

Anders Johansson
Journalist and member of the Swedish South Africa Committee—Africa correspondent of *Dagens Nyheter*
Regional reporter of *Dagens Nyheter*
(Eskilstuna, 19 November 1996)

Tor Sellström: Why did you get involved with South and Southern Africa?
Anders Johansson: I believe that it has to do with my background and upbringing in an small Christian community in Västergötland. My parents belonged to the Free Baptist Union, a very small church with about 2,000 members. It was both an informal and a very strict church. All the men were pacifists, for example, so some of my relatives went to jail because they refused to do military service. This little church also sent missionaries to South Africa, Northern Rhodesia and Mozambique. Some of them were my relatives and they stayed quite a lot in my home. I got firsthand information from Africa from them. That, I believe, started my interest in Southern Africa.
TS: The South Africa Committee that you started in 1963 was situated in Jönköping, often called the 'Jerusalem of Sweden'. Do you think that your church connections facilitated the setting up of the committee?
AJ: No, not really. I had started to work as a journalist at *Jönköpingsposten* in 1960, when I was only about seventeen and a half. I was interested in international affairs in general and in Africa in particular. The South Africa Committee was set up in February 1963, just before the launch of the boycott campaign by the National Council of Swedish Youth (SUL). I had then done part of my non-armed civic service at the Arlanda International Airport in the spring of 1961. During my first ever visit to Stockholm, I attended a meeting on South Africa in May 1961. The speakers were Victor Vinde, Arvid Svärd, Gunnar Helander, Per Wästberg, Charles Kauraisa from Namibia and Herbert Tingsten. Tingsten received the biggest applause when he said that "it is not the negroes in South Africa who should

thank us, but we who should thank them for the enthusiasm and anger that they inspire".

TS: Would it be fair to say that the anti-apartheid opinion in Sweden started in the liberal camp?

AJ: Yes, I would agree with that. Several of these people were prominent Liberals. The Social Democrats joined later.

TS: When you started the Jönköping South Africa Committee, which issues did you raise?

AJ: It was the apartheid system and the oppression in South Africa. The more ideological and political implications of that came later. This was also the era of non-violence. You had Albert Luthuli in South Africa, but also Martin Luther King in America. It was the spirit of the early 1960s.

TS: But ANC took a decision to initiate armed struggle. Was that a problem in your solidarity work?

AJ: I remember that we had a lot of discussions about that. The different South Africa Committees in Sweden had several meetings where we discussed how we could prepare the public opinion for the forthcoming violence in South Africa. You had this background of non-violence put forward by Luthuli. At the same time you had ANC speakers in Sweden who talked about a revolution. We discussed how we could prepare the public opinion for this change. In the Swedish South Africa Committee we discussed various statements—which we at that time did not make public—to the effect that we supported the liberation movements on their own conditions.

TS: Being a pacifist yourself, was it not a problem for you?

AJ: It was a great problem, of course, both with my Christian background and being a pacifist. It created a lot of contradictory emotions.

TS: At a very early stage, you and the different South Africa Committees established close relations with ANC. Did you not have contacts with PAC?

AJ: No, our contacts were mainly with ANC. The first ANC person that I remember—and who I met personally—was Duma Nokwe. Later there was Raymond Kunene from the ANC London office and, of course, Billy Modise, who was a very influential student in Lund and who participated in our public meetings and internal discussions. He was a major source of inspiration. We also had contacts with Abdul Minty, Ruth First and others. One contact led to another and it was not difficult to create a network. It was, however, mainly with ANC. Going through my files, I found that I had written a letter to PAC, asking for information about their struggle, but apparently I did not even get a reply.

TS: Many of the early ANC visitors to Sweden, such as Duma Nokwe and Arthur Goldreich, were also prominent members of the South African Communist Party. Did they appear publicly as members of the Communist Party or only as ANC?

AJ: As I remember, only as ANC. However, I do not recall any conflict regarding membership of the South African Communist Party. Besides, the main organizer of solidarity activities on a national scale apart from the Swedish South Africa Committee was SUL, which included the Communist Youth so, in principle, you could not have anything against that. But, for us they were ANC.

TS: So the question of Communism was not a divisive factor?

AJ: No, not among the local South Africa Committees. There were a lot of radical people, mainly in the Lund committee. In Jönköping, we mainly cooperated with the Lund committee, where there were some Communist members. But that was not the issue. We looked at what different individuals achieved in the solidarity work. For example, we had a conflict regarding the way the South Africa Committees should be organized in relation to SUL, which was a national organization including all kinds of people, from non-political organizations to the Communist Youth League. In the South Africa Committees, we wanted to build a strong unity between individuals who wanted to participate in solidarity work. In Jönköping, I think that we managed that. We both had organizations and individuals, mainly young students at the local secondary school, as members.

TS: You founded the Jönköping South Africa Committee just before the launch of the SUL campaign on 1 March 1963. The campaign was for a consumer boycott of South African goods. Did you not raise the issue of total sanctions against South Africa?

AJ: Yes, we did. We tried to hit at different Swedish companies, such as the Transatlantic shipping company in Gothenburg. The work developed from a consumer boycott to the demand for sanctions, but it is difficult to make a division between the two, because they were inter-connected. There was, for example, a close connection between the imports by different companies, how they were shipped to Sweden and sold to the consumers. However, what we described as our political enemies in Sweden were at that time often the trade unions, who sided with the companies against the South Africa Committees. There was a kind of unholy alliance between the trade unions and the export companies, and, of course, the trade unions also influenced the Social Democratic government in the beginning.

TS: Does this also mean that you did not have Social Democratic activists in the local South Africa Committees?

AJ: Yes, we did, but they were in opposition to the party leadership, where you had people like Torsten Nilsson and Kaj Björk. They were the people that we mostly had to argue with about sanctions. They kept a very strict legal line, maintaining that sanctions had to be imposed by the UN Security Council and not by individual governments, which we demanded.

TS: Did you find Olof Palme more receptive to your demands? Was he involved with South and Southern Africa?

AJ: Yes, he was. I think that he was the main force behind the change within the Social Democratic Party, for example, on the issue of Cabora Bassa later in the 1960s. We did not have many discussions with him, but he must have been quite influential for the change.

Quite early, we also saw the need of direct discussions between people coming from Southern Africa—not only South Africa, but also Rhodesia, for example—and we set up meetings between them and Social Democratic politicians such as Sten Andersson, Arne Geijer and Anders Thunborg, who was then the party secretary for international affairs and a member of the Swedish South Africa Committee.

TS: So your strategy was that the visitors from Southern Africa should meet the political leadership in Sweden?

AJ: Yes, of course. That was necessary. They were the people in power and they had to be influenced.

TS: At a very early stage, you corresponded with a number of ANC leaders and managed to have articles by them published in the Swedish newspapers. I am thinking of people such as Ronnie Kasrils, Ruth First and Joe Slovo. How did this come about?

AJ: It was through a network of contacts. I met Ruth First for the first time in January 1965 and I also came in contact with Kasrils. Apparently, they got to know that I not only had a platform on the South Africa Committee, but that I also was a journalist. They asked me for help to get the articles published and I did as much as I could. Sometimes we succeeded and sometimes not.

TS: One of the articles, I understand, was by Joe Slovo on the joint ANC-ZAPU 'Wankie campaign'?

AJ: That is right. It was published as quite a big feature in the Sunday edition of *Dagens Nyheter*. Actually, I managed to have articles by ANC people published in *Aftonbladet* in 1965, so it was not only in *Dagens Nyheter*.

TS: So, leading South African Communists wrote in Swedish Social Democratic and Liberal newspapers?

AJ: Yes, but we never introduced them as Communists. I do not even think that they used their correct names, but Ruth First was, of course, an authority on South African affairs by herself, not as a member of the Communist Party.

TS: During the first half of the 1960s, which were the forces in Sweden that were against the solidarity work?

AJ: The trade unions were quite a big force. Some of them were against us during the Cabora Bassa debate in the late 1960s. But the picture was not black or white. There were companies who cooperated with us and gave us information, for instance, in Jönköping. Among the trade unions, the Seamen's Union and others also gave us information about ships coming and going.

A major issue in 1964 concerned the Swedish missions in South Africa. On behalf of the Swedish South Africa Committee, we tried to organize a conference between the churches and the local South Africa Committees to discuss the fact that they cooperated with the regime in South Africa to be allowed to stay there and that they received assistance from the South African government for their social work. But the initiative failed. The most conservative mission societies, like the Swedish Alliance Mission and the Holiness Union refused to participate. The Swedish Alliance Mission was the strongest mission society in the Jönköping area and quite a strong local force against us. For me personally, this process created a division between myself and the church of my childhood, the Free Baptist Union. I broke with them and that was it. I believed that they cooperated too closely with the South African regime.

TS: Did you join another church?

AJ: No, I lost my faith, I guess, over South Africa.

TS: In the late 1960s, the first generation of solidarity organizations, the South Africa Committees, withered and died. New organizations—the Africa Groups—were formed in the 1970s. Why did the South Africa Committees disappear?

AJ: In my own case, I decided in 1965-66 to leave the Swedish South Africa Committee. Not because of a lack of interest or enthusiasm, but as a journalist I wanted to be impartial. Officially, I resigned from the board of the South Africa Committee in 1967. Working at *Dagens Nyheter*'s foreign news desk, I believed that you could not be a journalist and at the same time be active in an organization. However, by then I had established quite a good network with Africa. The same year, I was sent to cover the Six Day War between Israel and Egypt. I stayed for a month in Cairo, where there were a lot of important Southern Africans, like Andreas Shipanga from SWAPO of Namibia. He put me in touch with other interesting people from Southern Africa.

People were dropping out for several different reasons. Many activists in the South Africa Committees were students. They later got jobs and families, or were involved in other organizations. However, the main reason was, of course, that Africa became overshadowed by the developments in Indochina.

TS: Through the South Africa Committees, you had early contacts with Namibia. Do you recall your first contacts with SWAPO?

AJ: I think that it was in the mid-1960s. I do not remember exactly, but it must have been before meeting Andreas Shipanga in Cairo. I was quite influenced by some of the first members of the South Africa Committee in Lund. They were very clearsighted and saw at an early stage that SWAPO was a stronger force than SWANU. I wrote articles in that spirit in *Dagens Nyheter* and according to Shipanga I could be 'SWAPO's man in Sweden'. I do not know if that is true, but quite early we formed an opinion that SWAPO was a force to reckon with in Namibia.

TS: Later in the 1960s you got very involved with Mozambique, becoming the first Western journalist to visit the liberated areas in 1968, together with Eduardo Mondlane. How did you get in contact with FRELIMO?

AJ: I had met Mondlane in Stockholm in September 1965. At that time, I worked for a short time at *Aftonbladet*. I approached him as a journalist and interviewed him. Eduardo Mondlane and his wife Janet came quite often to Sweden. They became good friends with the then chief editor of *Dagens Nyheter*, Olof Lagercrantz. We met, and in January 1968 I went to Dar es Salaam to cover the official visit by Prime Minister Tage Erlander to Tanzania. I got an interview with President Nyerere and his permission to cross the border into Mozambique with FRELIMO together with Mondlane on his first visit ever to the liberated areas. Samora Machel and several other important FRELIMO leaders went on this mission. I was the first journalist to go there. Before me there had only been a Yugoslavian film crew.

TS: You published your impressions from that visit widely throughout the world?

AJ: Yes, *Dagens Nyheter* had a department which helped me with that. I also used my earlier contacts to distribute the information. I think that it was of particular interest at the time, because the view formed by the Portuguese propaganda was that FRELIMO was not a very important force and that they had no liberated areas in Mozambique. My articles had a news value. They turned the Portuguese propaganda upside down.

TS: At the same time, the Swedish company ASEA was bidding for the Cabora Bassa hydro-electrical project?

AJ: That came somewhat later. The main issue there was to prove that the electricity from Cabora Bassa would not only go to

South Africa, but also to Rhodesia, and I think that we were able to do that. Collecting different press cuttings and other information, I managed to put together a picture where it was apparent that Rhodesia was involved.

Together with some friends in the Lund South Africa Committee—Ulf Agrell and Lars-Erik Johansson—I had formed a 'South African Information Service', which we used as a cover to get information from official sources in Salisbury and Johannesburg. We wrote to different organizations and individuals in the name of the South African Information Service. That is how we managed to receive some interesting—and, as it turned out, important—information.

TS: As you recollect, how did other international journalists view the official Swedish support to the liberation movements in Southern Africa?

AJ: I do not think that it was a big issue, because it was not public. They did not know about it. Of course, Sweden was regarded as a friend of the Southern African liberation movements. That was obvious, but the extent of the support was not apparent. They regarded us as sympathizers.

TS: And the liberation movements, how did they look upon Sweden?

AJ: I think that some leaders could be critical, but, generally speaking, it was not the case. I remember many hot discussions where I—as an individual—criticized the Swedish government from a radical point of view, but was attacked for being critical of a friendly person like Olof Palme. I think that they in general were quite happy with what they received, but I sometimes wondered how close the relations really were. I recall, for example, that ANC during Olof Palme's visit to Zambia in 1971 had difficulties in making contact with him. They asked me, a private journalist, to act as middleman to set up a meeting between Oliver Tambo and Palme. I do not think that Palme did not want to meet Tambo, but, somehow, the Swedish diplomats' contacts were not what they should have been. It ended up with me contacting Pierre Schori, who organized a meeting between the two leaders.

TS: In 1976, the Social Democratic Party lost the elections and a non-socialist coalition government was formed. It continued the Social Democratic policy of support to the liberation movements and introduced the first sanctions law against South Africa in 1979. Why did it take such a long time to introduce sanctions? How come that the investments ban was introduced by a non-socialist government?

AJ: At that time, it was already in the pipeline and there was a great consensus among the Swedish politicians. The movement had started with the Liberals. The Social Democrats became active later. It was perhaps a surprise to the Africans that the assistance did not stop or was not reduced under the new government, but there was such a great force behind it in Sweden. I do not think that it was ever in question. In addition, perhaps the non-socialist parties were keen not to be seen as lagging behind the Social Democrats regarding the liberation process in Southern Africa.

Yes, it took a long time to introduce sanctions. At some stage, there were strong forces, like the trade unions against it and there were also the legal arguments about what the United Nations should do and not do. That has always played an important role in Swedish foreign policy.

TS: How would you describe the relationship between the NGO solidarity movement and the Swedish government?

AJ: I think that the early network was important. You had individual members of the South Africa Committees who later rose within the political establishment. It was mainly the case on the Social Democratic side, with people such as Birgitta Dahl and others. Quite early, they were active in these circles and later got important positions and responsibilities, and influenced the position taken by the Swedish government.

TS: The only country where there was a debate regarding the Swedish support to the liberation movements was Angola. The Liberal party advocated support to both FNLA and MPLA. How would you explain that Sweden only supported MPLA, which was considered to be close to the Soviet Union?

AJ: I was never really involved in Angola and I do not think that I have a good answer. However, the picture was not black or white. *Expressen*—a liberal paper—collected at a very early stage medicines for MPLA and later Liberals like Olle Wästberg tried to get the same paper to support FNLA. I also think that the old network played a role here. For example, if our ANC friends told us that MPLA was an important force, we trusted that.

TS: Finally, in the case of Zimbabwe you get the impression that ZAPU never really had a strong base in Sweden. It was less prominent than ZANU. Do you think that that is correct?

AJ: I think that it to a very great extent is correct and that it had to do with what they did on the ground. ZAPU had quite a strong leadership, but ZANU proved inside Zimbabwe that they were doing most of the fighting. Nobody could take that away from them. In exile, they also had strong representatives, while perhaps ZAPU's spokesmen were not always that good.

Tomas Ledin
Musician and solidarity organizer
(Stockholm, 18 March 1997)

Tor Sellström: You were one of the leading Swedish rock artists behind the gala in support of ANC in Gothenburg, Sweden, in November 1985. What was the background to the gala? Who took the initiative?

Tomas Ledin: If I remember correctly, the initiative came from Mikael Wiehe together with Björn Afzelius and Dan Hylander. Dan Hylander was the one who called and asked me if I was interested in a meeting with them and Lindiwe Mabuza, the ANC representative to Sweden. The Swedish rock scene was—in the media anyway—divided between commercial rock n' roll and alternative, more political rock n' roll. I was in their eyes in the commercial world, so they wanted to create a bridge. If we were the foundation, we could together get everybody involved. This was the idea.

It was a year or two after some really big concerts in England and the United States, such as the 'Live Aid' project initiated by Bob Geldof. There had been a lot of talk in Sweden that something should be done. We should use our influence as artists to both raise money, and awareness about an issue. I think that the idea that we should stage a gala for ANC and against apartheid came from Mikael Wiehe. I was aware of the situation in South Africa, of course, but I did not know in detail what ANC really stood for. I told them that I was quite interested, but that I wanted to do some research so that I really could stand up for the idea. I remember that I called *Expressen* and spoke to a political journalist who had been to South Africa and really had the knowledge. I realized quite soon that if we were going to make a difference, ANC was the right organization to support.

TS: What was significant about this gala was that it was not just for South Africa in general, but for ANC?

TL: Yes. There were, of course, those who said that it was too much to the left and that one should not go along with something so political. But through my talks with this journalist I felt that I had no problem in supporting it. It was for a very humanitarian cause. It was important to create a platform that a lot of artists could support. The strategy was that Mikael Wiehe and I jointly could bring a lot of artists together if we had a platform that was humanitarian.

I think that if you stand up for something, you must know why you are there. Then you can really work for it. My situation at that time was that I had stopped recording, touring and writing. I was very much working behind the scenes as an organizer. It was only towards the end, when everything looked so much fun, that I decided to be one of the artists and perform a couple of songs.

TS: You wrote the lead song, 'Mountains are to be moved'?

TL: Yes, Mikael Wiehe and I wrote it together. The first thing was to get all the artists to the studio and record it. It was quite easy. There were only a few who said that they did not want to participate. I do not think that it was for political reasons, but more for personal artistic reasons.

TS: I understand that you did this for free?

TL: I used all my powers to do this for free. We recorded the single in Polar Studios—which we own—so it was not a problem.

Also the people who made the cover and the art design worked for free and those who made the record worked for at least lower fees. For the actual concert, we went to EMA—the biggest concert promotor in Scandinavia, which also deals with a lot of the artists—and they said: 'OK, we will do this for free'. The whole idea was that everybody should work for free, so that we could raise as much money as possible.

TS: Do you know how much money you eventually raised?

TL: I think that it was around ten to twelve million Swedish Kronor.

TS: Was this money given to ANC without any strings attached?

TL: Yes, it was. A foundation was formed so that all the money could go straight to ANC. What was great was that during the work artists kept calling, wanting to join. More artists were added all the time, which, of course, was good for the spirit of the project.

TS: There were also some Danish artists?

TL: Yes, Sanne Salomonsen. I asked Mats Ronander if he wanted to join. They were living together at the time and Sanne said: 'I want to be there too'.

TS: How was the initiative received by the music industry and the press?

TL: It was, of course, discussed in the papers and by some people in the record business. Journalists who write about pop and rock music said that it was impossible: 'These artists cannot be on the same stage. They stand for different things in attitude, life style and political views, so this concert will not work'. But after the show everybody just loved it, even the journalists.

The concerts in Gothenburg were taped for TV, so we could sell the rights to get more money. We also got people to record the songs, so we could mix them. The problem was that we wanted to release the album the same day, which was impossible, of course. But Dan Hylander and I worked with two engineers around the clock. Twelve hours each and then we changed. We mixed the whole album in 48 hours. Then you have to consider that we taped two whole evenings and that we had to pick the right takes, which was a lot of work. The album was actually in the shops a week later and it sold very well. A couple of years ago, it was also released on CD and it is still selling.

TS: After the gala, you and some other Swedish artists—Py Bäckman, Eva Dahlgren and Dan Hylander—were invited by ANC to visit Tanzania, Zambia and Zimbabwe?

TL: I think that it was SIDA that made the invitation and wanted us to go. From what I understand, they wanted us to meet—in the flesh, so to speak—ANC people in Southern Africa. We were not aware of the significance until we came there. We then understood that it was important to keep spirits up. It was in every aspect a fantastic experience. It was also very moving, because we were not aware that what we had done in Sweden had had such an impact.

TS: Did you visit the ANC SOMAFCO school in Morogoro, Tanzania?

TL: Yes. It was a strange experience, because we landed in Dar es Salaam and nobody was there to pick us up. It took hours. It was really hot and we wondered what was going on. In the evening, a couple of guys came and presented themselves as being from the ANC. We took our trunks and went into a minibus and went away. We were told that we were going to a hotel in Dar es Salaam to stay one night before going to Morogoro. But instead they drove away from Dar es Salaam. After half an hour we got a little scared: 'What is going on here?' Then, suddenly, they stopped the car. I thought: 'Jesus, are they really ANC people? How do we know? Did they show any documents? No.' They stopped the car. It was completely black, totally silent and they did not say a thing. We got really scared. Maybe they were South Africans? For a moment, all of us thought that we were going to be taken out of the car, shot and left by the roadside. But then they turned around and said: 'We are really sorry. We have not arranged for the hotel. We do not have the money. So we are going up the coast, where you can stay really cheap'. And we said: 'No problem!'

They took us there and said that they were going to come back the following day, but they did not show up. We stayed there for two days. Nobody showed up. It was really difficult with telephones and communications in general. Finally, we managed to call the Swedish embassy. It was on a Saturday and they said that we had to wait until Monday, but we had air tickets for Tuesday, so we had to leave real fast for Morogoro. We said: 'Well, we are calling Pierre Schori right now and you'd better arrange this, otherwise he will get really upset'. An hour later we had a car. We never called him, of course. We just used his name to get the car.

Then we drove ourselves, without a map or anything, to Morogoro. I was driving and it was a bumpy road, I tell you. The distance was around three hundred kilometres and it was pretty hot. We drove and drove and drove and stopped to buy a coke and things like that on the way. We finally reached Morogoro and asked around for SOMAFCO. Not many people knew about it, but somebody told us: 'You should take that road. Go down there to the right'. Suddenly there was something over the road and under a tree there was this guy sitting really relaxed with a machine-gun. Then we understood that, okey, this is it. We stayed at SOMAFCO for a couple of days. We were very well received. They really took good care of us.

TS: What had happened then? Were they not informed in Dar es Salaam?

TL: There was some mix-up. For us it was just an adventure. At SOMAFCO we stayed in nice rooms. We had dinners and went into classes where they wanted us to talk about the gala. We visited the hospital. They did not have any malaria tablets, so we left everything that we had.

TS: From there you went to Zambia?

TL: No, we came to Zambia first. Zambia, Zimbabwe, Tanzania and Kenya.

TS: Were you received by the ANC leadership in Zambia?

TL: Yes, they took very good care of us. They arranged a big party and we went outside Lusaka to visit the ANC farm. I was videotaping during the whole trip. When I came home, I got some help from a guy to put it together. We had a twenty minute documentary on our trip on Swedish television.

TS: What did the ANC representatives say about your initiative? Did they appreciate the importance of the gala for the solidarity work in the Scandinavian countries?

TL: Very much so. When we came to Harare, there was a big and very formal dinner. The ANC Chief Representative to Zimbabwe, Reddy Mazimba, attended the dinner. They gave speeches to welcome us. I understood that the speeches were addressed to us, but also very much to all the ANC people who were there, so that they would understand that there were people working somewhere else on the earth for their cause. I felt this throughout our trip.

TS: ANC advocated a total cultural boycott of South Africa. The ANC gala was, of course, an alternative to any contacts with South Africa, but do you remember if the boycott was understood and observed by your fellow cultural workers in Sweden? Was this something that you discussed?

TL: Before the gala, I think that a lot of artists, including myself, were aware that there was a boycott, but many of us released records for different areas. You do not really have a clear picture of the countries where they are released. For example, if England picks up and distributes an album you do not always know in what countries England in turn will release it. I think that many artists really did not know, but after the gala everybody was aware of the problem and really checked it up: 'If this album is going to be released in England, I want to know that it is only for England'. The awareness was really much higher after the ANC gala.

TS: After your visit in 1986, there followed an exchange between Scandinavian and Southern African artists?

TL: Yes, the Frontline Rock project, with Mikael Wiehe, Peps Persson, Dan Hylander, Py Bäckman and others. I was supposed to join them, but I could not for some reason that I do not remember. But when they came to Sweden, we did a tour in which I took part. The idea was that there should be different Swedish artists for every concert. I was in Sandviken, my home town. It was fun.

TS: After that first involvement with ANC, were you able to follow the events in South Africa? Did you meet Nelson Mandela when he visited Stockholm?

TL: Yes, when he was released, I helped with the organization of the gala in the Stockholm Globe. ANC contacted me and I helped them to get in contact with EMA. We formed a group that organized the gala, with Stellan Skarsgård as master of ceremonies. I did not meet Mandela then, because I was behind the scenes to get things working. He walked by me, I remember. But when he got the Nobel Peace Prize, Mikael Wiehe and I were invited to Oslo and we actually met him. We were invited to his hotel room, which was quite something, to say the least. He was aware of the work we had done.

Mikael and I were invited to Mandela's presidential inauguration in South Africa. It was really a historical and moving moment. When Mandela was installed—when it actually happened—the sun was moving and a shadow over the place where we were sitting was slowly disappearing, so you really felt the change. For Mikael Wiehe and me it was quite spectacular. I had Sten Andersson to the right of me and a couple of rows above were Fidel Castro and Yasser Arafat. From our part of the world, it was Mikael and I. Quincy Jones was there from the US, and I remember Lindiwe Mabuza coming running to us: 'Tomas and Mikael, you have to come here. You have to meet Quincy'. It was quite something.

TS: Was that your first visit to South Africa?

TL: Yes. ANC took really good care of us. We went to some townships, celebrating the victory with the ANC people. We also went to a huge rally outside Johannesburg, where all the religious leaders held a ceremony. There were a hundred thousand people there. It was really moving, because the Jewish leaders, the Catholics, the Hindus, all of them, gave the message that 'we have to forgive'. Coming from Sweden we were not used to that attitude or to the emotional feeling that was there, so we were really moved. It was fascinating to see that in all the different levels of society the message was 'we have to forgive'. Even when you opened the newspaper and saw an advertisement for a new Honda car: 'This is the car for the future, for the new South Africa and we have to forgive'. If you went to get money in a bank, the same thing: 'This is money for the new South Africa. We have to forgive'.

When we were there, I realized that the church had been extremely important for the change of mind of the people, getting everybody moving in the same direction. The struggle was waged on a political level, on a religious level and also on a business level, from what I understand. That is quite remarkable.

I really fell in love with the country. South Africa is beautiful, but it also has vibrancy. You can feel the dynamics and there is a belief in the future and in change. I returned there six months later, on a holiday trip to Cape Town. I was fascinated, seeing how different groups were looking for new ways of living, finding patterns how to meet and how to live together. Basic things, like how do you behave or act when you go to the beach. Suddenly, there were totally different groups coming to the beach and a lot of funny situations occurred. It was a very exciting time to be there. The vitality is what I remember most.

I went to South Africa with my family. I even brought my parents. It was a great experience for all of us. It was fantastic.

In addition, Dali Tambo got to know that I was in South Africa. I was invited to his TV-show 'People of the South' together with Miriam Makeba and Barney Simon, who runs the Market Theatre in Johannesburg. I sang a song in Swedish: 'Here comes the new time'. It was really a special feeling to sing in Swedish on a South African TV show.

Sören Lindh
Africa Groups in Sweden
(Stockholm, 4 February 1997)

Tor Sellström: You have been actively involved in the Swedish solidarity movement with Southern Africa for about thirty years. How did your involvement begin?

Sören Lindh: It started around 1967, when I was a tutor for a student group in Uppsala. That is where my interest in Africa began. A year or so later, I was quarrelling with my father about international solidarity. I was angry with him and his friends, because they did not care. Going back to Uppsala, where I lived at the time, I asked myself: 'What do you do yourself?' The conclusion was: 'Nothing', so I conceived an organization that could fit into the government agency where I worked, the Swedish Agency for Administrative Development (*Statskontoret*). The main idea was to raise financial support and maybe have some information activities, but no big meetings. That was in November 1968. A handful of colleagues bought the idea and our organization still works.

It was conceived as a group in support of FRELIMO. Support for Vietnam was not politically realistic at this government agency. But I had read some articles by the Swedish journalist Anders Johansson from *Dagens Nyheter* about FRELIMO. So we chose the liberation movement in Mozambique. The organization was formed on a 'take it or leave it' basis: 'FRELIMO it is. If you do not like it, leave it!' That meant that we could avoid a lot of internal fights about what to support. Either you were in or you were out. And, as I said, the organization has survived for about thirty years.

TS: Did you have any previous contacts with FRELIMO?

SL: No. The idea was to mobilize people to do useful things. Then, of course, we got in touch with FRELIMO's representative in Sweden at that time, Lourenço Mutaca. It was just after the Cabora Bassa campaign, so it was not anything new or special.

TS: How was the initiative received by your colleagues?

SL: It was positive. A number of people joined. I think that we quite soon were about 15-20 people out of a total of some 300 employees. On the other hand, we tried to get the administration to draw money from the salaries every month—which usually was done if it concerned the Red Cross, Save the Children or similar organizations—but they said that they could not do that. Instead, we had to set up a special fund-raising account with a bank to which the members automatically transferred their contributions. It proved a bit difficult over the years, but it has worked.

Our main activity was fund-raising, but at the beginning of the 1970s we could also draw on the progressive wave of 1968. We had a number of meetings and small exhibitions at the agency. That boosted the activities and by 1972-73 we started to finance the shipment of used clothes to FRELIMO in Tanzania. The clothes went to Mtwara and from there into Mozambique. We also organized meetings with Marcelino dos Santos and others when they came to Sweden. Our activities went up and down, but they were quite good. Of course, all the time we were looked for by people from the Portuguese security police and others. There were instances when we had to adjourn meetings for a while and ask people to leave the room.

TS: Were these people Portuguese?

SL: No, they were Swedes, but of the type that security organizations would recruit and use as middlemen. But we were informed by our friends among the Portuguese deserters in Sweden when people from PIDE were monitoring the Africa Groups' demonstrations.

TS: How was your FRELIMO group linked to the broader Swedish solidarity movement with Southern Africa?

SL: In the beginning, there were no links. It lasted for about one year, but by the end of 1969 we got in touch with some people who belonged to the first Africa Group in southern Sweden and with others who wanted to set up a similar organization in Stockholm. Some of them were linked to the Swedish UN Association and later formed the Stockholm Africa Group. We were in touch with them, but we did not work together very much until 1971, when I joined. The Stockholm Africa Group really started to work at around that time. Before that it mainly functioned as a study circle. We also contacted those who had been working with the Cabora Bassa campaign against ASEA's participation in the project. They had a fund-raising account and a few pennies, but also a tradition of information which we took over. We also talked to the Social Democratic Youth League, which made a Swedish version of FRELIMO's publication *Mozambique Revolution*. Eventually, we formed a sub-group within the Stockholm Africa Group, called FRELIMO-Sweden.

TS: Did the Social Democratic Youth League form part of FRELIMO-Sweden?

SL: No. They could not link up with us formally, but we talked and made an agreement with FRELIMO to send *Mozambique Revolution* to us instead. We then set up a subscription service and activated our fund-raising account. I think that it set a standard for the Africa Groups' external work, with fund-raising and information activities. Later, we highlighted the Wiriyamu massacre in Mozambique. In preparation for the Stockholm conference on the environment, we also highlighted the genocide in South Africa and in Angola.

TS: In 1969, the Swedish parliament paved the way for direct humanitarian support to the national liberation movements in Southern Africa. How would you explain that a broad parliamentary majority in a neutral, Western country was in favour of liberation movements that waged armed struggles and were supported by the Soviet Union and/or China?

SL: Well, I have not thought of it very deeply, but if you look at it superficially you can see that it took place in the aftermath of the first South Africa boycott campaign. There was at the time a debate around the question that the West must do everything in its power to prevent Southern Africa from becoming Communist. I would not say that this was the reason for the Social Democrats' solidarity, but I imagine that some on the non-socialist, bourgeois side had that position. What was different in the case of Sweden—and maybe in the other Nordic countries—was that we did not have a business community that was actively and aggressively against us. I do not presume that they were foresighted enough to say: 'This could be of use for us in the future'. I do not think that. But, on the other hand, they did not really care. They did not harass the government or the solidarity movement unless we stepped on a very touchy toe.

TS: In your view, was the Swedish official support then given to influence the liberation movements ideologically, or was it granted as humanitarian assistance without any strings attached?

SL: We did not think about these things at the time. If you look back, there were, of course, people within the social democratic movement that wanted to influence them. I think that it goes for Sweden and for the social democratic movement in general. It was very clearly the case in the trade union field. Looking back, there must have been such strategies. But, we did not bother very much at the time. We did our work as well as we could and that was that. As FRELIMO put it, 'do not get sectarian, we would like to get as broad support from Sweden as possible'. We said: 'Fine, we will organize that'. So, we opened up. I think that it goes for the work on Angola as well. We entered into relations with a number of organizations and political movements, from the far left to sections of the Liberal Party. We worked with them when they were prepared to do so and set ourselves up as the information centre for Southern Africa of the NGO sector. Those who cared to ask would get the information. In retrospect, I can say that the information was very good.

TS: It was not until in 1975 that the Africa Groups recognized ANC as the leading force in South Africa. What factors could explain that the solidarity movement was so late?

SL: There could be a number of factors, some relevant and some really irrelevant. I think that the most relevant was that we were working in a political situation in Sweden where the focus was on Vietnam and later—from 1973—on Chile. We had to say: 'OK, we work with Africa, even if it may distract one or two activists from 'the main focus'. This was at the time of the 'focal point discussion', according to which all attention should be given to Vietnam. But we said that it was important to also cover other areas of the globe. In our case, we gave priority to the armed struggle in the Portuguese colonies. That was it. That also meant that we staved off demands to recognize this and that organization in other areas, although we were, of course, in solidarity with their struggle.

One of the more irrelevant reasons was that a couple of the leading Swedish activists had been staying for longer periods in Africa, where they had met people from the other liberation movements. Some of these persons were marked by exile and maybe not the ones that they should have met, because they did not encourage any political enthusiasm. These Swedes saw them as 'café revolutionaries', who it was not worthwhile supporting. Nobody in the Africa Groups really cared to question that position, because we could not do anything practical about it at that time, anyway. I think that it was one reason that held us back.

Another reason—whether relevant or irrelevant, I do not know—was that from 1973 the Trotskyists became very active in the Africa Groups. A few local groups were dominated by them and there were attacks on all the liberation movements, except ZANU. In their view, ZAPU, SWAPO and ANC were Stalinist, whatever that meant. For us who did the actual work, it was not very important to take on that fight. It would have required a big effort, so we said: 'Let it be'. But after 1975, when liberation had been achieved in the Portuguese colonies and we had to look for new areas, we took the decision to support ANC and SWAPO, as well as not to choose between ZANU and ZAPU. There were heavy fights between us in the mainstream and the Trotskyists. One of my arguments that I remember in that discussion was: 'OK, we might have objections to some features of SWAPO, but if we turn the question around and ask ourselves where the Namibian activists and progressives are, we will find that they are in SWAPO. Fine. Let us then support SWAPO and hope that the progressive forces will take over'. That was the level of discussion at that time.

TS: Would it be fair to say that the fact that the Swedish government and SIDA already had close relations with the liberation movements in South Africa, Zimbabwe and Namibia made it more difficult for the solidarity movement to recognize them?

SL: No. FRELIMO, PAIGC and MPLA also had support from the government and the Social Democratic Party. However, what we could see from the movements' representatives in Sweden was not always encouraging, for example, the infighting between ZANU and ZAPU. We tried to be as pragmatic as possible, appraising whether they had a genuine popular backing and if they could wage the struggle and so on. If they were productive on the home front and appreciated by the people. In the case of Zimbabwe, that was a bit difficult to assess. I think that it is why we had some difficulties with them and why we ended up supporting both ZANU and ZAPU.

TS: Talking about Zimbabwe, one gets the impression that the liberation movement with the weakest constituency in Sweden was ZAPU. Would you agree with that?

SL: Yes, I think that it is correct. ZAPU was the weakest for a number of reasons. When we talked to them, they had a clear analysis of the situation, but when we started to look at what was happening on the ground we could not find anything. So, we did not campaign very much for them. I also think that they were saying a lot of things that antagonized Social Democrats, Liberals and Trotskyists. This was in contrast to ZANU. ZANU floated around. You could not see any analysis, but they could on the other hand at times point at victories and advances here and there. I think that more enemies and a weak home ground worked against ZAPU in Sweden.

TS: At the beginning of the 1970s, the Maoist left in Sweden advocated support to UNITA in Angola, upholding that MPLA, FNLA and UNITA should be recognized and assisted as part of a united front. How did the Africa Groups look upon this?

SL: Well, we laughed a bit about it. We also smiled about the Liberal youth. They went for FNLA, but they also had a tendency to look favourably at UNITA. The Africa Groups did thorough homework on the Angolan organizations. We had already made an analysis in 1972, but did not publish it as it might provoke quarrels within the left. The time to take it up came in 1974. That is when we produced our booklet on UNITA, FNLA and MPLA, which is still a strong historical document. It influenced not only the left, but a number of organizations.

TS: In the case of Sweden, the government and the solidarity movement eventually supported the same liberation movements in Southern Africa. However, the situation was different on the trade union front. Notably, LO and TCO never advocated support to the South African Congress of Trade Unions (SACTU), while the Africa Groups strongly campaigned in its favour. Why did the Swedish trade union movement not support SACTU?

SL: I think that it was influenced by the so-called constructive engagement approach. The International Confederation of Free Trade Unions (ICFTU)—to which both LO and TCO belonged—had a very strong tradition of anti- Communism. If others were not too dogmatic about that, the trade unions were. In 1976, there was, for example, an ICFTU meeting in Mexico. For that meeting, the Swedish LO and TCO produced a report on the trade union situation in South Africa. I remember that they said that 'ANC had vanished, but that its spirit lingered on'. They also very clearly said: 'No support to organizations that do not exist. Like SACTU'. The interesting thing is that the report was first published in English for the Mexico meeting, so it was apparently meant for external consumption. Only later was it translated into Swedish.

Now, who was the secretary of the LO/TCO report? It was Åke Magnusson, a liberal who had been working with the student movement, channelling support to FRELIMO. That is where I first met him. I found him strange. He did not really fit in. Later, he joined the business side, actively working against sanctions and has become the head of the International Council of Swedish Industry. He also "infiltrated" the church, because the Swedish Ecumenical Council used him as well. But they realized that they were betting on the wrong horse. They corrected their position, but LO/TCO never did.

TS: LO and TCO supported internal trade union organizations like FOSATU, which was a driving force behind the constitution of COSATU. In retrospect, would it be fair to say that the support to FOSATU and other South African trade unions made a difference?

SL: What we did was that we gave selective support to internal trade union organizations. We talked to ANC and others and they told us that they had people in those organizations. We were not against giving money to internal organizations as such and we adjusted our campaign accordingly. But we said: 'Give money to SACTU as well'. That was our main message.

We also had to do our homework on the trade union situation. We used ANC's *News Briefings* and other sources to follow what was happening and realized from the beginning that it was a dangerous terrain unless it was very clear what you were doing. The interesting thing about the SACTU campaign is that we got allies within the Swedish trade unions. I had, for instance, contacts with the chairman of TCO, Lennart Bodström. He was concerned. Interestingly, he later became Minister for Foreign Affairs.

The fight we had around SACTU also left the Trotskyists behind. They could not cope. We were doing things. We were pushing and lobbying and they could only say: 'We have to think'. However, it was a situation where you had to act, which meant that it was about the last we saw of the Trotskyists within the Africa Groups.

TS: Did the emphasis on SACTU alienate the solidarity movement from organized labour in Sweden?

SL: We alienated ourselves from the official establishment of the trade unions, but we went to the shop stewards and to the local branches and said: 'Some people in South Africa are working openly, but in disguise. Others are working underground. If you would like to have a balanced situation, how do you channel the support? To both sides'. That made sense to a lot of people. We had unions supporting our view. Then they had to face the fact that SACTU was a member of the World Federation of Trade Unions (WFTU), but most of the people who were active and interested in international affairs did not care about that.

But, of course, it alienated us to a certain extent. However, we would have been their opponents anyway, launching the sanctions campaign in late 1976. We then talked to a number of people who had been active in the sanctions campaign in the 1960s. We learned from their mistakes and also from their advances. An interesting thing was that the initial opposition to the idea of a boycott against South Africa came from the trade unions and other Social Democrats. They said: 'We tried it. It did not work. Do not try to do what we did, because we know that it will not work'. We were a bit surprised, but formed other alliances. The last to come on board was the Social Democratic Youth League. We had all the political youth movements except the Moderates on board before we formally asked the Social Democrats to join the Isolate South Africa Committee (ISAK).

TS: Looking at the trade union scene in South Africa at the time, there were emerging unions that later became extremely important, such as the National Union of Mineworkers. They were largely influenced by the Black Consciousness Movement, with leaders such as Cyril Ramaphosa. Why did the Black Consciousness Movement never receive any support from the Swedish government or the solidarity movement?

SL: Well, what did they do? Where did they belong? I refer to the discussion we had on SWAPO: 'There are progressives, but there are also a lot of other people and it is very difficult to see who is who'. We could perhaps see them as John the Baptist, coming before Jesus, but they were not Jesus.

TS: The Swedish solidarity movement—the Africa Groups and ISAK—was very strong and united. How would you asses its influence on the Swedish government?

SL: We opted at the start for a maximum platform, with full sanctions and support for all the liberation movements in the ISAK programme. We got more or less 100 per cent support for that. So we had a strong basis, which meant that we could be very active regarding information, press releases and so on. At the beginning of the 1980s, we had a bourgeois government in Sweden. We harassed them and embarrassed Foreign and Prime Ministers alike with our questions. We were very well informed and that made us respected.

I also think that we were instrumental in helping the Social Democrats to take stronger actions against South Africa, going from an investment ban to full sanctions. For example, we found that according to the GATT treaty, a government could ban goods irrespective of other commitments if they were produced by prison labourers. We could easily show that many South African grapes, oranges and other agricultural products fell under that clause. We got support for our position. The Social Democratic member of parliament Maj-Lis Lööw read some of the statements and comments that we made in one of our booklets to the parliamentary records. Eventually, the government said: 'If we ban agricultural trade, why should we continue in other areas?' I think that our campaign helped them to a more comfortable position.

TS: Was this situation similar in Denmark, Finland and Norway?

SL: Finland was always exceptional. They did not have a strong grassroots organization. There was an activity as part of the Peace Committee, which was broader and wider than in Sweden. But it was quite a bureaucratic organization, with very few who had any international experience.

When it comes to Denmark and Norway, I guess that they did not have such a strong presence in the Southern African region as we had. We also had much more financial support. We received a number of grants from the government, available to all NGOs. We used them, which was not the case to that extent in Denmark and Norway. I also think that their political platforms were not that strong. They did not have the inner circle of organizations that we had in Sweden. It was, for example, not by chance that ISAK had its office close to us over the years. Even organizations that politically were quite far from us accepted our leading role as "the experts". I think that it partly was due to the fact that we tried to be factual and pragmatic. We always tried to be on firm ground.

TS: Nevertheless, your publication *Afrikabulletinen* did not sell very well?

SL: I think that it has to do with history. From the beginning, we did not aim at becoming a mass movement. We did not want to take away support and activists from the Vietnam or the Chile campaigns. We remained in the expert, lobbying area. Looking back, you could say that we carried that too far and that we were not seen as an organization in itself. That is bad. We should have gone out to became more of a mass movement. On the other hand, we have a strong and active core of long term members.

TS: The Africa Groups and ISAK would over the years increasingly receive official funds to carry out their activities in Southern Africa. Was there a discussion regarding possible loss of autonomy due to the funding from SIDA?

SL: It is hard to say how it affected us. We said: 'These are not grants and gifts from the government, but taxpayers' money that belongs to us. It is the people that rule and the people say: Do not interfere with what the NGO is doing. Just look if they are doing what they have promised to do'. We were quite strong on that point.

When we took up projects, we also very soon found that SIDA wanted us to do things that they could not do, some good and some bad. So, in a number of cases we were setting the terms, not the other way around. But I am also sure that there were occasions where we yielded, not in a political way, but by accepting principles from SIDA. It would be amazing if we did not. But I think that, generally, we said that 'it is our money. We do what we want and don't you try to turn us away from what we think is correct'.

TS: In general terms, how would you then characterize the relations between the soli-

darity movement and the Swedish government?
SL: I think that we have influenced the position of official Sweden. We have been boasting about the fact that we did things together and it has been to our advantage.

Our recruitment organization was set up in 1976. We had not done a thing in the Southern African region before in terms of development work, but we managed to survive the first mistakes and learn a lot from them. Eventually, we set up good machinery and were quickly regarded as professional by those who cared about development assistance at SIDA and the Ministry for Foreign Affairs. They came to respect us.

TS: You have been involved with Swedish solidarity work for Southern Africa for about thirty years. Where, do you think, did the Swedish solidarity movement make the greatest impact?

SL: Well, many things have gone so wrong for the region that it is hard to say that there have been any victories. I remember that we said to the people training to go to Southern Africa that the economy would end up in a mess. Unfortunately, we were much more correct than we hoped to be.

One of the very important things that we did was our work in Mozambique from 1976 to 1981-82. It was extremely good, and I think that we helped to establish a solidarity experience that hopefully will surface again with the younger generations. The spirit and collaboration were very good. Also at the practical level it was a victory, no matter what happened afterwards. Another achievement was the first ISAK boycott campaign, where we got the full support of the member organizations because they saw that we did a good job. Our research work won the respect of the Christian movement. These are important aspects. But there are lots of others.

Stig Lövgren
SIDA—Responsible for procurement to the liberation movements
(Sollentuna, 21 February 1996)

Tor Sellström: As head of SIDA's procurement division you were closely involved with Swedish official assistance to PAIGC of Guinea-Bissau and to the Southern African liberation movements. When did you start working at SIDA?

Stig Lövgren: I came to SIDA in 1969 and became almost immediately involved in support to the liberation movements, beginning with the first procurement programme for PAIGC. At that time, we were a section within SIDA's country division and we only became an independent division in, I think, 1978. I became head of section in 1974 and then head of the procurement division.

TS: I understand that the support in the beginning was exclusively in the form of food items and other basic articles?

SL: That is right.

TS: How did you assess the needs of the liberation movements? Of PAIGC, for example?

SL: In the beginning, Amílcar Cabral himself would come to Stockholm. He stayed in a hotel under an assumed name for security reasons and was working with us at SIDA to establish a list of articles, goods, equipment etc. that they needed. It was a very simple procedure and not very controversial, because at that time the list just covered food, medicines, hospital and school equipment and so on. We did not question their needs very much. After all, the funds allocated in those days were not that big and Curt Ström, who was the official in charge at SIDA, was of the opinion that we should not question too much.

TS: People from Sweden had also been to the liberated areas of Guinea-Bissau?

SL: At that time, perhaps Birgitta Dahl had been there. I think that she was one of the few persons from the Swedish side that had any previous contacts with PAIGC.

TS: In the early days, the Swedish solidarity movement would criticize SIDA and the Swedish government for being 'paternalistic' by supplying goods instead of unconditionally giving the same amount of money as cash support. How did you look upon this? Do you think that Amílcar Cabral, for example, was happy with the support?

SL: Absolutely. I remember quite well that he said that this was the best form of aid that Sweden could give. What possibility did they have to convert funds into the goods that they needed? Everything that they needed for the war they received from the socialist bloc, but they did not have any resources when it came to food, medicines, school equipment etc. for the civilian part of the struggle. They were totally dependent on countries like Sweden for these items, because they could not procure them on the international market. They had no use for money at the time. That came later.

TS: The Swedish support was humanitarian or civilian, that is, non-military. How did you draw the line between non-military and military supplies?

SL: This was very much discussed during the early years. Curt Ström, especially, was always very nervous that we might send things that could be used for military purposes. I remember very well one meeting with Amílcar Cabral at SIDA. We were discussing the lists that we had prepared earlier and which Ström should approve. When we came to machetes, he was very concerned and said that they could be used to kill people. Amílcar Cabral then took up a pen and said: 'This is a weapon too...'. By then we had already approved the procurement of, let us say, ten thousand pens of that same kind for the PAIGC schools. I think that Cabral had a point there.

There were other interesting episodes. We supplied a lot of food, especially tinned food, to PAIGC. At one stage, we bought something like a hundred tons of tinned fish—quite a considerable quantity—from a Swedish factory. The supplier—Strömstad Canning—asked me if we wanted a special label for the consignment. I thought that it was a good idea, so I contacted Onésimo Silveira, who was then the PAIGC representative in Sweden. He became so enthusiastic! It was not until later that I realized why he became ecstatic. He decided on a label with the PAIGC flag and with the text 'From the liberated areas of Guinea-Bissau'. Years afterwards, I was told that they had arranged for these tins to appear in different places in the areas where the Portuguese still held power. They even distributed some of the tins in Bissau, the capital. You can imagine what an effective psychological weapon this was. If I had raised this issue with the management of SIDA, I am not absolutely sure that the label would have been met with approval. I still do not know whether this was in accordance with the UN recommendation or not.

So, we were, as a matter of fact, quite heavily involved in the struggle. It does not necessarily mean that we were supplying weapons, but it was very difficult to draw the line. The main problem concerned trucks to the liberation movements. It was discussed many, many times. The basic reason why trucks were finally supplied was the fact that the goods that were provided by SIDA had to be transported in one way or the other from the ports to the stores at the PAIGC bases. After all, we found that it would be reasonable to provide a limited number of trucks at the same time as we were supplying large quantities of goods. But, generally speaking, after a few years this discussion was not so important and in the end we did not pay any attention to it. After all, we did not supply weapons or ammunition.

TS: Some countries that supported the liberation movements politically refused to supply vehicles. It was argued that they could be used by the liberation armies?

SL: Yes, but we supplied Land Rovers and other four-wheel drive vehicles. After a few years, there was no discussion about that. We even provided both Volvo and Scania vehicles specifically designed for the Swedish army, but made available in a civilian version too.

TS: There was also the question of non-essential goods, for example, the incident when SIDA supplied cigarettes to PAIGC?

SL: Yes, they got their own cigarettes as well, which were also produced in Sweden. The PAIGC people designed exactly what the package should look like. They were called *Nô Pintcha*. We discussed with the Ministry for Foreign Affairs well in advance of the decision whether cigarettes should be provided or not. After some hesitation we came to the conclusion that it would be reasonable to provide a limited quantity. One evening after work, I walked down Rådmansgatan and saw the headlines outside a tobacco shop: 'SIDA is distributing cigarettes as humanitarian assistance!'. There

was quite a strong reaction by the anti-smoking lobby, but it was no big deal.
TS: But the cigarettes were used to generate income for PAIGC. Were they not sold in the people's shops that PAIGC had?
SL: That is right. And that was the case with most of the bulk items that we provided, like canned food, fabrics for women's dresses, radio sets, batteries, torches, kerosene lamps etc.
TS: Did other liberation movements have similar shops?
SL: I did not come across any. I think that these shops were rather special to the liberated areas in Guinea-Bissau. The rural people would supply rice and other basic articles to PAIGC, for which they in turn received some sort of coupons that they could use in the shops.
TS: Was that part of the understanding between the Swedish government and PAIGC?
SL: Yes. The idea was very fundamental and much appreciated. It was absolutely natural that they used Swedish aid in that way.
TS: Against this background it is difficult to understand the criticism against SIDA for being paternalistic?
SL: Yes, of course.
TS: Perhaps people did not know what you were doing?
SL: No, of course not. We did not advertise it very much either. From SIDA's point of view this was not something that we gave much publicity.
TS: What were the main items that SIDA supplied?
SL: Food was the biggest item. Then there were medicines, mostly essential drugs, and simple hospital equipment, which was very important. Another group of items was school equipment: slates, textbooks, maps, pens and pencils.
TS: Was it the same for all the liberation movements?
SL: Yes, these items became normal and basic ingredients for all the movements. Cooking oil, beans and tinned food were the biggest component. Vehicles became more and more important. Hygiene articles like soap were also extremely important. We bought huge quantities of washing-soap, toothbrushes and toothpaste.

TS: How could you check that the goods came to proper use? Did you visit the liberated areas and the refugee camps?
SL: Basically, we did not and could not visit the liberated areas. We tried to, but in most cases they politely found some excuse for not letting us go there. Basically for security reasons, of course. But I was rather close to the liberated areas. I was making follow-up trips to PAIGC and visited one of their camps just on the border between the Republic of Guinea and Guinea-Bissau. I was able to see how the goods were handled from the point where they were discharged in the port of Conakry and taken to the central warehouse, which SIDA, by the way, had provided. A big pre-fabricated building that was very nicely erected by the PAIGC people themselves. From Conakry, the goods were then transported by truck to the PAIGC northern base. It took three or four days. It could also take two weeks if the roads were bad. There were a lot of ferries that they had to take and sometimes the ferries were not working. It was a very time-consuming operation.

At least in this case we felt pretty sure that the goods were properly taken care of and that they reached the final users. But I am afraid that the picture was not that good when we speak of MPLA of Angola and FRELIMO of Mozambique.
TS: At a very early stage you participated in SIDA's discussions with MPLA?
SL: Yes, I think that they started in December 1971. Curt Ström, Marianne Rappe and myself made a trip to all the major liberation movements. We left in early November and were away for about a month. We started with PAIGC in Conakry and then went to Lusaka. There was a meeting scheduled with the MPLA leaders, but nobody seemed to be there when we arrived. We were later told that we had to wait for one of the commanders from the province in Angola bordering with Zambia. I remember that the MPLA leader we were waiting for was Comandante Daniel Chipenda. He later became a controversial figure within MPLA and eventually joined Holden Roberto's FNLA. The MPLA people in Lusaka did not dare to discuss with us, because everything had to be decided by Chipenda himself.

Chipenda had to take a domestic flight to Lusaka, but he did not have any money. We had to provide him with a ticket. After a few days, he turned up and we had a meeting with him. But he was not prepared for the discussions either. Frankly speaking, he did not seem to know very much about us and what the purpose of our meeting was. So, the start with MPLA was really slow. It took a long time before we came on speaking terms. They also had a rather weak representative in Stockholm by the name of António Neto.

I often got the impression that the political decision taken by the Swedish government that Sweden should provide assistance to MPLA in itself was the most important. They did not seem to care very much about the content of the assistance. I am afraid that during these first years the technical side of the support to MPLA was not very effective.

TS: Was it also not controversial? For example, the Liberal Party argued in favour of support to FNLA.

SL: Yes, that is right. That made the whole picture more complicated.

TS: But, of course, there was no liberation movement with such logistical problems as MPLA?

SL: Yes, perhaps they had the worst problems. We visited a camp that they had outside Lusaka. There was some sort of a central warehouse. When the goods arrived, they had been transported from Dar es Salaam all the way through Tanzania and Zambia. And in Lusaka they were only half way to their final destination.

TS: There was no railway in those days. Two thousand kilometres on dirt roads only from Dar es Salaam to Lusaka?

SL: Exactly. In the MPLA camp we could also see that a lot of goods and equipment were being spoiled. Either it had been damaged during the transport or it had just been lying there. They lacked organisation and people that were able to handle these questions. This was particularly sad when you compared with PAIGC, which for us was some sort of ideal organization. The PAIGC people were also very social. Very friendly and nice. Most of them were Cape Verdians and I think that you can say that they were more used to the kind of discussions that we had. The MPLA people were more suspicious. Not the top people, but, generally speaking, the atmosphere was not at all the same.

TS: Did you meet Agostinho Neto?

SL: I met him once at SIDA, but he did not know very much about these matters. His mind was not with procurement. Amílcar Cabral, on the other hand, was extremely engaged in this kind of detail, because he felt that it was something that he had to attend to.

TS: You also started early with FRELIMO?

SL: Yes, that is right. I think that I started in 1970, but Swedish aid to FRELIMO had started before in some modest way. Our cooperation with FRELIMO was very much linked to Janet Mondlane, the widow of the former FRELIMO leader. She used to come to Stockholm as a fund-raiser and partner in this cooperation. She was heavily engaged in the procurement side and seemed to know quite a lot about their requirements. She was very able and interested in these matters. We had an excellent cooperation.

When we made our trip to the liberation movements in 1971, we met the FRELIMO people at the Mozambique Institute in Dar es Salaam. The experience was a little bit similar to the one with MPLA, because at that time we did not have any prior contacts with them other than through Janet Mondlane.

TS: In the case of FRELIMO, there was one particular incident with Scania trucks supplied by SIDA?

SL: Yes, I remember it quite well. As part of the annual procurement programme we were delivering two trucks to FRELIMO. They also received a lot of goods and, as in the PAIGC case, we found it reasonable that they should have some means of transport to handle them. On ships, trucks are normally transported on deck and these trucks were also loaded in that way. What I remember is that the ship was not scheduled to call on Beira in Mozambique, but that it had to go there for one reason or another. Such things happen. The fact that the ship had to go to Beira and probably take on some cargo made it necessary to temporarily off-load the trucks and put them on the quay in order to open the hatches. It was noted by the stevedores that the trucks were marked 'FRELIMO' and we were told by the shipping company that they reacted immediately. It was then decided by the Portuguese authorities that the trucks should not be allowed to continue to the end users, which, of course, was something that we became very upset about.

I was quite criticized for being 'so naive' as to send trucks with the open marking 'FRELIMO'. But, first of all, Beira was not part of the normal route. Secondly, what Sweden was doing was in accordance with recommendations by the United Nations, namely to provide humanitarian assistance, and I felt that this should not be hidden. It was something that was internationally accepted. However, this was a unique event. It did not create any problems other than at that particular time. The FRELIMO takeover was not far away and I suppose that the trucks became useful tools in the country's development, at least in the end.

TS: Apart from this incident, did you have any problems with freight to the liberation movements? Did you experience any sabotage by the South Africans in the case of shipments to SWAPO or ANC?

SL: No, they never had the possibility of getting in contact with the goods. Of course, some goods were shipped by boats that were calling on South African ports, but the goods were stored inside the ships. No, I do not remember that we had any problems with that.

TS: How was the relationship with ZANU and ZAPU from Zimbabwe, SWAPO from Namibia and ANC from South Africa when it came to procurement matters?

SL: I had the impression that they were better organized and that the goods that we provided came to more efficient use. In the beginning, the support to these movements was very modest and mainly on a cash basis, namely support to cover the living costs in the host-countries, such as Zambia, Tanzania etc. But it became more and more important over the years and it gradually changed to include the supply of goods. SWAPO, for instance, became a major recipient—like an independent country—during the last few years in Angola, where they had a camp outside Luanda. I think that they were very efficient.

TS: You did not only procure goods, but you also supplied the liberation movements with courses in procurement, storage and handling?

SL: That is right. They became interested in these matters. I think that they realized that if you try to procure goods efficiently and try to locate the best sources of supply, you get better value for the money. They became a bit impressed with what we were doing, because they normally received much more goods and equipment than what they were expecting, due to the fact that we could do good business by comparing different sources of supply and so on.

They became very interested and said that 'once we are independent, we will have to take care of this ourselves. We would like to learn some of this already now'. We at SIDA also felt that we should try to teach them how to handle the goods, how the goods should be stored and accounted for and so on. That, of course, was partly selfish, because we wanted to make sure that they were handling the goods properly. However, it was interesting to note that they were looking ahead, saying that they would need the knowledge one day and therefore would already like to start in exile.

TS: So, you acted as some sort of tender board for them?

SL: Yes, that is exactly how we tried to act. We invited bids from different parts of the world and from different sources of supply. If we had the possibility, we let the movements study the material and propose ideas. Especially those movements that had representatives in Sweden took a very active part in the procurement work.

TS: One could perhaps say that this was part of pre-independence planning?

SL: Exactly. That was also the case with PAIGC, although we did not arrange any courses for them, as we did for SWAPO and ANC. But I can assure you that they learned from these experiences. I was part of the first Swedish official delegation to Bissau after liberation and we were invited to a dinner with the President, Luís Cabral, whom I regard as a personal friend. During the dinner he invited me to come to Bissau and take up a job as the one responsible for all imports and public procurement in the country. I politely said that it was very tempting, but that I could not do that. Later SIDA arranged training courses for the procurement people in Guinea-Bissau.

TS: Was SIDA's procurement to the liberation movements tied to Swedish goods?

SL: No, not at all.

TS: How about sanctions and South Africa? Did you procure from South Africa?

SL: No, it was absolutely clear that there should be no contacts whatsoever with potential suppliers in South Africa. That was part of our basic policy.

TS: Did you purchase goods for FRELIMO or MPLA in Portugal?

SL: No, of course not.

TS: On the shipping side, did you transport the goods on Swedish ships or on any ships?

SL: There were very limited transport possibilities to Conakry. As a matter of fact, we had some problems in finding a shipping line with regular sailings for PAIGC, but we used a Danish company which had a regular service to some West African ports, among them Conakry. With respect to the other liberation movements, Dar es Salaam was the main port and there were no problems getting the goods there. We mostly used a Soviet shipping line called *Besta Line*. They had an excellent service. For Luanda we used the Swedish line *Transatlantic*.

TS: Did the shipping companies know that they transported goods for the liberation movements?

SL: Well, they must have known. I cannot recall that the matter was ever discussed. They did not raise any questions. They were not hesitant at all, as far as I remember.

TS: Did you enter into any agreements with the host countries, that is Guinea-Conakry, Tanzania or Angola? Or did this fall within the general scope of SIDA's accreditation to these countries?

SL: Yes, in the case of Tanzania and Zambia it did. I never heard of any discussions on the matter. It was quite natural that these activities were going on, but I cannot exclude that there might have been some special arrangements through the Ministry for Foreign Affairs. Regarding PAIGC, I know that we had to enter into a special arrangement with Guinea-Conakry in order to get things moving. I was also engaged in this. The price Sweden had to pay was the provision of a complete printing press for the education sector in the Republic of Guinea. It was set up in Conakry and we even sent an expert there to assist with the installation and the starting up of the printing press. I do not know whether this was wasted money or not, because the conditions in that country were not very easy. We set it up, but I do not recall that we had any contacts with the Conakry government afterwards. However, I doubt that the printing press could operate efficiently for a long time without continued technical assistance.

TS: SIDA purchased a lot of items for the liberation movements on the Swedish market. In your experience, how did the Swedish companies look upon the assistance to these movements?

SL: I cannot say that they cared very much about that. They looked at it commercially. However, Luís Cabral was once in Sweden for a period of time and I arranged a trip for him to some of 'their' suppliers in the Lake Mälaren region. One day we visited a factory in Gnesta which had supplied huge quantities of bars of soap for washing clothes to PAIGC. Cabral talked to all the people in the factory and explained how important this particular line of supply was for PAIGC's activities. They were all gathered together and he talked to them for half an hour. I think that it was something that the people at the factory must remember. I personally remember it as a very nice moment.

TS: And later, of course, he became the President of Guinea-Bissau.

SL: Yes, that is right.

TS: When it comes to some important Swedish companies, it could perhaps be said that SIDA actually brought them into cooperation with the liberation movements. I am thinking of Scania and Volvo, where you not only supplied vehicles, but also arranged training courses?

SL: Yes, when the movements became more organized and the conditions so allowed, both Scania and Volvo arranged courses in Dar es Salaam and in Luanda. Particularly in the case of SWAPO, where they even assisted in setting up a mechanical workshop in Angola.

But I am afraid that a lot of trucks were more or less regarded as consumption material—even by PAIGC—because of the extreme conditions. And, of course, they did not have the facilities to attend to the trucks. They did not last very long, but that was mostly due to heavy damage, even caused by gun-fire and landmines.

TS: How did you deal with the problem of spare parts?

SL: The trucks were supplied with basic spare parts. A truck is a fantastic machine. Once you provide it with oil, it will work year after year. But, of course, if you break the axles or the wheels it is destroyed. One thing that I regret very much is that instead of supplying the liberation movements with Swedish trucks, we should have supplied them with Russian trucks. At the time, you could get almost three Russian trucks for one Swedish truck. That was really a waste of money. They should not have received so many of these very technical and sophisticated Swedish machines, but such simple trucks as possible.

TS: Did they not insist on having Swedish trucks?

SL: Well, yes, but their preference for Swedish trucks was to be seen as a gesture towards Sweden.

TS: When it comes to the ANC settlement in Morogoro, Tanzania, and the SWAPO settlement in Kwanza Sul, Angola, SIDA was involved in huge projects, covering various aspects, such as the supply of water, agriculture, bakeries, mechanical workshops etc. Did you also work with these projects?

SL: At that time, the assistance to the movements had become similar to SIDA's country programmes. It was properly planned and involved the different sector divisions at SIDA. In the early years, the sections were not involved and not even very keen to become involved. As a matter of fact, in the beginning I tried to involve the sector divisions. I remember in particular the problems that MPLA had with the production of a SIDA financed textbook for their schools. The translation into Portuguese and the printing of the book was very costly, so I tried to encourage the people at SIDA's education division to look into the question and come up with a judgement whether this was reasonable or not. But they were not really interested and did not want to be engaged too deeply as the division had not been able to carry out a prior feasibility study. I am afraid that this particular book was another complete failure as far as the MPLA support was concerned.

TS: Looking back over the years when you were responsible for SIDA's procurement for the liberation movements, what gave you the greatest satisfaction?

SL: I think that we by and large were successful in providing value for money. I am basically a military person. I am a naval officer and my speciality is logistics. When I came to SIDA in 1969, I immediately became engaged in procurement to the liberation movements and found that it was both something that I knew and was interested in. The representatives of the movements were really amazed that they could get so much out of the rather limited funds available. What has given me most satisfaction is that Swedish aid was very valuable to them.

TS: What were the biggest disappointments?

SL: The greatest disappointment was the slow start in the cooperation with MPLA. I became extremely frustrated, because I felt that we did not come anywhere and they seemed not to care. Time just went on and on and nothing really happened. The specifications and the lists we received were so unrealistic. We tried to establish a close cooperation with the MPLA representatives in Stockholm and they were supposed to be in contact with their leaders. However, it did not work very well. It was very frustrating.

Åke Magnusson
Chairman of the Student Development Fund—Secretary to the 1977 Swedish committee on sanctions against South Africa
Executive Director of the International Council of Swedish Industry
(Stockholm, 27 January 1997)

Tor Sellström: How did your involvement with South and Southern Africa begin?

Åke Magnusson: As many others, my first contact was really at the beginning of the 1960s, when the anti-apartheid movement began the consumer boycotts. In the Gothenburg harbour you could watch people with different banners, asking us not to buy South African fruit as a contribution to the struggle against apartheid. I think that this really was my first contact, besides the fact that my grandfather was a missionary. The mission society of which he later became the director operated in Zululand. I remember some of the books he wrote.

TS: Was that with the Church of Sweden Mission?

ÅM: No, it was with the Swedish Alliance Mission, based in Jönköping. But my first involvement—at least when it comes to contacts and awareness—was with the consumer boycott movement, which was fairly strong at the beginning of the 1960s.

TS: Then you got involved in the student movement at Gothenburg university?

ÅM: Yes. That was in the second half of the 1960s. However, I think that it is correct to say that the South African issue was not very dominant in the student movement. It was rather the issues of Vietnam and to some extent Eastern Europe that dominated.

TS: What about Mozambique and the question of Cabora Bassa?

ÅM: Yes, Cabora Bassa was a big issue around 1968. Also Rhodesia was to some extent an issue, with the sanctions and the different activities that ZANU and ZAPU developed in Sweden. In those days, we probably had a greater knowledge of Rhodesia and Mozambique than of South Africa, although you may argue that the South African apartheid question was very dominant for the Cabora Bassa debate, as was the question of distribution of electricity to Rhodesia.

TS: Having been involved with South Africa in various capacities, which factors do you think explain both the strong and politically broad Swedish solidarity opinion over the years?

ÅM: I think that there are many contributing factors. One—and a very important one, indeed—is simply that some key journalists and publishers developed an early interest and also a fairly good knowledge about the problems. Not only Per Wästberg, but a few others as well. I think that their commitment—due to the importance of the media—created and maintained a public opinion. It was really critical. Mainly liberal newspapers and individual journalists and editors played a key role in maintaining that interest.

Secondly, apartheid was a symbol of those social and political systems in the world that most of us strongly dislike and feel distaste for. South Africa was extreme, because there were absolute, clear-cut colour lines. I think that it made the conflict enormously obvious and easy to describe, at least in a simplistic way. Therefore, it easily caught the attention of people. It was, literally speaking, a black and white issue. Simplistic as it was, and still is, it was easier to describe than, let's say, the Indian or the Malaysian caste systems or the feudal pressures in China.

Thirdly, I think that in this country we are American-inspired. It played a significant role that the South African issue—being a colour issue—was dominant in the United States in the 1960s and the 1970s. We were also influenced by the fact that colour is an important issue in the world in general. The US news coverage and political attention to those issues had an influence.

Fourthly, rightly or wrongly, some people argue that Sweden needed a very obvious Third World solidarity example. It fitted in, so to speak, with the general mood of many Swedes in those days. The Third World was important, but we had to make it obvious. The internal, very tragic conflict in South Africa—of which we have not yet seen the final outcome—could fill a gap, or a vacuum.

Fifthly, I think that the political parties in Sweden without doubt needed to find issues in foreign affairs. In those days, there were many big domestic issues that were discussed, but in the international field there was also a need to raise a conflict to create a profile. There again, the Liberal Party belonged without doubt to those forces that at a really early stage—at the beginning of the 1960s—called for economic sanctions. The Social Democratic Party did not give up their opposition to sanctions until the second half of the 1970s. Their view was that binding sanctions should be decided by the UN Security Council, rather than introduced unilaterally.

TS: How would you explain the relatively late involvement by the organized Swedish labour movement? Was it because of the UN factor or was it due to concerns regarding job security?

ÅM: My view would be that it is very much explained by the UN factor. Being fairly close to government circles and government thinking, the trade unions realized that there was chaos in many countries in the world. In order to avoid chaos in the international order, the road set up by the UN had to be obeyed. I think that it really played a significant role. That is not to say that they were as legalistic as Östen Undén, but it was more of that than the Liberal viewpoint. The fact that the Liberals—mainly the Liberals and to some extent the Communists—criticized the co-operative movement played a negative role from a Social Democratic point of view when it came to sanctions. It tied up the positions. At an early stage, the Social Democrats defended the right to free trade.

Indeed, a certain type of conservatism in the labour movement could be explained by the job factor. In some cases it was quite obvious. But I also seriously think that in the labour movement—at least those parts of the movement that I have been attached to or worked for—there is a serious belief that sanctions, irrespective of the moral or symbolic element, constitute a bad and inefficient way to change social conditions and structures in a foreign country. There is an inherent scepticism towards sanctions and isolations.

There are different ways of looking at sanctions. You can look at them as a tactical weapon or as a strategic weapon. Seeing them as a tactical weapon is a way of saying that we use or demand sanctions in order to pressurize. We do not believe in isolation, but we use the threat. The strategic thinkers believe that isolating a country is a way of getting the system down on its knees. I seriously think that there was scepticism in the labour movement towards the strategic thinking.

TS: In 1969, the Swedish parliament paved the way for direct, official humanitarian support to national liberation movements in Southern Africa. All the movements supported by Sweden waged armed struggles and were supported militarily and politically by the Communist camp. How would you explain that non-socialist parties in Sweden, like the Liberal and the Centre Party, added their voices to this support?

ÅM: I have two comments. One line of 'defence' was to say: 'This is nothing but humanitarian support. We do not provide weapons, nor ammunition. Only humanitarian goods, like food, first aid kits, trucks etc.' Regarding trucks, the question would then come: 'Could they be used for transporting military equipment?' The Swedish attitude was that the trucks were used to transport foodstuffs, refugees and wounded people. There was a kind of humanitarian Red Cross labelling of the support. That was one way of defending it.

The other was to say: 'Yes, we do support these movements. We know and recognize that they are supported by the Communists, but that is precisely the reason why we support them. We do not want these movements to be linked for ever to the Communist camp in the world. We support them because we do not want them to become traditional Eastern European Communists'. So, there were two lines of defence for this support. They have not often been made clear. A lot of the Swedish government's aid was de facto very confidential and secret. In recent years, some people have criticized this, asking: 'Why did you not tell us in public?'

TS: Do you think that the Swedish support actually counterbalanced the Communist influence, for example in the case of ANC?

ÅM: In the case of ANC, it is my firm impression—which later has been substantiated—that the Swedish cash support in particular was very significant. Sweden supplied thirty to fifty per cent of the total cash that ANC received. I seriously believe that it had a great impact and influence.

TS: When the Social Democratic Party lost the elections in 1976, it was succeeded by a non-socialist coalition government, including the conservative Moderate Party. Many people—also in the liberation movements—believed that it would put an end to a progressive Swedish policy towards the liberation movements. Instead, the assistance was increased and the first sanctions legislation was introduced by the Liberal Ullsten government in 1979. How do you look upon this?

ÅM: In part, the Social Democrats had given the impression to the liberation movements that they were the only ones in Sweden behind the policy of support, materially and politically. But the Social Democrats had informed their friends badly, because it was well known that the Liberal Party for years had demanded strong sanctions and increased support to the liberation movements. Their annual congresses had repeatedly, even without a vote, asked for such actions.

There were a couple of factors that came together in 1976. One was that the Social Democratic Party lost power, which I would argue gave the party a possibility—or at least made it easier—to turn around when it came to unilateral sanctions. For fairly obvious reasons, it is easier to do that in opposition than when you are in power. I am not saying that opposition parties are more irresponsible, but it is easier to make policy shifts when you are in opposition.

Secondly, the non-socialist coalition government consisted of the Centre, the Liberal and the Moderate Party. It was obvious that the Liberal Party—and to some extent the Centre Party—had sanctions and tougher measures on the agenda. In fact, you may argue that the Liberal Party had the sanctions issue as *the* international question. They did not say very much about Vietnam, Russia or Latin America. It was South Africa.

Thirdly, I would argue that the Moderate Party at a very early stage realized that there was a clear parliamentary majority in favour of sanctions. They did not find it worthwhile to try to fight this situation. They simply wanted to de-escalate the issue in order to keep the coalition together. It was a minor question for them, so, why not give the Liberals and the Centre Party a few things. In return, they could organize Sweden internally. This might sound like a cynical analysis, but I think that that is how politics operates.

In those days, I worked for the government, being the secretary of the parliamentary committee that prepared the sanctions legislation. I remember when we tabled our report to Staffan Burenstam-Linder, the Moderate Minister of Trade. His only question—if I recall it correctly—was: 'Are you sure that this proposal has no legal loopholes?' I was the one who firmly said: 'No, Sir, there is no problem with this legislation', which I am not sure was the correct answer.

TS: Before that you served as assistant secretary to the LO/TCO mission that visited South Africa in 1975. The visit and the recommendations made by the mission were heavily criticized by ANC, sectors of LO/TCO and the Swedish solidarity movement as they went counter to the 'isolation strategy' and advocated support to existing trade unions in South Africa. Do you think that the recommendations based on the 'new strategy' were conducive to a strengthening of the labour movement in South Africa?

ÅM: Without any doubt. The most important factor for the change in South Africa was not overseas interventions, sanctions or other measures. Certainly, sanctions—particularly financial sanctions—played a role, but the important factor was that South African labour organized itself in close cooperation with ANC and to some extent with PAC and other political organizations. It would not only be unfair, but unintelligent to suggest that the liberation of South Africa would have come about without that. The great majority inside South Africa actually achieved the change by themselves.

I have never believed in strategic isolation of a country. I think that history shows that it does not work. If I am wrong, please show me the examples. Look at China, Iraq, Libya and a couple of other countries.

The liberation, or the political change, of South Africa was—although to some extent assisted by ANC in exile—really due to the rising of organized labour. That was evident in the 1970s and totally obvious in the 1980s. Politically, COSATU was ten times more productive and creative than—with all due respect—what was done in Stockholm.

However, I must admit that financial sanctions played a crucial role at a certain stage. They had a kind of trigger effect, but were not the general cause. Financial sanctions were mostly carried out by US banks. The South Africans could not get credit lines, but had to run the country on a cash basis. I truly believe that the white South Africans could have carried on, maintaining relative stability for another ten, maybe fifteen or twenty years. However, due to the financial sanctions they fell under pressure from big business.

TS: When you went to South Africa with LO/TCO in 1975, you visited a number of Swedish-owned companies. Did they in any decisive way differ from comparable South African companies regarding working conditions, union rights, salaries and so forth? If so, did your visit have an impact in this regard?

ÅM: The first part of the question is very easy to answer, because we did not visit any comparable South African companies. However, my impression is that—generally speaking—the Swedish companies did not differ very much from the South African except with regard to the attitudes of management. When you talked to the management at the Swedish companies, they were very open. Some were scared, but still open. If you said: 'This locker room looks dirty', they would not argue, but immediately say 'Yes, it is, and that will be changed'. I know for sure that the management at the company headquarters in Sweden—and I am pretty sure also the local management in South Africa—realized the importance of as good a working environment as possible. It implied—and this was the difference—negotiations with the employees.

Depending on how you look at change and how you believe that change in societies is coming about, you may argue that the fact that Swedish companies made a couple of progressive moves did not really change the system very much. But, step by step, it certainly changed the working environment. Not dramatically, but in a way that was noticeable for the employees, at least for a couple of thousand blacks. SKF—the second or third company in the metal sector—took a policy decision to negotiate, not via the central council system, but directly with the employees. I think that it contributed to the change that followed later on in the South African society and in the work places. In some cases, Swedish companies were actually in the forefront. I am not saying that it was key to the abolition of apartheid, but it certainly played a role in creating space.

To make it very clear, none of the trade unions that we came in contact with in those days—whether Communist, liberal or conservative—rejected us. There was a clear difference when you talked to ANC officials and when you talked to the COSATU base. The demands for sanctions and isolation were certainly not coming from organized labour. They wanted an active, dynamic presence rather than withdrawal. I know for sure that in most of the cases they did not want us to withdraw and that is the main reason why the five or six Swedish metal companies actually did not close. The metalworkers' unions really wanted them to stay.

TS: In exile, the South African Congress of Trade Unions (SACTU) was strongly represented. In your view, would it be fair to say that the support channelled by LO/TCO from 1977 onwards was given to strengthen the non-Communist unions in South Africa or was it given without ideological considerations?

ÅM: My very firm impression is that SACTU did not exist in South Africa. Of course, sections did, but SACTU was not anchored in the minds of the working population. It is true that SACTU played a role as an outside force—for instance, taking part at the UN—but inside SACTU did not have any significant role to play.

Whether the union movement in Sweden wanted to undermine SACTU by mainly giving assistance to other tendencies in the South African labour movement, I do not know. I would not be surprised if that was the case. LO/TCO had a lot of contacts with the European trade union movement and with the International Confederation of Free Trade Unions (ICFTU). Even if there was a bilateral assistance programme, the funds were partly channelled multilaterally via ICFTU and the attitudes towards SACTU were probably coloured by positions in Germany, Denmark and other NATO countries.

TS: The Swedish industrialist Peter Wallenberg was interviewed in *Svenska Dagbladet* before Sweden lifted sanctions and then in a TV programme after the democratic elections in South Africa. On both occasions, he said that sanctions had hit harder against Swedish industry than against South Africa. Do you think that his opinion is representative of Swedish business interests?

ÅM: What I think that he meant was simply that we should not underestimate the fact—particularly after October 1987—that Swedish commercial interests were forbidden in South Africa and that they earlier had not invested there. Looking at it from a business perspective, it had a significant negative impact. For a mining equipment company like Atlas Copco, sanctions influenced the market very much. The Anglo-American company Boart got a chance to grow substantially. In fact, they got about fifty per cent of the total market for mining equipment, while before sanctions they only had some twenty-five per cent. I think that it is fair to say that from a purely business point of view, sanctions played a very negative role when it came to market positions. Lost market shares can, of course, be recaptured, but in the mining equipment sector this is not so easy. The competitors—Finnish, Canadian and South African—are very strong.

TS: Another way of looking at it would be that this was an investment in the future. Do you think that the Swedish official position has created good-will for Swedish companies in the new South Africa, or would you say that it does not play a role and that Swedish business is treated as any other on the market?

ÅM: One must first recognize that South Africa at the business level is still dominated by the same establishment as before. The manager is still white. It may take a generation to change that situation.

I think that the solidarity factor has created good-will for Sweden in certain circles, but that is not to say that we win any particular favours. In a way, I do not think that we should ask for that either. When Nelson Mandela was here in 1992, we had a lunch meeting hosted by Peter Wallenberg. Mandela then said that Swedish industry would be rewarded for supporting the struggle and that he would love to do business with friends rather than with enemies. My very firm impression, however, is that there has not been a business pay-off. That should not be the case either, because it would be bribery and corruption.

I remember a discussion a year ago when I reminded one of the South African telecommunication union leaders that Ericsson's competitors Alcatel and Siemens had not supported the struggle, but that they had exploited the South African consumers to the extent that they paid three times more for telephone connections than the world average. He then said: 'That is history'. A short answer to the question would thus be that we have not, in business terms, noticed any particular favours because Sweden supported the anti-apartheid struggle. However, the doors seem to be open. We are fairly popular. That, I think, is a better basis than waiting for political pay-offs as a result of what we did in the past.

Ernst Michanek
Director General of SIDA and Chairman of the Consultative Committee on Humanitarian Assistance—Vice Chairman of the International Defence and Aid Fund
(Stockholm, 19 March 1996)

Tor Sellström: As Director General of SIDA from 1965 until 1979, you have probably more than any other Swede been assisting the process of national liberation in Southern Africa. When and how did your personal contacts with Southern Africa begin?

Ernst Michanek: I do not remember exactly, but it could have been in 1951, when I had one of my first international contacts as a Swedish delegate to a meeting of the United Nations' Economic and Social Council in Santiago de Chile. What had happened in South Africa in 1948 with the establishment of the apartheid regime was, of course, of such great international consequence that it must have been brought up at that meeting.

At that time, I was already connected to the beginnings of Swedish aid, because in 1948, I think, I had become a member of the board of the Swedish Institute, where the Department of Technical Assistance under Sixten Heppling had begun its work in 1946. In 1954, I became the chairman—a royal chancellor, as it was then called—of the department at the Ministry for Foreign Affairs that dealt with multilateral assistance through the United Nations.

TS: In retrospect, would you say that it was difficult to mobilize the Swedish opinion around the issue of South and Southern Africa?

EM: No, on the contrary. In my opinion, it was not the government that took the political initiative in these matters. Even less so in the case of matters of a controversial nature. The whole build-up of the Swedish public opinion on Southern Africa came from below. The thinking that developed in the student movement was, for example, very important in this regard. I had experience of this, not least in Uppsala during the war. I was the first Nordic *ombudsman* of the Swedish National Union of Students (SFS) in the 1940s and the international relations of SFS were more or less conducted by that office together with the international *ombudsman*, who at that time was Curt-Steffan Giesecke. The idea of assisting foreign students was, of course, both very important and inspiring.

TS: Some prominent Swedish intellectuals were at an early stage also actively involved?

EM: Absolutely. People like Ivar Harrie, Herbert Tingsten and others.

TS: In your central positions in the Ministry of Labour and in the Ministry of Foreign Affairs, were you also in contact with these early opinion makers on South and Southern Africa?

EM: I entered the Ministry of Social Affairs and Labour on 1 January 1948 and during the first year I was really orientating myself, looking around, reading and trying to prepare my business. I did not have much time for other matters. In 1949, I published the first issue of *Socialboken*, which almost became general reading for all students of social and labour policies. Thus, at a very early stage I became somewhat of a teacher and it was in that capacity that I established my best contacts with the opinion makers.

TS: If we jump to 1965, when SIDA was established and you became its first Director General, would you say that that was the time when the official Swedish involvement in Southern Africa began?

EM: Well, it really began earlier. There was perhaps not much in terms of money, but what was later referred to as the Committee on Humanitarian Assistance already existed. It was established in 1964—one year before SIDA—under the Agency for International Assistance (NIB), but I think that it already by then had existed in some form or the other. The Central Committee for Swedish Technical Assistance to Less Developed Areas (CK)—the predecessor to NIB and SIDA—certainly had many contacts that led to the future programme of humanitarian assistance. It had several beginnings. The public opinion in these matters had been built up by non-governmental forces and by the press.

During the years immediately after the Second World War, or rather, during the latter part of the war, there was so much that pointed in this direction, so I think that there are roots further down in history. In fact, I have discussed the background of the Swedish involvement in Africa in some articles and speeches over the years. Not infrequently have I said that our concern as a nation for the developing countries had a high degree of concretisation in what took place in Ethiopia in 1936, when a Swedish Red Cross ambulance was bombarded by Mussolini's air force. My own memory starts at that time. I was then a young boy of seventeen, a pupil at the Fjellstedt School in Uppsala, and I think that we very well understood what was going on in certain parts of the world. There are many factors like that which should be taken into consideration when we talk about the background to Sweden's involvement against apartheid.

TS: Would it be fair to say that there was a strong liberal current, as well as influence by the churches, in this early Swedish opinion?

EM: Yes, indeed. The whole Christian community and—in general—the liberal forces were very active. Particularly the churches, because they had much more experience than anybody else when it came to developments in the Southern parts of the world. Ethiopia was particularly important in this regard.

TS: You mentioned the Consultative Committee on Humanitarian Assistance, which, I understand, was established to advise both NIB/SIDA and the Ministry for Foreign Affairs. How was the committee set up?

EM: Ulla Lindström was the Minister of Development Cooperation when I was appointed Director General and she felt that the chairman of the committee should be the head of SIDA. Within its own ranks, the government administration had very little experience of this kind of activity. On some occasions, I got the impression that officials in the Ministry for Foreign Affairs understood 'aid' as helping helpless Swedes in far away countries to get home. Speaking about aid, they thought of Swedes coming to the embassies to look for assistance...

The members of the Committee on Humanitarian Assistance had already been appointed when I became the chairman. Ulla Lindström had appointed them in 1964, or perhaps in 1963. The composition of the committee was carefully thought out. Since we were dealing with matters that were not necessarily well looked upon by the governments in the countries concerned, she wanted almost all the so-called grassroot organizations in Sweden to be involved. The committee should represent a cross-section of the Swedish society. A good deal of the work had to be undertaken under different degrees of secrecy. Against this background, it was important that the leaders of, in particular, the youth movements were knowledgeable about the work, without at the same time having the right to publicly speak about it.

In the committee, we had an absolutely wonderful cooperation and very open discussions on all kinds of matters. For example, when we were to recommend which liberation movements to support, it was a prerequisite that we had an open discussion. We had to come to conclusions on very difficult political issues and I remember only very few situations where there were real differences of opinion. The committee was well composed and served an enormously important purpose all the time. All the major political forces were represented, including the conservatives. I do not remember if they ever opposed a decision. I do not think that they did, because my personal conviction was that we as far as possible should avoid disagreements. The normal situation was that we reached agreement by consensus.

TS: In 1969, the Swedish parliament—through a statement by the Appropriations' Committee—paved the way for Swedish humanitarian assistance to the Southern African liberation movements. Such assistance was subsequently extended through SIDA. Why was the assistance given directly to the liberation movements and not via the OAU, for example?

EM: One reason was, of course, that our contacts primarily were with people in the field and not with any official body. We had to try to avoid being involved in administrative red tape and, in fact, I do not know if the OAU at that time—or later—would have been capable of doing anything that would not have implied more administration than aid. We also had to be very strict with the aspects of reporting and accounting.

To be of any importance in the struggle against colonialism and apartheid, it was absolutely necessary to work with revolutionaries and warriors and you could not do that without being rather radical in your own thinking. We had long discussions about this, not least with the Committee on Foreign Affairs of the Swedish parliament. The conclusion was that Swedish political decisions in these matters needed the backing of a position taken by important bodies of the United Nations. At the same time, that also motivated our actions against the regimes in question. It took many years to convince the international community that national liberation was a question referred to in the Charter of the United Nations and, thus, that both national governments and the United Nations should act accordingly. However, at the time there were sufficiently big majorities on very clear resolutions passed by different bodies of the United Nations for us to take action. Perhaps not by the Security Council, but often by the General Assembly, the Economic and Social Council and others. In my opinion, that was the key. But Sweden took the conclusions much further than most others did.

TS: In this connection, do you think that the early personal relations between many Swedish political leaders and leaders of the Southern African liberation movements made it easier for Sweden to take this stand?

EM: Yes, that was, of course, very important. For example, the position of a person like Olof Palme was—in addition to his own international family background—very much formed by his work within the international student movement in favour of victims of war and the like. We were, probably, early because we had people with this kind of experience in central positions, both in non-governmental organizations and in the government. For me, my own experiences were important. When I was a school-boy in the late 1930s and as a student in Uppsala during the Second World War, Sweden had, in fact, received thousands of refugee students from the neighbouring countries and many of us were closely connected to them. At an early stage, it was therefore easy for us to draw the conclusion that in order to be efficient in what we set out to do, we had to move beyond what ordinary diplomacy was ready to achieve.

TS: The Southern African liberation movements supported by Sweden also received support from the Soviet Union and/or China. How did you look upon this?

EM: Well, when it comes to my own personal convictions regarding what to do and whom to work with, it is of relevance that I had my experiences from the war years. We had to take a rather heart-breaking decision on the question of what kind of allies the government of the Soviet Union or the Communist Party were. Towards the end of 1939 or at the beginning of 1940, I had lined up at the recruitment office for the Swedish voluntary force in Finland, but I was too young and was not accepted. However, I was totally ready to join the war against the Soviet Union in whatever capacity. At that time, I had two friends from my school who fell in Finland, as soldiers on the side of the Finnish army. However, only a year later we had to widen our thinking when the Soviet Union became an ally. We therefore had to be pragmatic in these matters.

TS: With the exception of Zimbabwe—where Sweden supported both ZANU and ZAPU—SIDA channelled assistance to only one movement in each country in Southern Africa. However, in the case of Angola this was questioned in some political milieus which advocated Swedish support to both MPLA and FNLA. Was this a difficult case to settle?

EM: The Liberal Party and other parts of the liberal movement supported FNLA. We assessed the situation in Angola very carefully and had all kinds of connections to find out whom we should support. We had sympathies with the final objective of both MPLA and FNLA, but as they were fighting each other we had to discuss whether to support both movements or only one of them. Together, at the table, we came to the conclusion that the arguments in favour of MPLA were much stronger than the arguments for FNLA. There were counter-arguments against FNLA. We had to take a hard political decision.

There was a similar situation in Rhodesia, now Zimbabwe, where there also were contradictions between the different parts of the liberation movement. In that case, I was myself active, talking to Joshua Nkomo and Robert Mugabe on several occasions. That went on for years until we—after some trial and error—told each of them that 'unless you find a way of working together, we cannot support either of you'. That was more or less the beginning of the Patriotic Front between ZAPU and ZANU. I think that we almost demanded that the front should be created. Of course, within the front the infighting continued and SIDA's board of directors met with Joshua Nkomo—waving his stick like a marshal; very grandiose in his appearance—in Lusaka and with Robert Mugabe in Maputo. Their way of talking about each other—particularly about each other's lack of efficiency—was tremendous. However, the situation was very, very delicate, so we had to take a position. Outside the military field, Sweden was by far the largest and most important financial supporter of both ZAPU and ZANU.

Stockholm was a very important meeting point between the Zimbabwean liberation movements and international actors. I think that we played a prominent role in this connection and whatever decisions we took had been considered very thoroughly. In the case of Zimbabwe, we came to the conclusion that we had to steer in a way that we otherwise did not like to do. It was sometimes rather unpleasant, but necessary.

TS: In the case of Zimbabwe, did you also consult with African leaders such as Julius Nyerere and Kenneth Kaunda?

EM: Of course. David Wirmark and I had more than one important meeting with President Kaunda on how to deal with this matter. We also wanted to inform him about our thinking and keep him in the picture.

TS: If we return to Angola, you find that UNITA had quite good relations with Sweden in the latter part of the 1960s. Was the question of Swedish humanitarian support to UNITA ever discussed at that time?

EM: The position of Zambia was important in this connection. Whatever we might have thought about UNITA at that time, we simply could not support an organization that was impossible from the point of view of some of our co-operating partners.

TS: How about PAC? Why did they not receive bilateral Swedish humanitarian support?

EM: Well, I do not remember to what extent we had friendly feelings about PAC in the beginning. My memory is probably influenced by later events. PAC was, after all, a break-away group from ANC. During my close relations with IDAF over so many years I understood what it meant to uphold principles of the kind that John Collins had made his at an early stage, namely that you must support whoever is under the burden of apartheid and not take positions of a political character. However, in my position as a member of the board of IDAF I personally had to act against PAC. Of course, I had entered the IDAF board only after I had left SIDA. In any case, we had to put an end to the support of PAC, which had developed into something rather bad, with people murdering each other even in the circles that we were dealing with. If an organization was disrupting the struggle against apartheid in the way that PAC did, then I had to be very firm.

One of the results of my position was that some of the leaders of the PAC at the beginning of the 1980s produced a booklet in London of around a hundred stencilled pages, called something like *The curve in the South African spy ring*. It was particularly dealing with two people, namely, primarily, Horst Kleinschmidt, the Director of IDAF, and Ernst Michanek, as his main supporter, or the other way around if you like. Both of us were, in fact, depicted as supporters of the South African police. It was quite incredible, but it was also unpleasant to know that such a publication was being circulated in many quarters. Of course, the PAC leaders hated us enormously, because in the past they had had their opportunities at the expense of IDAF and therefore also of the Swedish government. This was cut off. I should not use any derogatory words about them, because I pitied them a great deal. But what they could do with the money that they received had nothing at all to do with the struggle against apartheid in South Africa. It was far too much to be accepted.

TS: However, PAC was recognized by the OAU and also received support from some governments, like Norway?

EM: Yes, but we could not understand why the OAU held that position, although we could understand why Nyerere found it reasonable, or acceptable, to give PAC a place and support the organization in Tanzania. However, to give another example of our trials in this matter: When I was the chairman of two important UN institutions, namely the Technical Assistance Committee of the United Nations and of the governing body of the International Labour Organisation (ILO), the ILO initiated support of a project in Tanzania for the training of PAC freedom fighters. But as far as I could understand from my different viewpoints and positions, what PAC did was not in any way worth the money. I thought that it was totally wrong to support such a project. If it ever existed in practice, it was so far from the blueprints that it would have been completely out of order to support it.

TS: In addition to ANC and PAC, there was also in South Africa Gatsha Buthelezi's Inkatha movement. Did Inkatha ever receive Swedish official assistance through SIDA?

EM: Yes, we supported Inkatha, for example through assistance via Ravan Press in South Africa, which on behalf of Buthelezi had particular pages published in South African newspapers as instruction and training material for the illiterate part of the population, particularly in Soweto. That started very early and I was later closely connected to this activity.

I know Gatsha Buthelezi very well. He was often in Sweden. He came to my office and to my home and I had secret meetings with him in several places. There is a long history between Sweden, Inkatha and ANC.

Inkatha and ANC also held bilateral meetings between themselves here in Sweden that were never given any publicity.

TS: The break between Inkatha and ANC only occurred in 1979, after a meeting in London?

EM: Yes. I had a very important role to play in the setting up of that meeting in London. On the basis of earlier discussions—including meetings in Stockholm—Oliver Tambo and Gatsha Buthelezi reached an agreement and also laid down how to treat the different parts of the agreement. However, for reasons that I could discuss for a long time without coming to a conclusion, the tragedy was that Buthelezi in the plane from London to Johannesburg openly and clearly broke the fundamentals of the agreement by talking to journalists about what had taken place in London. That created a lot of bitterness in ANC.

Like Nelson Mandela, Oliver Tambo knew Gatsha Buthelezi very well from his younger days, but he could never understand why Buthelezi did what he did. For long years and on many occasions, Inkatha had tried to become clean through different missions to Stockholm and many meetings all over the place. It was very painful to me personally, as well as to the Church of Sweden and others who had been involved, to come to the conclusion after some time that we could not continue our cooperation with Buthelezi. Oliver Tambo told me several times: 'I cannot understand Gatsha. How can he do a thing like that?'. But he did not say: 'I cannot see the man' or 'I hate the man'. Not at all. Instead, he said: 'How can we get together again?'. That was important. However, the racial position that PAC had taken had a parallel within Inkatha and that was, of course, impossible for ANC to accept. Non-racialism is one of the main backbones of ANC's ideology.

TS: You have mentioned the International Defence and Aid Fund (IDAF). The activities of IDAF and some other important British-based organizations—such as the Africa Educational Trust (AET)—were almost exclusively financed by Sweden and the other Nordic countries. Did the Swedish government not approach the British government to share the financial burden?

EM: Of course. I had a central position in our relations with the British, but I think that we probably did not talk to them in sufficiently hard terms. We only showed them what we thought that they should do. However, they knew exactly, at least during the times of Labour governments. In spite of that, they contributed absolutely nothing. Well, I remember that John Collins once said that the British government had given IDAF five thousand or five hundred pounds or something like that. It was tragic all through. The same goes for AET. However, because these organizations were based in London, it is probably so that even many beneficiaries believe that they were supported by the British, when in actual fact the support came from Sweden and the other Nordic countries.

TS: Were the British or other Western governments embarrassed about the fact that they did not play a more honourable role? Or did they criticize Sweden?

EM: I think that we did not have the time to waste on meaningless discussions with the British or others, for example, the US government. We had many friends in these administrations and we rather enjoyed having a nice relationship with them, using their premises—their territory, as it were—without asking for anything more than just that. I do not remember any criticism against us and I think that it probably was based on certain feelings of shame or envy on their part. We also had the support of the United Nations in a wonderful way. When it comes to IDAF, I counted each year the number of governments that gave it financial contributions through the United Nations and at the peak of the activities they were not less than fifty. However, many of them strongly emphasized that they did not want to be mentioned by name. They wanted to support, but not officially.

TS: Is there anything that you would like to add?

EM: I would like to underline that the struggle was not ours. The struggle in Southern Africa was waged by the oppressed and colonized peoples through their liberation movements. What we could do was to strengthen them. That was the aim of our assistance and that was in itself based on a great deal of discretion. For example, if we were to be embarrassed by indirectly being connected with the Soviet Union, should our Western partners not have been ashamed of being connected to all kinds of oppressors and colonialists? We were in a position to create connections that otherwise would not have been created and we had to try all possible means to do that, assisting behind the scenes to bring adversaries together for the building of peace.

Hillevi Nilsson
Africa Groups in Sweden
(Stockholm, 4 February 1997)

Tor Sellström: Did your involvement with Africa start with Angola?

Hillevi Nilsson: No, it did not. The first time that I became involved with Africa was when I was thirteen. I lived in Nyköping and was a candidate for confirmation. The Swedish missionary Barbro Johansson came there to tell us about Tanzania. We then formed a small group which tried to collect clothes and other things for her work in Tanzania. That was in the 1950s.

My next contact was with South Africa at the beginning of the 1960s. I then lived in Stockholm during the first Swedish boycott of South African goods. I participated but not in an organized way. When I later went to university, I became involved with the FNL Groups and the Vietnam movement. Had there been an organization working for Africa, I would perhaps have been involved with that. I was a member of the Baptist Church and my husband and I conducted Sunday school classes where we also talked about the missions. Discovering the bad things the missionaries had done, we started to read a lot about Africa. It was mainly about Kenya and South Africa, and a bit about what was then called Rhodesia. However, when we became involved with the FNL Groups, the doors to the Baptist Church were more or less closed.

At the end of the 1960s, I got into contact with the journal *Kommentar*. They had formed a study group on Africa in which I participated. In the beginning, we were mainly dealing with Rhodesia, Kenya and Ethiopia. At that time—between 1969 and 1971—I met quite a few representatives of different liberation movements who came to *Kommentar*. We interviewed them and published their stories. That is also how I for the first time got into contact with MPLA. It was when Daniel Chipenda visited Stockholm in 1970. He came to introduce the representative of MPLA to Sweden, António Alberto Neto. Soon thereafter, Agostinho Neto also came to Sweden, after the Rome conference. I met them and interviewed them.

In early 1971, a group called Verdandi was planning a trip to Zambia to write a book about the country. They had done something similar on Tanzania before. They contacted *Kommentar*'s study group on Africa and asked if there was anybody who wanted to go with them and take care of the chapters on foreign policy and mass media. The foreign policy chapter should include Zambia's relations with the different liberation movements that were represented there at that time. Elisabeth Hedborg and I—both members of the study group—decided to go with them. At that time, I already had contacts with the Stockholm Africa Group. That was my first visit to Africa.

TS: Was it during this trip in 1971 that you first visited the MPLA camps in western Zambia?

HN: Yes. We went around interviewing people from the liberation movements at the Liberation Centre in Lusaka. Chipenda then asked us if we wanted to go with MPLA to the border. It caused a discussion within the Verdandi group, because they did not want us to be away for ten or fourteen days out of the four weeks that we had. That was a lot. But we solemnly promised that we were going to do our part of the book and could thus join MPLA.

TS: In 1969, the Swedish parliament agreed to direct Swedish official humanitarian support to the national liberation movements in Southern Africa. How did you at *Kommentar* look upon that?

HN: I would say that the position of both *Kommentar* and the different Africa Groups in Sweden was that Sweden had two faces, a hard one and a soft one. We very much thought that it was a decision by the Social Democratic Party and not by the other parties. That is how we interpreted it.

TS: Did your background in the church not indicate that a strong solidarity opinion—at least on South Africa—was expressed by the liberal centre in Sweden?

HN: Well, of course I knew that and many others did as well. But with regard to the church, I think that it mainly had to do with very special persons like Gunnar Helander, who had an African experience and had written good pieces on Africa. My own experience from the church was that I was excluded because I advocated ideas similar to his. So, I did not really trust the church in these matters.

It should also be said, I think, that the left at that time took action from the basis of a general feeling of security in the Swedish Social Democratic welfare state. Even if we were attacking the Social Democrats, we were a bit proud of being Swedes in relation to the Third World. More than anything else, the criticism was made in order to make the Social Democrats go further. To push them, although we at the time did not really see it like that.

TS: Following upon Agostinho Neto's visit to Sweden in 1970, the Swedish government decided to grant humanitarian assistance to MPLA. Did you notice any reaction to this decision during your travels with MPLA in 1971 and 1972? Was it known to the MPLA cadres that they received government support from Sweden?

HN: Well, in 1971 we did not notice it, although the very invitation made to us by Chipenda perhaps was because of the Swedish support. As I see it afterwards, it could have been. But, of course, we did not understand that at the time.

However, in 1972, we did notice the support. Some things had already been delivered. They were also aware that it was purely humanitarian aid. For example, MPLA had asked for boots, but they could not get that, because boots were considered to be military. They got sandals instead. Things like that. They talked about it. At the level of group commanders they would know about the Swedish support and also laugh a bit about the sandals.

There was also an interesting episode regarding tinned herring from Sweden. It came to Dar es Salaam in great quantities and then it was transported—as all MPLA's supplies—all the way to Zambia's border with Angola and from there on people's heads into the country. Anyway, there were quite a lot of thefts in the harbour of Dar es Salaam and MPLA became suspicious about the tinned fish from Sweden because the harbour workers who had eaten it got sick. They had eaten it all! They did not take the herring out of the sauce, and got diarrhoea. So, MPLA tried the fish on us all the way from Dar es Salaam into Angola to see if we were going to get sick also. And then we had to show the people inside Angola that we were eating the fish without getting sick.

TS: In your view, what factors could explain that the Swedish government decided to give humanitarian support to MPLA at that stage?

HN: Well, if I had been asked that question in the early 1970s, I would have said that it was because of the good work by the Africa Groups. Today, I am not so sure that it was the only reason. But we had made a study on the different movements in Angola and I think that some people in the Social Democratic Party read it. I also think that the Swedish government perhaps was influenced by Julius Nyerere. I think Agostinho Neto had really good contacts with Nyerere and Nyerere had good contacts with Olof Palme and the Swedish Social Democratic Party on the whole.

TS: It was probably also influenced by Amílcar Cabral and—before his death—Eduardo Mondlane?

HN: Yes, of course. I do not know so much about Eduardo Mondlane, but Amílcar Cabral definitely.

TS: At that time, there were quite important representatives in the Liberal Party who supported FNLA. Why, do you think, did the Swedish government never give assistance to FNLA?

HN: One factor was, of course, that it was the Liberal Party that advocated that, while the Social Democratic Party had its own way. There was some party politics involved, I think. But not only that. Around that time, there was also an investigation made by the OAU Liberation Committee, which drew the conclusion that FNLA was not very active inside Angola.

TS: The Liberal Party also demanded the expulsion of Portugal from EFTA. Do you remember if this demand was high on MPLA's agenda?

HN: Their point was that the Swedish companies should withdraw from Portugal. That was the point they made to us and other solidarity groups in Europe. For example, there was a big boycott campaign against coffee from Angola which MPLA supported. That campaign started in Holland, but it never grew strong in Sweden. We imported very little coffee from Angola, almost nothing. It was difficult to get the campaign going here. It was very strong in Holland and in Canada.

TS: A third movement in Angola was UNITA. The Swedish Social Democratic Party initiated relations with UNITA and Jonas Savimbi visited Sweden in 1967. After that, the relations seem to have died completely. What could have happened?

HN: I do not think that it was because of difficulties to contact UNITA here in Sweden. There was a UNITA representative in Sweden, Stella Makunga. It rather had to do with what happened to UNITA itself, both inside Angola and in relation to Zambia. When UNITA attacked the Benguela railway, they got into problems with Zambia. It was also, I think, difficult to contact them in Angola. As far as I have understood, they were not very successful in the 1960s.

TS: The Maoist influence in the Swedish extra-parliamentary left was very strong at the end of the 1960s. That would have presented a fertile ground for UNITA. Which political organizations in Sweden were the strongest supporters of UNITA?

HN: It was the Communist League Marxist-Leninists (KFML) and the Clarté Association. They were really strong advocates of UNITA and it was with them that Stella Makunga had most of her contacts. But when KFML split, the 'revolutionaries' in KFML(r) supported MPLA. At that time, the Africa Groups did not see themselves as a kind of mass movement, but rather as study and information groups. We lobbied a lot among the left groups and at one stage—I think that it was in 1971—we also got the KFML to take part in demonstrations for MPLA. But it was only on one occasion.

TS: You visited Lusaka at the beginning of 1974 and had the opportunity to discuss the Chipenda rebellion directly with Agostinho Neto. In this connection, how did you experience the position of the Swedish embassy in Lusaka?

HN: I was in Lusaka at the beginning of January 1974. I did not meet many people from the Swedish embassy. A group from the Stockholm Africa Group was in Dar es Salaam for a holiday. I met Neto and he asked me if I would go with him to Lusaka for a meeting. There were problems and he wanted—as he said—the MPLA cadres to explain the situation to the Africa Groups through me. When I came to Lusaka, there was a rather big meeting in the MPLA camp. Dilolwa was the main person explaining the situation to me. It was complicated. Chipenda and the so-called Eastern Revolt had attempted a coup in 1973. They tried to murder Neto, as a matter of fact. The problems escalated when the Zambians supported Chipenda. He had a lot of support in Zambia. He had been based there and he was their main contact in MPLA.

Kurt Kristiansson was the SIDA representative in the Swedish embassy in Lusaka. Chipenda's wife was a very good friend of Kristiansson's wife. They met every week. MPLA told me that Chipenda through Kristiansson had managed to cut off the Swedish government's support from October or November 1973. MPLA wondered if this was done on instructions from the Swedish government, asking me to meet either Kristiansson or the Swedish ambassador, Iwo Dölling. But they were not there. It was Christmas time and they were on holiday. I met somebody at the embassy, who just said: 'I do not want to talk about this. You have to talk to the ambassador'. I was rather nervous, because I had never been dealing in the diplomatic corridors. Anyway, I then proposed that I would take the matter to Sweden and that Saydi Mingas and I would go to the Ministry for Foreign Affairs and talk to Bengt Säve-Söderbergh. Returning to Sweden, we did so. At the Ministry for Foreign Affairs they said that the aid had not been cut off from Sweden. It had been done in Lusaka. Still, it was a difficult situation. If the Zambian government did not allow goods to MPLA through the border, what could they do?

By the way, the reason why Neto called on me to go to Zambia was that the Africa

Groups in around October 1973—when we found out about the difficulties with the Eastern Revolt and Zambia's support to Chipenda—wrote an open letter to Kaunda and also sent it to the newspapers in Zambia and Tanzania.

TS: The Swedish solidarity movement with MPLA was very strong, also involving material support to the liberation struggle. You sent, for example, radio communication equipment to MPLA, which was requested by Agostinho Neto and played a very important part. How did you organize that?

HN: Well, some things of this kind were done, but it was not anything big. There was a materials group in the Stockholm Africa Group, with two or three engineers. They bought some components, and built things. However, in 1975 I think that they perhaps made a more important contribution. This small group then built an alarm for the National Bank in Luanda. The situation was very fluid in 1975, with attacks from FNLA, and MPLA was worried that they would take over the bank. MPLA wanted an alarm connected directly to the police and to MPLA. It was built by the Stockholm Africa Group, and transported to Luanda. It still functioned some years afterwards.

TS: At that time, you and your husband, Lars Nilsson, went to Angola to work for MPLA?

HN: Yes, in 1975, before independence. We stayed there for nine years.

TS: Before going to Angola, you worked at the MPLA office in Stockholm, which covered all the Nordic countries. In your view, how did the Nordic governments differ in their policies vis-à-vis MPLA and Angola?

HN: Sweden was the best, followed by Denmark, Norway and Finland. Finland was worst. Iceland did not do much, but what they said was not so bad.

TS: How about the solidarity movement?

HN: I would say that the strongest solidarity movement was in Sweden. In Denmark and Norway it was more or less the same. The Norwegian Council for Southern Africa had a good part, but there were also those who were very influenced by the Maoists. In Denmark, it was mainly the World University Service. And in Finland there was a good group called the Africa Committee, although it was a bit particular because it formed part of the Soviet-influenced World Peace Council. Nevertheless, the Africa Committee also had activists.

TS: In February 1976, Olof Palme published an article in *Dagens Nyheter* in which he strongly supported MPLA. Later that year, Palme served as a middleman between Neto and Castro on the one hand and Kissinger on the other regarding the conflict in Angola. Do you think that there was a close relationship between Palme and Neto?

HN: No, not really. I think that their contacts rather resulted from the close relationship between Neto and Nyerere and the close relations between Palme and Nyerere. I think that Nyerere was the middleman. But it is very difficult to say if Palme and Neto were close or not. I do not really know.

TS: You have been actively involved in Swedish solidarity work with Southern Africa in general and Angola in particular for more than twenty-five years. Looking back, which initiatives were the most important for MPLA and Angola?

HN: I think that we perhaps did the most important things at the beginning of the 1970s. Information was an important part of this. The fact that we tried to analyze the different organizations in Angola. Lobbying in favour of MPLA was another important part.

TS: How did you obtain your information?

HN: We got some from Portugal and from people in West Germany, Canada and the United States. We also got information from Tanzania. From people who were studying at the university of Dar es Salaam and others who had close contacts with MPLA and the OAU Liberation Committee.

TS: It seems that *Kommentar* played an important role in this context. Would you agree with that?

HN: Yes, I agree completely. In the case of Angola, the South Africa Committee in Lund had, however, already started this kind of assessment around 1967. It was mainly Dick Urban Vestbro and Rolf Gustavsson who worked on this. They also had contacts with Anders Johansson, although that was more on Mozambique.

TS: In your view, how did MPLA look upon the Swedish solidarity movement?

HN: Well, I did not really understand its importance for MPLA until Neto came to Sweden in April 1974. He was really worried at that time. We had a meeting with the Africa Groups at our place in Vällingby. Rolf Gustavsson was present, as well as people from the different Africa Groups in Sweden and from *Kommentar*. Neto then asked us straight out: 'What are we going to do? You are the only ones that we can trust in this situation. We cannot trust the Soviet Union, the Swedish government or anyone. What are we going to do? Can you as a solidarity movement tell us?' But, of course, we could not answer. He was foreseeing what would happen later, when they tried to isolate MPLA from the independence discussions. But those who eventually resolved the problem were not the solidarity organizations. It was the people in Luanda.

Anyway, I think that one important contribution by the Africa Groups and other international solidarity organizations was that MPLA could rely on us and discuss with us.

TS: What could the Swedish solidarity movement have done better?

HN: We could have done much better around and after Angola's independence. Until then, we had been very flexible, but somewhere in 1976-77 the flexibility withered away. I take a lot of the blame for this. My husband and I were perhaps at the wrong place at the time. We should have stayed in Sweden if we wanted better work done by the Africa Groups for Angola. We were simply consumed by the situation in Luanda. For example, in 1976 there was a delegation from the Africa Groups coming to Angola from Mozambique. They had made an agreement with Mozambique and they wanted to make it a blueprint for Angola. It did not work, of course. The situation was very different. Lasse and I should have been much more active, telling them so. MPLA became a bit irritated. I think that it was natural. You cannot just come from FRELIMO and say: 'We want the same agreement with you.'

We could also have done much better during later years. Nevertheless, we did something important for MPLA before the elections in 1992. That was a difficult situation. Many in MPLA thought that they would lose the elections. But I think that it was of some importance that we had our old funds for MPLA, which were then used to buy MPLA flags. The real importance of this, however, was that somebody outside Angola still had the guts to believe in MPLA.

TS: How would you, finally, characterize the relations between the solidarity movement and the Swedish government?

HN: Well, a lot of things have changed over the years, but there is something that has not and that is that the mainstream in the Africa Groups always wanted to be a kind of lobby group towards SIDA and the Ministry for Foreign Affairs. We believed—and still do—that there are many good people who know a lot at both SIDA and the ministry. So I would say our main task has always been and still is to provide solidly reliable studies and information on Southern Africa as a basis for lobbying.

Pierre Schori
Social Democratic Party—International Secretary—Under-Secretary of State for Foreign Affairs
Minister of International Development Cooperation
(Stockholm, 28 June 1996)

Tor Sellström: When and how did your long involvement with Southern Africa begin?

Pierre Schori: My first contact was in 1965, when I started to work at the headquarters of the Social Democratic Party in Stockholm. At that time, the party had relations with SWANU of South West Africa, today Namibia. There were a number of SWANU students in Sweden and you could say that they opened the eyes of both the party and of the public opinion to the situation in that part of the world. They participated in meetings and at our annual First of May rallies. We also had a person by the name of Tom Nässbjer engaged in certain projects on South West Africa. So, my first contact was with SWANU, although at that time I did not know where South West Africa was. Zedekia Ngavirue, who is now Namibia's ambassador to Brussels, had to show me on the map.

We had a very personal relationship. We were more or less of the same age and we all lived in students' homes. When I came to Stockholm, I stayed in Bernt Carlsson's room, on the floor. We went jogging together, Zedekia Ngavirue, Charles Kauraisa—who later became a Rössing man in Namibia—Bernt and myself. They were not used to jogging, but Bernt and I told them: 'If you are going to be guerrilla soldiers, you must be in good physical condition!' From that time I also remember an article that Kauraisa sent to Peking Review. It was entitled 'Long live the correct line!' and was signed Charles Kauraisa, Studenthemmet Nyponet, Stockholm, Sweden.

TS: You participated in the first international conference on South West Africa, held in Oxford, England, in March 1966?

PS: Yes, I did. The Swedish delegation to the conference was very big. Olof Palme was the chairman. This was when Palme said that he had noticed that the International Court of Justice was not competent to take a decision on South West Africa. He said that the court was very 'impotent'. At the time of the Oxford conference, the International Defence and Aid Fund, IDAF, had just been banned in South Africa, but Palme declared that Sweden was going to continue to support it.

TS: It was around that time that the Social Democratic Party and the Swedish government shifted the support from SWANU to SWAPO. What motivated this change?

PS: Well, there was an initial transition period, but we came to believe that SWAPO had more roots and that it was more anchored in the people. Of course, via the OAU the African states were at that time also in favour of SWAPO, and in the late 1960s and the beginning of the 1970s it was natural for us to follow the advice of the OAU Liberation Committee. I visited the committee several times.

There was no particular incident behind this development. It was simply based on reality. But we kept our contacts and our friendship with the SWANU people, because they had played such an important role by opening the eyes of the Swedish public to the African question. The first close contact that the Swedish Social Democratic Party had with any liberation movement in Southern Africa was really with SWANU. They came to Sweden as refugees, worked to raise an opinion and kept us informed. Initially, SWANU also formed part of the South African United Front together with the ANC and the South African Indian Congress. So, there was coordination between SWANU and ANC.

TS: Would it be fair to say that Tanzania and Zambia played important roles as bridge-builders between Sweden and the Southern African liberation movements?

PS: Yes, especially Tanzania, where Olof Palme, Ingvar Carlsson, Thage G. Peterson and other leading social democrats who were active in the Social Democratic Youth League (SSU) at an early stage had initiated support to the TANU Youth League. For many of them it was their first international involvement and it stayed with them all the time. You always remember your young loves, so to speak. And, of course, Tanzania's role in the OAU Liberation Committee and Nyerere's international standing also helped us very much.

TS: In 1969, the Swedish Parliament paved the way for direct Swedish official support to the Southern African liberation movements and humanitarian assistance was subsequently extended through SIDA. These movements were backed by the Soviet Union and/or China and waged an armed struggle. How did you look upon this?

PS: At an early stage, we saw that there was a contradiction in the Western approach to the liberation struggle. On the one hand, some of the Western countries cooperated closely with the apartheid state and the colonial powers and simply ignored the liberation forces out of economic interests. On the other, the West stood for democracy vis-à-vis the Soviet Union. During the Cold War, there was a worldwide power struggle and it was both obvious and logical that the super powers involved themselves in Southern Africa, trying to extend their influence and make the best out of the situation. At the same time, the liberation movements looked for support wherever they could get it. Sometimes they got that support from the Soviet Union and sometimes they did not.

Some of the movements—like Amílcar Cabral's PAIGC, for example—were very proud and did not accept any support that had strings attached to it. In that situation, support from Sweden was very handy. It had no strings attached and we knew—through studies and contacts with these people—that they were not Communists. Instead, the main ideological force was nationalism. They wanted to get rid of dictatorships and colonialism. Over the years, we heard many stories from the liberation movements about the problems that they had with the Soviet Union regarding political conditions and so on. The support from the Soviet Union was, so to speak, a necessary evil for the liberation movements. Of course, at the same time they appreciated it, because—as Nyerere said—'you cannot fight the colonial powers' jet-fighters and tanks with bows and arrows'. But, I would not support the expression 'Soviet-backed movements' and they themselves would never use that. You could as well call them 'Swedish-backed'.

TS: How about political pluralism? The Socialist International, for example, supported political parties that embraced political pluralism. With the exception of Zimbabwe, the Swedish Social Democratic Party—both in and outside government—advocated support to one liberation movement in the countries in Southern Africa. Why?

PS: Well, we closely—but not slavishly—followed the recommendations of the OAU Liberation Committee, because we thought that the Africans were the best judges of their own situation. The United Nations General Assembly also followed the recommendations by the OAU. In some cases, like in Namibia—where we had old links with SWANU—we tried to make SWANU and SWAPO work together. Sometimes they did that from their own free will and sometimes due to our friendly advice. In other cases, like in Zimbabwe, we refused to give unilateral recognition to one movement. We thought that both ZANU and ZAPU were authentic movements and that there was no reason for us to follow the demand of one or the other. When one of them asked for unilateral support we said that 'we do not give you unilateral recognition, because that is not up to us to do. We see two movements and we hope that you can work together.' But we understood that we could not force them to work together just because we stood for pluralism in Sweden. So, in some cases we made our own choice.

TS: Would it be fair to say that the Social Democratic Party and—by extension—the Swedish government looked upon the Southern African liberation movements as governments-in-waiting?

PS: Yes, that was the attitude that we took all along. In those days, Olof Palme and I worked very closely together. Writing his speeches, we always went a bit further than the Ministry for Foreign Affairs. We had the same approach on Latin America under the dictatorships in Chile and Uruguay, where we told the political refugees that came to Sweden: 'We see you as the true representatives of the democratic forces of your countries. The others are going to disappear.' For us it was a matter of identifying those that we believed were the forces of the future and of democracy. Of course, in a liberation struggle the forces of liberation and of democracy are not always identical. But, unless there are obvious anti-democratic forces from the beginning, that is a question that has to be dealt with later. In Vietnam, we all along stood against invasion and aggression and supported the right of the people to self-determination, in accordance with international law. This did not mean that we supported the Communist Party.

TS: In the case of South Africa, was it difficult to extend exclusive support to ANC in a situation where other actors—both in Sweden and internationally; Nyerere, for example—also advocated support to PAC?

PS: No, it was not difficult. Old, personal links influenced us, of course. We knew that Oliver Tambo and the other ANC leaders were truly democratic and that they had a vision of the future South African society as a mixed, pluralist and tolerant society. As for PAC, we saw them as an opposition and resistance movement against apartheid. But, their vision was more blurred. Contrary to ANC, they never approached us other than for very political purposes or for funding. For some reason they never tried to develop a political dialogue with us. Maybe they thought that it was a lost case, but they did not even try. They visited Sweden a couple of times, but it was always a matter of trying to incriminate ANC. We had more faith in ANC. We knew them better and we trusted them.

When Nyerere and others asked us to see PAC, we did so. We never refused. And although Sweden did not extend bilateral assistance directly to PAC, some humanitarian assistance went to them through the United Nations system.

TS: In the case of Zimbabwe, it appears that ZAPU enjoyed less general support in Sweden than ZANU. How would you explain this?

PS: I think that it also had to do with personal contacts. In general, there developed a relationship of trust and respect with the political representatives who first came to Sweden. In the case of Zimbabwe, we did not choose between ZAPU and ZANU, but I think that when Joshua Nkomo came to Sweden it was often through the churches, while Robert Mugabe was more of the pure freedom fighter.

I also think that it had to do with the way in which the leaders of the liberation movements dealt with the international scene. Amílcar Cabral of the PAIGC was a master of diplomacy. At an early stage, he saw the importance of creating personal links and, in addition, he carried an extremely good message. He was a formidable person and a great international figure. Herbert Chitepo of ZANU also represented his movement very well.

Finally, the image of the liberation movement also had to do with the quality and the personality of the people that they sent here as representatives. In general, they sent good representatives.

TS: Would it be correct to say that Amílcar Cabral brought the Swedish Social Democratic Party into contact with MPLA of Angola?

PS: I think that Cabral was important for the ideological analysis of the situation in Southern Africa in general and for the liberation struggle against colonialism in particular. He helped us to understand that it was not an East-West confrontation. Of course, it was something that we could understand ourselves, but he developed it very clearly. Anyone who met Cabral knew that he was an authentic leader who fought for freedom. And he had a vision beyond liberation.

The liberation movements from the Portuguese-speaking colonies had a coordinating organization called CONCP. They organized meetings and at one time I was asked to chair a meeting. That was in Rome in 1970. I was very honoured. There I met Agostinho Neto, who was another person of Cabral's standing. In a way you could say that Amílcar Cabral initiated our contacts with MPLA, but we had developed those contacts even earlier. For example, I remember when we tried to mediate between Neto and President Senghor of Senegal. Senghor said: 'Well, I think that Neto is a very good poet, but I do not like his politics.' After that I went to Neto and told him that I had talked to Senghor. He then said the same thing: 'Well, I think that Senghor is a good poet but a bad politician.'

TS: Was this mediation difficult for the Social Democratic Party? Senghor's party was an observer member of the Socialist International, while Neto's MPLA was quite close to the Soviet Union?

PS: Well, the Senegalese did not count very much in our relations with the liberation struggle. Senghor had his own ideas and he was not very influential.

TS: At an early stage, you established contacts with Eduardo Mondlane of FRELIMO and asked for his opinion regarding the political scene in Portugal. What was the background to that?

PS: When we had supported the liberation movements in the Portuguese-speaking colonies for a number of years, we found that they lacked substantial international support, except from the Soviet side for technical and strategic reasons. We realized that there would not be a change for many years, because Portugal was strong and there were no international sanctions against her. On the contrary, Portugal was a member of NATO. We then thought that there must be a change within Portugal and that was the reason why I was sent there in 1967. I carried out under-cover work and made a kind of X-ray of the political opposition The first ever, I think. That was also when I met Mário Soares for the first time, in his lawyer's office. He had defended many of the liberation movements in court.

Before I finalized my report, I asked Mondlane about people and political forces in Portugal that he thought would be of importance. My report was written to the Socialist International and was entitled 'Portugal: Colossus on Clay Feet'. In the report I described the different political forces in the country and my recommendation was to support the small Socialist Party, which at the time was called *Acção Socialista*. It had only about fifteen to twenty active members around Mário Soares, but they had a vision for the future and contacts with democratic people all over the country. My recommendation was to invite them to the congresses of the member parties of the Socialist International. Mário Soares then started to be invited and when the dictatorship fell in 1974, he was the only politician with solid international connections.

TS: In 1974-75, at the time of the coup in Portugal and of the independence processes in Angola and Mozambique, things were often strained between the Portuguese Socialist Party on the one hand and MPLA and FRELIMO on the other. This must have been a delicate situation, as you had been supporting both the build-up of the Socialist Party and the nationalist struggle of the two liberation movements?

PS: Yes, but I trusted Mário Soares all along. It was inevitable that Portugal with her colonial background had to take responsibility for tens of thousands of Portuguese at that time. It was a duty. There was also the refugee problem of the *retornados*. The political situation in Portugal was difficult and could have turned against the government, bringing the conservatives back into power. It was also a national, domestic question for Portugal and we fully understood that. What we tried to do was to get the different parties together. For that purpose, I acted several times as a go-between, sending messages back and forth between Soares and some African leaders. I think that it was important. For me personally, it was a positive experience. I trusted both sides and Mário Soares really tried to work things out. Of course, at some stage he was very disappointed, with Samora Machel for example. He thought that Machel was an extremist, but then he changed his mind.

TS: Turning back to Sweden and to the Swedish labour movement, you find that LO—the Swedish trade union congress—was much more cautious than the Social Democratic Party when it came to relations with the liberation forces in Southern Africa. How could this be explained?

PS: The policy that LO developed during the turbulent years in the late 1960s and at the beginning of the 1970s was to work through the International Confederation of Free Trade Unions (ICFTU) in Brussels. Of course, there you had all kinds of views represented. Those of the former colonial powers and also the policy of the United States, which was very aggressive at the time. In that context, it was difficult for the Swedish labour organization to get its views through. However, they had chosen to work through the international confederation as a point of principle. We talked a lot about this, but it was not until later that the policy was modified. We then created our own Solidarity Fund and—still later—the Olof Palme International Center, through which the Swedish labour movement could channel direct, bilateral support.

In the case of South Africa, the cautious position was also explained by the fact that SACTU was not considered to be entirely trustworthy by the ICFTU. SACTU was affiliated to the World Federation of Trade Unions (WFTU) and therefore LO could not co-operate with them.

TS: Did you at any time experience any threats against Sweden because of its support to the Southern African liberation movements?

PS: There were protests by the Portuguese. They organized demonstrations outside the Swedish embassy in Lisbon and they also threatened to boycott Swedish goods and so on, but it did not work. The reaction was not very strong and it had no effect.

TS: Denmark and—particularly—Norway followed Sweden and supported the Southern African liberation movements. Do you think that their membership in NATO limited their space for manoeuvre?

PS: No, I do not think so. I think that Denmark and Norway worked as much as they could inside NATO, sharing views on these issues. Of course, to a certain extent they had to be loyal to the overall goals of the alliance, but we were very much on the same level. We worked together, for example when it came to organizing visits by African leaders to the Nordic countries.

TS: Humanitarian assistance to the liberation movements was, of course, support for human rights. However, there were cases of 'struggles within the struggle' in the liberation movements, often coupled with human rights' abuses. The so-called Shipanga affair in SWAPO is a case in point. How did you react to these developments? Did the Social Democratic Party or the Swedish government discuss them with the leaders of the liberation movements?

PS: When such excesses became clear, we raised our voices. For example, when the Social Democratic Party started to support SWAPO for the election campaign in Namibia, we raised it very strongly. But we did not know about human rights' abuses and we had no ways of certifying what was going on. The liberation struggle was a situation of war and we did not get very much information about it. It was like the French resistance during the Second World War. In that situation, it was natural for us to support the movement as such.

The Shipanga affair was a different story. It was a personal case. Shipanga had his own ambitions and his story was not entirely credible.

TS: Together with its sister parties in Denmark and Norway, the Swedish Social Democratic Party had close contacts with the International University Exchange Fund (IUEF), led by Lars-Gunnar Eriksson. The IUEF was infiltrated by the South African spy Craig Williamson and dissolved in 1980. Did the IUEF/Williamson affair tarnish the relations between Sweden and ANC? Did you discuss it with Oliver Tambo or other ANC leaders?

PS: No, I only recently discussed this with the Swedish documentary journalist Boris Erson. ANC never raised it with me or with anybody else that I know of. We were all fooled by Williamson and I can only deplore that he has not been charged and taken to a court of law. After the exposure of Williamson, some said that they had warned Lars-Gunnar Eriksson about him. That might be true, but apparently not clearly enough.

TS: Through the IUEF, the Nordic governments extended support to the Black Consciousness Movement and to PAC in South Africa, and it was not until 1978 that the organization recognized ANC. It would appear that Lars-Gunnar Eriksson and the IUEF had a different political agenda than that of the Swedish Social Democratic Party. How could this difference be explained?

PS: At the time, some ANC representatives used to ask why we supported different forces in South Africa. We thought that it was good to have a pluralistic approach. We did not want to focus entirely on ANC. The IUEF gave scholarships to democrats from different forces or to independents, which was very much in line with Lars-Gunnar Eriksson's policy. He had worked like that with Angola when he started in the international student movement. ANC questioned this approach, but after the Williamson affair they never raised it again.

TS: Do you think that the long period of Swedish involvement with the liberation struggle in Southern Africa constitutes a unique chapter in Sweden's foreign policy? Would a similar expression of international solidarity be possible today?

PS: Well, apart from POLISARIO and FRETELIN there are very few liberation movements left. Times have changed and you could say that our efforts were fruitful.

For Sweden, South Africa is without any doubt the great success story. What made it possible was the long, sustained effort, the broad popular involvement and the innovative and pioneering work of the government. Because it was the Swedish government which stood against the others and took a pioneer position. All of this has left a lasting impression on the Swedish society. Today, there are no colonial powers to fight, the Cold War is over and the third way between the super powers is no longer an alternative. We now see a North-South relationship where the focus is no longer on confrontation, but on confidence-building. However, if there had been a similar situation today, I am sure that we would have mobilized with the same force, dedication and popular involvement as we did in our solidarity with Southern Africa.

As a concluding remark, I would like to say that in the case of South Africa we have had a continuation of solid support, channelled in different forms. When Nelson Mandela came to Sweden for the first time in 1990, he asked the Social Democratic Party—given our old involvement—to help ANC with the preparations for the forthcoming election campaign. There were many with a lot of money who wanted to do that. All over the world. But Mandela wanted Sweden to be the main sponsor, politically as well as practically. We then set up one of the largest popular education projects ever in South Africa. According to the figures that I have, Sweden assisted with the training of some 80,000 people for the election process. And after the elections we have trained tens of thousands of municipal councillors. The continuation of our commitment can also be seen within the European Union, where Sweden is among those countries that fight for better terms for South Africa, radically opposing those who put narrow national economic trade interests in focus.

Bengt Säve-Söderbergh
SIDA—Head of the Africa section in the Department for International Development Cooperation, Ministry for Foreign Affairs—Secretary General of the International Centre of the Swedish Labour Movement (AIC)—Under-Secretary of State for International Development Cooperation in the Ministry for Foreign Affairs Secretary General of the International Institute for Democracy and Electoral Assistance
(Stockholm, 14 January 1997)

Tor Sellström: How did your involvement with Southern Africa begin?
Bengt Säve-Söderbergh: I was at an early age interested in what was going on in the world. When I was nineteen I signed on as a mate with Transatlantic's merchant ship *Klipparen*. It took me to South Africa and Mozambique in 1960, a few months after the Sharpeville shootings. I had the opportunity of looking at these countries from the perspective of a young mate working with stevedores in Durban, Port Elizabeth, East London, Cape Town, Lourenço Marques, Beira and other ports. I did that for a couple of months. I later spent one year in the United States, where I saw racial problems from another perspective. I think that my involvement probably was due to a combination of these experiences. I was also marginally involved in various boycott activities against South Africa in the 1960s.

In 1967, I started to work at SIDA, where after some time I got involved with Africa. From there, I went to the Ministry for Foreign Affairs. During my first two years, I was dealing with Eastern Africa and in 1972 I became the head of the Africa section. I was then only 32 years old. That position put me into direct contact with the Swedish support to the Southern African liberation movements. I came in at the right moment, when we started the support and we entered into relations with the different movements. After four years, I moved to the Trade Union Confederation (LO), where I formally was placed at the research department, but mainly was involved with solidarity work. After that, I was asked to set up the International Centre of the Swedish Labour Movement (AIC), which now is called the Olof Palme International Center. It was a joint solidarity organization for the labour movement, starting in 1979.

The Swedish government was very much involved with the liberation movements and we had no reason to duplicate what it was doing. However, there were a number of specific projects that we carried out. For example, I remember that we organized a seminar with SWAPO on elections in 1979. At the time, there was hope that something would move on the issue of Namibia. In 1980, I was an election observer in Zimbabwe, also extending financial support and delivering messages from Olof Palme. We had not been invited by the British or the Commonwealth, but by ZAPU and ZANU.

In 1983, a very important thing happened in South Africa—which went almost unnoticed by many people—namely the founding of the United Democratic Front (UDF). I realized that it was a very important event. In those days, there was still some hesitation among solidarity groups and also within ANC regarding the situation inside South Africa. But I immediately initiated working relations with UDF. If there is any crucial matter where I personally affected developments, I would say that it was with regard to UDF. The Swedish contribution to the UDF budget was probably between 60 and 70 per cent. The emergence and development of UDF was a key event in the mid-1980s. At that time, we also organized two months of continuous protests outside the South African legation in Stockholm. Every popular movement in Sweden took part. A few months later, I moved back to the Foreign Ministry, where, of course, I could follow and influence things quite a lot.

TS: Many of the early Swedish opinion makers against apartheid represented liberal newspapers or the church. I am thinking of people like Herbert Tingsten, Per Wästberg and Gunnar Helander. Would it be fair to say that the Swedish anti-apartheid opinion grew out of the liberal centre?

BSS: No. In all issues you always have the early people, those who pick up a question, who can write and are prominent in other fields. They may have different political opinions. I do not think that you can say that the early anti-apartheid opinion was predominantly liberal. For example, *Dagens Nyheter* is a Stockholm-based newspaper. There were others who wrote in the trade union papers. I am not at all trying to diminish the role of Tingsten, Wästberg or Helander. They made very important contributions. But looking at the process of how opinions are formed, it always starts with individuals. It takes more time for organizations. I would say that the Swedish anti-apartheid opinion grew out of a combination of people from various ideological leanings. That was also its strength.

TS: You worked closely with Olof Palme. How would you asses his role for the Swedish involvement in Southern Africa?

BSS: It was extremely important. Palme had a very strong personal conviction, born out of two considerations. One was, simply, decency and the other more political. Palme was a strong anti-Communist and he had great difficulties in accepting that the democratic world followed the East-West divide, rather than what was decent. I remember him saying that one of the reasons for our involvement was to show that you do not have to be a Communist to be against apartheid. I have also experienced that on several occasions. For example, when I was Under-Secretary of State, Chester Crocker once said to me that he was worried about our support to Communism. But I said: 'If anybody is supporting Communism in Southern Africa, it is you, Mr Crocker. Communism is often born out of frustration and you are frustrating people by giving the wrong signals'. At that time, I felt fairly proud to represent Sweden.

Olof Palme loved to mix the smaller problems in Sweden with the big problems in the world. It was often a conscious philosophy. Politics is about cleaning the streets in Stockholm, but it is also about survival in the world. I think that it was part of his strength and why the ordinary people felt elevated, because their problems became bigger than themselves, so to speak. I remember many instances where he would have a meeting with the Social Democratic parliamentary group on a domestic issue and some emissary would come from Guinea-Bissau or somewhere to talk about their problems. Palme would then say: 'Please, come and address our parliamentary group before our discussion'. He always did things like that.

In particular, I was very much impressed by him in 1984. At that time, the South Africans were hitting all over Southern Africa and ANC was facing their greatest problems in later decades. I was in charge of organizing a conference of the Socialist International in Arusha, Tanzania, and went there to prepare it with Salim Salim. I came back and said to Palme: 'The only negative thing that I can report to you is that the conference will take place one week before the party congress of September 1984. But if that can be dealt with, it would be immensely important if you at an early stage could announce your attendance, because then all the others would also attend. Your name is so important in this connection'. The 1985 elections were coming closer and most people advised him not to go to Africa one week before the party congress. But he said: 'Give me a week to think about it'. He came back a week later and said: 'I will not follow the advice given by most people. I will go. If friendships ever count, it is when your friends are in trouble and this time my old friend Oliver Tambo is in trouble'.

His friendship with Tambo had started in the early 1960s. There were some people that he became closer to than others and Tambo occupied a very special place. Like Amílcar Cabral of PAIGC and a few others.

TS: How would you explain that the Swedish government with strong parliamentary backing in 1969 embarked upon direct support to the Southern African liberation movements? These movements were also supported by the Communist countries and waged armed struggles.

BSS: I think that the easiest way is to say that it was a situation where you could show some decency. I do not think that there is more to it. The roots of the problem were fairly straightforward. The East-West dimension was maybe the subject of a few diplomats. Others said that we cannot do it because of this or that principle. But they were a fairly small minority. Most people felt that it was the right thing to do.

TS: Palme would perhaps have said that you do not have to agree with the ideology of the Vietnamese or the Angolans, but we must agree with their right to become independent?

BSS: Yes. That was the spirit of the time. The right to self-determination was a strong and easily understandable issue, also in relation to our own country. But it was not seen like that by the Cold War representatives. For example, in my conversation with Chester Crocker—having said that he supported Communism—I said: 'To you, Swedish foreign policy must appear to be in a mess. In South Africa, we support the Soviets; in Zimbabwe, we support the Chinese; and in Afghanistan, we support the Americans'. He became very confused.

In our support to the Southern African liberation movements, there were, basically, two things that we looked at. Were they doing practical things and were they building a strong organization? We were not out to deliver arms or beef up some movement for ideological reasons. No, we assessed whether they were constructive in the struggle against apartheid and colonialism and if they were doing practical things to support their people. Those were our criteria for support. Two very simple criteria, which also meant that it was mostly officials in the Ministry for Foreign Affairs and SIDA who informed our policy.

TS: In the case of Angola, there was more of an ideological debate regarding the different nationalist movements. However, Olof Palme strongly supported MPLA?

BSS: Of all the countries in Southern Africa—except South Africa—Angola was of interest to those who were looking for money. We knew that nobody really cared about Guinea-Bissau and some only marginally cared about Mozambique. Angola was the interesting case and therefore the hottest country in terms of the East-West divide. That probably conditioned Palme. He held the view that if you want to make your voice heard and you come from a small country, you sometimes have to raise it to make it a little bit louder. He had become an international person and if he had not used some of his strong words, the newspapers would never have quoted him. And we knew, of course, that Portugal worked very much with UNITA and the Americans and CIA with FNLA.

TS: Both you and Olof Palme had close relations with Agostinho Neto?

BSS: Oh, yes. Neto was sitting in my kitchen in Stockholm the famous evening of 24 April 1974. He had no idea of what was going to happen in Portugal. He was not informed about the revolt. The following morning he left for Canada.

Some of the people in MPLA used an Eastern Communist rhetoric, perhaps more so than in any other Southern African liberation movement. However, Agostinho Neto was different. He was more of a nationalist and an intellectual.

TS: In 1972, you became the head of the Africa section at the Department for International Development Cooperation of the Ministry for Foreign Affairs. That was at the time when the Swedish assistance to the Southern African liberation movements really started. It was something entirely new. How was it looked upon by the 'old guard' at the Foreign Ministry?

BSS: In those days, the Foreign Ministry still had quite a few remnants from the House of the Nobility. There were lots of old ambassadors with that background, remnants from an old era that is now gone. However, the important people followed what the government decided, although not always with enthusiasm. The whole concept of the Third World and the people of the 1960s entered the Foreign Ministry as something which the cat had dragged in. I was one of them. At the time, the Foreign Ministry was a fairly closed institution. Sometimes you would receive threats from parts of industry, saying that 'you are following policies which make our business very difficult'. Some of the old ambassadors would rather listen to that.

TS: In the case of Sweden, the humanitarian support was not implemented by the Ministry for Foreign Affairs but delegated to SIDA. Were there any problems connected with that?

BSS: The implementation was done by SIDA, but you had the Consultative Committee on Humanitarian Assistance and very close follow ups of the support. The committee had members from the Swedish parliament, representing various political parties. Those who were designated to know could find out just about everything. There were control mechanisms in place. There was nothing specific about it. The Swedish public administration is divided between small ministries and implementing agencies. I do not see this differently. There was a corps of very committed civil servants at both the Ministry for Foreign Affairs and at SIDA. They saw it as a privilege and a challenge to work with these questions.

TS: Were you satisfied that the reporting and accounting routines were adequate?

BSS: That depends on what you can demand. People were working in a war-like situation. The government of South Africa was trying everything—including the killing of people—to stop the support. As a consequence, you could not establish the same criteria as in the Swedish society. At the same time, you could, of course, not allow embezzlement of funds or cheating. That could not be tolerated.

Getting involved in activities like these always constitutes a risk. If you want change, you must take risks. But, on the whole, we judged on balance and demanded what was reasonable. There was also an educational aspect to it. ANC, for example, was not the best when it comes to accounting and reporting. I think that all organizations that are being built up—whether it is a liberation movement or a sports club—should be trained in these fields. It is also part of democracy-building.

TS: Sweden supported a number of international NGOs, like the International University Exchange Fund (IUEF). It would appear, however, that IUEF and its Swedish director, Lars-Gunnar Eriksson, had a different agenda, trying to support a 'third force' in South Africa. How did you look upon that?

BSS: There were all kinds of organizations. We supported church organizations and many others. IUEF was originally an organization that dealt with scholarships. It was later given some money to look into other contacts. We were never restricted to one movement. That was not our task. It was to find different ways. Through some channels, we would support the victims of apartheid and in other cases we supported organizations that were actively working against the system. IUEF was just one of many organizations.

Well, I was not very much part of that. I was rather looking at it with some suspicion. It was led by someone who was trying to find an angle of his own.

TS: As director of AIC, you were—as you said—involved in support to the United Democratic Front (UDF). Would you say that it was AIC's most important project in South Africa?

BSS: Yes. At that time, AIC shared offices with the LO/TCO Council. It was very convenient, because Cyril Ramaphosa and many others who were involved in both the trade unions and UDF were often there. So, I knew what the situation was.

With regard to the trade union movement, I was never a friend of SACTU. I do not know how many times we refused their requests. Gradually, ANC realized that certain doctrines and structures which they had copied from other countries were irrelevant and that the struggle must be waged inside South Africa. There was also a power struggle between those who were outside and those who were inside. I was convinced that nothing decisive would take place until you really had actions going on inside the country. So, to me UDF was very crucial. And, as I said, if there was one area where I played a personal role, this would be it. Seizing the moment and going full blast, although I initially had problems with some SIDA bureaucrats. This was new to them and they did not really know what to do.

TS: Who were the UDF leaders that you were in contact with?

BSS: Cyril Ramaphosa, Murphy Morobe and various others. I proposed UDF for the Let Live Prize of the newspaper *Arbetet* and Azhar Cachalia and Murphy Morobe came to Sweden to receive it. We arranged various activities with them. In those days, there was still, as I said, some hesitation about support to the organizations inside South Africa, also within ANC. But, I had a different view.

TS: In Sweden, there was a strong solidarity movement, led by the Africa Groups and the Isolate South Africa Committee. How did you see the relations between the solidarity movement and the government?

BSS: They were very easy and warm. There were some frictions, naturally, but they were marginal. The objectives and goals were the same. The solidarity organizations could also do things—mobilizing people, for example—that the government could not do. They had various practical activities. There was a debate on sanctions, but not on the practical support.

TS: Did you experience any strong and consistent political opposition to the Swedish policy in support of the liberation movements?

BSS: Internationally, yes, in some circles. In Sweden, by some marginal people, especially in the beginning. You had the reactionaries, who were saying: 'You are just trying to be the conscience of the world' and things like that. However, if you launch a new policy, you also have to be prepared for such reactions.

Carl Tham
Liberal Party, later Social Democratic Party—Director General of SIDA and Chairman of the Consultative Committee on Humanitarian Assistance Minister of Higher Education
(Stockholm, 14 January 1997)

Tor Sellström: How would you explain the broad and active Swedish opinion against apartheid South Africa from the beginning of the 1960s?

Carl Tham: Well, I think that the broader anti-apartheid mobilization did not really start in the 1960s, but more in the 1970s. In the 1960s, prominent leaders of Swedish industry, for example, not only said that South Africa was not our business, but also actively defended apartheid. Maybe we tend to forget that, but it was in fact the case.

In the early days, *Dagens Nyheter*, Herbert Tingsten and Per Wästberg played quite significant roles. Tingsten's book about South Africa and his editorials should be mentioned. The missionary movements played, of course, important parts. That may be the reason why the Liberal Party became involved at an early stage. As always in politics, there was also a question of personalities. For example, in the Liberal Party, David Wirmark was for many years working as secretary general of WAY. Although it later turned out that WAY was financed by CIA, I must say that it was rather benevolent. Wirmark was engaged in almost all African matters and a very close friend of all the leaders in exile. Of course, he also brought that back to the Swedish youth movement. There were also others in the youth movement who were rather active. A towering person was, of course, Per Wästberg, whose many books and articles had an enormous impact.

It was easy to mobilize the Swedes in favour of an anti-racist policy. Maybe it would have been more difficult today, but at that time it was not. I cannot really say why.

TS: Do you think that the early anti-apartheid opinion was a continuation of the anti-Nazi opinion or was it a new opinion?

CT: It was a new opinion. I have written somewhere that the whole Swedish mobilization regarding Third World issues—the intellectual part of it at least—partly was a reflection of bad conscience about the Swedish position during the Second World War and about the passive position that Sweden took on many international issues at that time. In a way, South Africa presented a possibility to show that Sweden was not just a small, insignificant country on the periphery, but that we had a moral force. In the Cold War climate, it also presented a possibility to demonstrate a policy which was not in accordance with either the NATO or the Soviet side. It was more of pure solidarity, so to speak, and I think that it expressed a feeling that we should not repeat the mistakes of the past.

TS: How did your own involvement with Southern Africa begin?

CT: It started in 1963, when I became the secretary of the Liberal Party Youth League. Ola Ullsten, who was the chairman of the Liberal Youth at that time, and the former chairman, Per Ahlmark, were very close friends of mine and they were both very much engaged in Southern Africa. Also Björn Beckman, who at that time still was the chairman of the Liberal Students Association. He was the main force behind the Rhodesia campaign in favour of Kenneth Kaunda in 1962. David Wirmark was, of course, also active in the campaign. We got a lot of support from *Dagens Nyheter*—especially from Per Wästberg—and other sources. The campaign was very successful and we collected quite a lot of money. The Swedish youth also conducted campaigns against South African fruits and other commodities. We went into fruit shops, demonstrated and so on.

TS: How were these demands looked upon by the leadership of the Liberal Party?

CT: As far as I remember the general situation, the party leaders were mildly positive. Later on in the 1960s, they became more actively involved, maybe not as a general reflection of enthusiasm, but perhaps because the liberal youth movement at that time was powerful and they had to accept that. The old leaders of the Liberal Party, Bertil Ohlin and Sven Wedén, had a very bad time in relation to Vietnam. They felt that the Swedish position was too critical towards the United States and were, of course, criticized because of that by the youth. To compensate, they became more active in the South African question. But they were genuinely involved. I worked for Sven Wedén for many years and he was honestly and seriously involved. He really looked upon apartheid as an evil policy.

TS: Would it be fair to say that the Swedish anti-apartheid and anti-colonial opinion in the early 1960s mainly was formed around a liberal centre and not in the socialist left?

CT: I am not really in a position to answer that. My position at the time was rather modest, but in the Liberal Youth we felt that we were in the front line so to speak. Perhaps due to the involvement of people from the various churches, we were somewhat more active than, for example, the young Social Democrats. When we had debates with the Social Democratic Youth League, they had a bad time when it came to South Africa, because they supported our demands for total isolation, but the government did not. That was a problem for them. On the other hand, the Liberal Party was also on the side of the government on this issue.

TS: At an early stage, the Liberal Party Youth League was also actively following the liberation struggle in the Portuguese colonies and Liberal politicians such as Per Ahlmark demanded Portugal's expulsion from EFTA. How serious was this demand?

CT: It was not just a youth demand. It was a position which was supported by the party congress. I guess that Wedén was not too enthusiastic to press the demand very hard, rather arguing that 'OK, the party has taken this position and of course we shall support it'. Portugal's membership in EFTA was after all rather embarrassing for the government and it became even more so at the end of the 1960s, when Olof Palme had become Prime Minister. It was not an easy issue for the Social Democrats.

TS: Do you think that Olof Palme played a major role for the radicalisation of the Social Democratic Party vis-à-vis Southern Africa?

CT: From my perspective—being an outsider at that time—I think that he played a very important role, not least because of his position on Vietnam and his political charisma. He was an outstanding political figure, not only in the Swedish context, but also internationally. His many critics rejected this view, but in the end I think that they recognized that it was true.

TS: In 1969, the Swedish parliament paved the way for direct official Swedish humanitarian assistance to the liberation movements in Southern Africa. These movements waged an armed struggle and received support from the Soviet Union or China. How do you, in general terms, explain that Sweden assisted the same movements as the Communist countries?

CT: I think that the position we took really is something that we should be proud of. I guess that the people who took the decision understood that it was controversial in the Cold War context. The tragedy was that the whole process of de-colonization became part of the Cold War. The Soviet support was, of course, not only—or not at all—given for more moral reasons. It was for strategic reasons that they supported these movements. The US policy was, similarly, based on Cold War considerations. If the United States and the leading Western countries had taken another position in the beginning of the process, also defending the values of democracy in Africa, much would have been different. But they did not. They looked upon the liberation movements only as Communist movements. Because of that position, the movements became more and more dependent on the Soviet Union and China.

When the Swedish support was attacked—which was not that common, but it happened—our answer was: 'Well, this is part of Sweden's support for national liberation and de-colonization. It also constitutes a support for those groups within the liberation movements who are not Communist'. The movements were, of course, a kind of umbrella movements with various groups and fractions. I frankly think that the Swedish support to ANC during all these years was of crucial importance to the groups inside ANC who were not Communist, at least to reduce their relations with the Soviet Union. Of course, the Soviet support was very important. After all, Sweden did not deliver any arms and they needed that, even if ANC never was a very strong armed force.

In the case of Angola, we supported the struggle for national liberation. Then we supported Angola as a nation which was invaded by South Africa and CIA-supported groups. Nowadays, when everything is blamed on the Soviet Union, the Swedish opinion tends to forget that Angola in fact was invaded by groups established in Zaire and supported by CIA. Everything was arranged by the Americans to attack the government in Luanda.

TS: Do you think that the close relations established between Swedish politicians and opinion makers and a number of Southern African leaders, such as Mondlane, Tambo, Kaunda and Nyerere, made it easier to see beyond the ideological discourse and understand the nationalist core of the struggle?

CT: Yes, I think that it played an important part. Kaunda was never a Communist and Nyerere was never a Communist. I think that we clearly saw that they had national—and, as we thought, rather nationalistic—aspirations and demands for the development of their nations. Maybe we were a little naive. We did not always see the hard core groups and the reasons behind the Soviet support, but I still think that we played a certain role. Particularly in relation to South Africa. Perhaps less so in the case of Angola.

In Angola, the Liberal Party advocated support to FNLA. I think that it was a reflection of a more anti-Communist position within the party, specifically by Olle Wästberg. He was very much involved with FNLA. I guess that Olle Wästberg was the one who demanded assistance to FNLA and that the party supported him. But the broader liberal opinion was very divided on this point.

TS: There were many—not least in the Southern African liberation movements—who thought that the Swedish policy would change when the non-socialist coalition government took over from the Social Democrats in 1976. Instead, the assistance to the liberation movements increased, and in 1979 the Liberal minority government under Ola Ullsten introduced an investment ban against South Africa. How would you explain this?

CT: I think that those who expected a decrease had not studied the Swedish political scene very closely. They had had contacts with the Social Democratic leaders and it was rather natural for them to think that if there was a non-socialist government there would be a change of policy. If they had studied what the Centre Party and the Liberal Party were saying, they would, however, have been much more confident. At that time, we looked upon the Social Democrats as not being active enough. That was our main position. Ola Ullsten of the Liberal Party and Thorbjörn Fälldin of the Centre Party were both very much engaged in these matters, so there was never a problem. Gösta Bohman of the Moderate Party understood that and accepted it. I do not remember any case where he at that time actually went against the Swedish support. The Moderate Party was mainly obsessed with two foreign policy and aid questions. One was Vietnam and the other was Cuba. Southern Africa was not really on their agenda until later. The whole political spectrum changed from the mid-1980s. If the 1976 government had been of the kind that we had in 1991, it would, of course, have been quite a different story.

TS: You served as Director General of SIDA from 1985 to 1994. You also chaired the Consultative Committee on Humanitarian Assistance. During these years, did you experience any strong and consistent political opposition to the official policy of support to the Southern African liberation movements?

CT: No, not at all. We never had any political problems of that kind in the Consultative Committee on Humanitarian Assistance. The committee was from the beginning never supposed to be a kind of parliamentary board. The idea was rather that it should be composed by experts. The proposal to give the committee a more parliamentary representation was raised towards the end of the 1980s, but I was somewhat reluctant to that. I could not see why it was necessary. After all, we already had very close contacts with the parliamentary Committee on Foreign Affairs. If we had opened the committee to a more parliamentary representation, we would also have had all the political parties involved and it would have become much bigger.

The Moderate Party had their representatives on the committee. The Left Party was, however, not represented. I think that it was a reflection of the old habit in Swedish politics not to accept the Communist Party, as it was still called, in foreign policy questions. It must be looked upon from that point of view. But I would like to stress that the Consultative Committee on Humanitarian Assistance from the beginning was not conceived as a parliamentary institution. It was the government and the parliamentary Committee on Foreign Affairs that took the responsibility. The Consultative Committee was a kind of board which looked upon the various issues involved. For each activity, the decisions were so well prepared that it appears as almost unbelievable today.

TS: I guess that due to the confidentiality involved it was a very appropriate way of preparing the issues?

CT: Absolutely. I think that it was a very good system. As far as I know—of course, there can be hidden things which I do not know about—it worked very well. The only major setback was the spy story with Craig Williamson. I was in government at that time, but I was not involved in that question. However, Ola Ullsten and Hans Blix were furious. It must also be asked how Mats Hellström and others could be so deceived. It is impossible to imagine. A lot of people were after all suspicious and warned them, but they did not listen to the professionals.

TS: The Swedish support to the liberation movements was in the field often administered by relatively junior SIDA officials, rather than by trained diplomats. In your experience, were there any problems—or advantages—connected with this? Was the delegation of this political support accepted at the Ministry for Foreign Affairs?

CT: Well, if you had put this money into the hands of the diplomatic corps, nothing would have happened. They had a totally different concept of what they should do. Even if the SIDA employees sometimes went too far—it happened that people were too enthusiastic—by and large the system was good. For diplomatic reasons I also think that it would have been next to impossible to manage the support from the Foreign Ministry side of the embassies. Nevertheless, if you look at South Africa, Birgitta Karlström Dorph was there for many years and she was after all at the Swedish embassy. The South Africans must, of course, have known that she was active with all this money all over the country. However, she acted on behalf of SIDA. If the support had been more formally linked to the Foreign Ministry—with decisions by the Minister—that would have been very difficult.

TS: You did not receive any complaints from Swedish ambassadors in Southern Africa regarding SIDA and the support to the liberation movements?

CT: There were conflicts sometimes, but not on a general scale.

TS: Were you satisfied that the administrative routines regarding reporting and accounting of the humanitarian support were appropriate and that SIDA exercised sufficient control over the funds disbursed?

CT: Well, during my period we had some administrative problems here and there. You can always improve on administrative routines, but the system in itself was sound and healthy. As far as I remember, we did not even have the suspicion of any misuse of funds. Sometimes a project could not be accomplished because of the overall situation and the money had to be re-allocated for another activity. After all, there was a kind of war-like situation, particularly in the 1980s. We were happy if the money came to the support of the people that we wanted to assist.

We had no indication of any misuse, that is, that money came into private pockets. I am not saying that it did not happen. Maybe it did, but we never received any indication to that effect. The only question discussed in this context is, of course, the Boesak affair, but SIDA never made any claims that Boesak put SIDA money into his own pockets. We were dissatisfied with his project, but never said that he used the funds for his personal benefit.

TS: Inside the liberation movements, there were struggles within the struggle. Particularly well known are the internal divisions in SWAPO in Zambia in the 1970s and the tensions and abuse in both ANC and SWAPO camps in Angola in the 1980s. Do you recollect if these problems were raised by the Swedish government or SIDA with SWAPO, ANC or the host countries?

CT: We did not know much about that. We knew, of course, that there were divisions, but we did not know about abuse of power in the camps. After all, we did not stay so much in contact with the camps and we had no reasons to be there either. The camps in Angola were rather dangerous places and due to the war-like situation we did not want to have our personnel there.

SIDA was mainly a financing institution. We tried to follow events, but the implementing agents were the people involved in the churches and other NGOs. We were very much dependent on them. If they had raised the issue with SIDA, we would certainly have acted, but as far as I remember that was never the case.

TS: Apart from general criticism, are you aware of any pressures on Sweden by the Western powers against the support to the liberation movements?

CT: Of course, in the early days Portugal complained a lot. When I was at SIDA, I never experienced any complaint, except on one occasion. In 1993, there was a big anti-apartheid meeting organized by the Olof Palme International Center here in Stockholm. Sten Andersson was supposed to speak, but he fell ill and asked me to appear instead. I made a rather powerful speech in Swedish. The idea of the meeting was to start a campaign to raise money for the ANC election campaign in South Africa. I later heard that the South African government complained to the Swedish Foreign Ministry about my speech. It was obvious to me that de Klerk supported the forces which were against ANC and that the whole process from 1991 with all the killings was part of a political struggle to weaken ANC. I said so in my speech. They did not like that and complained to the Foreign Ministry. When Lars-Åke Nilsson, who at that time was Under-Secretary of State for Foreign Affairs, subsequently visited South Africa there were again complaints from the South African government.

That was the only reaction I ever got from any government during my period at SIDA, but I guess that there were questions and pressures earlier, specifically by the United States during the Reagan administration. However, the point we made—maybe more bluntly from SIDA than from the Foreign Ministry—was that outside interference started with the Western powers. South Africa would never have been in a position to keep the apartheid system for so many years without the support from the Western countries. That was our position, but I guess

that the Foreign Ministry gave more diplomatic answers.
TS: Is there anything you would like to add?
CT: There was a rather particular situation during these years when we had so much money allocated to secret operations. It was a unique situation which never will be repeated. We also gave support to humanitarian activities in Palestine and other places, but there was never any support similar to the kind we extended to South Africa. South Africa was really unique and it is interesting to reflect on the reasons for this. It started with a few people, developed and was then established. If you want to be cynical, you could say that it was rather easy. You did not take any risks if you were against apartheid. Of course, we could be criticized by the United States and others, but not that much. In the mid-1980s, the United States also changed their mind about South Africa. There could be some criticism here and there in Europe, but it was of no crucial importance to Sweden.

However, Swedish industry made a lot of resistance towards that policy, which was the main reason why the Swedish sanctions laws were adopted so late. One should therefore not exaggerate our benevolence. I am quite sure that if the policy had been more dangerous to Sweden, it would have been much more controversial. When the critics say that we pursued a particular policy when it was rather easy to do so—without any risks—there is, of course, some truth in that. On the other hand, it is always better to do something than nothing. It is also important to remember that the moral engagement of the people in the NGOs really was pure and that it was a strong force. It was, I would say, a genuine, democratic solidarity movement and a very important part of the Swedish political landscape towards South and Southern Africa.

David Wirmark
Liberal Party—General Secretary of the World Assembly of Youth—Member of the 1977 committee on sanctions against South Africa—Ambassador of Sweden to Tanzania
Board member of the Swedish International Liberal Center
(Stockholm, 20 February 1996)

Tor Sellström: How did your involvement with Southern Africa begin?
David Wirmark: I was a young student in Uppsala and elected to participate as a representative of the Swedish youth in the first general assembly of WAY, the World Assembly of Youth, which took place at Cornell University, Ithaca, USA, in 1951. The theme was 'Youth and Human Rights' and I was participating in a commission that dealt with racial discrimination. There was a fellow delegate from Cameroon. His name was Etienne Noafu and he represented the Protestant youth, I recall. He made a very interesting *plaidoyer* for solidarity of youth the world over with the cause of equality and justice in South Africa. He also made a description of the South African situation in a document that was very detailed about the educational and the political system. It showed how things had gone backwards and that discrimination had become harder.

There was a system which only allowed the white population to attain full citizenship. Of course, we were very shocked. I already knew from newspapers and articles that there was racial discrimination in South Africa and that the situation was getting worse, but I did not know the details. That made me struggle later in support of South Africa and against racial discrimination.

Of course, we were also shocked by the racial discrimination in the United States. We met many black American youngsters who worked for various youth organizations. They told us that they hoped that the system would cease, but that it would take a long time. At that time, we also discussed technical assistance and development aid, because President Truman had presented his Point Four plan. This struck me very much and determined more or less what I was going to devote my life to.

TS: Were you then chairman of the National Council of Swedish Youth?
DW: No, that was a couple of years later, but when I came back to Sweden I was internationally concerned. At that time, a students' association at Uppsala University devoted to international affairs invited a Swedish diplomat, Paul Mohn. He had an idea of inviting a thousand young people from the poor countries in Asia, Africa and Latin America to Sweden to learn how the Swedish society and democracy functioned.
TS: Was that the famous Mohn Plan?
DW: Yes. Mohn was already rather old, but had wide international experience. He had been in Korea to supervise the armistice and before that—immediately after or during the war—he was responsible for administration in Greece. Particularly, I think that his period in Korea and Asia had made him interested in how we could make the youth of the developing world understand how a modern society functions and become aware of the rules and the values of the democratic system, local democracy etc.

Mohn wrote a pamphlet about this and one of the first speeches he gave in Uppsala—it must have been at the Foreign Policy Association—aroused a lot of enthusiasm. We took over the idea and the National Council of Swedish Youth proposed it to the Central Committee for Swedish Technical Assistance (CK), but I think that the older generation did not know exactly how to handle the proposal. They thought that it was interesting, but they also saw difficulties in implementing it. We never got full support from them. The interesting thing is that the Under-Secretary of State for Foreign Affairs at that time, Arne Lundberg, made a speech on the First of May 1952 where he also took up the idea. That made us advance, but what happened in the end was that some youth organizations themselves raised money and brought a few people to Sweden.

We in the Liberal Youth League had one or two people here. I recall that we had a Korean who studied economy. Of course, the idea was that they should go back to their own countries and work for them, but he married a Swedish girl and stayed here. He became a good economist at *Konjunkturinstitutet* (The National Institute of Economic Research). But there were others who went back. The Centre Party Youth League (SLU) invited several people from Ethiopia and I think that the Social Democratic youth had young people from East Africa here. Paul Mohn spoke of one thousand young people, but we could never implement such a huge programme. There was a debate in *Expressen*. One article was against the plan, stating that the idea of learning democracy by coming to Sweden was a little bit naive. We replied that we did not want them to only study democracy, but also to practise and do some further training within their professional field, so that they could develop their knowledge while they were here. We thought that both things were important.

It is interesting to see that the questions of democracy and human rights later came much more to the forefront than they were at that time. It was only the youth that brought them forward and wanted to have this programme implemented. It might be because of the fact that WAY had made the Universal Declaration of Human Rights the basis for our work. We were accustomed to these questions.

TS: Among the students who came to Sweden through the Liberal, Centre or Socialist youth, were there any from Southern Africa?
DW: Yes, in the Liberal youth we had one or two people from Zambia. The National Union of Students also invited foreign students to Sweden. They had, I think, six or eight medical students from Indonesia. Olof Palme was involved in that undertaking and I was involved from the Uppsala side, so we had some contact already then.
TS: As chairman of the National Council of Swedish Youth and, from 1958, as general secretary of WAY, you had contacts at a very early stage with some of the future leaders of Southern Africa. You met Joshua Nkomo from Rhodesia as early as 1958 and also Kenneth Kaunda around that time. Just after he went into exile you met Oliver Tambo and you also met Nelson Mandela at a conference during his African tour in 1962. Could you comment on the relations that you established with the leaders of Southern Africa?
DW: Yes, we became very friendly. I met Joshua Nkomo several times. Kenneth Kaunda as well. When Kenneth Kaunda became President, he always received me when I came to Lusaka. I came rather often to Zam-

bia in those years, because when I worked for WAY I travelled widely in Africa. Those were the years of liberation and I went to Africa on various occasions, for instance, every independence celebration. When Tanzania, Nigeria and Zambia became independent I was there and, of course, I met a number of leaders at the same time. Kenneth Kaunda is really a very close friend of mine. I met him in South Africa during the elections in 1994. We happened to stay at the same hotel. I did not know that he was there, but when I came down to the breakfast room I heard his familiar voice 'Oh David, are you here?'

When Oliver Tambo was smuggled out of South Africa, I immediately—in April 1960—sent him a ticket through Seretse Khama in Bechuanaland. Seretse Khama replied that he had taken care of Oliver Tambo and that he had given him the ticket. Oliver Tambo then came to the first Pan African Youth Seminar in Tunis, where he gave a fantastic speech about the struggle for freedom in South Africa. It was on the basis of non-violence, which was the ANC policy at that time. Luthuli's old policy. That laid the foundation for a friendship that went on for a very, very long time. Until the end. I saw him about one month before he died. I saw that his health was not as it should be. Of course, I knew that he had been in hospital in Sweden. I had met him there.

TS: You were a leading representative of the Liberal youth. Later on you were a Liberal member of parliament. Many of those who were active in the formulation of an opinion on South and Southern Africa in Sweden—people like Herbert Tingsten, Ivar Harrie etc.—came from the liberal camp. Would it be fair to say that liberals were the first to articulate an anti-apartheid and pro-liberation opinion in Sweden from the late 1950s?

DW: Yes, I think so. In the church, there were individual missionaries, in particular those who went to South and Southern Africa and saw the discrimination on the spot. Some of them—not all of them—became horrified and decided to devote themselves to efforts and programmes to struggle against this. On the liberal side it was natural, because liberalism is about freedom, and colonialism and racial discrimination are negations of freedom.

I was very much influenced by Julius Nyerere. He came to a seminar that we had in Dar es Salaam. Kenneth Kaunda was also there. Julius Nyerere addressed the seminar, arguing against the British thesis that you need to be prepared to become independent. He quoted Nehru, saying that he did not accept that you first needed a certain standard of education. Education is important for every individual, but independence is something more than just the technical standard you have in terms of education. It concerns an important political element, namely political human rights. He was refusing the argument that you need a period of preparation before democracy. He said that the best preparation for democracy and freedom is freedom itself. I thought that it was very well put, because it went very well with my liberal belief.

In the case of Zambia, it was a Liberal group in Sweden that made the collection of funds for Kaunda's first election campaign in 1962, preceding independence. In that, for example, the Liberal Party chairman Bertil Ohlin and other personalities, both older and younger, participated. Among them was also Gunnar Myrdal from the Social Democratic Party, if I recall correctly. There was a mixture of political beliefs among those who supported the fund.

The Liberal Party Youth League was certainly the first political organization to take a clear stand on the Algerian struggle and freedom for the Algerian people. This we did in concordance with liberals in France, for instance, the group around Mendès-France and the journal *L'Express*. Of course, in Britain you also had important liberal newspapers, like *The Guardian* and *The Observer*, which played important roles in the debate and continue to do so, as also liberal politicians have done in Britain. I think that we in Sweden have been more or less part of the British progressive liberal tradition for the liberation struggles.

TS: In 1969, the Swedish Parliament paved the way for direct government support to liberation movements in Southern Africa. All of these movements waged an armed struggle and some of them had a formal alliance with a Communist party. Most of them were considered to be in the 'Soviet camp'. How did you in the Liberal Party look upon this?

DW: Of course, we knew that there were links between members of the liberation movements and the Communist parties or the Communist camp. But we were also convinced that they were not true Communists. They did not act like Communist party organizations. They were true national liberation movements. We never had any hesitation about ANC, for instance. All the time we also wanted that ZAPU of Zimbabwe should have some support. We were not guided by the question of whether they cooperated with the Communists. The important thing was that we were convinced that they wanted a free society and respect for human rights. They did not want a racial society. ANC had taken a very clear stand. They did not want the blacks to have more rights than the whites. They did not want to reverse the system, but a society where all citizens were equal.

TS: Do you think that the very early and close personal relations between leading opinion makers—like yourself—and the leaders of the liberation struggle in Southern Africa, like Mondlane, Tambo, Nkomo, Nujoma etc., played a role regarding the understanding of the ideological orientation of the struggle?

DW: Yes, I believe so. Definitely. It had repercussions in two directions. It was important for the understanding in Sweden of the national liberation movements and their significance, but it also, I think, had the effect that the leaders of the liberation movements saw that they could get real, and perhaps even more efficient, support from the non-Communist world. This was an argument when they later on negotiated for political liberation. The fact that they got support from true democrats in the Nordic countries had an importance, both for ANC and the other liberation movements. Many of the leaders have said so to me. Nujoma, Nkomo and Kaunda have said so, and, of course, the Tanzanian leaders. I was ambassador to Tanzania between 1979 and 1985, but even before that time I knew Julius Nyerere and his colleagues very well. In particular, Rachidi Kawawa, who was Vice President but also others in the Tanzanian government, like Salim Salim and Oscar Kambona, who was at the time Foreign Minister, but then fell out with the party and with Julius Nyerere. They were very close to me.

TS: Do you think that the Nordic countries were able to broaden the diplomatic space for the liberation movements in the polarized East-West divide?

DW: Yes. There was a time when the Soviet Union was very active in Africa and that created difficulties for the liberation movements. We were not in favour of the various Communist initiatives, for instance in Ethiopia and Angola, although most of us had to accept that MPLA had essential support from the Soviet Union. My line—and also that of the Liberal Party—was that it was not really up to the donor countries to decide which political inclination the liberation movements should have, other than in a broader sense. It should be democratic and respect human rights, but whether it should have a more socialist or another leaning was not for us to decide. That is why we advocated that in certain cases one should support several liberation movements. For instance, in Zimbabwe we thought that both ZANU and ZAPU should get support and they also got that when the non-socialist parties came into government. In Angola, we advocated that in accordance with what had been agreed between the African leaders, both MPLA and FNLA should get support. But Sweden went on with exclusive support to MPLA and did not change its stand. South Africa was a different case. There I became convinced from reports by, among others, Kenneth Kaunda that ANC was the main representative and that we did not need to extend support to PAC.

TS: Was the difference that the Social Democratic Party tended to support only socialist liberation movements, while the Liberal Party supported nationalist movements independent of their ideological outlook?

DW: Well, I would not go as far as to say that they only supported liberation movements with a socialist outlook, but they did not want to support more than one movement in each country. I think that they argued in favour of that. As I said, in principle we argued for letting the Africans themselves decide within a rather liberal framework. In the case of Zimbabwe, Angola and South Africa we would at an early stage probably have advocated support to the two movements that we have been speaking about, but in the end it was only in Zimbabwe that it was implemented.

I think that political reality was part of the decision in the other two cases. In the case of Angola, UNITA was impossible according to my and others' belief by the fact that they had so openly welcomed South African support. But we argued for FNLA for a long time. Olle Wästberg went there and wrote a book about the struggle. There were quite a few Swedes who had contacts with the FNLA side. Of course, in all camps one could see that some rather harsh methods were used, but I think that there was no major difference between, for instance, MPLA and FNLA in terms of the methods.

I would also say that if you had taken the liberal viewpoint you might have had a freer trade of opinions, which would have been positive. On the other hand, many of those that I thought were the best among the Africans advocated the one party system. So did Nyerere, Kawawa and others in Tanzania and so did Tom Mboya in Kenya. He wrote a very famous article in the American journal *Foreign Affairs*, defending the one party system. His main argument was that the tribal differences made it very difficult to make a multi-party system work.

I never bought that argument. I had various articles published by SIDA on this question. I have also written other things on the question of whether the developing world can have full democracy in our sense. My argument was that it is possible. It is not easy, but it is possible. One should strive for that. I was always against those who said that these were bourgeois or Western freedoms, because according to me human rights and fundamental freedoms are the same all over the world. They are universal and, therefore, if people want them, they should be allowed to. I found in Africa—also in the one party states—that many of my friends came to me and complained about the lack of freedom at a personal level. They either wanted to go to a country in Europe to have a period of greater freedom of expression or to change the system. I am also convinced that the British electoral system—the single constituency principle, where the winner takes all—is not very conducive to a fully fledged interplay of opinions and full democracy. I think that a proportional system could have helped to form a greater understanding of the need for an opposition and how to deal with an opposition.

TS: So you think that there is something in the statement that support to one 'sole and authentic' liberation movement was partly detrimental to a well functioning parliamentary democracy upon independence?

DW: One has to emphasize that it may be *one* cause, but I would say that in the case of South Africa I had no grudges about only supporting ANC. I think that they had such a solid base in the struggle for human rights that they will not be averse to the opposition or to other parties. In fact, I think that South Africa might well be the case that paves the way for a more open system in other countries in Africa. Even Nyerere has recognized that the one party system had its drawbacks. Well, I think that it would not have harmed to support several liberation movements in one country, but one should not invent a movement in order to get a better democracy. It is the people who decide which their movements are. In the case of Mozambique, for example, FRELIMO was the only liberation movement, so why should one worry? It was up to them to decide the movements and also about the future democratic system, but what one has to attack is the philosophy of making a virtue of the one party state, because I do not think that it has a virtue.

TS: Was the question of armed struggle in your view a difficult issue when it came to the anchoring of support in the Swedish public opinion and in parliament?

DW: Within the Liberal Party, we had a discussion on this. Of course, there were those who said that we could not support movements that used violence. In the case of ANC of South Africa, they changed their policy and entered into a period of armed struggle. The majority line within the Liberal Party was that it was up to them to decide which method they wanted to use. We knew that the apartheid government used violence to a great degree and it was in our view difficult to criticize ANC's stand. But we made it clear that we could not support the military struggle. We could not give aid to arms and military equipment.

TS: When the non-socialist coalition succeeded the Social Democratic government in

1976, it not only continued the support to the liberation movements, but increased the assistance. It also introduced the first sanctions' legislation against South Africa. Was the Swedish government ever the object of international pressure from the West—the United States and Great Britain, particularly—to end the support?

DW: I have no recollection of any pressure from the West on Sweden to change the policy with regard to the liberation movements. I think that the other Western countries simply knew that we were right and that we had a case.

When I was ambassador to Tanzania, there was nobody who tried to get us less involved with the liberation movements. Instead, what was important was that the various major powers—the United States, the UK etc.—in the Tanzanian context were very interested in the Swedish viewpoints and what we understood to be the viewpoints of the Tanzanians, because they knew that we had very good contacts with them. We had a close cooperation between the Nordic countries, but also with the Dutch and the Canadians, although they were not so outspoken as we were. I recall that we had a celebration for both ANC and SWAPO every year in Dar es Salaam. The Swedish ambassador was always invited to speak. I still have my speeches from that time. Once I also represented all the ambassadors to the President of Tanzania at a diplomat gathering at State House. I spoke about South Africa and I could go quite far. The pressure was not on us. It was rather the other way around, that the others were pressurised.

TS: As ambassador to Tanzania, you were the head of a Swedish mission that was responsible for a lot of support to ANC. Do you think that there was a sound distribution of responsibilities between the political and the aid offices in the Swedish embassy?

DW: Yes, I have no complaints. I thought that it worked well and that the SIDA personnel was competent. Of course, the major cause was that in a country like Tanzania we had very good SIDA representatives. The heads of SIDA were always selected with great care and we were consulting regularly. They knew of my interest in the liberation movements and they knew that I had been a member of the board of SIDA for a long time. There was no attempt to play one side against the other. I would say that it worked well. The decisions about the support were also mainly taken in Sweden.

TS: Is it your understanding that there was a satisfactory system in place when it comes to financial control of the funds disbursed to the liberation movements?

DW: Yes, I believe so. As far as I know, we had no complaints during my time.

TS: SIDA used a flexible system of quarterly payments in advance. Do you think that it worked well?

DW: I think that it was necessary to have a flexible system in order to make things work well. At the same time, it was necessary to check that the money really was used for the purpose that it was said to be used for. In most cases, this could be done satisfactorily afterwards, but, we were, of course, also involved in the planning of various programmes. It was not only that money was paid out at an early stage. We were also involved with the planning side and the liberation movements were open to us. I was often invited by ANC to Morogoro for discussions. They also received SIDA missions and various other people.

TS: One important issue is the question of liberation and liberty. We know of crises within the liberation movements, such as the Shipanga crisis in SWAPO, abuse in ANC and SWAPO camps in Angola, human rights violations in MPLA etc. Did you discuss these matters with the leaders of the liberation movements?

DW: Yes, I discussed them with those persons that I was most involved with. For instance, I took up delicate questions with Oliver Tambo, but I did not take up the issue of the Angolan camps, because it happened after my time.

TS: The so-called Shipanga affair involved three friendly actors from the point of view of Sweden, namely SWAPO, Zambia and Tanzania. Shipanga was never sentenced, but kept in jail in Zambia and in Tanzania for a long period. Did Sweden or the Nordic countries put any pressure on SWAPO or the host governments to have him tried in a court of law?

DW: I was not involved in that and I am not sure that it was the case. If there were things that I thought were not correct during my time in Tanzania, what would happen was that I first took them up with somebody among the Tanzanians that I knew was involved with the liberation struggle and then with the movement itself. But I had never any orders from home to do so. If they were taken up at the official negotiations, it must have been by the Ministry for Foreign Affairs or SIDA.

TS: Internationally, and perhaps particularly in Southern Africa, Olof Palme has to a large extent come to personify Sweden, the Nordic countries and a commitment to liberation. Did Palme earlier than others in the Social Democratic Party support the liberation process in Southern Africa?

DW: That I really do not know, but he had contacts with the liberation movements and when he committed himself to the liberation cause, he did so with all his mind and all his force. I recall when he came to Tanzania. That was when the Socialist International had a conference in Arusha in 1984. He invited me to participate. He knew my views since a very long time back. He also made a state visit to Tanzania at the same time and I helped to prepare his official speech. But he really came to life when he made his intervention in Arusha. That was his life, but, of course, he was limited by his social democratic policy.

We liberals had argued for more funds to the various countries in Southern Africa. More than the Social Democratic government, and Palme knew this. When I was in parliament, he visited Zambia where he made a famous speech about the border of decency with Rhodesia. I put a question to him in parliament and said: 'If this is the border of decency, should you not increase the support to Zambia?' He had some difficulty in giving a reply to this question, because he knew that we had argued for more aid to Zambia than his own government. I also see from the memoirs of Ulla Lindström that she at a certain time had to argue against him regarding the level of aid. She advocated more aid than he, so I am not sure that he always was heading the movement for more support. But it was clear that he was convinced and that he found this very important.

TS: Is there anything you would like to add?

DW: I would say that Southern Africa is a region where Swedish politics has played a role. We have made our impact and the Nordic countries have made an impact. We should be proud of that, because we really have had a significance and everybody has respected that. The British have respected it and the Americans have respected it. The Americans were never in Africa and American politicians were never very loyal to the colonial system. They wanted freedom for Africa, because they also thought that freedom was the best way of combatting Communism. As far as I know, we never had any criticism from the US because of our policy of support to Southern Africa. In individual cases, like in Angola, they might have thought that we landed wrong with our exclusive support to MPLA, but that is how it was. I think that our support to ANC in South Africa was well understood because of the political realities. Some of my best friends in the United States were very convinced that ANC was the organization to support and that it was the most representative. However, the most important thing is that we made a difference in terms of South Africa. We should play those cards well. We should not forget that role.

Per Wästberg
Founder of the Swedish Fund for the Victims of Racial Oppression in South Africa—Swedish South Africa Committee—Board member of the International Defence and Aid Fund—Vice President of Swedish Amnesty International—Member of the Consultative Committee on Humanitarian Assistance—Chief editor of *Dagens Nyheter*
Member of the European Academy of Arts and Sciences
(Stockholm, 28 February 1996)

Tor Sellström: You were one of the first, and perhaps the most important, opinion maker on South Africa in Sweden. How did it start? What factors were behind the early Swedish commitment against apartheid?

Per Wästberg: I must underline that my view when I returned from Rhodesia and South Africa in 1959 was quite narrow. I wrote a great number of articles simply because I was so upset. At the time of writing these articles, my only experience of any Swedish commitment was Herbert Tingsten's book on South Africa, which, I think, came out in 1954. I had also read one of Gunnar Helander's books. When I came home in the autumn of 1959, I took the initiative of establishing the Fund for the Victims of Racial Oppression in South Africa. In this connection, I came for the first time in contact with others, who—by themselves or sometimes because of my articles—had become interested in Southern Africa. One of them was Olof Tandberg.

Already before going to Rhodesia in early 1959 I had been contacted by him. Olof Tandberg had in 1956 been visiting South Africa for the Swedish National Union of Students (SFS) and he had met Neville Rubin, who was then a student of law at the University of Cape Town and very much engaged in anti-apartheid work. He was the son of Leslie Rubin, who, I would say, at the time was the most dominant anti-apartheid politician with an official role. He was a Liberal, senator for the Africans and close to Alan Paton. Through Olof Tandberg I got a few addresses in South Africa. I had also read Nadine Gordimer's first novels. That was my background.

Coming home, I again established contact with Olof Tandberg and through him with Björn Beckman, who was then a student. We were very committed. There was also a very young man, Anders Thunborg, who was the international secretary of the Social Democratic Party. He had been excited by my articles, but had also close contacts with the World University Service.

That was one of the groups which in early 1961 formed the Swedish South Africa Committee. It was parallel to the Fund for the Victims of Racial Oppression, which had been established as a kind of *bona fide* fundraising operation. We were extremely energetic in trying to have signatures by leading Swedes from all over the political spectrum. I regret to say that the only person that could be regarded as conservative among the signatories was the bishop of Karlstad, Gert Borgenstierna. Otherwise, all the conservative politicians and all the people from the business sector refused to sign, while Bertil Ohlin and others from the Liberal Party, as well as leading Social Democrats and representatives of the trade unions were all right. So, it was a rather broad sector, but as opinion makers we were all the time suffering from the fact that the conservatives were so reluctant to take sides. I think that they thought that the struggle—especially after Sharpeville—was led by too many lefties. It was seen as a left engagement.

The great dividing point was, of course, the massacre at Sharpeville in March 1960. It came after my articles and had an extraordinary impact. After that, South Africa was no longer 'my field', as it in a way had been before. The issue became more public. Television took it up. I was called there to speak, day after day. I either spoke straight out as a commentator or was interviewed. And suddenly people like Canon Collins, Robert Resha and Oliver Tambo turned up in Sweden. They were also interviewed by me on television, because there was nobody else at the time. In the beginning, I was more or less the only commentator. The Sharpeville massacre led to demonstrations. I think that

Sharpeville—more than anything else—started a kind of demonstration culture here in Sweden, which later flowered with the Vietnam movement. That had been very rare in the 1950s, although in November 1956 there were demonstrations against the Russians in Hungary, but they were not that big.

The South Africa Committee organized demonstrations and we very soon lined up, in an ad hoc way, with those who were better organizers, that is, the National Council of Swedish Youth (SUL), the Social Democratic Youth (SSU), the Liberal Youth and the students. We were more or less acting like a small steering cabinet. We were quite few and did not have a membership. You could not become a member of the South Africa Committee and that is why it was so short-lived, I think. Gunnar Helander, myself and others were out speaking for the Fund for the Victims of Racial Oppression and the money we got went there. We had donations and Helander organized church collections. Then there was the question of where to send the money. In the beginning, some of it was sent to SACHED (South African Council of Higher Education) in South Africa. Neville Rubin provided that link and we were guaranteed that the money was coming to good use, and so it was. A few years later SACHED was, I think, the very first organization in South Africa that SIDA supported.

Already at the time of Sharpeville I got to know about Canon Collins and the British Defence and Aid Fund. I then went to London. I think that it was in the autumn of 1960, when Tambo had fled with Ronald Segal. I met Patrick van Rensburg for the first time at Canon Collins' house. He was devoting all his time to the potato boycott after the revelations of child slavery on the Bethal farms by Joe Slovo and Ruth First in *Fighting Talk* and *New Age*. After that visit, more or less all the funds were channelled to IDAF, except for a small amount of petty cash with which we helped people who came to Sweden, for instance the *Golden City Dixies*. They were the first to seek asylum in Sweden. They played at Gröna Lund and Gunnar Helander and I were suddenly called there by the director and the police. They had defected after a concert and somebody had to establish their *bona fide*. Helander and I signed almost like a pledge that they were all right—not spies or anything—after having talked to them for quite a long time. Peter Radise was their leader. Anyway, the Fund was based on collections from churches and private individuals until SIDA started to support Defence and Aid from 1964. We then renamed it the Swedish Defence and Aid Fund and all the money went straight to IDAF in London.

TS: You mentioned the Swedish National Union of Students, SFS. At one stage in the 1950s, Olof Palme was the chairman of SFS. Do you remember if he had an involvement with South or Southern Africa at that time?

PW: Well, not with me. In 1959, when I returned, Palme's commitment was very much with the American blacks and with India. I do not know if he had his eyes on South Africa. I think that it came slightly later, with Sharpeville. He had possibly also read Tingsten's articles.

TS: If you look at the names of those who signed that first appeal, you find a strong group of people representing a liberal tradition. In the journalistic field opinion makers like Ivar Harrie, Herbert Tingsten, Torgny Segerstedt and others were also of that tradition. How did they react to the fact that ANC later on embarked upon armed struggle? Was that a divisive issue?

PW: Not in a serious sense. When the United Nations declared that South Africa was a threat against peace it became a non-issue. Also, when Nelson Mandela turned up in London in 1962, he went to Canon Collins and said: 'You are a Christian organization and we will need your support if we turn to violence.' And Collins said: 'It is OK. We understand you. We will support you nevertheless.' Which Amnesty International refused to do and which I think that Nelson Mandela up to this day cannot forgive them for. I took it up with him at one point and he said that he could not understand that.

Especially Oliver Tambo had close relations to John Collins. It was not a father-and-son relationship, because they were of the same age, but, nevertheless, it was something like that. They were extremely close. And Trevor Huddleston and Oliver Tambo were almost the same person. Trevor Huddleston would like to die only to see Tambo in heaven. For Oliver Tambo, I think that IDAF and all it stood for, as well as John

Collins as a person, represented the very best in the liberation struggle. But Mandela does not mention IDAF in his autobiography. One of the reasons, I think, is that it was written by an American ghost writer who apparently cut out an extraordinary amount of 'boring' stuff about organizations, committees, councils and so on. The other thing is the Winnie Mandela trial. IDAF financed a lawyer, but it was not enough in Nelson's view, I think. They should have done much more and come out openly for Winnie at the time. I do not know what he thinks today.

TS: So the ANC leadership—the Robben Island generation—would have known about IDAF?

PW: Yes. They would have known on Robben Island. Certainly. There was, however, one question where there were conflicts between IDAF and ANC and that was Robert Resha's anti-Soviet stance. The main problem was that Canon Collins defended Robert Resha when he was expelled for not obeying the Communist sector within ANC, with J.B. Marks sitting on the money in Moscow. Suddenly Resha got no pay. He was frozen out. He was a lovely person. I got to know him well. If I am not mistaken, he was the first ANC representative to come to Sweden and talk on Swedish television and also, I think, on the First of May 1961.

I think that the question of violence—because of the support of IDAF and of other church people, also in Sweden, and of the explanations given by a number of us who supported ANC—did not come up as something divisive. Of course, later, when there was big SIDA support to ANC, questions were raised in parliament and everywhere about weapons. I think that one of the consequences of this was that ANC's accounting became better than that of many of SIDA's programme countries. The South Africans had tried to falsify invoices, saying that there were weapons involved.

TS: Would it be fair to say that one of the reasons why many Swedish politicians could see beyond the Communist dimension and the question of violence was that they had early personal relations with the nationalist leaders from Southern Africa?

PW: I think that that is very true. One also has to take into account the role played by Nyerere, who came on the political scene in 1961, and Kaunda. They were socialists, humanitarians and against violence. There were quite a few Swedes who met them. Nyerere came to Sweden a number of times between 1961 and 1965. Nyerere and Kaunda acted as bridge-builders and South Africa was seen to be at the end of the decolonization process.

The conservatives were not uninterested and they did not really put up great resistance. One of the reasons why the Consultative Committee on Humanitarian Assistance had representatives from different political parties, including the Moderate Party, was that they should see where the money went, which, of course, was a secret. But that was much later. I think that the Dag Hammarskjöld tradition and Sweden's involvement in the UN also played a role. There were so many factors behind our confidence in these people. There was much more confidence in Nyerere, Tambo, Mondlane etc. than in Nkrumah, Sekou Touré and the other West African leaders.

TS: You were close to many of the Southern African leaders. How do you think that they saw the Nordic countries at the beginning of the 1960s? Did they view them as Western capitalist countries or as socialist countries?

PW: They saw us, I think, as Western, but social democratic. Most of them saw us as an ideal, while the Russians were necessary for them and they felt attracted to the Americans because of their freedom tradition. England was the colonial power. Also, we were a small country and they were small. That was a kind of link. And, again, Hammarskjöld was such a name in Africa, especially after being killed on African soil.

There was also the Swedish missionary tradition. An amazing number of Africans in South Africa, Zimbabwe and Tanzania had come into contact with Swedes—and with Finns in Namibia—through the missions. Oliver Tambo came here every year, sometimes several times a year. Clearly, he recognized in the Swedes people who were on the same wavelength. He had a missionary background and was a Christian. He had the most civilized behaviour. He was not a Che Guevara or anybody in fatigues. He was just a firm, but a very nice and civilized chap. The same goes for Mondlane, with his American background. Well, almost anybody. I think that there was a sort of chemistry which had to do with certain values.

The difficulty in the early years was that we were so unused to meeting these people on a formal basis. There was much hush-hush so as not to disturb the Portuguese embassy, the British or the South Africans. It meant that on his visits Mondlane was taken by Palme and others to different restaurants or to my place, because they just could not be seen inside the Ministry for Foreign Affairs. This was also true of others. They were never let in officially. SIDA was a bit easier, generally. Of course, SIDA was separate from the ministry. It also took some time before direct public support to the liberation movements was accepted. In the beginning, it had to go through NGOs and this was very much the conservative viewpoint. They warned that they would oppose assistance unless it went through NGOs or through the Red Cross. Guinea-Bissau was such a case.

Amílcar Cabral was, of course, the idol of many. His visits to Sweden made a very big impression. I do not remember how many times he was here. Agostinho Neto—whose umbrella I kept for a very long time; it was forgotten in my place—was much shyer. A difficult person, I think. You could not think of him as a popular speaker.

TS: The Swedish government supported the so-called authentic liberation movements. In addition, support was channelled to ZANU. In your view, why was Swedish assistance never extended to other liberation movements, such as FNLA and UNITA of Angola or PAC and Inkatha of South Africa?

PW: On the whole we supported the first movements and not the breakaway groups, except for ZANU. In the case of FRELIMO it was not complicated. There were dissidents within FRELIMO and they came here, but they did not make enough impression. With regard to Angola, I think that everybody who had met Holden Roberto and other representatives of FNLA—often dressed in smart suits—could not trust them a bit. Even if Roberto tried to seduce the Liberals and also managed to some extent. I have met him a few times. I immediately thought that this was a person that you should not have any deep relations with, regardless of ideology.

He was a tribal man, I would say. It was recognized.

TS: You wrote a strong article on Angola in *Dagens Nyheter* at the beginning of 1975.

PW: Yes, against David Wirmark, who was trying to argue in favour of FNLA.

TS: His position was to support both movements?

PW: Yes. My brother, Olle Wästberg, also went around parts of Angola with Roberto and FNLA.

Regarding UNITA, I think that in the beginning several of us were giving them a chance, which was never the case with FNLA. At one stage, Jonas Savimbi came to Sweden and I remember how Pierre Schori and I—only the two of us—sat with him in the basement of the restaurant *Aurora* in Stockholm, very isolated. There was nobody else. I think that we talked for five hours. Savimbi was, of course, here in order to get support. I was not totally impressed and to Schori's credit I must say that he was even less impressed. But we both recognized that Savimbi—in contrast to Roberto—was a forceful, persuasive talker and a personality. Not unsympathetic. Very civilized, one thought at the time.

When it comes to Namibia, I think that SWAPO in the early stages was seen as a tribal Owambo group. SWANU was more of a broadly based intellectual organization. But it never became a serious issue, because the involvement was weak with both SWANU and SWAPO and, finally, when SWANU was no longer there, there was no alternative.

In Zimbabwe, I think that very much was due to the fact that Mugabe was seen as a forceful intellectual. Although he was a Marxist, he was a Western intellectual that one recognized and talked to, while Nkomo, especially, was eating too many desserts. Sithole was an extraordinary drunkard and Muzorewa was a sell-out, more or less. While Mugabe was in jail he could communicate all the time. This was the paradox. He gave orders. Herbert Chitepo was the main ZANU figure in exile and he was a very likeable man.

Regarding South Africa and PAC, there was no question of ever supporting an organization that was more or less fraudulent and that could not take care of money. They had Robert Sobukwe in the beginning and then, if you like, Steve Biko on the black consciousness side, but PAC as an organization was never reliable. There was infighting and they were killing each other. They were absolutely impossible. The Unity Movement was impossible too. Buthelezi also came to Sweden. I met him twice, in Uppsala and Stockholm. He gave me a book and I saw to my horror that it was signed by Buthelezi, 'your brother in the struggle' or something like that. That was in 1977, I think. I especially remember one meeting, a long session and a dinner that we had at the Hammarskjöld Foundation in Uppsala with Ernst Michanek and Sven Hamrell. I suppose that we met on a kind of neutral ground, because Michanek was either the chairman or the vice chairman of the Hammarskjöld Foundation.

Buthelezi was very civilised and softspoken, making the argument that he was ANC inside the country. This was at the time when there were relations between Tambo and Buthelezi. What he asked for, I remember, was that SIDA should finance an Inkatha journal of gardening and agriculture in Zulu through which he could smuggle political messages. Inkatha, I think, had just been founded. He talked about Inkatha in enticing terms, saying that this was a new peace movement that could not call itself ANC, but, in fact, was ANC. We were slightly seduced, but it came to nothing and again I think that Pierre Schori, who was then international secretary of the Social Democratic Party, was more sceptical than Michanek and I. He totally ruled Inkatha out as too tribal and too uncertain. He was very firm.

TS: Questions regarding Swedish humanitarian support were discussed in the Consultative Committee on Humanitarian Assistance, where you from the very beginning were a member. How do you see the role of the committee vis-à-vis the Ministry for Foreign Affairs and SIDA?

PW: When Ernst Michanek was offered the position as Director General of SIDA instead of Minister of Social Affairs, he contacted me. We had never met, but I had been very impressed by him from newspaper articles and television programmes on social issues. He did not know much about Africa at all. I gave him a list of books. He was one of the most receptive persons that I have ever met. Very soon he seemed to know everything. He immediately had the idea of a committee to deal *in camera* with all the sensitive issues in order not to get into trouble with embassies and the political parties.

It started as a very loose committee, with Stig Abelin, Leif Kihlberg and Tord Palmlund as SIDA officials and Gunnar Helander, Sven Hamrell and myself as outside experts. It was quite small and extremely informal. I do not know if there even were any minutes from the very first meetings. I cannot remember us having a secretary. We just chatted. It was like sitting at a coffee table. We traded information, simply. Then gradually, but only slowly, it was widened, but I think that at this early stage there was no representative from the Ministry for Foreign Affairs. I cannot say at what stage somebody from the ministry came in. I was absent from 1976 until 1982, when I was chief editor at *Dagens Nyheter* and not allowed to have any official appointments.

TS: Were the committee members appointed by the government?

PW: Yes. The security aspect was very much underlined in the 1970s, but, in retrospect, it is extraordinary how the support was conducted on simple personal trust.

TS: As a writer and an influential representative in international cultural organizations, how did you look upon the cultural boycott of South Africa?

PW: I think that I from the beginning recognized that a cultural boycott was a much more complicated affair than other boycotts. We drew a strict line, perhaps too strict, in accordance with the wishes of ANC. But when it came to free cultural expression, it was more difficult. There were some crucial episodes. One was when Astrid Lindgren phoned and said that they would like to translate *Pippi Långstrump* (Pippi Longstocking) and several of her books into Afrikaans. Should she allow this? At the time, I simply said that it depended on herself. One could argue that Pippi Långstrump was a revolutionary, especially in the conservative Afrikaner context. On the other hand, hardly any black family would be able to buy these books. I think that the end result was that she did not allow it. Then Peter

Weiss, a revolutionary and Marxist writer, phoned me and said that the Market Theatre in Johannesburg, which was then just starting, would like to put on his famous play *The Murder of Marat* about rebellion against a totalitarian society. I said that my interpretation of the boycott would be that he should allow it, because the Market Theatre was a multi-racial theatre. Eventually, the play was performed and was a great success.

I took the question of the cultural boycott up with Oliver Tambo time and time again. I thought that it was tricky and he also realized that from the beginning. The absolute boycott was lifted by a lecture by Oliver Tambo in honour of John Collins. It must have been in 1982 or 1983, when Tambo in a very subtle manner said that cultural expression and art for the benefit of the people should be allowed. That was a turning point. I think that cultural boycotts are always very tricky, but I also think that Sweden followed the boycott of South Africa more strictly than any other country.

List of Acronyms

AAC	All-African Convention (South Africa)
AAM	Anti-Apartheid Movement (United Kingdom)
AAPC	All-African Peoples' Conference
ABF	Workers' Educational Association/Arbetarnas Bildningsförbund (Sweden)
AET	Africa Educational Trust (United Kingdom)
AGIS	Africa Groups in Sweden/Afrikagrupperna i Sverige
ANC	African National Congress (South Africa)
Anti-CAD	Anti-Coloured Affairs Department (South Africa)
ARM	African Resistance Movement (South Africa)
CANU	Caprivi African National Union (Namibia)
CCHA	Consultative Committee on Humanitarian Assistance (Sweden)
CD	Christian Democrats (Sweden)
CIA	Central Intelligence Agency (United States)
COD	Congress of Democrats (South Africa)
CODESA	Convention for a Democratic South Africa
CONCP	Conferência das Organizações Nacionalistas das Colónias Portuguesas/Conference of Nationalist Organizations in the Portuguese Colonies
COREMO	Revolutionary Committee of Mozambique/Comité Revolucionário de Moçambique
COSATU	Congress of South African Trade Unions
COSEC	Coordinating Secretariat of ISC
CP	Centre Party (Sweden)
CPC	Coloured People's Congress (South Africa)
CPSA	Communist Party of South Africa
CPSU	Communist Party of the Soviet Union
CSA	Church of Sweden Aid/Lutherhjälpen
CSM	Church of Sweden Mission
CUF	Centre Party Youth League (Sweden)
DFFG	United FNL Groups/De förenade FNL-grupperna (Sweden)
ECA	UN Economic Commission for Africa
EEC	European Economic Community
EFTA	European Free Trade Association
ELCIN	Evangelical Lutheran Church in Namibia
ELCZ	Evangelical Lutheran Church of Zimbabwe
ELOK	Evangelical Lutheran Ovambo-Kavango Church (Namibia)
EU	European Union
FNLA	National Front for the Liberation of Angola/Frente Nacional de Libertação de Angola
FPLN	Patriotic Front of National Liberation/Frente Patriótica de Libertação Nacional
FPU	Liberal Party Youth League (Sweden)
FRAIN	African Revolutionary Front for National Independence/Frente Revolucionária para Africana Independência Nacional
FRELIMO	Mozambique Liberation Front/Frente de Libertação de Moçambique
FROLIZI	Front for the Liberation of Zimbabwe
GRAE	Revolutionary Government of Angola in Exile/Governo Revolucionário de Angola no Exílio
ICFTU	International Confederation of Free Trade Unions
ICJ	International Court of Justice
IDAF	International Defence and Aid Fund
IRCZ	International Refugee Council of Zambia
ISAK	Isolate South Africa Committee (Sweden)
ISC	International Student Conference

IUEF	International University Exchange Fund
IUS	International Union of Students
IUSY	International Union of Socialist Youth
KF	Co-operative Union and Wholesale Society (Sweden)
LO	Swedish Trade Union Confederation/Landsorganisationen i Sverige
LP	Liberal Party (Sweden)
LPC	Left Party Communists (Sweden)
LWF	Lutheran World Federation
MAC	Anti-Colonial Movement/Movimento Anti-Colonialista
MANU	Mozambique African National Union
MCP	Malawi Congress Party
MK	Umkhonto we Sizwe (South Africa)
MP	Moderate Party (Sweden)
MPLA	Popular Movement for the Liberation of Angola/Movimento Popular de Libertação de Angola
NAC	Nyasaland African Congress
NATO	North Atlantic Treaty Organization
NDP	National Democratic Party (Zimbabwe)
NEUM	Non-European Unity Movement (South Africa)
NIB	Agency for International Assistance (Sweden)
NRANC	Northern Rhodesia African National Congress
NUSAS	National Union of South African Students
NUSWAS	National Union of South West African Students
OAU	Organization of African Unity
OECD	Organization of Economic Cooperation and Development
OMA	Angolan Women's Organization/Organização das Mulheres de Angola
OPO	Ovamboland People's Organisation (Namibia)
PAC	Pan-Africanist Congress of Azania (South Africa)
PAFMECSA	Pan-African Freedom Movement for Eastern, Central and Southern Africa
PAIGC	African Party for the Independence of Guinea Bissau and Cape Verde/ Partido Africano para a Independência da Guiné e Cabo Verde
PCC	People's Caretaker Council (Zimbabwe)
PCP	Communist Party of Portugal
PCR	Programme to Combat Racism of WCC
PDA	Democratic Party of Angola/Partido Democrático de Angola
PIDE	International and State Defence/Policía Internacional e de Defesa do Estado
PLUA	Party for the United Struggle of the Africans of Angola/Partido da Luta Unida dos Africanos de Angola
RF	Rhodesian Front
RMS	Rhenish Missionary Society (Germany)
SABRA	South African Bureau of Racial Affairs
SACHED	South African Committee for Higher Education
SACO	Swedish Confederation of Professional Associations
SACP	South African Communist Party
SACTU	South African Congress of Trade Unions
SADCC	Southern Africa Development Coordination Conference
SAF	Swedish Employers' Confederation
SAIC	South African Indian Congress
SAUF	South African United Front
SDF	Students Development Fund (Sweden)
SDP	Social Democratic Party (Sweden)
SDS	Students for a Democratic Society (Sweden)
SECO	Swedish Union of Secondary School Students
SFS	Swedish National Union of University Students
SI	Socialist International
SIDA	Swedish International Development Authority
Sida	Swedish International Development Cooperation Agency
SKP	Swedish Communist Party/Sveriges Kommunistiska Parti

SKV	Left Association of Swedish Women
SLU	Swedish Rural Youth League
SOMAFCO	Solomon Mahlangu Freedom College (ANC/Tanzania)
SRANC	Southern Rhodesia African National Congress
SSAK	Swedish South Africa Committee
SSU	Social Democratic Youth League (Sweden)
SUL	National Council of Swedish Youth
SWANLIF	South West Africa National Liberation Front
SWANU	South West Africa National Union
SWANUF	South West Africa National United Front
SWAPA	South West African Progressive Association
SWAPO	South West Africa People's Organization
SWAPO-D	SWAPO-Democrats
SWASB	South West African Student Body
TANU	Tanganyika African National Union
TCO	Central Organization of Salaried Employees (Sweden)
TCRS	Tanganyika Christian Refugee Service
TUC	Trades Union Congress (United Kingdom)
UANC	United African National Council (Zimbabwe)
UDENAMO	National Democratic Union of Mozambique/União Democrática Nacional de Moçambique
UDF	United Democratic Front (South Africa)
UDI	Unilateral Declaration of Independence (Rhodesia)
UFP	United Federal Party (Rhodesia)
UGEAN	General Union of Students from Black Africa under Portuguese Colonial Domination/União Nacional dos Estudantes daÁfrica Negra sob Dominação Colónial Portuguêsa
UN	United Nations
UNAMI	African National Union of Independent Mozambique
UNDP	United Nations Development Programme
UNEA	National Union of Angolan Students/União Nacional dos Estudantes Angolanos
UNETSPA	UN Educational and Training Programme for Southern Africa
UNHCR	United Nations High Commissioner for Refugees
UNIN	United Nations Institute for Namibia
UNIP	United National Independence Party (Zambia)
UNITA	National Union for the Total Independence of Angola/União Nacional para a Independência Total de Angola
UPA	Union of the Peoples of Angola/União das Populações de Angola
UPNA	Union of the Peoples of Northern Angola/União das Populações do Norte de Angola
UPRONA	União Progressista Nacional de Angola
WAY	World Assembly of Youth
WFDY	World Federation of Democratic Youth
WFTU	World Federation of Trade Unions
VUF	Left Party Youth League (Sweden)
WCC	World Council of Churches
WUS	World University Service
ZANC	Zambia African National Congress
ZANU	Zimbabwe African National Union
ZAPU	Zimbabwe African People's Union
ZIPA	Zimbabwe People's Army
ZWT	Zimbabwe Welfare Trust

Name Index

Aall, Cato, 279
Abdallah, Anna, 144, 145, 146, 246
Abelin, Stig, 253, 356
Abrahams, Kenneth, 98, 122, 123
Abrahams, Ottilie, 59, 98
Agrell, Ulf, 157, 227, 299
Ahlfors, Kid, 46
Ahlmark, Per, 46, 341
Ahtisaari, Martti, 30, 67, 80, 98, 115
Alexander, Neville, 123, 126, 127
Allmér, Göran, 275
Altman, Phyllis, 132
Amathila, Ben, 62, 75, 76, 77, 90
Andersson, Sten, 116, 227, 228, 297, 303, 344
de Andrade, Mário, 17, 18, 19, 278
Antunes, Luís, 26, 274
Appalraju, Jaya, 103
Appolus, Emil, 26
Asmal, Kader, 132
Auala, Leonard, 91
Axelsson, Roland, 96, 164, 252

Bakkevig, Trond, 184
Banana, Canaan, 206
Banda, Rupiah, 103, 226, 238
Beckman, Björn, 341, 352
Berggren, Birgitta, 137, 256
Bergknut, Knut, 133
Bergman, Tore, 262
Bessinger, Nico, 72
Beukes, Hans, 72, 75
Bhebe, Ngwabi, 210, 263
Biko, Steve, 182, 187, 188, 203, 356
Bildt, Carl, 272, 274, 275
Bjurner, Anders, 215
Björk, Kaj, 297
Björklund, Ellen, 221
Blix, Hans, 343
Blomquist, Lennart, 221
Blomqvist, Stig, 11, 100, 101, 165, 167, 168, 266
Bodström, Lennart, 307
Boesak, Allan, 149, 344
Bohman, Gösta, 274, 343
Boraine, Alex, 107
Borgenstierna, Gert, 352
Botha, P. W., 57, 82, 109, 180, 240
Botha, Roelof ('Pik'), 11, 57, 80, 111, 132, 147, 200, 273, 284
Boutros-Ghali, Boutros, 117
de Bragança, Aquino, 53
Brandrup, Poul, 199, 201
Bratt, Eyvind, 124, 125

Brezhnev, Leonid, 142
Brink, André, 139
Brisman, Johan, 164
Britton, Ronnie, 75
Brundin, Gertrud, 31, 32, 33
Burenstam-Linder, Staffan, 319
Buthelezi, Gatsha, 199, 200, 258, 266, 280, 288, 324, 325, 356

Cabral, Amílcar, 17, 18, 19, 22, 78, 244, 245, 280, 309, 310, 312, 314, 327, 332, 333, 338, 355
Cabral, Luís, 314
Cachalia, Azhar, 340
Canjimi, Lucas, 26
Carlsson, Bernt, 23, 97, 331
Carlsson, Ingvar, 38, 76, 142, 180, 292, 331
Carlsson, Paul, 100
Carolus, Cheryl, 196
Carrilho, Júlio, 51
Carrington, Lord, 214, 243
Castro, Fidel, 123, 241, 242, 303, 329
Cedergren, Jan, 164, 217, 218, 219
Chikwanda, Alexander, 228, 238
Chimurenga, 215
Chipenda, Daniel, 17, 250, 312, 326, 328, 329
Chissano, Joaquim, 16, 38, 118, 180
Chitepo, Herbert, 41, 56, 213, 215, 217, 227, 229, 230, 241, 242, 333, 355
Chiwale, Samuel, 26
Chokwenda, Claude, 226
Christiansen, Steen, 228
Clutton-Brock, Guy, 218, 265
Collins, John, 74, 131, 132, 133, 176, 202, 218, 285, 287, 288, 324, 325, 352, 353, 354, 357
Crocker, Chester, 116, 337
da Cruz, Viriato, 19, 20
Cunhal, Álvaro, 20

Dabengwa, Dumiso, 209
Dahl, Birgitta, 299, 310
Danell, Magnus, 283
Davidson, Basil, 19, 67
Davis, Don John, 123, 126
Dix, Tove, 96
Douglas-Home, Alec, 91
Dreifaldt, George, 90
Dumeni, Kleopas, 91
Dölling, Iwo, 328

Ebrahim, Gora, 118
Ehnmark, Anders, 277, 278

Ekéus, Rolf, 259
Engström, K.G., 85
Eriksson, Lars-Gunnar, 23, 34, 97, 120, 132, 187, 188, 198, 199, 200, 201, 202, 203, 204, 250, 285, 335, 339
Erlander, Tage, 76, 157, 286, 298

First, Ruth, 202, 286, 291, 296, 297, 353
Fockstedt, Sven, 167
Ford, Martha, 72
Forsse, Anders, 279
Fraser, Malcolm, 243
Fredriksson, Gunnar, 279
Funde, Eddie, 769
Fälldin, Thorbjörn, 55, 228, 271, 343

Gaoseb, Godfrey, 91
Garoeb, Moses, 72
Garthon, Per, 227
Geijer, Arne, 230, 292, 297
Geingob, Hage, 83
Genscher, Hans-Dietrich, 69
Giesecke, Curt-Steffan, 321
Giose, Gerald, 122, 126, 127
Goldreich, Arthur, 296
Gomomo, John, 127
Gorbachev, Mikhail, 204
Gordimer, Nadine, 139, 352
Gqabi, Joe, 177
Granstedt, Pär, 269
Guevara, Ernesto ('Che'), 123, 143, 354
Gustavsson, Rolf, 330

Hagård, Birger, 11, 26, 35, 272
Hallencreutz, Carl Fredrik, 8, 209
Hammarskjöld, Dag, 186, 278, 354
Hamrell, Sven, 277, 356
Hangala, Leake, 95
Hani, Chris, 143
Hansson, Ruth, 221
Hansson, Tommy, 275
Hareide, Dag, 70
Harlin, Tord, 266
Harrie, Ivar, 111, 114, 273, 277, 284, 321, 347, 353
Hartling, Paul, 66
Haste, Hans, 92
Hedborg, Elisabeth, 326
Helander, Gunnar, 77, 92, 111, 114, 132, 157, 277, 278, 281, 289, 295, 327, 337, 352, 353, 356
Hellberg, Carl-Johan, 66
Hellström, Mats, 202, 343
Helmuth, Paul, 63, 65
ya Henda, Hoji, 28
Heppling, Sixten, 321
Hermansson, Carl-Henrik ('C.H.'), 289
Hishongwa, Hadino, 67
Hjelm-Wallén, Lena, 292

Hodgson, Rica, 131
Hodgson, Spencer, 105, 133
Holmberg, Åke, 283
Hove, Byron, 263
Hove, Richard, 224, 227
Huddleston, Trevor, 284, 353
Höglund, Cecilia, 184

Ihamäki, Mikko, 101
Israel, Joachim, 75, 76, 92, 277, 278, 279, 285
Iyambo, Nickey, 95

Jernberg, Inger, 85
Johannes, Axel, 72
Johansson, Anders, 39, 53, 159, 295, 304, 330
Johansson, Barbro, 76, 156, 326
Johansson, Lars-Erik, 157, 299
Johansson, Lena, 138, 164
Johnson, Eyvind, 285
Jonsson, Josef, 254
Jorge, Paulo, 15
Jämtin, Ola, 96

Kadungure, Ernest, 217
Kamanga, Reuben, 241
Kambona, Oscar, 145, 348
Kameeta, Zephania, 72
Kandjii, Ambrose, 93
Kangai, Kumbirai, 213, 214, 233
Kapuuo, Clemens, 80, 82
Karlsson, Urban, 290
Karlström Dorph, Birgitta, 142, 149, 184, 344
Kasrils, Ronnie, 297
Katjavivi, Peter, 13, 26, 71
Katjiuongua, Moses, 59, 60, 93
Kaukuetu, Uatja, 75, 76, 92, 156
Kaunda, Kenneth, 11, 12, 35, 64, 222, 225, 226, 228, 230, 232, 238, 240, 242, 262, 270, 278, 324, 329, 341, 342, 347, 348, 354
Kauraisa, Charles, 75, 92, 93, 295, 331
Kawawa, Rachidi, 348, 349
Kgotsisile, Baleka, 170
Khama, Seretse, 347
Khoapa, Ben, 187
King, Martin Luther, 296
Kirkpatrick, John, 79
Kissinger, Henry, 182, 225, 242, 329
Ki-Zerbo, Joseph, 249, 278
Kleinschmidt, Horst, 324
de Klerk, Frederik Willem, 109, 113, 115, 116, 117, 118, 240, 288, 344
Kohl, Helmuth, 148, 163, 185
Kotane, Moses, 145, 161
Kozonguizi Fanuel, 59, 76, 77, 92, 93, 156
Kristiansson, Kurt, 328
Kulunga, Francisco, 26

Kunene, Raymond Mazisi, 296
Källberg, Sture, 290

Ladouceur, Paul, 202
Lagercrantz, Olof, 298
Lara, Lúcio, 17, 18, 31
Larsen, Lars, 133, 144
Leballo, Potlako, 145
Ledin, Tomas, 300, 303
Legum, Colin, 278
Legum, Margaret, 278, 279
Lekota, Terror, 152
Lidman, Sara, 75, 157, 175, 176
Lilja, Ingrid, 232
Lindstrøm, Bjarne, 108
Lindström, Ulla, 76, 322, 351
Lundberg, Arne, 346
Luthuli, Albert, 76, 77, 93, 157, 190, 282, 285, 286, 287, 296, 347
Lövgren, Stig, 309
Lööw, Maj-Lis, 308

Mabhida, Moses, 143
Mabuza, Lindiwe, 134, 166, 169, 170, 300, 303
Machel, Graça, 21
Machel, Samora, 16, 41, 46, 47, 53, 54, 56, 57, 142, 222, 298, 334
Machungo, Fernanda, 51
Magnusson, Åke, 307, 315
Maharaj, 'Mac', 195
Mahlalela, 265
Mahomo, Nana, 77
Makatini, Johnny, 246
Makeba, Miriam, 139, 141, 303
Makhurane, Phineas, 224
Makunga, Stella, 328
Malmer, Lennart, 39
Mampane, Reddy (aka 'Reddy Mazimba'), 142, 148
Mandela, Nelson, 57, 92, 110, 111, 113, 121, 122, 123, 142, 156, 161, 174, 175, 176, 190, 197, 222, 276, 287, 294, 302, 303, 320, 325, 336, 347, 353, 354
Mandela, Winnie, 354
Manuel, Trevor, 149, 196
Marks, J. B., 145, 161, 354
Martin, David, 242
Maseko, Tim, 133
Matthews, Z. K., 41
Mbeki, Thabo, 103, 104, 108, 109, 120, 136, 137, 153, 171, 189, 190, 194, 247
Mbita, Hashim, 218
Mboya, Tom, 349
Mbuende, Kaire, 76
Mbulu, Letta, 140
Meir, Golda, 34
Mendès-France, Pierre, 347
Meroro, David, 72

Michanek, Elisabeth, 256
Michanek, Ernst, 279, 285, 288, 293, 294, 320, 324, 356
Milner, Aaron, 230
Mingas, Saydi, 328
Minty, Abdul, 132, 296
Mlambo, Johnson, 118
Mobutu, Sésé Séko, 24
Modise, Billy, 103, 134, 156, 186, 226, 238, 286, 296
Modise, Joe, 122, 142, 143, 1477
Mohn, Paul, 346
Mokoape, Aubrey, 187
Mokoape, Keith, 180
Mokoena, Raymond, 103
Monare, George, 256
Mondlane, Eduardo, 17, 39, 40, 41, 42, 43, 45, 46, 47, 52, 53, 54, 64, 78, 177, 229, 246, 270, 280, 290, 292, 293, 298, 327, 333, 334, 342, 348, 354, 355
Mondlane, Janet, 41, 54, 252, 280, 292, 298, 312
Moonsamy, Kay, 161, 164, 252
Morobe, Murphy, 340
Mothopeng, Zephania, 119
Motlatsi, James, 11, 100, 165, 267, 268
Moyo, Canaan, 224
Moyo, J. Z., 56
Mthembi-Mahanyele, Sankie (aka 'Rebecca Matlou'), 168
Mudenge, Stan, 228
Mudge, Dirk, 80
Mueshihange, Peter, 65, 99
Mugabe, Robert, 26, 208, 214, 215, 217, 222, 223, 231, 232, 260, 264, 265, 266, 323, 333, 355
Mugabe, Sally, 205, 264
Muller, Hilgard, 80, 81
Mushimba, Aaron, 72, 84
Mutaca, Lourenço, 56, 304
Mutandare, Geoffrey, 267
Mutasa, Didymus, 147, 216, 265
Muyongo, Mishake, 24, 86
Muzenda, Simon, 215, 217
Muzorewa, Abel, 207, 208, 215, 221, 258, 262, 264, 265, 280, 355
Mwaanga, Vernon, 241
Myeni, Musa, 199
Myrdal, Alva, 65
Myrdal, Gunnar, 277, 347
Möllander, Anders, 164, 252

N'Zau Puna, Miguel, 23, 275
Naholo, Festus, 89
Naicker, M.P., 103
Naidoo, Indres, 173, 179
Naudé, Beyers, 110, 181, 186
Ndlovu, Edward, 224, 225

Nengwekhulu, Randwedzi ('Harry'), 187, 188, 199
Neto, Agostinho, 16, 17, 18, 20, 22, 24, 27, 29, 30, 78, 177, 241, 242, 250, 312, 326, 327, 328, 329, 330, 333, 338, 355
Neto, António Alberto, 18, 312, 326
Neto, Mateus, 32
Neto, Ruth, 21
Ngavirue, Zedekia, 76, 78, 92, 97, 286, 331
Nhanhla, Joe, 199
Nhongo, Rex, 147, 234
Nilsson, Hillevi, 28, 326
Nilsson, Lars, 28, 329
Nilsson, Lars-Åke, 344
Nilsson, Torsten, 65, 297
Nkobi, Thomas, 104, 132, 137, 143, 161, 164, 171, 201, 248, 252, 254, 255, 256
Nkomo, John, 223, 268
Nkomo, Joshua, 177, 201, 208, 210, 212, 222, 231, 232, 264, 265, 266, 323, 333, 347, 348, 357
Nkrumah, Kwame, 64, 240, 356
Noafu, Etienne, 347
Nokwe, Duma, 92, 298
Norberg, Carin, 84, 86
Norling, Jan-Erik, 165, 166, 167, 270
Nthite, Peter, 176
Nujoma, Sam, 33, 69, 89, 91, 94, 116, 177, 201, 289, 295, 350
Nyanda, Siphiwe ('Guebuza'), 180
Nyathi, Isaac, 225
Nyerere, Julius, 35, 54, 64, 89, 142, 145, 222, 232, 241, 246, 298, 324, 327, 329, 331, 332, 333, 342, 347, 348, 349, 356
Nzo, Alfred, 148, 249
Näslund, John, 268
Nässbjer, Tom, 279, 331

Ohlin, Bertil, 341, 347, 352
Opdahl, Øystein, 34
Oswald, Dennis, 105, 144, 146

Padmore, George, 278
Pahad, Aziz, 103, 195
Palme, Lisbet, 22, 247
Palme, Olof, 10, 12, 16, 17, 18, 19, 20, 22, 23, 26, 29, 30, 31, 32, 33, 35, 39, 43, 45, 48, 52, 54, 55, 56, 57, 64, 65, 69, 72, 73, 76, 86, 93, 94, 97, 135, 141, 142, 153, 154, 176, 177, 190, 194, 198, 203, 211, 217, 224, 229, 238, 239, 242, 245, 246, 247, 248, 274, 279, 281, 286, 290, 292, 293, 297, 299, 323, 327, 329, 331, 332, 337, 338, 341, 342, 346, 351, 353
Palmlund, Tord, 356
Paton, Alan, 277, 352
Pereira, Aristides, 19
Peterson, Thage G., 331
Pietersen, Count, 119
Pillay, Bobby, 179, 180
Pityana, Barney, 186, 199
Pohamba, Hifikepunye, 90, 94, 252, 254
Pokela, Nyati, 119

Radise, Peter, 141, 353
Ramaphosa, Cyril, 100, 165, 168, 267, 268, 269, 308, 339, 340
Ramphele, Mamphela, 186, 187
Ranger, Terence, 210
Rappe, Marianne, 311
Reagan, Ronald, 142, 345
Rebelo, Jorge, 45
Reddy, Freddy, 104
van Rensburg, Patrick, 353
Resha, Robert, 33, 352, 354
Ribeiro de Carvalho, Joaquim, 51
Ribeiro-Kabulu, Alberto, 27
Roberto, Holden, 16, 30, 250, 280, 312, 355
Rocha, Carlos ('Dilolwa'), 229
Romare, Jan, 66
Rubin, Leslie, 352
Rubin, Neville, 352
Runeborg, Anna, 143
Russel, Bertrand, 176
Rylander, Berit, 90, 96

Salazar, António, 55, 115
Salim, Salim Ahmed, 337, 348
Sandén, Per, 61, 66, 70
Sangumba, Jorge, 26
dos Santos, José Eduardo, 27, 241
dos Santos, Marcelino, 8, 13, 17, 47, 278, 304
Savimbi, Jonas, 23, 24, 25, 26, 35, 241, 274, 275, 276, 328, 355
Schleimann, Jørgen, 277
Schoon, Jeanette, 202
Schori, Pierre, 23, 39, 42, 53, 69, 76, 97, 158, 199, 202, 203, 228, 274, 278, 286, 299, 302, 330, 355, 356
Segal, Ronald, 77, 278, 353
Segerstedt, Torgny, 353
Sekeramayi, Sydney, 103, 226
Semenya, Caiphus, 140
Senghor, Léopold, 278, 333
September, Dulcie, 123, 126, 127
September, Reg, 103, 123
Sevefjord, Birgitta, 164
Shevardnadze, Eduard, 116
Shikongo, Hendrik, 90
Shipanga, Andreas, 26, 61, 62, 65, 89, 97, 98, 122, 242, 249, 261, 288, 298, 335, 350, 351
Shiri, Jonas, 208
Shubin, Vladimir, 11, 248
Sidelmann, Peder, 18
Silveira, Onésimo, 310
Sisulu, Walter, 92, 174, 190, 197

Sithole, Ndabaningi, 231, 262, 263, 355
Slabbert, Frederik van Zyl, 108
Slovo, Joe, 20, 133, 199, 287, 297, 353
Smith, Ian, 56, 206, 210, 211, 218, 219, 222, 225, 240, 242, 258
Soares, Mário, 20, 35, 334
Sobukwe, Robert, 356
Sorsa, Kalevi, 66, 67, 243
de Sousa, Noémia, 20
Stendalen, Anders, 165, 166, 266, 267
Stolt, Ulla, 93
Storhaug, Kari, 132, 285
Strachan, Garth, 192
Strauss, Franz Josef, 69
Ström, Curt, 114, 309, 310, 311
Sundbom, Anne-Marie, 22, 23, 63, 99
Suzman, Helen, 175
Svensson, Evert, 285
Svensson, Per, 151
Svärd, Arvid, 295
Säve-Söderbergh, Bengt, 329, 336
Söder, Karin, 274
Söderström, Erling, 222
Söderström, Hugo, 264

Tait, Peter, 267
Tambo, Dali, 303
Tambo, Oliver, 9, 10, 38, 54, 77, 105, 121, 122, 123, 134, 136, 139, 140, 141, 142, 145, 147, 153, 155, 161, 171, 177, 180, 188, 189, 190, 191, 199, 203, 211, 238, 247, 249, 270, 280, 286, 287, 288, 289, 290, 293, 294, 299, 325, 332, 335, 338, 342, 347, 348, 350, 352, 353, 354, 356, 357
Tandberg, Olof, 92, 285, 352
Tekere, Edgar, 265
Tham, Carl, 164, 340
Thatcher, Margaret, 90, 150, 243
Thomas, Franklin, 55
Thunborg, Anders, 279, 297, 352
Tikly, Mohammed, 133
Timol, Mohamed, 180
Tingsten, Herbert, 75, 76, 77, 111, 112, 114, 157, 273, 277, 284, 295, 321, 337, 340, 347, 352, 353
Tito de Morais, Manuel, 51
Tjongarero, Daniel, 72
Toivo ya Toivo, Andimba, 30, 99, 101
Tongogara, Josiah, 49, 56, 215
Toresson, Bo, 196
Touré, Sekou, 354
Tshombe, Moise, 97, 273
Tungamirai, Josiah, 233

af Ugglas, Margaretha, 272, 289
Ulenga, Ben, 11, 100, 168, 269
Ullsten, Ola, 16, 318, 341, 343
Undén, Östen, 317

Valentim, Jorge, 34
Vance, Cyrus, 116
Veloso, Jacinto, 8, 52, 179
Verwoerd, Hendrik, 112, 227
Vestbro, Dick Urban, 330
Vieira, Sérgio, 54
Vinde, Victor, 295
Vorster, John, 81, 225, 240
Vraalsen, Tom, 247

Walan, Magnus, 151
Waldheim, Kurt, 24, 80
Wallenberg, Peter, 320
Wedén, Sven, 341
Wedin, Åke, 269
Weinberg, Eli, 257
Weiss, Peter, 357
Wickman, Krister, 65
Wieslander, Anna, 156
Williams, Freda, 95
Williamson, Craig, 11, 119, 120, 132, 187, 188, 195, 197, 250, 261, 281, 285, 295, 335, 343
Wirmark, David, 30, 289, 324, 340, 341, 345, 355
Wästberg, Anna-Lena, 132, 262, 285
Wästberg, Olle, 32, 300, 342, 349, 355
Wästberg, Per, 76, 77, 92, 132, 157, 262, 277, 278, 281, 285, 294, 295, 316, 337, 340, 341, 352

Xuma, A. B., 284

Zhou, Sifas, 263
Zuma, Jacob, 179, 180, 195

Örn, Torsten, 66